*The Origin of Table Manners*

Claude Lévi-Strauss

# THE ORIGIN of TABLE MANNERS

*Introduction to a*
*Science of Mythology: 3*

TRANSLATED FROM THE FRENCH BY
JOHN AND DOREEN WEIGHTMAN

HARPER COLOPHON BOOKS
*Harper & Row, Publishers*
*New York, Cambridge, Hagerstown, Philadelphia, San Francisco*
*London, Mexico City, São Paulo, Sydney*

A hardcover edition of this book is published by Harper & Row, Publishers.

THE ORIGIN OF TABLE MANNERS. Translated from the French *L'Origine des Manieres de Table*. Copyright © 1968 by Librairie Plon. English translation copyright © 1978 by Jonathan Cape Limited and Harper & Row, Publishers, Inc. All rights reserved. Printed in the United States of America. No part of this book may be used or reproduced in any manner whatsoever without written permission except in the case of brief quotations embodied in critical articles and reviews. For information address Harper & Row, Publishers, Inc., 10 East 53rd Street, New York, N.Y. 10022.

First HARPER COLOPHON edition published 1979

ISBN: 0-06-090698-7

79 80 81 82 83 10 9 8 7 6 5 4 3 2 1

# Contents

6 CONTENTS

# Illustrations

# Table of Symbols

$\left\{\begin{matrix} \triangle \\ \bigcirc \end{matrix}\right.$     man
           woman

$\triangle = \bigcirc$     marriage

$\Rightarrow$     transformation

$\rightarrow$     is transformed into

$\left\{\begin{matrix} : \\ :: \end{matrix}\right.$     is to ...
           as ...

$/$     contrast

$\equiv$     congruence, homology, correspondence

$\left\{\begin{matrix} = \\ \neq \end{matrix}\right.$     identity, or equality (according to the context)
           difference, or inequality (according to the context)

$\left\{\begin{matrix} \cup \\ \cap \\ // \end{matrix}\right.$     union, reunion, conjunction
           intersection
           disunion, disjunction

$f$     function

$x^{(-1)}$     inverted $x$

$\simeq$     isomorphism

$\left\{\begin{matrix} > \\ < \end{matrix}\right.$     larger than ...
           smaller than ...

$\Sigma$     summation

$+, -$     these signs are used with various connotations, depending on the context: plus, minus; presence, absence; first or second term of a pair of opposites.

# FOR MATTHIEU

*Hoc quicquid est muneris, fili charissime, universo puerorum sodalitio per te donatum esse volui : quo statim hoc congiario simul et commilitonum tuorum animos tibi concilies, et illis liberalium artium ac morum studia commendes.*

Erasmus, *De Civilitate Morum Puerilium* (*Conclusio operis*).

# Foreword

Although the present work may appear to begin abruptly, it forms a separate whole, like each of the two previous volumes in the series. Anyone wishing to read it first has only to skip the six introductory lines referring back to *From Honey to Ashes* and to start directly on the Amazonian myth with which the enquiry then opens. This myth, No. 354, will prove to be a particularly useful guide-line since it has to be held on to until the end of the book, in which it plays the part of reference myth. It therefore occupies a strategic position comparable to that of the very first myth ($M_1$), with which the analysis of *The Raw and the Cooked* began, and which it also pursued right to the end.

It may well be that the myth of the Tucuna Indians, which provides the theme of the present work, offers an easier approach for the uninitiated reader, since this is probably the myth of which I have given the most thorough analysis, conducted simultaneously or successively from several different points of view – textual, formal, anthropological, semantic, etc. In this respect, the first part of the book has a didactic significance. Through the treatment of one definite example, it provides an introduction to my method, so that the reader can gradually familiarize himself with its procedures and judge its value by the results obtained.

But there is an additional reason. By following through one particular myth step by step we encounter many others which throw light on it, and enable us to perceive the organic links connecting them all. And, since the mythological universe of a given society, or of a group of societies bound together by geographical and historical ties, always forms a closed system, we inevitably meet up again with the myths which were studied at the beginning of the enquiry. So, when the reader reaches Part Five of this volume, he will find (p. 214) that the myth indexed as No. 428 links up with No. 10 in *The Raw and the Cooked*. He will subsequently verify, in Part Six, that myth No. 495 coincides with a group of myths ($M_1$, $M_{7-12}$, $M_{24}$) which served both as starting point and connecting link in the initial volume of the *Introduction to a Science of Mythology*.

Consequently there is no reason why the reader should not start the series with Volume Three and then return to the first, since the end of the present work leads back to the beginning of Volume One. Then, if he is still interested, he can embark on Volume Two. Similarly, it would be possible to begin with the second volume, then go on to the first, and finally to the third. In fact, the series can be approached in various ways, corresponding to the following formulae: 1,2,3; 2,3,1; 2,1,3, or 3,1,2. The only sequences which might complicate the reader's task are 1,3,2, or 3,2,1. In other words, the reading of the third volume after the second presupposes a knowledge of Volume One, although it is possible to read the second volume before the first, provided Volume Three is put last.

There are two explanations for this anomaly. In the first place, the first and second volumes on the one hand, and the first and third, on the other, fulfil complementary functions. As I explained in *From Honey to Ashes*, that book follows the same course as the preceding volume, but on the reverse side, as it were, instead of the obverse. *The Origin of Table Manners*, in its turn, also brings us back to the starting point of *The Raw and the Cooked*, but, through the choice of a different itinerary, compels us to cross the vast spaces separating the northern and southern hemispheres of the New World.

In the second place, the task undertaken in Volume Three is more complex than the one that the other two volumes aimed at accomplishing. Here I make the first attempt at a movement which is carried out simultaneously on three levels. The procedure will be analysed in detail on pp. 465–70 but to prevent the reader from becoming confused, it will be helpful to give a general outline of it at this early stage.

To begin with, from a strictly geographical point of view, certain mythic patterns, previously illustrated by South American examples, will have to be followed up into North America, where they reappear in modified forms, and the modifications will have to be explained.

But, as we move into the other hemisphere, further differences come to light, and they are all the more significant in that the armature of the myths remains unchanged. Whereas the myths already studied made use of spatial contrasts, such as the high and the low, heaven and earth, sun and mankind, the South American examples which offer the best basis for comparison chiefly use temporal contrasts, such as the slow and the fast, regular or irregular periods of time, day and night, etc.

In the third place, several myths examined in this volume differ from the others from what might be called a literary point of view, both as regards style and form of narrative. Instead of a firmly constructed story, we get a loose pattern of episodes within episodes, all closely copied from each other and with no immediate indication of why they should not be more or less numerous than they are.

Yet, on analysing a myth of this type, which serves as reference myth throughout the book (M$_{354}$), we see that a succession of similar episodes is less uniform than might at first be supposed. The series conceals a system, the properties of which transcend the formal plan initially adhered to. The episodic-type narrative reflects the extreme forms of transformations deriving from other myths, but whose structural characteristics become gradually blurred as they succeed each other and move further away from their original anthropological reference points. In the end there only remains a weakened form, containing a vestigial energy which enables it to repeat itself a certain number of times, but not indefinitely.

Leaving aside the American field for the moment, if we reflect on comparable phenomena in European civilization, such as serialized novels, episodic tales or detective stories written by one and the same author with the same hero and the same characters appearing every time in a similarly constructed plot – i.e. literary genres which have remained very close to mythology, we have to ask ourselves whether the transition does not constitute an essential point of articulation between myth and the novel, and whether it does not supply a hypothetical model of the change-over from one to the other.

On the other hand, in the Tucuna reference-myth, there is one outstanding episode in which a human wife, after being cut in two, survives in part by clinging to her husband's back. This episode, which cannot be interpreted according to the syntagmatic sequence, and on which South American mythology as a whole fails to shed any light, can only be elucidated by reference to a paradigmatic system drawn from North American mythology. The geographical shift is thus empirically necessary, although it still remains to be justified on theoretical grounds.

The simple fact that the myths of the Northern Plains Indians establish an equivalence between the clinging woman and a frog adds a dimension to all the observations contained in the previous volume and prompted by myths of tropical America in which the heroine is a frog. So, in this new context, I am taking up again and amplifying previous analyses with increased results which in themselves constitute a guarantee that a generalized interpretation of myths covering both hemispheres is not an illegitimate undertaking. In spite of their geographical remoteness from each other, once they are treated as reciprocal variants, all these North or South American myths illustrate a transformation which is, one might say, of a rhetorical nature: the clinging woman, in the literal meaning of the term, being none other than a female character who, in French colloquial parlance also, is referred to metaphorically as *'collante'* ('sticky' = 'clinging'). This confirmation from afar through myths originating in very different and widely separated communities and through picturesque expressions current in French popular speech (but of which any language could offer the same or different examples), seems to me to constitute a form of anthropological evidence not unworthy of those used in more advanced sciences. It is often asserted that the natural sciences alone, and not the social sciences, are in the privileged position of being able to repeat their experiments in identical conditions in different settings and at different times. We, no doubt, cannot organize experiments, but the varied range of human cultures allows us to seek experimental evidence wherever it happens to be.

At the same time, we obtain a clearer picture of the logical function and semantic position of another imaginary figure, who is symmetrical to the clinging woman and often accompanies her: he is male, instead of female, remote instead of close, but his insistence is just as real and no less insidious, since this is a character with an immensely long penis which allows him to overcome the obstacles caused by distance.

After solving the problem posed by the concluding episode of the reference myth, I turn my attention to a different but no less obscure episode of the same myth: it concerns a canoe journey the meaning of which can be elucidated with the help of the Guiana myths, which make it clear that the passengers are really the sun and the moon in their respective roles as steersman and oarsman, and thus obliged to remain both in close proximity to each other (in the same boat) and yet apart (one at the back, the other in front): *at the right distance*, therefore, as the two celestial bodies must in fact be, in order to ensure the regular alternation of day and night; and as day and night themselves must be at the time of the equinoxes.

It can thus be established that an Amazonian myth is linked on the one hand to a frog-wife, and on the other to two masculine characters personifying celestial bodies; and lastly, that the clinging-wife theme can and must be interpreted with reference to a frog, thanks to the consolidation, into a single group, of myths originating partly in South America, partly in North America.

It so happens that precisely in those regions of North America to which I have had to refer, i.e. the northern and central plains and the Upper Missouri basin, certain famous myths explicitly bring together all these themes in a single story, in which the brothers, Sun and Moon, in their quest for ideal wives, quarrel over the respective merits of human women and frogs.

After summarizing and discussing the interpretation of this episode put forward by the eminent mythographer, Dr Stith Thompson, I give my reasons, which differ from his, for taking the episode not as a late, local variant, but as a systematic transformation of the other known versions of a myth attested over an enormous area, from Alaska to eastern Canada and from districts south of the Hudson Bay to the shores of the Gulf of Mexico.

In analysing all the ten or so variants of the quarrel between the two heavenly bodies, I bring to light an axiomatic system of an 'equinoctial' type, to which the myths sometimes make explicit reference, and thus confirm hypotheses, previously suggested by the separate consideration of the South American myths, about the transition from a spatial to a temporal axis. But I also note that this transition presents a more complex aspect than that involved by a mere change of axis. The poles of the temporal axis do not appear as *terms*: instead, they are types of intervals between terms which can be contrasted according to their relative durations – they may be respectively longer or shorter – so that they already form systems of relations between terms which are not always the same distance apart. The new myths, compared to those studied in the other volumes, display greater complexity. They bring into play relations between relations, and not simply relations between terms.

In order to develop the structural analysis of mythic thought, I realize then that recourse must be had to several types of models, although it is possible to switch from one to another and the differences between them are interpretable in terms of the specific contents of certain myths. In the instance which concerns us here, the decisive transition seems to occur in connection with the astronomical code, in which the constellations – characterized by a seasonal, therefore slow, periodicity and structured by the contrast it emphasizes between the various modes of existence or techno-economic activities – are replaced in the newly introduced myths by individual celestial bodies such as the sun and moon, the diurnal and nocturnal alternation of which defines a different kind of periodicity, at once shorter and in principle unaffected by seasonal changes. This periodicity within a periodicity, because of its serial nature, contrasts with the other periodicity containing it, and is not marked by the same monotony.

The local character of the astronomical code does not prevent it interlocking with several others. Thus it brings into operation an arithmetical philosophy, to the elucidation of which the sixth part is almost entirely devoted. The reader will perhaps be surprised, as I myself was at first, that the most abstract speculations of mythic thought should provide the key to other speculations relating to forms of concrete behaviour, from the customs of war and the practice of scalping enemies to recipes for cooking; it is no less surprising that the theory of numeration, the theory of head-hunting and the art of cooking should come together to constitute a moral system.

So, at the same time as I propose to widen my field of enquiry and to establish a foothold in North American mythology, which will be the main theme of the fourth and last volume of the series, I achieve several results with theoretical implications. In dealing with an enormous group of myths, I simultaneously consolidate form and content, quality and quantity, material circumstances and moral values. Lastly, I show that the reductions, as they occur in the myths, follow the same lines as those along which, on an entirely different level, a fictional style emerges at the very heart of mythology itself. In spite of its formal character, this new style is linked to transformations affecting the content of the stories.

The reader familiar with the two previous volumes will no doubt notice a slight alteration in method, which is to be explained by the fact that I have been obliged to cover a greater number of myths emanating from widely separated areas, and to conduct my analysis simultaneously on various levels, between which there are also considerable gaps. To use a metaphor drawn from electronics, I have sometimes had to broaden the scanning of the mythic field – for instance, in order to compare myths from both North and South America – at the risk of distending the cycles. So, instead of subjecting a comparatively limited number of myths from adjacent, or not too widely scattered, areas to systematic scanning with periods of more or less the same constant range, in this volume I study certain myths thoroughly, while in the case of others, drawn from much further afield, I make do with more cursory treatment or merely brief reference. This reversion to what might be called, with only a slight straining of the technical meaning of the terms, amplitude modulation, in place of the frequency modulation the norms of which were more consistently respected in the previous volumes, should not be taken to indicate that I have definitively abandoned my former practice; it is a temporary obligation imposed upon me by the gradual transfer of the enquiry from South American to North American myths. But since, in the next volume, I shall limit the investigation to one clearly defined, although extensive, sector of the northern hemisphere, I shall be able to return to a more sustained form of close analysis, the results of which will provide retroactive confirmation of the bold simplifications I may have been led into from time to time by the very broadness of the investigation.

The present work, like the previous volumes, would not have reached publication so soon, but for the help of several people to whom I owe a debt of gratitude. The notes made by M. Jean Pouillon during my 1963-4 lectures have been a great help. Mlle Jacqueline Bolens translated the German sources; Mlle Nicole Belmont helped me to assemble the documentation and to make the indexes. Mme Evelyne Guedj undertook the heavy task of typing the manuscript. Mlle Monique Verkamp of the cartography section of La Maison des Sciences de l'Homme drew the maps and diagrams. M. Roberto Cardoso de Oliveira of the National Museum in Rio de Janeiro was good enough to send me the text of a hitherto unpublished word-list by Curt Nimuendaju and to add his own valuable commentaries, based on his research among the Tucuna Indians. In the body of the book I make other acknowledgements relating to more specific points. Lastly, the Smithsonian Institute in Washington, D.C., and the University Museum in Philadelphia have kindly supplied several illustrations, both black and white and coloured. To one and all I express my thanks.

# PART ONE  THE MYSTERY OF THE WOMAN CUT INTO PIECES

*The person concerned was an eccentric and fairly high-class American lady, who was said to indulge in strange fantasies.*

Guy de Téramond, *La Femme coupée en morceaux*, Paris 1930, p. 14

# 1    *At the Scene of the Crime*

The performers (in other words, the reader) are requested to refer back on the score to the third variation, $M_{241}$, *From Honey to Ashes*, II, *i*. This myth told the story of a baby-snatching frog, which perished because of a feast of honey – honey being an exquisite food on the border-line of poison. The same themes are found combined, in a much weaker form and in episodic fashion, in a Tucuna myth, thanks to which our investigation can start off on a new tack.

$M_{354}$. *Tucuna*. '*The hunter Monmanéki and his wives*'

In the days of the first people fished for by demiurges ($M_{95}$, RC, p. 171), there lived an Indian whose only occupation was hunting. He was called Monmanéki. On the way, coming and going, he often passed a frog which would dart into its hole at his approach, and each time the man would urinate into the hole. One day he saw a good-looking girl standing before the hole. Monmanéki saw that she was pregnant: 'Because of you,' she said, 'you always pointed your penis in my direction.' He asked her to come to his house and live with him. His mother also thought the girl pretty.

Husband and wife went hunting together, but they did not eat the same food. Monmanéki ate meat, but (for his wife) he used to catch a kind of black beetle that formed her only diet. When his mother saw these beetles she said, (not knowing about her daughter-in-law's tastes): 'Why does my son soil his mouth with such filth?' She threw them out, putting peppers in their place. When Monmanéki called his wife to the meal she placed her little pot on the fire and began to eat from it but the peppers burnt her mouth. She ran and hopped into the water in the form of a frog. A rat reproached her with having abandoned her little boy, who was weeping bitterly. She said in reply that she would have another child. However at night she returned to the house and stole the infant from his grandmother's arms.

Monmanéki again went out to hunt. In the fruit cluster of a bacaba palm (*Oenocarpus* sp.) an arapaço bird was sitting. 'Give me a gourdful of your drink,' said Monmanéki in passing. When he returned he saw a pretty girl who offered him a gourdful of bacaba palm wine. He took the girl home to be his wife. She was very pretty, but her feet were ugly. On seeing her, the hero's mother exclaimed that he could have made a better choice. The woman was annoyed and did not wish to remain with Monmanéki.

He returned to hunting. One day he had a sudden fancy to squat down to defecate directly over the spot where an earthworm was burrowing. She poked out her head and said: 'My, what a lovely penis!' Monmanéki looked and saw a girl with an extremely good figure. He copulated with her and took her home with him, where she gave birth to a child. When Monmanéki went hunting, he told his wife to leave the child with its grandmother while she herself went out to weed the plantation. But the child wailed so much that the grandmother decided to carry it to its mother in the plantation. There the earth woman had clipped the roots of the weeds (as earthworms do when moving underground), and they were already wilting, but the old woman did not notice this and criticized her daughter-in-law for laziness. She took a sharp-edged river-shell, and so cut off the lips of the earth woman who was gnawing the roots just below the surface. Only at night did the unhappy wife return to the house. When her son cried, she asked her husband to give him to her, but she could no longer speak properly. Humiliated by her disfigurement, she disappeared.

Again Monmanéki went hunting. A band of macaws flew over his head and he shouted to them to give him some of their maize beer. When he returned, a macaw-girl was waiting for him with the beverage. He took the girl home as his wife. One day the hunter's mother threw down a quantity of corncobs that hung from the rafters and asked her daughter-in-law to prepare maize beer. She herself left for the plantation. Using only one ear of corn, the girl roasted it and made enough beer to fill five large jars. When the mother returned, she tripped over the heap of unused corncobs and accused her daughter-in-law of having done nothing. The latter had gone off to bathe in the river, but heard the reproaches and refused to enter the hut. When her husband returned, she told him she wanted to retrieve her comb which she had thrown on the roof-thatch. (This is where Indians keep objects of everyday use.) Climbing up the ridge-pole, she began to sing: 'My mother-in-law has scolded me, now drink the beer alone may she!' The old woman realized her mistake and apologized, but the daughter-in-law refused to listen and resumed her macaw form. (Perched on the main beam), she cried to her husband at daybreak: 'If you love me, follow me! Look for the a:ru-pana laurel, the splinters of which, falling into the water, are transformed into fish. Make a canoe from the trunk and follow me down river to Mount Vaipi!' And with this she flew away to the east.

Monmanéki ran to and fro all the next day like a crazy man searching for the a:ru-pana laurel. He tried several trees with his axe until finally the splinters of one turned into fish when they fell into the water around the foot of the tree. Each day when he returned from work he brought back such a quantity of fish that his brother-in-law,[1] who was lazy and incompetent, began to spy on him. The effect of this indiscreet action was to prevent the splinters changing into fish. Monmanéki guessed the reason and called out to his brother-in-law to come and help him. When they finished the canoe they pushed it down the slope. While the brother-in-law was standing in shallow water, Monmanéki suddenly upset the canoe on top of him. The brother-in-law passed the night under the canoe singing and crying. The next morning Monmanéki released him and then invited him to accompany him down the Solimões. Monmanéki was seated at the stern and his brother-in-law was at the prow. Thus they drifted downstream without paddling. When they arrived among the people with whom the macaw-girl was staying all the inhabitants ran to the bank to see the canoe and its occupants, but Monmanéki's wife hid behind the others. The brother-in-law, transformed into a monan bird, flew up and alighted on her shoulders. The canoe continued downstream a short way, but suddenly its prow turned up perpendicularly and Monmanéki, after changing into an aiča bird, flew onto the woman's other shoulder. The empty canoe continued to drift at the mercy of the current and finally entered a large lake where it turned into an aquatic monster, dyëvaë, which is the lord of fish in the Solimões, more especially of the shoals of piracemas (Tupi: 'fish-birth'?), which go upstream periodically to spawn.

After this adventure, Monmanéki married a girl of his own people. Every time she went to the landing-stage, which was some distance from the house, her body divided into two sections at the waist: her abdomen with the legs remained lying on the bank, while her chest,

[1] In Tucuna, the same word, čaua-áne, may mean the husband's brother, the wife's brother and the sister's husband (Nim. 13, p. 155).

head and arms entered the water. The odour of flesh would attract the matrinchan fish and she would catch them with her hands and string them on a liana. Then her torso would crawl on its hands to the bank and adjust itself on the lower part, from which the spinal cord protruded to the length of a finger.

Monmanéki's mother was greatly astonished at the amount of fish brought by her daughter-in-law. One day when she was preparing maize beer, she ordered the young woman to fetch water from the river. However, as the daughter-in-law delayed, the old woman became impatient and went to the landing-stage herself. Seeing the lower half of the prone body she immediately pulled off the pro-truding spinal cord. When the upper half hoisted itself back on to the bank, it tried in vain to adjust itself to the lower half, and finally climbed up to a branch overhanging the path. When night fell, and his wife had not yet returned, Monmanéki lit a torch and went to look for her. As he passed beneath the overhanging branch, the upper half of the woman sprang onto his shoulders where she became stuck. She would not let him eat but, snatching the food from in front of his mouth, ate it herself. He grew thin and his back became filthy with the woman's faeces.

Monmanéki thought of a trick to get free. He said he had to dive into the water to inspect his fish weir and that if his wife did not keep her eyes closed the whole time the piranhas which infested the river might well tear them out. In order to make the warning more con-vincing, he scratched her face with a piranha jaw which he had secretly brought along. The woman took fright and decided to stay on the bank, thus momentarily freeing her victim. Monmanéki took advantage of this to dive into the water and swim away. Not knowing what to do, the upper part of the woman perched on one of the posts of the weir. After a few days, she began to sprout parrot-feathers 'and like a tame parrot, began to speak to herself'. Hidden in the bushes, Monmanéki watched her fly away, still chattering, further down the Solimões towards the mountains (Nim. 13, pp. 151–3).

At first glance, there would seem to be no reason why the story should not be continued. It is made up of successive episodes, each of which recounts the failure of a marriage entered into by a hero, whose only aim seems to be to vary his conjugal experiences. Why, in this case, should the fifth wife also be the last? South American mythology offers a great many instances of stories of this type in which certain episodes, constructed according to the same pattern, follow each other in even greater numbers. However, when it is looked at from a formal point of view, the structure of $M_{354}$ is seen to be both open and closed. Open, because Monmanéki, after his last mishap, might well marry again; and closed in the sense that the last marriage has certain original features which set it apart from the other four, as if the myth were envisaging the two extreme solutions of a single problem between which a number of intermediary forms were available, offering several correlational and oppositional relationships with each other, as well as with the extreme forms.

The hero's first four marriages are exogamous. They are so, one might say, in hyperbolical fashion, since they bring together a man and several female animals, which are still further removed from a human husband than a mere foreign female bride would be. In contrast, the last marriage is endogamous, as is clearly brought out by the text: 'Then, Monmanéki married a girl belonging to the same people as himself.' But it should be noticed that the last marriage in the exogamous series acts as a point of articulation between the two types, a fact which the myth expresses with an astonishing variety of means.

The first three episodes each contain two sequences: 1) meeting and marriage; 2) separation caused by the hero's mother. Only the fourth and fifth episodes carry the story beyond this point. But they too begin to diverge, from the beginning of the second sequence: in the fourth episode, as in the preceding one, the old woman separates her daughter *from her son*; in the fifth, she separates her *from herself*, since she prevents the two halves of the woman's body from joining up again. But the symmetry emerges more clearly only later. Either the woman runs off and her husband follows her, or she follows her husband (we have seen how tenaciously) and it is the husband who escapes. It is true that the fourth marriage is still exogamous, whereas the fifth was endogamous, but, in the first instance, the man agrees to go and live with his wife's people, although it had not occurred to him to do so previously. He succeeds only temporarily in doing so, by changing into a bird and perching on his wife's shoulder, which shows that she has retained her human form (in spite of being originally a bird). As for the endogamous woman in the fifth episode, she definitively gives up living with her own people only *after* changing into a bird. And the mountains downstream where she takes refuge are the same as those to which her fellow-wife has already fled (this fellow-wife is a macaw-woman, instead of a parrot-woman, and she is wild whereas the parrot-woman behaves like a tame bird). The two women are mistresses, one of fish, the other of fishing. In this last respect, in both episodes there is a lazy partner: in the one case, he is a male who, unlike his brother-in-law, is incapable of fishing, and in the other, the lower half – the most female of the two halves – of the heroine's body, which, unlike the upper half, is no good at fishing.

Other links between the last two episodes will appear later. For the moment, the few I have assembled are enough to show that the fourth episode, relating to an exogamous marriage like the previous episodes, but constructed in exactly the same way as the succeeding one, is the pivotal point of a narrative which has in consequence a two-fold structure, at once binary and ternary.

| episodes: | 1 | 2 | 3 | 4 | 5 |
|---|---|---|---|---|---|
| marriages: | exogamous | | | | endogamous |
| narrative structure: | 1st part | | | transition | 2nd part |

This having been established, let us begin by studying the exogamous marriages. They take place, in succession, with four creatures which come alternately from 'below' (animals living in holes) and from 'above' (birds):

            2) *arapaço bird*        4) *macaw*

    1) *frog*           3) *earthworm*

The term arapaço (arapassu, uirapassu), which comes from the Tupi, *Nasica* sp. (Nim. 13, p. 57), refers to several climbing birds which feed on grubs, as in this case, or the sap of trees. The South American myths associate them with the middle world, along with woodpeckers whose mode of life they share, since they nest in the hollows of the tree-trunks over which they clamber in their search for food. The arapaço bird in the myth we are studying is perched on a palm-tree and is relatively lower than the macaw, since the hero sees the latter flying in the sky. Similarly, the frog which takes refuge in its hole is relatively lower than the worm, which the myth describes as in the process of burrowing, and then as crawling along at ground level. From this point of view, the second term of each pair seems, in the same functional respect, to be more strongly marked than the first.

Moreover, a short Hixkaryâna variant (M$_{355}$; Derbyshire, pp. 100–

Figure 1. The arapaço (arapassu) bird. (From Ihering, p. 363.)

103), reduced to the single episode of the frog, attributes to the latter behaviour which is at once mysterious and reminiscent of the activity of the worm in the plantation. So both underground animals might well be acting as combinatory variants capable of illustrating the same function in slightly different contexts.

When the hero relieves himself in the frog's hole, the latter does not move. When he does likewise in the other hole, the worm sticks out her head to see what is going on. The arapaço bird is perched on a tree, whereas the macaw is in flight. Two animals, then, remain motionless while two are in motion. It might easily be supposed that this third pair of oppositions is redundant, since the other two provide adequate differentiation between the four animals. But only the third pair turns out to be relevant for the description, on the same level as the preceding terms, of the canoe carved out of a tree trunk that the hero uses to rejoin his fourth wife, and the wooden stake on which the fifth wife perches before leaving her husband for good: that is, we have an opposition between a hollow, horizontal trunk moving on the surface of the water, and a solid, vertical trunk standing motionless in the water. In this respect, the canoe, when it is pointed vertically, is being carried along by the current, and provides a transition between the boat (which it is ceasing to be) and the stake (of which it is a prefiguration). Lastly, the canoe contains a brother-in-law who is useless on two counts: first, he is imprisoned under the hull, and secondly he is the passive travelling companion of another man. Symmetrically, the stake, as opposed to the canoe, excludes half a body which is useless on two counts: first, it lies passively on the bank, then it does not accompany on her journey the same woman (as the one of whom it is however a part):

|  | frog | arapaço | worm | macaw | canoe | stake |
|---|---|---|---|---|---|---|
| high (+)/low (−): | − | + | − | + |  |  |
| (+) or (−) in relationship to the high and the low: | + | − |  | − | + |  |
| moving (+)/motionless (−): | − | − | + | + | + | − |

I do not include in the diagram the complete system of oppositions relating to the canoe and the stake, as they have just been formulated. This system, too, has all the appearance of being redundant but, as will be seen later, the reason is that it gives in codified form not merely the characteristic features of two objects, but an important part of the message which it is the function of the group of myths to which $M_{354}$–$M_{355}$ belong to convey.

The analysis, after being confined in the first instance to the first four episodes of the exogamous marriages, is, then, striking down to a level at which the relevant characteristics become common to the narrative as a whole. This continuous presence of a logical substratum is now about to become clearly evident.

The exogamous marriages are brought about by four incidental causes, two of which are connected with the excretory, and the other two with the nutritional, functions, in each case, however, associated either with copulation in the physical sense (and in both instances the woman conceives) or with a union of a more 'moral' nature[2] (since the woman plays the part of *food-supplier* to her husband). Monmanéki urinates on the frog and defecates on the worm; and he receives sap from the palm tree from the arapaço bird, and maize-beer from the

---

[2] TRANSLATORS' NOTE: The author intends the adjective to be understood in the old sense it had in the expression 'moral philosophy' as opposed to 'natural philosophy'.

macaw. The beer is cooked, as is made clear in the story: 'Through roasting only one ear of corn the woman had enough beer to fill five large jars . . .' Beer and excrement are more 'cooked' – in the sense of being more elaborated – than sap and urine; and the first two terms denote more solid matter than the others. We therefore obtain a triple entry diagram:

|  | RAW: | COOKED: |
|---|---|---|
| EXCRETION: | Urine | Faeces (*from man to woman*) |
| NUTRITION: | Sap | Beer (*from woman to man*) |

In both the instances given in the upper row, the woman is guilty of *physical* confusion between *excretion* and copulation: she becomes pregnant and produces a child. In both the instances given in the lower row, the reverse happens three times: the husband is guilty of a '*moral*' confusion, this time between *nutrition* and copulation; the girl he meets has only to supply him with food for him to make her his wife, although he does not fertilize her.

If we now examine the fifth and last episode, we note that the same relationships persist, while at the same time being duplicated. First, the wife's body is divided into two halves. The lower half is feminine through physical contiguity (it includes the sexual organs), and male through similarity (it fixes onto the other part by means of a tenon inserted into a mortise). According to the same kind of reasoning, the upper half is female in a figurative sense, although, from the sociological point of view, it engages in the masculine activity of fishing. According to the first sequence, the two halves copulate metaphorically when they fit one into the other; and the half which might be called masculine by social contiguity feeds the feminine part of her husband (his mother, who receives the fish, as the myth is careful to explain). Conversely, in the second sequence, the same half copulates with the man metaphorically (it clings onto him, but from behind), while it feeds, in the literal sense, on the food the husband tries in vain to consume. Consequently, whereas the major contrast in the four exogamous episodes appears either between excretion and copulation, or between nutrition and copulation, in the endogamous episode it occurs in the two-fold form of auto-copulation and exo-alimentation, then in the form of exo-copulation and auto-alimentation, each time in opposition one to the other.

For humans, the beetles which form the frog's only food are a form of filth, that the hero's mother classes with excrement. The frog commits the opposite mistake of eating peppers as a main food, whereas they are used by humans as seasoning. As we say metaphorically in French, 'they remove her mouth' (*ils lui emportent la bouche* = burn her mouth); this is, literally, the fate of the worm/wife when her lips are cut off. The frog-wife was ravishing from top to toe; the hero's mother had no reservations to make about her beauty. The arapaço-wife, who succeeds her, is half pretty (the upper half) and half ugly (the lower half): the dendrocolaptidae have, as a matter of fact, elongated toes with strong curved nails. The third wife, who was entirely pretty to begin with, becomes ugly after being disfigured by her mother-in-law. So here, the pretty/ ugly opposition changes from being spatial (affecting the parts of the body) to temporal. Lastly, just as the first wife was physically perfect, but had the moral defect of feeding on filth, the fourth is morally perfect and capable of performing miracles: a virtue which goes unrecognized by her mother-in-law, who accuses her of being lazy (= morally ugly), whereas she had admired the first wife's physical beauty. So the first and fourth episodes play entirely on the opposition between the physical and mental or moral; the second and third subordinate it to a further one between the spatial and temporal aspects that the same opposition is capable of adopting.

In this case too, the final episode reverts to, and provides a link between, the two axes. When the two halves of the woman are considered simultaneously, one is lazy (it lies motionless on the bank, while the other is busy in the water) and one is industrious. On each occasion, therefore, the qualities invoked are of a moral nature. But the second half also changes its physical nature in time: it is at first food-providing, then excrement-producing. Consequently it is confirmed that the sequence of the first four episodes gives rise dialectically to the terms of a system, which the final episode integrates within itself and turns into a structured entity.

If the analysis is taken one degree deeper, it can be seen that at this new level the integration begins as early as the fourth episode. The fact need cause no surprise, since it has already been shown that this particular episode acts as a point of articulation between the first three and the final one. Previously, it had been constructed in the same way as the first three; from now on, the formal characteristics it possesses in common with the final episode will come out more clearly.

The frog lives on beetles, a food which is not eaten by humans. The arapaço bird collects the sap of the palm tree, a food also consumed by humans. Unlike humans, the earthworm eats weeds, thus encouraging (passively, not actively like the bird) the production of vegetable foods. The macaw/woman's attitude towards food is more complex: she *over*produces maize-beer, consumed by humans, but it is a *second* degree food, in so far as the preparation supposes the maize to have been previously cultivated (an operation in which the woman takes no part whatever). *Actively* responsible for the *increase* in beer in the first sequence, she becomes *passively* responsible (by revealing the secret of obtaining them to her husband, who does the rest) for the *existence* of fish. The latter do not yet even constitute a food, since they have to appear before it occurs to anyone to eat them.

The fifth episode begins, indeed, after the creation of the fish. It is no longer a question of creating them, but of catching them: this is a function in which the legless woman *sur*passes humans, but by offering her own body as bait, that is, the *first* degree of food: a *condition* of fishing, in the same way as beer played the part of a *consequence* of agriculture. The legless woman, who is *actively* responsible for the increase in fishing in the first sequence, becomes, in the second, responsible for its *continuation* in a *passive* form (thanks to the weir that the fish come up against), when she agrees to free her husband to enable him – so he claims – to carry out the rest of the operation without her help. The abandoned woman then changes into a babbling parrot, which utters *meaningless* remarks and is a doubly pejorative counterpart of the previous wife, since the latter recovers her macaw nature by singing *meaningful* words intended for her mother-in-law, and revealing an *effective formula* (for the creation of fish) that her husband can profit by.

Let us now take the final step in the analysis. It will be remembered that the first and third wives are consumers of food, the second and fourth producers of food, and that the fifth, after being a pure producer of food, later becomes a pure consumer. What phenomena does this series of operations cover?

|  | GATHERING: | CULTIVATING: | FISHING: |
|---|---|---|---|
| *Unconsumable*: | beetles | weeds | splinters |
| *Consumable*: | sap of palm tree | maize-beer | fish |

Hunting constitutes the hero's essential activity. A Taulipang myth (M₃₅₆: K.-G. 1, pp. 81–91) testifies to the fact that the psittacidae – parrots, parakeets and macaws – are masters of maize-beer. If we consider that the hero gathers beetles, the frog's food, while on his hunting expeditions, that weeds grow in gardens when they are cultivated, and that splinters result from the hollowing out of the canoe which is itself a means of fishing, an ordered relationship emerges all the more clearly between these various terms in that the first quoted – the black beetles, that humans look upon as filth but are converted into food by the frog – has a counterpart in the final term of the series, the excrement which fouls the hero's back, and into which the legless woman has converted the food which should have provided sustenance for her husband. The series of 'alimentary' terms assumes this final form:

| HUNTING | GATHERING | CULTIVATING | FISHING | RECAPITULATION |
|---|---|---|---|---|
| game | sap | beer | fish | FOOD |
| *beetles* | *peppers* | *weeds* | *splinters* | EXCREMENT |

The position of the weeds, between agriculture and fishing, seems strange. It should be noted, however, that the men, who among the Tucuna alone have the right to plant maize, start by soaking the seeds to be sown in water, and are thereafter subject to strict taboos concerning several species of fish, especially the herbivorous ones. They are also forbidden to touch any of the plants which are used as fish poison (Nim. 13, pp. 21–2).

It is clear from the above analysis that the narrative, in spite of its linear appearance, develops simultaneously on several levels which are interlinked in ways both numerous and complex enough to turn the whole myth into a closed system. If we take a surface view of the myth, the easiest level of interpretation is sociological in character, since the narrative groups together the hero's matrimonial experiences. But in trying to reach ever deeper levels, we have finally come upon the analytical description of modes of life which entertain reciprocal relationships with each other. Among these modes of life, two in particular seem to be more strongly marked: they are hunting and fishing.

When the myth begins, the hero is a hunter pure and simple, since fish, and *ipso facto* fishing, no longer exist. The text stresses the fact in the very first sentence by setting the story in the period when the primordial fish, after being caught from the river, had immediately changed into terrestrial animals and humans (Nim. 13, pp. 128–9). The two leading characters, who are respectively mother and son, belong to this first human race. As for fishing, it is clear that it occupies an essential place: it provides the theme common to the two most extensive episodes, and it enters into the fourth, which, as we have seen, is the one on which the whole story hinges. The myth deals with three kinds of fish: matrinchan, piranha and piracema.

The first two kinds belong to the same zoological family, the chara-cinidae. The myth describes both as being carnivorous: the matrinchan (*Characinus amazonicus, Brycon* sp.) is attracted by the smell of the legless woman's flesh (cf. however, Ihering, under 'piracanjuba', who main-tains that this southern relative of the Amazonian *Brycon* sometimes eats fruit, seeds and other vegetable substances); the piranhas (*Serrasal-mus* sp., *Pygocentrus* sp.) attack men. But they differ in that only the latter are cannibalistic. This accounts for the legless woman's change of attitude: she offers her torso as a bait to the matrinchan, but avoids all contact with piranhas. So, although the two types of fish are in correla-tion with each other through zoological proximity, they stand in opposition to each other dietetically.

Piracemas, on the other hand, are not defined in these two connec-tions, but only in a third. The term piracema has no taxonomical value. It is applied indiscriminately to all those species which swim up-river to spawn (Rodrigues, *Vocabulário*, p. 30; Stradelli 1, p. 602); and, in this instance, no doubt to the shoals of fish which swarm up the Solimões in fantastic numbers and enter the tributaries to spawn in May and June (Nim. 13, p. 25). The subsidiary opposition between cannibalistic and non-cannibalistic characinidae occurs, therefore, within a major opposition between periodic and non-periodic fish. The significance of this point is now about to become clear.

Yet although structural analysis brings out the hidden pattern of hunter Monmanéki's story, this pattern is still only perceptible to us on a formal level. The narrative content remains arbitrary. What, for instance, can be the origin of the strange notion of a woman capable at will of cutting herself up into two pieces? A Guiana myth ($M_{130}$), which was briefly discussed in *The Raw and the Cooked* (pp. 232–3), throws some light on this paradigm, since it too deals with fishing and, like $M_{354}$, has as its leading characters a husband, a wife and a mother-in-law. According to $M_{130}$, hunger drove the older woman to steal a fish from her son-in-law's net. In order to punish her, he asked the pataka fish to gobble her up. But they were unable to get through the upper part of the thorax, the arms and the head. Thus reduced to a legless bust, the old woman became Berenice's Hair, the Kalina name of which, ombatapo, means 'the Face'. This constellation appears in the morning, during October, at the end of the main dry season, and causes fish to die. (Ahlbrinck, under 'ombatapo' and 'sirito' §5, b). The species mentioned (*Hoplias malabaricus*), known as huri along the Pomeroon river in British Guiana, is caught during the dry season. It is a carnivorous fish and is killed with a cutlass, when it lies sleeping on river beds where the water is only a few inches deep (Roth 2, pp. 192–5). The Kalina believe that a man's soul, after death, has to cross a narrow bridge; if it falls into the water, two cannibalistic fish tear it in half. Later, the two pieces join together again (Goeje 1, p. 102).

Unlike $M_{354}$, $M_{130}$ provides an explanation for the cutting up of the woman. We are told how and why she comes to be in this state. This prototype of Monmanéki's final wife conceals an inner logic. May it not also have an external logic? Is there any apparent reason why Berenice's Hair should be represented by a legless woman?

$M_{130}$ has certain elements in common with $M_{28}$, a Warao myth which purports to explain the origin of the Pleiades, the Hyades and Orion's belt, represented respectively by the hero's wife, his body and his severed leg (Roth 1, pp. 263–5; RC, p. 109 *et passim*). These myths can therefore be seen to belong to a vast paradigmatic set, which also includes, notably, $M_{136}$, about a mother-in-law who feeds her son-in-law on fish instead of stealing them from him; however, she draws them from her womb, and this makes them a form of filth comparable to menstrual blood. The man arranges the murder of his mother-in-law; all that remains of her is her intestines in the form of aquatic plants. In another Guiana myth, the intestines of a man with a severed leg rise up into the sky, where they become the Pleiades, a constellation heralding the arrival of fish ($M_{134}$–$M_{135}$, RC, pp. 243–4),

In passing from the Tucuna myth to the Guiana myth, the sociological armature remains the same, although there is permutation of the sexes between two terms: (*mother – son, wife*) ⇒ (*mother – daughter, husband*). But, in the different instances, the parts of the body and the constellations to which they give rise, are not the same: the leg, with or without the thigh, becomes Orion; the intestines, the Pleiades; the torso, head and arms form Berenice's Hair. No one myth achieves this triple division completely. They merely separate from the body either the intestines, or one of the lower limbs, or the torso along with the head and arms. But if we confine ourselves to the Tucuna and Kalina myths in which the heroine is a legless woman (the others have been discussed elsewhere, cf. RC, *loc. cit.*, HA, pp. 263–6, 273–5, 317–18), we see quite clearly what the point is: the legless woman separates herself from the rest of her body voluntarily in $M_{354}$, but not so in $M_{130}$; in other words, she gives up a part which includes the abdomen (with the intestines) and the legs, that is, the anatomical symbols of the Pleiades and Orion, which are nevertheless interlinked as constellations since they are seen together in the sky. The upper part of the body thus becomes the anatomical symbol of Berenice's Hair, whose right ascension is the same as that of the Great Bear and the Crow, a group of constellations which, taken as a whole, is in phasal opposition to the other group. The Pleiades, whose rising occurs a little before that of Orion, promise an abundant supply of fish; the rising of Berenice's Hair revokes this promise, since it takes place when fish disappear from temporary lakes and small rivers because of the absence of water. The Tucuna hunter's legless wife fulfils the same function, when she is definitively deprived of her lower half and becomes a parrot instead of a star. She does not fish again, although previously her function had been to keep the Indians supplied with fish:

BAD FISHING
(October:                    *woman's . . .    head and torso*
Berenice's Hair):

GOOD FISHING
(June: Orion                 *man's . . .    leg . . . intestines*
and Pleiades):

A similar type of opposition exists further south. The Caduveo, for instance, attribute the origin of the forest and the savannah to two children, who were born respectively from the upper and lower halves of a baby whose mother had severed it with murderous intent. The twins stole and scattered seeds, which germinated and grew into trees that were easy or impossible to uproot, according to which brother had sown them. The 'lower' one thus became the creator of the forest, the 'upper' one the creator of the savannah. A little later, the brothers stole beans cooked by a dirty old woman whose sweat was dripping into the pot. The 'upper' brother was afraid of being poisoned but the 'lower' one had no qualms and tasted the dish, which he found delicious ($M_{357}$: Baldus 2, pp. 37–9). So, in two instances, the brother from the 'upper' part proved to be timid and ineffectual, whereas the one from the 'lower' half was bold and efficient. This corroborates the respectively negative and positive values of the half of the body symbolizing Berenice's Hair and of the half symbolizing the Pleiades and Orion, in the mythology of the Guiana Indians.

Lastly, it will be noted that, in Guiana itself and the Amazonian basin, a second opposition confirms the one I have just indicated. Orion and

Berenice's Hair are situated together over against the sun as 'its right hand' ($M_{130}$) or its 'support' ($M_{279}$). The Pleiades, on the contrary, are over against the moon, a combinatory variant of the lunar halo ($M_{82}$), to which Orion is in opposition when, in the form of a jaguar, it devours the moon at the time of the eclipses (Nim. 13, p. 142):

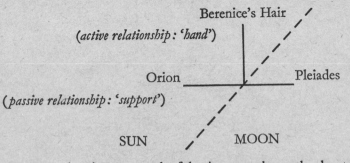

We have seen that, in areas north of the Amazon, the myths about the origin of Berenice's Hair and the bad fishing season reverse the Guiana myths dealing with the origin of Orion (or the Pleiades) and the good fishing season. But it is also true that the Tucuna myth is a reversal of this last mentioned group, in the fourth episode where the legless wife embarks on a supernatural and somewhat sinister fishing expedition, by using her mutilated body as bait, with the result that she catches enormous quantities of fish. In real life, such an abundance of fish only occurs during the months of May and June (the period of the morning rising of the Pleiades), when shoals of migratory fish swim up the river into the tributaries. The myth refers to this phenomenon, but attributes it entirely to the hero, whose canoe stands up on end in the water (a transformation of the severed leg in the sky) and changes into another celestial being: not a constellation like the leg, but the eastern rainbow; such, indeed, is the true identity of the aquatic monster produced by the metamorphosis of the canoe and which, as the myth explains, is also the master of fish (Nim. 13, p. 120 and n. 16).

So, in addition to its seasonal code which is obvious, $M_{354}$ also employs a latent astronomical code. Having realized this, we must pay particular attention to a detail in the fourth episode, which has not yet been discussed. When the wife's pursuers catch up with her in their canoe, she hides behind the crowd of people assembled on the river bank, so that her husband and the brother-in-law accompanying him can only approach her in the form of birds, which each perch on one of her shoulders. It seems hardly possible to interpret this sequence solely in terms of the chain of syntagmatic links. But perhaps some light may be thrown on it with the help of the astronomical paradigm, as happened with the dismembered woman whose case raised a similar difficulty.

The old heroine of $M_{130}$, a doublet of the legless wife in $M_{243}$, suffers her sad fate in spite of the warnings of a domesticated bird (petoko, *Pitangus sulphuratus*), a member of the Tyrannidae family, whose cry is interpreted by present-day Indians as an invitation to dive (Ahlbrinck,

Figure 2. *Pitangus sulphuratus*. (From Brehm, *Vögel*, Vol. I, p. 548.)

under 'ombatapo', 'petoko'). For Brazilian peasants, the cry means: *bem-te-vi*, 'I can see you'. The petoko eats flesh, fish and insects and likes to perch on the backs of cows to feed on blood-bloated ticks (Ihering, under 'bem-te-vi'; Brehm, *Vögel* I, p. 549).

In a Guiana myth about the origin of Orion, which I discussed in the previous volume and which exists in several variants ($M_{278}$–$M_{279a-d}$;

*HA*, pp. 278–82), two brothers-in-law pursue their sister's murderous husband. The husband creates three birds which warn him of the danger. In a version recorded by Penard and reproduced by Koch-Grünberg (I, p. 269), these birds are the 'caracara preto' (*Ibycter americanus*), a bird of prey, and two grain-eating birds of the *Cassidix oryzivora* species. In spite of their scientific name, birds of the *Cassidix* family seem to have a very varied diet, which includes parasitic insects found on large mammals and much sought after by other birds belonging, similarly, to the Icteridae family. Throughout the continent, from north to south, it is as if American mythology had methodically located the genera or species of this family of birds in order to attribute to its most diverse representatives, acting as combinatory variants of one and the same mytheme, the functions of watchers, protectors or advisers. The Icteridae of South America correspond to the meadowlarks (*Sturnella magna*), bobolinks (*Dolichonyx oryzivorus*) and blackbirds (*Agelaius* sp.) of the North. They will have to be mentioned again later.

The versions published by Ahlbrinck (under 'peti', §9) mention two birds, *Ibycter* sp. and *Crotophaga ani*, which eat parasites found on the tapir (Goeje 1, pp. 56–7) and are therefore, from the alimentary point of view, congruous with the bem-te-vi in $M_{130}$.

If the bird into which the hero of the Tucuna myth or his brother-in-law is changed were also a *Crotophaga*, a point about which we are unfortunately ignorant, this would give us a guiding line which might put us on the track of an astronomical paradigm, since the Tucuna ($M_{358}$) believe that this dark blue, or black, bird was born from leaves which an incestuous brother used to wipe his face after his sister had rubbed genipa juice over it (Nim. 13, p. 143). As in most versions of this myth, which is known throughout the American continent and beyond (cf. *RC*, pp. 296–7), the juice-stained brother becomes the moon. The Tucuna version therefore associates the genus *Crotophaga* with the spots on the moon, in other words with its relative dimness; and it will be remembered that the macaw/wife in $M_{354}$ disappeared (i.e. 'became eclipsed', *s'est éclipsée*) when the two birds caught up with her. The Bakairi believe that the sun's eclipses are due to a *Crotophaga* which covers the luminary with its wings (Steinen 2, p. 459). In the context I have just quoted from, Nimuendaju alludes vaguely to the bird in $M_{358}$ as being 'a forest turkey, an anum [*Crotophaga minor*, Gm.], or some other black-coloured bird'. But *Crotophaga minor* is the same bird as the *C. ani* (Brehm, *Vögel*, II, p. 125) and the term 'turkey' is hardly appropriate to it, since the crotophagae all belong to the Cuculidae family. On

Figure 3. *Crotophaga minor.* (From Brehm, *Vögel*, Vol. II, p. 126.)

the other hand, the anúguassú or large crotophaga, *C. major*, which is 45 centimetres long, is more like a wild turkey in size and its habits also fit in better with the fourth episode in $M_{354}$, which ends with the appearance of the migratory fish: 'When the fish swim up the rivers, on evenings when piracema are present, the *anu-peixe*, as they are sometimes called, accompany the migration and feed on the fish they catch' (Ihering, under 'anúguassú').

Were the geographical gap not so great, it would have been tempting to compare these particulars with those of a Puelche myth ($M_{359}$), which I will summarize very briefly. Two black birds cause darkness by eating the sun's son. In order to capture the birds, the moon, then the sun, assume the form of a decaying carcass. The moon fails; the sun succeeds in capturing one of the birds but not the other, which has swallowed two of the child's small bones, thus making it impossible for him to be resurrected. The sun then summons the animals in order to decide on the respective lengths of day and night, and also of the seasons. When general agreement has been reached, the moon and the sun (who are brothers) go up into the sky, but the moon makes so much noise that the armadillos are irritated and come out of their burrows to scratch his face: this explains the origin of the markings on the moon (Lehmann-Nitsche 9, pp. 183–4).

For the time being, it is enough simply to mention this myth as one that will be referred to again later. As will subsequently appear, the problems dealt with in the present work make it necessary to have recourse to myths belonging to the southern and Andean regions of South America. On the other hand, we cannot fail to be struck by the simultaneous presence, in $M_{359}$, of several themes which could more easily be illustrated by reference to myths from the northern regions of North America: e.g. the discussion between the animals about the respective lengths of day, night, and the seasons, the preventing of resurrection through the eating of the corpse and the refusal to give back a tiny bone (this theme extends from the Coastal Salish to the Ojibwa), and the double theme of the origin of death and seasonal periodicity associated with a celestial configuration of a very particular type, which sets, on either side of the luminary – sun or moon – two stars, two planets, or two meteoric phenomena (parhelia).

This cursory survey, which testifies to the presence of the same mythic motifs in areas very remote from each other, will seem less speculative if it is realized that the Tucuna myth I am now discussing has a surprising affinity with themes which occur in northern regions of North America and even in Siberia (cf. Bogoras 1). The Koryak, the Eskimo, the Tsimshian and the Kathlamet all have versions of the story about a man who marries a succession of animal creatures and loses them one after the other, often through a misunderstanding caused by their different, non-human diet. For example, the duck-wife in the Tsimshian myth ($M_{354b}$; Boas 2, pp. 184–5) collects a large pile of mussels, but the tribal chief, offended by the sight of this plebeian food, orders it to be thrown into the sea, as a result of which the duck-wife flies away. There is an obvious similarity with the beginning of $M_{354}$.

But there is more to it than that. Like $M_{354}$, the North American versions are careful to place the story in the very earliest stages of human life: 'Once, a very long time ago, the inhabitants of this coast married female animals, such as birds, frogs, snails, mice and many others. This happened on one occasion to a great chief ...' (*ibid.*, p. 179). Similarly, a version belonging to the eastern Cree begins as follows: 'There was a man once in olden days who tried every female animal one after the other to see which was the smartest to work that he might keep her to live with him. So he tried the deer (caribou), the wolf, the moose, the fisher (pecan), the marten, the lynx, the otter, the owl, the jay, the beaver ...' ($M_{354c}$; Skinner 1, pp. 104–7). The hero of $M_{354}$ lives alone with his mother; the hero of a Menomini version lives alone with his eldest daughter, and when he loses his beaver-wife, he goes crazy with despair and behaves in a way curiously reminiscent of the actions of the hunter, Monmanéki, in the Tucuna myth, after the disappearance of his macaw-wife: 'He was so overcome by sorrow that he gave himself up to die (of hunger)' ($M_{354d}$; Skinner–Satterlee, p. 377).

In the next volume, I shall discuss in greater detail the problems posed by the astronomical codes in the myths of both North and South America. At this point, I would just like to note that the greenish halo round the sun, which the Tucuna regard as the sign of an epidemic (Nim. 13, p. 105), might well be a parhelion; that mount Vaipi, where the end of the fourth episode of $M_{354}$ takes place, is the abode of the immortals (*ibid.*, p. 141); and lastly, that the three-part configuration suggested by the two birds perched on the shoulders of a supernatural personage who is trying to 'be eclipsed', bears a remarkable resemblance to one which is used systematically in North American myths. Actually, astronomical triads are also found in Amazonia and Guiana.

*$M_{360}$. Taulipang. 'The two daughters of the moon'*

In olden times, the moon, who was a man, lived on earth with his two grown-up daughters. It so happened that Moon stole the soul of a beautiful child whom he admired, and imprisoned it under an up-turned pot. A shaman was sent to look for it. Moon thought it prudent to hide under another pot, but before doing so he asked his daughters not to reveal his hiding-place. However, the shaman broke all the pots and discovered the soul and the thief. Moon decided to withdraw into the sky with his daughters, to whom he entrusted the task of lighting the way of souls, that is, the Milky Way (K.-G. 1, pp. 53–4).

The informant explains in connection with this myth that the daughters are two planets who have each had a son by their father. They recur in another myth, which makes it clear that the two planets concerned are Venus and Jupiter.

*$M_{361}$. Taulipang. 'The two wives of the moon'*

Kapei, the moon, has two wives, both called Kaiuanóg, one in the east, the other in the west. He lives alternately with each. One feeds him well and he grows fat; the other does not look after him and he becomes thin. He moves backwards and forwards between the two, putting on weight with the first wife, then returning to the second, and so on. The women are full of jealous hatred of each other, and so live far apart. 'It will always be so!' proclaims the good cook. This is why Indians today have several wives (K.-G. 1, p. 55).

The triad formed by two minor stars situated to right and left of a major luminary would seem to be homologous with that illustrated in $M_{354}$ by the two birds perched on the heroine's shoulders. The resemblance will appear even more striking when it is noted that, just as one of the celestial wives is a good cook and the other not, the two birds in the Tucuna myth are transformations of a husband who is a good hunter and marvellous fisherman, and a ne'er-do-well brother-in-law. The configuration described by the myths of Guiana and Amazonia recurs in the extreme south of the continent among the Ona of Tierra del Fuego whose demiurge, Kwonyipe, changed into the star Antarès, part of the Scorpio constellation, where he can be seen with two stars, his wives, one on his right the other on his left, while his opponent, Chash-Kilchesh, shines in solitary splendour a long way away to the south, as the star Canopus (Bridges, p. 434). Here, now, are other triads present in myths the message of which belongs to the same group as the one transmitted by $M_{354}$.

$M_{362}$. *Macushi. 'The origin of Orion's belt, Venus and Sirius'*

There were once three brothers, only one of whom was married. One of the bachelors was handsome, and the other so ugly that the good-looking brother resolved to kill him. He made him climb up an urucu tree (*Bixa orellana*) on the pretext of gathering seeds, and took advantage of the fact that he was sitting astride a branch to run a stake through his body. The wounded man fell to the ground and died. His murderer cut the legs off the corpse and went away. A short while later, he came back to the scene of the crime where he met his sister-in-law. 'What use are these legs', he said, 'except to feed the fish?' He threw them into the water, where they changed into surubim fish [giant catfish]. The rest of the body was left lying, but the soul went up into the sky and became the three stars of Orion's belt – the body in the middle with a leg on each side. The murderer changed into Caiuanon, the planet Venus [cf. $M_{361}$: Kaiuanóg was the name of the moon's two wives], the married brother into Itenha, Sirius – in other words, two stars in the vicinity of the position occupied by the brother upon whom they would be condemned to gaze for ever as a punishment (Rodrigues 1, pp. 227–30).

A second myth is a continuation of the above:

$M_{363}$. *Macushi*. 'The origin of certain stars'
An Indian, called Pechioço, married a toad-woman called Ueré. As she never stopped calling: 'Cua! Cua! Cua! ...', he became angry and struck her a blow which cut off her thigh just above the hip. When the leg was thrown into the water, it changed into a surubim fish, while the rest of the body went up into the sky to rejoin Epepim, the victim's brother (Rodrigues 1, p. 231).

Epepim is said to be none other than the ugly brother in $M_{362}$, who became Orion's belt. Barbosa Rodrigues seems to identify the husband who committed murder with the star Canopus. Koch-Grünberg believes him to be Sirius, known as pijoso among the Taulipang and Macushi. It would follow from this that the star Itenha, which is referred to in $M_{362}$, could not be Sirius (K.-G. 1, p. 273). In order to settle the difficulty, we would have to know which star is concealed behind the name of the toad-woman, following a reference by Barbosa Rodrigues ($M_{131b}$; p. 224, n.2) in connection with a different myth: 'Ueré refers to a star'. Despite these uncertainties, $M_{363}$ nevertheless brings us back to the Tucuna myth which acted as our starting point: a frog-woman is cut into two pieces and her lower half takes on the form of a species of fish (either by metamorphosis or absorption). The same thing also happens in $M_{130}$, a variant of $M_{354}$. On the other hand, the legless woman in $M_{354}$ is a combinatory variant of a frog-woman who steals a child (her own, in fact; I shall come back to this point on p. 60); in the group under discussion, the moon plays the part of a baby-snatcher ($M_{360}$).

Koch-Grünberg (*loc. cit.*) was certainly right to relate these myths to those which explain the origin of Orion, the Hyades and the Pleiades. We must not, however, overlook certain differences which seem significant. Since the Guiana myths concerning the origin of these three constellations ($M_{28}$; $M_{134-136}$; $M_{279a,b,c}$; $M_{264}$; $M_{285}$) have been discussed at some length in previous volumes of *Introduction to a Science of Mythology*, I will restrict myself here to illustrating their modalities by the following diagram:

|  | ORION | HYADES | PLEIADES |
|---|---|---|---|
| $M_{28}$: | leg | body | // wife (*Warao*) |
| $M_{285}$: | // husband | // male tapir | wife (*Carib*?) |
| $M_{264}$: | leg | // female tapir | // body (*Carib*) |

That is, reading from top to bottom: the leg and body of a mutilated husband and his wife (the wicked sister-in-law stays behind on earth); a mutilated husband, the seducer with the woman he seduced (this time the severed leg is outside the system); finally, the leg and body of one and the same hero, disjoined by an egotistical female tapir (who is therefore a non-wife). These commutations can be more conveniently represented as follows:

| $M_{28}$: | leg | | body | | wife |
|---|---|---|---|---|---|
| | (*Orion*) | | (*Hyades*) | | (*Pleiades*) |
| $M_{285}$: | | | body | male tapir | wife |
| | | | (*Orion*) | (*Hyades*) | (*Pleiades*) |
| $M_{264}$: | leg | female tapir | body | | |
| | (*Orion*) | (*Hyades*) | (*Pleiades*) | | |

The leg is always Orion, the wife always Pleiades and the tapir always Hyades. Only the mutilated body seems to be commutable with any other of the three constellations. In the case of: *Orion* = *leg*, the culprit, whose behaviour on either occasion is the reverse of that of a wife, is either outside or inside the system. In the case of: Hyades = tapir, the animal is male or female, a seducer (sexual) or an anti-seducer (alimentary). In the case of: Pleiades = wife, the latter is either well-disposed or antagonistic towards her husband. We thus obtain at least the rough outlines of a system.

Let us now examine a second group of myths belonging to the same family but in which the wife changes into a terrestrial animal, such as an agouti, snake or armadillo, and not into a constellation. She can therefore be omitted from the diagram:

|  | ORION | HYADES | PLEIADES |
|---|---|---|---|
| $M_{134}$: | | | husband's entrails (*Akawai*?) |
| $M_{135-136}$: | leg | | husband's body (*Taulipang-Arecuna*) |
| $M_{265}$: | husband's body | | husband's brother (*Vapidiana*) |

This group, in which the brother replaces the wife in the rôle of the Pleiades, when the body (the part containing the entrails) replaces the leg in the rôle of Orion, serves as a transition to a third, also characterized by the disappearance of the woman or her transference to the rôle of victim, and the intervention of one or two brothers, as well as by the absence of all mention of the Pleiades, which emphasizes the absence of any mention of the Hyades in the previous group (Figure 4).

Consequently, at the same time as the Hyades, then the Pleiades, disappear from the system, two phenomena can be observed. First of all,

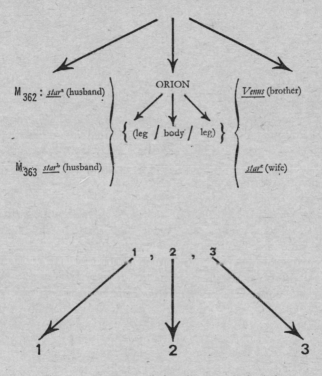

Figure 4. Astronomical and anatomical triads

the astronomical triad, which constitutes the unvarying element, is confined to Orion's belt, which it analyses out into three distinct stars. Next, a second triad, emerging from the first by a process of reduplication, extends beyond the Orion–Hyades–Pleiades system. Of the latter it retains only the central part of the Orion constellation, that is, the belt, with two stars some distance away on either side; in $M_{363}$ they are anonymous, and in $M_{362}$ they consist of one anonymous star and the planet Venus. The planet Venus is also the star which accompanies the moon in $M_{360}$–$M_{361}$, myths which describe an external triad similar in extent to the one in $M_{362}$–$M_{363}$ but symmetrical from the formal point of view with the internal triad by means of which these last myths describe Orion's belt, a constellation which, we must not forget, is 'on the side of' the sun and thus opposed to the moon (see above, p. 39). What part, then, do the Pleiades play in Macushi theory? Their origin goes back to a myth which is entirely different, but one well-known in North America and in which the Hyades reappear in the form of an animal jaw ($M_{132}$: cf. *RC*, p. 242 and n. 16). This myth exists also among the Kalina, who regard Orion as the celestial avatar of a man who has lost a leg ($M_{131c}$; Ahlbrinck, under 'sirito', 'peti').

What conclusions are to be drawn from this discussion? We note the coexistence, in the Guiana hinterland, of two traditions also present in the northern regions of North America: on the one hand, the tradition relating to an astronomical triad composed of two minor terms symmetrically framing a major term; and on the other hand, the one ascribing the origin of the Pleiades to seven characters who ascend into the sky and are, more often than not, greedy or hungry children. Elsewhere in Guiana, this second tradition (also found further south, cf. *RC*, pp. 241–3) is replaced by another, which uses the concept of the triad, borrowed from the first tradition, in order to give a joint explanation of the origin of the Pleiades, the Hyades and Orion. I do not wish to maintain that one formula is more archaic than the other. As was already noted in *The Raw and the Cooked* (p. 243, n.17), the Warao-Carib pattern also exists among the Eskimo. We are therefore dealing with two independent transformations which presumably emerged from the same basic material, one in the Arctic and the other at the Equator. But it is immediately obvious how important the discovery of such coincidences can be for theoretical anthropology. Provided structural analysis is carried far enough, the social sciences, like the physical sciences, can hope to reach a level at which the same experiments might be seen occurring in the same way in different areas and at different periods. We should thus be in a position to check and verify our theoretical assumptions.

This stage has not yet been reached, and for the time being it is enough to have been able to confirm, although in too roundabout a way, that the Tucuna myth $M_{354}$ and the Kalina myth $M_{130}$, when seen from a particular angle, continue to appear as a negative transformation of those linking the absolute origin or the relative abundance of fishing with several differentials, simultaneously made manifest on the sociological, meteorological and astronomical levels. If this point is accepted, it is possible to express much more simply the relationship linking the Guiana myths concerning the origin of certain constellations and good fishing, with the fourth episode of $M_{354}$ which deals with the origin of fish.

These Guiana myths tell the story of a *hero mutilated*/by his sister-in-law ($M_{28}$), his wife ($M_{135-136}$, $M_{265}$, $M_{285}$), his brother ($M_{134}$) or his brother-in-law ($M_{279}$)/ in spite of climbing up a *tree*, or in spite of trying to escape in a *canoe* ($M_{279}$)/, a mutilation which, directly or indirectly, causes abundance of *fish* in the water/ and the presence of the Orion constellation in the *night* sky. The second sequence of the fourth episode in $M_{354}$ presents a symmetrical construction, in that it concerns a *tree*, a future *canoe*/, *mutilated* (=felled and hollowed out) by the *hero*/in spite of his *brother-in-law* (who hinders the work by spying on him)/; a mutilation which brings about abundance of *fish* in the water/, and the presence of the rainbow in the *daytime* sky/. What it comes to is that the double transformation: *Orion* ⇒ *rainbow*, *night* ⇒ *day* reflects the circular permutation of *hero* → *tree*, *tree* → *brother-in-law*, *brother-in-law* → *hero*. It will be noted that, although in $M_{279}$ the hero who is mutilated by his brother-in-law succeeds in escaping in a canoe, in $M_{354}$ the brother-in-law is imprisoned underneath a canoe, that is, a tree which has been mutilated (felled) by the hero. But in $M_{134}$, $M_{135}$, it is the hero's wife who is imprisoned in a hollow tree.

If the 'louro chumbo', from which the canoe is made, belongs to the family of the lauraceae, as Le Cointe suggests it does (p. 260) – unfortunately without stating the genus – it is also possible to see some relevance in the various kinds of tree in which the hero undergoes his martyrdom: the urucu (*Bixa orellana*) in $M_{136}$, $M_{362}$; the avocado pear tree (*Persea gratissima*) in $M_{135}$, $M_{285}$:

> Then many ripening fruits they saw
> Bananas sweet were there;
> But still the man would climb that tree
> Where he his favourite fruit could see
> The 'avocado' pear.

> (Brett 1, p. 193.)

The *Persea* belongs to the lauraceae family, which includes various species, the wood of which is heavier than water, and which are used for the making of canoes, (Spruce, Vol. I, pp. 100, n.1, 160–61, 413; Silva, p. 184, n.19; Lowie 10, p. 9; Arnaud), in particular the false avocado tree, known as abacati-rana in Tupi (Tastevin 2, p. 689).

The reason why the avocado tree and the urucu tree are presented as being in opposition to, and in correlation with, each other is not clear, unless it is that the Bixa and the Lauraceae are among the oldest cultivated trees of tropical America. Even tribes which practise agriculture in a very rudimentary fashion give particular care and attention to the anatta trees (urucu), and the avocado tree seems to have been cultivated in Columbia from a very early period (Reichel-Dolmatoff 3, p. 85), and in Mexico from the El Riego period (6,700 to 5,000 B.C.; McNeish, p. 36). The two kinds of trees supply the stick used for making fire by friction or gyration (Bixa *in*: Barrère, p. 178; Lauraceae, *in*: Petrullo, p. 209 and pl. 13, I; Cadogan 4, pp. 65–7). Perhaps, too, an opposition should be established between the *seeds* of the urucu, which fulfil an essentially cultural function, since they supply the red dye which, as is well-known, plays an important rôle in native ornamentation, and the *fruit* (as opposed to the large, uneatable stone) of the avocado, which is highly appreciated not only by man, but also by all the animals, including the chief carnivorous ones (Spruce, Vol. 2, pp. 362–3, quoting Whiffen, p. 126, n. 2; Enders, p. 469): 'It is a well-known fact that all animals eat the avocado-pear of which even the cat family are passionately fond … I have been told that animals of every species are attracted by the fruit, and gather together under the tree' (Spruce, Vol. 2, p. 376). The urucu belongs to the domain of culture, while the 'laurels' seem to have a supernatural connotation, at least in Warao dialect in which the name of the laurel (hepuru) is derived from the word denoting the Spirits of the woods, hepu, hebu. The laurel therefore appears as the 'tree of the Spirits' (Osborn 3, pp. 256–7). Finally, the Tucuna word for the 'louro chumbo', a:ru-pana, is derived from a:ru, the name of a *Thevetia* (Nim. 13, p. 56). The Thevetial belong to the Apocynaceae family, but one at least, which bears edible fruit, although the sap of the tree is poisonous (Spruce, Vol. 1, pp. 343–4), is known as *neriifolia* (i.e. with rose-laurel leaves). In other words, it too is a member of the Apocynaceae family, which our own botanical terminology (*neriifolia*) links also with the laurel tree.

In spite of the uncertainty about the place given in the myths to trees of the lauraceae family, all the considerations put forward so far point to the same conclusion: to be interpretable, the Tucuna myth about Monmanéki, the hunter ($M_{354}$), must transmit the same *message* as the myths about the origin of Orion and the Pleiades, while at the same time employing the *vocabulary* used by the Kalina myth about the origin of Berenice's Hair to transmit an *opposite message*. So, in moving from one group to another, the code remains the same, the vocabulary changes and the messages are reversed. However, this applies only to the central part of $M_{354}$ which, it will be remembered, is concerned with the absolute origin of fish and the relative abundance of the catch. The sequel of the story raises different problems, which must now be broached.

# 2 A Clinging Half[1]

Without moving outside Guiana mythology, save in the exceptional case of $M_{357}$, which at least also belongs to tropical America, I have succeeded in solving the first part of the enigma posed by the divided woman. But what meaning is to be attached to the sequel, the episode in which the woman's upper half clings to her husband's back, starves him by devouring his food and defiles him with excrement? South American mythology offers very few examples of this story. Here, to begin with, is an Amazonian variant:

$M_{364}$. *Uitoto.* '*The rolling head*'

An Indian who liked to hunt at night aroused the anger of the spirits of the woods. They decided to take advantage of the hunter's absences to break into his hut every night. There they proceeded to dismember his wife's body and then to put it together again on hearing the noise by which the man usually announced his return. Because of this treatment, the woman's health began to deteriorate.

The hunter became suspicious and resolved to catch the spirits unawares. The latter fled, abandoning their victim who was no more than a heap of blood-stained bones; the head which had become separated from the body was rolling about all over the place. It jumped on to the man's shoulder where it remained, as a punishment, it said, for his having exposed his wife to the spirits' anger.

The head never stopped snapping its jaws open and shut, as if it wanted to bite. It ate all the food, so that the man was starved; and it covered his back with excrement. The unfortunate man tried to dive into water, but the head bit him cruelly and threatened to devour him if he did not return to the surface to allow it to recover its breath. Finally, the man made the excuse that he had to set up a fish-trap deep down in the water. The head, being afraid of drowning, agreed to

[1] TRANSLATORS' NOTE: The French word *moitié* can also have the meaning of 'better half', but the pun is impossible in English since, as will be obvious, the adjective 'better' would contradict the sense.

perch on a branch and wait for him. The man swam off through the opening of the trap, but the head rejoined him after he reached his hut. There it claimed to be the fire-woman, took up abode in the hut and asked for the manioc spatula. The hero changed them both into the species of parrot which can be heard singing by moonlight (Preuss 1, pp. 354–63).

A short episode from a Guiana story recounts one of a series of adventures experienced by a certain hero:

$M_{317}$. *Warao. 'One of Kororomanna's adventures'* (cf. *HA*, pp. 385–6)

The hero next came across a man's skull lying on the ground and what must he do but go and jerk his arrow into its eye-ball (*sic*). The skull, which was really an evil spirit, called out to him: 'You have injured me, so now you will have to carry me!' Kororomanna had to get a strip of bark and carry the skull wherever he went, as the women do with their hods, and he had to feed it too. If he shot bird or beast he always had to give a bit to the skull with the result that the latter became so heavy as to break the bark-strip support. Kororomanna took advantage of this to escape. All the ants came out of the abandoned skull (Roth. 1, p. 129; a lengthy variant exists in Wilbert 9, pp. 61–3; cf. also $M_{243}$ *ibid.*, p. 34 and *HA*, p. 188.)

$M_{364b}$. *Shipaia. 'The rolling head'*

There was once a woman whose head detached itself from her body during the night. Her husband noticed this, and after rolling the body up in a hammock buried it. Thereupon the abandoned head took up its position on the man's shoulder. He was unable to eat because it devoured all his food. Finally, he claimed that the weight of the head made it impossible for him to climb a tree and gather the fruit it demanded. It left him for a moment; he fled. The head tried different mounts – a deer which died, then a griffon-vulture which flew away, causing it to fall on the ground where it broke into pieces. The latter changed into rings which devoured the fingers of those who tried to wear them (Nim. 3, Vol. 16–17, pp. 369–70).

These versions are interesting but complicate, rather than simplify, the problem. They belong to a mythological group, evidence of which is to be found from the Arctic circle to Tierra del Fuego, and whose paradigm, especially if it includes the origin of swarming creatures or unevenly viscous substances such as ants, termites, mosquitoes, frogs, maize gruel, scum on the surface of streams, fishes' eggs, etc., makes it necessary to refer to examples from both North and South America. I shall return later to the 'rolling head' problem, but shall be able to limit its incidence by approaching it from a particular angle. To deal with it at this point would not really serve my purpose, especially since, by extending the paradigm to North America – which, as we have just seen, will be inevitable in any case – I can present the problem of the clinging-woman in much simpler terms, and provide a solution that can be quickly verified without reference to myths so numerous that their analysis would require a separate volume.

Since there is no avoiding the issue, let us take a look, then, at the North American myths in which the clinging figure is extremely well illustrated first of all by masculine characters.

M₃₆₅. *Blackfoot*. '*The legless man or the man cut in half below the waist*'

A young warrior agreed to carry back to camp on his back a com-panion who had lost both legs in battle. Every time food was given to the wounded man, it dropped through the lower half of his mutilated body. The warriors had to swim across a river, so they put the cripple on a raft that they could tow along; but they got tired and let the raft float off down the river (Wissler–Duvall, p. 154).

M₃₆₆. *Iroquois (Seneca)*. '*The clinging man*'

One day, the hero (of a very long myth) met a cripple who was lying prostrate with his feet in the water. Moved by his moans, the hero decided to take him to a dry place. The man had difficulty in getting onto his back and, having secured a hold, refused to get down. In order to free himself, the hero tried first of all to rub his back against the trunk of a hickory tree (*Hicoria* sp.), then to expose his tormentor to the heat of a large and very hot fire at the risk of getting burnt himself; finally he threw himself, together with his burden, over a very high and steep cliff. Abandoning all hope of ever being free again, he decided to hang himself, and the other man too, by putting both their necks into the same noose of a bark-rope tied to an Ameri-can lime-tree (*Tilia americana*). The attempt failed. Finally he was freed by a magic dog (Curtin–Hewitt, pp. 677–9; cf. L.-S. 13).

Here, now, are some feminine characters:

M₃₆₇. *Cree (Sweet Grass)*. '*The child born from the clot of blood*'

At a time when humans were indistinguishable from animals, a very voracious grizzly bear was reducing the skunk and her husband the badger to starvation. Husband and wife decided to run away. The bear had left them only a little buffalo blood. Skunk put it in the pot, where it changed into a miraculous child who soon grew up and killed the bear along with his sons.

Later, in a contest of magic, he overcame another bear who was reducing a village community to starvation. As a reward for his victory, he was given the bear's daughter in marriage. The other daughter became jealous and persuaded an old woman to cling to the hero's back, and he, in order to free himself, was obliged to change back into a clot of blood. The old woman at once changed into *pig-vermilion*[2] and into a phosphorescent mushroom. All the other inhabitants of the village became bears, wolves, foxes, lynxes and coyotes. And when the hero returned to his own people, he found they had changed into badgers, polecats and other edible animals (Bloomfield 1, no. 17, pp. 99–120).

In a different version ($M_{368}$; *ibid.*, no. 22, pp. 194–218), the question of the matrimonial connection comes to the fore. The hero does not succeed in getting married. Only an old woman is prepared to be his wife. Furious at being spurned, she clings to his back, crushing him under her weight and not allowing him to eat any food. He is half-dead when a stranger sets him free. Although the latter wears his fur garments with the hair on the outside, and is clumsy and ugly, the hero calls him 'brother-in-law' and gives him his sister in marriage. Later the whole family change into mice.

## $M_{369}$. *Assiniboine. 'The clinging woman'*

Long ago there lived a handsome young man who did not care for women, although they were all eager to marry him. One of them, a particularly good-looking girl, was living alone with her grandmother. She proposed to the youth, but he refused her just as he had refused the others. She complained to the old woman. The latter lay in wait for the boy and, when he passed close by her, she pretended she could not walk. He consented to carry her on his back for a short distance. But when he tried to put his burden down, she stuck tight even when he ran against trees. He began to cry and women came running to see what was the matter. But the old hag cried: 'Don't bother me! I am

[2] This is a native compound-word and the terms seem to refer to this etymology, although Bloomfield does not commit himself to an explanation.

his wife!' The hero's father made a solemn promise that whoever pulled the old woman off could marry his son. All the women tried, but all failed. Two good-looking girls who had remained in the background then approached the hero, who had collapsed out of sheer exhaustion and was lying on his stomach. One went to either side and began to pull (cf. M354, 361). At the fourth attempt they pulled the old woman off and killed her. The youth's back had been fouled by the woman's urine. After he had had his wounds doctored by his protectresses, he was quickly restored to his former condition and married them (Lowie 2, p. 180).

According to the informants, this story is supposed to symbolize the tenacity of the frog's nuptial embrace (*ibid.*, n.2). I propose to leave aside less rewarding intermediary versions (M369b: Dakota, Beckwith 2, pp. 387–9; M369c: Crow, Simms, p. 294; M369d: Skidi-Pawnee, G. A. Dorsey 1, pp. 302–3) and to go straight on to the opposite end of the Plains where the same interpretation is current:

M370. *Wichita. 'The clinging-woman'*

Once there was a young war chief who decided to organize an expedition against prairie chickens (*Tympanuchus* sp.). At that time, these birds formed a race of deceivers, all the more dangerous since they were ambidextrous and shot their arrows with either hand. On returning from a hunting expedition, the hero, as was his wont, waited to cross the river until all his companions were safely on the other side. While he was waiting at the river, there came along an old woman who asked him to help her. He willingly agreed to carry her on his back. However, she insisted that he should take her to the edge of the village, where they arrived when it was getting dark. Once again the old woman refused to get off, and she explained to the hero that she had made up her mind to marry him in order to punish him for having always refused to take a wife. Resigned to his fate, the hero agreed on condition that she got off his back. The old woman would not hear of it. She said she would never get off: she was there to stay.

So the hero had to eat and sleep with his burden. The old woman urinated and defecated on him and the man realized that his life was about to come to an end unless he was set free.

Everybody tried, but to no avail. Finally the turtle agreed to organize a ceremony during which he removed the old woman, a

Figure 5. The prairie chicken (*gélinotte des prairies*). (From Brehm, *La Vie des animaux*, Vol. 4, p. 329.)

limb at a time, by shooting arrows at her. She was then clubbed to death and the hero's back was healed. The old woman's name means: 'Something-that-will-stick-onto-anything.' Today it signifies the green tree-frog.

Fearing that another disaster might occur, the Indians split up into families and dispersed. Some turned into fowls of the air, some into beasts of the woods and plains. The chief's family became eagles (G. A. Dorsey 3, pp. 187–91).

The Sanpoil who are Salish from the Columbia river region also have a story about a clinging-woman. When the man succeeded in getting rid of her by exposing her to flames which covered her in blisters, she changed into a toad (M$_{371}$: Boas 4, p. 106).

Consequently, we possess a good deal of evidence, culled from the most diverse regions of North America, to show that the clinging-woman is a toad (or, according to M$_{369b}$, a spider of the species which carries its children on its back). Let us return now to Guiana for a while to make sure that our incursions into North American mythology have not led us into foreign territory.

In Kalina, the anurus, a large common frog, is called poloru. Taken in its figurative sense, the word means 'cramp', (poloru yapoi, 'I have cramp in my legs'): literally: 'the frog has grabbed me, has got me'; ëseirī yanatai, ëseirī polorupe na, 'my leg is stiff, numb', literally 'is a frog' (Ahlbrinck, under 'poloru'). It must not be forgotten that the clinging-woman in $M_{354}$ embodies the final variation undergone by a character who made her initial appearance in the form of a frog. This clinging-woman is also a legless woman. It would therefore seem that the thought processes of the Yabarana, a tribe belonging to the interior of Venezuela, follow a very similar pattern since, in a myth to which I shall return ($M_{416}$), the first human beings are described as being legless men and women, who took in food through their mouths, and eliminated through their throats excrement which gave rise to gymnotes (*Electrophorus electricus*; Wilbert 5, p. 59; 8, p. 150; 10, p. 56). It is well known that the electricity discharged by these fish produces cramp and sometimes even paralysis (cf. Goeje 1, p. 49).

Let us now examine the frog-woman theme from another angle. It will be remembered that the woman in $M_{354}$ steals a child who is in fact her own son. In North America, this curious action is also performed by a frog-woman who is at first completely dumb, but who talks for half the year after she has assumed her animal form ($M_{372}$; Ballard 1, pp. 127–8). With the help of numerous intermediary myths, it would be possible to show that the stealing of her own child by the frog represents, in North America, the lowest level of thieving, of which the frog is also guilty, the stealing of someone else's children, whom the batrachian covets because they are more beautiful than her own:

$M_{373}$. *Assiniboine. 'The baby-snatching frog'*

A certain Indian had many good-looking children. Those of the frog, who lived near by, were ugly. So the frog stole the Indian's youngest child and reared it. The latter were astonished: 'How is it that this child is handsome and all the rest of us ugly?' 'Oh!' replied the mother, 'I washed him in red water!' At last the father recaptured the kidnapped boy. Frog was scared and went into the water. That is why frogs live there now (Lowie 2, p. 201).

Certain Klamath variants are also known ($M_{373b}$; Barker 1, pp. 50–3; Stern, pp. 39–40) and a Modoc variant ($M_{373c}$; Curtin 1, pp. 249–53) in which the frog steals a deer's child. As a matter of fact, the theme of the baby-snatching frog or toad occurs over an extremely wide area in northern America, stretching from the Tahltan, who are Athapaskan belonging to the north-west of Canada ($M_{373d}$; Teit 7, pp. 340–1), to the central and eastern Algonquin.

A systematic study of this group would take us much too far, since it also overlaps with several others, which I shall merely indicate. First of all, the cycle of the bear-woman's children and the deer-woman's children ([frog/deer] ⇒ [deer/bear]; cf. Barrett 2, pp. 488–9, 442–3, etc.; Dangel). Next, the cycle dealing with the origin of the moon-demiurge who was stolen by milt-girls, which ranges from California to Puget Sound and the Columbia River basin ($M_{375}$; Dixon 2, pp. 75–8; 3, pp. 173–83; Adamson, pp. 158–77, 265–6, 276, 374–5 etc.; Jacobs 1, pp. 139–42). Lastly, the fatal struggle between a lunar divinity and a frog-woman in the cosmology of Southern California (C. G. DuBois, pp. 132–3, 145; Strong 1, p. 269).

Without claiming to provide a thorough analysis of these aspects, I would like to suggest the following sketch of one possible transformation:

$$
\left[
\begin{array}{l}
M_{241}: \left\{ \begin{array}{l} \text{2 women make} \\ \text{a vegetable} \\ \text{husband for themselves;} \end{array} \right. \\[2ex]
M_{375}: \left\{ \begin{array}{l} \text{a man makes 2} \\ \text{animal women} \\ \text{for himself;} \end{array} \right.
\end{array}
\right.
\left.
\begin{array}{l}
\text{husband eaten} \\
\text{(in the } \textit{alimentary} \\
\text{sense) by an ogre;} \\[2ex]
\text{women 'eaten'} \\
\text{(} \textit{sexually} \text{) by} \\
\text{their father;}
\end{array}
\right\}
\begin{array}{l}
\text{symplegades} \\
\text{(swinging doors)}
\end{array}
$$

$\not\equiv$

$$
\left[
\begin{array}{l}
M_{241}: \left\{ \begin{array}{l} \text{child stolen from} \\ \text{2 sisters by a} \\ \text{frog who marries} \\ \text{him,} \end{array} \right. \\[3ex]
M_{375}: \left\{ \begin{array}{l} \text{child stolen from} \\ \text{2 women (mother and} \\ \text{daughter) by two} \\ \text{sisters who marry} \\ \text{him,} \end{array} \right.
\end{array}
\right.
\left. \begin{array}{l} \\ \\ \text{having made} \\ \text{him grow up} \\ \text{by magical} \\ \text{means.} \end{array} \right\}
\left\{ \begin{array}{l} \text{Hero 'enlightened'} \\ \text{about his origin by} \\ \text{otters whose sense} \\ \text{of smell is } \textit{offended} \\[1ex] \textit{Blinded} \text{ Blue-Jay} \\ \text{'enlightens' the hero} \\ \text{about his origin} \ldots \end{array} \right.
$$

If, as will presently be shown, there exists an Ojibwa myth ($M_{374}$) which is a transformation of the Warao myth $M_{241}$, which in turn is a transformation of the Salish myth $M_{375}$, we must also note an important transformation, which occurs between $M_{374}$ and $M_{375}$ and which would deserve special investigation:

$$M_{374} \left[ \text{ conjoining cradle } \right] \Rightarrow M_{375} \left[ \text{ disjoining swing } \right].$$

Finally, mention must be made of the theme of the double which echoes itself, and is present independently in the Warao myth ($M_{241}$ where it is the cannibalistic jaguar) and in a myth of the coastal Salish (intestinal worm). A mythological system, which reproduces $M_{241}$ in $M_{375}$, reverses it with equal precision in another myth of similar origin ($M_{375b}$; Adamson, pp. 264–7) in which the hero is captured by an elderly mistress and learns from her who *is not* his *father*, instead of who his *mother is*.

Although these variants contain many elements characteristic of South American myths, particular attention must be paid to those emanating from the Algonquin, since in their case the comparisons are obvious enough for the two groups to be superimposed. In Penobscot, the toad is called mas-ke, which means 'smelly', 'dirty', because of the repulsion Indians feel towards toads (Speck 2, p. 276). Maski'.kcwsu, the toad-woman ($M_{373c}$), is a foul-smelling Spirit of the Woods who seduces men and kidnaps children. Clad in green moss and bark, she hangs about the camps and begs children to come to her. Should one go near her, she takes him in her arms and caresses him; but although her intentions are good, she produces a lethal effect: the child falls asleep never to wake again (Speck 3, pp. 16, 83). These beliefs form a background, common to the whole of North America, and against which the Ojibwa myths stand out with particular clarity:

*$M_{374a}$. Ojibwa. 'The Old-Toad-Woman steals a child'*
An Indian seduced by magical means, and finally married, a woman who had always rejected him. One day when the man was away, their baby was lost while the wife was out seeking firewood. Husband and wife decided to set off to look for him, each one going in a different direction. After a while, the woman reached the wigwam where the Old-Toad-Woman lived. She was the mother of two ugly children and it was she who had stolen the baby. The child had grown rapidly in stature, because the toad-woman had made him grow up magically by giving him her own urine to drink. And although she was prepared to give hospitality to the visitor, she made water on the food she offered her.

The boy had no recollection of what had happened. He took his mother for a stranger and paid court to her. She succeeded in revealing who she really was, by idenitfying the portable cradle in which her son had been carried off, and showing where the cradleboard was bitten because her (pet) dogs had tried to prevent the kidnapping. The husband, who had now caught up with his wife and son, killed a deer which he hung at the top of a balsam fir (*Abies balsamea*, cf. $M_{495}$); he sent the toad-woman to fetch it. It took her a long time to climb the tree and bring down all the meat. Taking advantage of her absence, the husband and wife smote the frog's children and, as a final gesture of scorn, stuck bladder bags full of grease into their mouths. When she saw this, the toad-woman wept bitterly (Jones I, p. 378; 2, part II, pp. 427–41).

Schoolcraft (in: Williams, pp. 260–2) had already transcribed this myth in a version ($M_{374b}$) which he published several times, and which is a particularly interesting version, not only because of its age but also because it differs in some points from those recorded later by Jones. Schoolcraft's version, which dates from the first half of the 19th century, bears a striking resemblance, as regards its details, to a group of Warao myths to which I have just referred ($M_{241, 243, 244}$) and in which a leading character is also an old frog-woman who kidnaps children. It was discussed at length in the previous volume (*HA*, pp. 180–214), but it must be referred to again in order to justify the comparison.

The heroine of $M_{241}$ is a young woman who lives with her sister in the forest, where, unaided by any man, they attend to their own needs. Such also is the heroine's situation in $M_{374b}$ (which, on this point, is a reversal of $M_{374a}$: *captured husband* ⇒ *captured wife*), since she lives alone with her dog. Each heroine, however, is supplied, one with vegetable foods ($M_{241}$), the other with meat ($M_{374b}$) by a supernatural being who agrees to become her husband, gives her a son and disappears shortly afterwards in circumstances about which $M_{374b}$ is less explicit than $M_{241}$.

In one instance, the women flee in order to escape from the ogre who has killed their husband. In the other, the child disappears mysteriously and the young woman, accompanied by her dog, sets out to find him. The flight or the search leads the mother to the house of an old frog-woman, who has stolen, or who hurriedly steals, the child, and who changes him into an adult by magical means. Also, on each occasion, the frog forces, or pretends to have forced, her adopted son to feed his mother (whom he does not recognize) on defiled food.

In North as in South America, the recognition scene occurs in a dual form. First, it is an animal which takes the initiative either because it has been offended by the smell of the hero's *excretions* ($M_{241}$) or gratified with the gift of a bowl filled with the mother's milk, that is, a *secretion*. The otters in $M_{241}$ are uncles (or in $M_{244}$ aunts), the mother's brothers or sisters; the dog in $M_{374b}$ is a 'brother' of the son. In *HA*, p. 202, I drew attention to the real or mythic rôle of 'fishing dog', a part allocated to otters by Guiana natives.

Secondly, the two groups of myths stress that revelations made by the animal protectors bring about what is virtually a state of anamnesis in the hero: he relives all his childhood. In this respect, $M_{374b}$ is particularly eloquent: the hero tastes his mother's milk[3] and receives from her the fragment bitten off by the dog and which makes it possible to identify the cradle from among all those later shown by the toad-woman. A Naskapi version, about the origin of the beluga (*Delphinapterus leucas*), depicts the return to childhood in a much more literal manner: 'the boy ... became small again and his mother started off with him through the woods' ($M_{374d}$: Speck 4, p. 25).

In South America, there is a Mundurucu myth ($M_{248}$; *HA*, p. 202) which effects the same transformation on the homologous episode in $M_{241}$, since the otters literally bring the hero back to an infantile condition by making his penis ridiculously small.

It is quite in keeping with the initial sequence of each myth that the hero, to get the frog out of the way in order to escape, should have recourse to an agricultural ruse in $M_{241}$, and a hunting ruse in $M_{347a}$. In $M_{241}$ and $M_{274b}$, however, the frog pursues the fugitives. The Warao hero delays her by obtaining wild honey for her. His Ojibwa homologue creates magical obstacles, first by throwing the flint and steel of his tinder-box (*sic*) behind him. As these objects are possibly of European origin, we will ignore them. The North American counterpart of wild honey appears shortly after when the hero, using magical means, grows a field of *snakeberries*, of which the frog is so fond that she succumbs to greed and stops to eat them. She finally resumes the chase, but the dog, obeying its master's orders, leaps on her and tears her to pieces (cf. $M_{366}$). The fate meted out to her in $M_{241}$ is less cruel: as in $M_{374a}$, she will henceforth be heard weeping and wailing.

It is not easy to identify snakeberries, since this folk term refers to

[3] It would seem that Matthews (p. 85), who gives a very free paraphrase of Schoolcraft's text, was prompted to substitute wild grape juice for the mother's milk, for the sake of decency.

several plants. It is unlikely to be the *Maianthemum* known as *snakeberry* on the Pacific coast, and the berries of which were occasionally eaten in the area between Vancouver Island and Alaska; although rich in oil, they were not much liked (Gunther, p. 25). The central and eastern Algonquin have different names for this species: deer weed, deer berry and chipmunk berry (H. H. Smith 1, pp. 373–4; 2, pp. 62–3, 105, 121). According to Wallis (2, p. 504), the Micmac give the name *snakeberry* to the great American whortleberry, *Oxycoccus Vaccinium macrocarpori*. In connection with the Potawatomi and the Ojibwa, with whom we are more directly concerned, Yarnell (p. 158) applies the term to *Actaea rubra*. The late Jacques Rousseau, the distinguished Canadian botanist who so kindly gave me the advantage of his knowledge, listed various plants sometimes referred to as *snakeberry*, but also thought the one concerned must be *Actaea*, the berries of which are red or white according to the species, and attract the attention by being at once shiny and poisonous in appearance. This evidence is supported from other sources: '*Baneberry, Snakeberry, Necklace Berry, Actaea rubra* and *A. pachypoda* (or *alba*) ... have such beautiful cherry red or ivory white fruit that it must be known that these berries are sometimes poisonous ... and cause dizziness and other symptoms indicative of their toxic nature' (Fernald–Kinsey, under *Baneberry*). Like the European Actaea, known as St Christopher's herb in French folk medicine, the American species had numerous medicinal uses depending on their varying degrees of toxicity. The Arikara gave *Actaea rubra* to women in labour in order 'to frighten the baby' and so induce the birth. An infusion of *Actaea rubra* was used to break up blood clots, and poultices made from it cured breast abscesses. The mother was washed with an infusion of *Actaea rubra* in order to encourage the flow of her milk, and the newly born infant's mouth, eyes and nostrils were bathed with it (Gilmore 2, pp. 73–7).

What we are dealing with, then, is a wild fruit offered by nature to man in the form of miniature works of art, as pretty as necklace beads, but – according to the botanists – 'sometimes poisonous'; in both these respects, they are comparable to the various kinds of honey found in tropical America that nature offers to man in the form of an already prepared food and which, while constituting a most delectable form of nourishment, can also produce physiological disorders because of their permanent or occasional toxicity. Without even having to refer back to the demonstration of the fact that berries and milt (cf. the milt-girls in M375), sometimes reduced to a single, rotten berry, illustrate a borderline form of food (L.-S. 6, pp. 36–8), as honey does in its own way, since it is on the borderline of both food and poison (*HA*, pp. 52–9), the reader will understand that berries which are attractive to the eye, although suspect, can fulfil the same semantic function as honey which presents a similar ambiguity on a purely alimentary level.

Moreover, the Coast Salish see a kind of parallelism between wild berries and hymenopterous insects, such as bees, wasps or hornets. When Blue-Jay went to the land of the dead to visit his sister he received from her a basket which he opened too soon with disastrous results. Buzzing hymenopterous insects (bees) flew out from it. Had he been more patient, they would have changed into fir-cones and berries ($M_{376a}$; Adamson, pp. 21–3). One variant explains that Blue-Jay gambled for berries with the dead and won: 'If he had not won, we would not have any berries' ($M_{376b}$; *ibid.*, p. 29).

In a Californian version ($M_{373f}$; Dixon 2, p. 77; 3, pp. 175–7) the frog, in a reversed position – instead of being the kidnapper of a moon-boy, she is a mother whose children are stolen by the sun-woman – is a basket-weaver whose enemy delays her progress by magically conjuring up such slender willows that the frog forgets everything in order to gather them. So here too the delaying obstacle has a borderline quality, being situated at the point of intersection of nature and culture. The same kind of argument might be put forward in connection with the toboggan ride, an intoxicating sport which plays the part of delaying obstacle in $M_{374d}$.

The above equivalences indirectly confirm my argument. In the preceding volume I established that the baby-snatching as well as honey-loving frog in $M_{241}$ is a transformation of the female character who was crazy about honey, a seductive food; and that she in turn is a transformation of the metaphor of a woman sexually raped by an animal seducer, and restores the metaphor to its literal meaning. The same system of transformations appears in the mythology of certain eastern Algonquin of the Wabanaki group, where the baby-snatching toad-woman is confused with the ogress, called Pook-jin-skwess in Passamaquoddy and Bukschinkwesk in Malecite, who is so enamoured of a bear whom she summons by beating on a hollow tree, that she neglects her garden and her cooking; also, as in the South American versions, she unwittingly eats either her lover's penis or his whole body (Mechling, pp. 50 *et seq.*, 83–4; Stamp, p. 243).

The pieces of bear fat which the killers in $M_{374}$ scornfully stuff into the mouths of the frog's children after murdering them occupy, then, an intermediary place between the bear-lover (whose flesh will finally be eaten by his mistress, also a mother) and the berries. Another Ojibwa myth ($M_{374c}$; Schoolcraft in: Williams, p. 85) warns the hero to be on his guard against a certain seductive food. This is a transparent, tremulous substance resembling bear-fat, but which is really frogs' eggs. The eastern Algonquin ogress referred to in the preceding paragraph also possesses an affinity with batrachians:

$M_{377}$. *Passamaquoddy*. *'The baby-snatching ogress'*

Glooskap, the demiurge, was still quite young when the ogress Pook-jin-skwess fell in love with him. When she willed it she could assume many forms, man or woman or many of them, an ugly old hag or a troop of ravishing girls. As her own children were all ugly, she used to steal Indian children and bring them up as if they were her own. From her vermin there came forth porcupines and toads (Leland, pp. 36–9).

Since the North American baby-snatching frog is a transformation of a woman who takes an animal as her lover, it follows that wild fruits, of which she is also very fond, are the equivalent of the seductive honey which occupies the same position in South American myths in relation to a baby-snatching frog, and which, as a natural, alimentary seducer, is the literal equivalent of the erotic animal.

One problem arises however. The South American myths in which a frog-heroine is featured form an integral part of a honey cycle. As I showed in the preceding volume, this is because native thought sees both an empirical and a logical relationship between bees which nest in tree trunks where they make wax or resin cells, and certain tree frogs, particularly the cunauaru, which also build resin cells in hollow trunks where they lay their eggs. Comparable in respect of their mode of life, bees are the mistresses of honey without the water with which men must dilute honey before drinking it. Even in the middle of the dry season, the cunauaru frogs remain mistresses of the stagnant water in hollow trees which is necessary to protect their eggs, but they have no honey; this explains why, in the myths, they are shown to be so passionately fond of it. The fact that bees and frogs are in correlation with, and opposition to, each other is therefore the result of what I have elsewhere called an *empirical deduction* (*HA*, p. 38, n.6; L.-S. 14).

How can a myth directly linked with honey in tropical America occur in a northern region of North America and be identical down to the tiniest details, except that in North America it is concerned with wild berries, the semantic position of which, as we have seen, is similar to that of honey, but which are very different from the empirical point of view? The recurrence of the same myth among the Warao of the Orinoco delta and the Ojibwa of the Great Lakes area is already an enigma, and one which is further complicated by the fact that the southern version appears, objectively, to be more coherent than the northern one. Had the myth travelled from south to north, one could have understood that, in the absence of honey, wild berries might offer an acceptable substitute. But the peopling of America took place in the opposite direction, and it seems extraordinary that a northern myth should have had to wait until it chanced upon a ready-made vocabulary in tropical ethno-zoology to find a better means of expressing its message than the material it had had to make do with in the original fable.

But there is more to it than that. The Great Lakes area, where the myth originates, is the land of the maple tree, the sap of which the Indians can transform into syrup or granulated sugar, which bears a much greater resemblance to honey than berries do. In the sixth part of this book, I propose to study the place occupied by maple-syrup in the myths of the central Algonquin. For the moment, I need only draw the reader's attention to one aspect: there seems to be a much greater difference between tree-sap, which is no more than a refreshing drink, and syrup or sugar requiring a complicated process of preparation than there is between raw honey and fermented honey. Raw honey is a concentrated food, ready for consumption; on both counts it can act as a point of articulation between nature and culture. Neither the maple-sap which is still on the side of nature, nor the syrup or sugar which are already on the side of culture can, then, constitute a signifier suited to the demands of the story. The South American frog can be tempted by honey which is immediately available in the hollow of a tree; but the maple-sap would not be sufficiently enticing, and only in the distant past did the syrup flow spontaneously from the tree without its production depending on the arts of civilization ($M_{501}$). So the honey/berries alternative appears to be justified.

Had the North American Indians been familiar with, and made use of, varieties of wild honey on the same scale as their fellow Indians in the South, it would be possible to formulate the hypothesis that the transformation: *honey* ⇒ *berries* occurred in their area. According to information kindly given me by M. S. E. McGregor, head of the Apiculture Section of the U.S. Department of Agriculture and by

M. B. L. Fontana, an anthropologist on the staff of the Arizona State Museum, it would appear that Meliponidae were once found across the Mexican border and even in the southern part of the United States. According to recent evidence, huge nests made from some cardboard-like substance can be observed hanging from trees in the Mexican state of Sonora. These nests are the work of very small, stingless but highly aggressive bees which bite (*Trigona?*), and they contain a honey so thick that it does not flow from the combs: it has to be softened by heating before it can be removed (Terrell). Yet research has gleaned from the Cahita, who live along the Pacific coast in the north-west of Mexico, only a fragment of a myth in which honey plays a part (Beals, pp. 16, 220–1), and it is so meagre as to be uninterpretable. A wild honey produced by hornets or carpenter-bees which nest in the crevices of houses was used in cooking and in ritual ceremonies by the Pueblo Indians and their neighbours the Pima (Cushing, pp. 256, 304, 625, 641). The Californian Indians harvested small quantities of the honey of certain bumble-bees (Sparkman, pp. 35–6; C. DuBois, p. 155; Goldschmidt, p. 401) and traces of the same practice are to be found even in the state of Washington (Jacobs 1, pp. 19, 108; Adamson, pp. 145–50, 189). It is often impossible to know whether the honey referred to is real honey or more probably, the honey-dew of certain plants such as the *Agave parryi*, by means of which – according to the Pomo – the universal conflagration was extinguished and terrestrial water re-created (Barrett 2, p. 472). Before the arrival of Europeans, the Cherokee probably sweetened their food with the pods of the bean-tree (*Gleditschia triacanthos*; Kilpatrick, p. 192, n.39). Finally, European bees have sometimes reverted to the wild state; Indians of the south-west, who are honey-gatherers, find it difficult to believe that *Apis mellifica* appeared in America only about a century ago (McGregor).

There is no reason to suppose that the native honey-producing bees were not once present over much wider areas of North America than is the case today, nor is it impossible that the introduction of the European species may have caused their disappearance. Chateaubriand (1, p. 121; 2, I, p. 239) is no doubt repeating what he had been told by the settlers when he notes that they 'are often preceded, in the woods of Kentucky and Tennessee, by bees ... These peaceful conquerors, which are foreign to America, and arrived in the wake of Columbus, steal from this new world of flowers only those treasures which the natives had never put to use'. But he immediately contradicts the epithet 'peaceful' by adding that the bees got the better of the myriads of insects which attacked their swarms in tree trunks. Such insects, in addition to mosquitoes and sand-flies, might well have included meliponae, although he does not mention them by name, since they frequently indulged in robbery (*HA*, p. 81, n.8). Whether or not meliponae were found in central and northern districts it is difficult to say, in spite of the Cheyenne origin myth which describes how the First men 'lived on honey and wild fruits and were never hungry' (Dorsey 4, p. 34). The Arapaho, who are close relatives of the Cheyenne, seem to remember wild honey but deny ever having eaten it (Hilger 2, p. 178). And the use of honey by the Menomini to bait bear traps (Skinner 4, pp. 188-9) must be a relatively late practice, since the Iroquois told Kalm in 1748-50 that they had never seen bees, which they called 'English flies', before the arrival of the English (Waugh, p. 143).

Generally speaking, it must be accepted that there is an almost complete absence of any mythology of honey in North America. The contrast with the wealth of honey myths in South America – which provided the material for a whole volume – is so striking that the difference is significant. There remains the possibility that the myth featuring the baby-snatching frog was given its original form in the south of the United States, where meliponae may have once been present, and that it spread both to the south and the north. The presence of *Nectarina lecheguana* has been attested in Texas (Schwartz 2, p. 11). We should even accept it as a fact that there were meliponae further north, if the honey, which unidentified Indians (probably Kansas or Osage) used to gather in quantity from hollow trees at the very beginning of the 19th century (Hunter, p. 269), was not already produced by European bees which had reverted to the wild state. If so, it must be taken as significant that the myth about the clinging-woman, who is herself a frog indissolubly linked with the other frog for a reason which will presently be explained, is distributed along an axis which corresponds approximately to that of the Caddo settlement. Finally, the position of the Warao is no doubt relevant, since they were in the Orinoco delta, opposite the lesser Antilles (cf. Bullen) which could provide a series of stepping-stones to the greater Antilles and Florida. When it was supposed that the peopling of America took place hardly more than 5,000 years ago, this lapse of time was considered long enough to allow successive waves of migration from Alaska to reach Tierra del Fuego. Now that the peopling of America is believed to go back ten or twenty thousand years or even further,[4] the possibility of population shifts in

---

[4] After being greeted first of all with enthusiasm, earlier estimates were very soon

both directions should perhaps be considered. The case of the myths featuring a frog-woman is certainly not the only one which might lead us to infer that a late migratory wave may have occurred from south to north, rather than in the opposite direction. But, if several population shifts in both directions did take place, the isthmus should still bear some traces of them, and so far no evidence of even a single journey has been found. There remains the possibility of the sea-routes, including the one by way of the Antilles. The question has been raised many times, and has always been given despairingly negative answers (Sturtevant). The case cannot be closed, however, as long as several problems remain unsolved: for instance, that of the existence and destination of the 'yokes' or 'collars' made of stones found in the Antilles and on the Gulf coast and which are associated with carved stones bearing a strong resemblance to each other, and called in some places 'palmas', in others 'three-pointed stones'; also the striking similarities between the petroglyphs representing long-eared figures, along the North-West Coast and in Puerto-Rico.

Let us now leave historical speculation and return to the more solid ground of structural analysis. We are dealing with two paradigms – the clinging-woman and the frog-woman – whose area of distribution covers both North and South America. In either hemisphere, these paradigms are independently linked; it has been verified that both in the north and the south the clinging-woman is a frog. Lastly, we can see the reason for this union: one states literally what the other expresses metaphorically. The clinging-woman adheres physically, and in the most abject manner, to the back of her bearer, who is, or whom she would like to be, her husband. The frog-woman, an adoptive but excessive mother, and often, too, an aged mistress who cannot resign herself to the departure of her gallant, is reminiscent of a type of woman who, in modern speech, is referred to as 'clinging',[5] although we use the term figuratively.

The correctness of this interpretation is, moreover, brought out by

---

disproved, but they now appear more reliable since the discovery, in the Yukon basin and in Mexico, of deposits at least 20,000 years old and probably much older, containing tools made of bones, mixed with vestiges of extinct animal forms (cf. *Scientific American*, Vol. 216, no. 6, 1967, p. 57).

[5] TRANSLATORS' NOTE: *Collante* (from *colle*, glue) suggests a tedious person who cannot be got rid of; 'clinging' seems to be the nearest translation, although it tends to have the pleasanter sense of 'dependent' or 'helpless'. Here it must be given an aggressive connotation.

the English expression used to describe the clinging-woman in the myths. She is called *burr-woman*, which is not a mere catchword, arbitrarily fixed upon by folklorists. The idea is difficult to convey in French, since the language has no common-or-garden word like 'burr' for those parts of certain plants, mostly bracts but sometimes also leaves with curved prickles, which catch onto the clothes of passers-by. However, there exist versions of the clinging-woman myth which purport to explain the origin of these vegetable forms.

$M_{378}$. *Pawnee (Skidi). 'The origin of cockle-burrs'*

A man and wife who were being tormented by a voracious she-bear were saved, thanks to a mysterious child who emerged from a clot of buffalo's blood [cf. $M_{367}$]. He killed the she-bear, then decided to set out on his travels. One adventure led him to a village where he earned the gratitude of the people. He was offered all the young girls in marriage but none found favour in his eyes. To punish him for his indifference, a woman stuck onto his back and refused to let go. Magic animals came to the hero's aid and tore the woman off in pieces which changed into cockle-burrs (G. A. Dorsey 1, p. 87).

According to a variant in the collection ($M_{379}$, pp. 302–3), the hero has a passion for gambling (and because of this takes no interest in girls). He meets a lovely young person who asks him to help her across the creek. He puts her on his back, but she refuses to get down and claims to be his wife: 'Her body had grown into the boy's flesh so that she was stuck to him.' Soon she changes into an old woman. Four sisters come to help him and, using an ointment given them by the sun, they detach the woman and tear off her limbs one after the other with hooks that are also magic. The pieces of the body became cockle-burrs.

These myths are identical with $M_{370}$, which features a frog instead of burrs. According to the Assiniboine ($M_{369}$), the frog has a very tenacious nuptial embrace. By way of introduction to their myth about the clinging-woman, the Arapaho explain that the curved bracts of the American burweed (*Xanthium* sp.) 'represent the desire to get married, the search for a husband or a wife' (Dorsey 5, p. 66). Long curved bracts, known as 'woman-chasers', are used as models for the decorative patterns which young men paint on their faces and bodies during certain ceremonies (Kroeber 3, III, pp. 183–4).

$M_{380}$. *Arapaho. 'The deceiver who was too much loved'*

Having been rescued from an awkward situation by a troop of young girls [var: mice-women], Nihançan the deceiver asked them to delouse him. He laid his head on their laps and went to sleep. The women covered his head with cockle-burrs and left him. As he rolled about the embedded cockle-burrs adhered tightly, drawing his face out of shape. When he awoke, his head and face were hurting. On placing his hand on his head, he found that the cockle-burrs had collected so thickly that he set to work and cut off the hair very close.

What he had taken for women were really cockle-burrs: and the point of the story is that they wanted him for a husband (Dorsey 5, p. 66; Dorsey–Kroeber, pp. 108–10).[6]

The Mandan ($M_{512}$; Bowers 1, pp. 352, 365) tell a story in a similar vein about a shy virgin, whose clothes became covered one day with cockle-burrs. She went back into the hut in order to undress. A shadow passed over her naked body, making her pregnant by Oxinhede, Acting-Foolish (the Sun's Fool) . . .

I was not mistaken, then, in hoping that North American myths might shed light on the meaning of a South American myth, which, as I had surmised from the outset, poses the problem of matrimonial alliance, as do all the myths of the clinging-woman cycle. In $M_{354}$, Monmanéki the hunter appears at first to have a dilettantish approach to marriage. He is a kind of hyperbolic Don Juan who, not being content, as we say in French (but already using sub-specific differences) *d'aller de la brune à la blonde* (to flit from brunette to blonde), extends his amorous curiosity to a great variety of animal species, such as batrachians, birds and invertebrates. In this respect he resembles the hero of an Arikara version ($M_{370c}$). The Arikara are a North American tribe neighbouring on the Mandan but belonging, like the Pawnee and the Wichita, to the Caddo linguistic group.

Both are lucky hunters, and the Arikara hero, having once copulated with a buffalo woman, also excels at a game of skill. The game consists in throwing a small ring which had to be caught on a stick while it was still moving. In the myth, it is symbolic on three counts: copulation, war, and buffalo-hunting, which lies half-way between the two (Dorsey 6, pp. 94–101). However, the Tucuna and Arikara versions differ on two major points. One deals with the origin of fishing, the other with

---

[6] The Oglala Dakota believe cockle-burrs to be symbols of desire or jealousy (Walker, p. 141, n. 1). The Cherokee offer them in the form of a decoction to prospective initiates, for 'as the burrs stick and cling to anything that comes in contact with them, they will also be of material assistance in keeping the acquired knowledge in the mind' (Mooney–Olbrechts, p. 101).

buffalo-hunting. What is more important, the Arikara hero, apart from his brief incursion into bestiality, is chaste: he has never had any dealings with women, and the old woman clinging to his back reproaches him for his abstinence: 'Grandson, you might as well go home, for I am to stay with you always. Let the young men see you carry an old woman! That will teach you to be so proud that you do not look at the women!' On the contrary, the Tucuna hero's clinging-woman forces herself upon him to punish him for having been a woman-chaser: he is an *insufficiently shy husband*, taking the place of the *excessively shy bachelor* in the North American versions I have listed.

But, at the same time, one peculiarity of these versions is made clear. The difference I have just pointed out at the beginning of the myths is echoed by another corresponding difference at the end: most of the North American versions conclude with the separation of humans and animals, and the division of the latter into distinct zoological species (Cree: $M_{367, 368}$; Wichita: $M_{370}$). In the South American myth, the separation, which is of recent date, is mentioned only at the beginning. The Tucuna hero therefore treats the female animals as if they were still members of human society, whereas the Cree and Wichita heroes, in rejecting the human women, treat them as potential members of animal species, which they only become at the end. The present order of the world requires humans to intermarry, without being too demanding within these limitations (otherwise marriage would become impossible), since animals too are divided up into species whose members also intermarry among themselves, and not with those of other species, or with humans. The Arikara version acts as a point of articulation between these two extreme arrangements; the reason is that it deals with one particular animal species, the buffalo, and successful buffalo hunting is based on the notion of a complicity, intermediary between the complicity illustrated by the union (which is also a duel) of man and woman in marriage, and that illustrated by the duel (which is also a union) between traditionally hostile communities (cf. L.-S. 16).

Proof of this can be given. If the Tucuna myth about the clinging-woman is an inversion of the North American myths on the same theme, the inverted forms of the latter myths, in North America itself, should bring us back to the Tucuna myth. I have drawn attention to inversions of this kind, notably in myths belonging to the Wabanaki group, in which the frog-woman, who is fond of human children, sometimes changes into a human, the mistress of an animal seducer. The Penobscot, who distinguish between the two characters, making one strong and the other weak, tell (M381) of the amorous experiences of Pukdji'nskwessu, the jug- or scab-woman, who took a bear as her husband (cf. M377) and, on another occasion, a big stick which she tied round her waist tight against her. But when she tried to get back into her wigwam, she could not get rid of the stick: 'I am your husband,' said the stick, 'you tied me here, and I will have to stay. You can't get rid of me.' After that, wherever she went, she had to take the stick with her (Speck 3, p. 83). It is clear then that, apart from the sex inversion, this myth restores the armature of the Tucuna myth.

There are also cases where the North American myths are inverted in the opposite direction or along other axes. As an instance of the first type, a version belonging to the Coast Salish can be quoted (M382; Adamson, pp. 171, 377–8), in which the demiurge Moon, who has put on a hat which he cannot remove, offers to marry the first woman who can take it off. Only the ugly toad-woman manages to do so. In future, it can happen that ugly women will marry handsome men. This transformation is of special interest, since it can be broken down into two operations:

a) *clinging-woman* $^{(-1)}$ $\Rightarrow$ *toad-woman*;

(in other words, the inversion of the paradigm depending on the notion of contiguity:

*clinging-woman* $\Rightarrow$ *woman-who-delivers-from-a-clinging-hat*,

reconstitutes the paradigm based on similarity: '*clinging*'-*woman*). But this reversal from a literal to a figurative meaning involves a consequence:

b) *sociologically equivalent wives* $\Rightarrow$ *physically non-equivalent wives*,

that is, the restoring of an anatomical paradigm establishing individual differences between wives within that human society, which, in the 'straight' versions of the myth, the anatomical paradigm was intended to distinguish as a whole from the animal kingdom (while at the same time dividing the latter into different genera and species). Thus, from being exteriorized in nature, the anatomical paradigm changes into being interiorized in society, the biological foundation of which it reveals. The transition from the *literal* to the *figurative* meaning, which is ensured by the first operation, brings about by reaction the reverse operation: that which, beneath the illusion of *moral* order, discloses the underlying truth of a *physical* disorder.

What do the myths proclaim? That it is wicked and dangerous to confuse physical differences between women with the specific differences separating animals from humans, or animals from each other. This anticipatory form of racialism would be a threat to social life, which demands, on the contrary, that as *human beings*, women, whether beautiful or ugly, all deserve to obtain husbands. When contrasted in the mass with animal wives, human wives are all equally valid; but if the armature of the myth is reversed, it cannot but reveal a mysterious fact that society tries to ignore: all human females are not equal, for nothing can prevent them being different from each other in their animal essence, which means that they are not all equally desirable to prospective husbands.

It would be appropriate to examine, in greater detail than is possible here, other permutations leading to results of the same type. An Arapaho myth (M₃₈₃) relates how Nihançan, the trickster, insisted on accompanying young men on the war-path and on carrying the lower-part of a woman which helped to make their solitude more acceptable (inversion of clinging-woman). But he let the precious object fall. It broke into two equal parts and could no longer be used. By chance, Nihançan discovered a village entirely inhabited by women, a potential complement to the group of bachelor warriors, who, having been informed of this, decided to organize a race in which the fastest would have the prettiest women. On the pretext of giving them all an equal chance, they persuaded Nihançan to load himself with stones. He was easily the last to arrive and had to make do with an old woman (Dorsey–Kroeber, pp. 105–7). Among the Shoshone (M₃₈₄), the clinging-woman first appears as the feminine counterpart of the ingenious bachelors of M₃₈₃: she masturbates with an artificial phallus. Her nephew Coyote peeps to see what she is doing, and she puts her arms round him so tightly that he finds his muscles are gone on both sides of his back. After further adventures, which threaten Coyote's anatomical integrity by subtraction or addition, he finally loses his member in his sister-in-law's vagina: this explains the origin of a woman's smell (Lowie 4, pp. 92–102). Since there are so many versions of M₃₈₅, I single out only one, about young warriors returning from an expedition. In order to husband their strength, they climb on the back of a giant turtle which is going in their direction. But they cling on to it when it plunges into a lake, and are all drowned (from the Sioux to the Indians of the south-east, by way of the Crow, the Cheyenne, the Paiute and the Pawnee). The myth reverses the story of the clinging-woman along two axes:

*clinging-woman/clinging-men*, and: frog/turtle. A Guiana version ($M_{386}$) rectifies the situation, at least with regard to the second axis, since the animal which carries off the young men is a frog (Brett 2, pp. 167–71; cf. $M_{149a}$, RC, p. 264; K.-G. 1, pp. 51–3; Goeje 1, p. 116).

In the Guiana bestiary, the turtle acts as a mount for the moon, a hermaphrodite creature, like the Passamaquoddy baby-snatcher ($M_{377}$), from whose vermin came toads and who, as we have seen, is the North American equivalent of the Guiana frog. Symmetrically, the Indians of the north-west of North America make the frog ride on the moon's back, and link this astronomical paradigm with the sociological paradigm, the importance of which has been stressed in the preceding pages: according to the Lilloet ($M_{399}$; below, p. 103), the frog sisters clung to Moon's face after Beaver had caused a deluge in order to be revenged on the frogs who refused to marry him (Teit 2, p. 298; cf. Reichard 3, pp. 62, 68).[7]

So far, the astronomical paradigm has been left in the background; not that I underestimate its importance; the reader must already have been struck by the 'lunar' aspect of myths featuring a clinging-woman or a frog-woman. In fact, the problem appears so far-reaching that it calls for a separate analysis and will be the subject of the second part of this book. I shall conclude this first part with a number of more general observations confirming the hypothesis, already formulated in the preceding pages, that the myth group which has just been studied belongs to the same complex as the one studied in Volume Two, which was confined to tropical America and dealt with the origin of honey.

I stressed the fact that South American myths about the origin of honey were often concerned with its loss. I explained this peculiarity by

---

[7] I draw the attention of research workers to the fact that this complex system appears to be linked with pottery. The heroine of the Penobscot is a 'jug-woman'. The clinging-woman of a Ponca version ($M_{370b}$; J. O. Dorsey 1, p. 217) is a potter. According to the Jivaro of Peru, the night-jar (*caprimulgus*) was once the wife of the brothers Sun and Moon; but this attempt at polyandry failed: it explains the origin of conjugal jealousy and earthenware ($M_{387}$; Farabee 2, pp. 124–5; Karsten 2, pp. 335–6; Lehmann-Nitsche 8). It is well-known that the Mexican codices represent the moon as a jug. The Popol Vuh tells how, after their defeat, the people of Xibalba were reduced to being potters and bee-keepers (J. E. Thompson 1, p. 44).

The Hidatsa myths, which will be introduced later, feature a jealous woman who orders that no woman must even touch her husband or even brush against his clothes; she is a water-spirit, the mistress of pottery and more particularly of two ritual pots, one male, the other female, over which skin is stretched and which are used as drums for bringing rain – a function which also devolves on frogs – during the summer drought ($M_{387c}$; Bowers 2, p. 390).

a regressive process characteristic of myths in which the search for honey, as it is carried out today, is believed to be the residue or vestige of an easier and more profitable activity, the benefit of which was lost to mankind in circumstances the myths set out to describe. The fact is that honey holds pride of place in the hierarchy of native foodstuffs; and yet its perfection, to which human industry adds little or nothing, and the absence of regulations governing its gathering and immediate consumption (which is in such marked contrast to the very strict rules about hunting and agriculture, especially among the Ge) make honey a paradoxal substance: it is a food prized above all others, although man finds it, as it were, in the state of nature and although, in order to obtain it, he himself has temporarily to regress from the social state.

I also observed that in myths which take honey as their theme, the regression from culture to nature often makes use of devices of a metalinguistic order; confusion between the signifier and the signified, the word and the thing, the figurative meaning and the literal meaning, and between resemblance and contiguity. In this respect it is significant that similar devices can be found in those areas of North America to which I have had to turn in order to complete my paradigms:

$M_{388}$. *Menomini.* '*The frogs' song*'

There was once an Indian who made it a practice to listen to frogs and toads when they thaw out and sing in early spring. The batrachians however were indignant: the man thought mistakenly that they were happy; on the contrary, they were in deep sadness and, far from rejoicing when they croaked, they were wailing for their dead who had not wakened from their winter sleep. ... The Indian had completely misunderstood the situation and should be taught a lesson: now it was his turn to cry!

Sure enough, next spring, the Indian lost his wife and children, as a result of which he died. Ever since, Indians know that they must not go on purpose to listen to the cries of frogs in the early spring (Skinner–Satterlee, p. 470).

Like the characters in several South American myths, the central figure of which is sometimes also a frog (or a bee, but in that case replacing an inverted frog; cf. $M_{233-239}$, *HA*, pp. 153–80), the hero of $M_{388}$ commits the error of mistaking one thing for another; he interprets in terms of contiguity (the coming of spring) that which he ought to have understood by resemblance (the frogs' song is sad); he attributes to nature (seasonal periodicity) that which belongs to culture (funeral dirges). In short, like the hero in $M_{236}$, he dies because he has failed to grasp the difference between the literal and the figurative meanings.

The loss of the constituent categories of human thought and existence, which is so typical of the 'frog' myths and which was described in the preceding volume, causes the gradual distortion of a series of oppositions: between nature and culture; between the domestic hearth, where good cooking takes place, and vomiting, the result of bad cooking; between food and excrement; between hunting and cannibalism. A similar kind of regression can be observed at the beginning of $M_{354}$, which has served as my theme up till now. There too, in fact, a frog, a chance encounter with which starts the hero off on a series of adventures, is guilty of a triple confusion: first, between excretion and copulation, then between what is food (for her) and what human beings believe ought to be classed as excrement; and finally between condiment and aliment. These equivalences can be simplified by means of another Amazonian myth.

$M_{389}$. *Mundurucu. 'The origin of toads'*

A man whose love-making all the women avoided because his sperm burnt their vaginas consoled himself by masturbating over a gourd. Every time he ejaculated into it, he closed it up again and carefully hid it. But his sister found it and opened it: out came toads of every species, which had been born from the sperm. The sister also changed into a toad of the bumtay'a species. And when the man found the gourd was empty, he became a mëu toad (Kruse 2, p. 634).

There is no need to attach much importance to the zoological families mentioned in the myths, since, as Ihering rightly notes (under 'sapo'), Brazilian popular speech refers to almost every kind of batrachian as 'toad'.

The inversion: *distant woman* (frog) / *near woman* (sister) is echoed by another on the level of the physiological functions: *alimentation/copulation*. In $M_{354}$, the wife of an Indian (she has become his wife as a result of physical contiguity) ingests peppers, a hot food, and is turned back into a frog. In $M_{389}$, a woman (who resembles a wife psychologically, in the sense that she becomes involved in her brother's sex-life) is the sister of an Indian who ejects a secretion which stings like pepper and she becomes a frog. We thus arrive at the formulation:

a) $M_{354}$ $\left[ nutrition \ \cup \ peppers \right] \Rightarrow \left[ exogamous \ wife \ // \ frog \right] \Rightarrow frog$

b) $M_{389}$ $\left[ copulation \ \cup \ peppers \right] \Rightarrow \left[ endogamous \ wife \ // \ toad \right] \Rightarrow toad.$

This is tantamount to saying, as I admitted, that in respect of the batrachian mytheme the *copulation/nutrition* opposition has no relevance.

$M_{390}$. *Cashinawa. 'The greedy toad'*

Two women who had remained alone in the hut while the others were in the fields made insulting remarks to a toad who was singing in the hollow trunk of a dead tree. The animal emerged in the form of a small corpulent old man: 'I was crying,' he said, 'you reproached me for singing too much!' (cf. $M_{388}$). In order to pacify him the women gave him something to eat; he swallowed it all including the dish. When the men came back, they lit a huge fire and burnt the tree which was the toad's home. As he died the toad vomited up the dish which fell to the ground and broke into pieces (Abreu, pp. 227–30).

This dish-eating toad, who is a combinatory variant of the filth-eating frog in $M_{354}$, is also characterized by the tendency to confuse opposites. He mixes up food and receptacle, just as his feminine counterpart failed to distinguish between spices and inedible food, and copulation and excretion.

While we are still on the subject of the ambiguity of categories, let us go back briefly to a subject already dealt with. I have shown how myths or parts of myths, some dealing with a clinging-woman, others with a frog-woman, constitute two parallel series one of which expresses literally (a woman actually stuck to her husband's back) what the other expresses figuratively (a 'clinging' woman). The Mundurucu, a tribe not far removed from the Tucuna, whose mythology as we have just seen ($M_{389}$) is akin to theirs, have a myth in which the hero displays literally, in respect of a frog-woman, natural gifts comparable to the mental attitude which prompts the hero of $M_{354}$ to carry his search for a wife as far as the batrachians. Giving the term a metaphorical connotation, I described this hero as a woman-chaser. The other one is afflicted with a long penis, a symbol which decency prevents us from using, but one which none the less corresponds, on a sexual level, to a figurative expression which we use freely in French in a social context when we say of someone that he has *le bras long* (a long arm; i.e. 'is very influential'. Cf. in English, 'the long arm of the law').

M$_{248}$. *Mundurucu. 'The cure effected by the otters'* (cf. *HA*, pp. 203–5)

One day, in the forest, a hunter heard a female frog called Wawa singing: 'Wa, wa, wa, wa' in a croaking voice. He went up to the animal, which was sitting in a hole in a tree, and said to her: 'Why are you making that grunting noise? Be mine and you will grunt from the pain of my penis when it is inside you.' But the frog continued to sing and the man went his way.

As soon as his back was turned, Wawa changed into a beautiful young woman wearing a lovely bluish dress. She appeared on the path in front of the man and asked him to repeat what he had said. In spite of his denials, she reproduced his words exactly, and since she was willing and beautiful, the Indian agreed to take her as his wife.

They walked along the path a bit, and before long the man wanted to have coitus. 'All right,' said Wawa, 'but warn me when you are ready to ejaculate.' At that instant, Wawa changed herself back into a frog and went hopping off, stretching her partner's penis, which she held fast inside her vagina. He stood helplessly as she hopped away and stretched his penis out to an incredible length. After it had stretched to about fifty feet, the frog released her grip and disappeared. The unfortunate man would have liked to return home but his penis had become so long and heavy that he could neither drag it along nor carry it coiled round his shoulders or waist. Some passing otters found him in a state of utter despair. They asked what was wrong and said they would fix him up by applying a caratinga fish, after roasting it just enough to heat it. The penis at once began to shrink. 'Is that enough?' asked the otters. 'No, a little more,' said the man. A second application reduced his penis to the size of his little finger. The Mundurucu name for the caratinga fish indicates the connection with this story. And the reason why the caratinga is only half black is that it was only half roasted (Murphy 1, p. 127).

According to Murphy, the caratinga belongs to the *Diapterus* species of the Gerridae family (*ibid.*, p. 142) which, according to Ihering (under 'caratinga') has a very well developed spike in its anal region and might therefore suggest the idea of a fish with a long penis. Since Ihering maintains that the fish belongs to a marine and not a river species, I shall not try to use this aspect of the myth but merely draw attention to two analogies. The first one is with the Cashinawa $M_{000}$ and the Menomini $M_{388}$ since, in all three cases, the hero (or heroine) fails to understand the frog's song and ascribes to it a meaning different from the real meaning, imagining it to be a cheerful song and not a dirge, a harbinger of spring or an invitation to love. The second, more important, analogy is with the hunter Monmanéki in the Tucuna myth $(M_{354})$, whose amorous temperament throws him into the arms of a frog-woman, in consequence of a conjunction brought about by the jet of urine which extends his penis symbolically as far as the creature's 'hole', and enables her to win him.

There is, however, a difference. Monmanéki is an active woman-chaser, whose long metaphorical penis allows him to have all kinds of amorous adventures, whereas the hero of the Mundurucu myth $(M_{248})$ is afflicted with a real long penis, which, however, incapacitates him and causes him such discomfort that he is driven to the other extreme and is left in the end with a pathetically small penis. To accomplish this transformation the myth chooses the otters, in other words the masters of fishing (cf. HA, pp. 205-8) and a fish, whereas, in $M_{354}$, Monmanéki is himself the master of fishing and the creator of fish.

This group of correlations is all the more remarkable in that Monmanéki creates fish from wood chippings, a theme which is much in evidence elsewhere, but the main distribution area of which, like that of the man-with-the-long-penis theme, includes the most northerly tribes of North America: the Eskimo as well as Indians living on the North-West Coast and in the Columbia basin. The reindeer Eskimo believe that the man who created fish from wood chippings had a long penis. The Polar Eskimo, who call him Qajungajugssuaq, and those of Western Greenland say that he is afflicted with enormous testicles, which hang right down to the ground and cause him shame and embarrassment (Kleivan, pp. 17, 21; Holtved 1, p. 57). Although the long testicles cause their owner psychological embarrassment, the long penis, in the mythology of the Polar Eskimo, enjoys a physical auto-nomy which is conducive to activity (Holtved 1, p. 64), and this is also the case in several South American versions $(M_{49}, _{50}, _{77}, _{79}, _{80})$. Most of the versions belonging to the north-west of North America and the Plains, which I shall not discuss here, assign an intermediary rôle to the long penis: it has no physical autonomy, since it remains attached to its owner's body, but it allows the latter to indulge his whims in all kinds of ways. Whether real or metaphorical, the long penis can, then, according to circumstances, assume antithetical functions: it can be either an active means of having adventures, or a passive burden which paralyses and humiliates its owner. In this second function, the long penis is transformed, in Eskimo mythology, into long testicles (but thus remains in the lower register), whereas in the east, among the Iroquois who are familiar with the long penis theme, the testicles change into long upper eye-lids, thus moving into the upper register (Curtin–Hewitt, p. 213).

The presence of a fisherman with long testicles in a Warao myth ($M_{317}$; cf. below, p. 83), and of a man with a drooping nose in a Guarayu myth (Cardus, p. 76), provides evidence of the fact that transformation rules of the same type are observed in South America. The misfortune which befell the Mundurucu hero in $M_{248}$ recalls that of a Tacana Indian ($M_{256}$; HA, p. 207) who wanted to copulate with the moon and whose penis grew so long that he had to weave a basket to carry it in. The Tumupasa ($M_{256b}$), who are neighbours of the Tacana, tell how the sun surprised Lady Moon and her young sister, the planet Venus, in the act of stealing from his garden. The sun forced the moon to become his mistress and his penis grew so long that he had to carry it in a basket. One day Venus started stealing from the sun again. The latter pointed his penis in her direction, but the young girl mistook it for a snake and cut it in two with her knife. The sun died and went off into the heavenly vault (Nordenskiöld 3, pp. 296–7). Among these Indians of Lower Bolivia, the transformation: *long penis* ⇒ *long testicles*, may well have re-emerged in a weakened form in the character of the tapir, who is endowed not only with a large penis (cf. HA, p. 411) but also with three testicles. The Tumupasa believe ($M_{256c}$; Hissink–Hahn, p. 163) that these anatomical peculiarities are to be explained by the fact that the tapir copulated with his wife just when – as was her wont – she had devoured the waning moon, and without waiting for her to release it so that it could begin to wax again on the other side of the horizon.

South American rituals also bear witness to the link between the man with the long penis and the moon: 'When the moon is full ... young Mocovi boys pull their noses and ask him to lengthen this organ' (Guevara, in: Métraux 5, p. 20). The ancient Araucan worshipped the sun, the moon and batrachians all at the same time, no doubt because the sun's son, also called 'twelve suns', 'mareupu-antü', was himself a frog or toad. In its successive phases the moon, 'cüyen', personified a young girl, a pregnant woman and an emaciated old woman.[8] According

---

[8] Couto de Magalhães (p. 171) remarks, in connection with the Tupi: 'It would seem that the Indians believe each of the moon's phases to be a different being.'

to one chronicler's account, when the moon was full 'the dancers
tied to their sexual organs a finger-thick rope of wool, on which the
women and young girls pulled. This rite was followed by promiscuous
scenes' (Latcham 2, pp. 378–86).

In certain myths the long penis is the result of copulation, in others
its pre-condition (Hissink–Hahn, pp. 82–3): the moon is so far away
from the earth that her human lover would never unite with her, unless
she took care to provide him with a sufficiently extended member. The
moon's remoteness is physical, whereas the frog in $M_{354}$, $M_{248}$ symbol-
izes, through the effect of a metaphor, a woman who is socially too
remote. Once again, then, we are referred back to the astronomical
paradigm. Before tackling it, as I must do, I would like to summarize
what my procedure has been so far. A comparison covering both North
and South America has made it possible to consolidate myths which
seemed to belong to two distinct groups: those with a clinging-woman
as heroine and those in which the character is a frog-woman. The two
groups of myths transmit the same message, which in each instance
concerns a clinging woman, although the attribute may be literal in
one case and figurative in the other.

However, at the same time, a further result has been obtained, since
three themes have also been consolidated: the frog's lover, the man
with the long penis and the creator of fish. The Mundurucu link the
first and second, the Tucuna the first and third (while at the same time
assigning a place to the second, which, however, is expressed metaphorically); while the Eskimo, for their part, join together the second
and third themes. From this system of equivalences, a final stage in the
argument makes it possible to infer that the man with the long penis
and the clinging-woman, who are brought into correlation with, and
set in opposition to, each other in the same myths, have symmetrical
qualities: he can reach a mistress from a distance, and she can only be
a wife by sticking to her husband's back. Like the clinging-woman, her
masculine counterpart can have both a literal and a figurative meaning.
Consequently, the two successive operations which I have carried out
in order to consolidate myths or parts of myths, makes it possible to
link together groups I had, in the first place, consolidated separately.

In short, myths which appeared heterogeneous in content and geographical origin, can all be reduced to a single message, of which they
effect transformations along two axes, one stylistic and the other lexico-
logical. Some are expressed literally, others figuratively. And the
vocabulary they use relates to three separate categories: the real, the

symbolic and the imaginary. For it is a fact of experience that there are clinging women and woman-chasers, whereas the cockle-burrs and the snake-like penises are symbols, and marriage between a man and a frog or a worm belongs purely to the realm of the imagination.

# PART TWO  FROM MYTH TO NOVEL

*Dryads and water-nymphs can appeal to the imagination, provided they do not recur incessantly; I certainly have no wish to*

> *... Chasser les Tritons de l'empire des eaux,*
> *Oter à Pan sa flûte, aux Parques leurs ciseaux ...*
> *(... Drive the Tritons from their watery realm,*
> *Deprive Pan of his flute, or the Parcae of their*
> *                                          shears ...)*

*But what remains of all this deep down in the soul? What effect is there for the heart? What benefit can thought derive from it?*

> Chateaubriand, *Génie du christianisme,*
> *Livre IV, Ch. 1*

# 1 The Days and the Seasons

> *It is not impossible to maintain that much vaunted mythology, far from embellishing nature, destroys its real charms, and I believe that several distinguished men of letters are now of this opinion.*
>
> Chateaubriand, *Génie du Christianisme,*
> *Livre IV, Ch. 1*

In Part One, I showed that the Monmanéki myth concerning the origin of fish and fishing, belongs to a vast group which also includes Guiana myths about the origin of certain constellations: Orion and the Pleiades on the one hand, and Berenice's Hair on the other. The myths relative to Orion and the Pleiades are concerned with the appearance of fish in the spring, and the one relative to Berenice's Hair with their disappearance because of the severe conditions prevailing during the main dry season. The originality of $M_{354}$ lies in the fact that it transmits the same message as the first ones (the appearance of fish, first of all in the absolute when the hero creates them, then in the relative form of the seasonal swim upstream), while using the same vocabulary as the other (the legless woman).

It should be recalled that the Tucuna regard the moon and the Orion constellation as being antagonistic to each other; the latter, in the form of the demon 'venkiča', who is associated with the jaguar clan, causes lunar eclipses (Nim. 13, p. 142). We shall consider this character again later. For the moment, it need only be stressed that his clan connection refers to beliefs which are very widespread in tropical America and which, in the case of the region of origin of the myths I am dealing with here, exist just as much among the Carib and the Arawak (Farabee 1, pp. 101, 107) as among the Tupi. Along the Eastern coast, the latter used the name januaré, 'dog' (but cf. iauré, iaurété, 'jaguar') for a red star which pursues the moon in order to devour it (Claude d'Abbeville, ch. LI). The same belief has been recorded among the Guarani, the Chiriguano, the Guarayu and other southern Tupi.

Lastly, it will be remembered that, while Orion is antagonistic to the moon, together with Berenice's Hair it maintains a collaborational relationship with the sun (see above, p. 40). It can therefore be postulated that the myth about Monmanéki the hunter, which is an inversion of the myths about the origin of Orion in respect of its vocabulary and the myth about the origin of Berenice's Hair in respect of its message, has itself a link with both the moon and the sun. Because of the double inversion, this relationship would seem to be only diurnal and not nocturnal, as indeed the myth suggests by referring to a single meteoric phenomenon: the rainbow. I propose to verify this hypothesis in two ways, first indirectly and then directly.

Several Amazonian myths, such as Tucuna ($M_{403}$) and Mundurucu ($M_{255}$), present the sun and the moon as masters of fishing. The two luminaries therefore fill this rôle concurrently with Orion and the Pleiades, on the one hand, and Berenice's Hair on the other, although each team plays the part in its own way: Orion and the Pleiades are responsible for the *appearance* of fish, Berenice's Hair for their *disappearance*, while the sun and the moon ensure their *resurrection* which, as it were, neutralizes the opposition between the first two terms:

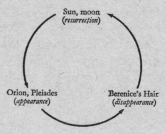

Sun, moon
(*resurrection*)

Orion, Pleiades          Berenice's Hair
(*appearance*)            (*disappearance*)

The diagram already shows that if, after setting off from Orion and the Pleiades supply the starting point of the transformation, as is sug-impossible to avoid passing through the sun and the moon as well, since they are situated on the return route. This, in fact, is what happens in the myth in question ($M_{354}$). To be convinced of this, one has only to suppose: first, that the Guiana myths about the origin of Orion and the Pleiades supply the starting-point of the transformation, as is suggested by the pan-American distribution of the myths associating the Pleiades with entrails and Orion with a severed limb (*RC*, pp. 216–17,

240-6); and then that $M_{354}$, which cannot be explained syntagmatically, is connected with a paradigm in which it occupies a derivative position in relationship to the myth about Berenice's Hair (cf. above, pp. 37-40); in other words $M_{354}$ is an inversion of $M_{130}$, and not the other way round. We can, then, set out the matter as follows:

$$M_{134-136} \left[ (\text{Orion–Pleiades}) : (\text{fish} (+)) \right] :: M_{130} \left[ (\text{Berenice's Hair}) \right.$$

$$\left. : (\text{fish} (-)) \right] :: M_{354} \left[ (\text{Berenice's Hair} (^{-1}) : (\text{fish} (+)) \right]$$

It is easy to understand why the very notion of a constellation should disappear during the transformation, since the latter takes place in three stages, only the first of which has to do with reality. The myths dealing with the origin of Orion and the Pleiades do no more than state the empirical coincidence of a celestial event and a zoological occurrence: it is nowhere stated that constellations give rise to fish, whereas, symbolically at least, Berenice's Hair aims at exterminating them, and in order to conjure up the reverse phenomenon, while using the same vocabulary, it would be necessary to imagine an anticonstellation (but without claiming to be able to describe it). This being so, only one problem remains. Why, as the constellation gradually fades out, must the sun and the moon make their appearance? We shall see that the outline of the two luminaries can be glimpsed through the fog caused by the dissolution of the constellation, although only vaguely and as if behind frosted glass. This brings us back to the problem of the presence, in $M_{354}$, of an astronomical code left in a latent state. The problem can be broached directly, when formulated in this way.

Of all the myths of the New World, none perhaps is more widely distributed, from the extreme north to the southernmost regions, than that which attributes the origin of the sun and moon to an incestuous relationship, voluntarily or involuntarily entered into by a brother and a sister ($M_{165-168}$), (RC, pp. 296-9), that is, individuals united by *too close* a tie. In central and northern Brazil, an axis perpendicular to the preceding one, and roughly following the course of the Amazon, illustrates in successive stages – if followed in an east–west direction – the fusion between this myth and another, which is also extremely widespread and recounts the adventures of a severed head. I have quoted other examples of it ($M_{317}$, $M_{364}$, $364b$), but now let us first discover it in its pure state in the mythology of the eastern Tupi:

$M_{391}$. *Tembé*. *'The rolling head'*

Some hunters were camping in the forest after having slaughtered a large number of animals and their barbecues were collapsing under the weight of the game. Heads, pelts and entrails were lying strewn on the ground. A young boy was in charge of the smoking while the other men hunted. Suddenly there appeared a stranger who, with a look of displeasure, inspected the game, counted the hammocks and fled. When the hunters returned, the boy told them of the stranger's visit, but none of them paid any attention to it. Later, during the night, he repeated the story to his father, whose hammock was near his own, and managed to alarm him. They both took down their hammocks and went off to the forest to sleep. Shortly after they heard cries of nocturnal animals, human moans and groans and the cracking of broken bones. It was the Curupira and his band, the protective spirits of game, who were slaughtering the disrespectful hunters.

When day dawned, the two men returned to the camp where, amid the blood-stained hammocks and bones, they discovered the severed head of one of their fellow-hunters, which begged them to take it with them. The father told the boy to go on in front, and he tied the head to the end of a creeper in order to drag it along. Every time he gave way to fear and tried to abandon the head, it rolled up to him imploring him to take it with him. On the pretext that he had an urgent need to defecate, the man ran ahead and dug a pitfall in the middle of the path, covering it over with leaves. As the head grew impatient, the hunter's excrement replied in his place that he had not finished. 'When I lived among humans,' the head remarked, 'excrement did not talk.' It moved forward and fell into the pitfall. The man lost no time in covering it over with earth, and went back to the village. During the night, the head which had managed to free itself could be heard howling. It had changed into an enormous bird of prey, which devoured the first Indian it encountered. A shaman managed to kill it with an arrow which went in at one eye and came out by the other (Nim. 2, pp. 290–1; Baldus 2, pp. 47–9; variant in: Wagley–Galvão, pp. 145–6).

The episode of the head with pierced eyes, which concludes the myth, makes it possible to introduce a Mundurucu myth, which was no doubt recorded as an isolated story but which is clearly a continuation of $M_{255}$, already referred to in the course of the preceding pages.

After the two brothers-in-law had been changed by the celestial divinities, one into a handsome and distinguished man because he had not committed incest with his 'mother' (the moon), the other into an ugly cripple as a punishment for the opposite behaviour, the story relates how enemies killed them and carried off their severed heads:

$M_{255}$. *Mundurucu.* '*The origin of the suns of winter and summer*' (continuation and conclusion; cf. *HA*, pp. 205-6)

The heads were placed on top of posts and a small fat boy was given the task of guarding them. He himself was unaware that he had inherited shamanistic powers and was the first to show surprise when the heads began moving and talking. 'They are getting ready to rise into the sky,' he cried to the elders of the tribe. But, in spite of his protestations to the contrary, everybody thought he was telling lies.

The warriors adorned the heads with red urucu paint and decorated them with feathers. At noon, the heads, accompanied by their wives, were seen to rise skywards. One couple rose rapidly, but the other ascended slowly because the wife was pregnant. The warriors shot arrows at the heads and all missed, except one shaft bent by the fat boy which put out both eyes of the head which had belonged to the ugly man. The two heroes, both children of the sun as a result of their stay in the moon's womb, appear as the visible sun. When it is sunny and bright, the beautiful man is in the sky and his eyes shine a bright red. When it is dark and cloudy, it is because the ugly man, whose wife is the visible moon, is in the sky: he is ashamed to show his ugliness and his eyes are dull and lifeless. He hides, and humans do not see the sun (Murphy 1, pp. 85-6; cf. Kruse 3, pp. 1,000-1,002).

This myth brings together three themes: incest, which in this case takes place with a mother; the story of one or more severed heads; and lastly, the alternation of the seasons, defined by the opposition between a bright and a dark sky, homologous with the alternation between day and night, since the winter sun's wife is the moon. Continuing our east-west prospection, we shall encounter these three interlinked themes again, but only after a doubly significant transformation:

maternal incest is replaced by sororal incest, and periodicity changes
from being seasonal to being monthly:

$M_{392}$. *Kuniba*. '*The rolling head and the origin of the moon*'

A young Indian woman was visited every night by a stranger whose
face she rubbed on one occasion with the bluish-black juice of the
genipa. In this way, she discovered that her lover was her brother.
The culprit was driven out; as he fled, enemies killed him and cut off
his head. Another brother, who was trying to rejoin him, offered the
head shelter. But it never stopped asking for food and drink; the
man resorted to craft, abandoned it and fled. It managed to roll as
far as the village and attempted to get inside his hut. As it was not
allowed to enter, it considered in turn several possible metamor-
phoses: into water, stone, etc. Finally, it chose to be the moon, and
rose into the sky unrolling a ball of thread as it went. In order to be
revenged on his sister who had denounced him, the man, now
changed into the moon, inflicted the curse of menstruation on her
(version recorded by Nimuendaju, in: Baldus 2, pp. 108–9).

Baldus rightly compares the above myth with the Tembé myth
($M_{391}$). The Kuniba, who are now extinct, spoke Arawak and used to
occupy territory along the left bank of the middle reaches of the
Jurua, which was relatively close to that occupied further west by the
Cashinawa, who themselves belonged to the Pano linguistic family.
Koch-Grunberg (3, p. 328) had already drawn attention to the affinity
between the Tembé myth and a Karaja myth ($M_{177}$; *HA*, pp. 396–7)
and, as Baldus (2, p. 108) following Nimuendaju observes, the discovery
of a Kuniba version still further strengthens the impression that, in the
minds of the Amazonian tribes, the severed head theme and that of the
moon's origin were interlinked. No doubt it would be possible to quote
examples of the same link in the mythology of North American tribes:
Iroquois (Hewitt 1, pp. 201, 295–6, etc.) and Pawnee (G. A. Dorsey 2,
pp. 31–8), but in these cases the theme of fraternal incest is absent, since
most of the myths in this group, whether belonging to North or South
America, associate it with only one of the other two themes, that of the
moon's origin, and make no mention of the severed head episode (cf.
for instance, the obscure Bororo version $M_{392b}$, in: Rondon, pp. 164–5).
This creates a difficulty which can be overcome by studying the
Cashinawa myths.

$M_{393}$. *Cashinawa. 'The origin of the moon'* (1)

Two tribes were at war. One day, an Indian met an enemy and tried to run away. The other man, to calm his fears, gave him a large bundle of arrows. He then invited him to go with him to his village, in order, so he claimed, to visit his wife who would certainly be delighted to welcome a stranger. Full of joy, the Indian picked up his arrows and donned his feathered head-dress. On the way his companion and he stopped to eat fruit which blackened their teeth. When they arrived outside the hut, the guest hesitated, feeling frightened. His guide encouraged him, and he tidied himself up: he smoothed out his hair with a comb and put on his ornaments and bracelets. An excellent hammock was hung up so that he could rest, and the wife served a copious feast which the two men were unable to finish. The guest was told to wrap up what was left and take it back home with him. When he came to take his leave, his host, as polite as ever, insisted on accompanying him part of the way. As, at the same time, the host picked up his weapons and a large, extremely sharp bush knife, the other man became uneasy. He was told that the knife was to cut wood and make a digging stick. But the Indian, laden with his food, did not get far: the other man chopped his head off; the body remained upright, swayed for a moment, and then fell. Seeing that the eyes continued to blink, the murderer stuck the head on a post planted in the middle of the path, and went off. One of the victim's compatriots came along. At first, he was terrified at the sight of the head with its long hair flapping in the wind. It was not dead: its eyes were shining, its eyelids flickering, its tears flowing and its lips moving, but it was unable to reply to any of the questions put to it. The compatriot went back to seek help in the village. Well-armed warriors set out to look for the head; the murderer, who was not far away, climbed into a tree to follow what was happening. When the head's fellow-Indians had finished mingling their tears with its own, they buried the body and put the head in a basket. To no avail: the head gnawed the bottom with its teeth and dropped out. After various other attempts to deal with it, someone had the idea of clasping it tightly in his arms, but it bit the bearer viciously.

Losing heart, the men abandoned the head and fled. It rolled behind them, hurling reproaches. They had to cross a river; the head crossed too. The fugitives climbed into a tall fruit tree overhanging the bank; the head saw them and took up its position at the foot of the tree. It demanded fruit; they threw down unripe fruit, but it insisted on ripe fruit which was no sooner swallowed than it came out through the severed throat [cf. $M_{317}$, $M_{354}$]. It was not deceived when they threw fruit into the river in the hope that it would drown. However, one man had the idea of hurling the fruit some distance away and this caused the head to move off far enough for the men to climb down and continue their flight. They were all safely inside their huts by the time the head, still rolling, reached the village.

It beseeched them with tears to let it in and give it back its belongings. They agreed to throw it its balls of thread through a tiny opening. 'What shall I become?' the head wondered. 'Vegetables or fruit? People will eat me up. Earth? People will walk on me. A garden? People will sow seeds in me, plants will ripen and people will eat them. Water? People will drink it. A fish? People will eat it. Fish poison? People will pull it up and dilute it with water, thanks to it they will eat the captured fish. Game? People will kill it and eat it. A snake? But men will hate me, I shall bite them and they will kill me. A poisonous insect? I shall bite people and they will kill me too. A tree? People will fell me and when I have dried out, they will cut me up into fire-wood in order to cook food, which they will eat. A bat? I shall bite in the dark and you will kill me. The sun? But I shall be able to warm you when you are cold. Rain? I shall fall, the rivers will swell, you will catch fish which are good to eat, or I shall make the grass grow and game will feed on it. The cold? When it is too hot, I can make you cool. Night? You will be able to sleep. Morning? I shall be the one to wake you up so that you can get on with the day's work. So what shall I be? I have an idea! With my blood I will make the rainbow, the path of the enemies; with my eyes I will make the stars; and with my head the moon. And then your wives and daughters will bleed.' 'But why?' asked the frightened Indian women. And the head replied: 'For no reason.'

The head collected its own blood in a bowl and sprinkled the sky with it. As it flowed, the blood marked out the path of the strangers. The head pulled out its eyes, which became countless stars. It handed over the balls of thread to the vulture, which used them to pull the head up to the highest point in the sky. The Indians all came out of their huts to gaze at the rainbow and, when night fell, at the full moon and the stars which were shining for the first time. Then the women began to have periods, their husbands copulated with them and they became pregnant (Abreu, pp. 458–74).

There are two further known versions of this myth. One (M₃₉₃ᵦ) briefly tells how the head of a warrior who had been decapitated during a nocturnal attack changed into the moon. It states more clearly than the subsequent one, which I have just summarized, that women only obtained the ability to conceive after the simultaneous appearance of the moon and menstrual periods. At birth, all the children (or possibly – since the wording of the myth is not easy to interpret – those conceived during the full moon) would have 'very black bodies' (Abreu, pp. 454–8). Is this to be interpreted as a reference to the so-called 'Mongolian spots' which are of frequent occurrence in South America, and would be thus associated in the native mind with moon spots? I shall come to this question later.

The other version grafts the episode of the head which turns into the moon onto a story that seems different, at least at first sight:

*M₃₉₄. Cashinawa. 'The origin of the moon' (3)*

Once there was neither moon, stars, nor rainbow, and the night was totally dark. This situation changed because of a young girl who did not want to get married. She was called iaça [cf. Tupi jacy, 'moon']. Exasperated by her obstinacy, the mother sent her daughter away. The young girl wandered for a long time in tears, and when she tried to return home the old woman refused to open the door. 'You can sleep outside,' she cried. 'That will teach you not to want to get married!' The young girl ran frantically about in all directions, beat on the door and sobbed. The mother was so infuriated by this behaviour that she took a bush knife, opened the door to her daughter and cut off her head, which rolled onto the ground. Then she threw the body into the river.

During the night the head rolled and moaned round the hut. After wondering about its future [cf. M₃₉₃], it decided to change into the moon. 'In this way,' it reflected, 'I shall be seen only from afar.' The head promised the mother not to bear her any ill-will, provided she gave it its balls of thread; by holding one end between its teeth, it got the vulture to take it up into the sky. The eyes of the decapitated woman became the stars and her blood the rainbow. Henceforth women would bleed each month, then the blood would clot and children with black bodies would be born to them. But if the sperm clotted, the children would be born white (Abreu, pp. 475–9).

Apart from the stylistic device of eliminative enumeration to which I have already drawn attention (*RC*, p. 272 and n. 36), because it appears in a whole series of South American myths and is found in the west and north-west of North America, from California to the Arctic Circle by way of the Columbia basin, and even east of the Rockies (Assiniboine: Lowie 6, pp. 3–4; Blackfoot: Josselin de Jong 2, p. 36), these Cashinawa myths raise several problems that I propose to study in turn.

Before doing so, I would like to digress for a moment. The fact that I am limiting my inventory to the Cashinawa does not mean that the rolling-head theme is absent further west. It occupies an important place in Andean mythology, and its southern area of distribution can be traced from the Tacana of Eastern Bolivia to Tierra del Fuego. However, from the Tacana onwards, the triple connection with which we are concerned begins to become blurred. The severed head theme is separated off from the other two dealing with the moon and an excessive attitude towards marriage, expressed positively by incest or negatively by celibacy. The Tacana, however, prefer to believe in the existence of a whole race of cannibalistic heads, tijui, resulting from the transformation of hunters killed by falling from the tops of trees ($M_{395a}$; Hissink–Hahn, p. 244), or by the attacks of coatá or guariba monkeys (*Ateles* and *Alouatta*; $M_{395b,c}$ *ibid.*, pp. 125–44, 242–3). Sometimes the severed heads give rise to the chima or chonta palm (*Guilielma* sp.), the fruits of which resemble hairy heads and provide food for fish (*ibid.*, pp. 68–72); then, after being thrown 'to the end of the world', they become a star which is visible in the morning.

The *star//fish* disjunction refers us back to North America where the decapitated wife's husband becomes a star, whereas the severed head, which is initially cannibalistic, but subsequently becomes either one of the Pleiades (Eskimo: Holtved 1, pp. 16–18) or a sturgeon, beluga, 'white fish', or again the eggs of these fish (Cree: Bloomfield 2, pp. 271–9; Ojibwa: Schoolcraft in: Williams, pp. 212–13; 268–73; Naskapi: Speck 4, pp. 24–5, $M_{374d}$). On the other hand, a Cavina version of $M_{395}$ (the Cavina are neighbours of the Tacana) attributes the origin of the rolling head turned meteor to self-dismembering (Nordenskiöld 3, pp. 294–5), a variant which is also found in the north-west of North America, from California to the upper reaches of the Columbia river. Over an even greater area, which includes the preceding one, the rolling head story is said to derive from the one about the animal seducer ($M_{150-159}$). A woman who takes an animal lover offers an exact counterpart to the hunter Monmanéki in $M_{354}$; he is a man who takes a female animal as his wife. Lastly, it should be noted that an Arawak myth from Guiana ($M_{396}$; Roth 1, pp. 175–6), which belongs to the pan-American mythic cycle of the ogre who is killed on the pretext of being made more beautiful, attributes the origin of goat-suckers (night-jars) to brains scattered from a crushed head (cf. the bird of prey in $M_{391}$). The central and western Algonquin and several of their southerly neighbours, possess a myth ($M_{397}$; Jones 3, p. 13, 130) in which the goat-sucker, by violently breaking wind, causes a rolling rock to burst open: this rock is homologous both with the rolling head and the clinging-woman, which is not surprising, since in America the goat-sucker is a symbol of oral avidity (L.-S. 17) and can therefore behave in a manner which is the reverse of anal retention. Similarly, the rolling-head, one of the forms taken by a promiscuous woman in the North American myths, is an inversion of the clinging-woman figure, who in turn is one of the forms taken by the wife of a man who, according to circumstances and area, may be too much ($M_{354}$) or too little ($M_{368-369}$) of a woman-chaser.

Consequently, there can be no doubt that if one went right round America from the Arctic Circle to Tierra del Fuego it would be possible to offer a generalized interpretation of all the 'rolling-head' myths, into which one could easily fit those I am dealing with here and which come from a much more restricted area extending from the Tembé to the Cashinawa. I may some day undertake this long peregrination. For the time being, as I have already explained, I prefer to isolate the sub-set in which the three themes of the rolling head, the reprehensible marriage (or the rejection of marriage, which is no less reprehensible) and the origin of the moon are clearly linked. If we approach the problem by way of the astronomical paradigm, it will be possible, with the help of the Cashinawa myths, to amplify and elaborate the analysis of those South American myths on which attention has been centred from the beginning of this book.

Compared with $M_{354}$, the Cashinawa versions enrich the sociological paradigm in two ways. Instead of telling the story of a man who looks for a wife either too far away or too near, they feature either a man ($M_{393}$) or a woman ($M_{394}$). The man behaves as a *too-trusting traveller*, who treats his enemies as if they are affines. The woman, on the other hand, is *home-loving* and *too-distrustful*: being driven from home fills her with despair, but in rejecting marriage which, among the Cashinawa, is usually between cross-cousins (Métraux 15, p. 677), she treats as enemies the people near to her and who are her potential affines.

When interpreted in this way, the two main Cashinawa versions can be placed at the respectively masculine and feminine extremities of an axis (which can be imagined as running horizontally) and which establishes an oppositional relationship between the too-trusting behaviour of a man who is presumably married (since he carries off food for his family), and the over-shy behaviour of a young girl who refuses to be

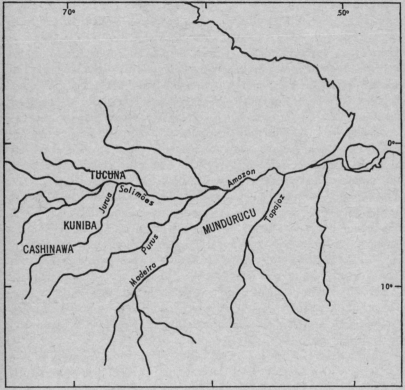

Figure 6.  Tucuna and other tribes

married. On this axis, therefore, the opposition between the sexes is relevant. The equally relevant opposition between kinds of behaviour is defined by deficiency; in order to escape their identical fates, the shy virgin ought to have been more trusting and the trusting visitor more shy (Figure 7).

There is a Tucuna myth already summarized ($M_{358}$) which has the same oppositional relationship with $M_{354}$ as the two Cashinawa versions have with each other: the two Tucuna myths can, therefore, be placed at either extremity of an axis perpendicular to the previous one. The hero of $M_{358}$, is an incestuous brother: although of the same sex as the venturesome husband, the hero of $M_{354}$, he differs from this husband in that his behaviour is excessive in a reverse direction: the two heroes assign themselves respectively one or several goals in their amorous enterprises, and these goals are either too near (the hero's own sister, within the social group) or too far (animal wives, beyond the pale of humanity). Along this new axis, the opposition between the sexes is no longer relevant. The opposition between the attitudes remains, although these are now characterized by excess and not by deficiency.

The Kuniba version ($M_{392}$), which is identical in its first part with $M_{358}$ and with $M_{393}$ in the second, is equidistant from both. But because of its conclusion (the moon originating from a severed head) it can be placed on a line connecting $M_{393}$ to $M_{394}$ (since both have the same conclusion) but outside the axis in reference to which these two myths are in opposition to each other.

Going back over the same ground by way of the shy virgin story, we encounter now a series of mainly Mundurucu myths, which lead back by successive stages to the story of the venturesome husband: the virgin secluded during the puberty rites and who takes a dog as her lover ($M_{398}$: Murphy 1, pp. 114–16); and the young unmarried girl who has a love-affair with a snake ($M_{49}$; RC, p. 124). The Mundurucu regard this myth as an inversion of the story of the married man who abandons his human wife for an animal mistress, a female sloth, since it contains a specific reference to the story ($M_{286}$: Murphy 1, p. 125; Kruse 2, p. 631; HA, p. 306). This last myth must link up with $M_{354}$, since the sloth-woman is afraid that her lover's legitimate wife may jeer at her black teeth (cf. the hero's mother in $M_{354}$, who jeers at the black beetles, the staple diet of her frog-daughter-in-law); and when they lose their beloved animals (sloth-woman or macaw-woman), both heroes give way to despair.

The use of certain Mundurucu myths to ensure the transition from the character of the shy girl to that of the venturesome husband can be justified in two ways. The Mundurucu, like the Tucuna, are an Amazonian tribe; and alongside the Kuniba myth and in symmetrical fashion, another Mundurucu myth ensures the transition between the incestuous brother figure and the too-trusting visitor. This is $M_{255}$, which also combines the three themes with which we are concerned: the origin (of the husband) of the moon, since the story deals with the winter sun; the severed head; and lastly incest – in this case, with a divinized moon. No doubt, the divinized moon is a mother, not (the brother of) a sister, but I shall return to this interpretation of the origin of the sun and moon as being brought about by incest between relatives – a transformation of incest between full brother and sister – and which also occurs between father and daughter, in a Tacana myth ($M_{414}$:

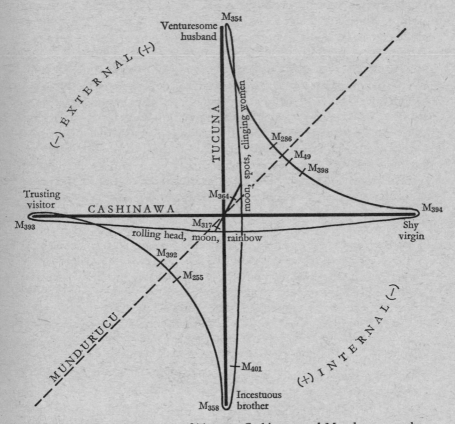

Figure 7. Group structure of Tucuna, Cashinawa and Mundurucu myths

Hissink–Hahn, pp. 79–80). The distribution of the Mundurucu myths along a diagonal line, as shown in Figure 7, seems all the more significant in that these Indians do not develop the rolling-head theme in their myth; perhaps because, being traditionally head-hunters and greatly attached to their trophy-heads, which they used to decorate very lavishly, they attributed a positive, and not a negative, value to severed heads, at the same time as they transferred that value from the mythic to the ritualistic level. The question is not without interest, especially since Mundurucu mythology is peculiar in establishing a correlation, not between the head and the severed leg, but between the head and the humerus, the head being that of a dead, decapitated, enemy and the arm-bone that of a dead comrade; so important was it to take away the arm for mummification and burial on the return to the village that Mundurucu Indians adopted the practice of amputating the limbs of men who were too seriously wounded to get back alive (cf. Murphy 1, pp. 53–8).

But let us return to the diagram. If the myths constitute a closed group, we should be able to trace the curve of the intermediary types by joining up, outside the axis along which they are in opposition to each other, the venturesome husband figure with that of the incestuous brother. Let us try to effect this link. Both in South and North America, there are many instances of the incestuous brother becoming the moon, and having his face blackened in places by his sister with soot or genipa juice. We can move up, then, from the incestuous brother to the origin of the moon spots. In the opposite direction, as we know – since that is how $M_{354}$ proceeds – it is possible to move down from the venturesome husband to the clinging-woman. There exists a series of North American myths in which the clinging-woman becomes a frog attached to the face of a moon-hero: the spots on the moon show the outline of the frog's shape. It is because of the already acknowledged impossibility of constructing the paradigm of the clinging-woman without reference to North American versions that these northern myths have to be brought into play:

$M_{399}$. *Lilloet.* '*The origin of moon spots*, (cf. above pp. 76–7)

Beaver and his friend Serpent wished to marry their neighbours, the Frog sisters. But the frogs thought them so ugly that they rejected them. In revenge, Coyote brought about a flood. When the last inch of dry land was under water the frogs leapt and jumped on Moon's face, where they may still be seen at the present day (Teit 2, p. 298).

$M_{400}$. *Cœur d'Alêne.* '*The origin of moon spots*'

Once the hero Moon invited his neighbours to a great feast. Toad came along and found the house full. In vain she begged to be given a small place where she could sit down, but was sent away.

In revenge, Toad made a heavy rain which penetrated Moon's

house. The guests, who had been chased outside into the night, saw a light coming from Toad's house. They wanted to shelter there, for inside everything was quite dry. Then Toad jumped on Moon's face, people tried to pull her off and didn't succeed. The marks on Moon may still be seen there (Teit 3, pp. 123–4; cf. Thompson; $M_{400b}$ in: Teit 4, pp. 91–2, in which the guest is Moon's young sister).

It would be possible to quote many more examples of myths emanating from the same, or other neighbouring, regions, and in which the theme of the clinging-woman (herself a transformation of a frog) is transformed into the theme of the origin of moon spots, then of the moon itself. The mythological curve is thus completed so that, starting from any version, it is possible to discover all the others arranged in the 'natural' order of the transformations which produce them. It must furthermore be noted that this complex curve – whose two outlines, if drawn in the planes of the two perpendicular axes, follow the imaginary surface of a sphere – defines a diffused semantic field in which it would be possible, at any point inside the sphere, to locate the position of myths already studied, or of other known, or even potential, myths.

I shall restrict myself to two examples. $M_{317}$ in one episode, and $M_{364a,b}$ more generally, link up the rolling-head and the clinging-woman themes. They are therefore situated, ideally, inside the sphere, along a horizontal axis perpendicular to the other two. This axis passes through their point of intersection and terminates at the complex curve at two opposite points, which correspond respectively to the rolling-head and the clinging-woman.

Let us now examine a curious similarity of detail between $M_{393}$ and $M_{286}$, two myths very remote from each other in the diagram, where they do not even occupy symmetrical positions. On the way to the enemy's village, the trusting visitor and his perfidious host eat a vegetable substance which blackens their teeth. When a married woman welcomes him and provides a feast for him, the stranger's teeth are therefore of the same colour as those of the female sloth, the mistress of a married man in $M_{286}$, who is afraid that her lover's wife will not give her a warm welcome, precisely because of the colour of her teeth. There exists, then, a theme correlating the enemy visitor (to whom his host almost offers his wife) and the female animal visited by a man (who abandons his wife for her sake). In other words, they are two human or animal prototypes, each carried to the extreme limit – human but an enemy, animal but a concubine – although in opposite directions; sociological or zoological, cultural or natural. However obscure this theme may be, it can be traced as far as the Jivaro. These Indians of upper Amazonia have a myth about the origin of the moon, in which the latter, weary of being importuned by the sun, her brother, takes advantage of the fact that he is painting his face red to escape to the sky, where she paints her own face black ($M_{401}$: Stirling, p. 124). From this point, it is easy enough to get back to $M_{286}$, since, in subsequent episodes of the Jivaro myth, the sloth is the incestuous son born to the sun and the moon, after their reconciliation, and the ancestor of the Indians. It will be remembered that the Jivaro, like the Mundurucu, to whose mythology $M_{286}$ belongs, were head-hunters and that in the absence of human heads they made do with those of sloths (*ibid.*, pp. 56, 72–3).

When defined in terms of a limited number of oppositions such as *male* or *female*, *near* or *distant* relationships, and *shy* or *trusting* attitudes denoted by their *deficiency* or their *excess*, several myths can, then, be arranged in a closed set. However, this must not cause us to neglect the fact that, when viewed from other angles, they remain spread out over a hyper-space, also occupied by other myths whose properties have not been fully dealt with in the preceding analysis. While the $M_{393-394}$ set and its variants are connected with the same sociological paradigm as the $M_{354-358}$ set, also with its variants, at the same time they depend on an anatomical paradigm, the study of which I broached in connection with $M_{130}$, $M_{135-136}$, and $M_{279a,b,c}$, myths which had been brought to my attention by $M_{354}$, my starting point.

These myths attribute the origin of certain constellations – Orion, Hyades and the Pleiades – to the dismembering of a body. $M_{393-394}$ offer a similar explanation of the origin of the moon, the rainbow and the stars in general, instead of confining themselves to individual constellations. As a consequence, the pattern of the dismembering also changes. So, in these newly introduced myths, one can see the persistence of a significant parallelism between three kinds of division: a sociological division defining and delimiting the categories of the near and the far; an astronomical division which isolates or assembles diurnal or nocturnal phenomena; and lastly an anatomical division which chooses between various ways of dismembering the human body. Consequently, the set of myths with which we are dealing illustrates, with examples of each kind, several modalities of a triple transformation.

It can be analysed from two different viewpoints: binary and analogical.

From the binary point of view, we can agree that the eyes are a metonymical variant of the head (in which they are contained), and the leg a metonymical variant of one of the lower limbs (of which it is a part). This simplification will allow us temporarily to disregard, in $M_{393-394}$, the transformation affecting the eyes (which are a smaller representation of the head) and, in the group of myths concerning the origin of Orion, to leave out of account the fact that one and the same transformation sometimes concerns a lower limb up to the hip (which may be included), and sometimes only the leg (a smaller representation, as it were, of the lower limb). I shall also take advantage of the text of $M_{393-394}$, in which mention is made of a long trail of blood, to include this trail in the category of elongated bodies.

Once this is accepted, the anatomical transformation can be represented in the following way, the $+$ and $-$ signs indicating respectively the first and the second term of each opposition:

|  | Origin of Orion and the Pleiades: | | Origin of the moon and the rainbow: | |
|---|---|---|---|---|
|  | LOWER LIMB | ENTRAILS | HEAD | BLOOD |
| *elongated/ rounded* | $+$ | $-$ | $-$ | $+$ |
| *hard/soft* | $+$ | $-$ | $+$ | $-$ |

In respect of the first disjunction: (*thigh+leg*) // *entrails*, which concerns the lower part of the body, and the second disjunction: (*head+eyes*) // *blood*, which concerns the upper part, the disjunction mentioned in $M_{310}$, and which gives rise to Berenice's Hair, illustrates a mixed formula: it divides the character into two parts at waist level, that is, in the middle. It follows, from this observation, that the cycle of transformations can also be interpreted analogically, by gradually moving the section from low to high.

At one pole of the set, the severed leg (or thigh) and the scattered entrails give rise to Orion and the Pleiades, constellations which herald the coming of fish. The character who is cut in two at waist level becomes, in respect of the lower half: fish ($M_{362}$), food for fish ($M_{130}$), or neutral with regard to fishing ($M_{354}$). The upper half becomes a negative

($M_{130}$) or positive ($M_{354}$) means of fishing. If we continue in an upward direction, the severed head, whether greedy or cannibalistic, succeeds or does not succeed in attaching itself. If it succeeds, it constitutes a border-line form of the legless woman, and like the latter, plays a 'clinging' role. If it fails, the severed head and the spilt blood, definitively separated from the parent body, give rise to the moon and the

| MUTILATION (LOW) | MUTILATION (MIDDLE) | | | MUTILATION (HIGH) |
|---|---|---|---|---|
| Orion-Pleiades ($M_{135, 136,}$ $279a, b, c$) | Berenice's Hair ($M_{130}$) | Berenice's Hair ($-1$) ($M_{354}$) | Clinging-woman ($M_{354}$ etc.) | Rolling head ($M_{393, 394}$ etc.) |
| rejection accepted | | | adhesion enforced | rejection submitted to |
| Constellations (nocturnal objects) | | Sun (diurnal object) . . . | . . . Moon, stars (nocturnal); rainbow (diurnal) | |
| Seasonal periodicity: abundance or famine | | Daily periodicity: day and night | Monthly periodicity: procreation and death | |
| Internal social antagonisms (jealousy, family quarrels, adultery) | | External social antagonisms (inter-tribal conflict, war) | | |
| Misuse of marriage (domestic adultery) | Perversion of marriage (too near or too far) | | Rejection of marriage either (+): incestuous siblings or wife practising bestiality; or (−) shy boy or girl | |

rainbow. These celestial beings bring about, one menstruation and procreation (life) and the other no less bloody happenings, but of quite a different kind (death), since the Cashinawa, who are the tribe concerned, refer to the rainbow as the 'path of the enemies'.

The table (above) makes it unnecessary to give a lengthy commentary. The reader will notice in the first place that the point at which

$M_{354}$ stands explains both how the theme of the rainbow's origin already appears in it (as in the myths to the right of it), and why the astronomical references to the nocturnal sky, evidence of which is still present in the armature, cannot generate a clear message. These references, which come from the myths on the left, use only an imaginary constellation as their vehicle of expression. Secondly the Cashinawa versions – which bring out very clearly the opposition between life emanating from the group (by means of feminine fertility and procreation), and death inflicted on it by enemies (because war is sociologically bloody for men, whereas fertility is physiologically bloody for women) – help us to understand why, even in the North American versions of the clinging-woman myth, the latter's victim is a young warrior opposed to marriage: he refuses to partake in a life-giving activity, being exclusively devoted to the inflicting of death.

A social group in which transgression of the normal marriage laws takes the form of incest ($M_{255}$, $M_{366}$, $M_{392}$), or bestiality ($M_{370c}$ and several North American versions from $M_{150-159}$, which have not been numbered), or occurs because the young girls in the group ($M_{394}$) or the boys ($M_{367-370}$) persist in remaining single, has no means other than war of settling its relationships with strangers ($M_{255}$, $M_{393}$). Even its relationships with nature will be characterized by excess in hunting ($M_{391}$) or fishing ($M_{354}$), comparable to the warlike excess. By treating game as if it were an enemy and by thus abusing natural resources ($M_{391}$), the hunters are guilty of a denial of periodicity, and more particularly of that seasonal periodicity which, provided it is not disregarded, ensures the annual reappearance of fish or game. No doubt, it already implies some degree of privation, since abundance of food all the year round is not inconceivable but even desirable. So, it is understandable that the myths should regard seasonal periodicity as the result of misconduct: the abuse of marriage, a fault which presupposes the existence of marriage and therefore constitutes a less serious disadvantage than its rejection.

In the myths, the constellations are born or result from marriages between humans, which are abused or subverted by an act of betrayal: theft or adultery, often imputable to a supernumerary character, such as a husband's brother or a wife's mother or sister (HA, pp. 301–4). The sun and moon, on the other hand, result from non-human marriages, or marriages considered as such: it may be a case of incest 'contrary to culture', or of union with an animal, and therefore contrary to nature, although the South American myths, on the whole, consider that such a union accounts for the origin of fish ($M_{150}$ etc.) or of fish poison ($M_{145}$), the means of catching fish, of which the sun and moon are the masters ($M_{255}$), and the arrival of which is heralded by the constellations of Orion and the Pleiades ($M_{134-136}$). This angle of approach makes it possible to complete the set.

It follows that, in the myths, marriage between the moon and a human being, or between the moon and the sun by inversion of the incestuous formula ($M_{256b}$; Nordenskiöld 3, pp. 296–7) is considered as being at the extreme limit of the possible: the conjunction requires an excessive lengthening of the man's penis if the moon is female, or, if the moon is male, it produces a miraculous child, who, because of his inflammable and exploring temperament, might almost be said to personify a long penis ($M_{247}$). A simultaneous study of the lunar myths of the north-west of North America and of the Guiana-Amazonian area would show in similar fashion that the female moon is a baby-snatcher (a transformation of the clinging-woman), whereas the male moon is a kidnapped child; the kidnapping is done, however, by milt-girls, who are in turn a transformation of the 'wooden bridegroom' found in certain Guiana myths ($M_{241}$); he is the father of a child stolen by a frog, whose rôle is played in the Salish versions by the milt-girls.

Thus the moon, which is often a hermaphrodite when it does not actually change its sex, provides the theme of a mythology of ambiguity. The sun is too close to the moon for them to unite without doing wrong but man is too far away for his remote union with the moon not to expose him to certain dangers. The nocturnal luminary oscillates perpetually between these two possibilities of social inertia or avid curiosity for the exotic; considered from the point of view of sexual relationships, the only choice they leave open is between incest and licentiousness.

These two, unequally serious, forms of misconduct each correspond, then, to a shortening of the periodicity cycle. This would be incomprehensible, if the perverted marriage did not adversely affect a spatial periodicity which, on the sociological level, constitutes the equivalent of the temporal periodicity characteristic of astronomical phenomena. In his quest for a mate, a human may look either too near or too far. And, according to whether the periodic return of a particular celestial body occurs every year, every month or every day, it offers a suitable model for the representation of the fluctuating values of endogamy and exogamy. The abuse of marriage is opposed to the rejection of marriage, just as the seasonal constellations can be opposed to the moon, whose phases are monthly; on the other hand, the presence or absence of the moon, alternating with the presence or absence of the sun, reflects the shortest observable form of periodicity (which in this sense is 'incestuous'), namely that of day and night.

As it happens, the Cashinawa myths expressly link up these two short modes of periodicity: when the moon makes its first appearance, it starts the women's monthly bleedings; and according to whether it is new or full at the moment of conception, the masculine sperm or the feminine blood will clot in the uterus and the children will be born with skins as light as day or as dark as night:

*Daily periodicity:*

*Monthly periodicity:*

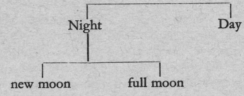

The native text is so difficult to interpret that I hesitate to try to give a precise definition of the correlation between the phases of the moon and the pigmentation of children. Whatever the truth of the matter, all the myths of the group I am attempting to construct use a double entry system of astronomical references. They establish a correspondence between diurnal and nocturnal phenomena and they refer to different cycles of periodicity. Whereas, in $M_{393-394}$, the moon has the rainbow as its diurnal equivalent, in a Guiana myth ($M_{149a}$), to which I shall return later, the diurnal sun produces the Milky Way, a nocturnal phenomenon, when he entrusts his daughters with the task of lighting the way of the dead:

This double correlation of the Milky Way as a nocturnal mode of the sun, and of the rainbow as a diurnal mode of the moon, confirms the equivalence, already independently established (*RC*, pp. 246–7) between the rainbow and a dark patch in the Milky Way, that is, an inverted Milky Way. Consequently all the astronomical terms are duplicated:

the Milky Way exists positively (standing out brightly against the dark sky) and negatively (the Coal Sack standing out against the light background of the Milky Way): the moon may be full (bright) or new (dark); and the sun itself can appear in two contrasting modalities: the bright summer sun or the dark winter sun ($M_{255}$). Lastly, it is well-known that the Indians think of the rainbow as having two aspects, one eastern and the other western, or again, one higher the other lower (RC, p. 247).

The myths use this complex code in such a way that each celestial phenomenon, when viewed from one or other of the two aspects, suggests different forms of periodicity and so fulfils a two-fold function. This already emerged clearly from the native comments on the rainbow that I summarized in *The Raw and the Cooked*: the Tucuna draw a distinction between the eastern and western rainbows, linking one with fish, the other with potter's clay, that is, two natural products which have a seasonal harvest time. $M_{354}$ is no less explicit on this point: it associates the eastern rainbow with the periodic migrations (known as 'piracema') of the fish which swim up the river every year to spawn. On the other hand, the western rainbow, the master of potter's clay, is connected with a shorter periodicity: clay is only collected during the first night of the full moon, otherwise the pots would be in danger of breaking and the people eating out of them would catch serious diseases (RC, pp. 247-8). Consequently, the dual nature of the rainbow allows it to act as a link between two valencies of periodicity, one annual, the other monthly.

Similarly, the sun, the two aspects of whose dual character, diurnal and seasonal (winter sun and summer sun, $M_{255}$), are stressed alternately in the myths, links the annual and daily valencies of periodicity. What, then, is to be said about the moon? It displays a double periodicity, daily like the sun's, or again monthly, but never seasonal like the periodicity of the constellations (Figure 8).

There is, then, a break at one point in the periodic cycle. The constellations are completely on the side of the solidly built structure formed by the annual and seasonal periodicities, characterized by the alternation of rain and drought, plenty or famine and the arrival or departure of fish. The moon, on the other hand, is completely on the side of the short, serial periodicity, which can occur in the two forms, daily or monthly, but without entailing changes comparable to those brought about by the seasonal cycle. The seasons are in opposition to each other, but the days are all alike, and the phases of the moon follow each other in an immutable order, winter and summer alike. Only the

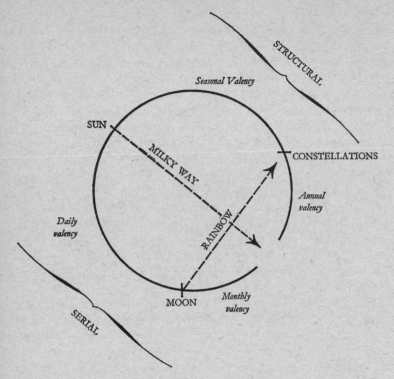

Figure 8. Forms of periodicity

sun which is daily, like the moon, and annual, like the constellations, enjoys the full privilege of being related to both aspects.

One can see, then, the complementary functions which devolve upon the rainbow and the Milky Way in a system of this type. If a seasonal connotation is attributed to the rainbow's eastern mode and a monthly connotation to its western mode, it can connect, on the diurnal level, terms which are doomed to remain disjoined on the nocturnal level. The rainbow, therefore, resolves a contradiction. The Milky Way, for its part, and on the nocturnal level, neutralizes the contradiction, since it brings together synchronically, throughout the whole year, and in the form of a scattering of (bright) stars and Coal Sacks (dark), the opposition between the light and the dark that the moon, alternately new and full, illustrates by a monthly periodicity which unfolds diachronically, but repetitively, from one end of the year to the other. At the same time, the respective affinities of the rainbow and the Milky Way with the sun and moon are clarified. The dual nature of the rainbow forms a bridge, thrown out, as it were, by the moon in the direction of seasonal periodicity, which would otherwise remain inaccessible to it. With the Milky Way, the sun spans the gulf opened up by the system between monthly periodicity and annual periodicity, since only the sun, by bringing together both aspects through its daily connivance with the moon and its seasonal connivance with the constellations, can bridge this gap.

# 2 *The Daily Round*

> *Yes, even if man were to reject the Divinity, the thinking being, unaccompanied and unobserved, would be still more august in the midst of lonely worlds than if he appeared there surrounded by the petty deities of legend; the empty desert would still be in keeping with the range of his ideas, the sadness of his passions and the bitterness of a life devoid of illusion and hope.*
>
> Chateaubriand, *Génie du Christianisme, Livre IV, Ch.* 1

When, as has just been the case, a distinction is made between two kinds of periodicity, one with long annual or seasonal cycles, the other with short monthly or daily cycles, the first characterized by diversity, the second by monotony, it becomes possible to understand why, in moving from one form of periodicity to the other, myths relating to the origin of the constellations are regularly transformed into myths about the origin of the sun and the moon. However, during this transformation, there occurs another, which affects the structure of the narrative as well as the nature of the message. Let us begin by giving an example:

$M_{60}$. *Tucuna. 'The errors of Cimidyuë'* (cf. RC, p. 132, and $M_{129a}$, p. 223)
Cimidyuë's husband, who thoroughly disliked her, decided to lose her during a hunting expedition. He convinced her that the white sexual parts of the coatá monkeys (*Ateles* sp.) were the Kapok tufts on the butt ends of darts he had already fired into their bodies, and that it was therefore necessary to wait for the poison to take effect before collecting the animals when they fell to the ground. He meanwhile would go on ahead and kill other game. But the man went off and returned to the village, without whistling to his wife as he said he would.

She waited a long time at the foot of the tree. And as she did not know the way home, she decided to follow the monkeys and live on the sorva fruit (*Couma* sp.) they dropped. At sundown the monkeys assumed human form, and invited Cimidyuë to sleep in one of the hammocks in their hut; but the next morning there was no house and the monkeys again had animal form.

After wandering with the monkeys for a very long time, Cimidyuë arrived at their chief's house. Although of a race of jaguars, the lord of the monkeys had human form. She helped him to prepare sweet manioc beer for a beer drinking festival. The lord of the monkeys slept and snored through his nose, announcing that he would devour the heroine. Becoming anxious she woke him and this enraged him. He ordered them to bring him a large kernel of the čaivarú fruit, and with it he struck his nose until it began to bleed. Then he fell asleep again but soon began to snore in the same fashion. Again Cimidyuë woke him up, whereupon he began to maltreat his nose, furiously catching the flowing blood in a gourd and drinking it. Then he ordered more beer and everyone became befuddled.

The next morning the lord of the monkeys went off hunting; but first of all he tied a long rope to Cimidyuë's leg and kept hold of the other end. From time to time he gave the rope a tug to make sure the woman was still a prisoner. In the hut a tortoise was tied up in the same way. It explained that the lord of the monkeys was a jaguar who proposed to devour them both, and that they really ought to escape. They freed themselves from their rope, tied it to one of the house posts, and passed by Venkiča's house yard. Venkiča was the lord of the monkeys' brother, and happened to be sitting with one leg crossed over the other in front of his door. On the tortoise's advice, Cimidyuë took a cudgel and dealt the man a smart blow across the knee-cap. The blow hurt him so much that he jerked back his leg. 'Don't tell on us,' shouted the woman as she passed. Venkiča is visible in the Orion constellation.

When he returned from the hunt, the lord of the monkeys started looking for the two runaways. He asked his brother whether he had seen 'a fat girl' go by. Still crazy with pain, the brother said he didn't want to hear about fat girls; his knee was too painful for him to reply. The lord of the monkeys gave up the chase.

Cimidyuë, once more lost in the forest, met with further misadventures. A bird of the picidae family took her the wrong way while pretending to guide her back to the village. Next she mistook the inhambu, a bird of the gallinicae family, who was puffing up his feathers in order to preen them, for an old woman plaiting a basket inside a hut in which the traveller asked if she could spend the night. But the bird flew away and she had to sleep alone under the tree. When she tried to set out on her way again the following morning, the bird gave her the wrong direction.

The next night, Cimidyuë thought she could shelter from the rain under a huge ants' nest hanging from a branch. But the nest was a jaguar, which threatened to kill her. She fled and came to an area which she recognized as being the valley of the Solimões. That night she slept among the root buttresses of a kapok-tree. The animals which passed by, a huge lizard first of all, then a toad, jeered at her while pretending to offer her food. Finally, the lord of the kapok-tree, a blue butterfly, *Morphos menelaus*, woke up and announced amid yawns that he was going to eat pineapples in a certain Indian's garden. This Indian, whose name he gave, was none other than Cimidyuë's father.

Cimidyuë followed the butterfly to the river. Her father's hut was on the other side. So Cimidyuë had crossed the river without realizing she had done so. The butterfly uttered a magic formula which changed the woman into a red dragon-fly. The two insects flew together towards the opposite bank, which Cimidyuë would never have been strong enough to reach without her companion's help. In order to thank him, she crushed the best pineapples and the butterfly drank the juice. The father was astonished to see the crushed fruit. He hid with his wife, recognized his daughter and tried, but in vain, to hold her back.

Called upon to help, the villagers lay in ambush. For three days they waited for the insects to return. Finally, they succeeded in capturing Cimidyuë but the butterfly escaped. In spite of her protestations, they took the woman away. Her father gave her an emetic: she vomited violently and recovered her reason.

Some time later, Cimidyuë met her former husband at a feast. He had come dressed in a mask representing a small downy lizard and had straw bound to his head. He began singing a mocking song to his victim. She lit a piece of resin which she threw at the mask and the dry straw caught fire. The man ran off but could not rid himself of his bark costume. His belly burst with the heat and the porénë bird dyed its plumage with the blood (Nim. 13, pp. 148–50).

In several respects, this myth is reminiscent of the story of Monmanéki the hunter ($M_{354}$), also a Tucuna myth. Monmanéki is a *venturesome husband* who collects a succession of animal wives; Cimidyuë illustrates the symmetrical case of a *wife exposed to adventures* and abandoned by her husband to various animals, who treat her not like a woman but as an alimentary subject or object: the monkeys feed her, the lord of the monkeys and the jaguar try to feed off her, the lizard and the toad refuse to feed her and the butterfly receives food from her. This dialectic always remains, then, within the limits of the literal meaning, whereas, in the case of Monmanéki's animal wives, the dialectic operates at the point of intersection between the literal and the figurative meanings: the bird-women feed their husband literally, the frog- and earthworm-women are fed by him figuratively, since they mistake eliminatory postures (the reverse of nutrition, in the literal sense) for fertilizing postures (the equivalent of nutrition taken in the figurative sense).

At the end of the Monmanéki myth, we are left with a man, his mother and his wife; at the end of the Cimidyuë myth, with a wife, her father and her husband. In one instance, the wife 'holds' her husband, who escapes from her by means of water. In the other, the husband 'lets go' of his wife, who takes her revenge on him by means of fire. The toad-woman is divided in two at waist level; the husband who abandons his wife explodes at stomach level. On the one hand, the hunter's mother causes disasters by misjudging the virtues of her animal daughters-in-law; on the other hand, the father of a woman married to a hunter is helpful towards his daughter, who herself is mistaken about the animals she frequents. Finally, it will be remembered that the Monmanéki myth refers explicitly to the origin of the rainbow, and implicitly to that of Berenice's Hair, the function of which it reverses, whereas the Cimidyuë myth refers explicitly to the origin of the Orion constellation (while weakening the anatomical theme – knee fixed in a bent position instead of severed leg), and implicitly to the origin of the lunar eclipse, which the Tucuna attribute to the demon Venkiča playing the part of Orion (see above, p. 89).

Certain corresponding pieces of evidence suggest, then, that $M_{60}$ and $M_{354}$ belong to the same group. We cannot, however, ignore the fact that, when considered from the syntagmatic point of view, the two myths appear very different. Both have the form of an episodic narrative, although, as regards $M_{354}$, this point of resemblance is deceptive, since it has been possible to show that, underlying the serial form, is a structure the elements of which, when observed from various angles, always fit together precisely. No comparable result would be obtained in the case of Cimidyuë's adventures, since apart from a few isolated points which are, in any case, difficult to connect up with each other, a much less rigid inventiveness seems to be responsible for the number of the episodes, the order in which they are arranged and the types to which they belong; this inventiveness is about to break away from the constraints of mythic thought, if it has not already done so. In other words, the question arises whether the story of Cimidyuë does not illustrate a significant transition from the mythic genre to the genre of the novel, which admits a more flexible development, or does not obey the same fixed rules.

All the people who have recorded or studied the oral literature of the South American Indians have been aware of this contrast. Nimuendaju, who recorded Cimidyuë's story, places it in a separate category which he calls 'Legends of Odysseys and Adventures'. It is true that he also puts the Monmanéki myth in the same category, but the reason is, no doubt, that, not having subjected it to analysis, he did not see beyond the superficial resemblance that I too have pointed out, and so failed to detect the more deep-seated differences. Murphy (1, p. 94) groups certain Mundurucu myths under the special heading: 'Adventures and Sagas', and he refers to a certain myth ($M_{402}$) as a 'saga' (cf. Kruse, 2, p. 642: 'Journeys'), and observes that it corresponds to the Tucuna story about Cimidyuë and to a Tembé story ($M_{403a}$; Nim. 2, p. 299). There exist two variants of this last story, one in Wagley and Galvão ($M_{403b}$; pp. 140–42) and the other in Métraux, who recorded it in almost the same form among the Kayapo ($M_{404}$; 8, pp. 30–32), and in both sources it is given the title 'adventures', following the example of Roth (1, pp. 126–30), who gave the title 'The Adventures of Kororomanna' to a long Warao story, to which I have referred on many occasions ($M_{317}$). Its kinship with the Cimidyuë myth seems quite clear since, in one version, a hero called Keré-Keré-miyu-au, is also guided back to the family hut by a butterfly. Roth says that when he expressed surprise at this intervention on the part of an insect rarely mentioned in the myths, his informant replied that the butterfly was always a good friend of the Indians: does it not come and join in the feasts, and get so drunk it cannot fly away?

I would like to digress here for a moment. The helpful behaviour of the butterfly in $M_{60}$ and $M_{317}$, which contrasts with the unhelpful rôle assigned to the other creatures by the two myths, whereas in most myths they are helpful, can cause surprise for a reason additional to the one put forward by Roth. Throughout the whole of the Guiana-Amazonian region, butterflies, especially those of the *Morpho* genus, have an evil connotation. 'A creature associated with shamans and the spirit of evil ... (the butterfly) mixes malaria in a gourd and spreads the disease over the whole countryside' (K.-G. 2, p. 328). This is a reference to a Cubeo belief, which is also the subject of the following quotation: ... the *morpho* butterfly with its beautiful blue wings, is a creature of sorcerers and of evil ... When a sorcerer is cooking a brew that will kill a victim at a distance, the *morpho* butterfly appears and encircles the pot. Finally it falls in and is consumed and at that moment the victim dies' (Goldman, pp. 224–5). The Tucuna who live along the Uaupés call the butterfly wãx-tĩ-turu, 'piece of Wãxti', in other words of Jurupari, the 'devil' of western Amazonia (Silva, pp. 332–4). According to the Aguaruna, the *morpho* butterfly, uampisuk, is a diabolical creature (Guallart, p. 85, n.68), the embodiment of the souls of young girls carried off by a devil. This last piece of information, taken from Wavrin (pp. 626–7), brings us back to the Tucuna who believed that the spirit of the kapok tree was the enemy of menstruating women (Nim. 13, p. 92); it is this same spirit of the kapok tree, which takes the form of a *morpho* butterfly in the Tucuna myth about Cimidyuë, but there it becomes the heroine's guide and protector.

It is perhaps not inconceivable that this reversal of the semantic value of the butterfly might be linked with the ritual use of narcotics or drugs taken in powder form, particularly paricá (Wassén 1, 2; Wassén–Holmstedt). This is a generic term applied to several preparations made from the seeds, bark or leaves of the mimoseae (*Piptadenia peregrina*) or myristaceae (*Virola* sp.) families. In the myths, interventions on the part of the dragon-fly are even rarer than those of the butterfly, in whose company Cimidyuë, having been changed into a dragon-fly, succeeds in crossing the river which bars the way back to her native village. The Tucuna took paricá in the form of snuff, and there is a carved wooden paricá platter of Maué origin in the Anthropological Museum in Vienna which has been said to show dragon-flies mating, and also butterflies (Wassén 2, fig. 12 and pp. 45–6). But the two insects joined together at the rear are so unlike that the scene would seem rather to represent a butterfly pulling a dragon-fly along, as in the Cimidyuë myth. Similarly, the Tucuna platter in the Anthropological Museum in Oslo (Wassén 2, fig. 41) could be taken as representing a butterfly with, above it, a dragon-fly with folded wings, if the chief figure did not have the angular nose characteristic of the *Cebus* monkey in Tucuna masks (as Wassén

Figure 9. *On the left:* Tucuna slab in the Oslo Anthropological Museum
*On the right:* Maué slab in the Vienna Anthropological Museum.
(Museum photographs.)

rightly notes), whereas butterfly-masks have a kind of elongated proboscis (Nim. 13, p. 82 and pl. 17b) (Figure 9).

Most of the other paricá platters originating from the Amazonian area represent a creature which can be identified as a snake or a cayman, the animal which replaces the butterfly as ferryman in the Tembé-Tenetehara, Kayapo and Mundurucu versions of the myth under discussion (RC, p. 253, n. 24). I shall interpret this episode in Part Seven, However, the carved animal displays a tongue which, according to the myths, the cayman does not possess (*HA*, p. 228); and among the Kachúyana in the river Trombetas area, Frikel (1, p. 8) noted an object of a similar type representing 'water-jaguars' and a being called Kurahi, korehi or antchkire, about whom he could obtain no information. At the same time, the distribution area of the myths we are concerned with coincides only partially with that of paricá. In spite of these uncertainties, one cannot but be struck by the fact that all relate the wanderings of the hero or heroine among deceitful or evil animals, many of whom are huge (like the inhambu bird which Cimidyuë mistook for an old woman's hut and which she even tried to enter). What we know about rites involving paricá does in fact suggest that they are chiefly intended to establish friendly relations between humans and giant animal spirits, called worokiema by the Kachúyana (Frikel 1, *passim*), and hekura by the Surára (Becher 2, pp. 91–6), to frighten these spirits, to neutralize their evil power, to appropriate their beneficent influence and to allow humans to become identified with them. This seems to be precisely what the two travellers are trying to do, for the most part in vain, when they find themselves wandering in a strange and threatening world, cut off from their own country by a river which sometimes they do not even remember having crossed on the outward journey ($M_{60, 403a,b}$).

So great is the freedom of invention shown in these myths and so powerful their dreamlike charm, that it would be a pity to summarize them. On the other hand, they are too long to be quoted in full. I shall therefore limit myself to one or two references. After losing his way among demons in the form of howler monkeys and after deceiving them in various fashions ($M_{317}$; *HA*, pp. 385–6), Kororomanna, the Warao hero, realizes he is lost. During his wanderings, he meets with various adventures: he encounters a seductress with a snake-husband; a female demon, whom he destroys after killing her baby; ogres who capture him in a trap, and from whom he manages to escape; a human skull which clings to him and persecutes him (see above, p. 55); and a fisherman who dries up a river by collecting the water in a pocket formed by lifting up his long testicles (see above, p. 83) and who imprisons the hero in a block of wood. After being eventually set free on making a gift of tobacco, and being himself presented with an enormous quantity of fish put up in a very small bundle, Kororomanna manages to find the right path back to his mother and wife, with the help of a series of animals who show him the way (Roth 1, pp. 126–30).

Several episodes of the Mundurucu version ($M_{402}$; Kruse 2, pp.

642–6; Murphy 1, pp. 95–102) coincide with those in the Warao myth: the hero is seduced by an ogre's wife; he deceives another ogre by offering him pieces of monkey instead of his own flesh and liver ... But the story begins differently. A young boy called Perisuát is taken a long way away from his village by his maternal uncle, who has changed into a tapir; believing the animal to be dead, the boy innocently plunges his arm into the tapir's anus right up to the shoulder, in order to remove the entrails from the carcase before cutting it up into pieces. No sooner has the animal agreed to free his prisoner than it is killed by hunters. Perisuát escapes from them by changing into a bees' nest. He crosses the Tapajoz on the back of a cayman which tries to gobble him up, and has unpleasant encounters with various creatures: birds, caterpillars, several male and female jaguars, more caterpillars, a tapir and his daughters who want to marry him, as well as all kinds of supernatural beings: an ogre with a pointed leg, another who catches him and from whom he is delivered by insects and a squirrel, and monkeys who are really 'the mothers of rain' ... A jaguar, whose wounds he tends, finally shows him the right road, and when he arrives at his own village he has become so fierce that he kills his own pet birds. As a result of his long stay in the forest, his skin has become pallid and infested with vermin. His grandmother washes and nurses him. In an attempt to cure him, she smears him with urucu, but the sickness is too far advanced and Perisuát dies.

As I have already explained, the Tembé-Tenetehara versions ($M_{403a, b}$; Nim. 2, p. 299 *et seq.*; Wagley–Galvão, pp. 140–42), the Shipaia versions ($M_{403c}$; Nim. 3, pp. 390–93) and the Kayapo versions ($M_{404}$; Métraux 8, pp. 30–32) are very similar. In the Shipaia version, an Indian whose hand has been caught in a hole (cf. $M_{402}$) is clubbed by a hairy spirit who carries him off in a basket full of ants. He manages to escape from this prison, then from a hollow tree which has also captured him. A soft-hearted cayman agrees to take him across a river. Then the hero sleeps in one of the three hammocks which the inhambu bird claims for his sole use, he stares a jaguar straight in the eye for a whole night, and is given hospitality by a couple of tapirs; the male tapir is such a heavy sleeper that his wife has to beat him repeatedly to wake him up.

In other versions, the hero who has lost his way during a war expedition or a goat-sucker hunt, begs several animals to take him across to the other side of a river, but without success. The cayman agrees to do so, but only because he intends to gobble him up. The hero escapes thanks to a stilt-bird, which hides him in its crop underneath the fish it has just swallowed. In the Kayapo version, the hero meets in turn a deer, a tapir, a monkey and a coati, which accuse him of having injured them during his hunting expeditions; they promise to take him back to his village, but either lead him astray or abandon him. Finally his brother, who happens to pass by, puts him on the right road. The Tembé-Tenetehara versions have the cayman and stilt-bird episode as the sequel to a series of unpleasant adventures with creatures such as the toad, the humming-bird and the cannibalistic snake. Only the wild pigs prove to be friendly. With them the hero wanders about looking for seeds and wild fruit until one day he finds himself by chance in his mother's plantation. One version explains that from then on he always keeps himself to himself, sleeping in a corner of the hut, chanting the story of his adventures and singing songs he learned among the pigs, for he himself is now a pig. Others state that he throws himself into his mother's arms with such impetuosity that he is unable to detach himself again. Irremediably disjoined or conjoined, the hero, who has been lost and is now found, becomes, then, either an animal or a clinging-man. He thus combines in his own person attributes which the venturesome husband of $M_{354}$ found in his series of wives, since most of them were animal women, apart from one human who played the part of 'clinging-woman'.

In the entire series of myths, Cimidyuë is the only woman, the other central characters being all masculine. The heroine tries to go back to her father; the heroes return to their mothers. This does not necessarily reflect an opposition between the patrilocal organization of the Tucuna and the matrilocal organization of the Warao and, recently at least, of the Mundurucu (Murphy 3); the Tembé-Tenetehara also were patrilocal. Consequently, the oppositional structure remains significant, independently of the ethnological data: even when disguised in this way, it is still the relationship of remoteness or proximity *between the sexes* which makes it possible to code the relationship between distances or periods of time.

Cimidyuë, whom the myth describes as a 'fat girl', paralyses the leg of the demon Venkiča, personifying the constellation of Orion. She is therefore reminiscent on two counts of the 'fat boy' in the Mundurucu myth $M_{255}$, who blinds a personification of the winter sun (see above, p. 95). The sun, being ashamed of its infirmity, hides behind clouds, but the demon Venkiča, maddened by his disability, has as his mission to bring about eclipses of the moon. So, weakened manifestations of the sun and moon (weakened, since they suffer eclipses) appear to be linked to equally weakened forms of the mutilation which give rise to these stars in the same or neighbouring myths: the eyes are blinded instead of the head being cut off, and a knee is paralysed instead of a leg or thigh being severed. No doubt, an explicit astronomical reference is to be detected only in the Cimidyuë myth. It should not however be forgotten that this myth – the only one in the set in which the main rôle is given to a woman – belongs to the *corpus* of Tucuna mythology; it is, therefore, a much more direct and immediate transformation of $M_{354}$ than the other versions. The latter belong to different tribes and, according to the perspective I have adopted, they are also more remotely situated. If the Cimidyuë myth were the only one at our disposal, we should almost be entitled to say that, after starting from the myths about the origin of Orion and the Pleiades, and moving on to those about the origin of Berenice's Hair which are an inversion of them, and then on to $M_{354}$, which in turn represents an inversion of the preceding myths, we are brought back by the story of Cimidyuë to the origin of Orion, but in a very weak form in respect of the anatomical theme, and with a different coding as regards astronomy. It will be remembered that, in order to explain the arrival of fish, the Tucuna, unlike their Guiana neigh-bours, reverse Berenice's Hair, a nocturnal constellation, and have recourse to the rainbow, the diurnal equivalent of a constellation. In this system, the Orion constellation has no part to play, except with regard to the moon: and even then, its special function is to bring about the moon's eclipse, that is, its connection is with a moon which is first diminished and then obliterated. Consequently, just as the Tucuna create a double inversion (in respect of period and function) of Berenice's Hair to come back to Orion, they transform the character and powers of Orion to come back to the moon, which is *present in its absence* – as is already the case, in their mythology, with Berenice's Hair. This is tantamount to saying that, in Tucuna mythology, where the positive moon is the result of too close a sexual union (the incest in $M_{358}$), the negative moon (= the moon in eclipse) is the result of disunion between a married couple (Cimidyuë and her husband) who ought to have remained in close contact. Similarly, at the end of the myth, a too-close terrestrial fire wickedly starts a conflagration and causes an abdominal explosion which, as we shall see later in connection with another myth ($M_{406}$, p. 137), contrasts with a cerebral explosion, which creates celestial fire with its beneficent warmth. So, the two-fold itinerary uniting sun, moon and constellations in their positive and negative manifestations adopts the means of a two-fold anatomical coding, in which high or low mutilations correspond to diurnal explosions ($M_{406}$) or nocturnal explosions ($M_{396}$, $M_{60}$), which in turn, and as the case may be, affect the low and the high.

Finally, one would have to enquire whether the 'fat girl' character is not a transformation of the celestial woman who in the mythology of the Guiana Arawak became wedged in the aperture leading to the upper world, and who in Warao mythology turns into the morning star (Roth 1, pp. 141–2; $M_{243}$ in: Wilbert 9, pp. 25, 35; cf. *HA*, p. 188). Thanks to the moon in eclipse acting as intermediary, we can thus move on from the 'obstructing body' to the severed head, from which results on the one hand an 'unstoppered body', and, on the other, the full moon. It would seem that there is not enough material available to complete the circle, unless one ventures as far afield as the Lepcha of Sikkim, who have a myth which is curiously similar to the Mundurucu story ($M_{255}$) and in which a *toad*, the murderer of one of the sun brothers, replaces the 'fat boy', who also blinds one of the suns with his arrows. In the Lepcha myth (Stock, p. 269 *et seq.*), the other sun withdraws under a black veil and causes a prolonged night, which continues until the introduction of a comic god who, as in ancient Japanese mythology, cheers the sun up and restores light to mankind.

The Cimidyuë myth, then, effects a discreet transition between the stellar and the lunar codes. The Orion constellation, which is explicitly mentioned, has no seasonal function and its personification by the demon Venkiča merely denotes a lack of moon. In the Cimidyuë myth itself, as well as in several others belonging to the same group, the transition is also demonstrated in a different way which confirms the emergence of very short forms of periodicity.

In reading these stories, one cannot but note that they are very careful to make the unfolding of the narrative coincide with the alternation of day and night, since each of the hero's or heroine's adventures is located within a period of twelve or twenty-four hours. Cimidyuë's story ($M_{60}$) is full of transitional formulae such as: the following day ...; at nightfall ...; on that particular night ...; the next day ...; for three days ...; etc. This procedure comes out even more clearly in Perisuát's story ($M_{402}$): the following day ...; in the morning ...; night fell ...; he walked all day and far into the night ...; the whole day ...; that night ...; the following morning ...; at the end of the fourth day ...; the fifth day ...; rain fell for a whole day and all night until half-way through the following day, etc. Of the fifteen episodes in the same myth which are preserved in the Kruse version, six refer to a twelve-hour period corresponding to the duration of night. The Tembé and Kayapo myths ($M_{403a}$, $_{404}$) are vaguer, but we possess only brief versions of them, and in the Tenetehara version (the Tenetehara are related to the Tembé, $M_{403b}$), it is possible at least to detect four successive nights. Although the Warao myth ($M_{317}$) is rich in details, it does not show a clear division into daily periods: several adventures take place during the same night and day; while another adventure extends over several days. However, we shall see that, in this myth, short periodicity is indicated by a different device.

On the way back, Kororomanna meets, in succession, six animals, each of which is carrying a particular fruit or vegetable which comes from the hero's mother's garden. Goeje (1, pp. 104-5) must be given credit for linking this enumeration with the method adopted by the Kalina to describe the moon's phases: 'They imagine that the moon first of all roasts the game it has killed during the day. The bigger the game, the later the moon is in appearing, since the cooking takes longer. The day when the moon is full will therefore also be a day when a small animal, such as a rat or a mouse, is killed. On each succeeding day, the size of the game increases; the moon roasts in turn a porcupine, an agouti or paca, a caetetu pig, a queixada pig (bigger than the caetetu), a deer, an ant-eater, then another species of deer ... On the final day of the last quarter, the moon roasts a tapir, and people say that it has stopped roasting a tapir when it is no longer visible' (Ahlbrinck, p. 319). Although the Warao hero has far fewer encounters, the latter occur approximately in the same order as the Kalina series:

| Kalina: | rat | porcupine | agouti or paca | | caetetu | queixada | deer | | tapir |
|---|---|---|---|---|---|---|---|---|---|
| Warao: | rat sweet potato | | agouti manioc (root) | paca yam | | | deer manioc (leaf) | ant manioc (leaf) | tapir pineapple |

The same can hardly be said about the animal series in the other myths, which seem much more arbitrary and repetitious. However, Guiana ethno-zoology cannot be reduced to our categories and when, for instance, jaguars appear at different moments in the narrative, we must take into account the fact that the Indians subdivide this species, and other species too, into clearly-defined varieties, each one of which is supposed to feed off a particular kind of game. So just as the animals encountered by Kororomanna are characterized by two categorical signs, that is, by their zoological species and by the botanical species on which they feed, so jaguars are described according to the particular animal they choose to hunt, and the call of which they can imitate: according to an Arawak saying, 'everything has tiger' (jaguar) (Roth 1, p. 367).

I do not mean to assert that the lists of animals given in the myths always, and in all circumstances, conceal a hidden principle of organization. But, in this particular instance, they bear a formal resemblance to those used to describe the daily evolution of the moon's phases, which throughout the whole of South America are so often associated with separate creatures (see above, p. 83). The analogy gives weight to Goeje's remark that 'there is something reminiscent of the zodiac in these stories' (1, p. 104, cf. also pp. 16–18); this is all the more true in that the Guiana Indians believe each constellation to be a spirit which reigns over one particular species of game. Yet I hesitate to follow the Dutch scholar, when he includes in the same group the famous myth about Poronominaré ($M_{247}$), in which the organization of the animal kingdom by a lunar divinity occupies a predominant place, as it does in the myths of the Salish of North-West America, which are very similar in several respects in spite of their geographical remoteness. Poronominaré is a 'coureur des bois', who systematically goes in search of adventures instead of being subjected to them after losing his way. He drives forward, whereas characters like Cimidyuë wander at random in their search for the road back home, and only very exceptionally in these myths are the absurd encounters with weird animals expressive of any positive contribution to the natural order. The relation suggested by Goeje exists perhaps between the two types, but only if their respective themes are transformed along a different axis from the one I have chosen to deal with. Also, to reduce these myths merely to a zodiacal formula reflecting the annual course of certain constellations would be to disregard their intrinsic originality. It is probably true that, in native thought, each animal species is associated with a constellation whose rising or culmination heralds the hunting, fishing, or breeding season. But in this instance, we are dealing with a succession of animals which make their appearance within a relatively short space of time and at the ideal rate of one per night. At the same time, the behaviour attributed to them ceases to have any concrete zoological reference. In a masquerade, reminiscent for us of the paintings of Hieronymus Bosch, they mingle with imaginary beings such as the rolling head, the man with

the sharpened leg or long testicles, the demons who walk backwards
and the talking excrement. All of these turn up unexpectedly in the
narrative, detached from their relevant mythic paradigms, without
which they become impossible to interpret. What is more important,
the animals themselves make disconcerting statements or behave in a
disconcerting manner: the huge toad in the shelter of whose body
Wirai ($M_{403b}$) tries to sleep, spends the night waking him up and asking
him to lie down under some other part. Perisuát ($M_{402}$), stretched out
at the foot of a tree, cannot sleep because a bird nesting on the other
side of the tree rails all night about misbehaving adolescents. Other
birds ($M_{402}$, $M_{60}$) assume the form of a cosy hut, and conjure up or
dispel the mirage at will. A monkey, who is also a man and a jaguar
($M_{60}$), vigorously hammers away at his own nose ...

I have no desire to suggest that these mythic themes, by their very
nature, defy any attempt at interpretation. Even those with which we
are already familiar and which here take on the appearance of quotations
or *collages* through being removed from their original context, must be
connected with the most surprising by links which 'structural analysis
could probably elucidate, if it modified its angle of approach. But, to
achieve such a result, it would be necessary to take into account other
dimensions of the myth: it would be essential to have a better knowledge of the aspects of the astronomical code and, going beyond the
story, to study the narrative style, the syntax, the vocabulary, and
perhaps the phonology. The transcriptions that would be necessary for
this purpose are not available, and in any case the task would be beyond
my competence. However, I should like to make it clear that the
inability to proceed further is relative to the particular approach which,
with intent no less than by necessity, I have chosen to adopt, and it
does not exclude the possibility of using another interpretative technique along different lines. Moreover, even though I am obliged to
recognize a certain freedom of invention in these myths, I can at least
demonstrate the necessity of this freedom with the help of the tools I
normally use.

After a long series of transformations, the theoretical point of departure of which was to be found in myths about the origin of certain
constellations (although I did in fact begin by considering an intermediary type illustrated by $M_{354}$), I succeeded in isolating the set $M_{60}$,
$M_{317}$, $M_{402-404}$. From these constellations I moved on to others, then to
the logical symbols of constellations without any actual existence (this
was the case in $M_{354}$), and finally to the sun and the moon. In the myths,

this progression is accompanied by another occurring in the same order and moving from the notion of a long – annual or seasonal – periodicity to a short, monthly or daily, periodicity, the two kinds being in opposition to each other in the same way as the constellations are opposed to the moon, and forming polarities between which, for reasons I have already described, the sun occupies an intermediary position and exercises an ambiguous function. Now something irreversible occurs as the same narrative substance is being subjected to this series of operations: like laundry being twisted and retwisted by the washerwoman to wring out the water, the mythic substance allows its internal principles of organization to seep away. Its structural content is diminished. Whereas at the beginning the transformations were vigorous, by the end they have become quite feeble. The phenomenon was already apparent in the transition from the real to the symbolic, and then to the imaginary (see above, p. 84), and it is now manifest in two further ways: the sociological, astronomical and anatomical codes, which before functioned visibly, are now reduced to a state of latency; and the structure deteriorates into seriality. The deterioration begins when oppositional structures give way to reduplicatory structures: the successive episodes all follow the same pattern. And the deterioration ends at the point where reduplication replaces structure. Being itself no more than the form of a form, it echoes the last murmur of expiring structure. The myth, having nothing more to say, or very little, can only continue by dint of self-repetition.

But, at the same time, it becomes more extended, for two reasons. In the first place, there is no reason why episodes unconnected by any internal logic should not accommodate other additional episodes of the same type, theoretically *ad infinitum*. The myth therefore appropriates elements from other myths which are all the more easily separable from their sources in that they themselves belong to very rich paradigmatic sets, whose underlying coherence is often concealed by their complexity. Then – and this is a more important point – the need to fill increasingly short episodic periods makes it necessary to extend the myth, as it were, from within. Each period requires its own particular little story, and the diminished contrast with other stories of the same type nevertheless generates a differential feature, which serves to signify that story.

This being so, it is understandable why these exotic narratives should be so strongly reminiscent of a genre no less widespread than their own, but associated with the powerful technical resources and popular demands of industrial society; I am referring to the serial story, the *roman-feuilleton*. Here, too, is a literary genre which draws its inferior substance from better models, and becomes poorer the further it moves away from the originals. In the myths, as in the *roman-feuilleton*, creation proceeds by imitations which gradually distort the nature of the source. But there is more to it than that: the analogous construction of the episodic myth and the *roman-feuilleton* results from their respective sub-servience to very short forms of periodicity. The difference is that, in the one case, the short periodicity arises from the nature of the signified and that, in the other, it is imposed from without as a practical require-ment of the signifier: the visible moon, by its apparent movement, and the popular press, by its circulation, are subject to daily periodicity and, in the case of any story, the same formal constraints apply to the need to signify the one or to be signified by the other.

However, it would be wrong to forget that although the paths of the episodic myth and the *roman-feuilleton* may intersect, myth and serial story move along their courses in opposite directions. The *roman-feuilleton*, the ultimate and debased state of the novel as a literary genre, links up with the lowest forms of myth, which are themselves a first attempt at fictional creativeness in its pristine freshness and originality. With its 'happy ending', which rewards the good and punishes the wicked, the *roman-feuilleton* achieves a rough equivalent of the closed structure of the myth, transposed on to the caricatural level of a moral order with which a society caught up in history believes it can replace the logico-natural order it has abandoned, or which has abandoned it. But the stories we have just been considering depart from the mythic paradigm in that they do not really finish: the story they tell is not a closed one. It begins with an accident, continues with a series of dis-couraging and inconclusive adventures and ends without the initial deficiency having been remedied, since the hero's return solves nothing; having been indelibly marked by his arduous journey through the forest, he becomes the murderer of his partner or his pet animals, and is himself either doomed to an incomprehensible death or reduced to a state of wretchedness. It is, then, as if the myth's message reflected the dialectical process that had produced it, and which is an irreversible decline from structure to repetition. The hero's reduced destiny expresses, in terms of content, the modalities of a form.

Is this not precisely what constitutes the novel? The past, life and the dream carry along with them dislocated images and forms, by which the writer is haunted when chance or some other necessity, contradicting the necessity by which they were once engendered in the actual order of reality, preserves in them, or rediscovers in them, the contours of myth. Yet the novelist drifts at random among these floating fragments that the warmth of history has, as it were, melted off from the ice-pack. He collects these scattered elements and re-uses them as they come along, being at the same time dimly aware that they originate from some other structure, and that they will become increasingly rare as he is carried along by a current different from the one which was holding them together. The *dénouement* or 'fall' of the plot,[1] which from the very beginning was internal to its development, and has recently become external to it – since we are now witnessing the fall or collapse *of* the plot, after the 'fall' *within* the plot – confirms that because of the novel's historical position in the evolution of literary genres, it was inevitable that it should tell a story that ends badly, and that it should now, as a genre, be itself coming to a bad end. In either case, the hero of the novel is the novel itself. It tells its own story, saying not only that it was born from the exhaustion of myth, but also that it is nothing more than an exhausting pursuit of structure, always lagging behind an evolutionary process that it keeps the closest watch on, without being able to rediscover, either within or without, the secret of a forgotten freshness, except perhaps in a few havens of refuge where – contrary to what happens in the novel – mythic creation still remains vigorous, but unconsciously so.

---

[1] TRANSLATORS' NOTE: The author appears to be playing on the literal and rhetorical meanings of *la chute*: 'fall', 'collapse' and 'end', 'ending', 'resolution' (cf. 'dying fall'), and he is no doubt referring to the rejection of the concept of plot in the 'New Novel'.

# PART THREE  THE CANOE JOURNEY OF THE MOON AND THE SUN

*It is a terrifying thing to see the Indians venture forth in bark boats on this lake where the tempests are terrible. They hang their manitous at the sterns of the boats and shoot forward through snow-storms and amid high waves. These waves are on a level with, or higher than, the open tops of the boats, which they seem about to swallow up. The hunters' dogs, standing with their front paws on the edges of the boats, howl dismally, while, in complete silence, their masters strike the water rhythmically with their paddles. The boats move forward one behind the other: at the prow of the first boat stands a chief who repeats the monosyllable OAH, the first vowel on a high short note, the second on a long, muffled note; another chief stands in the last boat, manipulating a huge oar which serves as a rudder. The other warriors are seated cross-legged in the bottoms of the boats: through the mist, snow and waves all that can be seen is the feathered-headdresses of the seated warriors, the straining necks of the howling dogs and the shoulders of the two chiefs, pilot and augur: they look like the gods of these waters.*

Chateaubriand: *Voyage en Amérique*, pp. 74–5
(cf. *Mémoires d'Outre-Tombe*, Livre VIII, Ch. 1)

# 1  *Exotic Love*

In order to find his macaw-wife, Monmanéki, the hero of M₃₅₄, accompanied by his brother-in-law, set off eastwards on a canoe journey. The hero took up his position at the back and put his brother-in-law in front. Then, without using the paddles, they drifted downstream ...

It is an interesting fact, although one little commented upon, that myths involving a canoe journey, whether they originate from the Athapaskan and north-western Salish, the Iroquois and north-eastern Algonquin, or the Amazonian tribes, are very explicit about the respective places allocated to passengers. In the case of maritime, lake-dwelling or river-dwelling tribes, the fact can be explained, in the first instance, by the importance they attach to anything connected with navigation: 'Literally and symbolically', notes Goldman (p. 44), referring to the Cubeo of the Uaupés basin, 'the river is a binding thread for the people. It is a source of emergence and the path along which the ancestors had travelled. It contains in its place names genealogical as well as mythological references, the latter at the petroglyphs in particular.' A little further on (p. 46), the same observer adds: 'The most important positions in the canoe are those of stroke and steersman. A woman travelling with men always steers, because that is the lighter work.[1] She may even nurse her child while steering ... On a long journey the prowsman or stroke is always the strongest man, while a woman, or the weakest or oldest man is at the helm ...'

This being so, it may seem surprising that M₃₅₄ should reverse the rôles: the hero goes to the stern and he puts his brother-in-law in front, although the myth depicts the latter as a lazy ne'er-do-well. We should not forget, however, that, as is also made clear in the myth, the current is carrying the boat along, so there is no need to paddle. The only

---

[1] 'Stroke' and 'steersman' are the English terms. Indian canoes have no tiller (*barre* in French), therefore the French term for steersman, *l'homme de barre* or *barreur*, could not be used. The French Canadians solved the problem by applying the noun *gouvernail*, 'rudder', to the man instead of the thing. They referred to the crew member at the stern as *le gouvernail du canot*, and to the crew member at the bows as *le devant du canot* (Kohl, p. 33).

activity which counts is the steering done with the oar. But what is the meaning of this canoe journey in which, according to circumstances, the value of the respective positions changes? Other myths, also belonging to the Tucuna or originating from neighbouring tribes, bring out the importance of these questions:

$M_{405}$. *Tucuna. 'The canoe of the sun'*

A solitary youth was fishing when the sun arrived in a canoe and asked him if he had caught anything. The boy answering in the negative, the sun invited him to join him for, he said, they should have caught something by this time. The youth sat in the prow while the sun steered. The sun asked his passenger which was the 'Pathway of the Sun'. Then the youth realized that he was in the sun's company, although the sun had made the boy insensitive to the heat. They paddled along. The boy thought that they were still paddling down here on earth but they were already up in the sky. A pirarucu fish (*Arapaima gigas*) one metre long appeared. The sun seized the fish, threw it into the canoe and baked it with his heat.

Some time later they halted in order to lunch in the canoe. The youth finished his share first. The sun pressed him to eat more, but the boy was obliged to decline. The sun ordered him to bend his head forward and then slapped him on the back of the head. At once a great number of cockroaches fell out of the boy. 'That was the reason that you felt stuffed,' said the sun. The boy regained his appetite. They ate the entire fish. The sun collected the scales and bones, put the fish together again and threw it alive into the water (Nim. 13, p. 142).

This myth links up with several others. With $M_{354}$, in the first place, since the couple formed by the sun, master of fishing and resuscitator of fish, and the apathetic and ineffectual young fisherman, reconstitutes – with an additional enlightening astronomical reference – the couple formed by Monmanéki, creator of fish and master of fishing and his ne'er-do-well brother-in-law. It will be noted that in both cases the character endowed with supernatural powers takes up his position in the stern, while the other is in the bow.

Secondly, $M_{405}$ is reminiscent of a Mundurucu myth already studied in the previous volume ($M_{255}$; *HA*, pp. 205–8) because it attributed the origin of the winter and summer suns to two brothers-in-law, put to the test by two divinities, the sun and moon, masters of fishing and resuscitators of fish (see above, p. 93). During the encounter, one of the men lost his penis metaphorically (it was not much of a penis anyway), while the other became metaphorically (and probably in actual fact, if the recorded versions had been less prudish and more explicit) a man with a long penis. After acquiring strength and beauty, the former married a woman socially remote from him; whereas the latter, because he had committed incest with a mother, that is a woman close to him, became an ugly cripple. I am still dealing, then, with the same semantic field as was worked out in the first part of this book, although I have now chosen to look at it in a new perspective. Let us now turn to the Guiana myths.

*M106. Warao. 'The story of the beautiful Assawako'*

There was once a boy called Waiamari who lived at his uncle's house. The uncle's youngest wife made advances to him while they were both bathing in the river. 'Incest! Shame!' shouted the boy. The uncle, hearing the angry shouts up at the house, called out to his wife not to trouble the boy. The latter thought it better to leave his uncle's house and he went off to take up his abode with his elder uncle, whose name was Okohi. His departure aroused the first uncle's suspicions, and he went to reproach the young man for having attempted to seduce his own aunt. They started fighting and the uncle was thrown down twice. At this moment, Okohi interfered in order to save further strife, and thought it best to take Waiamari away with him on his journey. Waiamari prepared the canoe and painted the sign of the sun on the bow of the boat, while on the stern he painted a man with a moon alongside him.

Uncle and nephew got away the next morning, the nephew paddling in the bow and the uncle steering. They were intending to cross a big sea and as the paddle-blades swept along the water sang: 'wau-u! wau-u! wau-u!' At last they reached the opposite shore and went up to a house where the good and beautiful Assawako lived. The latter received them graciously and asked the uncle to let his nephew accompany her to the field. When they reached there, Assawako told the young man to rest himself while she gathered something for him to eat. She brought him yellow plantains and pineapples, a whole bundle of sugar cane, some watermelons and peppers. The boy ate the lot and spent a very happy time with his companion. On the way back she asked him whether he was a good hunter. Waiamari never said a word and soon rejoined her with a full load of armadillo flesh. She was proud of him and as an Indian woman always does, she resumed her place behind him. Just before reaching home, she promised him they would find a drink in the house and asked whether he could play a certain musical instrument. 'I can play a little,' the boy replied. So he was given a whole jugful of drink to prime him for playing the music, and he played beautifully. They sported all night.

Next morning Okohi made ready to leave. Of course Assawako would have liked Waiamari to remain with her, but the latter said: 'No! I cannot leave my uncle. He has always been good to me and he is getting old.' The young woman burst into tears. He was very sorry also and they both tried to find a little comfort in music.

Okohi and his nephew returned to their own country. After bathing and cleansing his skin, the old man gathered all his family round his hammock and spoke to them as follows: 'When I was young I could stand travelling day after day as I have just done, but I am old now and this is my last journey.' So saying, his head burst and out of it there came the sun's warmth and heat (Roth 1, pp. 255–6).

In connection with this myth, Roth (1, p. 255, n. 2; 2, p. 611) recalls that even up to very recent times, Indian canoes were decorated with the sun and moon. The custom must have extended well beyond the area he is referring to: in Martinique, R. Price saw and described canoes decorated on the bow and stern, and sometimes in the middle too, with painted patterns representing the rising sun (on the bow), or made up of concentric circles or multi-coloured rosettes. These paintings, which were a common sight a hundred years ago, and which perhaps still are at Sainte-Lucie, are said to bring the fisherman good luck. It is just possible that they originated in a mythic system of the same type as the one I am now analysing, and that the sun and moon represented on the bow and stern of the canoe are ideally its passengers. The Yaruro of Venezuela say that the sun and his sister, the moon, travel in a boat (Petrullo, pp. 238, 240). Similarly, in a passage in the Jivaro origin myth: 'Nantu, the moon, and Etsa, the sun, then constructed a canoe of caoba wood and in it went out into the river, where a second son, Aopa, the manatee, was born' ($M_{332}$; Stirling, p. 125). The Amazonian Tupi believe the four terminal stars of the Southern Cross to be the corners of a fishing dam, and the others to be fish already caught. The Coal-sack represents a *peixe boi*, the Portuguese name for the manatee, and the two stars of the Centaur represent fishermen preparing to harpoon it. It is said that the younger, who is now standing in the bows of the canoe ready to throw the harpoon, was formerly at the stern. The old fisherman had found the weapon too heavy and they changed positions (M$_{407}$; Stradelli 1, under 'cacuri'). Here again, then, but transposed into a constellation, we find the old and young fishermen, one effective, the other ineffective, forming the canoe couple which has already been featured in several myths. These myths can now be compared with the following one:

M$_{149a}$. *Arecuna.* '*The frog catcher*' (cf. RC, p. 264)

There was once a huge tree at the top of which lived the toad Walo'ma. In spite of the latter's threats, an Indian called Akalapijeima had resolved to catch him. After several vain attempts, he thought he had succeeded but the toad swam away with the man to an island where he abandoned him. The island was very small and it was very cold there. The only shelter the Indian could find was under a tree where griffon-vultures perched and spattered him with excrement.

He was covered with droppings and extremely foul-smelling, when Kaiuanóg, the morning star, came along (the planet Venus; cf. M$_{361}$). The man asked her to take him up into the sky, but she declined because when, according to the native custom, he had put his manioc loaves to dry during the day on the roof of his hut, he had dedicated the offering to the sun. The moon, who next appeared on the scene, refused to help and warm him for the same reason.

Finally, Wéi, the sun, arrived and agreed to take him in his canoe; he also ordered his daughters to clean his protégé and cut his hair. When the latter's beauty was restored, Wéi suggested that he should marry one of his daughters. The man was unaware of his rescuer's identity and, in all innocence, begged him to call the sun to warm him because, now that he had been washed and installed in the bow of the canoe, he was suffering from the cold. It was early morning and the sun had not yet begun to shed his beneficial rays. Wéi asked his guest to turn round and he put on his feather diadem, his silver head-dress and his ear-rings made from beetles' wing-sheaths. The canoe rose higher and higher into the sky. It became so hot that the man complained. Wéi gave him protective clothing and then he felt comfortable.

The sun, who still wanted him for his son-in-law, promised him one of his daughters, and forbade him to pay court to other women. As it happened, they were approaching a village. While Wéi and his daughters were visiting a hut, Akalapijeima, although he had been ordered not to leave the canoe, got out of it. The griffon-vulture's daughters gathered round him and, as they were very pretty, he made advances to them. When the sun's daughters returned, they hurled reproaches at him, and their father became angry: 'If only you had listened to me, you, like me, would have remained eternally young and beautiful. But, things being as they are, your youth and beauty will be short-lived!' Whereupon each one went off to retire for the night.

The next morning, Wéi set off early with his daughters. When the hero awoke among the vultures, he had become as ugly and old as the sun had predicted. The sun's daughters scattered throughout the sky in order to light up the Milky Way, which is the way of the dead. Akalapijeima married one of the vulture's daughters and grew accustomed to his new life. He is the ancestor of all the Indians and, because of him, his descendants only enjoy youth and beauty for a limited period, after which they become old and ugly (K.-G. 1, pp. 51–3).

Goeje, who suggests 'big skull' as the etymology of the hero's name, gives a variant in which the latter jumps onto the back of a frog, who carries him off to an island. The rain, the sun and the wind in turn refuse to help him. Finally the moon agrees to take him in its canoe ($M_{149b}$; Goeje 2, p. 266; cf. 1, pp. 43, 83, 116). The two versions are obviously linked with the Guiana set mentioned in connection with $M_{386}$, and which, in the light of certain North American parallels ($M_{385}$), I suggested might be considered as a group symmetrical with that of the clinging-woman. It is also clear that $M_{149a, b}$ are inversions of other myths which have already been studied, since the opening sequence begins with a disjunction of the hero in order to achieve conjunction with the metonymic filth of the vultures (they produce it), and to which filth – after the sun's vain attempt to rescue him – he returns metaphorically by allowing himself to be seduced by the vulture's daughters. The order of the sequences adopted by $M_{405-406}$ is therefore changed on two counts. On the one hand, in two successive sequences of the same myth, a syncretic process brings together filth in the literal sense ($M_{405}$; the cockroaches covering the back of the hero's neck), and metaphorical filth ($M_{406}$; the invitation to commit incest). On the other hand, $M_{406}$ considers first of all a sexual union which is too close (with the aunt), then one which is too remote (with Assawako, the beautiful stranger), whereas $M_{149a}$ begins with the second kind (the hero goes off with the sun's daughters) and ends with the first (he returns to the vultures' filth).

Attention must also be paid to the various sanctions entailed, in the myths, by the hero's behaviour. When considered at group level, these sanctions are found to be of two types. Some concern fishing, others periodicity, which can be either seasonal or biological.

Let us begin with fishing. From a close marriage (with a fellow Indian), $M_{354}$ moves on to a miraculous catch of fish, but one obtained by a demoniacal method, which consists in the fisher-woman's body (flesh presented as a bait) being brought into *physical contiguity* with the fish. From a distant journey (in the sun's canoe), $M_{405}$ moves on to an equally miraculous catch of fish, but this time angelical in character, since, in order to restock the rivers, all that is necessary is to shape the bones and skin of the fish, after the flesh has been eaten, *in the likeness* of the whole animal: the simulacrum, when thrown into the water, at once comes to life. In this way, the sun's fish are immortal, as his human son-in-law in $M_{149a}$ might have been. So, it is clear that the two kinds of sanctions merge into each other, although, according to the particular myth concerned, they may affect either the product of the operation (the fish) or the fisherman himself (the passenger in the canoe).

Since the myths present the alternatives of resuscitation and putrefaction, it should be noted that the second term also admits of two meanings: *physical filth*, in the form of cockroaches which prevent a successful catch of fish (the hero fails to catch any), and spoil his enjoyment (the hero has no appetite), or in the form of excrement with which the clinging-woman in $M_{354}$ (who is too close) defiles her husband's back while at the same time preventing him from eating, that is, again, from enjoying the catch of fish; and *figurative filth*, subsequent to an over-close marriage, such as is punished by the 'shame' of incest ($M_{406}$) or premature old age and ugliness ($M_{149a}$). It is possible, however, to see certain differences between the three myths. Monmanéki the hunter, the hero of $M_{354}$, *accepts* a series of wives who are too remote, then one who is too close. Waiamari, the hero of $M_{406}$, *refuses* a wife who is too close, then another who is too remote. Akalapijeima, the hero of $M_{149a}$, *refuses* a wife who in the circumstances would *not* have been too remote, and *accepts* one who is too close. In the first instance, the diabolical catch of fish is lost (unlike the catch of fish in $M_{405}$, which is angelical because of the immortality of the fish); in the third and last instance, it is the fisherman's immortality which is lost, leading to the shortened periodicity of human life. But what happens in the second case?

First, it should be noted that $M_{406}$ is the only myth in the group to envisage, albeit by omission, a third solution to the matrimonial dilemma facing the hero because of the advances of a perverse woman who is too close and of another woman who is too remote, although endowed with every physical and moral virtue. Waiamari does not become the lover of his aunt, the wife of his benefactor; nor the husband of his benefactress, whose lover he agrees to become only for one night: he returns to his own people and no doubt gets married, although the myth does not say so; it must not, however, be forgotten that the Warao are in favour of endogamy within the matrilocal group (Wilbert 9, p. 17). This matrimonial formula, which, in their view, constitutes a happy medium, allows them to shift the other two formulae in the direction of proximity: a close marriage is confused with incest, and a remote marriage becomes simply exotic, whereas the Tucuna, who are patrilineal and were once strictly patrilocal (Nim. 13, p. 96) but exogamous, regard the too-remote marriage ($M_{354}$) as a distended union: that of a human with an animal.

The Warao hero's good behaviour leads to the transformation of his old uncle Okohi (Hokohi, Wilbert 9, p. 64) into beneficent light and warmth. It would therefore seem, that the Warao, like the Mundurucu (Murphy 1, p. 86, n. 16), distinguish between the visible sun and the real sun, who is a personified divinity. The Bororo make the same distinction and I could quote other instances, but the case of the Mundurucu offers a special interest. They combine the initial distinction between the real sun and the visible sun with an additional distinction (latent in the Warao myth) between the summer sun, which is 'warm and luminous', and the winter sun which is 'dark and veiled by clouds' ($M_{255}$; Murphy 1, p. 86). The transformation of old Okohi therefore takes on a two-fold aspect: from transcendent sun to immanent sun and from aperiodic sun to periodic sun.

That is not all. Roth (1, p. 255, n. 1) notes that the Warao word okohi means the hottest part of the day, and that it refers to the warmth and heat of the sun, as distinguished from its power of producing light. The moon and the sun both have the power to give light, but only the sun is also able to radiate warmth. Consequently, strange as this may seem to European minds, the sun is included in a broader category of luminaries, of which it is a particular instance. It is a fact that, in several languages of North and South America, the same word is used for both the sun and the moon, and accompanied, if need be, by a suitable qualification: e.g. 'day' star, or 'night' star. The Warao, who have two separate terms, nevertheless subordinate the sun to the moon: the moon 'contains' the sun (Wilbert 9, p. 67). This logical priority of the moon over the sun is found in several communities. The Surára, who consider the moon as their demiurge, attach little importance to the sun because, they maintain, the sun is alone in the sky, whereas the moon enjoys the company of countless stars closely associated with it. Mountains too, being many in number, occupy a place in the hierarchy of divinities immediately after that of the moon, for which they act as mediators (Becher 1, pp. 101, 104; 2, p. 91 *et seq.*). This conception of the sky in which – as Chateaubriand writes so poetically, 'day prepares immense emptiness, as if to make ready a camp to which night will silently bring an army of stars' (3, III, iv, 5; 2, I, 6), also emerges from the Cashinawa myths ($M_{393-394}$); linguistic evidence of it can be found much further south, for instance among the Southern Guarani, whose word for the stars, yacitata, is a compound of yaci, 'moon', and tata, 'fire' (Montoya).

The Cubeo, who live along the Uaupés river, apply the same word, avya, to the two celestial bodies. However, their interest is in the moon and not in the sun: 'they say that the sun is merely the moon giving light and heat during the day ... But as sun, avya lacks anthropomorphic character. The interest of the Cubeo in the moon rather than the sun, seems related to their concept of nightfall as the sacred time. Almost all ceremonies are night ceremonies, whereas day-light is the time for work' (Goldman, pp. 258-9). The Serenté of the central plateau call the sun bdu and the moon wa, although instead of the first term they tend to use sdrako, meaning 'solar light and heat' (Nim. 6, p. 84). In spite of the distance between them, the Toba of the Chaco and the Cubeo have remarkably similar attitudes: 'The attention of the old men is concentrated on the moon ... they say that the moon is "our brother and cousin" ... the moon's phases illustrate the various ages of human life.' According to a tradition, there is a kindly old-man-moon, who is murdered but immediately comes back to life again. The new moon is a young moon, the full moon an old moon. The first crescent a 'little man', and the last a 'dying man' ... The Emok describe the sun, nala, as having two aspects: lidaga, 'light giving' and n:tap, 'which warms' ... In mythic traditions, the sun does not play an important part ... ' (Susnik, pp. 22-4). Like the Toba, the Cubeo believe the moon to be masculine: he is a god who deflowers virgins and is responsible for menstruation. These miscellaneous indications show how useful it would be, for the study of both the North American and the South American Indians, to chart the distribution of this complex and recurrent ideology, in which the moon is given priority over the sun, the latter appearing rather as the moon's diurnal and meteorological mode, although it is conceived of as being, at one and the same time, substantively more rich (it emits heat as well as light) and more restricted in extent. At any rate, this ideology explains why, in the myths with which we are concerned, the sun, although the more respectable partner ($M_{405, 406, 149a}$) or the more efficacious ($M_{354}$), takes the back seat in the canoe, which, as has been seen, is the one usually occupied by a woman or an old man, in other words by the less strongly 'marked' of the two terms. And although, in $M_{407}$, the old man first of all sits in the bows[2] he quickly resigns himself to giving up the place to the younger man.

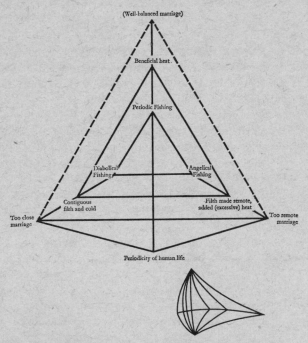

(Well-balanced marriage)

Beneficial heat

Periodic Fishing

Diabolical Fishing

Angelical Fishing

Contiguous filth and cold

Filth made remote, added (excessive) heat

Too close marriage

Too remote marriage

Periodicity of human life

Figure 10. Structure of 'celestial canoe' myths

[2] The place of the solar motif in contemporary canoe decoration from the West Indies to Venezuela.

We see, then, that, in the group of myths thus constituted, an astronomical dimension is added to the techno-economic, sociological and seasonal dimensions already indicated. These form a series of closely interlocking reference systems. If I may venture the image, they can be likened to a plant bulb, at the top of which the theme of the reasonable marriage, one which is neither too remote nor too close and which the myths leave as a potentiality (perhaps because they believe it to be Utopian), indicates the direction which an unlikely shoot might take, were it to germinate.

In Figure 10, the reader can, if he wishes, single out the courses corresponding to each of the myths we have considered. He will then see that $M_{354}$ describes the most complex network, since it links together marriages which are too remote and one which is too close, contiguous filth, diabolical fishing (which it loses) and periodic fishing (which it obtains). This wealth of relationships provides retrospective justification for my choice of $M_{354}$ as the guiding line for my enquiry.

It will, however, be noted that the symmetrical form given to the diagram in order to make it more intelligible distorts the mythic message. On either side of the vertical axis, constituted by terms bringing together forms of stable periodicity, there is a distribution of aperiodic forms. But those which are on the right in the diagram are aperiodic through excess, those on the left, aperiodic by deficiency. The former result from over-remoteness (even the excessive heat, which is a result of the hero prolonging his journey with the sun), the latter from over-proximity. A more faithful representation of the mythic structure would, therefore, distort the diagram in the way shown in the additional line drawing at the bottom.

Without denying the obscure or conjectural nature of these remarks about a journey by water with the sun and moon as canoeists, I am tempted to apply them to the interpretation of canoe-scenes engraved on bone, which were found some years ago in the grave of a Maya priest or dignitary discovered at Tikal. One of the discoverers describes them as follows: 'Two divinities paddling, one in the bows the other in the stern of a canoe, with, as passengers, the Iguana, the spider-monkey [*Ateles* sp.], a gesticulating priest, a being who is half-man, half parrot, and a hairy animal who can be provisionally referred to as "shaggy dog". In another version of the same scene, one of the divinities and the gesticulating priest are sitting at the centre of the canoe, while the animals are arranged in pairs fore and aft. The divinities are looking

Figure 11. The canoe journey. Bone drawings found at Tikal.
(From Trik, p. 12. Photo, University Museum, Philadelphia.)

straight ahead and their eyes are abnormally big; the one steering the
canoe has a squint, a characteristic feature of the solar god' (Trik, p. 12).
'. . . in Maya art squinting eyes constitute one of the sun's chief
attributes' (J. E. Thompson 2, p. 133). It may be added that the divinity
in the stern seems to be the elder of the two, as is also the case of the
sun in the South American myths we have been studying. Lastly, both
figures have a so-called 'Roman' nose, which is characteristic of
Itzamná, the god of the sky, a toothless old man, the master of day and
night, and closely associated with the moon and the sun between whom
he appears in the high-relief sculptured figures at Yaxchilan (Krickeberg, Vol. I, pl. 39; cf. also Spinden 2).

I shall disregard for the moment the problem raised by the paddlers'
changing places from one scene to the other; there will be occasion to
discuss it later in connection with other myths. What is more important,
in my view, is the fact that the Tikal engravings seem to fuse together
in a single scene the canoe journey made by the sun and the moon (of
which M354 contained a weak echo in the form of the journey of the
hunter Monmanéki and his brother-in-law) and a second aspect of the
same myth: although the animals are not the same in the two cases, it
is as if the Maya god were transporting in his canoe the zoological
harem which the Tucuna hero set out to assemble. These two themes –
the canoe journey and the animal passengers – are found together in
certain myths belonging to the northern regions of North America:

### M₄₀₈. Hare Indians. 'The boatman'

The demiurge, whose names Kunyan and Ekka-dékhiné mean respectively 'the judicious one', and 'the one who goes through every kind of difficulty on water', had two wives, one close, his own sister who was as sensible as he was; and the other very remote: an evil mouse who very nearly caused his death. He met with numerous adventures during which he brought about a flood which destroyed mankind. In collaboration with the raven, he created a new generation of men (the bird created a new generation of women), who emerged from the bellies of two fish.

Ekka-dékhiné also built the first boat and set off on a journey downstream along the Mackenzie river. On his way, he met and invited into his canoe a frog and the pike who was trying to eat it, then another frog and an otter who were quarrelling over the skins they were busy tanning (Petitot 1, pp. 141–56; cf. Loucheux, *ibid.*, p. 30).

It will be noted that the northern Athapaskan share with the Venezuelan Warao the belief that men and women were created by two different divinities, one of whom, according to the Warao, was precisely Kororomanna, the creator of the male section of mankind (M₃₁₇ and Roth 1, p. 126). Similarly, the Athapaskan share with the Tucuna the belief that the cardinal points were reversed in the days before the east took the place of the west, and vice versa (Petitot 1, pp. 230–31; Nim. 13, p. 134).

The Iroquois, also a North American tribe although belonging to the north-east, associate the river journey made by a small collection of animals with the origin of the sun and moon. The latter do not actually travel themselves: the demiurge and his servants go to fetch them in the east for the good of mankind. The episode forms an integral part of a cosmological system too complicated to be explained in detail. I shall merely mention in passing that an evil twin, wishing to be born from his mother's arm-pit, causes his mother's death in childbirth, and, tired of waiting for her to come back to life, he cuts off the corpse's head. His grandmother (the dead woman's mother) hangs the head from the tree of the east where, according to an Onondaga version, it becomes the sun and, according to a Mohawk version, the moon. The virtuous twin, distressed by the fact that the people he has created are deprived of daylight, or plunged into too dark a night, undertakes a canoe journey eastwards, accompanied by four animals: a spider, a beaver, a hare and an otter. While the demiurge and three animals go off to make an onslaught on the tree, the beaver remains in the canoe: his function is to turn it round quickly, as soon as his companions come back. Ever since the travellers took possession of the sun/moon, the latter accomplishes its regular course every day and every month, thus ensuring alternate day and night. According to the various readings, the woman's head becomes the sun, and her body the moon or vice versa ($M_{409}$; Hewitt 1, pp. 201–8, 295–7, 315–20 and passim).

One of the animals in the myth acts, then, as the pivot around which the boat revolves, as it were, in order to face back towards its starting-point. This, perhaps, explains why one of the characters in the Tikal engravings, as well as in several myths, sits in the middle of the canoe. Thus, among the Micmac, who are eastern Algonquin: 'The man takes his seat in the stern and the woman in the prow, and the dog sits up in the middle of the canoe' (Rand, p. 146).

An Onondaga version of $M_{490}$, which appears more sophisticated, says that the sun was born from a grandfather's body. At a later stage, the demiurge attributes the rôle of the sun only to the head, while entrusting the body with the task of producing diurnal warmth during the summer. Symmetrically, he transforms his mother's head into the moon, which plays the part of nocturnal luminary, while the body ensures nocturnal warmth during the summer. Consequently, we observe here the same dissociation between the lighting and heating functions of the sun and moon as was already noted in connection with the South American myths (p. 142). It would be particularly interesting to study this aspect in greater detail, since other examples of dissociation occur in the same context: there is dissociation of the demiurge and the first man, who had the same name as the demiurge in the other versions, and of the animal passengers, which are separated out into four effectual and two ineffectual, a division which is not found else-where (Hewitt 2, pp. 512–16, 540–45, 551–5 and passim).

The Iroquois inhabited territory in the middle of the area stretching from the Great Lakes to the East coast, and where, as in Venezuela and the West Indies, bark canoes were usually decorated with stars or con-centric circles, sometimes with the addition of rosettes. The Malecite and Passamaquoddy believed that these circles represented the sun, the moon or the months (Adney–Chapelle, p. 53; cf. pp. 68, 122 and fig. 75, 125–9, 133, 135–7). When travelling, the Ojibwa or Chippewa of the Great Lakes area would often leave behind them messages in the form of drawings; these messages had no mythic significance, since they referred to actual happenings and the animals represented indicated the clan relationships of the travellers. Nevertheless, I would like to give an example, because of the invariable connotations associated with the front and back positions in the canoe, and which correspond to the significance I have attributed to these positions (figure 12).

Figure 12. Chippewa charcoal drawing on a wooden tablet is used to convey a message, which is that two families are travelling by canoe. The eponymous animal of the father's clan is represented at the front of the canoe, that of the mother's at the stern. Between them can be seen the children. Their eponymous animal is a smaller representation of the father's (the society being patrilinear). In the canoe on the left is a man of the bear clan, his wife belonging to the cat-fish clan and their three children; the one on the right contains a man of the eagle clan and his wife belonging to the bear clan with their two children. (From Densmore 2, pp. 176-7.)

Certain converging data suggest, then, that the myths of the Iroquois and neighbouring tribes are related to the same paradigm as the myths of South American origin which combine the idea of a distant undertaking (warlike or matrimonial, accepted or rejected) and that of corporal mutilation or explosion resulting, as the case may be, in the appearance of a celestial body in motion, or a warm, diffused light. These myths, whether they belong to the Cashinawa, to Amazonian or Guiana tribes or even to the Iroquois, bring into play the same pairs of contrasted terms: *fission* or *explosion*, affecting the *upper* part of the body (head) or the *lower* part (headless body, abdomen), and giving rise, on the one hand, to the *moon* or the *sun*, on the other to *light* without heat or *heat* without light, to both heat and light, or to their opposite (as is the case in $M_{396}$, where the goat-suckers emerging from a crushed head express night in its privative aspect: without light and without heat). The similarity between the Iroquois and Cashinawa cosmological systems is particularly striking; the Iroquois combine in the same myth, and express by means of the opposition between the dioscuri, two functions which the Cashinawa assign to characters featured in separate myths: the shy virgin and the trusting visitor; the former is withdrawn and stubbornly opposed to social contacts, like the evil Iroquois twin who wants to keep the light emanating from his mother's head solely for himself, and the latter is responsive to the attractions of the world and of human companionship – even that of an enemy – like the good twin who is ready to undertake a distant journey in order to set the celestial bodies in motion. However, one difference can be noted; the negatively endowed Cashinawa heroes become a sterile moon, whereas the moon freed by the Iroquois demiurge is fertile. In this respect, each group of myths forms an exact counterpart to the other. Reduced to no more than a severed head, the shy virgin and the trusting visitor of the Cashinawa myths only decide to become the moon after long hesitation and after rejecting in turn all the courses which would be advantageous to mankind, among the most important being their ultimate transformation into edible fruit or vegetables (see above p. 96). They think of the moon as a luminous star which, because it gives out no heat, is sterile; they choose this moon because they do not want to serve any useful purpose. The Iroquois demiurge, on the contrary, is not satisfied with a moon which has been reduced to a severed head and whose only function is to illuminate the night sky. He also reconstitutes his mother's body and addresses it as follows:

'So now, mother, I ordain for thee that thou shalt have a duty and that the purpose of thy duty shall be that thou shalt attend to the earth here present, also all kinds of grasses, some that habitually put forth fruit and also the grown clumps of bushes, some that habitually put forth fruit; also the forests of all kinds of trees, some that habitually put forth fruit; also the many other things that habitually grow on the earth here present, mankind and game animals. . . . Thou shalt have thy duty when it will become dark on the earth; at that time thou in thy turn (that is, alternating with the sun) wilt cause it to be hot, and thou wilt cause it to be light, and thou shalt cause dew to fall. Also thou shalt continue to assist thy grandchildren, as thou addressest them in mind, who will continue to go about on the earth' (Hewitt 2, pp. 542–3).

The Iroquois believe that the moon is female and the sun male, and that the latter takes precedence over the former. Yet in all the dialects, a single word is used for both: gaä'gwā in Onondaga, karakwa in Mohawk, with the general meaning of 'disc' or 'luminary', accompanied, if need be, by a qualifying term. Thus we have andá-kā-gă-gwā, 'day luminary' and so-á-kā-gă-gwā, 'night luminary' (Morgan, Vol. II, pp. 64–5). I would not venture to assert that the Tucuna terms for the sun, jakẹ, and the moon, tawsmakẹ (Nim. 15) are formed from one root. The Cashinawa certainly have a special word, ôxö, to designate the moon, but in their language – as is also the case in other South American dialects – the word for the sun, ba-ri, does not seem to be clearly distinguished from the word meaning daylight and summer heat (Abreu, pp. 553–4). On the other hand, we know that several of the tropical American languages follow the Iroquois and Algonquin pattern and use a single term for both sun and moon. It is worth noting that the Iroquois, like the tribes who speak these languages, believe the butterfly to be the prototype of maleficent creatures (Hewitt 2, p. 505), a belief which is also found among the Salish who live on the opposite side of North America (Phinney, pp. 53–4).

This last comparison is significant since the Salish speaking tribes, although unlike their Kutenai and Klamath neighbours (Boas 9, pp. 68–9; Gatschet, passim; Spier 2, p. 141) and most of the Algonquin and Iroquois, they do not as a rule use the same word for the sun and the moon, believe that the sun and moon are two brothers, one of whom is sometimes no more than a pale replica of the other. In other words, as in South America, we have here two extreme cases (with, however, certain intermediary forms): either the sun and the moon are of different sexes, although they are referred to by the same name, or the sexes are identical and the names are different.

It is chiefly in those regions of North America where these symmetrical procedures are to be observed side by side that the motif of the canoe journey is given prominence and the same attention paid to the position, age and sex of the travellers, as has already been noted in the South American myths. I prefer not to list myths which will be studied in detail in the next volume, and to which I propose here to make only the briefest of references. In a Modoc myth (Curtin 1, p. 4), two brothers sit in the stern, two others in the bow, and the fifth along with his sister in the middle. In several myths found among the Coast Salish, a grandfather and a grandson set off in the same canoe on a distant matrimonial expedition (Adamson, pp. 117–20; cf. M₄₀₆); or the two passengers are a brother and a sister, in which case the man sits in the front, the woman at the back, for 'following the custom, the woman would always take the stern and steer'. During the journey, the sister is made pregnant by a bead hanging from her nose or by the surrounding mist, and is accused of committing incest with her brother; in other words the closeness of the passengers *in the canoe* contrasts with the closeness brought about by the journey itself between people who were originally remote from each other (Adamson, p. 254; Boas 10, p. 51). In another group of myths, the deceiver takes advantage of a canoe trip, during which he sits in front and puts his 'daughters' at the back ('but the girls could not paddle well and the boat went zig-zag') to commit incest with them (Adamson, p. 159; Boas 5, pp. 154–7; E. D. Jacobs, p. 143). These references are particularly interesting since, as already noted (see pp. 61, 109), the 'milt-daughters' created by the trickster in the Salish myths represent an inversion of the 'wooden husband' featured in an important Guiana group ($M_{241-244}$). They thus replace the frog as kidnappers of a lunar hero who later learns his true origin, in the one instance (Salish) from a bird he has blinded, and in the other (Warao) from otters whom he offends by producing a foul smell. Finally, along with the ancient Maya, the Salish share the belief that the sun squints, this being the reason why the moon, his brother, and he once decided to change rôles (cf. $M_{407}$). Sun is cross-eyed, be-cause after moon's disappearance, his mother and grandmother made him from the urine wrung out of the latter's swaddling-clothes so that he could act as a substitute for his brother: 'As he was a cross-eyed child, he is not as hot as his brother was when he travelled as the Sun. Had Moon decided to travel in the daytime, it would be much hotter than it is now, for he has stronger eyes than the Sun' (Adamson, pp. 272, 283 and *passim*). The inland Salish hold similar beliefs: 'The sun is a one-eyed man ... so it is never as hot as it was when Robin (the American bird *Turdus migratorius*) was chosen to be the sun' (Teit 6, p. 177; Ray 2, pp. 135–7). 'Formerly, the moon was an Indian ... whose face was as bright as that of the sun, if not more brilliant ... it was his young sister who darkened it' (Teit 4, p. 91; 6, p. 178; $M_{400}$, $400b$). There is, then, a paradigm, found in both North and South America, and in which certain homogeneous but unequally marked elements – a head, severed, blinded, or blinded in one eye, and a squinting – or a normal gaze – are used to regulate and qualify the summer sun and the winter sun, the excessive sun and the moderate sun, the diurnal sun and the nocturnal sun, in their reciprocal relationships.

These hasty references to North American material have not been made for the purpose of using up extra notes. As I am dealing with communities whose myths will provide the subject-matter of the next volume, in which I shall try to show that these myths are at once transformations and repetitions of those which provided the starting-

point of my enquiry, it was worthwhile making the reader aware of the
point at which I was beginning, in however fleeting and confused a
manner, to realize their importance. The comparison may appear
superficial and arbitrary. But, in so extended a study, it is impossible to
lay out all the proofs simultaneously. The reader can, if he so wishes,
regard the preceding pages as a digression, although he will eventually
come to see that they are the starting point of a whole demonstration.

Whether the chief character is a venturesome husband ($M_{354}$), an
incestuous brother ($M_{392}$), a trusting visitor ($M_{393}$) or a shy virgin
($M_{394}$), he or she is always defined in the myths in relation to two kinds
of marriage, close and remote respectively, one kind sometimes being
chosen in preference to the other, sometimes both being accepted or
rejected at the same time. Every time a canoe journey is featured in the
system, its purpose is to remove the hero from the too-close woman
(an incestuous aunt in $M_{406}$; the vulture's daughters in $M_{149a}$), or to
bring him closer to the remote woman (the macaw-wife in $M_{354}$; the
beautiful Assawako in $M_{406}$), or to do both at the same time, or the
reverse:

| Marriage | $M_{149a}$ | $M_{354}$ | $M_{406}$ |
|---|---|---|---|
| close/remote | + − | + − | + − |
| accepted/refused | + − | + + | − − |

A Machiguenga myth, which was summarized and discussed in the
previous volume ($M_{298}$; *HA*, pp. 315–16), clearly belongs to the same
paradigm, although it replaces the journey by water by an overland
journey. The hero goes off on a distant expedition in the hope of finding
a foreign wife for his son by a previous marriage, so as to prevent him
from making love to his stepmother. As in $M_{393}$, the strangers whom he
hoped would become his affines, behave in a hostile manner; and, as in
$M_{392}$, the suspected incest is only too real. The astronomical coding
which I detected in these myths is retained in $M_{298}$ by means of regular
transformations: *severed head* ⇒ *disembowelled body*; *moon* ⇒ *comet*; *rainbow*
⇒ *shooting stars* (for a more general statement of the transformational
structure of the group, cf. *HA*, p. 317, n. 20). This approach provides
us with additional proof of the fact that the myths establish a correlation
between the sociological opposition of close and remote marriages and
an astronomical opposition: that between light and darkness; these are
terms which can be conceived of as existing in a pure state, absolute

daylight contrasting with absolute darkness, or in a mixed state, day-light being then tempered by the rainbow or the sun's winter haze, and the darkness of night by the moon and the Milky Way, of which the comets and shooting stars are erratic equivalents.

However, the myths go even further. The reconciling of light and darkness occurs not only in the same period of time, as can be observed when the colours of the rainbow or rain-laden clouds mitigate or temper the brightness of daylight, or when the moon and stars light up the nocturnal sky. Such synchronic mediation is complemented by diachronic mediation, illustrated by the regular alternation of day and night, which is in opposition to a theoretical state in which one would prevail to the exclusion of the other. It can be shown that mythic thought applies this matrix in its totality, without separating off its different aspects:

|  | *day*: | *night*: | *mediation*: |
|---|---|---|---|
| *synchronic axis*: | absolute | absolute | tempered one by the other |
| *diachronic axis*: | exclusive | exclusive | alternating one with the other |

The Cashinawa believe that, before the creation of the moon, a dark night prevailed, 'without moon or stars' ($M_{394}$, Abreu, p. 475). In another myth, this *absolute night* is contrasted with the *exclusive daylight* which prevailed on the earth before the first night occurred:

*$M_{410}$. Cashinawa. 'The first night'*
Formerly, perpetual daylight prevailed. There was neither dawn, nor darkness, nor sun, nor cold. Consequently, human beings had no set time for carrying out their various activities; they ate, worked and slept whenever they felt like it. At any given moment, each individual did what he liked. Some could be seen working, while others were eating, relieving nature, drawing water from the river or weeding the plantations.

When the spirits, masters of dawn, night, sun and cold, resolved to release these powers for the first time, pathetic scenes were observed: the hunter in the forest and the fisherman at the riverside were caught unawares and immobilized by the onset of darkness ... A woman, who had gone to draw water from the river, broke her jug on a tree, to which she clung, sobbing, all night long because she could not see her way home. Another woman, who had gone off alone in order to relieve nature, collapsed on top of her excrement. A third, who was urinating, remained in a squatting position until the following day.

But now people sleep during the night, get up at dawn, work and eat at set times; everything is regulated (Abreu, pp. 436–42).

A variant of similar origin ($M_{410b}$; Tastevin 5, p. 171) relates how men first obtained too short a night, which did not allow them time to sleep, then too long a night, during which the forest invaded the fields, and finally a night of the right length lasting as long as the day.

The Carib-speaking Yupa, who live along the frontier of western Venezuela and Colombia, also deduce the concept of a tempered night from that of exclusive day:

$M_{411}$. *Yupa. 'The origin of the moon's phases'*

In former times, there were two suns. One rose as soon as the other set and perpetual daylight prevailed. But it so happened that one of the suns fell into a pit full of red-hot cinders while trying to embrace a woman called Kopecho who was dancing round the fire to seduce him. When he emerged, he had changed into a moon, and ever since day alternates with night. To be revenged on Kopecho, the moon-man threw her into the water where she became a frog.

Every month, the stars rush at the moon-man and beat him, because he has refused to allow his daughter to marry a star-man. The moon-man's family consists of stars which remain invisible because he keeps them in seclusion. The moon's phases reflect those of the fight between him and the stars (Wilbert 7, p. 863).

I propose to disregard certain analogies, striking though they may be, between the Cashinawa–Yupa group and myths on the same theme found in North America from Southern California to the Columbia river basin: the plurality of suns maintaining perpetual light, the search for a proper balance between day and night, and summer and winter; and the eliminatory enumeration of the parts of the body and their functions terminating in the sexual organs of the incestuous couple who, thus instructed, give birth to the first race of men (Tastevin 5, p. 170; to be compared with a Diegueño-Luiseño-Cahuilla series, etc., which extends northwards as far as the Coast Salish). They had, however, to be mentioned in passing since, in South America itself, the Yupa myth has a remarkable affinity with Araucan beliefs which also belong to the area west of the Cordillera and to the western shore of the New World. Moreover, the Yupa live in the Sierra de Perija, and so themselves belong, geographically, to the Andean zone.

The first point to note is the recurrence among the Yupa and the Araucan of a complex linking together the plurality of suns, a female seducer and the frog. The name given by the Araucan to the sun's son – mareupuantü – could mean 'twelve suns', an interpretation which would be even more directly reminiscent of the multiple suns and moon of Klamath and Joshua mythology than the Yupa myth (cf. $M_{417d}$, p. 341; Gatschet, Part I, pp. 105–6; Frachtenberg 2, pp. 228–33). However, Lehmann-Nitsche (9, p. 191) rejects this interpretation of the sun-child's name, which also has the meaning of frog or toad (Latcham 2, p. 378). The Yupa female seducer, who is subsequently thrown into the water and changed into a frog, is reminiscent of a supernatural creature called Shompalwe in Araucan. She is mistress of fish and lakes, in which she drowns young men (Faron 2, pp. 68, 73–4), and is also presented as a green frog, goddess of the water (Cooper, p. 748). It should not be forgotten that the Kogi of the Sierra Nevada de Santa-Marta, in Colombia, regard the words for toad and vulva as homonyms, and that they have the same mythological complex associating multiple suns, the frog and the replacement of too hot a sun by a tempered sun ($M_{412}$: Reichel-Dolmatoff I, Vol. II, pp. 26–32; Preuss 3, pp. 154–63). Evidence of this belief is found from the north-west coast of North America to the Machiguenga of Southern Peru ($M_{299}$; HA, pp. 320–21), who are also sub-Andean.

The selfish father of the Yupa myth, a celestial character who refuses to give his daughters in marriage and keeps them in seclusion, has an exact counterpart in Araucan mythology:

$M_{413}$. *Araucan*. '*The long night*'

Old Tatrapai's nephews wished to marry their cousins. The old man forced them to undergo ordeals from which they emerged triumphant. But rather than free his daughters, Tatrapai preferred to kill them. The suitors took their revenge by imprisoning the sun in a pot, thus creating a night which lasted four years. Old Tatrapai died of hunger, and the birds, whose existence was also threatened, offered the heroes substitute wives, whom they refused one after the other. Finally, they married one-eyed women offered by the ostrich, or set off to look for their brides in the country of the dead. According to a third variant, the brides were brought back to life by the blood which spurted from their father's severed head (L.-N. 10, pp. 43–51; Lenz, pp. 225–34).

The pampas-dwelling Araucan associate the ostrich (actually part of the Rhea family) with the Milky Way (Latcham 2, p. 402), which the Arawak of Guiana believe to be the final transformation undergone by the sun's daughters just after they had been offered in marriage by their father, and an eligible son-in-law had refused to marry them. In this respect, $M_{413}$ is already an inversion of $M_{149b}$, just as it is an inversion of $M_{394}$ although along a different axis; in this Cashinawa myth, the blood which streams from the severed head of a daughter who is opposed to marriage, and for this reason murdered by her mother, later becomes the rainbow; in $M_{413}$, the blood streaming from the severed head of a father who was opposed to his daughter's marriage, brings them back to life, although it was the father who had murdered them in the first place. We can therefore begin to discern the outlines of a system.

There would be too much to say on the subject of the celestial one-eyed wives, and I shall merely stress that this theme has the same area of distribution, from north of the Rockies to the sub-Andean southern regions, as all the others to which I have already drawn attention. It is found among the Kodiak (Golder, pp. 24–6, 30) and the Klamath (Gatschet, Part I, pp. 107–8; Barker 1, pp. 71–3); and further on we shall encounter North American transformations which are of paramount importance for my demonstration. In South America, the same theme occurs among the Bororo (one-eyed moon) in a myth already quoted and which would confirm the sub-Andean affinities of this community, were such confirmation necessary ($M_{392b}$; Rondon, p. 164), and among the Jivaro who, like the Yupa and the Kogi, believe the sun's wife or wives to be one or several evil or stupid frogs (Wavrin, pp. 629, 635).

Without attempting to follow up simultaneously all these various lines of enquiry, I feel I should summarize the ground already covered. After setting out to discover what significance the myths attach to the canoe-journey made by the sun and moon, I confirmed that this motif is situated in a two-dimensional semantic field. Along the spatial axis, there is an opposition, in respect of their relationship of reciprocal remoteness, between a close marriage and a distant marriage, either accepted or rejected, and which constitute sets of alternatives between which the canoe journey, as it were, makes it possible to arbitrate.

Along the temporal axis, the choice is between eternal day and the long night, and the arbitration occurs synchronically through attenuated modes of light and dark: the rainbow, winter clouds, moon and stars, and the Milky Way; and diachronically through the regular alternation of day and night.

Furthermore, in exploring this field, we have just seen that the myths orientate the spatial axis in two ways: it is thought of as being either horizontal or vertical. Horizontal, of course, when the canoe-journey takes the hero from the near to the distant pole, thus removing him from a domestic environment where he can only be either a confirmed bachelor ($M_{394}$), or an incestuous lover ($M_{392, 406}$), in order to transport him to exotic surroundings where, if he is unmarried, he meets distant princesses ($M_{406, 149b}$), or, if already married, treacherous hostesses ($M_{393}$). However, the Yupa myth ($M_{411}$) clearly raises this axis to a vertical position: the nocturnal sun dies in a pit full of red-hot cinders because he tries to embrace a woman who promptly changes into a water-frog, that is, because he tries to enter into a distant marriage. And when, after becoming a moon in the sky, he refuses to marry his daughters, the stars, to suitors who are also stars and chooses to keep them in seclusion rather than release them, he is behaving like an incestuous father prompted by a secret desire for a close marriage, like old Tatrapai, the hero of $M_{413}$, who, under the influence of a similar

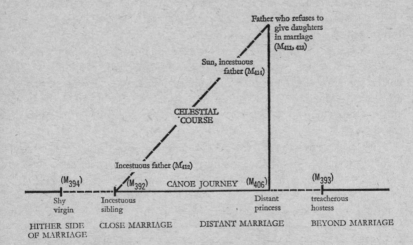

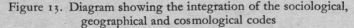

Figure 13. Diagram showing the integration of the sociological, geographical and cosmological codes

feeling, forces his nephews – although, as suitors, they are the 'right distance' away, since in theory at least, the Araucan were in favour of matrilateral marriage with cross-cousins (Faron I, p. 191) – to look for their betrothed in the land of the dead, or to enter into more distant marriages (Figure 13).

At the risk of considerable simplification, it might be said that the horizontal axis is more evident in the myths belonging to the tribes of the Amazon and Orinoco valleys, and the vertical axis more so in those of the mountain tribes or the tribes living close to the cordillera. I would add that certain Andean or sub-Andean myths are situated along a doubly oblique axis, in the sense that, through the incestuous father theme, they link up the myths about the incestuous brother (horizontal axis) with those about the selfish father (vertical axis), while at the same time folding back the astronomical code, as it were, over the socio-logical code. In the Kogi myth ($M_{412}$), the maleficent sun commits incest with his daughter, the planet Venus, who, moreover, is a trans-formation of a boy; since then, they have travelled a certain distance from each other to avoid meeting. Coincidence between the two codes is also evident in a previously quoted Tacana myth ($M_{414}$; Hissink–Hahn, pp. 79–80), in which the sun and the moon, who are respectively father and daughter, acquire their celestial nature as a result of the father's amorous initiative, and in order that they should henceforth remain apart. As in the other myths of this group, in which the origin of the sun and the moon is attributed to incest, a distant astronomical configuration (the characteristic of the sun and the moon being never to appear together) represents a condemnation of a close sociological configuration.

In the Orinoco basin, there is a group of myths which attempt to integrate the two axes. An old version of a myth originating from a now extinct Carib-speaking tribe survives in the form of a few brief but significant details:

$M_{415}$. *Tamanac. 'The girls who were forced to marry'*

Amalivaca, the ancestor of the Tamanac, arrived at the time of the great deluge in which all the Indians, with the exception of one man and one woman who had taken refuge on the top of a mountain, had been drowned. While travelling in his boat, the demiurge carved the figures of the sun and moon on the *Painted Rock* of the Encaramada. He had a brother called Vochi. Together they levelled the earth's surface. But in spite of all their efforts, they were unable to make the river Orinoco run both ways. Amalivaca had daughters who were very fond of travel. So he broke their legs in order to force them to be sedentary and to populate the land of the Tamanac (Humboldt, Vol. VIII, pp. 241–2; cf. Gilij, III, I, Ch. 1; Brett 2, pp. 110–14).

Compared to those previously studied, this Tamanac myth occupies what might be called a strategic position. First of all it is an inversion of $M_{413}$, in which a father was anxious to prevent his daughters getting married; the Tamanac demiurge, on the contrary, forces them to get married. The daughters afflicted with ambulatory mania are the opposite of the shy, home-loving virgin of $M_{394}$. As women, they correspond much more to the venturesome husband of $M_{354}$, and to the too-trusting visitor of $M_{393}$: like the former, they are paralysed, but from within not from without, and not because of entering into too-close a marriage but through being prompted by the reverse intention; like the latter, they have been amputated, but below, not above. The motif of the canoe journey integrates the sociological and astronomical codes so completely that their spatial and temporal modes are simultaneously revealed by the carving of the figures representing the sun and the moon on the rock face along the river (whereas, in $M_{406}$, the sun and moon decorate the boat itself) and by the demiurge's plan to force the river to flow both ways, which would equalize the times of the journey upstream and downstream. This is a translation, into spatial

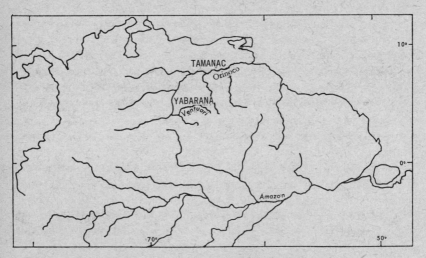

Figure 14. Tamanac and Yabarana

terms, of the regular alternation of day and night that the other myths in the group try to establish (cf. also Zaparo, in: Reinburg, p. 15). I shall return to all these points later, since the Tamanac version is too brief to provide a solid basis for the demonstration. The Tamanac have long since disappeared, and even the memory of their chief divinity has faded from the minds of neighbouring peoples. In the early years of the 19th century, Humboldt noted that the name of Amalivaca was 'known over an area of 12,500 square miles'. Schomburgk, who travelled the same ground less than fifty years later, was surprised to obtain no information concerning Amalivaca: 'even his name appears to be now unknown here' (quoted by Roth I, p. 136).

The situation would have been irredeemable, but for the fact that, as sometimes happens in mythology, a story one might have thought lost for ever reappeared a hundred and fifty years later, in a transposed but quite recognizable form, among a community living quite close to the former territory of the Tamanac and speaking a language belonging to the same family. This was a tribe which, in 1958, numbered hardly more than fifty individuals, whose traditional culture seemed to have been seriously impaired:

*M416. Yabarana. 'The origin of day and night'*

At the beginning of time, the only people who existed were a solitary couple. The man and the woman had bodies different from ours, without any lower limbs and terminating at the lower part of the abdomen. They ate through their mouths and eliminated waste through the wind-pipe at the level of the Adam's apple. Electric eels (*Electrophorus electricus*) sprang from their excrement.

In addition to these two human beings, who were anatomically incapable of reproduction, there lived on the earth two brothers endowed with supernatural powers. The elder was called Mayowoca, the younger Ochi. One day, Mayowoca set off to look for his brother who had got lost during one of his numerous expeditions. He came upon the legless man fishing by the edge of a stream, just as he was pulling out on to the bank a superb piranha fish, which was still alive and quivering. The man was about to club his catch to death, when Mayowoca recognized it as his brother who had changed into a fish in order to steal the fisherman's golden hook.

Mayowoca at once changed into a vulture and attacked the legless man, spattering his club with excrement. Ochi took advantage of this to jump back into the water, and his elder brother assumed the form of a humming-bird which made off with the hook. Then, reverting to his original form, he embarked on a vigorous argument with the man in order to obtain possession of a mysterious basket from which could be heard snatches of bird-song. The legless man had succeeded in capturing the sun-bird. It should be explained that, at that period, the sun shone motionless at the zenith. Day and night were as yet unknown.

But the man noticed the golden hook attached to the side of Mayowoca's head, just where the human ear is now. Furious at having been robbed, he rejected all the proposals regarding the basket. Mayowoca then made him a supreme offer: 'I see', he said, 'that half your body is missing. You have no feet on which to walk, and you drag yourself along with the help of a stick. In exchange for the sun-bird, I will give you a pair of feet and then you will be free to go anywhere in the world.' The legless man had such difficulty in moving from place to place that he agreed to the bargain, on condition, however, that his wife was granted the same favour.

Mayowoca called the woman and set to work. By dint of vigorous massaging and modelling of potter's clay, he completed the missing parts. The man and woman jumped on to their new feet and cautiously began to walk. Henceforth, not only were humans able to travel but they also acquired the ability to procreate.

When the man handed the basket over to Mayowoca, he warned him never to open it, because, if he did so, the sun would escape and never be found again. So precious was the cage that its owner should never show it, nor entrust it, to anyone.

The demiurge set off in great jubilation, balancing the cage on the open palm of his hands which he held close together. He never wearied of listening to the marvellous song of the sun-bird. As he was walking cautiously along, he came upon his brother Ochi who was washing the wounds he had received when he was a fish, and which are still visible on the head of the piranha in the form of black stripes. They continued on their way together and went into the forest.

Presently, as they were hungry, they stopped at the foot of a fruit-laden tree, which Mayowoca asked his brother to climb. The latter, however, had noticed the basket and the mysterious song emerging from it. Feigning exhaustion, he remained on the ground while Mayowoca gathered fruit. Hardly had the elder brother disappeared among the foliage when Ochi, ignoring his brother's injunctions, opened the basket. The sun-bird flew away; its tuneful song turned into a horrible cry, clouds piled up, the sun disappeared and the entire earth was wrapped in a night as black as jet. Torrential rain fell for twelve days on end, flooding the ground with black, filthy, cold and foul water ...

The two humans nearly died. They were saved by a hill which had remained above the water-level. No bird sang, no beast roared. All that could be heard was the howling wind and driving rain, and, between the waters and the still blacker sky, the faint voice of Ochi, bemoaning his mistake as he crouched on top of a mountain. Mayowoca could no longer hear him, for he had changed into a bat which flew very high in the sky, blinded by the darkness and deafened by the storm. Ochi made himself a bed of earth and created around himself all kinds of quadrupeds so that he could feed off them. Mayowoca, with the same intention, created monkeys and birds at a higher level, above the storm.

Years passed. Finally, Mayowoca sent the conoto bird to look for the sun. When it reached the zenith in a state of exhaustion, the sun was no longer there; so it glided down with the wind, which carried it to the end of the earth. By a miracle, the sun was there, like a ball of fire. Weary of being shut up in its cage, the sun had fled to the zenith and thereafter moved from one end of the world to the other, without being able to escape beyond. This was the beginning of the alternation of day and night. At night, men cannot see the sun, because it is passing underneath the flat earth; in the morning it re emerges on the opposite side. To avoid being burnt, the conoto bird took hold of the sun with the help of a tuft of woolly cloud and threw it down to earth. A white monkey received the parcel, unravelled it and put the sun-bird back in its cage.

The sun climbed once more to the zenith where it stopped for a moment. Then, Mayowoca called his brother and told him that, from then on, they would live separately, Ochi in the east and he himself in the west, with the hostile earth between them. Mayowoca next set about organizing the world which had been rendered uninhabitable by the flood. By the sheer force of his thought, he caused trees to grow, rivers to flow, and animals to be born. He opened up a mountain, whence emerged a new race of people to whom he taught the arts of civilization, religious ceremonies and the preparation of the fermented beverages which allow communication with heaven. [A son was born to him, but an ogre tried to devour the child.] Finally he rose up into the clouds, from a place where the imprint of his two feet is still to be seen.

Thus the third world was created. The first had been destroyed by fire in order to punish men who were then given over to incest. The second world perished in the flood, caused by Ochi's imprudent releasing of the sun bird. The third world will be brought to an end by the mawari, who are maleficent spirits in the service of the demon, ucara. The fourth world will be Mayowoca's world, in which the souls of men and all other beings will enjoy everlasting bliss (Wilbert 8, pp. 150–56).

In spite of its length, there is no doubt that this late version is incomplete, since the informant lists at the end episodes that he does not give in full and which would have been more appropriately placed at the beginning. Furthermore, it is not clear what happened to the first couple during and after the flood, nor why the sun-bird had to be put back into its cage after its escape had instituted the regular alternation of day and night.

These uncertainties notwithstanding, the resemblance between the respective names of the demiurges in $M_{415}$ and $M_{416}$, in both of which they are subjected to the ordeal of a flood which destroys mankind and then entrusted with the reorganization of the world, suggests that the two symmetrical episodes of the original legless couple and the demiurge's daughters with broken legs should be treated as inverted sequences. Amalivaca broke his daughters' legs in order to prevent them travelling hither and thither and to force them to remain in one place, so that their procreative powers, which had no doubt been put to wrong uses during their adventurous wandering, should henceforth be confined to increasing the Tamanac population. Conversely, Mayowoca bestows legs on a primeval and, of necessity, sedentary couple, so that they can both move about freely and procreate. In $M_{415}$, the sun and the moon are fixed or, to be more exact, their joint representation in the form of rock carvings provides a definitive gauge of the moderate distance separating them and the relative proximity uniting them. But, since the rock is motionless, the river below should – supposing creation were perfect – flow both ways, thus equalizing the journeys upstream and downstream.

Anyone who has travelled in a canoe knows that a distance that can be covered in a few hours when the journey is downstream may require several days if the direction is reversed. The river flowing two ways corresponds then, in spatial terms, to the search, in temporal terms, for a correct balance between the respective durations of day and night (cf. $M_{410}$); such a balance should also be obtainable through the appropriate distance between the moon and the sun being measured out in the form of rock carvings. Consequently, $M_{415}$ adopts the same procedure on the astronomical as on the sociological level: it places the diurnal and nocturnal luminaries, man and woman, at the right distance from each other once and for all, but immobilizes them; and it is the river which moves. $M_{416}$ adopts a symmetrical but reverse procedure; originally, the sun occupied a fixed position at the zenith, and the primeval couple was immobile. Considered in its positive and negative aspects, the work of creation consists in both cases in rendering them mobile.

There is no mention of a canoe journey in $M_{416}$, nor of its inverted expression, also present in $M_{415}$ in the form of the attempt to make the current 'double', which would neutralize, as it were, the temporal inequality between the upstream and downstream journeys. The contemporary myth replaces the river sequences by another of similar inspiration: the legless man catches the younger demiurge who has changed into a piranha fish in order to steal a hook.

This consequence is directly linked with $M_{354}$, the starting point of the present work, and in which the piranha fish provides the hero with an excuse to get rid of the legless woman – who is also a clinging-woman – whereas, in $M_{416}$, the hero uses it as an excuse to acquire the hook (= clinging-instrument) belonging to a legless man. But that is not all. The river sequence of $M_{416}$, which could appear merely anecdotal, acquires its full significance in Tupi-Guarani mythology where it often occurs. Furthermore, the destruction of the world as a punishment for incest (but by means of flood and not fire) also belongs to Tupi-Guarani mythology (Cadogan 4, pp. 57–8).

The two demiurges in the myths of the southern Guarani are the sun and the moon; in the course of their activities ($M_{13}$; RC, pp. 74, 111), they change into fish in order to steal the hook from an evil, cannibalistic spirit. The clumsy younger demiurge falls prey to an ogre (and not to an ogress, as I mistakenly wrote in The Raw and the Cooked), who eats him up under the horrified gaze of his brother – an episode which is also preserved in a Yabarana story (Wilbert 8, pp. 154–6), which belongs to the same set as $M_{416}$. However, the elder demiurge was careful to gather up the fishbones, and thanks to them was able to bring his brother back to life. The process of devouring followed by resuscitation is perpetuated in the phases and eclipses of the moon, and, incidentally, the moon's spots are the result of an incestuous affair with a paternal aunt. She stained the face of the nocturnal visitor so as to be able to recognize him. Whenever rain has fallen since then, he has been trying to wash away the spots. The sun's eclipses are also due to the struggles of the elder demiurge with the ogre Charia (Cadogan 4, pp. 78–83).

The Tupi-Guarani cosmology exists in several different versions. However, this single version serves to fill the gaps in the astronomical coding of $M_{416}$, the sociological coding of which is clarified by $M_{415}$. The Tupi and the Guarani no doubt think of the mythical twins as the sun and the moon. In this respect they differ from the Yabarana, who imagine the sun to be a bird, and recount the episode of the devouring by the ogre in terms which seem to indicate that Mayowoca's son personifies the moon. The separation of the demiurges in the east–west directions suggests rather an affinity with the rainbow, a meteoric phenomenon which the natives of equatorial America often divide into upper and lower (according to the positions occupied by the demiurges during the flood), or into eastern and western, as happens at the end of the myth. I have already quoted a myth belonging to the Katawishi, a Catukina-speaking tribe of the upper Teffé, between the Purus and Jurua rivers (RC, p. 247):

*$M_{417}$. Katawishi. 'The two rainbows'*

The Katawishi believe there are two rainbows: Mawali in the west and Tini in the east. Mawali and Tini were twin brothers. After the departure of the Amazons, the men were left on their own and it was Mawali who made new women. The two brothers created the flood which inundated the whole world and killed all living people, except two young girls, whom they saved to be their companions. It is unwise to gaze at either of them: to look at Mawali is to be doomed to become flabby, lazy and unlucky at hunting and fishing; to look at Tini makes a man so clumsy that he cannot go any distance without stumbling and lacerating his feet against all the obstacles in his path, nor pick up a sharp instrument without cutting himself (Tastevin 3, p. 191).

Tastevin mentions that the word mawali or mawari means a god, wicked or otherwise, in several dialects (*ibid.*). This is certainly so in Yabarana, in which mawari means 'evil spirit' (see above p. 164). There is probably a connection with Arawak yawarri, which signifies both the opossum and the rainbow (RC, pp. 249–50), especially since the Tucuna, whose territory lies between the Arawak of Guiana and the Katawishi, distinguish between the eastern and western rainbows (see above pp. 40, 112), and speak of two demiurges, one an opossum-god (*RC*, pp. 173, 183), who eventually separate, one going to the east, the other to the west.

Like the Tamanac and Yabarana dioscuri, the Katawishi twins create a flood which destroys mankind and have very fixed ideas about how young girls should behave. The Tamanac demiurges turn a pair of wandering daughters into sedentary women, whereas the Yabarana dioscuri do the opposite in duplicated form: they make a sedentary *couple* into *wanderers*. As for the Katawishi twins, they have dealings with two kinds of women: with Amazons who are also wanderers, since they abandon the twins, and with two fellow country-women whom they save from the flood to be their companions: consequently these women become sedentary. Lastly, the future relationships between humans and demiurges are defined in terms of virtues, in a manner symmetrical with that which enables the other myths to contrast close and distant marriages. To gaze at one of the rainbows causes flabbiness, laziness and bad luck in hunting and fishing, i.e. leads to deficiencies analogous to those which, in the other myths, account for the origin of incest. To gaze at the other rainbow leads to accidents, such as falls and injuries, which are the usual penalty for imprudent and venturesome behaviour. A moral coding is added to the astronomical and sociological codings.

So it is not at all surprising to discover, in the same region but this time among the Carib, a fourth coding, which I have already had occasion to refer to and which is anatomical in inspiration:

M₂₅₂. *Wawai. 'The first act of copulation'* (cf. *HA*, p. 203)

Before any people existed in the world, a pregnant tortoise-woman, who had lost her way, tried to take refuge with the jaguar. The latter killed and ate her, except for the eggs she carried in her belly and from which emerged two children, Mawari and Washi.[3] An old woman brought them up. When they were fully grown, they became bearded and hairy. But they had no sexual organs, since in those days these only grew in the form of a small plant in the forest. Having been

---

[3] It must be noted that the Waiwai language distinguishes between mawari, the name of one of the dioscuri, and yawari, the word for opossum. Similarly in Kalina: mawari and awaré (see Ahlbrinck, under these two words). It follows that the connection I suggested above, on the basis of the respective connotations that the myths assign to the corresponding signifieds, must not be taken as certain. For the words designating opossum and the rainbow, cf. Taylor.

informed of this by a bird, they licked one of these plants one day and then lay down to sleep. While they slept, an unnaturally long and big penis grew out of each one. They now felt the desire for a woman and had sexual intercourse with an otter who pointed to the river and told them to go and find wives over there. However, the women advised the dioscuri not to have sexual relations with them, because they had toothed vaginas (tiny pirai fish in their vaginas). Washi could not refrain from enjoying his wife and nearly died, but in the process his amputated penis acquired a normal size. Mawari preferred to begin by giving his wife magic drugs and this caused the piranha teeth to fall out (Fock, pp. 38–42).

So, the tradition is from no penis at all, which makes even a close marriage impossible, to the acquisition of a penis of reasonable length, by way of the intermediary stage of an over-long penis which could only be of use in a distant marriage. The Waiwai myth thus expresses, in anatomical terms, what certain myths state in sociological or astronomical terms, while others make simultaneous use of two or three coding systems. In all cases, each myth can be defined by the itinerary it chooses to follow through the various registers of a total semantic field, the different aspects of which are now becoming discernible:

ASTRONOMICAL CODE
{
absent moon, eclipse, phases ......... fixed sun
long night ... regular alternation of
                night and day ... long day
............... Milky Way – rainbow...............
}

GEOGRAPHICAL CODE
{
near ............ canoe journey ............ distant
downstream ... river flowing
                both ways ... upstream
}

ANATOMICAL CODE
{
legless woman ............... wandering woman
man without penis ...... man with long penis
}

SOCIOLOGICAL CODE
{
...... incest, endogamy ...... exogamy .........
celibacy ............................. promiscuity
}

ETHICAL CODE
{
shyness ...................................... boldness
}

The above rectangular matrix, which I have considerably simplified in the interests of legibility, represents the common chess-board on which each myth plays out its game. But all the possibilities must be looked at together, if one is to understand the reasons for certain transformations, which at first sight seem puzzling. Thus, Tucano cosmology, which explains the regular alternation of day and night by dividing women up into two categories: 'serious women' and 'loose women or prostitutes' (Fulop, Vol. 3, pp. 121-9), includes a long story ($M_{418}$; Fulop, Vol. 5, pp. 341-6) in the course of which, as in the Yabarana myth ($M_{416}$), a cage is imprudently opened and birds set free. They at once turn into yurupari, i.e. sacred flutes, which the women take possession of and are thus enabled to reduce men to slavery, in spite of the fact that these musical instruments now constitute the symbol and means of the subjection of women to men. The transformation would be incomprehensible if we did not know that, among the tribes living along the Rio Negro and the Rio Uaupés, the word yurupari also means a son which a mortal bore to the sun, so that he (the son) could put an end to the ascendency of women and decree strict laws which they would henceforth have to obey ($M_{275, 276}$; *HA*, pp. 271-3). Consequently, at the same time as the sociological code evolves from the level of matrimonial alliances to that of political relationships (but always in the perspective of sexual opposition), the metaphorical link between the astronomical and social orders changes into a metonymical link between women and the sun's son, as embodied in the flutes. The latter are the *cause* of the disciplined behaviour of the women, just as the regular alternation of the diurnal and nocturnal luminaries is an *image* of a well-regulated matrimonial alliance: not too close, as it would be if the women were incestuous, nor too distant as the result of uncontrollably amorous dispositions which would turn them into gadabouts or Amazons; instead, securely protected against both these risks, they prove to be modest wives, obedient to their husbands' orders. For the Tucano, the dilemma was especially acute, since they practised strict tribal exogamy and obtained wives by sister exchange with related tribes, or even by capturing girls from enemy tribes (Fulop, Vol. 3, p. 132; Silva, p. 408 *et seq.*). The example of a well-ordered sky might perhaps not have been enough to discipline outsiders who must often have proved recalcitrant. And, in these difficult conditions, the terror inspired by the flutes was no doubt to be preferred as a means of ensuring that the wives from outside were not at the beginning shy virgins or incestuous sisters, and did not later turn into treacherous hostesses or dissolute women.

# 2 *The Stars in their Courses*

When considered from a more general point of view, the myths we have just been examining are seen to be trying to resolve a contradiction of which river-dwelling communities in an equatorial area must have been particularly aware. On the temporal level, night alternates exactly with day since, in that part of the world, the two periods are of the same duration. So daily experience offers a constant image of a successful mediation between two states which are at least theoretically conceivable: one in which there would only be day ($M_{410-411}$), and another in which there would only be night ($M_{413, 416}$); or even between two states in which the duration of one period considerably exceeded that of the other.

On the spatial level, however, it is the mediatory state which belongs rather to the realm of theory: for a canoe-journey to be of equal duration upstream and downstream, the rivers would have to flow in both directions at once. But no such situation exists in empirical reality. In fact, although the distance remains the same, it may take a whole day or even several days to go back up a stretch of river that one came down in only a few hours. This is particularly true in the case of rivers broken up by waterfalls and rapids; the force of the current carries the canoe downstream at tremendous speed, but makes long spells of porterage necessary when the journey is being made upstream. In the myths in which one of the dioscuri tries to make rivers flow both ways, the other ruins his attempt by creating rapids and waterfalls, the chief causes of the discrepancy in the lengths of the two journeys.

Consequently, the spatial axis and the temporal axis relate to structures which, from a logical point of view, must appear symmetrical and inverted. Along the temporal axis, the mediatory state is precisely that provided by experience, and only by conjecture can we reconstitute an original state of immediation, in the two forms suggested by myths with a diurnal or nocturnal preliminary, between which, moreover, there is no parity (*HA*, pp. 419-21). Along the spatial axis, the opposite happens:

the absence of mediation is the only datum; with the supposition of the river flowing both ways, the imagination reconstitutes a reverse initial state. Consequently, in either case, the poles of each axis correspond to to each other logically, and one is real, the other imaginary.

The paradox becomes more noticeable along the sociological axis, which now appears as a function of the other two: the marriage rules, whether endogamous or exogamous (and more or less rigidly so in either case) make it necessary to consider carefully the *distance* to be travelled in the search for wives, but with the aim of perpetuating the species, that is, of ensuring the periodicity of the generations which, in the final analysis, is measured by the *span* of human life. So it is not

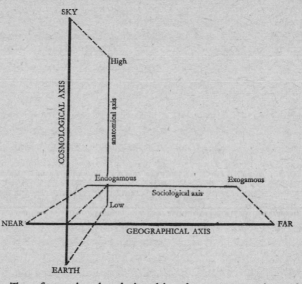

Figure 15. Transformational relationships between cosmic and human coordinates

surprising that myths dealing with the impossible arbitration between the near and the far, should frequently take as their theme the shortness of human life, which was instituted by the demiurges at the same time as the reasonable distance between the sun and moon, the inevitable discrepancy between upstream and downstream canoe-journeys, and the degree of mobility permitted to women. According to the oldest known version of M₄₁₅, the demiurge gave up trying to make the rivers flow both ways but broke the legs of his roving daughter, who 'era amante de camminate', and decreed man's short span of life (Gilij,

Vol. 3, pp. 4–5). Another more recent version adds that he made rock carvings without leaving his large canoe and 'smoothed away the rocks and cliffs' (Brett 2, pp. 111–13), thereby diminishing the obstacles which impede progress, especially during the upstream journey. At the other end of the continent, among the Ona and Yahgan of Tierra del Fuego, the demiurges are concerned with regulating alternation between day and night, ordering the universe, instituting man's short span of life, and teaching humans the art of copulation and procreation (Gusinde, Vol. 2, *passim*). In all cases, the astronomical, geographical, sociological and biological codes are interlinked.

It would be more accurate to say that the astronomical axis, which is vertical since it concerns the sky and the earth, and the geographical axis, which lies horizontally between the two poles of the near and the far, are projected on a reduced scale in the form of axes, which are also perpendicular to each other: an anatomical axis, the two poles of which are formed by the high (head) and the low (legs), and the sociological axis, along which endogamous marriage (near) is opposed to exogamous marriage (far) (Figure 15).

The ideological armature of the myths of equatorial America seems, then, to be linked to a substructure in which native thought sees a contradiction between a temporal axis of the equinoctial type and a spatial axis along which the direction of the journey causes disparity between identical distances. But, this being so, it may appear surprising that the 'double current' theme should also occur in areas of North America, where the solstice rather than the equinox would be the relevant phenomenon. In one sense, the recurrence confirms my thesis, since it is to be observed in those areas where the recurrence of the complementary theme of the canoe journey has already been noted; on the one hand, among the Iroquois (Cornplanter, p. 29; Hewitt 2, p. 466); on the other hand, along the Pacific coast, from Puget Sound (Haeberlin, p. 396) and the Quinault to the North (Farrand, p. 111) to the Karok (Bright, p. 201) and the Yurok: 'At the beginning of time, the Klamath itself flowed up one side, down on the other. Then the creator made the river flow down only, the salmon climb up only' (Erikson, pp. 269, 271). These tribes of North Western California were essentially river-dwelling communities (Kroeber 1, pp. 9, 98–100). The Iroquois, although famous for their highly-developed agricultural system, lived in a region of large lakes and innumerable streams and rivers on which, in olden times, they travelled more often, and much further afield than is supposed today (Morgan, Vol. 2, p. 83).

Consequently, from this point of view, the 'double current' theme, because of its area of distribution, confirms the homogeneity of the group, in spite of the distance separating the tribes. This approach also consolidates the correlation between ideology and infrastructure. Along the temporal axis, however, the infrastructure is not equinoctial in character, since the North American communities just quoted all live between 40° and 50° North. But it is a striking fact that those in the west, at least, should share with their northern neighbours – as far as, and including even the Eskimo – what is tantamount to an obsession with diurnal and nocturnal periodicity, in addition to seasonal periodicity. I have made reference to this (see above, pp. 155–6). This is the case with the Chinook who live along the estuary of the Columbia river to the north of the Yurok and the Karok (Jacobs 2, part 2, pp. 395–6; Sapir 1, p. 173; Boas 7, p. 12), and with the Sahaptin and the Coast Salish (Adamson, pp. 132–3, 188; Jacobs I, pp. 3–5 etc.). But, compared with the South American myths to which they are similar in many respects, those originating from the above-mentioned communities present one outstanding difference: they are not so much concerned with making night and day equal as with preventing their respective durations becoming equal to that of the seasons. In other words, it is less a question of the *relative inequality* of day and night as of their *absolute duration*. On the other hand, the myths systematically refer to magical devices which act sometimes as accelerators, sometimes as brakes, but are always intended to obtain seasonal equality: over a vast territory stretching from the Arctic circle to California, string games are used to slow down the sun's course, or may be in danger of prolonging the winter months, which must then be shortened by cup-and-ball games.

The Eskimo on Baffin Land delay the sun's disappearance by means of string games; with cup-and-ball games they hasten its return (Boas 8, p. 151). The Sanpoil believe they can shorten the year when they play cup-and-ball in winter (Ray 2, p. 161). In Klamath, to catch the ball in the cup is known as 'putting one of the sun's eyes out' (Barker 2, p. 382; cf. above, p. 152); the Modoc, neighbours and kinsmen of the Klamath, play string games in order to 'kill the moon', that is, in order to shorten the current winter months (Ray 3, p. 132). The Shasta play cup-and-ball in winter 'so that the moon should grow old and the winter be short ... In winter too, the children play string games but only when the moon is waxing ... in order to hasten its progress. On the other hand, when the moon is waning, they play cup-and-ball with the backbones of salmon so that it may die more quickly' (Dixon 7, p. 446). So, all these operations, which might also be described as 'lame', since they shorten on one side and lengthen on the other (cf. *HA*, pp. 459–63, where I gave a similar interpretation of the ritual or mythical lameness or limping which plays an important part in these areas), offer, in respect of seasonal periodicity, a positive equivalent of the canoe, the valency of which, in respect of daily periodicity, becomes negative when it 'limps': in other words, when the journey is longer in one direction than in the other. So, expressed in spatial terms, the equinoctial paradox corresponds to the solstitial paradox, which tribes geographically very remote from each other express in temporal terms. In spite of the diversity of their environments, their aim is to safeguard a common ideology, in one quarter by speculative operations inspired by a particular technical skill (the art of navigation), and in another by technical operations (including games) which, needless to say, are doomed to remain speculative. For just as rivers cannot flow in two opposite directions at once, it is impossible, in northern latitudes, to make the seasons of equal length.

In the previous volume, I emphasized one aspect of the theory of periodicity as it occurs in the thought processes of South American Indians, by showing that the starting point of their myths was daily periodicity, based on an actual experience of mediation. At the same time, the myths try to go back to an absence of mediation, the concept of which remains purely theoretical, although it may be thought of in two distinct modalities. According to circumstances, a myth may opt for one of two hypotheses: at the beginning of time, there was either night without day or day without night. But these nocturnal or diurnal preconditions are not logically equal: along the temporal axis, one corresponds to a disjunction between the sun and the earth, and the other to their conjunction. When projected along the spatial axis, the same configuration acquires a sociological significance: according to the ideal distance that each society seeks to establish between the two spouses, they will have been more or less close to each other, that is, relatively conjoined or disjoined, before actually being united in marriage.

Two Guiana myths quoted by Goeje (1, p. 108) from Van Coll and Penard confirm the systematic character of this link. According to one (Arawak: $M_{420a}$), the sun and moon were formerly human beings who kept light shut up in a basket. The sun wanted to marry an Indian woman, but he was too high up to come down, and so the girl had to climb into the sky. No sooner had she got there than she made haste to open the basket, and light poured out of it. It is obvious that this myth systematically reverses $M_{411}$ by means of a series of transformations:

*love-affair* ⇒ *marriage*; *descent of the sun* ⇒ *ascent of the human being*; *origin of nocturnal light* ⇒ *origin of diurnal light*. The other myth, which is Kalina in origin ($M_{420b}$), relates how the sun, the master of light, was obliged to release it, in order to keep a more effective watch over his unfaithful wife. 'Thus he became the visible sun, which henceforth would cause day to alternate with night ... If there had been no sin, night would not have existed, only perpetual light.' The Warao say two old people were in charge of daylight. Their son would only give it to the younger of two sisters, who was still a virgin ($M_{420c}$: Roth 1, p. 266; Wilbert 9, pp. 64–7).

While, from Amazonia to Tierra del Fuego, the myths associate chastity with daylight and sensuality with night, they are agreed in considering the regular alternation of day and night as the normal condition of conjugal relationships. A Mundurucu myth ($M_{421a}$; Murphy 1, pp. 88–9) and a Kayapo myth ($M_{421b}$; Métraux 8, pp. 18–19), both constructed on this theme, bring us back to an Amazonian Tupi myth which was summarized and discussed in the previous volume ($M_{326a}$; *HA*, pp. 416–21). It must be referred to again, since it brings out, even more clearly than those already discussed, the underlying cause of the link between the two themes: the canoe journey and the regular alternation of day and night. As will be remembered, $M_{326a}$ tells of a time when perpetual daylight prevailed. The daughter of the Great Snake had married an Indian, but refused to sleep with him because she considered darkness necessary for love-making. The husband dispatched three servants in a canoe to fetch night from his father-in-law, who held it prisoner beneath the waters. The father-in-law was quite willing to give the servants night encased in a palm-nut, on condition that they did not open the nut until they got home. Prompted by curiosity, the two servants who were acting as paddlers wanted to discover the cause of the noise they could hear coming from the nut; the steersman tried at first to dissuade them, but finally gave in. The three men assembled in the middle of the canoe and opened up the nut; night escaped and covered the earth. The Snake's daughter had to intervene, and she established the regular alternation of daylight and darkness.

We have already encountered astronomical triads. The three servants recall the three ugly, old, black-skinned hags who according to the Kogi ($M_{412}$; Reichel-Dolmatoff 1, Vol. 2, p. 29) persecute the sun and try to establish perpetual night, especially since an Amazonian myth of uncertain origin associates all the themes I have just mentioned with similar characters.

$M_{104}$. *Amazonia*. *'The origin of night'* (cf. *RC*, p. 178)

At the beginning of time, night did not exist. The sun travelled continuously back and forth across the sky, men did not work, and they slept in broad daylight. Three scatter-brained and rebellious young girls one day saw a female water spirit snatch an Indian called Kadaua from under their very eyes. They tried to hold him back, but the current carried them away and all the people in the village who had rushed to the rescue fell into the water after them and became blind, all except three old women who had remained on the bank.

The latter spotted Kadaua, who was floating along with one of the girls and shouted to him to bring her back. He waded ashore, handed the rescued girl over to the old women and went back to look for the others, who were deliberately keeping a long way from the bank. The old women took advantage of this to urge the girl to escape. They explained to her that Kadaua had never loved any woman, that they themselves had once been in love with him and that he had turned them into decrepit old women. The young girl listened, but did not reply. Meanwhile, Kadaua was trying to catch up with the other girls, who no longer recognized his voice and swam away from him. In the end, they drowned.

Kadaua returned, weeping. On coming out of the water, he saw that his pretty protégée was weeping too. In reply to his questions, she explained that she was afraid that, like the three women before her, she might grow old when he approached her. Kadaua protested that he had never been their lover; they in turn accused him of indifference to women. After that, the old women rushed at the heroine and tore out all her hair. The young girl plunged into the water, followed by Kadaua, while the old women turned into opossums.

Kadaua was swimming so closely behind the young girl that he could touch her heel, but she maintained her lead. They swam like this for five lunar months. Kadaua gradually lost his hair, but the fugitive's hair, when it started to grow again, was completely white. Finally, they collapsed together on a bank. 'Why are you running away from me?' he asked. She replied that it was because she was afraid of her hair turning white. Since the irreparable had happened, she could allow him to overtake her; but what had become of Kadaua's hair? The latter then noticed that he was bald. He blamed the water. The young girl replied that the water had indeed 'washed the blackness' out of her hair, and that from now on they would have to live and appear in this state. Kadaua should go back to his own country where his mistresses would laugh at his bald pate!

The man saw the situation in a different light. 'Since it's your fault,' he told his companion, 'that the water shaved off my hair, you can make it grow again!' 'Certainly,' she replied, 'but on condition that you give me back my black hair, as it was before your mistresses tore it out!'

Quarrelling as they walked along, they arrived at a large hut with no one in it. Here they cooked and ate the food (? uareá) which happened to be there, and while they were doing so, the owners appeared. They were the young girl's father and mother, but they refused to recognize her because of her white hair, and they made spiteful remarks about her companion's bald head. The latter felt so depressed that he slept for two days. Two more days passed, and the two couples set off for Kadaua's village, in the hope that the three aged mistresses would be able to cure the young people. However, the hut in which the old women were crying 'Ken! Ken! Ken!,' as opossums do, was so foul-smelling that they dared not go inside. Kadaua set fire to the hut, and there was a strong smell of burning: 'You will burn my hair,' protested the young girl. At that moment, daylight vanished and a dense night spread everywhere, while the heat caused the opossums' eyes to explode.

Immediately, bright sparks rose into the sky and remained there. Kadaua leapt into the hut in the hope of finding his companion's hair; she followed him and her parents did likewise. All four were burnt in the flames. Their bodies exploded and flew up into the sky, where ever since a fire and glowing embers embellish night (Amorim, pp. 445–51).

The interpretation of this myth raises several difficulties. In the first place, it tells a very complicated story. Furthermore, its exact origin is unknown. The fact that it was recorded in nheêngatu, that is in Amazonian Tupi, proves nothing, because this *lingua geral* was in current use in the vicinity of Manaus, among tribes belonging to several linguistic groups, such as Arawak and Tucano. We have only to glance through Amorim's collection, in which he assembles Amazonian myths of various origins without stating exactly what these origins are, to discover that themes like those of the three thoughtless girls and the adolescent lunar hero, who is impotent because he is a hermaphrodite, form an integral part of a mythological heritage shared by related or enemy tribes, between whom matrimonial exchanges or the abduction of women have created all kinds of bonds. In addition to the uncertainty of the anthropological context, some doubt prevails regarding the special genre to which most of the myths recorded by Amorim, Stradelli, and to a lesser extent Barbosa Rodrigues, belong. These authors still had access to versions belonging to a learned tradition, which had no doubt been evolved from hybrid materials by associations of wise men about whom almost nothing is known, except that they were graded according to a strict hierarchy, and that relatively esoteric versions of the same myths presumably corresponded to different levels of the hierarchy (cf. *HA*, pp. 271–2).

I shall therefore put forward my arguments cautiously, and do no more than emphasize certain aspects. It is clear that the two female triads in $M_{104}$ are reminiscent of the masculine triad of servants in $M_{326a}$, since all are associated with the origin of night. They also bring to mind an observation made by Stradelli (1, pp. 503–6) about a feminine nocturnal triad composed of supernatural creatures: Kerepiyua, Kiriyua and Kiririyua, who were respectively 'mother of dreams', 'mother of sleep' and 'mother of silence'. The Tupi believe Kerepiyua to be an old woman who came down from the sky, 'but the Baniwa, Manao, Tariana and Baré etc. tribes maintain that the woman who comes down from the sky is not old but a young legless girl, called Anabanéri in Baniwa, who prefers to travel along star beams or by the rainbow way … '. This mutilated character is reminiscent of others whom we have already encountered.

Like the masculine hero of all these myths, Kadaua finds himself between two kinds of women, and two forms of marriage. The originality of $M_{104}$ consists in duplicating this image, which was a dual one to begin with. At the beginning of the myth, Kadaua is lured by a supernatural creature, the mother of the waters, towards a *distant* and irrevocable marriage, while brazen fellow-countrywomen try to keep him *near* them. The spatial expression of the relationship between the near and the far is followed up by another on the temporal level: it contrasts the three old women from whom Kadaua is moving *away* and the three young girls *towards* whom he is moving, the movement being now in the temporal register. For, by sending the old women away from him, the hero changes them into opossums, that is – as I showed in *The Raw and the Cooked* (pp. 164–88) and as is confirmed by the episode of the foul-smelling opossum – from aged into putrid creatures; and in bringing the young girls closer to him, he transforms one of them into an old woman, and the other two into corpses. As will be shown presently, the second part of the myth combines both aspects.

The process of ageing which is speeded up so that it takes place within a space of five lunar months occurs during a chase through water, which is the opposite of a journey by canoe: the two characters, a man and a woman, are immersed in the water and not floating on it in a boat. The woman is in front of the man, instead of sitting behind him (cf. above, p. 135). Finally, most important of all, the man whose hand is just touching the woman's heel ought to be able to catch up with her, yet does not manage to do so, whereas in the canoe journey (and on this point, the evidence in $M_{326a}$ is of capital importance) the guilty passengers assemble in the centre of the canoe, whereas they ought not to do so. The three thoughtless travellers gather around one of their number, who consequently plays the part of spatial mediator. The uncatchable woman swimmer, because she refuses to be the object of temporal mediation (the ageing process, between youth and death), is the sole survivor of a female trio of thoughtless swimmers.

The reason for these reversals is clear: as myths with a diurnal preliminary, $M_{104}$ and $M_{326a}$ establish a similar opposition between the hypothesis of the long day and that of the long night, but they present a different conception of mediation between the two terms: in $M_{326a}$ mediation is diachronic and consists in the regular alternation of day and night; it is synchronic in $M_{104}$, where the absolute night which might have prevailed is tempered by the conjunction (which is not alternation) of the burnt and the rotten – as soon as it comes into existence thanks to the concomitant creation of the moon and the Milky Way.

Consequently, $M_{104}$, belonging as it does to the learned category, can be placed without further ado at the point of intersection of several myths. If the analysis were continued, it would probably confirm that the opossums shouting 'Ken! Ken! Ken!' inside a blazing hut are transformations of the nocturnal animals in $M_{326a}$ which cry 'ten! ten! ten!' inside their nut prison, from which fire also brings them forth, together with darkness. In $M_{416}$, the sun-bird's cage is an undoubted reversal of the previous theme, since the heroes of the three myths are examples of sexual impotence: legless cripples ($M_{416}$), a hermaphrodite ($M_{104}$) and a husband who cannot sleep with his wife because she rejects him ($M_{326a}$). From Tierra del Fuego to Amazonia, the deficiency from which they suffer is presented as being in relationship with a primordial state in which perpetual day prevailed (cf. $M_{421a, b}$ and the Ona myth $M_{419}$ in: Bridges, p. 433; Lothrop, p. 101; Gusinde, Vol. I, p. 586).

Finally, $M_{104}$ shares with another previously studied myth ($M_{149b}$) an armature, at once synchronic and diachronic, which links the theme of premature ageing, that is, man's mortality, with the theme of darkness tempered by the presence of nocturnal luminaries, such as the moon, the stars and the Milky Way. A hero whose name could denote baldness (see above, p. 140), and another who is soon to become bald, are fought over by the sun's attractive daughters and the vulture's foul-smelling daughters, or by young mistresses and female opossums (also foul-smelling). Both heroes travel by water, having been carried off either by a monstrous toad or a water spirit. Marriage with the sun's daughters brings the human prolonged youth; marriage with the man inflicts premature ageing on his young wife. In both instances, the outcome is the result of a victory won by the foul-smelling creatures. The sun's daughters are abandoned by the hero and change into the Milky Way; the heroine of $M_{104}$, together with the hero who has remained faithful to her, changes into the night stars.

No one myth is completely explicit but, by shuffling them round one over the other until they coincide, I have made them reveal, as through a grid, the common message of which each conceals a fragment or an aspect. I now propose to summarize this message in explicit terms, as it occurs in $M_{415}$, which was the starting-point for the preceding discussion. It can be said that Amalivaca and Vochi, being unable to neutralize the opposition between *close marriage* and *distant marriage* by the 'double current' method, first determined the *reasonable distance* between the sun and moon (an insurance against *incest*) by means of a rock carving; then, by breaking their daughters' legs, they succeeded in fixing them in *relatively close* marriages, although the daughters themselves tended towards *too distant marriages*.

Similarly, the disjointed messages contained in other myths can serve to consolidate each other. If, after rejecting incest with the aunt (instead of committing it and thus causing darkness, $M_{13}$), a lunar hero had agreed to marry a too distant princess, daylight would have been *light without heat* ($M_{406}$), like night, when it is lit with a pale glow by those distant and abandoned princesses, the sun's daughters ($M_{149}$). By coming back to his own people, and so making an *outward* and a *return* journey, the hero allows the sun to appear in the form of the *warm light* of day ($M_{406}$); in other words, the sun is now established at the *right distance*, like the sun's companion who, in order to avoid suffering from cold or heat in the canoe ($M_{149a}$), must sit neither *too near* nor *too far* ($M_{405}$).

When I first dealt with $M_{149a}$ (*RC*, p. 264), I noted that this myth stood in a paradoxal relationship to those with which *The Raw and the Cooked* was chiefly concerned. As a frog hunter, the hero figure is a reversal of the man looking for macaws' nests in the reference myth ($M_1$), since in real life batrachians do not perch at the tops of trees. We know that the Bororo and Ge myths, in which the hero looks for birds' nests, deal with the origin of cooking fire, and that they form a parallel series with other, mainly Ge, myths which associate the origin of man's mortality with that of cultivated plants. $M_{149a}$, the aetiological function of which is the origin of man's mortality, links both groups crosswise. Its beginning is symmetrical with one group, and its end identical with the other.

At this point a curious fact should be noted. All the myths just referred to deal with the relationship between sky and earth, whether the theme is cultivated plants resulting from the marriage of a star with a mortal, or cooking fire which disunites the sun and the earth, once too close to each other, by coming between them, or man's shortened life-span, which is always in all cases the result of disunion. The conclusion seems to be that the myths conceive of the relationship between the sky and the earth in two ways: either in the form of a vertical and spatial conjunction, terminated by the discovery of cooking, which interposes domestic fire between sky and earth; or in the form of a horizontal and temporal conjunction, which is brought to an end by the introduction of the regular alternation between life and death, and between day and night.

The Arawak of Guiana attribute the sun's eclipses to a fight between it and the moon; they try to separate the combatants by uttering terrifying cries (Im Thurn, p. 364). Similarly, when only one part of the moon is visible, or when it is in eclipse, the Kalina interpret such phenomena as a battle waged against it by the sun (Ahlbrinck, under 'nuno' §4, 7). There is an Amazonian story ($M_{422}$; Rodrigues 1, pp. 211–12) to the effect that the sun and the moon were once engaged, but marriage between them came to seem impossible: the sun's love would set fire to the earth, the moon's tears would flood it. So they resigned themselves to living separately. By being too close to each other, the sun and the moon would create a rotten or a burnt world, or both these effects together; by being too far apart, they would endanger the regular alternation of day and night and thus bring about either the long night, a world in which everything would be inverted, or the long day, which would lead to chaos. The canoe solves the dilemma: the sun and moon embark together, but the complementary functions allocated to the two passengers, one paddling in the front of the boat and the other steering at the back, force them to choose between the bow and the stern, and to remain separate.

This being so, ought we not to recognize that the canoe, which unites the moon and the sun and night and day, while maintaining a reasonable distance between them during the *time* of the longest journey, plays a similar part to that of domestic fire in the *space* circumscribed by the family hut? If cooking fire did not achieve mediation between the sun and the earth by uniting them, the rotten world and the long night would prevail; and if it did not ensure their separation by coming between them, there would be a conflagration resulting in the burnt world. The canoe fulfils exactly the same function in the myths, but transposes it from the vertical to the horizontal, from distance to duration.

In short, the transformation which causes the ideological superstructure to change as we move from the Brazilian plateau to the Guiana–Amazonia area – centring in the latter on the canoe and fishing, and in the former on cooking fire and cultivated plants – corresponds all the more closely to the differential characteristics of the infrastructure in that fishing or agriculture are the technical activities most rigidly subject to seasonal periodicity. The latter is half-way between daily periodicity, which has shorter cycles and that of human life, which has longer cycles.

I would like to digress here for a moment in order to demonstrate indirectly the formal homology that I have thus recognized between the canoe and the domestic hearth. $M_{104}$ appears to be a myth about baldness and the whitening of hair through age, afflictions which are very rarely found among American Indians, and of which few examples are to be found in anthropological literature. It is all the more remarkable, then, that myths dealing with baldness should have almost the same distribution in tropical America and in the north-western areas of North America as other themes common to both hemispheres, and that in both regions the explanation put forward is the same: the immersion of hair in water or in an aqueous environment which causes it to rot. In South America, the Uitoto have a story about a man who became bald through contact with decayed corpses in the belly of a snake which had swallowed him ($M_{423a}$; Preuss 1, pp. 219–30) and there is, in the Chaco, a Choroti myth on the same theme ($M_{423b}$; Nordenskiöld 1, p. 110). The Yupa of Venezuela believe that dwarfs in the chthonian world are bald because human dejecta fall on their heads ($M_{423c}$; Wilbert 7, pp. 864–6).

The theme of the man who becomes bald after being swallowed by a monster is present in Siberia and exists also in North America from Vancouver Island to the State of Oregon (Boas 2, p. 688; Frachtenberg 1, p. 31). According to the Hare Indians, the master of fishing had a bald head (Petitot 1, p. 231). The Yupa, as I have already indicated, believe baldness to be caused by layers of dejecta falling on the head; the same idea occurs in Chinook mythology (Jacobs 2, part 2, pp. 326–8; cf. too the Sahaptin versions in: Jacobs 1, pp. 186–8; and the Nez-Percé versions in: Phinney, pp. 106–12). These brief references by no means exhaust the problem. Among the Cashinawa of South America, a bald or partly bald character represents thunder (Tastevin 4, p. 21) and also among the Pawnee in North America (G. A. Dorsey 1, p. 14); lastly, an Ojibwa myth, about which I shall have more to say later, features a bald woman who becomes the beneficent moon after the sun has given her back her hair ($M_{499}$; Jones 1, pp. 375–6; 2, part 2, pp. 623–53). However, in listing these references, my intention was merely to correlate them with a particular detail of the Araucan origin myth, which must be summarized at this point, according to the versions arranged and compared by Lehmann-Nitsche (11, pp. 28–62).

### $M_{424}$. *Araucan.* '*The origin of baldness*'

In very ancient times, a flood destroyed mankind. According to certain versions, it was a punishment for debauched living [cf. $M_{416}$]. In all versions, it is attributed to a snake monster, the master of the ocean, who was called Caicai because of his cry. In order to escape from the rising water and the prevailing darkness, the humans, laden with supplies of food, climbed a three-peaked mountain of which another snake, the enemy of the first, was the master. He was called Tenten, also because of his cry; he may perhaps have assumed the appearance of a poor old man in order to warn humans of the danger threatening them. Those who could not climb fast enough were drowned; they changed into fish of various species, which later fertilized women who came to catch fish at low tide. This was how the ancestors of clans bearing the names of fish came into being.

As the survivors gradually made their way up the side of the mountain, the mountain itself became higher, or, according to other versions, floated on the surface of the water. For a long time Caicai and Tenten engaged in a struggle for mastery. Finally, the mountain won, but he had lifted the humans so near the sun that they had to protect their heads with the dishes into which they had packed their provisions. In spite of these improvised parasols, many perished and several became bald. This is the origin of baldness.

By the time Caicai admitted defeat, there were only one or two surviving couples. Thanks to a human sacrifice, they brought about the subsidence of the waters, and repeopled the earth.

I shall refrain from using as an argument the phonetic resemblance between the cry of the snake, master of the mountain (tenten, trentren, thengtheng), and the opossums' cry in $M_{104}$ (kenkenken), or the cry uttered by the nocturnal beasts in $M_{326a}$ (tententen). But no doubt a linguist would draw interesting conclusions from a study of the onomatopoeic value of words denoting conjunction and disjunction in various South American languages: in the Amazonian myths, tenten, or tintin on the one hand, and wehweh on the other; and in this myth, caicai and tenten, by means of an inversion which is all the more notable in that $M_{424}$, if interpreted as a myth about the origin of baldness, is also an inversion of Amazonian myths of the same type: it attributes the affliction to the burning heat of the sun and not to the putrefying effect of water. Let us confine ourselves for the moment to this last aspect. According to $M_{104}$ and other myths, baldness is a result of immersion in water during movement along the horizontal axis. According to $M_{424}$, it results from close proximity to the sun caused by elevation along the vertical axis. In the first instance, baldness might have been avoided if active travellers (they swim vigorously), instead of diving into the liquid element, had travelled in a canoe, which is a wooden vessel. In the second, baldness seems to be avoidable for passive travellers (the mountain acts as a lift), who are escaping from the flood and protecting themselves from the sun's proximity by means of a set of wooden vessels. Actually, pottery was not unknown among the Araucan of olden times, although they made their dishes and plates of wood. Consequently the missionaries to whom we owe the first versions of the myth ridiculed the absurdity of using dishes made from inflammable material as a protection against a red hot sky (Lehmann-Nitsche 11, p. 34, n. 3; p. 36, n. 2; p. 41, n. 3). But on the contrary, this technological peculiarity seems to fit in well with a mythic inversion which attributes the same protective rôle against baldness of solar origin to wooden culinary dishes as the Amazonian myths – if my hypothesis is correct – attribute implicitly to the monoxylous canoe, in respect of baldness of aquatic origin. This approach, then, would seem to confirm the equivalence between the canoe and domestic fire as respective mediators between the near and the far on the horizontal level, or between the low and the high on the vertical level.

The affinity between the Araucan myths and those belonging to the Guiana area – an affinity already suggested by Lehmann-Nitsche, although on different grounds – would appear even clearer, if it were legitimate to argue on the basis of analogous beliefs found in both areas. For instance, according to the Indians of Guiana, certain rows of stones represent ancestors who were petrified while imploring the sun to return during the course of a long night (Frikel 2). However, I dare not presume that, in these American languages as in French, stones are particularly suggestive of ancestors who have become bald, since in French we say of a bald man: *il n'a plus rien sur le caillou* (he has nothing left on the pebble).

The study of myths dealing with the origin of cooking ($M_1$, $M_{7-12}$) led me to suppose an opposition between the rotten world resulting from the disjunction of the sky and the earth, and the burnt world, resulting from their conjunction. In Araucan mythology, these two worlds correspond to those of Caicai and Tenten. And all the other myths which have been discussed so far are imbued with this fundamental opposition, which they diffract, as it were, along several bands, each one of which carries a particular shade of meaning. On the one hand, then, we observe too remote marriages, or shy single men or women, venturesome husbands, flirtatious girls or animal wives, over-trusting visitors and perfidious hostesses, all of whom illustrate aspects of communication when it becomes dangerous or impossible.

On the other hand, we find too-close marriages, incestuous parents, and clinging-women, that is, modalities illustrating over-rapid communication. In opposing the man with the long penis, the moon's favourite ($M_{256}$), to the man without a penis, the sun's favourite ($M_{255}$), the myths are resorting to an anatomical dialectic congruous with the previous ones, many examples of which were quoted in the first two volumes of this series: characters who are pierced or blocked, or piercing or blocking; in the latter case, becoming too heavy or too fat and playing the part either of commutators or interrupters ...

All these oppositions are logically graded in pairs. The contrast between the rotten world and the burnt world belongs to the cosmic order, which itself admits of two main modalities, one astronomical and one geographical, according to whether its component parts are distributed along a vertical axis opposing sky and earth, or along a horizontal axis opposing the near and the far. Next, the poles of the vertical axis can be plotted on the reduced scale of the human body, limbs and organs of which are then divided between the high and the low; and these limbs and organs can also be classified as being either sexual or alimentary. In the second case, the opposition between the sexes has no relevant function and leaves the way clear for different contrasts: the apertures of the digestive tube can be divided into upper and lower, and, separately or together, can be either open or closed. In the second instance, the opposition between the sexes requires to be expressed by appropriate lexical means: the vulva can be closed or gaping, the penis can be too short or too long.

When the myths look at things from the human point of view, the primary opposition is between nature and culture, which coincides with the geographical pole of the cosmic dichotomy. However, the category of nature itself admits of two modalities, one biological, and the place of which is already marked, the other technological, and which coincides with one of the terms of the opposition emerging from the category of culture. The other, sociological, term gives rise in its turn to

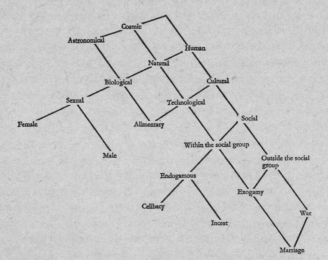

Figure 16. The structural network of a system of mythic oppositions

the opposition *within a group/outside a group*, from which, by means of further bifurcations, we arrive at endogamy, exogamy or war; or to celibacy, incest or marriage, etc. (Figure 16).

All the oppositions we have been dealing with since the beginning of this book can therefore be distributed at the points of intersection of a network with a discernible structure and which further analysis, incorporating other myths, could extend in new directions, while filling in gaps here and there. In the last resort, the differences that can be noted between the myths are to be explained by the levels at which the latter select the oppositions they use, and by the original way in which each myth folds the network back upon itself, horizontally, vertically or diagonally, in order to make certain pairs coincide and to reveal, in a certain perspective, the homology existing between several oppositions.

However, it must also be emphasized that, for the purposes of diagrammatic expression, I have flattened and simplified the network, since its complete representation would have demanded extension into other planes. For instance, the astronomical axis can be spatial or temporal, and in both these forms it remains superimposable upon the geographical axis, which in turn admits of two aspects: the spatial, concerned with near or far distance, and the temporal, concerned with a quick or slow journey. From an alimentary point of view, the pierced characters can be pierced in two ways: they may have no entrails, so that food follows a normal course through the body – from the mouth to the anus – but too *rapidly* (temporal axis); or they may have no body (the rolling head, the legless woman, etc.), so that the course followed by the food, which is excreted at throat level, becomes abnormally *short* (spatial axis). The blocked characters, in their turn, appear to be either without a mouth (high) or without an anus (low). From the sexual point of view, similar dichotomies prevail, according to whether the person concerned is male (with too long or too short a penis) or female (with too open or too closed a vulva), and, as we know, these characters can also be given rhetorical connotations. So the technological contrast established by the myths between domestic fire and the canoe takes its place alongside other superimposable contrasts: the high and the low, the near and the far, the spatial and the temporal, the literal meaning and the figurative meaning.

Consequently, it may be said that, from a logical point of view, the transformation leading to the domestic fire boils down to the projection along the horizontal axis of a vertical mediatory structure, with the result that the *heaven/earth* poles of the one coincide with the *here/yonder* poles of the other (Figure 17). Moreover, a considerable number of myths provide direct evidence that the journey to the sky ($M_{187}$) constitutes the supreme adventure of a wandering hero who has been imprudent enough to go too far.

When formulated in this way, the transformation becomes virtually identical with itself, and there are communities which are fully aware of this, since they describe the basic units of their society in terms of 'boatcrews', rather than in terms of families or hearths. The Malays refer to the boat-shaped end of the scabbard of the kriss as the 'house' of the blade (Rassers, p. 35). They thus express symbolically a correspondence which finds full practical application in Siberia: the social

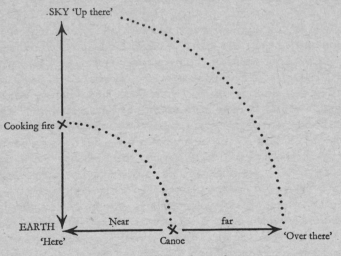

Figure 17. Cooking fire and canoe

unit of the maritime Chukchee is in the 'boatful', a crew whose members hunt and fish together. The Chukchee thus say of a village that it consists of so many boatsful, each composed of related families (Bogoras 2, pp. 544, 629). Similar observations have been made among the Eskimo (Boas 11, p. 601; Spencer, pp. 177–92 et passim). No less significant is the case of those tribes of New Guinea, each clan of which has its own large hut and big boat, which its members use respectively and exclusively for sleeping in at night and for travelling and meeting in by day. The hut itself is often boat-shaped, and both hut and boat are given a name, which never varies but is passed on to the new dwelling built to replace the old one and to the new boat succeeding the one that has had to be discarded. In certain areas of the Delta, a single word has the meaning of both 'clan' and 'boat': the phrase used to ask a stranger which clan he belongs to means 'what is your boat?' The boat, then, constitutes the chief social unit, a role which elsewhere devolves on the common house where members of the group assemble (Wirz, p. 146 *et passim*).

Finally, the fact that when they travel by boat, South American Indians are always careful to take with them a few glowing embers in a calabash or palm shuck and see that they remain alight, surely transmutes the canoe into a domestic hearth, mobile no doubt, but counteracting by its relative security the dangers and uncertainties of the journey, and thus providing an approximate equivalent of the house.

In fact, however, the domestic hearth and the canoe belong to a more complex system than is shown in Figure 17, which illustrates only one stage of the demonstration. To move from one axis to the other, it is not enough to superimpose a vertical structure on a horizontal structure with which it is in all other respects homologous; a topological transformation of the whole into the part must be carried out. A primary system, consisting of two poles joined by a mediatory term, becomes its own mediation; or, in other words, it becomes a mediatory term for a higher-ranking system, notwithstanding a complex structure which transposes the whole picture of the old system onto a reduced scale.

What, actually, is the initial situation? At the start, the myths about the origin of cooking postulate a vertical axis, the poles of which are the sun and the earth. Between these two, the discovery of cooking fire creates a middle term: when present, cooking fire mediates the opposition between sky and earth; when absent, it leaves the polar terms with two alternatives: conjunction which would result in the burnt world, the supreme manifestation of day, or disjunction which would result in the rotten world, the supreme manifestation of night.

The presence in the same canoe of the sun, the day star, and the moon, the night star (sitting at either end of the boat, thus leaving the middle place for a third figure, who, since he is obliged neither to row nor to steer, theoretically has his hands free and could, as anthropological evidence shows, watch over the smouldering embers) constitutes in itself the establishment of a relationship between day as a moderate *conjunction* between sky and earth – congruous with the geographical category of the near – and night, another moderate form, but of the *disjunction* between sky and earth, congruous with the category of the far. *Consequently, it is the very occurrences of conjunction and disjunction that the canoe is keeping apart.* If day and night, conjunction and disjunction, were too close, there would be incest between the sun and the moon, eclipses and a subversion of daily periodicity, all of which phenomena correspond, on the geographical level, to the loss of the opposition between the near and the far. Conversely, if day and night, conjunction and disjunction, were too far apart, the result would be either perpetual or absolute day, or perpetual or absolute night, with, in both cases, a divorce between light and darkness, or the disappearance of their mutual tempering by moonlight or starlight at night, or by the graded colours of the rainbow during the day, according to whether the myths adopt a diurnal or nocturnal, diachronic or synchronic perspective. Finally, on the geographical level, there would be a loss, not of opposition, but of mediation, between the categories of the near and the far.

In moving from myths about the origin of cooking to those about the origin of the alternation or mutual tempering of day and night, we have, then, passed from the study of a first degree set to that of a second degree set. Instead of a straightforward opposition between terms, we are now faced with another, more complex, opposition affecting two modes in which the first opposition can be expressed. The new myths I have introduced do more than contrast terms. They oppose the various ways in which these terms can be in opposition to each other. They are therefore opposing oppositional modalities, and thus illustrate the transition from a logic of judgement to a true logic of propositions.

This additional complexity would be impossible to interpret, if it did not have recourse to yet another dimension. The myths about the origin of cooking could probably take place in time, but, as regards their internal medium, they only conceptualized space, whereas the myths about the origin of day and night conceptualized both space and time. Consequently, the notion of space evolves by being inserted in a multidimensional continuum: from being absolute, space, now made indissociable from time, becomes relative. It is no longer to be defined by the static opposition between the high and the low, but by the dynamic opposition of the near and the far, which is determined by social, instead of cosmic, coordinates.

Thus, in mythic thought the category of time appears as the necessary means for revealing relations between other relations already given in space. The genre of the novel, which, as has been seen, has its source in seriality following on the reduction of differential features, also derives from an increased complexity in the logical nature of the separated terms. This development demands a temporal dimension which, as historical duration, is doubly opposed to synchronic space, while at the same time making it possible to overcome its contradictions. When envisaged from this formal point of view, the dilemma facing mythic thought is not unlike the one with which music is confronted. In both cases, the reduction of the gaps between the significant terms requires – if the latter are to remain distinct – that they should be chosen at greater distances from each other. This dialectic of the near and the far, common to both myth and music, presents them both with the same alternatives: the myth either has to become fictional (and music to stay romantic) by remaining faithful to short intervals; or it can remain mythic (or would-be structural, in the case of music) by a return to the practice of wide intervals, which are made all the more conspicuous in that the distance between them, instead of being already inherent in the nature of the system, is an effect of artifice: wide intervals are obtained by systematic rejection of short intervals.

If, after our excursion into fictional mythology, we find ourselves again concerned, in $M_{415}$, with forms relating indisputably to structural analysis, could the reason not be that, in this myth, Amalivaca resolves to break his daughters' legs, in the same way as serial music proceeds, when it resorts to wide intervals to clip the wings of melody?

Let us return to the canoe. It serves in the myths as the vector of a medium solution between the two extreme forms of an opposition which, for lack of an intermediary term, would be abolished by the conjunction or disjunction of its poles. All those who have travelled by canoe know from experience the technological imperatives which make this type of boat ideally suitable to fulfil the role on the formal level. Any canoe journey of a certain duration requires at least two passengers who perform complementary functions: one paddles while the other steers. The steersman must sit at the back and so, in order to keep the balance, the paddler must sit in the front. During the journey neither must move, still less change position, since to do so would impart a sudden movement to the canoe causing it to capsize. It follows that the two passengers must not, at any moment, come *too near* each other; but, being associated in a common undertaking, they must not be *too far apart* either. The limited space in the canoe and the strict navigational rules tend to keep them at the *right distance* in relation to each other, together and separate at one and the same time, as the sun and the moon must be in order to avoid excessive daylight or excessive darkness which would scorch or rot the earth.

That is not all. The canoe, being *included* within the journey, carries out a topological transformation of the semantic function that the myths attribute to the journey. It could almost be said that the canoe interiorizes the journey within a privileged space, whereas the journey exteriorizes the canoe within an indeterminate period of time. Thus they both act as operators, one spatial and the other temporal, their function being to ensure the arbitration of the near and the far, the opposition between which emerges in the myths in the triple form of incest and impossible marriage, the stay-at-home temperament and the thirst for adventure, and continual or absolute day or night.

The schema of the canoe journey makes it possible, then, to carry out two operations simultaneously: one, which is logical in character, totalizes oppositions selected at various levels, and yields a total product consisting of a system the terms of which, being opposed to each other, form a new opposition. The other, which is semantic in character, totalizes in analogous fashion spatial registers (vertical and horizontal), temporal registers (journey and calendar), sociological registers (celibacy and marriage, endogamy and exogamy, kinship and war) and anatomical registers (mutilations and explosions, openings and closings, physiological deficiencies) and yields a global product, the properties of which are summarized in the sun–moon pair. But here we encounter a problem which must be solved, if we are to understand the reason for the surprising semantic oscillations which characterize the notion and function of the two luminaries (L.-S. 18), in accordance with different periods, regions and tribes.

I have said that the canoe is an operator; what kind of operator? When it takes the sun and the moon aboard as passengers it forces them to remain at a fixed distance apart. The journey transports this standard of measurement over a course the various points of which are traversed in succession by the canoe. This movement of a segment of discontinuous space over continuous space makes it possible to effect the summation of the unlimited series of inversely proportional values taken on during the journey by the distances of both the near and the far. At the moment of departure, the canoe is so near the bank that the 'near' distance is virtually nil; on the other hand, the unforeseen risks of the expedition make the 'far' distance virtually infinite. But once the journey has begun, with every day that passes the near recedes and the far draws nearer. By the time the canoe arrives at its destination, the initial values of the two terms have been reversed. The return journey brings about the same operations the other way round, and the fixed measure of the canoe, by eliminating their extreme products in favour of zero or infinite values, allows only their mean product to be extracted.

If we consider that these extreme products correspond respectively to what I have called the burnt world and the rotten world, and if it is accepted, in accordance with what has gone before, that the canoe achieves the summation of all the values taken on during the journey by the conjunction (∪) and the disjunction (//) of the near and the far, it can be stated that the canoe is a spatial operator which ensures the compatibility, along the temporal axis, of the burnt world (conjunction of sky and earth, the point of balance of which would be day) and the rotten world (disjunction of sky and earth, the point of balance of which would be night):

$$\left[\begin{array}{c} SKY \cup EARTH \end{array}\right] \left(\sum_{far \;//\; near}^{near \;\cup\; far}\right) \left[\begin{array}{c} SKY \;//\; EARTH \end{array}\right]$$

But, in fact, the logical structure of the system is still more complex, since the sun and the moon, the reciprocal alternation of which maintains the balance between the burnt world and the rotten world, themselves function as operators, effecting, along the semantic axis, summations analogous in form to that brought about, along the logical axis by the canoe and the journey. This point must be examined more closely.

Considered in relation to the spatial axis, the sun illustrates the conjunction of sky and earth, resulting in drought, sterility and conflagration, that is, the burnt world. On the temporal axis, however, it conjures up a purity and an asceticism which are expressed by the disjunction of the sexes: according to the myths, continuous light rules out love-making. Symmetrically, the moon, according to whether it is absent or present, ranges across a semantic field half of which is occupied by the disjunction of the sky and the earth, along with the over-long night generating hostility, cannibalism and corruption, while the other half is occupied by the conjunction of the sexes, since the night must be long enough to permit sexual union, the source of fertility. Consequently, the sun and the moon each express in their own way the total sum of the successive values that a relationship can take on along a semantic axis, before being reversed into its opposite along the other axis:

$$\text{SUN} = \left[ \sum \begin{array}{l} sky \cup earth \text{ (spatial axis)} \\ \\ male \parallel female \text{ (temporal axis)} \end{array} \right]$$

$$\text{MOON} = \left[ \sum \begin{array}{l} sky \parallel earth \text{ (spatial axis)} \\ \\ male \cup female \text{ (temporal axis)} \end{array} \right]$$

If we agree to use the symbol of intersection: ∩ to express the point of balance at which, in spite of their contradictory nature, two relationships of conjunction and disjunction $r$ cease to be incompatible and prove to have something in common, the journey made by the sun and moon can be regarded as an operation to which the canoe subjects the two luminaries, and the product of which is the mythic universe; this universe consists of the sum of all the spatial and temporal relationships which each of them integrates in its particular way:

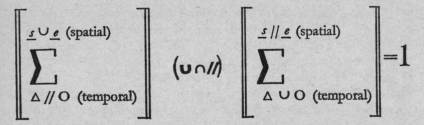

$$\left[ \left[ \sum \begin{array}{l} \underline{s} \cup \underline{e} \text{ (spatial)} \\ \\ \triangle \parallel \text{O (temporal)} \end{array} \right] \right] (\cup \cap \!/\!/) \left[ \left[ \sum \begin{array}{l} \underline{s} \parallel \underline{e} \text{ (spatial)} \\ \\ \triangle \cup \text{O (temporal)} \end{array} \right] \right] = 1$$

In other words, the canoe mytheme effects the intersection of the conjunction and disjunction which it declares to be present, at the same time as it keeps them apart. This logical operation assigns average values to conjunction and disjunction, while keeping both in the same semantic register. Conversely, the sun and moon, which can be seen to be operators functioning also as terms in a different operation, totalize the series of variable values of conjunction and disjunction, without leaving out the most extreme, but by referring them to different semantic registers. The result is that all these contrary operations cancel each other out. Provided we stand far enough back, a mythic field which appeared extraordinarily rich and complex when subjected to a close and detailed study will, seen from a distance, seem completely empty: the opposition between the sun and moon, provided it remains an opposition, can take on any meaning. Initially, mythic thought forms a closed system; it can only acquire depth by sacrificing its redundancy.[1] It sees itself as constantly discovering new oppositions, but these force it to recognize the equivalence of terms it had already used for the formulation of different oppositions. As the content becomes richer and more complicated, the formal construction loses its rigorous nature, or rather survives only by becoming schematic. In the case of the sun and moon, the increasing confusion of content tolerated by so many myths, and which allows the two bodies to be interchangeable, since in the beginning the sun was the moon and the moon the sun, can no longer be made up for, except by the different modalities in which the sun and moon give abstract expression to the same or different meanings. Being now both subject to the same instability, the two luminaries can only remain distinct from each other *through the particular ways each has of being unstable*. Each can, no doubt, signify anything, but the sun can only do so on condition that it is *all one thing* or *all the other*: a beneficent father or a cannibalistic monster. And the moon, for its part, can only maintain its original correlational and oppositional relationship with the sun on condition of being either *one thing and the other*: a demiurge who is at once a legislator and a trickster; or *neither one nor the other*: a sterile, virgin girl, or a hermaphroditic personage, or an impotent or dissolute man.

---

[1] In the sense that communication theory gives to this term, which means the aspects of the message predetermined by the structure of the code, and thereby not subject to the free choice of the encoder of the message.

# PART FOUR   EXEMPLARY LITTLE GIRLS

*'Very well, forgive me,' he went on. 'But the fact is
that it is horrible, horrible, horrible!'
'What is horrible!' I asked him.
'Our utterly mistaken attitude to women, and our
relations with them.'*

L. Tolstoy *Kreutzer Sonata*, Ch. 3

# 1 · *On Being a Young Lady*

> ... *among the duties of a woman, one of the most
> important is cleanliness; it is a special and essential
> duty, imposed by nature. There is no more disgusting
> object in the world than a filthy woman, and a husband
> who becomes disgusted by her is never wrong.*
>
> J.-J. Rousseau, *Emile* Book V

It would be true to say that, since the beginning of this volume, we
have been discussing one single myth. All the others introduced in the
course of the argument have been brought in with the avowed intention
of arriving at a better understanding of the one which served as our
starting-point: the Tucuna myth, $M_{354}$, which tells the story of the
conjugal misadventures of Monmanéki the hunter.

By dividing the myth into sequences not always clearly indicated by
the plot, and by relating each sequence to paradigmatic sets capable of
giving them a meaning, we eventually found ourselves in a position to
define the fundamental characteristics of a myth which turns out to be
representative of several others. These characteristics are four in number. First, the myth compares and contrasts animal wives and a human
wife. Next, the first animal wife is the literal embodiment of a frog,
whereas the last and only human wife is a figurative representation of a
frog. Thirdly, the figurative frog plays the part of a clinging-woman:
she refuses to let go of a husband whom she disgusts and who wants to
be rid of her; conversely, the frog in the literal sense, whose husband
has no wish to be rid of her, is separated from him (figuratively, however) by a mother-in-law who is revolted by her daughter-in-law's diet.
Lastly, by means of the canoe-journey sequence, which brings together
two brothers-in-law with contrasting characteristics – one is active, the
other ineffectual – I showed that the myth belongs to a vast group concerned with the sun and the moon, considered in terms of periodicity.

As it happens, there is, in North America, another group of myths presenting the same characteristics, and in which indeed they are even more marked, since in these myths the moon and the sun occupy a prominent position, instead of their presence being merely suggested in the guise of human figures, as is the case in $M_{354}$. This only serves to make the link-up between the two groups more convincing. It would be possible to find, and compare, myths belonging to both hemispheres in which the sun and the moon are given equal importance and play approximately the same roles. But this would merely face us with the traditional choice presented by this kind of comparison: are the resemblances to be explained by independent invention or by diffusion? There is no need to prove that many mythic themes travelled from one part of the New World to another, since previous researchers have assembled a wealth of instances. The task I have undertaken is quite different; it consists in proving that myths *which are not alike*, or in which the similarities seem at first sight to be accidental, can nevertheless display an identical structure and belong to the same group of transformations. It is not, then, a question of listing common features, but of demonstrating that, in spite of their differences, and perhaps even because of them, myths which seem at first to present no similarities, proceed according to the same principles and originate from a single group of operations.

Let us begin by summarizing one episode, which is present in several myths and requires lengthy analysis. Two brothers, the sun and the moon, quarrel over the respective merits of human and animal wives, the animal wives being in fact frogs. Since they are unable to reach agreement, each decides to choose as he pleases. The frog-wife disgusts her in-laws, not by what she eats, as in $M_{354}$, but by the manner in which she eats. The two sisters-in-law – who, in this respect, are congruous with the two brothers-in-law in $M_{354}$ – have opposite characteristics: one is active and neat in her person, the other lazy and slovenly. Infuriated by the reproaches levelled against her, the frog leaps onto her brother-in-law, moon, and refuses to let go, thus becoming a clinging-woman. Although the order of events is not the same and the semantic functions are permuted, all the features I discerned in the armature of the Tucuna myth can be recognized here.

These hidden analogies, which appear in different contexts thousands of miles apart, present an especially difficult problem, since the North American myths themselves are a regional variant within a vast group known as the 'star-husband' myths, of which Reichard (2) and S. Thompson have made a detailed study. Thompson's work, which is the more recent, lists eighty-six versions scattered everywhere in North America, except among the Eskimo and the Indians of the southwest. Many more versions could be added, if the themes were less narrowly defined.

The star-husband myth tells a story in episodic form. In its complete version, it includes numerous episodes, but they are rarely all present at the same time. The myth as a whole, therefore, remains a potentiality, and can hardly be illustrated adequately by any one of the recorded versions. To give the reader some idea of it, I propose to summarize the syncretic narrative evolved by Reichard (2, pp. 297–302), arranging in the appropriate order elements originating from all sources, but especially from the Plains Indians of North America.

One or two young Indian girls wish to have a star as their husband. The stars grant their wish and the heroine goes into the sky, where she is given a warm welcome by her husband and parents-in-law. However, she is warned never to dig up the root of a certain edible vegetable growing in the garden.

Out of curiosity or boredom, she fails to comply with this injunction. The root blocked up a hole in the celestial vault. Through the opening, the woman can see the earth below and her own village, the sight of which makes her incurably homesick. She patiently collects vegetable fibres or sinews[1] and joins them together. When she thinks the rope is long enough, she starts to climb down it with her baby.

The star-husband discovers that his wife has disappeared. He bends down to look through the hole; his runaway spouse is hanging in the void, because the rope is too short. She meets her death either because she lets go, or because her husband throws a stone at her. The baby at first feeds on the milk in his dead mother's still swollen breasts. He quickly grows up and becomes able to look after himself.

Sometimes the myth ends at this point, or even earlier, with the wife's death. In those versions which feature two women, the latter fall into a tree and cannot get down from it. These versions will be discussed later. In the Plains, the story leads on into another, which some myths place in an initial position and is known by a special title: 'the grandmother and the grandson'.

The orphan, or another hero who finds himself from the outset in a similar situation, steals produce from the garden of a solitary old

[1] The English word *sinew*, which all these versions use, refers to thin strips cut from the fibrous tissue covering the backbone of bison and deer. They are used as sewing-thread (W. Matthews, p. 125).

woman. She discovers him and adopts him. An equivocal relationship develops between the two characters; either the woman seduces the boy who has grown into an adolescent (cf. $M_{241-244}$), or she gives him a detailed account of the dangers surrounding them, although it is not clear whether her intention is to put him on his guard, or to encourage him to face them. The young man becomes a killer of monsters and negotiates with enemies, to whom he hands over his grandmother. Sometimes he kills her.

Once again the story may end at this point, or it may continue under the conventional title of the 'star's son'. According to the particular version, the hero may be the son either of a star, or of the sun or moon, or sometimes he himself becomes either the sun or moon. After fulfilling his terrestrial role as organizer of creation, and conqueror or victim of monsters, he ascends into the sky and becomes a celestial body.

The North American cycle, if limited to the first act, the one we shall concern ourselves with for the moment, has its counterpart in South America in the cycle concerning the star-wife of a mortal, which occasionally presents an inversion of the star's sex together with a reduplication of the earthly heroine ($M_{110}$), thus restoring the armature of certain northern versions. The South American forms were discussed in *The Raw and the Cooked* ($M_{87-93}$, $M_{95, 106, 110, 112}$; pp. 164–95), where I showed that they were related, on the one hand, to the origin of cultivated plants and, on the other, to man's mortality. It also became evident that the Ge myths about the origin of cultivated plants constituted a parallel series to the Ge and Bororo myths about the origin of cooking-fire, and that a third series of myths, mainly Ge and Tupi, about the origin of game occupied an intermediary position between the other two series. We moved, then, from the origin of cooking fire to that of meat; from the origin of meat to that of cultivated plants; and, finally, from the discovery of agriculture to man's mortality, the biological form of periodicity.

In the present volume, I am repeating the process, but by examining different myths and operating on a different level. From the origin of fish and fishing, we have moved on to that of the regular alternation of day and night, the astronomical form of periodicity, symbolized by a canoe journey, the canoe being, as I established at the end of Part Three, a transformation of the domestic fire – the origin of which was the subject of the very first myths I studied ($M_1$, $M_{7-12}$) – and which plays, along the vertical axis of the high and the low, the same mediatory rôle as devolves on the canoe along the horizontal axis of the near and the far. But at the same time as the spatial axis swings round from the vertical to the horizontal, it also changes from spatial to temporal. We thus return to the problem of the periodicity of human life, which is a transposition of daily and seasonal periodicity (see pp. 170–71, 178–80).

So, it would be wrong to minimize the structural analogies between stories found in both North and South America by arguing on the basis of the supposed anecdotal and contingent nature of the mythic imagery. We sense, on the contrary, that when myths which are both historically and geographically remote from each other say the same thing, this can only be because of a common organization by virtue of which they are analogous species within a given genus. Instead of allowing ourselves to be intimidated by the width of the gap to be bridged, we should, on the contrary, find encouragement in a logical and semantic similarity, amply demonstrated by what has gone before, and which will be confirmed by a more detailed analysis of the North American myths. The confirmation, in addition to being relevant to these myths themselves, will also shed new light on a great many still obscure areas of the South American myths already discussed.

Of the 86 versions of the 'star-husband' myth mentioned by Thompson, 69 feature two women, 27 quickly eliminate one of them and 10 have only one woman from the start. The variant beginning with a quarrel between the brothers sun and moon about the qualities of women, belongs to the first category, since each brother marries the woman of his choice: there are thus two rival wives. According to Thompson (p. 118), this variant exists only in the Plains. The nine known versions of it belongs to the Gros-Ventre, the Hidatsa, the Crow and the Arapaho.

The Gros-Ventre or Atsina split off from the Arapaho only a few centuries ago. Together with the Cheyenne, they represent an extreme southern extension of the Algonquin linguistic stock, which is represented to the north by the Blackfoot, the Cree and the Ojibwa, and stretches, unbroken, from the northern Rockies to the Atlantic coast. Into this cluster of related languages, the Siouan tribes, although chiefly concentrated in the south and east, drove two wedges: one towards the north formed by the Assiniboine, and the other towards the west, formed by the Crow, whose territory cut across that occupied by the western Algonquin.

The picture is complicated by the fact that the Crow and the Hidatsa separated recently enough for their traditions to be reminiscent of each other, although they subsequently evolved in different directions. Like

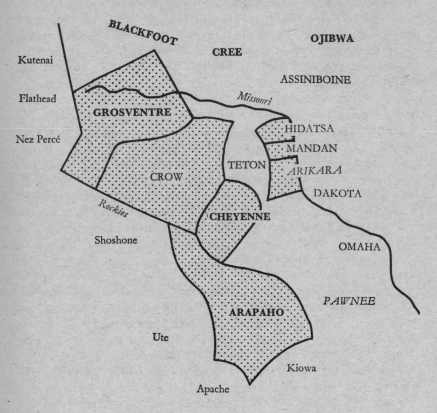

Figure 18. The distribution area of the story of the quarrel between sun and moon and the position of surrounding tribes

most of the Plains tribes, the Crow adopted a way of life based almost entirely on buffalo hunting, especially after the introduction of the horse. The Hidatsa, on the other hand, by coming into contact with their Mandan and Arikara neighbours, who were 'village' tribes, like the more southerly Pawnee, became sedentary; in addition to hunting, they practised agriculture. But we know very little about how exactly these transformations took place.

We have archaeological evidence to show that, long before the introduction of the horse in the 17th or 18th centuries, the Mandan, the Arikara and the Pawnee led a sedentary, agricultural existence; the same may also have been true of a section of the Hidatsa, a tribe which does not appear to be homogeneous. Among the Algonquin, the Cheyenne provide a typical example of an agricultural community which was still settled in the Great Lakes area three or four centuries ago, and which completely altered its way of life between 1700 and 1770, at the same time as it moved into the Plains (Jablow, pp. 1–10).

It is thought that the Gros-Ventre were still an agricultural community at the beginning of the 19th century. But, although the Mandan are Siouan Indians, who had been established in their historic territory several hundred years before the Crow and the Hidatsa, since the latter originated from the Lake Superior area at a time when they still formed a single group, their language is closer to that of the eastern Siouan.[2] The Arikara belong to the Caddo linguistic family, the chief area of which is situated much further south, among the Wichita and the Caddo proper. After breaking away from the Pawnee, the Arikara would seem to have formed the spear-point of a Caddo drive to the north. Their separation from the main branch dates, in all probability, from the end of the 16th or the beginning of the 17th century (Deetz, p. 5).

It is as if, over a vast area formed by the foothills and the eastern flank of the Rockies, three linguistic families had collided and overlapped. Perhaps the region was initially peopled by tribes of the Uto–Aztec linguistic stock, who, along with the Comanche and the Kiowa, survive to the south of the Arapaho and the main body of which occupies the Great Basin to the west of the watershed. They were probably driven back by the arrival of the Athapaskan (Apache and Navaho) from the north. The Sioux penetration would seem to have occurred later, when the French, after settling in Canada, supplied arms to their Algonquin allies from the Great Lakes region, who brought

[2] As is customary, I use the term *Siouan* to refer to the linguistic family, which includes, amongst others, the *Sioux* or Dakota tribes.

pressure to bear on the other tribes and forced them to leave. The quarrel responsible for the separation of the Hidatsa from the Crow occurred in the 19th century. And it was in 1837 that the smallpox epidemic reduced the number of the Indians and prompted the Hidatsa to move closer to the Mandan. But it still remains true that the presence of village communities in the Plains goes back at least seven or eight hundred years, if not more, even if their original habitat was, as is supposed, to the east of the Mississippi (Strong 2, Wedel 1, 2). As for the western Algonquin, there are considerable linguistic differences between the Arapaho and the Cheyenne, although they are neighbours; differences also exist between the Arapaho and the Gros-Ventre, on the one hand, and the Blackfoot on the other. However, contrary to what was thought until recently, these differences are no greater than those separating the languages spoken by the central and eastern Algonquin: 'The Algonquin family thus appears to be one group' (Haas, p. 523). It would seem, however, that this internal differentiation first started a very long time ago. Finally, west of the Rockies, the Kutenai, Salish and Sahaptin groups may have been settled on their territories for several thousand of years.

Since, in this mixture, it is impossible for the time being to sort out the relatively archaic features from those due to more recent upheavals, there would be little point in appealing to an inevitably hypothetical prehistory to discover whether the variant with which we are concerned was introduced by one particular group rather than another, or whether it came into being *in situ*. As I shall have occasion to show, the quarrel between the sun and the moon has a much wider area of distribution than is indicated by S. Thompson's study. He takes into account only examples that are closely integrated into the star-husband cycle. But, even from the geographical point of view, too much importance must not be attached to the barrier of the Rockies, although it marks the western frontier of the Algonquin linguistic area as well as the frontier of the respective territories of the Blackfoot, the Gros-Ventre, the Crow and the Arapaho. To the north, the ridges become less marked and the slopes are intercommunicating. It is therefore understandable that there should be no break between the great mythic themes of the Algonquin and those of the Kutenai, who are an isolated community, or those of the Salish-Sahaptin. Further south, where the mountains become a really formidable obstacle, one has only to compare the mythology of the Plains Indians with that of the Shoshone to be convinced that they both derive from some ancient syncretism. Fortunately, structural analysis can make up for the uncertainties of historical reconstruction. It will provide a more solid basis on which to interpret the recurrence of a single mythic pattern in the cultures of both North and South America, between which, at first sight, there would seem to be no obvious point of comparison.

It follows from the preceding observations that certain communities, differing in both language and culture, settled in their geographical locations at such variable periods that, when one comes to study their myths, there is no fundamental reason to adopt one order of approach rather than another. I am beginning the enquiry with the Arapaho, chiefly because they provide a great wealth of material:

$M_{425}$. *Arapaho*. '*The wives of the sun and moon*' (1)

While, on earth, two young Indian women were dreaming about which they would like to marry, the sun or the moon, the two luminaries, who were brothers, compared the respective merits of the women below. They both looked down to earth and viewed the inhabitants from afar. 'I cannot see prettier creatures than those human women,' said Moon; 'when they look at me, their faces seem charming, and I can't help but go after one of them.' But Sun protested: 'Oh! those ugly-looking creatures! I don't want them, their faces are horrible, showing wrinkles, and they have small eyes. For my part I am going to select one of the water animals for a wife!' (Water animals have larger eyes and their sight is not affected by the heat of the sun, therefore their faces are smooth in appearance.)

One morning there were four young women going out after a load of wood. One of them came close to a dead tree (*Populus* sp.). Moon himself appeared on the cottonwood as a porcupine. The young lady wanted some quills; she climbed the tree, but every time she tried to hit the porcupine with the stick her companions had handed to her, the animal changed position slightly. She was so engrossed in the hunt that she did not notice the tree was growing. The others anxiously called to her to come down. 'Oh, my companions,' she protested, 'this beast has splendid white quills and my mother will be delighted for she has none.' She continued to climb and soon she was lost to sight.

Suddenly the porcupine turned into a handsome young man who said he was Moon, whom the young girl had wanted to marry. She agreed to follow him and they reached the sky where the moon's parents warmly welcomed their new daughter-in-law. 'But where is the wife my brother chose for himself?' asked Moon. 'She is outside,' replied Sun timidly. His wife was a frog which was hopping along in front of the door and urinating at every leap. Overcoming his repulsion, Moon took the frog into the hut and gave each woman a piece of intestine to see which one would make the pleasantest noise as she ate. The human wife cheerfully started to chew, but the frog tried to cheat by cracking a piece of charcoal between her gums. A trickle of black saliva came from her mouth and Moon jeered at her. As soon as she had swallowed her piece of intestine, the Indian girl went off to draw water. The frog could not chew and dragged behind with her pitcher. 'Well, brother-in-law, your actions towards me are such that I shall be with you all the time.' She leapt onto Moon's chest where she can still be seen, with her pitcher, as a dark stain with a smaller one next to it (Dorsey–Kroeber, pp. 321–3).

As it is not my intention to make a general study of the 'star-husband' cycle, I will leave aside for the moment the next part of the myth. Similarly, I propose to quote only the first part of another myth:

$M_{426}$. *Arapaho. 'The wives of the sun and moon* (2)

Once upon a time there lived on the earth a chief, his wife and their two sons. The earth was without any object in heaven and therefore dark. The father decided that they should leave the people below and go above. Then the people were left on earth without any instructions how to live.

The sun and the moon were two stars. One day they had a discussion about the respective merits of human women and water animals. Moon praised the latter and Sun the former, because, he said, their bodies resemble ours. Moon first of all pretended to agree, and since his brother showed some misgivings he persuaded him to change his choice. Had he not said that human women were ugly, because their faces wrinkle when they look at you? Let him therefore take a water-wife; Moon would make do with a human wife.

The two brothers went down to earth. To the west was a camp near a river. Moon went towards it, and Sun went in an easterly direction where there was another camp. Moon followed the course of the river until he came abreast of the camp, and sat down in the brush at the edge of the path. Two women came along. They were entrancing with their long hair and their fine garments. As soon as he saw them, Moon changed into a porcupine and took up his position at the foot of a tree, to the west of the trunk. When the women came excitedly after him he began to climb. One woman started to follow him in spite of her companion's entreaties. The porcupine resumed his human form. The woman agreed to accompany him to the sky and to marry him.

The young man's mother admired her daughter-in-law's beauty. Shortly after Sun arrived and told the old woman to go and welcome his wife. The latter was a frog, who jumped and croaked. Moon inspected his sister-in-law with a critical eye: 'Her eyes are large, her face is large, her skin is rough, her belly is big and her legs are small.' And turning towards his mother: 'Which one do you prefer? Cook paunch for them, then point to the one who makes the greatest noise in chewing.' The frog put a piece of charcoal in her mouth, but she succeeded only in dribbling a blackish juice, while her pretty rival chewed noisily. Moon burst out laughing. Finally the frog said to him: 'I am not going to live with your brother, but the old woman quite likes me and does not want me to go. Therefore, my body shall be part of yours and shall be with you as long as you live.' (Dorsey–Kroeber, pp. 332–3.)

In a third version (M₄₂₇ₐ; Dorsey–Kroeber, p. 339), Moon has two wives, one human and one a frog. He organizes a competition to see which wife makes the greatest noise while eating, and to find out which one is provided with better teeth, that is, the younger. The human wife wins, but shortly after escapes. Moon takes back the old frog whom he has repudiated. This explains why a black frog can be seen attached to his person. In a fourth version (M₄₂₇ᵦ; *ibid.*, p. 340), the woman who follows the porcupine is married to Sun. His brother accuses him of inconsistency; had he not declared that human women were ugly when they looked at him? In fact, Moon is jealous. Sun kills his wife while she is trying to escape.

Even more effectively than M₄₂₅, M₄₂₆ restores a mythic configuration that I have gradually managed to bring to light through comparing a large number of South American myths. Before the right alternation of night and day was established, and when dense darkness still prevailed, mankind lived in confusion and without rules (M₄₁₀). A human had to go up into the sky and be changed into a moon, before absolute night could be replaced by tempered night (M₃₉₃, ₃₉₄). The balance between day and night and also between absolute or tempered modes of light and darkness is expressed sociologically by an opposition between two types of marriage, one near, the other distant ($M_{149a}$, $M_{354}$, $M_{406}$, $M_{415}$, etc.). As in $M_{354}$, human or animal wives illustrate the two types. In each case, the frog represents the animal wife who disgusts her parents-in-law, sometimes by the way she eats: *black* juice trickles from her mouth; and sometimes by what she eats: *black* beetles, the chewing of which would presumably produce the same result. Let us summarize then once more, properties which we find to be common to the armature of the Tucuna myth, and that of the Arapaho myths: a comparison between a human wife and one or several animal wives; the discrediting of the animal wife because of her alimentary behaviour; the equating (early on in the Arapaho myths, eventually in the Tucuna myth) of the frog-wife with a clinging-woman; lastly, the connection between these three themes and an astronomical pair consisting of the sun and the moon, whose implicit rôle in the Tucuna myth was established in Part Three of this volume. The North American myths present, then, explicitly terms of which only some appear openly in the South American myths. To discover the other terms, I have had to make a patient effort of deduction, since their necessity seemed no more than immanent. So, it is only after postulating the existence of a certain mythological system that I have been able to verify its objective presence in the data. The bringing to light of this system by a process of induction using North American examples marks the beginning of the experimental phase of my enquiry, which will provide confirmation of my initial hypotheses.

Whether explicit or merely implied, the cosmological references present in all these myths prove that the chewing contest, in spite of its farcical aspect, has serious implications. Among the Arapaho and in several other communities too, this myth, of which I have quoted a number of variants, is one of the foundation myths connected with the most important annual ceremony of the Plains Indians and their neighbours.

This ceremony, generally referred to as the 'Sun Dance', probably because its Dakota name means 'to stare at the sun', followed a different pattern according to the group. Nevertheless, it had a syncretic aspect, which can be explained by imitations and borrowings. In times of peace, invitations were sent out far and wide and visitors were impressed by certain rites, which they remembered and mentioned later. The number of episodes and the order in which they followed each other were not the same in all cases, but in broad outline the form of the sun-dance can be described as follows.

It was the only ceremony performed by the Plains Indians in which the entire tribe took part; other ceremonies involved only particular brotherhoods of priests and certain age-grade societies. After remaining scattered during the cold season in small groups established in sheltered spots, the Indians came together in the spring for the collective hunt. At the same time as the tribe recovered its full complement of members, abundance replaced scarcity. From the sociological, as well as the economic, point of view, the beginning of summer gave the whole group the opportunity to live together again as an entity, and to cele- brate its new-found unity with a great religious feast (Wissler 2, p. v). An observer who saw the sun-dance in the second half of the 19th century notes: 'the requirement of the Sun Dance is such that it requires every member of the tribe to be present: every clan must be present and in their place' (Seger, in: Hilger 2, p. 151).

So, in principle, the ceremony took place in summer. However, instances are on record when it was celebrated later in the year. The sun-dance was linked not only to the main seasonal cycles which regu- lated the collective life of the tribe, but also to certain incidents in the life of the individual. A member of the tribe would make a vow to cele- brate the feast the following year in recognition of his escape from some danger, or because he had recovered from an illness. Preparations had to be made a long time in advance; the complicated sequence of rites had to be organized, provisions had to be collected for the feeding of the guests and gifts collected to be given to the officiants in repayment of their services. Also, the new 'owner' of the dance had to receive his title from his predecessor, and, from the priests and other qualified dignitaries, the rights attaching to the various phases of the ritual. During these transactions, he solemnly handed over his wife to the man he called his ceremonial 'grandfather', and whose 'grandson' he became, for the purposes of a real or symbolic act of copulation, which took place out of doors at night in the moonlight, and during which the grandfather transferred a piece of root, representing his semen, from his own mouth to that of the wife, who then spat it into her husband's mouth.

Throughout the feast which lasted several days the officiants fasted and neither ate nor drank – the Plains Cree called the ceremony 'the abstaining-from-water-dance' (Skinner 6, p. 287) – and submitted to various mortifications. For instance, the penitents ran sharp wooden skewers into their dorsal muscles, and made them fast to thongs attached to the central pole, around which they danced and leapt until

the skewers were wrenched out, together with the flesh; or else they
trailed behind them heavy objects, such as buffalo skulls with horns
which dug into the ground. These objects were attached to their backs
in the same way, and with the same result.

First, the priests and chief officiants met in a tent set up apart from the
others, in order to proceed in secret with the preparation or renewal of
the liturgical objects. Then, groups of warriors went to fetch the tree-
trunks necessary for the erection of the framework of a huge lodge
roofed over with branches. The trunk intended to serve as the central
pole was hacked at and felled as if it were an enemy. It was in this public
lodge that the rites, songs and dances took place. In the case of the
Arapaho and the Oglala Dakota, at least, it would seem that a period of
unbridled licence prevailed, and was perhaps even prescribed, on this
night (Dorsey 5, p. 138; Spier 4, p. 475).

While the generic name given to this group of extremely complex
ceremonies probably exaggerates their solar inspiration, the solar
element should not be underestimated. In actual fact, sun-worship was
ambiguous and equivocal in character. On the one hand, the Indians
prayed to the sun to be favourably disposed towards them, to grant long
life to their children and to increase the buffalo herds. On the other
hand, they provoked and defied it. One of the final rites consisted in a
frenzied dance which was prolonged until after dark, in spite of the
exhausted state of the participants. The Arapaho called it 'gambling
against the sun', and the Gros-Ventre 'the dance against the sun'. The
aim was to counteract the opposition of the intense heat of the sun, who
had tried to prevent the ceremony taking place by radiating his warm
rays every day during the period preceding the dance (Dorsey 5, pp.
151-2). The Indians, then, looked upon the sun as a dual being:
indispensable for human life, yet at the same time representing a threat
to mankind by its heat, a presage of prolonged drought. One of the
motifs of the Arapaho dancers' body-paintings shows them being
'consumed by fire' (Dorsey 5, p. 171). An informant belonging to the
same tribe relates that 'in the past, during one sun-dance, it became so
hot that the pledger [officiant] was unable to continue the ceremony and
left the lodge. The other dancers followed, as they could not continue
the dance without him' (Kroeber 3, p. 301). But the sun was not alone in
being involved: the Thunder-Bird's nest was placed in the fork of the
central pole. The link with thunder, and more especially with spring
storms, emerges even more clearly in the mythology of the central
Algonquin, according to whom the dance, referred to elsewhere as

'the sun-dance', had replaced an ancient ritual intended to hasten the arrival of the rain-storms (Skinner 5, pp. 506–8; 6, p. 287). In the Plains, too, the dance fulfilled a dual purpose, which was to conquer an enemy, usually the sun, and to force the Thunder-Bird to release rain. One of the foundation myths concerning the dance describes a great famine which an Indian and his wife succeeded in bringing to an end by their knowledge of the rites and the recovery of fertility (Dorsey 7, pp. 650–51).

There is, then, a very close analogy between the sun-dance, as performed by the Plains Indians, and the ceremony of the great fast, as celebrated by the Serenté Indians to ensure that the sun continued exactly on its course and brought the drought to an end (RC, pp. 289–91, 295–6, 314, n. 18). In both cases, the ceremony concerned was the major one of the tribe and involved all its adult members. The officiants neither ate nor drank for several days. The ritual was performed near a pole which represented the path to the sky. Around this pole, the Plains Indians danced and whistled in imitation of the Thunder-Bird's cry. The Serenté did not erect their pole until they had heard the 'whistling', arrow-bearing wasps (Nim. 6, p. 96). In both instances, the ritual ended with the distribution of consecrated water. In the case of the Serenté, the water was contained in separate receptacles and could be pure or roiled;[3] the penitents drank the pure water but refused the other. The 'perfumed water' used in the Arapaho rite was sweet, yet it symbolized menstrual blood, a liquid not in keeping with the sacred mysteries (Dorsey 5, pp. 22, 35, 177–8).

I showed, in The Raw and the Cooked (p. 291), that the Serenté ritual of the great fast and the Bororo and Ge myths featuring the bird-nester ($M_1$, $M_{7-12}$) follow the same pattern. In the myths, the bird-nester climbs to the top of a tree and remains a prisoner there until the discovery of cooking-fire brings about mediation between the disjoined poles of the sky and the earth. Similarly, the officiant in the Serenté rite climbs to the top of the pole until he obtains fire from the sun to rekindle the flames of the domestic hearths, and a promise to send rain, that is, two forms of moderate communication between the sky and the earth, which the sun's hostility towards men threatened to conjoin with a consequent conflagration.

In North America, the same relationship of congruence can be observed between the myth in which the heroine dislodges a porcupine

---

[3] TRANSLATORS' NOTE: The American term, meaning 'turbid' or 'tainted'.

and the sun-dance rites. The Arapaho informants show themselves to be
perfectly aware of this relationship and list the points of comparison
between the two systems. One of the main rites of the dance consists in
the offering of a human wife to the moon. The central pole in the
ceremonial bower represents the tree climbed by the heroine in the
myth, and belongs to the same species (*Populus* sp.). A bundle of
branches, with a digging-stick inserted in it, is set in the fork left at the
top of the trunk after all the other limbs have been lopped off. This tool
is said to be the one used by the moon's human wife to remove the root
blocking the celestial vault, and which she laid across the opening so as
to attach to it the end of her rope made of sinew. These thongs can be
seen tied around the handle of the stick. The penitents, strung-up on
strips of leather by means of wooden skewers inserted in their backs,
represent the woman during her descent. And the pit-like altar inside the
ceremonial bower commemorates the hole dug by the heroine (Dorsey
5, pp. 27, 112, 114, 177). The same link between the sun-dance and the
star-husband myth exists among the Blackfoot (Reichard 2, p. 279) and
the Hidatsa (Bowers 2, pp. 292–3).

Special attention has, therefore, to be paid to Dorsey's version of the
myth, which he recorded during his investigation into the Arapaho
sun-dance. Although similar to $M_{426}$, this version is more philosophical
and learned in character than those we have studied so far. Because of
this, it must certainly be one of the foundation myths of the ritual, and
it states explicitly themes, the importance of which could be felt, but
which would have been much more difficult to define had it not been
available.

### $M_{428}$. *Arapaho. 'The wives of the sun and moon'* (5)

In former times, there used to be in the sky a big camp circle controlled by a man, his wife and their two sons. This family was
innocent, but generous in heart and industrious. Their tent was
formed of daylight and the entrance door was the sun; the tent was
fastened by means of eagle feathers.

The two boys were on the go all the time and would see many
kinds of people and animals. During their absence, the parents who
remained at home in the camp thought only about their family and
their belongings. They were sedentary and contemplative people.

One night, the two brothers who were resting together consulted
each other about looking for wives. They agreed to search for their
respective wives. The next night, Sun, who was the elder, addressed

his father in respectful terms, explaining that for their individual welfare and in order to lessen the toil of their aged parents, his brother and himself wanted to marry. They would be more often at home, and the father and mother would not worry so much about them.

The parents reflected and very solemnly gave their consent, along with much wise and prudent counsel. The camp was situated on the left bank of a stream, the Eagle River, which flowed from west to east. Before going off each on their separate ways, the brothers told one another of their plans. Moon intended to look for a human woman or a 'resurrected woman'; Sun wanted a water wife, for he maintained that humans looked homely and ugly about their faces: 'When they look up towards me, their eyes almost close with a mean appearance. I cannot bear to see their disgusting faces. Batrachians are much prettier. When a toad looks at me, she does not make faces like a human woman. She gives all her attention to me, without a single wrinkle about her eyes and she has a charming mouth: the way she sticks out her tongue shows she has a disposition to love dearly.' Moon protested that when human women looked at him they were handsome and benevolent, and that their ways and habits were decent. Whereupon, the two brothers took leave of each other.

The elder went downstream and the younger upstream. They set out the night of the disappearance of the moon, after the full moon. Their journey lasted six days. They had two days of cloudy weather, two days of rest (holy), and two days before the new moon.

Moon travelled westwards up the river until he reached a huge camp circle; he heard much noise of people and dogs. The air was fragrant, the scenery at the horizon was grand. Birds were singing everywhere, as well as reptiles (*sic*) and insects. The river he saw mirrored the trees and the sky. The inhabitants of the camp were engaged in games and various occupations.

Moon was admiring this idyllic scene, when he saw two young women gathering dead wood as they walked along the river-bank. Changing quickly into a porcupine, he attracted the attention of one of them. 'What a splendid porcupine!' exclaimed the young girl. 'Look at his long white quills. I want his quills. As it happens my mother is out of quills ...'

But the porcupine got the girl to follow him up a tall tree (*Populus* sp.). In vain her companion beseeched her to come down. When the porcupine resumed his human form and spoke, the woman on the ground could no longer see the other. Charmed by the glorious attire and beauty of her suitor, the young girl followed him up into the sky without hesitation, after which Moon hastily covered the opening so that his wife might forget the position of the entrance.

The young woman gazed at the celestial camp along the Pink River, which flowed from north to south. The tent of her parents-in-law was further upstream. After showing his young wife the magnificent spectacle of the earth far below, Moon presented her to his parents, who were delighted with her beauty and gave her a robe nicely ornamented with porcupine quills.

Moon, however, was surprised not to see his brother's wife, when the latter arrived from the east. Sun explained that, being shy, she had remained on the bank of the Eagle River. The old woman went after her: she noticed a toad leaping towards her, suspected the truth, and spoke graciously to the batrachian, who changed into a woman and agreed to follow her. As she suffered from incontinence, her father-in-law gave her the name of *Water-woman,* or *Liquid-woman.* Nevertheless she was given just as warm a welcome as the other one.

Sun was so fascinated by his sister-in-law's beauty that he kept on looking at her and paid no attention to his own wife. Moon looked at her with contempt, she was so homely and wrinkled. He was displeased with her, and Sun himself regretted his choice. At this time life was being discussed, objects of use mentioned, things were planned and substances named. The desires of men and women were pointed out and precautions were given. [*sic*].

So, the two women were provided with necessary articles by their parents-in-law, while the husbands went hunting to provide meat for the household. In their absence, the human wife devoted herself to the various chores and soon became an industrious housewife. The 'Liquid-woman', on the other hand, remained idly seated on her bed, with her head turned towards the wall, and was paralysed by her timidity. In vain did her parents-in-law encourage and reassure her: nothing did any good.

The hunters came back laden with meat, which their father ordered them to boil so that each daughter-in-law could be presented with a bowl of tripe. The human wife relished the food, chewing noisily and cracking it nicely. The toad woman slyly put a piece of charcoal in her mouth; but since she had no teeth, there was no sound from her mouth. While she was chewing away, black saliva dribbled from the corners of her mouth. Moon laughed vigorously.

The old man sent his sons to hunt in opposite directions. As usual they did not make the slightest objection. Their father thereupon undertook to instruct his daughters-in-law in agricultural tasks. His wife made digging sticks and explained how to use them. The earth had to be struck at the four corners of the vegetable; first, to the south-east, then, in turn, to the south-west, the north-west and the north-east; lastly, the root had to be lifted up on the west side. The human wife helped her mother-in-law as best she could. The other wife remained passive and did nothing.

When the brothers returned from hunting and the meal was being cooked, the old man gave a digging stick to each wife: 'This will be the instrument you use every day,' he said. 'You can use it in erecting the tents and digging up eating weeds and roots.' The two men listened attentively, since it was their wives who were being educated.

'Come over quickly,' the human wife cried suddenly, gasping for breath. The mother-in-law ran to her, felt her body and was astonished to discover a well-formed baby struggling for life under her limbs. Everybody was delighted with the new-born baby's beauty, apart from the toad-woman who sulked. 'You make me tired of your foolishness,' she shouted to her brother-in-law, who was gazing at her with a scornful frown. 'Because you criticize me inhumanely, I will be with you all the time. In this way people will see you plainly hereafter.' She leapt onto Moon's breast and adhered to it.

The old man then spoke to his younger son and explained that he had not finished instructing the women and giving them rules for their behaviour. It was a splendid thing to have children, but a woman should not give birth unexpectedly. When, therefore, had Moon's wife conceived this nice baby? They worked out the dates and went over the incidents which had taken place during the journey, and the details of the elopement. Moon and Sun had set out and returned at the same time: so at that time day and night were of equal length. On the other hand, Moon had brought back his wife on the very day of the elopement, and there had been a witness in the person of the wife's companion.

'I am very proud of your success,' said the old man, 'but I don't like this method of sudden deliveries, for it is not human. Ten moons should elapse between conception and birth. The last month in which the woman had her period is not counted. You then count eight months without a period, followed by a tenth month in which the confinement takes place accompanied by a discharge of blood. By counting in this way on all ten fingers, a wife knows that she has not been fertilized unawares by some wild beast. She can warn her mother and husband a long time in advance. Indians are descended from menstrual blood; that is why they are fond of boiling blood. In the beginning the child preceded the flow of blood; henceforth it will follow it after a ten-monthly interval. And each bleeding will last from the first to the last quarter of the moon, that is, the same period of time which elapsed between Moon's departure to look for a wife until his return' (Dorsey 5, pp. 212–21, 178).

Although this lesson in gynaecology exists in two versions, its meaning is far from clear, and I am not sure that I have summarized it correctly. The myth goes on to describe the escape of the human wife with her baby, the wife's death, the hero's childhood experiences and adventures, his death followed by his resurrection and his ascent into the sky where he becomes a constellation. I propose to leave these episodes aside for the moment.

The first part of the myth alone raises enough problems. What strikes one in the first place is its sententious and moralizing tone. The father of the sun and moon is a holy man, his wife is blessed with every domestic virtue, and the sons cannot do enough to express their love, respect and submission. So the myth presents a picture of the ideal family, such as might be imagined by the most scrupulous defenders of morality in a bigoted and conservative society. Yet we are dealing with Red Skins, not with the provincial middle-class in 19th-century France or England. This eventually becomes obvious, however, through the mixture of pompous moral maxims and crude outspokenness with regard to the biological functions. No European guide to etiquette would base its recommendations on a comprehensive system involving simultaneously cosmology, technology, the rules of social life and the reproductive faculties.

The celestial family's camp is situated on the left bank of two rivers. The one flowing from west to east belongs to the lower world, the one flowing from north to south to the upper world. According to the axis envisaged, the camp itself is either in one world or the other; according to $M_{428}$, it is in the upper one, but, as will be remembered, $M_{426}$ puts the same camp initially in the lower world.

At the beginning of the story, the sun and moon are leading a roving life. They are never, or hardly ever, in the camp. Since the myth makes a distinction between the fixed, visible sun and the wandering luminary, we can infer that the regular alternation of day and night did not yet exist and that light and darkness are present in confusion. M$_{426}$ asserts that, at this time, perpetual night prevailed. Among the arguments put forward by the brothers in favour of marriage, the most important is the one relating to a regular, sedentary life. Once they 'settle down', as the saying goes, the sun and moon are often together, instead of going their separate ways, and they help their parents. In relationship to each other, the brothers were then, at first, *distant*; marriage brings them *close*.

The search for wives begins when the moon is in the last quarter, and ends when it is about to enter the first quarter. During this time, the moon disappears from the sky, as if it were moving away westwards from the point of its recent setting. The sun goes towards the east, as it does every night when it returns to its starting point in the east (Mooney 4, p. 971). No doubt, these absences are not all of equal duration. But it has been accepted that the myth begins at a time when alternation between day and night did not yet exist. So the sun and moon can each remain absent for the same length of time, on a six-day journey corresponding to the interval between the first and last quarter. However, the journey takes only four days (because of the two days of rest), that is, it lasts as long as the henceforth prescribed time of the female monthly period.

Let us now study the journey made by the two brothers, which is, in two respects, an inverted canoe journey. The main characters are still the sun and moon, but they travel by land and not on water. Yet they both follow the course of a river: that is, they undertake a terrestrial journey the concept of which is not only contrary, but contradictory, to that of a river journey, a form it might well have also taken. It is true that Plains Indians hardly ever travelled by water. The rounded coracles peculiar to the Mandan, Hidatsa and Arikara (Denig, p. 579) were used chiefly for crossing rivers. I shall return to this point later (p. 295 *et seq.*). But apart from the fact that the Arapaho, like the other Algonquin of the Great Lakes area, may well have used canoes in the northern areas from which they originated, the myth puts forward a decisive argument to exclude the possibility of the river journey: the two brothers do not travel in the same direction. Supposing, then, that they had made the journey by water, one upstream, the other downstream, they could not have reached their respective destinations simultaneously, since the journey upstream would have taken longer. The myth states quite clearly that the sun and moon arrived at the same time; as the text puts it: 'the lengths of day and night were about the same' (Dorsey 5, p. 220).

If we compare, from this angle, the South American myths concerned with the canoe journey made by the sun and moon and the Arapaho myth under consideration, we cannot but conclude that, in order to arrive at the same result, that is, the regular alternation of day and night, the Indians of North and South America adopt opposite procedures. In the South American myths, the sun and moon travel together in a canoe in the same direction, and this obliges them to remain at a reasonable distance from each other, that is, they can neither move further away nor closer together. The Plains Indians represent them as travelling overland in different directions, and the alternation results from the fact that they cover equal distances. The two modes of representation are not incompatible, although one projects – in the unvarying form of a privileged space – the temporal properties of the identical courses followed by the moon and the sun from east to west, one after the other, one by night, the other by day. The Arapaho, on the other hand, lay out – in an extended space – the supposedly opposite courses followed by the sun and the moon, at night only. In South America, a diachronic perspective encloses the longer of the two periods of time within a contracted space. In North America, a synchronic perspective allows the shorter period to expand into an extended space. Symmetrically, the passengers in the canoe remain motionless within a small segment of moving space; and the travellers by land move within a total space which remains stationary.

The same oppositions are also to be found on the sociological level. In the South American myths, the canoe-journey actualizes the choice between close and distant marriages, or it may offer the third possibility of a marriage which is neither too distant nor too close. However, the land-travellers in the Arapaho myth neither choose nor reject, since one brings back a human wife and the other an animal wife: they conjoin the near and the far. Consequently, for the Arapaho, the regular alternation of day and night originates not, as in South America, from a middle course chosen from between two extremes, but from the juxtaposition of these extremes. It is a striking fact that this logical formulation should go hand in hand with a very special theory about eclipses, according to which the sun and the moon, when they disappear, are changing their respective places in the sky (Hilger 2, p. 91).

As he approaches the village where he hopes to find a wife, Moon's eyes and ears are charmed by the beauty of the landscape, the joyful hum of activity and the songs and cries of humans and animals. This idealized picture of native life proves that the concept of the 'noble savage' was not unknown to the savages themselves! The term thawwathinintarihisi, 'resuscitated woman', which refers to the human woman, presents a problem: it could allude to the belief in an era when humans, having become immortal, will be periodically rejuvenated every spring (Mooney 4, p. 818; cf. also pp. 785, 806, 959), or to the belief that certain humans are reincarnated ancestors. In support of the second hypothesis, it should be remembered that it chiefly concerns individuals who are born with teeth, or individuals whose upper teeth grow before the others (Hilger 2, pp. 5–6), a belief which is firmly entrenched in North America, since it is found even among the northern Athapaskan (Petitot 1, p. 276). In the rest of the myth, it is emphasized that Moon's wife has a fine set of teeth, a fact which establishes an additional affinity between her and her celestial and immortal parents-in-law. Although 'social order came into being at the same time as the sundance, whereas formerly the Indians had lived any way and without rules' (Hilger 2, p. 148), Moon's wife comes from a society which, while it may not be regulated, is at least living in harmony through the state of nature. Furthermore, as Sun says in $M_{426}$, 'the human body resembles ours'. So the human wife and the animal wife are different from each other both physically and mentally. Everything predestines the one for her vocation as wife and mother; everything precludes the other from such a vocation. Thus the human wife has no difficulty in reaching the state of culture, while the animal wife remains in a chaotic blur. It is not surprising that the unteachable woman should be a frog, since in the previous volume, we encountered the prototype of the ill-bred girl, in the form of a woman mad about honey – that is, a slave to nature – and, as we moved from the Chaco to Guiana, this honey-loving woman changed into a frog. Consequently, the South American frog, which is a transformation of an ill-bred human girl, is in opposition to a well-bred human girl in North America. But in both contexts, as I showed in *From Honey to Ashes* (pp. 285–6), the veil lifts to reveal a vast mythological system common to both South and North America, and in which the subjection of women is the basis of the social order. We can now understand the reason for this. The human wife's parents-in-law are not content just to present her with domestic utensils and to teach her the correct way to use them. The old man also proceeds to carry out a veritable physiological shaping of his daughter-in-law. In her pristine innocence, she did not have monthly periods and gave birth suddenly and without warning. The transition from nature to culture demands that the feminine organism should become periodic, since the social as well as the cosmic order would be endangered by a state of anarchy in which regular alternation of day and night, the phases of the moon, feminine menstruation, the fixed period for pregnancy and the course of the seasons did not mutually support each other.

So it is as periodic creatures that women are in danger of disrupting the orderly working of the universe. Their social insubordination, often referred to in the myths, is an anticipation in the form of the 'reign of women' of the infinitely more serious danger of their physiological insubordination. Therefore, women have to be subjected to *règles*.[4] And the rules instilled into them by their upbringing, like those imposed on them, even at the cost of their subjection, by a social order willed and evolved by men, are the pledge and symbol of other 'rules', the physiological nature of which bears witness to the correspondence between social and cosmic rhythms. In this sense, the time-gap of four days between the first and last quarter of the moon plays the same part as the spatial gap between the two canoe-passengers – the sun and the moon. The former determines the duration of menstruation, a standard measure of time which shifts from month to month and marks their succession. The old Arapaho informants said that they observed the periods in which the moon waxed or waned, but that, unlike other Indians, they did not feel any need to name the months (Hilger 2, p. 84). We have seen that the succession of day and night, which is also nameless, is measured by means of a spatial unit: the canoe moving along a certain course. The illusion of a theoretical coincidence between the phases of the moon and menstruation is borne out not only by the myth but also by the evidence of an informant: 'The proper time for the beginning of the ceremony was from seven to ten days after the new moon, and hence an equal number of days after the menstrual period' (Dorsey 5, p. 22). Several Plains tribes, although perhaps not the Arapaho, included in the sun-dance a rite during which the young women challenged the men to accuse them of sexual misbehaviour. This too provides a link-up between feminine morality and a ceremony intended to regulate the sun's course.

That any failure on the part of women to respect strict periodicity would represent as serious a threat to the orderly working of the universe as would the suspension of the alternation of day and night, or a disturbance in the seasonal cycle, is quite clear from the way in which the myths and rites try to establish an equivalence between the various

---

[4] TRANSLATORS' NOTE: *Règles*, in French, has the double meaning of 'rules' and 'monthly periods'.

types of calendrial periodicity. In addition to the central post, the ceremonial bower included sixteen others, arranged in a circle and supporting the framework. Two black-painted posts were placed at the
north-eastern and north-western corners of an imaginary quadrilateral
drawn within the circular plane, and two red-painted posts at the southeastern and south-western corners. These four posts symbolized the
Four Old Men of the Arapaho pantheon, the masters of the winds, who
embody respectively summer, winter, day and night (Dorsey 5, pp. 14,
96, 124). So, Indian thought sees the two kinds of alternation, 'sol-

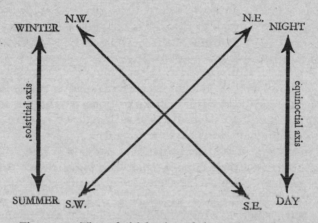

Figure 19. The solstitial axis and the equinoctial axis

stitial' and 'equinoctial', as being homologous. One and the same
arrangement of posts ensures both the regular succession of day and
night, and that of the months and seasons.

In the group of myths $M_{425-428}$, the sun and the moon are both
masculine. Mooney (4, p. 1,006) refers to other Arapaho traditions,
according to which the moon and sun are respectively brother and
sister. It is worthy of note that $M_{428}$, in the space of a few lines, transforms the luminaries from brothers into spouses (Dorsey 5, p. 228).
The sun-dance rites confirm the uncertainty about the sex of the sun
and moon and their relationship to each other (L.-S. 18). This explains
why the ceremonial copulation between the 'grandfather' or 'sur-
renderer' of the feast and the 'grandson's' wife admits of three interpretations. When the woman undresses and lies on her back, she is
offering herself symbolically to the moon shining above her (Dorsey 5,

p. 101). In this instance, the moon is a masculine character. But the copulation itself takes place between the 'grandfather', who represents the sun, and the woman, who then becomes the moon (*ibid.*, p. 177; Dorsey–Kroeber, p. 2). Lastly, it is stated that by the figurative means of the piece of root transferred from the grandfather's mouth to the wife's, and then to the husband's, the real copulation unites the grandfather and the grandson, who, at this point, personifies the moon:

|  |  | MOON |  | humans |  |  |
|---|---|---|---|---|---|---|
| 1) |  | △ | = | ( ○ | = | △ ) |
|  |  | sun |  | MOON |  | humans |
| 2) |  | △ | = | ○ |  | ( = △ ) |
|  |  | sun | humans |  |  | MOON |
| 3) |  | △ | ( = ○ ) |  | = |  | △ |

In other words, and provided the change of sex takes place, the moon is interchangeable between the three positions which constitute the invariant aspect of the system. If we note in addition that the sun can also be a male moon's sister and the female moon a male sun's wife; that the myths sometimes refer to the 'sun' as moon's father (Dorsey 5, p. 178), and, lastly, that the old woman who looks after Moon's son after his mother's death is herself mistress of night and sometimes identified with the moon (*ibid.*, p. 99), we can agree that the myths and rites do not attribute semantic valencies to beings and things in the absolute, but that the meaning of each term results from the position it occupies in systems which change because they correspond to a number of synchronic cross-sections made in a gradually unfolding mythic discourse.

No doubt, the ambiguity peculiar to the moon – the celestial husband of a human wife, according to the myth, or, according to the rite, the sun's terrestrial wife who inspires evil deeds (Dorsey 5, p. 124) – can probably be explained by its hermaphroditic nature, the formal necessity of which I established at the end of Part Three. The Arapaho myths describe the moon's hermaphroditic nature in concrete terms.[5] Moon is primarily a man who quarrels with his sister-in-law, the frog. She, in a rage, throws herself upon him and clings to his body, thus conferring on him a dual nature: his own, with, in addition, the moon-spots, which

---

[5] The Omaha say that men who adopt feminine costume and a feminine way of life are 'instructed by the moon' (Fletcher–La Flesche, p. 132).

are simply the frog with her pitcher, but which symbolize the menstrual flow. The frog herself looks like a pregnant woman (Dorsey 5, p. 177). Consequently, the male moon acquires a feminine appearance, because the frog is clinging to him.

# 2   The Porcupine's Instructions

> *Always justify the tasks you impose on young girls, but*
> *always make sure that they are given tasks. Idleness*
> *and intractability are the two most dangerous faults*
> *they are exposed to, and, once contracted, the least easy*
> *to cure. Girls ought to be vigilant and hard-working:*
> *that is not all; they must be subject to rules from an*
> *early age. This misfortune, if it is a misfortune in this*
> *case, is inseparable from their sex; if ever they escape*
> *from it, they will only endure other misfortunes far*
> *more cruel.*
>
> J.-J. Rousseau, *Emile*, Book V

The quarrel between the sun and the moon develops simultaneously in
three registers. The first, which is astronomical and calendrial, concerns
daily, monthly and seasonal periodicity. The second is sociological: it
relates to the suitable distance at which to look for a wife: the sun considers that human women are too close, since his heat makes them screw
up their faces, but the moon thinks they are the right distance away;
conversely, the moon considers the frog-women to be too far away,
while the sun proclaims that they are at the right distance. The third
register is concerned with the upbringing of young girls, a process
which is thought of as being tantamount to a psychological and physical
shaping; indeed, moral instruction is not enough; the female organism
must be moulded so as to allow it to fulfil its periodic functions:
menstruation, pregnancy and childbirth. These functions are all interlinked, since the menstrual blood, which is held in reserve during
pregnancy, forms the child's body. And, taken together, they are linked
to the main cosmic rhythms: menstruation (*les règles*) accompanies the
moon's phases; pregnancy lasts for a fixed number of lunar periods;
the alternation of day and night, the order of the months and the return

of the seasons belong to the same system. Since the varying ability of women to undergo moral and physiological training depends on their greater or lesser remoteness, everything is interconnected. If we stand back and view the Arapaho myths from a certain distance, they begin to appear rather like a cross between a picturesque and exotic Book of Genesis and a decorous version of L'Histoire d'O.[1]

It is not, however, from this angle that they have been studied by mythographers. The North American star-husband cycle, to which they belong, has been the object of painstaking research on the part on Reichard (2) and Thompson. Thompson's study, which is the more recent and the more complete, is rightly considered to be a model of its kind. Far be it from me to underrate it, since, but for it, I would have had great difficulty in carrying out my own research. However, since Thompson adopted the historical method, which is very different from mine, this is a good opportunity to put both methods to the test in relation to one example and to see what each can make of a given myth.

Like all the works of Stith Thompson, The Star Husband Tale is modelled on the work of the Finnish school and claims to demonstrate its validity (p. 95). It is well-known that the method of the Finnish school, which has an empirical and positivistic approach, is to begin by carefully listing all extant versions of any given story transmitted by the oral tradition. The story is then divided up into the shortest themes or episodes that can be recognized and singled out, through their recurrence in the same form in several versions, or through their unexpected appearance in one particular version among themes already recorded. The frequency with which these themes occur is calculated, and the conventional symbols used for drawing up the distribution chart are apportioned accordingly. By a comparison of the numerical values and their geographical distribution it is hoped to pick out those types which are relatively older and to establish the source from which they originated. The aim is to work out a kind of natural history of the folktale, showing where it came into being, at what period and in what form, and classifying the variants according to their place of origin and their order of occurrence.

In so far as it sets out to ascertain facts, this method is not open to criticism, since no analysis, structuralist or otherwise, is possible without a thorough preliminary knowledge of all the available data. The Finnish school, and its illustrious American representative, have introduced into anthropological research a meticulousness, an insistence on

[1] TRANSLATORS' NOTE: A famous, anonymous, erotic, sado-masochistic novel.

the exhaustive listing of variants, a scrupulous regard for the most minute details and an accuracy in geographical siting which make their research invaluable. All of this is beyond question. The difficulties start with the defining of the facts.

At no point does the historical method raise the question of what constitutes a fact in folklore. Or, to be more exact, it accepts as factual any element that the observer's subjective appreciation of the ostensible content of the narrative takes to be such. Little or no attempt is made to effect a reduction that would show how two or more themes, superficially different from each other, stand in a transformational relationship to each other, with the result that the status of scientific fact is not attributable to each particular theme or to such and such themes but rather to the schema which gives rise to them, although this schema itself remains latent. The method restricts itself to listing terms without establishing any link between them.

The fact is that the historical method considers only the absence, or the presence and geographical distribution, of elements which it leaves in a state of non-significance. But what is true of the rules of kinship is also valid for mythic narratives. Neither are limited to being simply what they *are*: they *serve a purpose* – to solve problems which are sociological in the one case and socio-logical in the other. This will be clearly shown by a comparison of the Arapaho myths with others belonging to the same group.

Basing his case on a comparative study of all the known variants of the star-husband cycle, Thompson (p. 135) infers the existence of a basic form or archetype combining all the themes with the greatest statistical frequency: *two young girls* (65 per cent) *spend the night out of doors* (85 per cent), *wish they had stars as husbands* (90 per cent). *As they sleep, they are carried off to the sky* (82 per cent) *by stars who marry them* (87 per cent): *a young man and an old man, whose respective ages are linked with the brightness or size of each star* (55 per cent). *The women disobey the injunction not to dig the ground* (90 per cent) *and unintentionally pierce the celestial vault* (76 per cent). *Unaided* (52 per cent), *they climb down by means of a rope* (88 per cent) *and return to their village safe and sound* (76 per cent).

It will be noted that only fifteen widely scattered versions, out of the eighty-six listed, present this basic form. This is a hardly surprising result, since physical anthropologists have reached similar conclusions whenever they have tried to define the typical Frenchman or American by putting together those features which occur with the greatest statistical frequency: such a method suggests only an artificial image

THE PORCUPINE'S INSTRUCTIONS 229

bearing very little resemblance to any actual individual, and which there is no reason to believe to be in any way representative of earlier generations. A statistical average expresses nothing but itself. It is only a way of re-ordering the facts, and gives us no information about any particular form that their objective combination may have taken in the past and may assume in various contexts at the present time.

If this difficulty is overlooked and one is prepared to believe, as Thompson does (p. 136), that the archetype must have existed over all or most of its present area of distribution before the appearance of any special developments, a second type of story can be singled out, and, from the logical and historical point of view, would seem to be derived from the first. Thompson calls this second type the 'porcupine redaction', no doubt in order to suggest that a methodology similar to the one used in dealing with written texts can also apply to the oral tradition. The Arapaho myths we are concerned with form part of the 'porcupine redaction', but in addition to the eight versions originating from this tribe (I have used only five, since the others repeat the same points), twelve have been recorded among the Gros-Ventre, the Cree, the Arikara, the Hidatsa, the Crow, the Cheyenne and the Kiowa, making twenty versions in all, distributed almost without a break over an area stretching between 55° and 35° North. If, in this case too, we select those features with the greatest statistical frequency, the following story can be constructed: *a girl* (100 per cent) *while performing a task* (84 per cent) *follows a porcupine* (95 per cent) *up a tree which stretches to the upper world* (95 per cent). *The porcupine becomes the moon* (45 per cent), *the sun* (25 per cent) *or a star* (15 per cent), *in the form of a young man* (30 per cent). *The girl marries him and bears him a son* (95 per cent). *She is warned not to dig* (80 per cent), *but disobeys and discovers a sky-hole* (85 per cent). *By her own efforts* (45 per cent) *or with the help of her husband* (25 per cent), *she descends on a sinew-rope* (85 per cent), *but it is too short. The husband sends down a rock with instructions to kill the wife and spare the son* (85 per cent). *Sequel: the adventures of Star-Boy* (*Moon-Boy or Sun-Boy*) (90 per cent).

Type II presents a denser, but much more restricted, area of distribution than that of type I, or basic form. Within the type II area, the still more limited distribution pattern of the quarrel between the sun and the moon includes eight versions out of the preceding twenty. These are found among the Gros-Ventre, the Hidatsa, the Crow and the Arapaho.

Thompson does not comment on these at any length, merely observing (p. 188): 'This elaboration serves to introduce the porcupine incident, and has a certain artistic value, though the chewing contest in the upper world hardly helps the story ... It looks like an addition, which has been widely adopted in part of the versions, without a clear-cut geographical pattern'.

Of the above-mentioned eight versions, those originating from the Crow and the Hidatsa (who formed a single community a few centuries ago) differ on one point. Instead of (or in addition to) the injunction imposed on the woman not to pull up a certain plant in the celestial garden, her young son is forbidden to hunt a particular species of bird – meadowlarks. One day, the boy disobeys; he fails to hit one of these birds, which then hurls abuse at him, telling him he is nothing but a slave. When urged to give an explanation, the meadowlark reveals that the hunter's mother was a human. The young man is then consumed with a desire to visit the earth and his kinsfolk, and it is he who persuades his mother to flee ($M_{429-430}$, see pp. 261–2, 283–6). According to Thompson (p. 138), the only purpose of the incident is to create a rôle for the son and to provide a reason for the woman's flight.

Although the basic form, or type I, exists in only fifteen versions, Thompson maintains that this archetype must once have existed over all or most of its present area of distribution. It follows that type II came into being within the type I area, of which it occupies only a part, that the quarrel between the Sun and Moon developed inside the distribution area of type II, and finally that the meadowlark episode, which has the most restricted distribution area of the four, developed within that of the Sun–Moon quarrel. Looked at from an historical and geographical point of view, the relationship between the four forms can be expressed by means of concentric circles (Figure 20): the meadowlark episode is contained 'within' the quarrel between the sun and moon; the quarrel is 'within' the porcupine redaction; and this redaction, type II, is 'within' the basic form or type I, since the latter is said to possess the two-fold privilege of being the oldest and the most widespread. It may be assumed, then, that each form, according to its greater or lesser antiquity, occupies an area the extent of which is related to the date of its first appearance.

There is nothing more to be said, once the analysis, which is intended to be objective, has reached this conclusion. The themes and episodes have no decipherable meaning, once they have been discovered, located, listed and dated. The porcupine redaction provides as good a means as any of transporting the heroine to the sky. The quarrel between the sun and moon makes it possible to introduce the porcupine episode, which the myths bring in in a variety of ways. The chewing

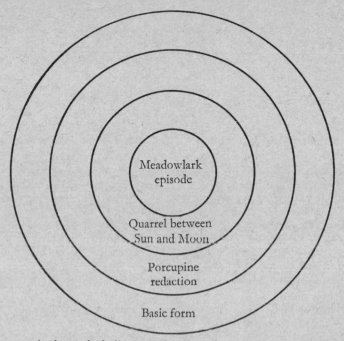

Meadowlark
episode

Quarrel between
Sun and Moon

Porcupine
redaction

Basic form

Figure 20. A theoretical diagram showing the distribution of the myths concerning the wives of the sun and moon, according to the historical school

contest adds nothing to the story. The reasons used to explain the meadowlark episode verge on the trite ...

Thompson next embarks on a study of an important variant, or type III, the distribution area of which extends through southern Canada and the region north of the Great Lakes from north-east Alaska to the coast of Nova Scotia. From west to east, this 'northern crescent' includes the following communities: Kaska ($M_{431}$), Tahltan ($M_{432}$), Tsetsaut ($M_{433}$), Carrier ($M_{434}$), Cree ($M_{435}$), Assiniboine ($M_{436}$), Ojibwa ($M_{444}$), Passamaquoddy ($M_{437}$) and Micmac ($M_{438}$). Linguistically, the first four communities belong to the Athapaskan group, and all the others to the Algonquin group, with the exception of the Assiniboine who are Siouan Indians forming an enclave in the preceding group (Figure 21).

Apart from the final episode, type III reproduces the basic form. Instead of making an uneventful landing on earth, the two young women, in escaping from the world above, fall onto the top of a tree, where they remain stranded. Various animals go by; the women call to

Figure 21. The 'northern crescent' and the distribution area of the Sun/Moon
quarrel

them for help and even promise to marry them. All the animals refuse, apart from the last one who, in ten of the thirteen versions listed, is a wolverine, and in the other three, a fisher, or a diving bird. As soon as they reach the ground, the women deceive their over-credulous rescuer. In the myths of the Micmac and the Passamaquoddy, the two Algonquin tribes situated at the eastern tip of the crescent, the story is slightly different. The women do not escape but are granted the favour of a magical means of transport by the celestial people, on the understanding that they close their eyes during the descent and only open them after hearing in turn the cry of the black-headed chickadee and that of two different species of squirrel. The women disobey, are punished and remain prisoners at the top of a tree. The one detail in this special development that Thompson singles out for comment (p. 140) is that the Micmac and the Passamaquoddy occupy a peripheral position in the distribution area of the type. After a few brief observations about three other local variants (types IV, V and VI), with which I do not propose to deal for the moment, Thompson (p. 144) puts forward his conclusions: the basic form, which is also the oldest, goes back at least to the 18th century. The porcupine redaction cannot be later than 1892, and type III probably came into being round about 1820–30. These estimates are surprising, to say the least, especially in the case of North American myths which, as I have established, are absolutely straightforward transformations of South American ones. Those of both North and South must correspond to patterns common to the two hemispheres, and their age should be calculated not in decades but millennia. Further convincing evidence is offered by the resemblance between the situation of the two women, stranded at the top of a tree while more or less helpful animals pass by, and that of the bird-nester in the Bororo and Ge myths ($M_1$, $M_{7-12}$) who manages to climb down with the help of a jaguar. The analogy cannot be accidental, since the bird-nester myth exists in a literal form in the north-west of North America, where it is also possible to find all the stages of a transformation which brings us back to the star-husband cycle. This, indeed, will be the subject of the fourth volume in this series.

Without in any way anticipating the final phase of my enquiry, I propose to prove at this point that the four variants, which Thompson takes as a basis for his reconstruction of the historical evolution of the star-husband cycle, do not differ from each other in the manner of material objects, whose unequal extensions in space and time are simply to be recorded. The situation is, rather, that they are dynamically interlinked, which means that they are in oppositional and correlational relationships with each other. These relationships both determine the distinctive features of each variant and are more effective in explaining their distribution than statistical frequency. To make the demonstration more convincing, I shall approach it by way of the two episodes which Thompson sees as playing hardly any part at all, since he considers them to be late, local developments: the episode of the meadowlark in type II, and the episode of the chickadee and the squirrels in type III. It will be remembered that they originate from two very widely separated areas; the first occurs among the Crow and Hidatsa, who are western Siouan, the second among the Passamaquoddy and Micmac, who are eastern Algonquin.

In the Crow and Hidatsa myths, the hero is expressly forbidden to shoot meadowlarks. But there is a reason for the ban, as is subsequently explained in the story, after the hero has disregarded it. When attacked, the bird speaks and reveals to the boy that he is of terrestrial origin. So, the hunting prohibition masks an acoustic one. Its aim is to prevent a male hero *hearing* what a bird might say to him, since, as soon as he is informed of his origin, he will want to go back down to earth from the sky.

In the Algonquin myths, the episode featuring the chickadee and the squirrels reverses this episode in every particular. The hero is replaced by two heroines. They are given an order, the declared aim of which is to allow them to go back to earth, not to prevent them doing so. The injunction takes an obvious form: they must not open their eyes (just as the Crow–Hidatsa hero must not 'see' the meadowlarks), but this form conceals another: *hearing* (instead of *not hearing*) the cries of certain animals. Finally, the cry is a *signal*, not a *message*.

No doubt, one or two indications suggest that the chickadee (*Parus* sp.) might also be a bearer of news. The Fox and the Kickapoo imply as much in their myths (Jones 3, p. 83; 4, p. 99), as do the Wabakani (Speck 5, p. 371). The same belief used to exist in Europe: 'Its cry heralds various things. In Estonian, tige "bad", was a name connected perhaps with the Lettonian conception of the bird as a prophetic creature' (Rolland, pp. 124–5). The Cheyenne and Blackfoot Indians limit the bird's prophetic powers to being the harbinger of summer, since its cry is 'mehnew', and in Cheyenne 'mehaniv' means 'summer is coming' (Grinnell 2, Vol. 2, p. 110). The Ojibwa, on the other hand, believe there will be a storm if the chickadee swallows the last syllable of its song: Gi-ga-be; gi-ga-be; gi-ga-me (Coleman, pp. 105–6).

These instances in which the chickadee plays the part of informer or adviser deserve analysis, since, as a general rule, this particular rôle devolves on the meadowlark.[2] Countless instances could be quoted, and they range from the Coast Salish (Adamson, p. 225), the Chinook (Jacobs 2, texts no. 14, 24, 27, 36; Sapir 1, p. 300), the Nez Percé (Phinney, pp. 205, 222, 227, 251, 381, 401, etc.), the Western Sahaptin (Jacobs 1, pp. 111, 121, 163), the Pomo (Barrett 2, pp. 350-51, 446-7), to the Mandan and Hidatsa (Beckwith 1, p. 27; Bowers 1, pp. 132, 370-73), the Cheyenne (Grinnell 1, p. 308) and the Pawnee (G. A. Dorsey 1, pp. 20-23). The meadowlark's cry is not so much a signal as a true language: 'Many are the words of the meadowlark which the Indian can understand,' say the Oglala Dakota (Beckwith 2, p. 381). The Crow and the Arapaho go even further, the Crow maintaining that 'the meadowlark speaks Crow' (Lowie 3, pp. 51, 69), while the Arapaho say, 'You know, meadowlarks speak Arapaho.' Although the Arapaho, unlike the Mandan, believe that the words spoken by the bird are nasty and even obscene, they feed their little children on the flesh and eggs of the bird 'so that they learn to talk quickly and know many things' (Hilger 2, pp. 41, 94; Kroeber 3, pp. 317-18). The Gros-Ventre of Montana believe that when a child is backward in talking or understanding, it should be fed on meadowlark's eggs baked near a fire ... Even today, it is said of a chatterbox that his mother must have given him meadowlark's eggs to eat (Flannery, p. 143). The Blackfoot claim to be able to understand the meadowlark's song (McClintock, p. 482; Schaeffer, p. 43). The same beliefs persist to the west of the Rockies among the Yana, who maintain that the meadowlark understands foreign languages, and among the tribes of the Puget Sound, who make their children eat meadowlark's eggs so that they will learn to speak well (Sapir 3, p. 47; Haeberlin-Gunther, p. 21, n. 46).

So, in spite of the rare instances in which their functions are reversed, it is hardly possible to compare the linguistic talents of the two birds. Those of the black-headed chickadee are exercised in a different area, as was already indicated by the meteorological rôle assigned to it by the Cheyenne and the Ojibwa, and confirmed by the Navaho and Menomini, who classify the chickadee as a winter bird (Franciscan Fathers, pp. 159-60; M₄₇₉, and p. 354 below). Unlike the meadowlark, which is a

---

[2] Conversely, however, the Thompson Indians believe that the meadowlark indicates proximity to land (Teit 4, p. 25 and n. 54, p. 104). According to a native witness, the Iroquois used to believe that whoever ate the flesh of the chickadee turned into a liar (Waugh, p. 133).

migratory bird (Audubon, Vol. 1, pp. 379–87; McClintock, *ibid.*; Grinnell 2, Vol. 2, p. 109), the chickadee is usually non-migrant. But its tongue is barbed with filaments, of which – according to the Shoshone – there are six; one falls off each month and grows again six months later, so that it is possible to tell, by capturing a chickadee, which month in winter or in summer it is. This is why it is wrong to kill chickadees (Culin, pp. 11–18). The belief is sufficiently widespread to be also found among the Mandan and the Hidatsa, who reckon the months of the year from the chickadee's tongue: they even supply a sketch in support of this practice (Figure 22).

Figure 22. The chickadee's tongue. (From Beckwith 1, p. 147.)

In *The Raw and the Cooked*, I encountered, and discussed, the *hearing/ not hearing* dilemma, in connection with South American myths dealing with human mortality. It is significant, then, that it should recur in North America, in connection with a bird symbolizing periodicity.

This bird (*Parus atricacapillus*) forms part of a triad, the two other terms of which are, in order of appearance, the red squirrel and the striped squirrel. Although both members of the Sciuridae family, these animals belong to two distinct types. The red American squirrel, or *chickaree* (not to be confused with *chickadee*, the popular name for the black-headed tit) is a tree-dwelling rodent: *Tamiasciurus hudsonicus*. The striped squirrel or *chipmunk* is a ground rodent: *Tamias striatus*. So, the animal series: black-headed chickadee, red squirrel and striped squirrel, corresponds to the stages of the descent to earth:

SKY |

| bird
|       *tree-dwelling* ⎫
|                     ⎬ animal
EARTH ↓       *ground* ⎭

The myths (M437a, b; M438a, b) are quite explicit on this point: after realizing that their human wives were yearning for the earth and their families, the sun and moon ordered them to sleep close to one another. At day-break they must not be in a hurry to open their eyes and put their heads out from under the blanket; they must wait at least until they heard the song of the black-headed chickadee, then the call of the red squirrel, followed by that of the striped squirrel. Only then could they get up and see where they were.

The younger of the two women was always impatient, and wanted to leave her bed as soon as she heard the chickadee, but the elder held her back. However, when the red squirrel called, there was no holding her: she jumped to her feet and the other did likewise. The two women then realized that they had come back to earth, but were perched on the top of a high hemlock-pine (*Tsuga canadensis*), from which they could not get down unaided. 'And it had come to pass in this wise: for as each song was sung by the birds and the squirrels, they had come nearer and nearer to the earth, even as the light of day drew near, but as they could not delay, they had been deserted' (Leland, pp. 146–7; cf. Prince, p. 63; Rand, pp. 161, 310).

In this respect, too, the meadowlark is opposed to the animal triad in the eastern myths. Each term of this triad denotes one stage in the descent from sky to earth, whereas in the Crow and Hidatsa myths the descent is represented by the one bird. The meadowlark (*Sturnella magna*) lives near the ground, running rapidly from place to place in search of food. It perches above ground only occasionally, to escape pursuit, and it sleeps on the ground. 'You can find the nest at the foot of some thick tuft of tall grass: it is a hollow in the ground where the bird has arranged a circle of grasses, fibrous roots and other vegetable substances; round about, in order to cover and conceal it, it has inter-twined the leaves and stems of the surrounding plants' (Audubon, Vol. I, p. 384). The Dakota myths describe this ground nest as being 'oval like a wigwam' (Beckwith 2, p. 382). As a bird, the meadowlark is a sky dweller, but its habits make it familiar with earthly things. Consequently, it is capable of differentiating between what belongs to the world above and what concerns the world below. There is nothing surprising about its denunciation of a human woman's son who had taken up his abode in the sky as an imposter. But the most important point is that its ambiguous nature creates a contrast with the carefully graded series of the three creatures in eastern Algonquin myths.

Let us summarize the argument as it has proceeded so far. At both extremities of the area occupied by the myth featuring the wives of the sun and moon, among the Crow and Hidatsa on the one hand, and among the Micmac and Passamaquoddy on the other, we have discovered forms which are opposed to each other in several ways. Among the north-eastern Algonquin, where the story ends happily, two heroines, after being carried off to the sky, must – before they can return safe and sound to their village – *see* the earth below (although they have been forbidden to look) and *hear* the calls of three creatures living at a greater or lesser distance from the ground. Among the Crow and Hidatsa, where there is only one heroine who dies, her son ought *not to have seen* the meadowlarks (which he is forbidden to hunt), and *not to hear* the revelation of his terrestrial *origin* (which is a message and not the signal of a terrestrial *arrival*, like the calls of the three animals in the other group). Finally, the animal triad in the Algonquin myths has an analytical function: each animal's cry indicates that the heroines are at a different distance from the ground. The meadowlark's function is, on the contrary, synthetic: because of its way of life, the bird belongs at one and the same time to the sky and the earth:

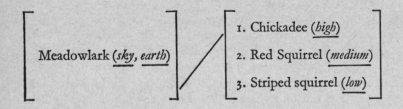

Let us suppose, as a working hypothesis, that these two forms, each of which occurs in a very small number of versions taken from two groups of Indians geographically very remote from each other and at the same time different both in speech and culture – Plains Siouan or woodland-dwelling or coastal Algonquin respectively – stand in a relationship of inverted symmetry to each other. Theoretically, they cor-

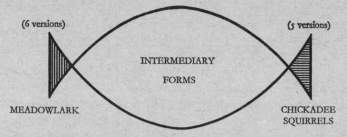

Figure 23. Theoretical diagram of the distribution of myths featuring the wives of the sun and moon, according to the structural method

respond to each other on either side of an intermediary zone which must now be studied (Figure 23).

The same kind of relationship prevails between Thompson's basic form – it will be remembered that empirical evidence of its existence is to be found only in the 'northern crescent', where it constitutes type III (see above, pp. 228–30) – and the Plains variants which begin with the quarrel between the sun and the moon. Other myths besides those belonging to the basic form begin with a discussion between two women about the luminary they would like to have as a husband. I do not propose to discuss them in detail, although the study of all the various commutations would no doubt prove fruitful, but, according to the particular version, one of the two luminaries may be dull, the other brilliant; one small, the other large; or again one red, the other blue, white or yellow. Similarly, one of the two women is sensible, the other foolish. The one who makes a reasonable choice obtains a young man – a warrior or a chief – as her husband. Her companion finds herself with an old man or a servant.

It is clear that this initial situation reproduces, in an inverted form, the quarrel between the sun and the moon. In the one case, two male, celestial characters discuss the respective merits of terrestrial women. In the other, two terrestrial women discuss the respective merits of celestial males. In either case, one character is sensible, the other unwise. The foolish character, whether male or female, makes a bad choice: a frog-wife with wrinkled skin, who is sometimes old ($M_{427a}$), suffers from incontinence and therefore leaks from below; or a rheumy-eyed old man ($M_{437, 458}$), who leaks from above. Again, then, we are dealing with two types which, in regard to each other, stand in a relationship of symmetry, not inclusion.

So true is this that there are myths displaying intermediary forms between these two extreme modes of the deceptive choice:

### M₄₃₉. *Arikara.* '*The deceptive choice*'

There was once a young warrior who wanted to be great. He used to go out and mourn all alone among the hills and implore supernatural aid. A bird led him to a place where a man all painted red appeared to him. It was the sun who demanded the supplicant's tongue. The warrior at once pulled it out and died.

The following night, the moon, who was also a man, brought the young warrior back to life, and took him under his protection. Moon explained that the sun was coming for him the next day and would take him off to his dwelling place where he would have to choose between two groups of weapons. He was to take the old weapons.

The young warrior took the old weapons. The sun was furious because these much damaged weapons would confer long life and greatness on whoever possessed them. He tried several times to kill the young man or asked his sons to kill him, but they were the ones who perished. 'No-Tongue' became very old and blind. The sun, satisfied at long last, took the old man up to his home (Dorsey 6, pp. 61–5, cf. the Mandan version in: Will 1, 2).

The deceptive choice theme occurs, then, in three forms: the sun and moon, who are men, choose dissimilar wives; human women choose dissimilar luminaries as husbands (sometimes, moreover, these luminaries are the sun and moon, a fact which completes the symmetrical relationship between the two types); or, thirdly, a human invited by the sun to choose between dissimilar objects, is told by the moon that he must not be misled by appearances.[3] This line of enquiry brings us back to the question of how to bring up young girls, two aspects of which question are represented by the extreme forms of the deceptive choice.

[3] Here I am merely touching on the deceptive choice theme, which has an important place in Plains mythology, where it takes on many different aspects. In the grandmother-grandson cycle, the old woman guesses the child's sex from the choice she asks him to make between feminine and masculine objects (M₄₂₉ₐ, M₄₃₀ᵦ; Lowie 3, p. 53; Beckwith 1, p. 122; cf. the illustration of this scene on the back flap of the French edition of the present volume). In this case, it is a terrestrial and not a celestial choice, a genuine and not a misleading one. In M₄₃₀ᵦ and other myths, the choice, a misleading one, which human women propose to the star's son, is terrestrial and has to be made by a celestial figure. It can be seen that the choice is sometimes concerned with natural qualities, such as the appearance of the sun and moon or feminine beauty, and sometimes with cultural qualities: new or damaged objects, objects used by men or by women, etc. This group of transformations would be worthy of special study.

A well-brought-up young girl must learn, among other things, not to trust appearances, and not to allow other people to judge her by her own appearance. In the one case, she makes a mistake; in the other, she encourages men to be mistaken about her.

There remains the 'porcupine redaction'. In order to interpret it, we must begin by enquiring into the position of the porcupine in North American mythology. What is its significance? Or rather, what are the myths trying to signify through its agency?

The American porcupine (*Erethizon dorsatum*) is a rodent, quite dif-

*on dorsatum.* (From Brehm, *Säugetiere*, Vol. 2, p. 567.)

ferent from the European hedgehog of the family of insectivores. Its body is covered with thick fur, which, over the back, tail, neck and belly, grows into stiff bristles and quills of uneven length. Its claws are so set as to enable it to climb trunks and perch in trees. In fact, it lives chiefly on bark, cambium and leaves; although it does not hibernate, in winter it settles in some hollow trunk, near trees which it abandons only after it has stripped them of all their edible parts. It is said to begin at the top and then move down to the branches and trunk (Brehm, *Säugetiere* 2, pp. 567–8; Hall–Kelson, p. 780).

The image of its rolled-up body bristling with quills has occasionally caused mythographers to suppose that the animal symbolized the rising sun and its rays (Curtin–Hewitt, pp. 655, 812). Yet, apart from one Arapaho and one Crow version, all the myths featuring the quarrel between the sun and moon identify the porcupine with the moon. It will be seen presently that the association with one luminary rather than another is a secondary feature, when we consider the more basic properties that ethnography can reveal, and which have little in common with the subjective interpretations put forward by certain commentators.

An initial semantic function of the porcupine emerges from certain myths of the eastern Algonquin, who see a correlation between this animal and the toad ($M_{377}$). According to the Micmac (Leland, pp. 108, 289), the two beasts were once witches, whom the demiurge punished by removing their noses. Since then they have been flat-nosed (Figure 24).The same Indians also believe that porcupines are a race of chthonian witches who try to destroy the human heroes by fire. However, the humans sometimes turn this means of destruction against their enemies, in which case it is the porcupines who die ($M_{440}$; Rand, pp. 6, 70–71, 320; Speck 8, p. 63).

As I have explained, porcupines settle in hollow trunks in winter. Among the Tsimshian of the north-west coast, it is forbidden to smoke them out of their lairs (Boas 2, p. 449). Although these Indians live a long way from the Micmac, we shall soon see that certain beliefs relating to the porcupine are common to the whole of northern America. On the other hand, it is true that the animal has a characteristic profile, with the forehead and nose forming an almost straight line, and that many myths describe frog-women or toad-women as having broad, flat faces. Although the porcupine does not hibernate in the strict sense, both animals seek shelter during the cold season. The Micmac say that the demiurge 'sleeps for six months like the toad' (Leland, p. 134). In the Algonquin myths, then, the porcupine and the toad form a feminine and periodic pair. In the Plains myths, the porcupine is an embodiment of the moon in its masculine aspect, and the frog, by clinging to the moon, confers on the latter a periodic and feminine aspect (see above, pp. 224–5). With only slight differences in the two cases, the relationships between the same terms bring together in similar fashion the moon, the porcupine and various kinds of batrachians.

We now come to a second aspect, which the preceding discussion has already hinted at. From the Pacific coast to the Great Lakes, there exists a group of myths ($M_{440}$ is simply an inversion of them) in which the porcupine, ostensibly master of the cold, in fact institutes daily and seasonal periodicity. As regards daily periodicity, we can quote an

Iroquois myth (M$_{441}$; E. A. Smith, p. 86), in which the porcupine has to settle a quarrel about the alternation of light and darkness between the striped squirrel, the champion of day, and the bear, the champion of night. Myths dealing with seasonal periodicity, habitat and mode of life are more numerous (cf. Teit 7, pp. 226, 245; the general discussion in: Boas 2, pp. 724–7). The Tahltan, Tsetsaut, Shuswap and Tsimshian, etc. say (M$_{442}$) that the beaver and the porcupine had a quarrel, because one can swim and the other cannot. Finding himself marooned on an island, the porcupine conjured up frost and ice so that he could walk ashore without getting his feet wet. The variants of this story are too numerous to be discussed in detail. They establish a series of oppositions between the two animals:

| | | | | |
|---|---|---|---|---|
| *Porcupine*: | west | climbs trees which he gnaws. | spends winter close to the ground, | associated with mountains, etc. |
| *Beaver*: | east | does not climb trees, which he cuts down. | spends winter underneath water, | associated with lakes, etc. |

Among several tribes in the Great Lakes area, the master of cold theme is linked to that of a foolhardy porcupine hunt, embarked upon by two young women: this second theme takes us back to the 'porcupine redaction':

*M$_{443}$. Menomini. 'The porcupine, master of cold'*

There were once two sisters, who were considered the swiftest runners and who decided to visit towards the setting sun another village situated so far away that an ordinary walker would have to travel two days to reach it. They set off in the morning and ran on the snow until nearly noon. At this moment they noticed the track of a porcupine leading to the hollow of a trunk lying across the trail.

One sister started to tease the animal by poking a stick into the cavity to make it come out. At last it came out and she pulled out all the long quills from his body, throwing them in the snow. The other sister remonstrated against such cruelty.

When the sisters continued their running toward the distant village, the porcupine crawled up a tall pine and began to shake his small rattle, singing in tune to its sound. Soon the snow began to fall. The more sensible of the two sisters turned round and saw the porcupine on the tree top. She feared that some harm would befall them and insisted that they should go back to their own village. The other sister wanted to go on. So they continued their journey but the depth of snow impeded their progress. They could hear the voices of the people in the village they were striving to reach, but exhaustion compelled them to stop and they perished in the snow. Ever since, people have never harmed porcupines (Hoffman, pp. 210–11; Skinner–Satterlee, pp. 426–7).

The Winnebago believe that there is a special relationship between the porcupine and the north wind (Radin 1, p. 503). According to an Iroquois belief, members of the porcupine clan are able to foretell whether or not the winter will be severe; and when lost in the forest, they are better able than others to locate the north (Curtin–Hewitt, p. 657). It is, then, an established fact that the tribes of the 'northern crescent' associate the porcupine with seasonal periodicity and believe it to be a master or precursor of winter.

Yet it is precisely in the northern crescent that the porcupine episode is absent from the myth featuring the wives of the sun and moon. We have just seen, however, that it appears in $M_{443}$, where the two sisters *are not* the wives of the sun and moon, although in a sense they are a transformation of them: they move *horizontally* and not *vertically*, and the heroine takes possession of the quills, the lure of which in another context leads to her own capture. She *throws away* the quills, instead of trying to *preserve* them carefully. On the other hand, the porcupine *makes his lair* in a *felled* tree, instead of *perching on* an *upright* tree; he *slows down a race* instead of *encouraging an ascent*. I established an opposition between the porcupine and the beaver: in the Kaska version of the myth concerning the wives of the sun and moon ($M_{431}$; Teit 8, pp. 457–9), the heroines are changed into beavers by means of a transformation that I shall return to later (p. 253).

The most important point of all is that certain northern crescent versions belonging to Thompson's type III contain a final episode which Thompson did not deem worthy of attention, in spite of the fact that it is an exact counterpart of the initial episode of the porcupine hunt in the myths of the Plains tribes. The point can be established by an examination of the following example:

$M_{444}$. *Ojibwa. 'The wives of the sun and moon'*
There was once a man, his wife and their two daughters. When the latter had come to maturity, their mother sent them far away. They set out with no particular destination in mind, sleeping every night in a clearing.

Here follows the discussion about the sun and moon, the carrying off of the young girls into the sky where they become the wives of the sun and moon, their escape at the instigation of the elder girl who is dissatisfied with her old husband, and their return to earth with the help of a compassionate old woman. But the elder girl opens her eyes too soon, the cord holding the basket breaks and the women fall into the nest of a bird of prey (fish-hawk) at the top of a tree. Various kinds of game folk walk past, but not one is moved to pity. Finally, the wolverine (*Gulo luscus*) comes along and they offer to marry him. He helps them to climb down; the elder sister sends him back up the tree to fetch the tape she has discreetly left behind in the nest, whereupon the women flee. The wolverine overtakes them and does all manner of things to them until he has them nearly killed. The younger sister manages to pound him with a stick and to bring her sister who had died as a result of her sufferings, back to life.

The heroines come upon a lake at which a diver (bird) is floating (*Colymbus, loc. cit.* p. 2: *Podiceps auritus*). They call him by his name, but he refuses to reply, because he is trying to pass himself off as somebody else: 'Arrayed-in-Wampum'. In order to convince the women, he secretly pulls off the beads he uses as ear-rings and pretends to spit them out; the supernatural character whose identity he is usurping has the power to secrete beads in place of saliva. The women are delighted and climb into his canoe. Diver allows them to paddle and sits in the middle. By the edge of the shore, the trio see in turn a bear, a caribou and a moose. Each time, Diver claims that it is his pet (animal), but when, at the women's request, he calls it, the beast takes flight. 'That is the way they always act when I am in company with women,' he explains. He goes after the moose and kills it. The women are very happy to have meat. Several other burlesque incidents intervene before the arrival at Diver's village.

There, the women discover that, contrary to all their husband's boasts, the latter's sisters are extremely homely and wear ear-rings made of dog-dung, not beads. In spite of their husband's instructions to the contrary, they go out in the evening and find the village beauties assembled around the real 'Arrayed-in-Wampum'. The imposter is there too, but all the women jeer at him, push him about and trample on his back.

Sickened by this spectacle, the two women go to 'Arrayed-in-Wampum's' wigwam, not without having placed two pieces of wood under their coverlets. Diver finds decayed wood full of ants in the place where his wives are accustomed to lie and is bitter. Diver goes off to look for his wives, whom he finds lying in bed with 'Arrayed-in-Wampum', who is his elder brother. He throws a pebble 'which has been heated red' into his open mouth and kills him.

When told that his brother is dead, Diver feigns despair and pretends to stab himself. But he has merely split open caribou intestines full of blood which he has attached to his belt, and as he swims away, he boasts of his crime. He is pursued and great leeches are set the ask of sucking the water out of the sea. Diver kills them with flints he has tied to his feet. The water pours out of the disembowelled animals and submerges the whole community (Jones 2, Part 2, pp. 151–67).

This myth calls for several observations. I have established that the versions containing the episode of the quarrel between the sun and moon are inversions of the celestial bodies' canoe-journey motif which is a characteristic feature of homologous South American myths. The version just quoted, which does not include the quarrel between the sun and moon, restores the canoe journey with the two wives of the sun and moon in the positions – fore and aft, since the women row while Diver sits in the middle – occupied by their husbands in other versions. This commutation is accompanied by yet another: the canoe sails past trickster animals (they flee when they are called) which are standing on the bank, instead of themselves being passengers in the canoe, as is the case in the North American myths which illustrate the journey theme more directly ($M_{408-409}$). Secondly, the animals *which are sailed past* correspond to *those which filed past* the foot of the tree in the eastern versions. Although they are referred to in $M_{444}$, this myth attaches greater importance to the others:

|  | 1. *moose*: | 2. *bear*: | 3. *marten*: |
|---|---|---|---|
| $M_{437a}$ | 'married since the autumn' | 'married since the spring' | 'married since the previous spring' |
| $M_{437b}$ | – | – | 'married since the beginning of spring' |
| $M_{438a}$ | – | – | |
| $M_{438b}$ | (*no details given*) | | |

(Prince, p. 65; Leland, pp. 148–9; Rand, pp. 162, 311)

It is not important to know whether the breeding season has been correctly observed in the case of each species. The proposals of the two women are evaded by each animal pretending to be already married, and the date of the marriage is moved back each time. So if the moose's marriage, which is the most recent, took place in the autumn, it follows that the women came back to earth shortly afterwards, that is, at the beginning of winter. Consequently, the episode of the trickster animals replaces that of the porcupine, which, because of the animal's rôle as harbinger of winter, would seem to fit in at the same period. Hagar (p. 103) deserves great credit for realizing the seasonal nature of the procession of animals in these myths; and this provides occasion to recall the zodiacal nature of the encounter of the hero or heroine with animals (who also play the part of tricksters) in a group of South American myths ($M_{60}$, $M_{317}$, $M_{402-404}$).

The seasonal character emerges prominently in the episode with which most of the Ojibwa versions conclude. While the character variously referred to as 'Arrayed-in-Wampum' or 'Spit-Wampum' is a diver (*Gavia* sp.), whose black beak is to be explained by the red-hot pebble incident (Speck 7, p. 52), the ludicrous brother, who has usurped his identity, is a little fresh-water grebe,[4] which the Ojibwa call Cingibis, Shingebiss: this is the 'fall duck who defied the severest blasts of wind to kill from the north-west, the master of fish on which it feeds and the possessor of a fire which never went out' (Schoolcraft 1, pp. 85–6; 2, pp. 113–15; 3, Vol. 3, pp. 324–6; Williams, pp. 224–5). A Timagami version ($M_{444b}$; Speck 7, pp. 47–53) presents the two heroines as scatter-brains, since they sleep in the open air in winter. After their visit to the sky and adventure with the wolverine, 'the break-up of the ice-pack begins'. The hole through which they travel back down to earth corresponds to the position occupied by the Pleiades, the culmination of which takes place in these latitudes after nightfall, towards the end of January or the beginning of February, and is believed by the Iroquois to mark the beginning of the year (Fenton, p. 7). In an Ojibwa version from the Lake Superior region ($M_{444c}$; Jones 1, p. 371), it is explained how Diver, who kills his brother, goes to spend winter in a marsh. The Master of winter tries in vain to freeze and starve him to death. Diver also gets the better of winter in a Menomini version ($M_{444d}$; Skinner–Satterlee, pp. 408–10). Seasonal periodicity is no less real in the Ojibwa myths than in those of the eastern Algonquin, but it seems to be differently phased. All the myths have a spatial axis, in so

---

[4] In the myths of the Micmac the rôle played by the first bird is reversed (Leland, pp. 164–6). The problem of the semantic valencies of the diver will be dealt with in the next volume.

far as the story takes place between the high and the low, and a temporal axis which, as the case may be, goes from winter to spring, or from spring to winter.

What has the argument proved so far? The myths of the Great Lakes area add a final episode – the grebe one – to the story about the wives of the sun and moon, and this episode itself concludes with the return of spring. On the other hand, in the myths of the Plains Indians, an initial episode – the porcupine one – precedes the story of the wives of the sun and moon, which consequently begins with the arrival of winter. So, the porcupine, who is the master of ice and cold, is in opposition to the grebe, who is the master of thaw and the rewarming of the earth. We thus obtain two symmetrical series:

|  | I | 2 | 3 |
|---|---|---|---|
| *Central Algonquin*: |  | Wives of sun and moon | Return of spring (*grebe redaction*) |
| *Plains tribes*: | Arrival of winter (*porcupine redaction*) | Wives of sun and moon |  |

This gives rise to a two-fold question: is there something which replaces the initial sequence in the Ojibwa series? Is there something which replaces the terminal sequence in the Plains series? Actually, the two queries can only be answered by raising a third, on which they are dependent: what is it that makes the porcupine a symbol of winter periodicity?

Although it seeks shelter during the cold season, the porcupine does not hibernate, and its thermic cycle presents a more or less unvarying character. The real answer is to be found elsewhere:

$M_{445}$. *Arapaho. 'The painted porcupine'*

Early in the autumn, there was a big camp-circle on the edge of a forest. The people were having a prosperous year. The women had plenty to do, scraping, tanning, painting and quilling hides. But porcupine quills were scarce among the women and they did not have enough quills to finish their embroidery. There was one woman, an excellent embroiderer, who did not have enough to finish her 'vow' (work). Her daughter, who was as good as she was beautiful and tenderly devoted to her parents, said that she had heard of a painted porcupine to which she intended to propose marriage, although she had no desire to have a home and family. But such a son-in-law would provide a constant supply for her mother, who for the moment need only collect as many quills as possible and make out with those.

The young girl went to the painted porcupine's house: 'I have come to offer myself to you,' she said, 'because times are hard: my dear mother is out of quills. I will be yours and you will help me and my parents.' At first the porcupine hesitated, but he had been touched by his pretty visitor and finally accepted. They made a happy couple.

One day, while they were sunning themselves outside their tent, the porcupine laid his head on his wife's lap and told her she could cleanse him, that is, pull out his quills and give them to her mother: 'At this time of year,' he said, 'I have plenty of quills: but in late summer I have very few. So bear in mind that I cannot furnish many during the hot season but am ever providing during the fall and winter.' The wife started to pull out the quills with which she filled bladder bags kept for this purpose. The mother was very pleased: 'Tell your husband that I fully appreciate his favour and kindness,' she exclaimed as she gathered up the bags filled with white, red, yellow and green quills.

The young woman told her parents about the ways of her husband and went back to him. Ever since then women have dyed quills for their embroidery (Dorsey Kroeber, pp. 250–51).

In the 'porcupine redaction' myths ($M_{425-430}$), the young girls wax enthusiastic on the whiteness, size and abundance of the quills. The painted porcupine points out to us, as well as to the heroine of $M_{445}$, that he possesses all these qualities only in autumn and winter, thus confirming my theory about the season at which the mythic narrative begins. At the same time we realize why, and in what way, the porcupine is a periodic animal: the quills vary in quantity and quality according to the season.

Among the Plains tribes, these characteristics take on an extraordinary importance, for two reasons. Quill-work, which is geometrical in style and appears to be purely decorative in inspiration, has a symbolic significance. The woman doing the embroidery gives much thought to the form and content of the messages she is transmitting. Her meditation, which is always philosophical in nature, may lift her into a state of grace in which she is visited by a revelation. Before starting work, she fasts, prays, celebrates rites and respects prohibitions. The starting and completion of the work are marked by ceremonies: 'The robe was set up again so as to resemble a buffalo and after being perfumed with incense, was touched as if to make it rise. Then it was spread out and five feathers were laid upon it, one at each corner and one in the centre. The women sewed the feathers at those places. Then Yellow-Woman announced the man for whom she had made the robe and he was sent for. He was Bird-in-Tree. He came in and sat with his eyes looking towards the door. Yellow-Woman spat on the blanket four times, moved it towards him several times, then gave it to him. Then both he and the robe were perfumed with incense. Then he gave Yellow-Woman his best horse; she kissed him for it. Then he went out with his new robe' (Kroeber 3, p. 34). So, the art of quillwork constituted the most refined and the noblest expression of material culture, and this explains why, among the Blackfoot, it was practised only by a small group of initiates (Dempsey, p. 53).

Secondly, quillwork, which was carried out exclusively by women, called for considerable skill. There were four kinds of quills: the large, coarse tail quills; then, in order of excellence, those taken from the back and neck, and finally the most delicate of all, those which came from the underbelly. Many difficulties had to be overcome, since the quills had to be softened, then dyed, after which there remained the business of bending, knotting, overlapping, sewing, plaiting, weaving or intertwining (Orchard). These skills were not acquired without suffering. The Menomini maintained that 'the art of quillwork was both irksome and dangerous ... The sharp tips of the spines ... were likely to wound the fingers ... and when they were being trimmed off, might fly into the eyes and cause blindness' (Skinner 14, p. 275).

To protect themselves from this danger the Blackfoot women rubbed their faces with magic paint before starting work (Dempsey, p. 52). The Arapaho tell similar stories: 'When an inexperienced woman tries for the first time to do quill embroidery, failure ensues. The points of the quills fall out and the whole embroidery becomes loose. One woman relates how, when she was young, she once helped the women to embroider a robe. She had never done this before and the line of embroidery which she was working was spoilt: the quills would not stay fast and the other women refused to work with her. She prayed that she might be able to work successfully and said that she would make a whole robe in this style. An old woman said that this was good. After this, the quills remained fast and she was able to embroider' (Kroeber 3, p. 29). It is not at all surprising that the embroiderers kept a little stick on which they made notches representing the number of robes they had made, and when they reached old age they could still describe in detail the pattern of each one and its particular symbolism: they had more heart to go on living when they recalled times past and the great works they had accomplished (*ibid.*, pp. 29–30).

Quillwork was not, then, simply an exceptional mode of culture in societies such as the Menomini, among whom the expression 'embroidered with quills' is used with the meaning of 'enriched' (Skinner 14, p. 140). It was also the highest skill women could hope to acquire, and one which provided evidence of their perfect upbringing. The heroine of $M_{425-430}$ is fascinated by the sight of the porcupine and wants the quills for embroidery, intending to give them to her mother. Thanks to this revealing detail, we know at once that she is a well-brought-up young girl; she even does something beyond the call of duty, since she tries to capture the porcupine, a task which, apparently, would normally have been carried out by a man (Orchard, p. 6). Furthermore, in twelve out of the nineteen versions of the porcupine redaction, the girls are gathering wood. The other versions are less explicit, apart from two in which the heroine goes to draw water or is making moccasins. Among the Arapaho, the gathering of wood was carried out by young girls and old women: 'When I was quite small,' a seventy-seven-year-old informant related in 1932, 'I helped my mother pack wood for a long distance. When I became a young woman, I was not permitted to pack wood on my back as that was the duty of older women' (Michelson 2, p. 599). On reaching marriageable age a young girl of good family ceased to perform household tasks; she learnt what we call accomplishments, chiefly embroidery, a noble occupation which is contrasted with 'dirty work' (Dorsey-Kroeber, p. 64). At this period in their lives, the virtue of young girls was closely guarded. The mother used to accompany them to the river or when they went to the brush to attend to nature's demands. For additional security, they wore a chastity belt made from rope which was wound round the body from waist to knee, a custom also practised among the Assiniboine (Denig, p. 590), the Cree (Mandelbaum, p. 245) and the Cheyenne, in which tribes young wives continued to wear this protection for one or two weeks after marriage; they spent their honeymoons in conversation (Grinnell 2, Vol. 1, p. 131; 5, pp. 14–15). Arapaho women also remained chaste even after marriage. Coitus between husband and wife was strictly forbidden during the daytime, and even at night a wife would cover her face with her left or right arm during coitus. Women who did not respect these rules were considered fast (Michelson 3, p. 139).

These closely guarded young girls were particularly attentive to their personal appearance. They would have baskets containing several beauty products, and spent hours painting their hair and faces with puffs made of porcupines' tails minus the quills. They were covered in jewels and put perfume not only on themselves but on their horses too. Having thus beautified themselves, they would observe a modest demeanour, keep their eyes lowered in all circumstances, and refrain from laughing and talking loudly (Michelson 2, *passim*).

As is explicitly stated in an Arapaho myth ($M_{446}$; Dorsey–Kroeber, pp. 64–5), these young, sumptuously adorned princesses who were exempt from all except the most refined tasks, appeared so remote that they could only be reached by an excessively long penis. They were, then, in a two-fold sense lunar creatures (cf. $M_{256}$, p. 83), corresponding to the Iroquois concept of the spots on the moon: a woman sitting endlessly doing quill-work; should she finish her task, the world would come to an end (Curtin 2, p. 508).

In the porcupine redaction, Moon chooses one as his wife. But she is too young to embroider, since she intends to give the quills to her mother and is herself still expected to gather wood. The heroine of $M_{425-430}$ must in consequence be regarded as an adolescent on the threshold of puberty. $M_{428}$ even states specifically that her marriage to the moon preceded the appearance of the first monthly periods, not only in her own case but also in that of humanity as a whole.

This detail is not without significance, since it allows a comparison between the moon's young wife and the Bororo bird-nester ($M_1$), who is presented in the myths as a boy who has not yet reached puberty, but is close to the age of initiation (*RC*, pp. 43–5, 56). In both cases, the central character is disjoined vertically at the top of a tree or a rocky peak, the final term or provisional stage of a descent or an ascent. The Algonquin versions emphasize the resemblance, since the heroines fall into a nest from which they are helped down by a fierce quadruped – the wolverine (cf. L.-S. 9, pp. 67–72) – to whom in exchange they make a sexual promise; on the other hand, the bird-nester in the Ge myths ($M_{7-12}$), who is also stranded in a nest, obtains the same assistance from the jaguar in exchange for an offering of food.

Although the nest theme does not appear in the Arapaho myths nor, generally speaking, in the myths of the Plains Indians, evidence of it is to be found in the liturgy of the sun-dance, in the form of the bundle of sticks representing the thunder-bird's nest which is placed in the fork of the central pole of the lodge, and into which is thrust a digging-stick symbolizing the heroine. The aim of the dance itself is often to obtain rain from the thunder-birds, and it will be remembered that $M_1$ is a myth about the origin of the rainy season. All the variants of this myth must, indeed, begin at the same period of the year, which can only be the season when macaws and parrots hatch their eggs and raise their young. But apart from the fact that sexual cycles have a weakened periodicity in equatorial and tropical areas, our knowledge of the habits of the psittacidae is very inadequate. Several Brazilian ornithologists, whom Mlle Aurore Monod and M. Pierre Verger kindly approached on my behalf, maintain that, in the central plateau area, the eggs are laid during a period varying between August, according to some experts, and December according to others. In the absence of reliable data, it can nevertheless be sensed that these myths form a vast set, definable through the interconnection between the spatial axis and the seasonal axis.

But, to return to the porcupine; it is a seasonal animal having a double affinity with the feminine sex. For young girls are also periodic creatures, and it is considered essential that they should be well brought up so as to be protected against disorders – physiological as well as moral – that are always possible. On the cultural level, their good up-bringing is judged by their skill in certain accomplishments, the raw material of which is provided by the porcupine's quills. Moreover, we have seen that the bringing up of young girls involves a discussion of physiology. Not only are they required to have good manners and to know how to embroider, they must also give birth within a prescribed period of time and must have regular monthly periods. The porcupine, the growth of whose quills gives a pattern to the activities of women as cultural agents, thanks to its periodic character also obviates the delays or disorders which may threaten the vital rhythms. The Ten'a Indians, Athapaskan of the extreme north, maintain that the porcupine 'has the easiest parturition: it lays its young without effort, just momentarily interrupting its walk or its gambols to deliver itself of them as if nothing had occurred ... A porcupine's foetus is given to a woman during sequestration: she then slips it within her skirt and makes it slide down to her feet, to obtain the porcupine's facility of delivery' (Jetté, pp. 700–702). The Ten'a live a long way from the Arapaho, but close to the Kaska who are familiar with the story about the wives of the sun and moon ($M_{431}$), and transform the porcupine episode by giving it a cultural overtone: in order to escape from the wolverine, the heroines obtain the help of a water-bird which takes them across a river in exchange for garters *embroidered with porcupine quills*. Symmetrically, in the Ojibwa, Micmac and Passamaquoddy myths, from which the porcupine episode is missing ($M_{444a-c}$, $M_{437-438}$), the heroines arrange for rotten, ant-infested tree-trunks to take their places as the wives of their ludicrous husband. Ants figure as master embroiderers in the mythology of the Blackfoot Indians ($M_{480}$; Wissler–Duvall, pp. 129–32; Josselin de Jong 2, pp. 97–101).

But is it true that, with the exception of the one or two disguised forms I have mentioned, the porcupine episode is absent from the versions found in the northern crescent, as Thompson suggests in his definition of type III?

*$M_{447}$. Ojibwa. 'The wives of the sun and moon'* (inverted variant)

There were once two sisters who lived alone with a dog who did their hunting for them. Winter came. The dog killed a fawn, and for a long time they had it to eat. When it was finished, the dog killed another fawn. It was a beast with a lot of meat and it was halfway through the winter before they ate it up. Then the three of them set out on a hunting expedition, but met with no success. They were attacked by wolves while crossing a frozen lake. The elder sister, who was very foolish, addressed a song of welcome to the wolves and this encouraged the dog to go out and meet them. The wolves slew the dog and fled. In their attempt to pursue them, the women lost their way. They had no dog, nor did they have anything to eat.

A porcupine came in sight. The foolish sister admired its lovely white quills and tried to take them. The animal invited her to sit down on the tree-stump in which he lived. The two sisters spent a long time discussing which one would expose her bottom first. Finally, the foolish sister agreed to do so, provided she could keep the nicest quills. She fitted her buttocks as far as she could into the hole, and the porcupine slapped her across the bottom with his tail, plunging his quills into her buttocks. The girl could no longer walk since her bottom was all swollen, and her sister had to draw her along in her toboggan. They came to a lake and saw a fish-hawk's nest in a tree. Still as foolish as ever the elder sister wanted to be in that nest. To the great despair of the younger sister, they both became wedged in it.

Several animals passed by, but they neither would nor could help them, although the girls promised to be their wives. The wolverine agreed: first of all he helped the elder, who made water on him while on his back, then the younger. After he had lain with the foolish maiden, the [poor thing] was nearly killed. The other sister freed her by striking the wolverine with an axe. This is why the wolverine still bears the mark on the small of his back.

The injured girl recovered slowly. When she was quite better the two sisters settled down to fish at the edge of a river. They were visited by Nänabushu, the Trickster; he pretended to be ill so as to stay with them. Having been informed by a mouse of their guest's guilty desires, the young sister fled. Shortly afterwards the elder fled too, and Nänabushu, who had feigned death in order to prevent his nurses leaving him, went after them. They escaped by ascending into the sky, where the foolish sister started a discussion as to which star would make the best husband. She preferred a star that could hardly be seen, but her sister chose the brightest. When they woke the following morning, the foolish sister was lying with a very old man, and the wise sister was lying with a handsome youth (Jones 2, part 2, pp. 455–67).

Several elements in this myth, and also in the 'straight' version of it (M444), are retained in the Ojibwa and Menomini cycles featuring the trickster (Jones 2, part I, pp. 133–9; Josselin de Jong 1, pp. 19–20; Hoffman, p. 165). These at times assume the form of episodic novels, their construction being similar to the kind of narrative that I mentioned in connection with certain South American examples (above, pp. 114–131). The Algonquin trickster travels through the air with vultures, who wickedly let him fall; he finds himself imprisoned in a hollow tree. In order to induce some women to release him by splitting open the trunk with an axe, he pretends to be a porcupine with magnificent quills. Then he steals their clothes and flees. Disguised as a woman and fitted out with a false vagina made from a moose's spleen, he persuades a shy bachelor to marry him, and pretends to give birth to a baby, which is in fact an animal acting as his accomplice. But the spleen starts to decay and the stench betrays him.

There can be no doubt that we are dealing here with part of the bed-rock of American mythology, although it would be needless to ponder on whether its reality is of a logical or of an historical nature. It has long been known that, within the trickster cycle, there is a close parallelism between the myths of the Chaco Indians and those of the Algonquin family. However, I want to draw attention to one very particular aspect of this parallelism. In the previous volume (*HA*, parts II, III), we arrived at the trickster cycle by way of the Chaco myths containing a heroine mad about a certain variety of honey which is gathered from hollow trees. In that connection, I showed that, like hunting and fishing poisons and like the mythic figure of the seducer, honey, a seductive but often toxic food, formed a point of intersection between nature and culture. The girl mad about honey – the South American prototype of the ill-bred young girl – makes the mistake of yielding to the natural lure of honey, instead of transferring it to culture. But does the porcupine in the Algonquin myths not fulfil exactly the same function as honey? It too is to be found in hollow trees, as a natural entity offering a ready-made material to culture: its quills. The formal analogy with honey is at once obvious, honey being either a delicacy or a poison, and so too with hunting and fishing poisons, which are highly successful but inedible means of procuring foodstuffs. Porcupine quills have the same ambiguous characters: they are precious objects which are coveted, yet dangerous because of their sharp points which prick the embroiderer's flesh. The Arapaho, coinciding on this point with the French King Louis XII, whose motto was a porcupine accompanied by the inscription: *Spicula sunt humili pax haec, sed bella superbo,* compared the quills to armed warriors imprisoned in bladder bags, the only membrane they cannot pierce (Dorsey–Kroeber, p. 378). The porcupine, who is a metaphorical seducer in the Algonquin myths, becomes an actual seducer in those of the Plains Indians, and on each occasion makes it possible to distinguish between a well-bred and an ill-bred young girl.

This kinship between myths of the northern and southern hemispheres when they are comprehended at the deepest possible level suggests that $M_{447}$ could be the prototype which gave rise to the other Algonquin versions, as well as to those of the Plains Indians. To bring back the quarrel between the two brothers sun and moon about terrestrial wives into an initial position, we have merely to invert, along two axes, the Ojibwa myth which presents the quarrel between the terrestrial sisters about celestial husbands in a final position. In both myths, the porcupine episode occurs at the beginning, but with all the terms inverted: the tree is *lying flat* and not *erect*; the porcupine is *inside* and not *outside*; a *foolish* instead of *sensible* girl, *crouches down* over the porcupine (from high to low) instead of *rising up* towards him (from low to high); the animal is *aggressive* and not *seductive* and *lacerates* his victim from behind instead of *deflowering* her from the front ... The opposition between the two sisters, one of whom is sensible, the other foolish, corresponds to the contrast between the human wife and the frog, and all the more so since the foolish girl, like the frog, suffers from incontinence: she urinates inopportunely. The two human heroines in the Plains myths (one of whom goes up into the sky, while the other remains on earth) come from the same village: one refuses to move, while the other moves in a vertical direction. The two heroines of the Ojibwa myths have no village, or no longer have a village; they are alone in the world or exiled ($M_{444}$), and they move first of all horizontally, one rashly, the other hesitantly. In this respect, $M_{447}$ seems to act as a transition between $M_{444}$ and $M_{443}$, in which the sisters are literally *'coureuses'* (runners),[5] just as the daughters of the demiurge are *coureuses* in both the literal and figurative sense in a South American myth ($M_{415}$), with which comparison is by no means arbitrary, as has just been shown. Lastly, it will be noticed that whereas, in the Plains versions and the 'straight' Algonquin versions, the story opens with the ascent into the sky and marriage with the two luminaries, these two events form the conclusion in the inverted version (see above. pp. 254–5).

To set against the Plains series, which I shall not try to complete as yet, we have, then, not one (p. 248) but two series belonging to the eastern Algonquin:

| | | | | |
|---|---|---|---|---|
| *Eastern Algonquin* | (1) | | wives of sun and moon (*at the beginning*) | grebe redaction |
| | (2) | porcupine redaction$^{(-1)}$ | wives of sun and moon (*at the end*) | |
| *Plains* (3) | | porcupine redaction, | wives of sun and moon (*in the middle*) | ..................... |

To complete the table of commutations, it would be interesting to compare the kinds of trees selected by the myths for the ascent or descent of the heroine or heroines. Unfortunately the species is not always stated. Among the Arapaho and other neighbouring tribes, both

[5] TRANSLATORS' NOTE: The French word *coureur*, *coureuse* means both runner and gadabout, libertine.

in myth and ritual, the tree would seem to be the cottonwood (*Populus monilifera, sargentii*), a species characteristic of the arid plains at the foot of the Rockies and which owes its name to the downy blossom-fronds it bears in spring: 'As it never grows out in the open but always close along the borders of the few streams, it is an unfailing indication of water either at or near the surface, in a region well-nigh waterless. Between the bark and the wood there is a sweet, milky juice of which the Indians are very fond: according to an informant, it is their *ice-cream*. The tree is held to be almost sacred' (Mooney 4, pp. 967-8). The Arapaho also consider this American poplar to be the prototype of deciduous trees (Kroeber 3, p. 347), and consequently congruous, in the vegetable register, with the porcupine, which is an embodiment of the moon. There is an Arapaho ritual object which has on one side a representation of a crescent moon supporting a cottonwood, and on the other a cedar (*ibid.*, pl. lxxviii and p. 353).

The cottonwood with its soft wood and periodic vegetation stands in opposition to the cedar (*Juniperus* sp.), which is also held to be sacred 'for its evergreen foliage, its fragrant smell, and its red heart wood and the durable character of its timber' (Mooney 4, p. 979). The *cottonwood/cedar* pair can probably be placed in a triangular system, in which the *willow* (*Salix* sp.) occupies the third point (Gilmore 1, pp. 57-8). It is the cottonwood which allows the heroine of the Plains Algonquin to make her ascent, and an evergreen conifer (*Tsuga canadensis*), congruous with the cedar, which offers the heroines in the eastern Algonquin myths a means of descent.

The Kiowa present a problem. These Indians, who live on the edge of the area in which the myth featuring the wives of the sun and moon is found and who do not belong to any of the great linguistic families in which it is current, associate this myth, as do their Plains neighbours, with the sun-dance. They perform the latter every year 'when the down appears on the cottonwoods', that is, about the middle of June (Mooney 2, p. 242). They therefore attribute a periodic and natural function to this species, and also assign a ritual function to it, since they use cottonwood for the construction of the bower (Mooney 2, p. 243; Spier 3) and also for the central pole (Parsons 2, pp. 98-9; Nye, p. 59). However, a native illustration, corroborated by Mooney (4, p. 979), undeniably depicts the mythic tree as a conifer (see the flap of the dust-cover of the French edition), although one version refers to it as a cottonwood but also changes the porcupine into a 'yellow bird' (Parsons 2, pp. 4-5). Without attempting to solve the difficulty, I merely note that the Kiowa sun-dance presents certain distinctive features: it excludes mortification and bloodshed. In the Kiowa version of the myth ($M_{448}$; Mooney 2, pp. 238–9), the porcupine takes the form of the son of the sun, and not of the moon which, incidentally, does not appear in the story.

So, this particular example, in which the inversions correspond to each other from one level to another, does not invalidate the general system of oppositions I have worked out. The 'inverted porcupine' redaction found among the Ojibwa and the Menomini acts as a bridge between the porcupine redaction of the Plains and the grebe redaction of the eastern and northern Algonquin. This becomes even more obvious when we observe that the inverted redaction displaces the operation of the seasonal cycle: the heroines set off on their wanderings at the beginning of winter and they encounter the porcupine in the second half of the season. When the elder sister recovers from her injuries, they take up their abode along the banks of a river in order to fish, i.e. after the spring thaw. It is at this point that the trickster appears and tries to usurp the affection of the two sisters, as happens in other eastern versions, where the trickster is the grebe, master of fish and spring. In both cases, the order of the episodes is merely reversed.

However, although the porcupine redaction of the Plains Indians has a correlational and oppositional relationship with the grebe redaction found among the eastern Algonquin, the two redactions differ on one point. In the Plains redaction, the porcupine performs two functions: a natural function as master of winter, and a cultural function as a supplier of quills, the raw material for embroidery. In the grebe redaction, the same two functions occur, but are shared out between different animals: the grebe, a non-operative character as regards culture, but supreme in terms of nature, since he presides over the return of spring; and the loon, or his *alter ego* called 'Arrayed-in-Wampum', 'Spit-Wampum' or 'Wampum-Head' (the loon's breast has a necklace of white feathers), who has no function with regard to nature in these myths, but is a pure embodiment of culture, symbolized by the shell pearls, known as *wampum*, comparable to the porcupine's quills,[6] and which he has the power to produce in limitless quantities. As a point of intersection between nature and culture, the porcupine expresses in a

---

[6] This practical affinity between quills and shells, added to the theoretical affinity between quills and honey, to which attention has already been drawn (p. 255), explains why, in a myth belonging to the same region, wild, inedible berries, which look like natural pearls, play the part assigned to honey in homologous South American myths (cf. $M_{374}$ and my remarks on p. 66, above).

synthetic form the same relationship as is expressed analytically by the disjoined characters of the grebe and the loon. Hence:

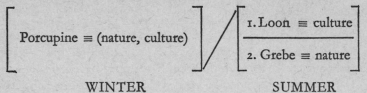

$$\left[ \text{Porcupine} \equiv (\text{nature, culture}) \right] \Bigg/ \left[ \frac{\text{1. Loon} \equiv \text{culture}}{\text{2. Grebe} \equiv \text{nature}} \right]$$

WINTER       SUMMER

This formal structure is the same as the one used to contrast the meadowlark in the Crow–Hidatsa versions with the chickadee, red squirrel, and striped squirrel triad in the Micmac–Passamaquoddy versions. I said (above, pp. 237–9) that one single animal, the meadowlark, being placed at the point of intersection of the sky and the earth, expressed synthetically the same relationship as was expressed analytically by three different animals positioned at varying distances from the sky and the earth. It follows that all the local forms, between which Thompson tries to establish relationships of historical derivation or geographical inclusion, can be integrated into a total and coherent system:

$$\left[ \text{meadowlark} \equiv (sky, earth) \right] : \left[ \begin{array}{l} \text{1. Chickadee} \equiv sky \\ \text{2. Red squirrel} \equiv halfway\ between \\ \text{3. Striped squirrel} \equiv earth \end{array} \right]$$

$$:: \left[ \text{Porcupine} \equiv (nature, culture) \right] : \left[ \begin{array}{l} \text{1. Loon} \equiv culture \\ \text{2. Grebe} \equiv nature \end{array} \right]$$

or more simply:

$$Plains \left[ (\text{Meadowlark} + \text{Porcupine}) \right] \underset{Algonquin}{\overset{Eastern}{\equiv}} \left[ \left( \frac{\text{Chickadee}}{\frac{\text{Squirrel 1}}{\text{Squirrel 2}}} \right) + \left( \frac{\text{Loon}}{\text{Grebe}} \right) \right]$$

The whole of this system can be fitted into another, even more general one, which develops an opposition between the two main groups of myths featuring the wives of the sun and moon, according to whether they begin with the quarrel between the men or the discussion between the women.

| 2 women moving | 1 elder 1 younger | elder foolish | mistake about husband's *age* | (*nature*) | descent allowed |
| 2 men moving | 1 elder 1 younger | elder foolish | mistake about woman's *upbringing* | (*culture*) | descent forbidden |

It only remains to reply to the second of the two questions posed on p. 248. I have confirmed that the porcupine redaction of the Plains Indians is reflected, as it were, in the Algonquin series in two ways: symmetrical – the inverted porcupine redaction, and asymmetrical – the grebe redaction. In one case, the characters remain the same, but horizontal replaces vertical, low high, behind before, good evil, etc. In the other, the characters too change, while summer replaces winter, thaw ice-bound water, etc. To complete the balance of the whole system, it is therefore necessary to find, in the Plains series, some image symmetrical to the grebe redaction, which it should be remembered, refers to the return of summer.

In Plains mythology, the story of the wives of the sun and moon is usually followed up by that of the grandmother and grandson, and the latter, more often than not, leads on to the story of the adventures of the sun's son (see above, p. 201). After his mother's death, the hero grows up in the care of an old woman who has received him into her home. He attacks monsters, destroying them one after the other, and then one day meets two men who are busy cutting up the corpse of a calving buffalo. The sight of the foetus on which the hair had not yet grown so terrified the hero that he took refuge at the top of a tree. The two strangers hung the foetus up on the trunk and their victim dared not come down. After some discussion, it was agreed that the foetus would be removed on condition that the hero handed his grandmother over to the two men who claimed to be in love with her. The versions differ as to the length of time – varying from four days to a whole year – that the prisoner remained at the top of the tree, but all imply that he was in a sorry state when he did come down.

The key to this strange episode, which occurs in the mythology of the Crow, the Hidatsa, the Mandan and the Arikara, can be found in the myths of these last mentioned Indians who assert that they were the originators of the myth ($M_{449}$; G. A. Dorsey 6, p. 60; 2, p. 56, n. 1): 'The reason why the boy was afraid of the foetus was that it was the time of year when female animals have not yet given birth to their young and the clusters of stars to which the boy's father belonged is never seen at this time to come up with the rest. The boy knew that his father could not be present to help him and he did not dare to do anything to help himself.'

A Crow version ($M_{429a}$; Lowie 3, pp. 52–7) maintains that the hero became the morning star, which hides during summer and rises before dawn in winter. Another version ($M_{429c}$; *ibid.*, pp. 57–69) develops the buffalo foetus theme: 'The hero stayed up in a tree all summer till the autumn when the foetus rotted and fell to the ground: then he also came down.' Disillusioned by this experience, the hero decided to change into a star and explained that no one would see him when the buffalo were calving but only after they had given birth to calves. Similarly, in a third version ($M_{429d}$; *ibid.*, pp. 69–74), 'he became the morning star and in the spring when the animals are about to have their little ones he does not come out: he is only seen afterwards.'

It would seem that this 'morning star' is not a planet; it forms part of a constellation in which the hero's mother, brother and dogs are also represented. They would appear during two months in the spring, then not any more for the next two months, then they would appear again. The interpreter thinks the stars referred to are the Pleiades (*ibid.*, p. 69). It will be remembered that in Ojibwa mythology the culmination of the Pleiades is supposed to be at the very spot in the celestial vault at which the wives of the sun and moon escaped (see above, p. 247). They are therefore disjoined from this constellation, whereas in the Crow versions they are conjoined with it. In this respect, too, symmetry is maintained between the various versions.

In computating their calendar, the Plains Indians, like some other tribes, were not satisfied merely with astronomical or meteorological reference points. They also took into account the growth of plants and animals. The Hidatsa, who are closely akin to the Crow and neighbours of the Arikara, fixed certain periods of the year according to the development of buffalo foetuses *in utero*. Furthermore it was forbidden to eat an unborn calf until after the hair was grown on its body. Before that it was covered in blood and unclean like a woman during her menstrual period ($M_{430b}$; Beckwith 1, p. 134). According to the Teton and the Cheyenne, also neighbours of the Arikara, the year began at the end of autumn, and the sequence of their months was: 'the moon the leaves fall off, the moon the buffalo cow's foetus is getting large, the moon the wolves run together, the moon the skin of the buffalo foetus commences to colour, the moon the hair gets thick on the buffalo foetus, the moon the buffalo cows drop their calves', etc. (Mooney 2, pp. 370–71).

The episode of the alarming foetus takes place, then, approximately in January. A Mandan version ($M_{460}$; Bowers 1, p. 203) confirms this by explaining that in order to punish her grandson's persecutors the old woman makes winter set in hard and cold. With the arrival of spring, according to certain Mandan and Crow versions ($M_{429c}$; Lowie 3, p. 65), or the following year, according to other versions, there begins another episode, treated at greater or lesser length in different contexts, but which, in the Mandan, Hidatsa, Arikara, Pawnee and Arapaho myths, as well as in one Crow version ($M_{429a}$), concludes the hero's terrestrial adventures. He pays a visit to hostile snakes, which he lulls into unconsciousness by telling them stories largely concerned with sleep. He kills them all except one, which, shortly afterwards or some time later, succeeds in crawling through his anus and in reaching his head, where it coils up. The hero wastes away and becomes a skeleton. His celestial father, moved to pity, creates heavy rain so that the skull is filled with water, which is brought to boiling point by the intense heat. This drives the snake out. The hero is brought back to life and joins his father in the sky, where he changes into a star.

Although in one Crow version ($M_{429d}$; Lowie 3, pp. 71–4), the snake episode would seem to come after the beginning of spring whereas the foetus episode occurs last, the story of the sun's son appears to take account of seasonal changes. Each episode refers to a period of the year: the beginning of winter, severe cold spells, spring, the rains and storms of early summer and the dry, torrid heat of late summer. Since the chief characters are luminaries associated with constellations, the myth follows, in celestial coding, the same course as the grebe redaction, in which the coding is based on the habits of terrestrial and aquatic animals. So we can now complete the diagram on p. 257 by putting the sun's son sequence after the Plains series, where it occupies a position corresponding to that of the grebe redaction in the eastern Algonquin series.

It has been confirmed that all types of the myth about the wives of the sun and moon, form pairs of opposite terms which can be organized into a system. It would be useless to try to interpret them separately: their meaning is differential, and can only be revealed in the presence of its opposite. In an area where the exponents of the historical method try to discover contingent links and traces of a diachronic evolution, I have uncovered an intelligible synchronic system. Where they itemize terms, I focus on relations. Where they put together unrecognizable

264 THE ORIGIN OF TABLE MANNERS

fragments or haphazard assemblages, I have pointed out significant contrasts. In so doing, I have simply been putting into practice one of Ferdinand de Saussure's teachings (p. 57): 'As one probes more and more deeply into the subject-matter of linguistic study, one becomes increasingly convinced of a truth which – it would be useless to deny – offers remarkable food for thought: namely, that, in this field, the link which one establishes between things exists *before the things themselves*, and helps to determine them.'

Nevertheless, it is impossible to evade the historical problem, since it is no doubt true that we must know what things consist of before we can reasonably ask ourselves how they came to be what they are; and also that it would be impossible to understand Darwin's researches, without reference to those carried out by his predecessors, Linnaeus and Cuvier. But myths, no more than living beings, did not belong from the start to a finished system; the system has an origin, into which we can and should enquire. So far, I have made a comparative anatomical study of several mythic species all belonging to the same genus. The point to determine now is how, and in what order, each one acquired its originality.

It will be remembered that the meadowlark episode, which is peculiar to Crow and Hidatsa mythology, has a place in the porcupine redaction and, together with it, constitutes a system in which the relevant relationships are expressed in an involuted form. I established a diametrical opposition between this system and another, exactly symmetrical, system, since the episode of the chickadee and the squirrels, which is peculiar to the Micmac and Passamaquoddy Indians, is an inversion of that of the meadowlark and has a place in the Ojibwa grebe redaction, which is in turn an inversion of the porcupine redaction. In this second system, the relevant relationships are expressed in an extended form. When projected onto the map of North America, this logical structure coincides approximately with the geographical distribution of the tribes in which the four types occur (Figure 25). The porcupine redaction and the grebe redaction occupy two opposite triangles which meet at the apices. A dotted line cuts through them to form two subsidiary triangles within the compass of the other two and corresponding to the respective areas of the meadowlark, on the one hand, and the chickadee and squirrels on the other. The point of intersection of the three straight lines forming this single structure is situated somewhere to the west of Lake Superior, along the boundary between the Prairie Ojibwa and the Siouan and Algonquin tribes of the Plains.

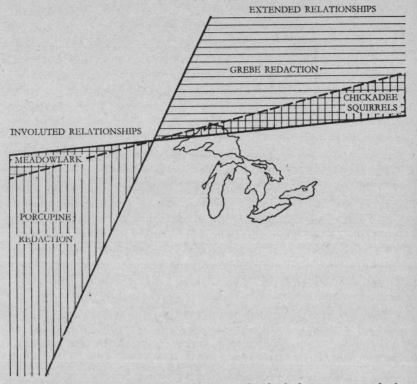

Figure 25. The interconnection between the logical structure and the geographical distribution of the myths about the wives of the sun and moon

The problem is, then, to discover whether there exists, on either side of the point of intersection, some significant difference between the modes of life, social structures, forms of political organization or religious practices which might explain the regular reversals brought to light by the comparison of the mythic systems.

The first contrast to spring to mind is the simple one between plains on the one hand, and woods and prairies on the other, since in theory it is accompanied by striking differences between the two ways of life. However, the contrast is not always clear-cut. The real Plains do not begin in the Great Lakes area, but much further to the west of the low-lands lying between them and the Lakes; this intermediary zone has no uniformity of character. The Plains themselves are not the same in the north and in the south. On either side of the Lakes, the Ojibwa occupy the forest to the north, and the more or less wooded prairies to the west and the south. The valleys of the Platte and Missouri rivers, which were inhabited by village tribes, offer no marked differences in climate and vegetation, except in a few localized areas, from the dry western steppes, where buffalo hunters lead a nomadic life for most of the year. Yet the mythic contrasts I am trying to explain are at once coherent, systematic and clear-cut: involuted relationships as opposed to extended relationships; winter as opposed to summer, at the beginning or the end; different positions of the marriage episode in the myth; the men's quarrel as opposed to the women's quarrel, etc.

Social organization might perhaps prove more rewarding. It was relatively simple and homogeneous among the Ojibwa and the northern and eastern Algonquin, where patrilinear descent and exogamous clans prevailed. But a kind of break in the system of family attitudes should be noted approximately in the longitude of 80°: taboos and stereotyped behaviour patterns were almost non-existent to the west of James Bay but abounded in the West (Driver 2). Let us however confine ourselves to the rule governing descent. Whereas it was uniformly patrilineal in the north-eastern triangle in Figure 25, it was reversed in the south-west triangle, where matrilineal systems prevailed among the Crow, the Hidatsa and the Mandan; furthermore, matrilocal residence would seem once to have been in force among the Arikara (Deetz), the Cheyenne, the Gros-Ventre and the Arapaho, although in historical times this was replaced almost everywhere by more flexible forms.

In all other respects, the area covered by the south-west triangle is far from being homogeneous. The village tribes had a closely-knit social organization, whereas that of the Plains hunters was extremely loose. The Crow, Hidatsa and Mandan, perhaps even the Arikara in the past, had a kinship system of the type known as 'Crow' (Bruner), based on the logical and genealogical primacy of the matrilineal lines. The kinship system of the Cheyenne and the Arapaho, who did not give preference to either line of descent, was based on the concept of generation. The Gros-Ventre had a hybrid system: unlike the Cheyenne and Arapaho, who were divided into non-exogamous groups, they classified relatives, as they did, into generation levels, while at the same time allocating them to patrilineal clans – at least this would seem to be what happened in the past (Grinnell 2). The Crow and Hidatsa had matrilineal phratries, the Mandan had moieties organized according to the same principle, whereas the Arapaho and Gros-Ventre had no moieties and there is no trace of the Arapaho ever having been divided into clans.

So it is not easy to see what possible correspondence there could be between the variations in the social structure and the observable differences found in the myths. In the myths of the patrilineal Ojibwa, it is the terrestrial women who move from place to place (see above, p. 257); but the Cree, who are also Algonquin speaking, and their immediate neighbours to the north and east, present no matrilineal characteristics, although the non-mobility of the women constitutes a striking feature of their mythology: the women always seem to be waiting for the arrival of some hypothetical husband (Bloomfield 1, pp. 130–42, 176 *et passim*). Conversely, in the Plains myths which contain the quarrel between the sun and moon, it is the men who set out to look for wives; yet these myths originate among neighbouring matrilineal tribes (Crow, Hidatsa, Mandan) or among tribes which had perhaps once been patrilineal (Gros-Ventre), or which did not hold to any particular line of descent (Cheyenne, Arapaho); or among which the rules of residence were of several types; or whose opposite ways of life contrasted village farmers with pure hunters; and who, lastly, belonged to at least three different linguistic families.

Actually, there is only one frontier-line which corresponds to the opposition between the two main mythic systems, and can no doubt help to explain it: the boundary defining the habitat of the porcupine, which covers a northern area from Alaska in the west to Labrador in the east, with two extensions to the south: one from the Great Lakes area to Pennsylvania, the other along the Rockies and the Cascade Range and extending as far as Mexico. This, at least, is the distribution shown in Orchard's map (Figure 26) and in those of Burt and Palmer, which are identical with each other (Figure 27; cf. Palmer, p. 272). It would, however, be wrong not to include also Hall and Kelson's map, which covers a greater variety of sub-species and attributes a much wider distribution area to *Erethizon dorsatum* (Figure 28). This point calls for some comment.[7]

In preparing their maps, the authors in question have used sporadic sightings and observations of isolated individuals from marginal communities. The method is certainly legitimate from the biological point of view, since even the presence of one single individual is enough to

[7] My remarks summarize the instructive observations obtained, through the agency of my colleague Pierre Maranda, then at Harvard University (now at the University of Laval, Quebec); from Miss Barbara Lawrence, of the Museum of Comparative Zoology, Cambridge, Mass. and, directly by correspondence, from Dr Richard G. Van Gelder, Chairman of the Department of Mammalogy at the American Museum of Natural History, New York. I would like to take this opportunity of expressing my gratitude to them.

Figure 26.
The distribution of *Erethizon dorsatum*.
(From Orchard, pl. II.)

Figure 27.
The distribution of *Erethizon dorsatum*.
(From Burt, p. 143.)

Figure 28.
The distribution of *Erethizon dorsatum*.
(From Hall and Kelson, Vol. 2, p. 782.)

Figure 29.
The distribution area of quill embroidery
(From Driver and Massey, map III.)

prove that the species is able to live in a given area. The anthropologist, on the other hand, is more concerned about the problem of relative density, and the point beyond which, for a native culture, the rarity of a species is virtually tantamount to its absence. Being a forest animal, the American porcupine certainly does not live on the Plains; but even there it can adapt itself to the wooded banks of certain rivers, a fact which explains why certain individuals have been found a long way from their usual habitat, an area corresponding, in Hall and Kelson's terminology, to the Canadian biological zone; it is significant, then, that even for them, the southern limits of this zone coincide with those attributed by the other authors to the genus *Erethizon*. Lastly, the southern extension, the confines of which were noted by Hall and Kelson and carefully indicated on their map, would seem to be a recent development which in no way contradicts anthropological observations regarding the Plains Indians' unfamiliarity with the porcupine.

Yet, even in this connection, the statement needs to be qualified. The Hidatsa, who used to occupy the most northerly part of the area with which we are concerned, were probably familiar with the porcupine. According to one piece of evidence, dating it is true from after the population shifts caused by epidemics and the infiltration of the whites, they used to hunt the animal along the Upper Missouri. One tributary flowing from Montana was called in Hidatsa a pá di a zis, 'the porcupine river' (W. Matthews, pp. 71–2, 144). In *La Pensée sauvage* (pp. 71–2), I pointed out the effect that the geographical position of the Hidatsa, along the edge of the Canadian biological area, may have had on their mythology, and it is a striking fact that an observation which was made in connection with the transformation of the wolverine from a terrestrial species into a chthonian animal, should again appear appropriate with regard to the transformation of the porcupine from a tree-dwelling species into a celestial animal. Even if we admit that the Hidatsa constitute a border-line case, the preceding discussion makes it clear that the porcupine is rare, if not absent, over almost the whole of the area where it plays such a major part in the myths. The paradox is even more marked when it is considered from the technological angle, since these same Plains communities from whose territory the porcupine was absent, were also the people who carried the art of quillwork to its highest point of perfection (Figure 29). First Orchard (p. 3) and then Driver and Massey stress this fact (p. 324): 'There was a high correlation between the presence of the porcupine in the environment and the use of its quills for decoration; the main exception to the rule is the

Plains area, where the porcupine was absent. Some tribes obtained the quills in trade, others made special trips to the mountains to obtain porcupines.'

So it is not inconceivable that the porcupine story may have come into being as an ideological reaction to the infrastructure. For communities where quillwork, in addition to the exceptional artistry it involved, the care it demanded and the richness and intricacy of its designs, was also a vehicle of philosophical expression, the porcupine might well assume the character of an animal made sublime by the very fact of its exotic nature, a metaphysical creature really belonging to 'another world'. On the other hand, for the Ojibwa and eastern Algonquin the porcupine was a very real animal, which they were fond of eating once the quills had been removed; they could, therefore, treat it in their myths as a natural being whose ambiguity was expressive of its two-fold character: as master of cold in a barely symbolical sense, and as a provider of riches in the form of succulent flesh defended by a prickly yet extremely valuable armour. If, as seems to be the case, the Plains Algonquin and their Siouan neighbours came from the northeast, where the porcupine was to be found, they may well, on losing the real animal, have reversed a mythological system which was originally very close to the one retained by the Ojibwa. This would confirm, from a different angle, the suggestion I made about the archaic nature of the Ojibwa myth, $M_{447}$, because of its underlying analogy with the South American cycle in which the heroine is a girl mad about honey. It will be recalled that, earlier in this volume, there was mention of an Ojibwa myth ($M_{374}$), corresponding in every detail to a South American group ($M_{241-244}$), which I had already related to the girl-mad-about-honey group, and the heroine of which is in both instances a frog (*HA*, pp. 180–214). Among the Warao of Venezuela, this frog is literally mad about honey; among the Ojibwa, the frog is mad about wild berries so beautiful that they are compared to beads (see above, pp. 65 and 259, n. 6). These same Ojibwa replace the porcupine by the master of the beads which are known as *wampum*, and there is good reason to believe that the ornamental use of these beads derives from an older embroidery technique in quillwork (Wissler 3, p. 13). A curious reversal must be noted at this point: in the South American myths, the frog happens to be mad about a kind of honey which I showed to be congruous with the North American porcupine. In the mythology of the Ojibwa and eastern Algonquin, the frog or toad congruous with the porcupine is mad about wild berries, which are congruous with beads, which in turn are congruous with quills. A young Indian girl is mad about these quills both in the Plains myths and in those belonging to the region of the Lakes. But in the first, she is the reverse of a frog and the frog is afflicted with the same incontinence that is attributed in the Lakes mythology to the human woman who is too fond of quills.

The anomaly can be explained, once it is realized that the heroine who is mad about honey is giving in to nature: she covets honey in order to eat it straight away, thus diverting it from its cultural function as a mediator of matrimonial exchanges. The heroine of the Ojibwa myth, on the contrary, is mad about the porcupine, and gives in so completely to culture that she turns her posterior into a pincushion: she wants the quills for embroidery and shows no respect for the animal's nature, since she wrests it from its winter sleep. A similar type of transformation can be observed among tribes of the extreme north-west, who are familiar with the porcupine but do very little quillwork or do not rate it so highly. For instance, in the myths of the Thompson, Lilloet and Shuswap Indians (M₄₄₂b; Teit 4, p. 83; 1, pp. 658-9), the porcupine, which helped with the organization of the animal kingdom, is rewarded with a generous gift of *dentalia*. In this region of America, those shells are used to make the finest ornaments and are considered as the Indians' most precious possession; according to the Thompson Indians, the porcupine's quills were once *dentalia*.

One final question remains to be answered. In linking the origin of the porcupine redaction with the absence of this animal in a new habitat, so that the origin becomes, as it were, a function of the absence, am I not reverting to a chronology similar to Thompson's? I rejected Thompson's chronology (p. 233) because it covered too short a span and thus failed to recognize that mythic forms common to both hemispheres must have their origin in a very remote past. Now I am referring to population shifts which took place a few centuries ago and came to an end only in historical times, since the first European travellers were able to witness them. The objection can be countered in the first place by pointing out that the settlement of the Plains goes back several thousands of years, and that the buffalo-hunters who, ten thousand years ago, roamed over territories subsequently occupied by the Arapaho, no doubt had a mythology certain features of which may have been passed on to generation after generation. Without claiming to establish definite links after such a lapse of time, we may suppose that certain village tribes such as the Mandan, who had been more or less settled for hundreds of years and who in the past had connections with the Algonquin, may have evolved myths which, for the reasons I have given, took a contrary line to those of their northern neighbours.[8]

But the main point is that my interpretation of the porcupine redaction respects the common structures on which attention has been concentrated, and is worked out at their level. To understand the origin of the porcupine redaction, I do not fall back on historical contingencies or on the improvisatory talent of some story-teller. The star-husband myth or, as I have preferred to call it, the myth about the wives of the sun and moon, is not to be reduced to a mere list of recorded types; it anticipates them all in the form of a network of relations which is operative, and through whose functioning the types are created. The fact that some appear simultaneously and others at different periods, presents problems the interest of which I do not underestimate. It must, however, be conceded that certain types, the concrete emergence of which seems to occur very late, cannot have sprung from nothing and did not emerge under the influence of purely historical factors or in response to external promptings. It would seem rather that they allow certain possibilities inherent in the system to be brought into actual existence and, in this sense, they are as old as the system is. I do not mean that the porcupine redaction already existed somewhere, and in this form, before the Arapaho and their neighbours adopted it. Such a hypothesis is by no means impossible, but even if the ancestors of present-day story-tellers imagined they were inventing it, or had obtained it through some mystic revelation, the new version had to respect the already existing constraints and guide-lines which limited the freedom of the narrative. For if, as I believe, the porcupine redaction is a reaction to an experience which contradicts another experience and corresponds to the need to modify a world-picture, so that it harmonizes with new living conditions and new processes of thought, it consequently follows that all the elements of the earlier system of representations must be transformed in a manner homologous with the change affecting the most directly challenged element.

In other words, if the presence of an animal as important as the porcupine as regards technology, economic activities, art and philosophy, is transformed into its absence, then in all those contexts in which it played a part – and in order that it should continue to play the

---

[8] The present volume was ready for the printer when Raymond Wood's important work on the pre-history of the Middle Missouri came to my notice. Wood gives the dating 1100–1400 A.D. for the oldest remains attributable to the Mandan, but he also establishes the existence of semi-sedentary farmers in the Missouri valley as early as the 8th century A.D.

part – the animal must be projected into a different world and, because of this, low must be changed to high, horizontal to vertical, internal to external, etc. Only in these conditions can a formerly coherent world-picture remain coherent. And if the porcupine theory operated according to extended relations, it will, in its new version, call for involuted relations. Whatever the historical contingencies may be, it remains true that all the forms are mutually implicit, and that their interrelations admit of certain contents and reject others, the process being still further restricted, incidentally, by the fact that the contents do not exist as free radicals: in other myths belonging to the same community or to neighbouring communities, and sometimes in the ritual, they were already inseparable from forms which predetermine their adaptability to these new uses. As regards the case under discussion, the point will be established in Part Six (pp. 376, 431).

# PART FIVE  A WOLFISH APPETITE

*It is above all important ... that children should not be turned into meat-eaters; for their characters', if not for their health's, sake; for however the experience is explained, it is certain that great meat-eaters are in general more cruel and ferocious than other men; this observation holds good for all places and all times.*

J.-J. Rousseau, *Emile*, Book II

*The Embarrassment of Choosing*

To the east of the Rockies, the porcupine redaction covers a continuous stretch of territory peopled by tribes who are dissimilar in language, way of life and social organization. We have just seen that the absence or rarity of the porcupine in this region of North America, constitutes the only relevant and available datum for understanding the mythology. The area under consideration is homogeneous only in the dual respect of the supernatural function attributed to the animal and its absence in real life.

However, in describing the internal organization of the myth about the wives of the sun and moon and in setting the different versions in some kind of perspective, I have not taken all the tribes into account, or rather I have not devoted the same attention to each. The Arapaho have been the main suppliers of examples in which the quarrel between the sun and moon occupies an initial position, with the porcupine episode immediately following it. But just as the grebe redaction, divorced from the story about the wives of the sun and moon, extends over a wide area to the north and west of the Ojibwa, so the story of the quarrel between the two luminaries extends beyond the area of the porcupine redaction, which it surrounds with weak forms, some linked to this story, others not. It is important to connect up these weak forms with the more typical examples that have been discussed.

The Arapaho and the Cheyenne share the same linguistic origin. It is also an accepted fact that they moved together from their earlier habitat and that they have lived side by side for a long time. However, the porcupine redaction has not been recorded among the Cheyenne, who tell the story of the quarrel between the sun and the moon, but without bringing in any conjugal problems. Each luminary lays claim to superiority, the sun as the shining and brilliant master of day, the moon as master of night. The sun and moon are brothers, but only Moon takes care of all things on the earth, and protects men and animals from danger: 'I can take charge of day as well as night and guide all things in the world. It does not trouble me if you rest,' he declares to the Sun, his brother. And Moon boasts of having wonderful beings on his side – he means the stars ($M_{450}$: Kroeber 4, p. 164).

This little tale takes us back directly to the South American theories about the logical primacy of the moon over the sun, first because the sun is alone in the sky, whereas the moon enjoys the company of countless stars, and secondly because, in a sense, a stronger opposition prevails between light and night than between light and day: the moon also has a diurnal aspect, since it emits light; the sun, on the other hand, has no nocturnal feature (see pp. 142–3; L.-S. 18). The Wichita, who are Southern Caddoan, apply the same oppositional structure to the stars; in their version of the myth about the wives of the sun and moon ($M_{415a}$; G. A. Dorsey 3, pp. 298–9), one heroine makes the wrong choice when she desires a brilliant star for her husband, for all she got was an old man who explained to her that the dim stars are fine-looking young men. Helped by a vulture, the woman succeeds in escaping. Since then people have refrained from invoking the stars and it has even been considered unlucky to count them. In a version found among the Miami, an Algonquin tribe living to the south of the Great Lakes, the large red star becomes a wrinkled old man, and the small white star a handsome young man ($M_{451b}$; Trowbridge, p. 51).

There are other obvious comparisons with South American myths. The Amazonian Tupi ($M_{326a}$), the Mundurucu ($M_{421a}$) and the Ona ($M_{419}$) believe night to be indispensable for conjugal copulation, whereas in a short Cree version ($M_{435}$; Skinner 1, p. 113) the wives of the sun and moon pine because their husbands disappear during the day. Generally speaking, and whatever the oppositional pole indicated, the quarrel between the sun and moon constitutes a frequent theme in north-western mythology, which – as will be seen in the next volume – contains the same myths as those with which this enquiry began. The Chinook ($M_{452}$; Jacobs 2, part 2, no. 61) emphasize that the bright summer sun encourages people to come out into the open and put on their best necklaces, whereas the moon sheds light only on defecation and illicit love-affairs. Similar views of the matter can be noted among the Thompson (Teit 4, p. 336), the Coast Salish (Adamson, pp. 271–2, 283–4, 378), the north-western Sahaptin (Jacobs 1, p. 195), and the Nez-Percé (Phinney, p. 87; as regards the area of distribution of the theme cf. Boas 2, pp. 727–8).

So the area covered by the story of the quarrel between the sun and moon extends almost continuously from the Fraser River basin in the north-west to the Prairies and wooded hills of the south-east. According to the Omaha and the Ponca ($M_{453a}$; J. O. Dorsey 1, p. 328), the moon quarrelled with the sun on the grounds that the latter was causing human beings to scatter and go astray, when the former was trying to assemble them. The sun protested that he was deliberately making them move about in order that they should increase and multiply. The moon, on the other hand, plunged them into darkness and caused them to die of hunger. In this case, then, the assembling of humans within a restricted space conjures up darkness, famine and sterility, while their dispersal suggests daylight, plenty and fertility. This dialectic of the near and the far refers us back to Part Three, where I discussed it in connection with South American examples.

The Canadian Dakota, who derive from a Siouan-speaking tribe bordering on the Cheyenne, nevertheless reverse the respective values attributed by the Cheyenne to the sun and moon: they maintain ($M_{453b}$; Wallis 1, pp. 40–44) that the sun is the mother of women, and the moon the father of men. Yet the female sun claims to be all-powerful, since the moon only shines intermittently, whereas the sun does not merely shed light: it warms or cools humans, according to its humour. Besides, it cannot be looked at directly, whereas the moon's light is too weak to dazzle. The moon can find no answer to all these arguments and admits defeat. I shall return later (p. 397) to an inversion which seems typical not only of the Sioux but also of the Algonquin of the Great Lakes region, and particularly of the Menomini.

Lastly, the Cherokee, a North Carolina tribe related to the Iroquois, develop the theme of the quarrel between the sun and moon in a different direction:

$M_{454}$. *Cherokee. 'The quarrel between the sun and moon'*

The Sun lived on the other side of the earth but her daughter lived in the middle of the sky directly above the earth, and every day, during her daily course, she used to stop at her daughter's for dinner.

The Sun hated the people on the earth because they screwed up their faces when they looked at her. Moon, her brother, protested that when they looked at him they always smiled. The Sun was jealous and planned to kill all the people by sending down rays which created a great fire. The people feared that no one would be left and went for help to the Little Men, who said the only way was to kill the Sun. They changed two men into snakes and sent them to watch near the house. According to some versions, the Sun died and was replaced by her daughter; according to others, the snakes mistakenly killed the daughter instead of the mother.

Sun grieved over the death of her daughter. The people did not die any more, but the world was dark all the time because the Sun would not come out. On the advice of the Little Men, the people sent an expedition to the Ghost country to bring the Sun's daughter back. The seven men would have to strike her with rods, she would fall to the ground and her body would be put into a box; but they should be very careful not to open the box until they were home again.

The seven men accomplished their mission, and started off towards the east, when the girl came to life again and begged to be let out of the box. But the men made no answer and went on. Then she called out again that she was hungry, then thirsty and lastly that she was being smothered. The men were afraid that she was really going to die now, so they lifted the lid a little to give her some air. She flew out, having changed into a bird.

For this reason, we cannot bring our friends back from the Ghost country when they die, as we would have been able to do if the men had kept the box closed, as they had been told to do. The Sun grieved and wept at losing her daughter a second time until her tears made a flood upon the earth and the people were afraid the world would be drowned. So they sent their handsomest young men and women to amuse her, so that she would stop crying. For a long time, she kept her face hidden and paid no attention to the songs and dances. But a drummer suddenly changed the song. The Sun was taken by surprise, lifted up her face and was so pleased at the sight that she forgot her grief and smiled (Mooney 1, pp. 252–4).

This story is very reminiscent of Japanese mythology, and is not the first case of its kind (cf. HA, pp. 378–81). But I shall dwell less on that comparison than on another (which raises fewer problems) with an important set of myths belonging to the American North-West. This group is concerned with the resurrection of the dead, and will be discussed in detail in the next volume. The recurrence of the same myths in regions of North America as far apart as the River Columbia plateau and the wooded slopes of the South-East proves, without the help of more exotic parallels, that we are dealing with certain fundamental patterns of American thought, which it is not at all surprising to find in both hemispheres. Like the heroes of the South American myths about the origin of Man's shortened life-span ($M_{70-86}$; *RC*, p. 147), those in $M_{454}$ ought not to have listened to the call of a ghost; whereas the messengers in $M_{326a}$ carry night in a receptacle, they carry the promise of day. In the Tupi myth, the opening of the box leads to the alternation of day and night, i.e. to the establishment of daily periodicity; in this instance, it destroys the possibility of resurrecting the dead and so institutes the periodicity of human life. The South American myths symbolize daily periodicity by means of a canoe-journey, which forces the sun and moon to remain together but at the right distance from each other. The hypothesis that the North American theme of the quarrel between the sun and moon in which the latter become *enemies* is symmetrical with the South American theme of the canoe-journey in which the sun and moon are represented as *partners*, is confirmed, then (although such confirmation is hardly necessary after the previous demonstrations), by the fact that, in the Cherokee myth, the quarrel between the sun and moon starts a series of disastrous events, the out-come of which is the institution, for human beings, of a limited span of life.

So, by widening the sphere of the quarrel between the sun and moon, we rediscover the major themes with which our enquiry started. Exactly the same result will be achieved if, instead of carrying the investigation into regions still further removed from the one where I first located this mythological motif, I undertake a study in depth. For this purpose, I propose to introduce the Gros-Ventre (Atsina) version, even though it is almost identical with those already encountered among the Arapaho. It should be remembered that the Gros-Ventre and the Arapaho were originally the same people and that they broke away from each other only a few centuries ago. However, the Gros-Ventre version at least has the advantage of reminding us of a mythic pattern with which Part Four opened, while at the same time presenting divergencies from that pattern which will provide a transition to other forms:

$M_{455}$. *Gros-Ventre. 'The wives of the sun and moon'*
The Sun and Moon disagreed about women. Moon said that women outside of the water and outside of the brush (human females) were the prettiest. 'No they are not,' replied the Sun. 'Whenever they look at me, they make faces; they are the worst-looking women in the world. The women in the water are the most beautiful: when they look at me they look just as if they were looking at their own people'

[cf. M₄₂₆]. Moon said, 'You think the Frog is a pretty woman? You surely have poor judgement of women. The frog has long legs; she is green with spots on her back and large, lumpy eyes. Do you find one like that pretty?'

Sun came down to earth and brought back a frog to be his wife. With each leap she urinated. Her mother-in-law asked what a ridiculous thing was that. Moon, who was shining in the sky, troubled a woman all night so that she could not sleep. Early in the morning, she decided to go and get wood with her sister-in-law. They saw a porcupine and the heroine wanted to kill it to use its quills for embroidery. She pursued the animal to the top of a tree, until they reached the sky. There the porcupine changed into a handsome young man; he took her to his mother's tent; the latter thought her a fine-looking woman.

So the old woman had two daughters-in-law. The woman did much for her but the frog little. Whenever the frog was sent anywhere, she hopped along. Forgetting she had a frog as a daughter-in-law, the mother was quite startled by her hopping. One day, the mother boiled the thickest part of a buffalo's paunch and shared it between the two women. She announced that she would choose as her favourite the one who made most noise in chewing. The human woman was easily the best, since she had good teeth. The frog tried to chew charcoal but the blackened saliva ran down from each side of her mouth. Moon was disgusted. He hated his sister-in-law because every time she moved she urinated. She should not move at all!

These insults directed at his wife exhausted Sun's patience. He threw the frog at his brother's face so that it would always remain stuck there. That is why there is black on the moon. Then the Sun took the human wife, and the son she had already had by the Moon. The human wife was unhappy and fled, taking her child with her. But the sinew rope she used to help her to escape was too short. The Sun saw his wife hanging below, swinging. He dropped a stone and killed her. She fell and the child remained near his mother even when she was rotten and when only her bones remained. He stole from an old woman's garden in order to eat. She caught him and adopted him. In spite of the woman's warnings, the hero paid a visit to female seducers who quickly changed into snakes. He killed all the reptiles apart from one which shot up into the boy's anus, thus causing his death. Moon sent down cold rain, which chased the serpent out. The son and the mother came back to life at the same time (Kroeber 6, pp. 90–94).

The myth follows the same course as the Arapaho versions, except (but cf. $M_{427b}$) that Sun takes possession of his brother's wife and throws his own wife onto his brother's face; between the sun and moon there is, then, an enforced exchange of wives. Consequently, the hero's real father is not the sun but the moon, a fact which leads later to a modification in the story: it is icy rain of lunar origin which drives out the killer snake, instead of thundery rain warmed by the sun's heat. The resuscitation of the mother at the same time as the son is reminiscent of a similar transformation in the Tupi and Carib cycle about the sun's twin sons, a cycle which is obviously parallel to this one ($M_{266}$; $HA$, pp. 221–2).

In the Gros-Ventre version we can detect, then, an incipient inversion affecting the respective rôles of the sun and moon. The Crow myths carry this inversion to its ultimate conclusion. It was probably the Crow invasion of the Plains which separated the Gros-Ventre from the Arapaho. In historic times, the Crow occupied a territory situated between the other two tribes. So far, I have alluded only briefly to their myths (pp. 230, 262). These must now be examined more closely.

$M_{429a}$. Crow. 'The wives of the sun and moon'

One day, Moon went to Sun to find out who was the best-looking girl on earth. Sun asked if he had already selected one. Moon replied that down in the world the best-looking girls were frogs. 'Not at all,' said Sun, 'the finest-looking are Hidatsa.' Each decided to marry the girl of his choice.

It so happened that three Hidatsa sisters were going out for wood. They saw a porcupine in a tree. The two elder girls wanted to get it for its quills, and asked their sister, who was also the prettiest, to climb up the tree and capture the animal. The Sun carried the young girl off to the sky and married her.

Moon brought back a frog and begged his mother to allow his wife to share the family tent. The old woman looked everywhere but saw nothing resembling a wife. The frog spoke and introduced herself; but she had a speech defect.

Sun organized a chewing contest. His mother boiled some buffalo guts and asked the two girls which piece they wanted. The Hidatsa girl started to eat in the dark. She was a good eater. The frog hid behind the bucket and tried to eat the bark of the fire-wood, in order to make a good sound. But she was a poor eater, and Moon threw her out three times. The fourth time, she jumped on Moon's back, saying, 'I'll live with you for ever!' The myth goes on to recount how the Sun's wife escaped and was killed, then continues with the story of the grandmother and grandson, and ends with the one about the luminary's son becoming the 'morning star' (Lowie 3, pp. 52-7; cf. above, p.262 *et seq.*).

An older version ($M_{429b}$; Simms, pp. 299-301) relates how Sun, the creator-demiurge, saw a beautiful human woman, whom he wanted for his wife and whom he succeeded in taking up into the sky with the help of a porcupine. No mention is made of the quarrel between the sun and moon, nor of the chewing contest. The same is true of two other versions, which do not specify the identity of the celestial husband. One explains that the adoptive grandmother is the moon; she hates the hero but brings his mother back to life ($M_{429c,d}$; Lowie 3, pp. 57-69).

Consequently, a two-fold transformation is visible in the Crow versions. In the first place, several details appear in a weakened form: the frog has a speech peculiarity and not a bladder disorder; she chews bark instead of charcoal; she clings to Moon's back and not to his face or chest. In other words: *low* ⇒ *high*; *internal* ⇒ *external*; *anterior* ⇒ *posterior*. Secondly, these changes are accompanied by an inversion of the matrimonial choices, since the sun marries the human woman and the moon the frog. This decline in the status of the moon, which plays the part of the foolish luminary, is still more marked when it changes sex and merges with the terrestrial, or perhaps even chthonian, grandmother, whose maleficent character is stressed in the Crow myths.

All this becomes explicable, when we remember the importance of the sun in Crow ritual. Although the Crow regarded religion as a private affair and had no priestly caste, the sun held an important place among a theoretically limitless number of supernatural beings, each of whom corresponded to particular mystic experiences. The revelations obtained from the sun were the most highly prized. Oaths were sworn in the sun's name and offerings were made to it. The sweat-bath was thought of as a prayer to the sun. For the Crow ... 'the sun then closely approaches our conception of a Supreme Being'. This did not mean, incidentally, that it always appeared as a benevolent being. It was conceived of as male and addressed by the term used to designate the elders of the father's clan. The moon figured far less frequently in Crow religious beliefs and practice. There was even some uncertainty about its sex; more often than not Moon was a woman (Lowie 7, pp. 318–20).

There seems to be no doubt that a devotional preference for the sun or the moon helped the Plains Indian tribes to express their identity in contradistinction to each other. Like other Siouan tribes, the Crow were sun-worshippers, whereas their Hidatsa cousins, who were also Siouan and spoke almost the same language, had chosen to worship the moon, like the village tribes whose way of life they had also adopted. A Hidatsa informant (who referred to himself as Gros-Ventre, because the same nickname was applied to the Hidatsa as to the Atsina-Gros-Ventre, kinsmen of the Arapaho) explained that 'the Sun is the helper of the Sioux against the Gros-Ventre but the Moon is for the Gros-Ventre; when there is an eclipse of the moon, the Gros-Ventre mourn but the Sioux go out and shoot arrows at it' (Beckwith 1, pp. 133–4). Similarly: 'The sun favours the Sioux, the moon the Mandan and the Hidatsa' (*ibid.*, pp. xvi, 188).

Although the Hidatsa are opposed to the Crow as regards the allocation of the wives, their attribution being the same as that of the western Algonquin, nevertheless they complete the mythic narrative on one point; they explain the choice made by the women for the purposes of the chewing contest:

$M_{430a}$. *Hidatsa. 'The wives of the sun and moon'* (1)

Moon thought the Hidatsa women looked pleasant. Sun said he was mistaken and that all of them had their faces screwed up. The women in the water (he meant toads) are the best looking. 'Alright,' said Moon, 'I will bring a wife for myself and you may bring yours. We will offer them cooked paunches and the woman that chews best, making a creaking sound with her teeth, we shall keep: the other one we'll turn away.'

The story continues with the porcupine episode and the discovery that the toad was incontinent. In the contest, the Hidatsa woman chose the thin part of the paunch, while the toad wanted the thick part. She surreptitiously chewed charcoal with her paunch, but did not succeed in making a noise. The charcoal began running down her breast and making her black all over. She jumped on Moon's back ... 'so that he could not reach her with his hands'. When you see the full moon, the spot in the centre is the toad (Lowie 5, p. 2. Version recorded in 1910–11).

$M_{430b}$. *Hidatsa. 'The wives of the sun and moon'* (2)

There was an earth-lodge up in the sky, and in this lodge lived an old woman who had two sons, Sun and Moon. Their duty was to light the earth with sunshine or moonlight. One day, Sun asked the Moon which nation he thought had the handsomest maidens. Moon said: 'The Gros-Ventre (= Hidatsa) are the handsomest. They live in earth lodges and do not burn from your rays, because they paint up and protect themselves from the heat. They bathe often and take care of themselves. Other peoples do not attend to these things, hence I consider the Gros-Ventre maidens to be the handsomest.' 'I do not agree,' replied the Sun. 'When the Gros-Ventre maidens look at me in the daytime they squint their eyes and turn away their faces, so that one side is in shadow. Now the frog maidens look straight at me without blinking their eyes or twisting their faces, and they are the handsomest maidens.' Sun and Moon agreed to bring back a woman of each species and to compare their beauty.

Moon went to a certain place where there lived a man, his wife and their three daughters: the two eldest were already married, and the youngest still unwed and as virtuous as she was beautiful. There follows the episode of the porcupine, coveted by the two elder girls. On their orders, the youngest climbed up after the animal and disappeared.

Moon's mother was proud of her son's choice. The frog, who remained forgotten on the threshold, croaked and grumbled. The old woman put Frog next to the pot. Moon organized a chewing contest. They would keep the woman whose teeth would cut into the intestine with a crackling noise, as if she were crushing ice, and send away the one who slobbered over her food and did not crack it neatly. Moon did not want to offend his brother. He conceived the idea that the contest would provide an excuse for sending the frog away, since he saw that the frog would not get on well in the house.

The mother cooked the tripe and the daughters-in-law chose each what part she would take. The Indian woman took the thin part, the frog the thick part. They cut up the meat with flint knives and started chewing. The Indian woman chewed and cracked loudly. Then the frog chewed and made a crunching sound. Moon pulled the pot aside and saw that Frog was chewing charcoal; she was slobbering and making a mess with her mouth. Moon threw her into the fire, but she leapt onto his forehead. In spite of his vain attempts to get rid of her, the frog finally landed on Moon's back, saying: 'You two do not want me here, but here I shall stay, where you cannot reach me, and I will never die.'

The Gros-Ventre say of the spots on the moon 'That is the frog on the moon.' It was not the green frog, but the big sand toad that the Sun took as his wife. This species is known as 'Grandmother', and the sun is called 'Grandfather'. These toads are held to be sacred and children are taught to honour them and talk and pray to them.

The myth goes on to tell the story of the grandmother and grandson, followed by the story of the sun's son (Beckwith 1, pp. 117–33; cf. Bowers 2, p. 333).

The fact that the human wife in the Crow version may be a Hidatsa Indian suggests that the Crow were aware of the importance of the myth in the religious thought of the Hidatsa, where it forms the basis of several ceremonies. Such was not the case among the Crow themselves because of their loosely organized religious life, which Lowie emphasizes and to which I have already drawn attention. On the other hand, it should be noted that, unlike the Blackfoot and the Arapaho and the western Algonquin generally, the Hidatsa connect the origin of the sun-dance not with the myth featuring the wives of the sun and moon, but with the myth about the accepted brother and the rejected brother (Lodge-boy and Thrown-away; cf. Beckwith 1, p. 137), which ought therefore to be included in my analyses.

I do not propose to bring them in for the moment, not because I find them difficult to accommodate, nor because I can agree with Lowie that the Hidatsa versions in which the two cycles interlock (such interlocking is surely also true of the Crow versions?) ... 'structurally, are monstrosities, due to the Hidatsa feature of explaining ritualistic origins by a loose connection with popular tales' (Lowie 5, p. 9; cf. 8, p. 415 et seq.). The truth is that the link between the two cycles is obvious, and can be proved by means of a very simple operation, which makes it possible to convert one into the other. However, the number of significant variants would be so great that a whole volume would be needed to summarize them and, by elucidating them with the help of other myths, to define their reciprocal relationships. After devoting so many years to the study of mythology, I shall probably never have the desire to write such a volume, although the plan and the title already exist in my files.

I shall confine myself, accordingly, to the wives of the sun and moon.

The Hidatsa versions give a precise description of the circumstances in which the chewing contest takes place. The mother-in-law serves up a dish of tripe to the women and they choose thin and thick pieces respectively. Why this distinction? One might be tempted to give an explanation based on purely practical reasons: the human wife, being more shrewd than her animal sister-in-law, takes the thin piece which is easier to chew, while the frog, being greedier perhaps, stuffs a thick piece into her mouth and cannot manage to swallow it. There are no arguments against such an interpretation, which has the merit of simplicity. However, anthropological analysis can provide a different and more subtle explanation, but one which involves so circuitous an approach that I can only put it forward as a stylistic exercise, without claiming to be able to establish its validity.

One of the finest masterpieces in all anthropological literature deals with the Hidatsa. G. L. Wilson had the inspired idea of allowing his informants to talk freely, and of respecting the harmonious and spontaneous fusion, in their stories, of anecdote and meditation, humble technological actions and intricate liturgical ritual; of hunting, cooking and fishing, on the one hand, and rites and myths on the other. The old story-tellers who told of the ritual eagle-trapping expeditions, which still took place in the second half of the 19th century, dwelt lyrically on the adventurous life led by the small group of trappers, who camped out and improvised their means of subsistence from day to day. The first deer they killed (*Dama hemionus*) provided meat, and its hide was kept to make a winter garment; the belly was cut off at the neck, turned inside out like a glove and immediately put to use as a water-bag. The informant illustrated the phases of the operation by two drawings

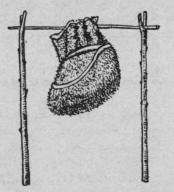

Figure 30.  The water-bag. (From G. L. Wilson, p. 110.)

(Figure 30) and added the following comment: 'The bucket was made of the paunch turned wrong side out. There were little cells, or hairs, as we called them, over the inside of the paunch, except where the white bands are marked in the sketch. These bands are hairless and here the walls of the paunch are thicker than anywhere else' (Wilson, p. 113).

Never having seen a buffalo's stomach, I cannot guarantee that the description applies exactly to this animal. But the Hidatsa versions of the myth do not specify what animal the paunch came from, and it does not seem that, in this respect at least, there are any major differences between the stomachs of *Bovidae* and *Cervidae*. The point to which I wish to draw attention is that, after the lapse of half a century, an informant still remembered a two-fold opposition which no doubt had some importance in his society: the *hairy* part of the belly is *thin*, but the *thick* part is *smooth*. So it may be that, in the myth too, the opposition between thick and thin conceals another opposition between smooth and hairy.

As it happens, this second opposition occupies an important place in the rites of tribes who, like the Hidatsa and their neighbours, wear robes made of buffalo hides. These fur robes are smooth on one side and hairy on the other. Furthermore, the surface which has been tanned by the women is often adorned with paintings and embroidery which emphasize its cultural character, whereas the wearing of the robe with the fur on the outside, *more animalium*, puts man on the side of nature.

That the Plains Indians conceive of the opposition in these terms is made clear by the circumstances in which, irrespective of climatic variations, they stipulate the wearing of the fur inside or outside. Among the Mandan and Hidatsa, the priest presiding over tortures and sacrifices had to wear his robe with the hair side out (Beckwith 1, p. 40), like the dancers in the great annual ceremony, okipa, who impersonated buffaloes (Bowers 1, p. 134; 2, pp. 206, 444–5). On the occasion of the transfer rites, the female officiants of the 'White Buffalo-Cow Society' wear their robes with the hair inside or outside, according to their function (Bowers 1, p. 325). It would be easy to quote other examples (for instance, the garment worn by the mysterious stranger in $M_{368}$ and $M_{503}$).

So it could well be that the frog's mistake in choosing the thick piece, lies in the fact that – since this piece is also smooth – she is opting for culture, whereas the wise choice *when you are the sun's guest*, ought to be in the direction of nature. As I shall try to show, this is the interpretation which can be inferred from the Hidatsa and Mandan myths. Before leaving the subject of the paunch, let me mention finally a South

American example, in which the same opposition reappears in a context similar to the one featuring the wives of the sun and moon, the only difference being in this case that the sun's wife ($M_{456}$; Preuss 1, pp. 304–14) is also celestial, and has her husband killed by a chthonian being who has become her lover. The sun's sons, then, lead a terrestrial existence until a woodpecker, whose life they have saved, reveals their true origin to them. The inversion is all the more remarkable, in comparison with $M_{429-430}$, in that the woodpecker, a bird belonging to the middle world half-way between the high and the low, is in this sense also a transformation of the meadowlark, which I have defined as an intersection of the sky and the earth.

The brothers kill their stepfather, who changes into a jaguar. The woman has to take revenge on her sons, and pursues them up into the sky. One of them becomes the visible sun and burns his mother with the heat of his rays. Being unable to protect herself in spite of having taken supplies of water with her, she dies and her charred body splits up into fragments as it falls; the legs become terrestrial plants; the *thick* parts of her intestines turn into creepers with strong roots, the *thin* parts into epiphytal plants with surface roots. As for the two brothers, they are permanently installed in the sky, and adorned with necklaces made, in the one case, of tapir teeth, and in the other of caudal vertebrae; they indicate to men the times for cannibalistic feasts and tapir hunts.

Through finding our way back to South America by this unexpected route, we have discovered proof that the quarrel between the sun and the moon exists also as a mythic motif in the southern hemisphere. So far, this essentially North American motif has appeared as a transformation of the canoe-journey of the sun and moon, in the sense that both motifs pose the problem of the most suitable distance to travel in the search for a wife. The Uitoto myth, however, mentions the quarrel itself, in a form which invites comparison with a Machiguenga myth that has already been summarized and discussed ($M_{299}$; *HA*, pp. 320–25), and in which the sun also burns up his mother by his heat. The mother, in this case, was an Indian who had become Moon's wife, and Moon sent his son into exile as a punishment. Consequently, as in the North American myths, the two luminaries, here transformed into father and son, quarrel over Moon's marriage to a human; and there is an Ojibwa myth ($M_{387a}$; Jones 2, part I, pp. 3–7, and p. 6, n. 1) in which the sun, by his birth, kills his human mother who had been fertilized by the wind.

Other South American forms of the quarrel illustrate it even more directly. For instance, there is a Jivaro myth ($M_{387}$), in which the sun and moon, both male, quarrel over the night-jar woman, whose favours they share; this is the origin of conjugal jealousy. Certain versions (Wavrin, pp. 635–6) change the wife or wives into a frog or frogs, who, like their North American counterparts, are inefficient housewives. In a Tumupasa myth ($M_{387b}$; Nordenskiöld 3, pp. 291–2), a toad-woman proves to be equally negligent. She does not succeed in being a suitable replacement for her husband's first wife and thus illustrates the failure of polygamy, whereas polyandry had provided the theme in $M_{387}$. Finally, let me quote a Guiana myth:

$M_{457}$. *Arecuna.* '*The quarrel between the sun and the moon*'

Formerly, Wei and Kapei, the sun and moon, were inseparable friends. At that time, Kapei had a pure and gracious countenance. He fell in love with one of the sun's daughters and went to visit her night after night. This did not please Wei, who ordered his daughter to smear her lover's face with menstrual blood. Since then, the sun and moon have been enemies; the moon avoids the sun and his face is stained (K.-G. 1, p. 54).

In spite of its brevity, this myth is interesting on several counts. Its suggested interpretation of the origin of the moon's spots places it half-way between $M_{354}$ – the starting point of the present volume – in which a woman who is a metaphorical frog defiles her husband's back with excrement, and the North American myths which present the moon's spots as being the image of a metonymical frog, clinging in its totality to the face, the chest or the back – that is, to one part of a character personifying the moon. It is thus possible to define a semantic field common to all these forms:

*Moon spots*

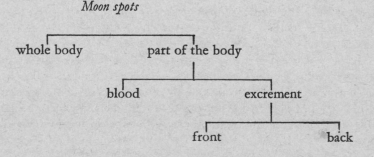

Each myth or group of myths confines itself to dividing up the field in its own way: *half a body, excrement, back* ($M_{354}$); *whole body, front* or *back* (the North American group concerning the quarrel between the sun and moon); *part of the body, blood, front* ($M_{457}$). The difference between $M_{457}$ and the North American group lies in the fact that in the Arecuna myth, menstrual blood, a part of the body, causes the Moon's spots, whereas in North America the whole body signifies menstrual blood, as is explicitly stated in $M_{428}$.

$M_{457}$ belongs to a family of Guiana myths ($M_{360}$–$M_{363}$), which I used at the beginning of the present volume as a way of introducing astronomical triads, equivalents of which were later provided by the motif of the canoe journey (pp. 175–80, 449). It may, then, be no accident that the concept of the triad should have reappeared in the Hidatsa myths which have led us to the present point in the argument; Moon has to choose between three sisters, the two eldest of whom are already married, whereas the youngest is unmarried.

The reader will recall the part played by triads in the South American myths featuring the canoe-journey: three servants ($M_{326a}$), three young girls and three old mistresses ($M_{104}$); or a central figure flanked by two acolytes ($M_{354}$, $M_{360}$, $M_{361}$, $M_{362}$, $M_{363}$ etc.). The figure 3 appears so rarely in the religious imagery of the American Indians that we cannot fail to be struck by its importance among the Mandan, southern neighbours of the Hidatsa, whom they preceded by several centuries along the banks of the Missouri. It seems that the Mandan influenced the Hidatsa much more than the Hidatsa influenced the Mandan (Bowers 2, pp. 476–89).

In the myths and rites of the Mandan and the Hidatsa, a very important place is given to a goddess of vegetation, 'The-Old-Woman-Who-Never-Dies', who either personifies or inhabits the moon. She also plays the part of the adoptive grandmother in the grandmother/grandson cycle which, in the myths of these two tribes, always follows the cycle featuring the wives of the sun and moon. For this reason, she is directly related to our argument. According to the Mandan, the rites and 'sacred bundles' (altars) dedicated to her belong to an archaic tradition which can be traced back to the first occupants of the region (Bowers 2, pp. 338–9).

Prince Maximilian of Wied, one of the first observers to study the Mandan, says that the old woman had six children: three boys and three girls. The eldest boy was day (the first day of creation); the second, the sun and the third, night. The eldest girl was the morning-star; the second was called 'Striped Gourd', the name of a star which revolves round the Pole-star; the third was the evening-star (Maximilian, p. 360; Will–Spinden, p. 133; Bowers 1, pp. 155–6). The morning and evening stars correspond respectively to east and west. Like their brother the sun, the three women are formidable characters: all four, but especially the sun and his sister, 'Woman-Above', who occupies an intermediary rank, are cannibals who also bring about miscarriages, madness, twisted faces, droughts, death, conjugal infidelity, convulsions, feeble-mindedness and other misfortunes (Bowers 1, pp. 296–9; 2, p. 330).

These facts indicate that the boys, the youngest and oldest of whom denote respectively day and night, have an 'equinoctial' aspect (cf. the illustration on the cover of the French edition), and the homologous sisters who denote east and west a 'solstitial' character, in the sense in which I have already used these terms (p. 223). Together they form a configuration similar to that of the four major posts in the Arapaho ceremonial bower. The Mandan did not perform the sun-dance but instead had an annual feast of a peculiar nature, known as okipa, which also took place in summer, in a permanent lodge and not one erected for the occasion. The lodge, kept closed throughout the year, had an oblong framework supported by six poles (Bowers 1, pp. 113, 124–5, fig. 14 p. 127). Six was the number of the children of the 'Old-Woman-Who-Never-Dies', and of the chief divinities of the pantheon according to Maximilian (pp. 359–60). It will be noted that the number of the children is a result of the fact that between the terms of each masculine and feminine pair, a third term is introduced and occupies the zenith either during daytime (midday sun) or at night time (satellite of the Pole Star).

The Mandan and Hidatsa also worshipped other triads. According to one myth ($M_{459}$) to which I shall return, the first three ancestors emerged from the depths of the earth with their sister. The 'People-Above' form a triad composed of the 'Old-Woman-From-Above' (not to be confused with the 'Woman-Above', the sun's sister), the mother of the two brothers, sun and moon. They are represented by a comparable number of emblems: ash sticks planted at an equal distance from each other, with the effigy of the Old Woman on the centre stick and those of the sun and moon on either side (Figure 31; Bowers 1, p. 303; 2, p. 325).

The way the sticks are arranged is reminiscent of the positions adopted by the celestial travellers in the canoe, and we cannot ignore the fact that the rites of the People-Above have as their foundation-myth the story of the quarrel between the sun and the moon ($M_{461}$; see below, p. 313). In Mandan, the actual ceremony is called HapminakE, which

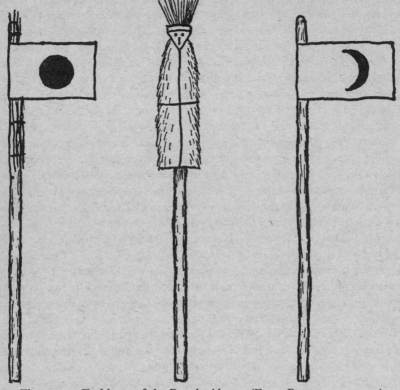

Figure 31. Emblems of the People-Above. (From Bowers 2, p. 325.)

means 'day-boat' or 'day traveller' (Bowers 1, p. 296). Let us pause for a moment to consider this point.

In a letter dated January 9th 1967, Prof. Alfred W. Bowers, whom I take this opportunity of thanking, kindly supplied me with details about the etymology of the term. In everyday conversation, he explains, the sun is called mi-nak-E, which also means a boat. In ceremonial language, the word hap(á)-mi-nal-E(i) or hap(á)-ma-na-ki-ni-de is used. The morphemes can be analysed as follows: hap(á) = 'day'; mi = 'stone, rock'; nak = 'round-shaped'; or hap(á) = 'day'; minak(E) = 'boat', which, when combined, mean the sun. The word can also be divided up into: hap(á) = 'day'; mana = 'wood'; ki = 'act upon, repeat an action'; ni (with a nasalized i) = 'walk, move'; dE = 'move, go from place to place'; this gives: 'a wooden object which moves during the day', or 'day-journey in a boat'.

Later, in connection with another myth (M$_{466}$, p. 335 *et seq.*), I shall discuss the assimilation of the sun to a rounded stone. For the moment let us keep to the boat-traveller image.

The Missouri valley tribes – the Mandan, the Hidatsa and the Arikara – were the only ones (Denig, p. 579) to possess rounded boats of the coracle type, made from elk[1] or buffalo hides stretched over a framework of willow branches. The known specimens are between 1.20 m. and 1.50 m. in diameter; some were too small to take a passenger, and were only used for ferrying loads. In the larger types, the paddler sat at the front (Adney–Chapelle, p. 220; Simpson, p. 175). These details, which are taken from specialized studies of American boats, do not always coincide with the evidence supplied by anthropology or mythology. According to the former, the Mandan boats could have a diameter of nearly 2 m., while it is clear from the latter that they were sometimes thought of as being very large: in myths which will be dealt with later (M$_{510-513}$), there is reference to boats capable of carrying twelve people for four days and four nights. Of course, this does not mean that such boats actually existed, but does suggest that we should treat with caution the frequent statement that these boats were only used for crossing rivers and even drifted one or two kilometres downstream before reaching the opposite bank (Neill, p. 252). The old Hidatsa informants describe long down-river journeys on the way back from eagle-trapping expeditions which had lasted until spring, or to make a surprise attack on an enemy downstream (Bowers 2, pp. 57, 265).

The most important point is that the myths describe a method of navigation differing in all respects from the one used in previously-discussed myths to justify the canoe theme. The boats of the Plains Indians have neither prow nor stern. Instead of the two passengers each sitting at either end, from which positions they dare not move for fear of the boat capsizing, the myths clearly state that they stand in the centre of the boat in order not to rock it (Beckwith 1, p. 83); and, quite normally, the boat swings round at every stroke of the paddle (Neill, p. 252; Will–Spinden, p. 113).

[1] In *La Pensée sauvage* (p. 80), I fell into the obvious trap of translating 'elk' by *élan*. But the *élan* (moose), a northern animal, is not found in the central and southern regions, where there are only various American members of the genus *Cervus*. The English word 'elk' and the French *élan* refer to the single species of the genus *Alces*, which is called 'moose' in America, where the word 'elk', having lost its European meaning, is applied to the large members of the genus *Cervus (canadensis, merriami)*, which, incidentally, in mythology act as combinatory variants of the moose, being the major *cervidae* in areas where there are no moose. The French word for the American moose is *orignac* or *orignal*, a term of Basque origin meaning 'deer', which was introduced into Canada.

I shall not carry partiality to the point of saying that the myths are right and the specialists wrong but, whether true or false, the description they give at least has the advantage of illustrating conceptions which fit in with those relating to the canoe journey, so that the combination of the two forms a coherent discourse. If we suppose that, because of their special navigational technique, the Mandan, like the Indians of the Amazonian basin and Guiana and the Iroquois, establish a connection between the course of the stars and human journeys, they must have their own way of envisaging the relations between these terms.

The informant quoted above says that the long journeys by water occurred on the way back from eagle-trapping expeditions when harvests had been poor and people were resigned to camping a long way from the villages until the return of spring. This empirical connection between journeying by water and journeying overland provides a first, partial explanation of the fact that one can replace the other in native thinking. However, the transference is based on much more profound reasons. Like the long canoe journeys in the case of other Indians, the overland eagle-trapping expeditions raised for the Plains tribes, especially the Mandan and Hidatsa for whom they had a religious character, the problem of arbitrating between the near and the far.

From the geographical point of view, first of all: the Mandan and Hidatsa only went eagle-trapping on rough ground adjacent to narrow sections of river country which formed a small part of the total area claimed by these two tribes (Bowers I, pp. 206–7). In native thought and topography, these regions occupied an intermediary position between the semi-permanent villages situated a short way from the cultivated fields and the plains where, during the nomadic period, the great buffalo-hunts took place. However, the way of life demanded by eagle-trapping was, strictly speaking, neither nomadic nor sedentary. The expedition sometimes travelled more than a hundred kilometres from the village, and its destination was always some hunting-ground belonging to the chief by virtue of a transferable title, kept within the clan. Furthermore, women and children were allowed to accompany the trappers, on condition that they had a separate camp. Thirdly, unlike agriculture and ordinary hunts, eagle-trapping was not a quest for food. The birds, which, after capture, were allowed to go free again or ritually smothered, were only valued for their feathers, which were used for making headdresses or other articles of clothing, or as items of barter. However, the Indians took the opportunity to hunt all the varieties of game in these little frequented regions. But the entire population of a village could not have taken part in the collective hunt in rough country where buffalo never came in great number and where it was difficult to surround them; in addition, there was always the fear of ambush. So, only small groups of eagle-trappers and warriors ever ventured into this territory.

Since the trapping expeditions took place in deserted and inhospitable regions, traditional enemies sometimes had unexpected encounters there. However, in political terms, trapping, in this context, also occupied an intermediary position between intertribal alliance and war. Although the Cheyenne and the Mandan were enemies, 'it was understood that the eagle-trapping season should not be marked by bloodshed between the two tribes, or the trappers would have bad luck ... There would be visiting between camps and good-natured joking about the potency of their respective sacred bundles'. There was supposed to be a similar treaty between the Arikara and the Sioux not to fight during the eagle-trapping season (Bowers I, p. 210).

Lastly, eagle-trapping occupied an intermediary place in the calendar. It took place in autumn, that is, after the great summer hunting-expeditions and harvests, but before the cold season forced the Indians to leave their summer villages, which were built on terraces overlooking the river, and to move down for the winter into wooded valleys. In order not to be caught by a sudden freezing of the river, it was imperative that the trappers should cease their operations immediately with the first appearance of cold weather. Before horses became numerous in the villages, it was customary to travel overland to the trapping sites where bull boats were made for floating back meat and hides to the village. If the cold became too severe, there was a danger of being ice-bound (Bowers 1, pp. 250-51).

Consequently, eagle-trapping was mediatory in five different ways: in space and in time, as well as in mode of living, economic activity, and intertribal conflict. For a few weeks, it allowed the participants to lead a life that was reasonably situated between the near and the far, winter and summer, a sedentary and a nomadic existence, the pursuit of materialistic or spiritual ends, and war and peace. Being a journey with a periodic rhythm and an ensured destination, the trapping expedition was suitable for coding the regular alternation of the days and the seasons:

$M_{458}$. *Mandan. 'The holiday of the sun and the moon'*

When Coyote, the demiurge, lived on earth, he took it into his head to pay the Sun a visit. So he started east, where the Sun comes up and when the Sun came out early in the morning it was in the form of a magnificently attired man. The following night, Coyote created, by means of his power, an exactly similar costume and walked along the path he had seen the Sun take the day before. At noon-day he stopped at the zenith, where Sun was in the habit of sitting to smoke his pipe. There he waited for the Sun. Up came the Sun as usual, and his curiosity was aroused by the footprints he had noticed along the road. At the sight of the demiurge, he became angry and shouted to him: 'What are you doing there?' Coyote explained that he came from the innermost part of the earth and gave light there. He had been told that he had a friend up on top of the earth who gave light to the heavens, and he wanted to get to know him and talk to him. Sun replied that he had always been alone and was well able to do without a friend. He gave Coyote a good beating and threw him out of the heavens head first. Coyote struck the earth and lay there unconscious. It was after sundown when he came to himself. He asked the earth what country he was in now, and the earth told him. Bruised, and limping along with pain, Coyote went in the direction of a spring. On the way, he met wolverines performing a ceremony. Coyote knew them. They welcomed him and doctored his wounds.

When he had recovered, Coyote asked the wolverines to help him to be avenged. They advised him to arm himself with an ash club, a snare made of vegetable fibres and a cottonwood tree reduced to the size of a stem of sand grass. Then Coyote and a wolverine named Black Snare set out to snare the Sun. They placed the grass blade where Sun was accustomed to sit and tied the snare to it. Sun arrived grumbling and angry, because the same footprints were there. The snare caught him, the blade of grass became a tree again and sus- pended him in mid-air. Coyote sprang out and beat him on the head with his club, but Sun's protectors had been careful to choose a club made from soft wood so that it would break without causing too much harm. Whereupon Coyote bound Sun head and foot, put him on his back and went off with him to the wolverines' hut. There they untied him, made him sit near the door and reproved him for his bad behaviour towards a visitor who wanted to be his friend. Sun was pleased with the songs and dances performed by the wolverines, and remained with them.

Moon looked everywhere for his brother Sun and finally he came near this lodge. Peeping in, he saw his brother sitting near the door.

Moon was asked to go in and offered food. They explained to him
how Sun happened to be there. Moon scolded the headman and
insisted that he should give up the place of honour to Sun, who was
proud, and that he himself should sit near the doorway. He added
that when they left they would leave behind symbols which would
take the place of their bodies. These symbols can still be found today
in the eagle-trappers' lodge: the Sun symbol is a snare on the wall of
the lodge opposite the door, and the Moon symbol is a snare over the
top of the door. Sometimes, because of this incident, Sun and Moon
are impersonated in the camps of the eagle-trappers.

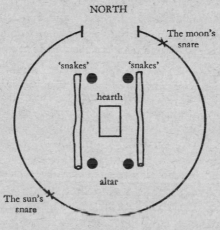

Figure 32. Plan of the eagle-trappers' lodge. (From G. L. Wilson, p. 143.)

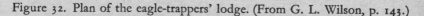

Sun and Moon liked the place so well that they found substitutes
to light the earth until the end of the trapping season. They told
Coyote that they would come back the following season when the
leaves began to turn yellow. Then everybody went their different
ways. The animals who had taken part in the eagle-trapping went
back to their places, and Sun and Moon went back to light the
heavens. Coyote roamed about as usual. One day he happened to be
lying thinking of the fine feasting at the time of the eagle-trapping, when
he saw a vine-leaf that looked as if it were already yellowing. Failing
to realize that this was the natural colour of the leaf, he got up and
went off to the camp and when he reached it sang a song. At the camp

all was empty. One of the medicine-plants said: 'It is not time yet.'
Then he was disappointed, and went away (Beckwith 1, pp. 269-72).

For an explanation of the wolverines (*Gulo luscus*) as prototypes of the
hunter, I refer the reader to *La Pensée sauvage* (pp. 66-72); here, I shall
content myself with pointing out a mythic armature of remarkable
symmetry. Chthonian wolverines are opposed to eagles, birds of the
upper air, in the same way (although less fully) as there is an opposition
between the sun, a celestial luminary, and Coyote – called also 'first
creator' – who claims to play the part of the sun of the underworld. At
the beginning of the myth, mediation between the extreme terms proves
impossible: Coyote can neither take the sun's place, nor become associated with him. In the second phase, he manages to persevere on earth
thanks to the help given him by wolverines, the masters of pitfalls dug
just under the level of the ground. Finally, in the third phase, Coyote
along with the wolverines succeeds in removing the sun from the zenith
and in bringing him closer to the low earth. But in order to do so, they
have to catch Sun in a snare: that is, they treat him *as if he were an eagle*,
whereas Coyote does what an eagle-trapper would do, *as if he were a
wolverine*.

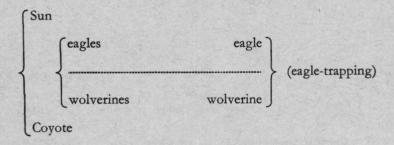

In this presentation of the issue, the snare fulfils a dual function. On
the one hand, as we have just seen, it acts as a mediatory term between
the high and the low; on the other hand, it overcomes a cosmological
contradiction. The antithesis illustrated at the beginning by the
characters of Coyote and Sun is changed into a relationship of compatibility on the techno-economic and temporal levels: as long as the eagle-
trapping expedition lasts, and because of it, nothing is impossible any
more and opposites can co-exist. However, this first assertion is not the
myth's chief aim. By presenting as axiomatic the principle that eagle-
trapping has the power to remove all contradictions, even the most

extreme the mind can conceive of, the myth is preparing the ground for a more essential task, situated on the temporal axis.

The change of axis is already apparent thanks to the link which can be observed between the liturgy of eagle-trapping and the Mandan and Hidatsa versions of the myth featuring the wives of the sun and the moon. In part at least, the myth is the basis of the trapping-ritual, but this part is different from the one on which, as has already been noted (p. 213 *et seq.*), the Sun-dance is based. In the case of the Sun-dance, the link was established through the agency of the central pole of the lodge, symbolizing the human woman rising into the sky. In the rites connected with eagle-trapping, use is made of tree-trunks, but they are placed horizontally on the ground, instead of being upright and vertical. In the lodge that the trappers made out of branches, two tree-trunks were arranged on the floor, where they lay parallel to each other on either side of the hearth (Figure 32). They were used as head-rests by trappers, when the latter lay down to sleep with their feet turned towards the wall. In placing the trunks in position, the trappers were remembering the snakes represented by the trunks (Wilson, p. 146), or the head-rests used by snake eagle-trappers, against which the Sun's son fought during his peregrinations (Bowers 2, pp. 293, 334). It can be seen that the liturgy of eagle-trapping relates to a terrestrial sequence in the myth, and not a celestial sequence, and that it signifies this sequence with the help of two horizontal poles and not an upright one. The analogy is brought out even more clearly when we observe that the hearth in the hunters' hut, which has the form of a hole in the ground, represents the pitfall. The sacred bundle in the Sun-dance also includes a pit, which, according to some evidence, represents the hollow caused by the sun's wife when she fell; in other words, it is the means of a *sky, earth* disjunction in this instance, and of an *earth, sky* conjunction in the other.

The arrangement given to the two fibre snares mentioned in the myth also respects the horizontal axis: one, associated with the Golden Rod (*Solidago*) and hanging on the wall opposite the door, symbolized the sun; the other, associated with sagebrush (*Artemisia*) and hanging near the door, symbolized the moon (Wilson, pp. 150–51). A painted red stick held each noose in place and represented the celestial owners, so that the sun and moon were physically present in the hunting hut. Although the latter was round-shaped like a hide boat, the sun and moon still occupied opposite positions, as they did in the canoe.

I have explained that the eagle-trapping season lasted from early autumn until the first frosts. Consequently it included the equinox, to which the myth alludes in two ways: firstly, by making the sun and moon diametrically opposed to each other, and secondly by making them change their respective places. It will be remembered that the wolverines made Sun sit first of all near the door, which is the despised side; he stayed there until Moon, who had been invited to sit on the honoured side, gives up his place to his brother. For their places to be interchangeable, night has, then, to be 'equal' to day at the time when the action is taking place.

So, the myth adds a new type of mediation to the types I listed in indicating the position of eagle-trapping in Indian philosophy:

| | | |
|---|---|---|
| 1) plains, nomadism | bad-lands | inhabited lands |
| 2) alimentary hunting | ritualistic hunting | agriculture |
| 3) animal foods | adornments | vegetable foods |
| 4) peace | truce | war |
| 5) summer village | hunting-lodge | village or winter encampments |

The myth now suggests:

| | | |
|---|---|---|
| 6) summer solstice | autumn equinox | winter solstice, |

in other words, three terms denoting respectively predominance of day, predominance of night, and equality of night and day.

The fact that in this 'equinoctial' function, the hunting lodge plays the part of a terrestrial variant of the aquatic canoe is also clear from the similarity, which had already impressed Maximilian (pp. 359–60), between the chief mythic themes of the Mandan and those of their Algonquin neighbours and other communities further east, among whom can be found the theme of rock-carvings invented by the cultural heroes (Fox, in: Jones 3, p. 137). We encountered the theme for the first time in a myth from the Tamanac of the Orinoco river ($M_{415}$, pp. 159–60), and I explained it in terms of a double transfer – from water to land, and from the diachronic to the synchronic – of the standard used to establish a reasonable distance between the sun and the moon, and therefore between day and night. When the Tamanac dioscuri claim to be able to make rivers flow both ways, a theme also found in North America, are they not trying to replace a situation of the solstitial type, in which the upstream and downstream journeys are unequal in duration, as day and night are of unequal length, by another situation, equinoctial in type, in which the two journeys last exactly the same length of time?

If, for the cultural heroes, the equinox represents an ideal formula they are trying in vain to generalize, this hypothesis can be suggested:

$$solstice:equinox::nature:culture$$

This equivalence sheds new light on a problem I have discussed elsewhere (L.-S. 18): this is the problem of the instability of the sexes of the sun and moon, which change not only from one community to another but also within the rites and myths of the same community.

According to the Arapaho foundation myth relating to the sun-dance (M$_{428}$), a young girl's upbringing is based on learning to comply with physiological periodicity. This periodicity can be irregular: like the solstice, it can be too long or too short; or it can be regular and therefore perfect, that is, equinoctial in type. According to the equivalence already indicated, irregular periodicity relates to nature, regular periodicity to culture; the myth, in its way, makes just this point.

If, on the other hand, it is a question of the education of terrestrial women by celestial men, it follows that the myth implicitly asserts a triple equivalence between: *earth, nature, femininity,* and: *sky, culture, masculinity*. So far so good. But then a difficulty arises: the regular and perfect periodicity which it is the function of male gods to instil into mortal women must, in the last resort, be embodied by these same women. Like the magic root which, during ritual copulation, is passed from the grandfather's mouth to the granddaughter's, culture is transmitted from father-in-law to daughter-in-law in the course of the myth and, furthermore, the transmission affects the mode of the future manifestation of culture. What man has taught her in the form of a lesson, woman will experience, in living, through the development of her physiological functions. The man, as it were, culturalizes what was formerly pure nature; the woman naturalizes what was formerly pure culture. Through being transmitted from man to woman, the word becomes flesh, a truth which is demonstrated *a contrario* by the frog in the myth, since being herself nature in its most recalcitrant form, she feminizes Moon when she fastens onto him. However, the marriage between a male, equinoctial being (it must not be forgotten that the sun and the moon get married at the equinox) and a female, totally aperiodic being (the frog suffers from incontinence) results in menstruation, the biological mode of periodicity.

According to the viewpoint adopted and the point in the myth on which attention is centred, the *nature/culture* poles swing round and take on opposite semantic charges. From the physiological point of view, man is aperiodic and woman periodic, but from the cosmological point of view the opposite is true, since the masculine demiurges are in possession of the 'rules' – in all senses of the word[2] – which they imprint on the bodies and minds of their charming pupils. Rather like physics, which for a long time had at its disposal two separate theories to explain the nature of light, both of them satisfactory provided no attempt was made to have recourse to both simultaneously – mythic thought uses an armature which it can interpret in two ways. From one myth to another, and sometimes from one episode to another within the same myth, it assumes the right to switch the meaning round:

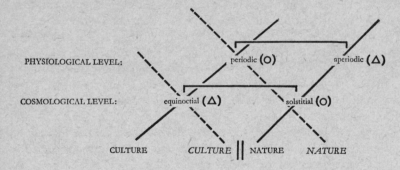

# 2  *A Dish of Tripe Mandan Style*

*Mulieres ornat silentium.*

Erasmus, *De Civilitate morum puerilium*, Bâle, 1530, Ch. IV

From the Arapaho to the Hidatsa, all the myths which start with the quarrel between the sun and the moon consider it meritorious on the part of the human wife to eat noisily. Before enquiring how the Mandan treat this theme, I remind the reader that we met it early on, at the beginning of the first volume of the *Science of Mythology*, in a Timbira myth ($M_{10}$: *RC*, p. 71), which, in this connection also, was a transformation of other myths belonging to the same group ($M_1$, $M_9$; *ibid.*, pp. 147–9), where the hero, in order to avoid a disastrous fate, must adopt the opposite behaviour: he must eat without making a noise. If we take $M_{10}$ and $M_{428}$ as examples for comparison, it becomes clear that the analogy between the myths of North and South America goes much further still:

$M_{10}$: A boy ⎫
⎬ under the age of puberty, guests ⎰ of a conjugal family (jaguar, pregnant woman),
$M_{428}$: A girl ⎭ of a domestic family (father, mother, and two sons),

$M_{10}$: that is, a TERRESTRIAL *couple*. ⎫
⎬ In order to rejoin them (by means of a tree where is/are perched
$M_{428}$: that is, a CELESTIAL *family*. ⎭

$$
\left[
\begin{array}{l}
M_{10}: \text{ macaws, whose } \textit{feathers} \\[1em]
M_{428}: \text{ a porcupine whose } \textit{quills}
\end{array}
\right\}
\text{provide material for adornments, coveted}
\left\{
\begin{array}{l}
\text{by a parent),} \\[1em]
\text{by an affine),}
\end{array}
\right.
$$

$$
\left[
\begin{array}{l}
M_{10}: \text{ the hero } \textit{climbs down.} \\[1em]
M_{428}: \text{ the heroine } \textit{climbs up.}
\end{array}
\right\}
\begin{array}{l}
\text{They are offered a meal}
\end{array}
\left\{
\begin{array}{l}
\text{of GRILLED } \textit{meat,} \\[1em]
\text{of BOILED } \textit{viscera,}
\end{array}
\right.
$$

$$
\left[
\begin{array}{l}
M_{10}: \\[1.5em]
M_{428}:
\end{array}
\right\}
\begin{array}{l}
\text{which makes it difficult for each one}
\end{array}
\left\{
\begin{array}{l}
\textit{not} \text{ to make} \\[1.5em]
\text{to } \textit{make}
\end{array}
\right\}
\text{a noise as they eat.}
$$

$$
\left[
\begin{array}{l}
M_{10}: \text{ The hero obtains cooking fire and weapons, } \textit{masculine} \text{ appliances.} \\[0.5em]
M_{428}: \text{ The heroine obtains domestic arts and the digging stick, a } \textit{feminine} \text{ appliance.}
\end{array}
\right.
$$

The boiled and the roast, which, as the preceding table shows, are opposed as a pair of terms, emerge independently and thousands of miles from each other. The same can be said of all the elements in the adjoining pairs. But, the fact that, in spite of the distance between them, these oppositions fulfil a relevant function, seems all the more indisputable in that the boiled/roast opposition can be found within the Plains area from which $M_{428}$ originates. The Cheyenne and the Arapaho lived side by side for a very long time. However, the Cheyenne myths do not contain the story of the quarrel between the sun and the moon, nor the one featuring the chewing contest. The divergence can perhaps be explained by the fact that the Arapaho considered feminine monthly periods to be of slight importance and did not celebrate female puberty (Kroeber 3, p. 15), whereas the Cheyenne were much more particular in this respect. Young girls, during their first period of menstruation, were not allowed to eat boiled meat, but only meat grilled on charcoal (Grinnell 2, Vol. I, p. 130). If, in this instance, as in others I have discussed elsewhere (L.-S. 5, pp. 257–68), it could be shown that one community deals in its ritual with a problem that a neighbouring community transfers to its mythology, the lacunae in Arapaho ritual and Cheyenne myth would appear complementary. The Arapaho heroine would seem to succeed in eating even boiled meat noisily, because she is a mythic character. But the Cheyenne young ladies, being real people, could hardly be trusted to do as well, and so have to be put on a diet of grilled meat which produces a crunching sound more easily. At the end of the present volume, I shall return to the subject of the customs enforced at puberty.

The table manners just referred to are too like those which we ourselves approve of or condemn for us not to wonder about the hidden motives which prompt myths on both sides of the equator to place them in opposition. In one context, the hero must make no noise when he eats; in another, the heroine must do exactly the reverse. The Mandan myths help greatly towards a solution of this problem, since they retain the theme, while at the same time approaching it in a fashion rather different from that of the neighbouring tribes. What is more, they produce modulations on it from one version to another, and these, seemingly divergent, treatments throw light on each other.

To link up the South American myths about the boy who goes after birds' nests with the North American ones featuring a girl who goes after a porcupine, at the beginning of Part Five I used the argument that each group of myths is connected independently with rites between which a parallel can also be established: the Great Fast of the Serenté and the Plains Sun-dance, both of which were intended to ward off the threatening sun and to obtain rain. Without even mentioning the rites, all the versions of the myth about the quarrel between the sun and the moon looked at so far confirm the existence of a temperamental incompatibility between humans and the sun. The sun dislikes humans, and always for the same reason: they screw up their faces and blink when they look at him, since they are unable to bear his heat and brilliance. Frogs are less affected, but in their case, there is an intermediatory element: the water interposed between sky and earth.

These themes are also present in Mandan mythology, where they are given exceptional importance. In this respect, the Mandan have a different philosophy from that of the other village tribes, rather in the way the Serenté differ from the other Ge tribes. I have already pointed out (p. 292) that the Mandan consider the sun and the members of his family to be demoniacal creatures, fire-raisers, cannibals and instigators of other kinds of disasters. The sole aim of the rites in honour of the People-Above was to placate these ogres: 'It was the Sun who brought death to members of war parties and carried their bodies to his mother's lodge where she prepared them for his meals. He would not, however, knowingly eat those he had sent dreams to, or those who had his sacred bundles and who gave feasts and offerings to him regularly.' These offerings consisted of pieces of torn flesh and severed fingers (Bowers 1, pp. 296–7, 167). Bowers says that he had great difficulty in collecting information about the rites connected with the People-Above, since they were performed during secret tribal ceremonies and the participants were reluctant to reveal their nature for fear of death.

Another important annual ceremony, known as okipa or 'impersonation' (of buffaloes), is officially intended to commemorate the flood which the ancestors escaped, and to encourage the breeding of buffaloes (Catlin, p. 352). The whole tribal pantheon, the animal kingdom and even cosmic beings appeared in the guise of dancers, gaudily painted, costumed or masked, and who entered in turn, either alone or in groups (cf. the cover illustrations of the French edition). During the first two days, these dancers hurled ever-mounting defiance at an invisible being called Oxinhede, 'Acting-Foolish'. He finally appeared on the third or fourth and last day (Maximilian, p. 375; Catlin, p. 360). He was scantily clad in a breechcloth made of buffalo hair and a small close-fitting cap of the same material, and he also had a necklace of maize straw and sometimes a mask. He was painted black, with white circles on his body, limbs and head to represent the stars. A red disc on his chest represented the sun and a red crescent on his back the moon. White teeth were painted round his mouth to give an impression of bared fangs. The two further items of his equipment were an artificial set of genitals made from a rod and two small pumpkins, and a long staff at the end of which hung an imitation human head. Small children were afraid of him because they had been told that he came from the sun and ate people. Whoever dreamt of Acting-Foolish was doomed to an early death.

The other officiants repulsed the monster, who tried, like one possessed, to break up the feast; he spread terror, predicted death for participants at the hands of their enemies and opposed the return of the buffaloes, which was precisely what the carefully performed dances were intended to ensure. Before driving him away, the people threw him all kinds of valuable articles. As soon as he saw this happening, he turned towards the sun and intimated to it, by signs, how well he was being treated, and that it was foolish of the sun to keep at so great a distance ... (Maximilian, pp. 375–6; Bowers 1, pp. 144–5, 153–5).[1]

No doubt the ritualistic saboteur was trying to draw the sun nearer to mankind, along with all the attendant disasters that such a conjunction might involve. So, in this case too, the holding of the sun at the correct distance (since it is a source of life provided it remains sufficiently far away) is brought into a functional relationship with the granting of beneficial rain.

The foundation myth relating to the okipa and to the corn (maize) rites (Bowers 1, p. 183) confirms this interpretation:

$M_{459}$. *Mandan. 'The young girl and the sun'* (extract; cf. p. 457 *et seq.*, pp. 471–2)

The first ancestors of the Mandan emerged from under the ground at a certain high point on the ocean shore. There were four of them, and they brought corn up with them. Their chief was called 'Good-Furred-Robe'. He had two brothers, the elder of whom was called 'Cornhusk Earrings', and the younger 'Uses-His-Head-For-A-Rattle'. The three men had a sister called 'Waving-Corn-Stalk'.

The chief was Corn medicine man and he taught the people how to raise corn and to celebrate the corn rites. He possessed a coat which only had to be sprinkled with water for rain to fall. Good-Furred-Robe taught the inhabitants of the earth to clothe themselves, build villages and cultivate the fields. He laid out the lodges in rows like rows of corn, and assigned the plots to each family. Then he distributed corn, beans, gourd and sunflower seeds to each family.

In those days the sister would be out in the fields all day overseeing the work. One day a stranger came and wanted to talk to her but she would not see him. He came four times to see her but each time she refused. That man was the sun. When he left for the last time, he said that the young girl would never harvest what she planted.

The next day when the sun came up the air was so hot that the corn wilted. After the sun had set, the young girl ran through the fields

[1] Catlin was present at the okipa in 1832 and recounted his experiences in a lavishly illustrated little book (*o-kee-pa*, Philadelphia, 1867). Maximilian arrived among the Mandan the following winter but did not actually witness the ceremony, as he explains on p. 372. He obtained his information chiefly from Catlin. The Mandan were decimated by smallpox in 1837 and soon ceased to form an organized tribe. The last okipa took place in 1890.

with her robe, singing the holy songs. The corn plants revived. Four times running Sun scorched the fields, but each time the young girl revived them with her robe and her songs (Bowers 1, pp. 156, 195).

I shall not insist at this point on the striking resemblance between certain versions of the myth and the origin myth of the Warao of Venezuela (M$_{243}$; *HA*, p. 188). The theme in all instances is the introduction of the civilized arts, particularly agriculture or the Warao equivalent of agriculture, i.e. the extraction of palm-tree pith, which, like maize for the Mandan, is a sacred food. The ancestors go up or come down, being attracted by the abundance of food discovered in the new world by their scouts. A pregnant woman spoils their undertaking, because she is too heavy or too stout. A few Indians reach the promised land, the others – among whom the master shamans, in the case of the Warao, or the master of corn in the case of the Mandan – remain prisoner, and their absence deprives mankind of help and protection. There follows a conflict with the water spirits (see: Maximilian, p. 366; Bowers 1, pp. 196–7; Wilbert 9, pp. 28–36; Osborn 1, pp. 164–6; 2, pp. 158–9; Brett 1, pp. 389–90).

Considered in itself, the Mandan myth calls for comment of a different order. It shows that the sun's 'cannibalistic' appetite extends to agricultural produce. The Serenté ceremony of the Great Fast had an overt link with agriculture: 'If the drought was too prolonged or too severe, the Serenté attributed the threat to their harvests to the sun's anger' (Nim. 6, p. 93). The Mandan had at least two Fasts equivalent to the Serenté rite, one of which lasted four days and was followed by mortifications that the warriors inflicted on themselves during the okipa (Catlin, pp. 355, 362–8, 380). Furthermore, the corn priests, who represented an appreciable fraction of the male adults (thirty-five persons), were subject to numerous prohibitions, some pertaining to food, during the period when the cultivated plants were growing. Several of these taboos were valid for the entire community (Bowers 1, pp. 191–6). Nimuendaju (5, pp. 89–90; 8, p. 62) describes similar provisions among the Timbira and the Apinayé, who are the northern and southern neighbours of the Serenté. It is true that, during the period, the Apinayé used to sing a daily hymn of praise to the sun. The Mandan refrained from doing so, being convinced of the sun's hostility. During a particularly hard winter, they prayed to the south wind, rather than to the sun, for an alleviation in the temperature (Bowers 1, p. 307).

Between the sun and the earth, then, water had to play the part of mediatory term. Good-Furred-Robe, the first corn priest, explained to the Indians that, to obtain plenty of rain and good crops, they should sing sacred songs every spring when the ducks and the other water birds came north. At this period a sweat rite was also obligatory. In a tightly closed sweat lodge, red hot stones were sprinkled with water. There were four of these, each one representing one of the Sun's visits to Waving-Corn-Stalk. According to an informant, these stones were their enemies just as the Sun had been their enemy. The officiant named the four enemies he wished to conquer ... And those entering the sweat lodge imitated wild geese and other water birds (Bowers 1, pp. 192, 195).

In all these rites, a system is apparent, reflecting the correlation between the myths and the social structure. The Mandan were divided into two matrilineal moieties, associated respectively with east and west. The names of the moieties, if they had any, are unknown, but all clan members participated in the construction of the ceremonial lodge: the clan on the east side erected their side of the lodge and placed offerings of yellow corn in each post hole. The west side clans erected the west side of the lodge and placed small mats of buffalo hair in the post holes (Bowers 1, p. 29).

The *corn/buffalo* opposition, symbolizing the social organization, corresponds to that between water-birds and the sun in the myths and rites already studied. Of these four terms, the birds on the one hand and corn on the other are more closely associated with water. Water therefore is related to each pair in its capacity as an ambiguous element which, as regards birds, belongs to the sky, and as regards corn, to the earth, since it should not be forgotten that corn comes from the chthonian world:

This diagram will prove extremely useful, since it shows water as occupying an ambiguous position which supplied the key to certain anomalies apparent in Mandan mythic thought. However, it is incomplete and does not claim to represent a total system, illustrating, as it does, only one aspect. Corn and buffaloes do sometimes appear together in certain rites and myths. The okipa feast, which is celebrated in summer at the time when the willow leaves are fully grown, encourages the breeding of buffalo (Catlin, p. 353). Yet it reverses the agrarian rites in so far as these connote *invoked celestial water*, whereas the okipa, as I have said, and as we shall see more clearly as we go along, connotes *rejected terrestrial water*.

The winter rites calling back the buffaloes reverse both the corn rites, based on the okipa myth, and the okipa ceremony itself: they take place in mid-winter, when the days are shortest; they consist of prayers addressed to the north wind, asking it to unleash over the plains storms which will drive the herds towards the valleys. Lastly, they demand absolute silence and the cessation of all activity. On the other hand, the foundation myths relating to these rites associate either buffaloes and corn, or the sun and birds. Consequently, the terms that have been noted remain the same, and the consideration of other rites or myths involves no more than the discovery and registering of new combinations. The complete system would add no new elements to the incomplete system; it would merely be an extension of it.

The task of constructing the total system would be enormous. But, as is true in the case of all mythologies, it is impossible to fully understand the Plains myths, especially those of the village tribes which are so rich and so complex, without undertaking a methodical classification so as to establish the reciprocal relationships between the myths: they may be symmetrical or anti-symmetrical, directly imitated one from another, with differently coloured backgrounds or outlines; mirror images, or negative or positive prints, displayed the right way round, or edgewise or reversed.

The Mandan tell the story of the quarrel between the sun and the moon in several ways. Among all the variants, two constitute what might be called the Rosetta Stone of this mythological set: being written in different 'languages', they allow the elucidation of a meaning that would otherwise remain inaccessible.

$M_{460}$. *Mandan. 'The quarrel between the sun and moon'* (1) (extract; cf. p. 439)

Sun and Moon once came down to earth. They wanted to get married, for their mother was getting old and feeble. Moon planned to choose a wife from among the 'corn-sheller villages'. Sun protested that these women had only one eye, and wrinkles all over their faces whenever they looked at him, whereas toads turned such pretty blue eyes upon him. 'Very well,' said Moon, 'you will marry a toad woman, and I will take a Mandan girl for my wife.'

Moon went close to a large summer village and saw two girls looking for fire-wood. Moon transformed himself into a porcupine and lured the younger of the two up into a young cottonwood tree, then into the sky. Red juneberries were growing in front of his door and red 'willows' in front of Sun's door. The mother went to bring in the two women but could not find the toad, who remained crouched under the brush. She passed water at each jump.

When the mother set dinner before them, the Mandan girl chose a thin part of the paunch and the toad a thick part. The old woman wanted to know who was the better eater and who made the loudest crackling noise with her teeth. The Mandan girl had sharp teeth and could eat like a wolf. But the toad tried in vain to chew charcoal so as to make a noise. Everyone laughed at her. She became very angry and jumped onto Moon's breast and stuck there. Moon cut her away with his knife and threw her into the fire. Thereupon, she jumped onto his back, between his shoulder blades where he could not reach her. This is how the black spots we see on the moon originated.

The myth goes on to tell the story of the woman's escape, her death, the son's adventures with the 'Old-Woman-Who-Never-Dies' who becomes his adoptive grandmother, the death of the hero followed by his resurrection and ascension into the sky, where he changes into a star (Bowers 1, pp. 200–5).

There is little to be said about this version, except that it includes the story of the wives of the sun and the moon as part of a much larger group concerned with the Old-Woman-Who-Never-Dies, the goddess of vegetation. I shall return to this (pp. 441, 453–4). In other respects, the story is told almost in the same terms as those used in versions we have already studied, and which also form part of the porcupine redaction.

On the other hand, the rites relating to the People-Above, whose maleficent character must not be forgotten, have their foundation in another myth, which differs greatly from the preceding story, both in spirit and in respect of several details:

$M_{461}$. *Mandan. 'The quarrel between the sun and moon'* (2)

'Three people go together in this story: the Old-Woman-Above and her sons, Sun and Moon.' So the story-teller begins.

A long time ago, a young girl called Corn-Silk (the word silk denotes the filaments surrounding the ear) wanted to marry the sun, and she asked a Holy Woman how she might reach him. The Holy Woman advised her to make the journey in several stages, and to spend each night with the mice.

On the first evening, the young girl asked the 'lodge mice' for hospitality. They gave her a supper of ground beans which they had just harvested. In exchange, she gave them buffalo fat which they were to rub onto their hands which were chapped from digging beans. She also gave them blue stone beads. On the second evening, the same scene occurred at the lodge of the white-breasted mice, and on the third evening at the home of the mosquito (long-nosed) mice. To the pocket gophers, who welcomed her on the fourth night, she gave, in exchange for the usual ground beans, buffalo fat and corn balls, which she also had with her.

On the evening of the next day, Corn-Silk reached the lodge where the celestial people lived. The Old Woman was struck by her beauty and bade her enter. Sun and Moon each owned a side of the lodge and the mother sent the young girl to Moon's side. When a Cheyenne woman came up from below, the Old Woman sent her off to the side where the Sun usually slept.

Sun realized that his mother was cheating him, and complained. She replied that Moon did not have many marriage proposals. When the time for supper came, the Old Woman gave Sun, who was a cannibal, a stew made from hands, ears and human skin. The Cheyenne woman and Sun ate heartily.

Each wife gave birth to a child. As Sun was trying to turn his nephew into a cannibal, Moon lengthened night so as to allow Corn-Silk to flee with the child. The latter grew up in his mother's village, against which the ten brothers of the Cheyenne wife waged war. Moon changed into a thunder-bird, fought his wife's people and killed the ten brothers; his son killed his cousin and cut off his head; this was the Sun's son, whose body he burned at the stake and whose head he offered to the Water Spirits. He became the Mandan war chief (Bowers 1, pp. 299–302).

I propose to discuss the second half of the myth in Part Six, and to consider for the moment only the beginning. Who is Corn-Silk? Doubtless a humble doublet of Corn-Stalk, the heroine of the origin myth (cf. $M_{459}$), who, incidentally, is called Corn-Silk in the homologous

Hidatsa myth (Bowers 2, pp. 339, 342). Several myths seem to call any female character Corn-Silk. It may even happen that two separate heroines are called by this name in the same myth ($M_{462}$). But it should not be assumed too quickly that the naming is arbitrary; rather should we bear in mind the remark made by Ferdinand de Saussure about the *Nibelungen* cycle: 'It is true that in going more deeply into things, we notice in this field, as in the related field of linguistics, that all incongruities of thought spring from inadequate reflexion on the nature of *identity*, or the characteristics of identity, when we are dealing with a non-existent entity like the *word*, or the *mythic person*, or a *letter of the alphabet*, which are merely different forms of the *SIGN*, in the philosophical sense.' And, in a note, he adds: 'imperfectly understood, it is true, by philosophy itself' (in: Godel, p. 136).

The reason why the Mandan heroines have the same name is that their adventures have certain features in common: the synonymity o the latter explains the homonymity of the former. Corn-Silk, whether she is a first ancestor or a humble village beauty, always has an ambiguous attitude towards marriage. One function of the heroine is to dismiss the Sun as a possible husband; he wanted to ally himself to humans by marrying her, and she thus becomes the cause of his hostility. The other function is to refuse all suitors near home; when her brothers or her mother reproach her for this, she slams the door and goes off to the far end of the earth to marry an ogre. Whether or not she succeeds in this undertaking, the consequences are equally disastrous: she brings back to the village war ($M_{401}$), incest, conjugal dissension and jealousy ($M_{462}$; Beckwith 1, pp. 63–80; Bowers 1, pp. 272–81), or a killer ogress who has assumed the form of a pretty little girl personifying winter storms and famine ($M_{463}$; Bowers 1, pp. 319–323). To put the matter in very simple terms, it can be said that when the sun tries to introduce himself as a husband, the heroine expels him in the form of an ogre; but when she expels herself as a wife, she introduces real or metaphorical ogres. Admittedly she also brings back corn, which has ceased to grow during her absence. Whether they found agrarian rites ($M_{459}$) or hunting rites ($M_{462, 463}$), the myths featuring Corn-Silk as heroine are playing on a two-fold opposition. As a seasonal product, corn is sometimes near, sometimes far. It is also one of many seasonal products, the first and foremost of which is game, which forces men to abandon corn to *pursue* buffaloes in the plains in summer or *lure* them into the valleys in winter. A purely agricultural life would keep the community in the village, and would therefore have an incestuous aspect ($M_{462}$). But the abandoning of the village implied by nomadic hunting and warlike expeditions to distant areas involves all the dangers of exogamous adventures. It is significant that these adventures take place in the land of the buffalo-woman, whose hostile kinsmen plot the destruction of their son-in-law (Bowers 1, pp. 276–81).

As in the other myths featuring the wives of the sun and the moon, it is clearly the problem of the near and the far which is posed in the Mandan versions. $M_{461}$, however, pushes it in two particular directions. Firstly, the sociological code is relegated to the background: the types of marriage mentioned in the myths suggest rather different ways of life. Corn-Silk tries to enter into marriage with distant and supernatural characters, who turn out to be hunters or cannibals, or both. Or, (as in $M_{462}$), she tries to seduce her own son, thus forcing him to accept a close marriage; on this occasion, she herself behaves like a supernatural character, the mistress of corn. The son of the master of hunting (and of nothing but hunting) avoids an incestuous relationship with his mother who is also the mother of corn (and of nothing but corn) by marrying two women associated respectively with corn and buffaloes. For the first time, a balance is established between agriculture and hunting, but it is precarious since the two women are not alike, one being tolerant, the other jealous. For harmony to reign, the vegetable wife has to sacrifice herself, while watching over the unfaithful hero from afar, and the hero has to overcome the dangers to which the animal wife has exposed him. Before corn is restored to him he must become an established hunter and warrior.[2]

Mandan thought makes no attempt, therefore, to define the middle terms between the nomadic and the sedentary life, hunting and agriculture or war and peace. On the contrary, it tries to prove that the extreme forms are irreconcilable and must be accepted as contradictory. This no doubt explains the tragic tone and sombre grandeur of the myths, and the tortures, apparently more cruel than among other tribes, which the penitents inflicted on themselves during ceremonies whose symbolism, more complex for this reason too, could not be limited to one register. We have seen that the okipa feast consisted simultaneously of prospective rites intended to ensure an increase in the quantity of game, and of the retrospective commemoration of the end of the flood, the pattern of this commemoration reversing that of other

[2] I am not, however, losing sight of the fact that the myth featuring the two wives and its variant known as the *piqued buffalo-wife*, exist among other Plains tribes. I am referring to them here only in respect of their connection with Mandan mythology as a whole.

prospective rites, which were celebrated at different periods in order to obtain rain and ensure abundant harvests. Similarly, the difference in tone between the two main versions of the myth relating to the wives of the Sun and the Moon would be incomprehensible, if we did not take note of the fact that $M_{460}$ belongs to the corn rites, and $M_{461}$ to the rites connected with the People-Above, who are the sworn enemies of gardens.

On her way to the sun's abode, Corn-Silk spends the night with four different kinds of rodent. The English word 'mice' used by the informant probably covers a great variety of families and genera which I shall make no attempt to identify. It should, however, be noted that the name of the 'lodge mice', the first to be visited by the heroine, suggests a relationship of contiguity and familiarity with humans,[3] whereas the fourth group, the pouched rats or pocket-gophers, are perhaps different from the others taxonomically (they could be either Geomydae or Heteromydae) and appear to show little liking for Indians: pocket gophers are said to pillage fields and gardens. The Plains Sioux fear them for a different reason: they believe that the animals can shoot grass arrows which cause ulcerous swellings on the face (J. O. Dorsey 2, p. 496), probably by analogy with the facial pouches in which the gophers store food. It can be accepted, then, that the heroine obtains help from a series of animals which are progressively less friendly and more hostile. She arrives in the end at the sun, who does more than just pillage gardens like the gophers; he destroys gardens and is a cannibal into the bargain. He is therefore unlike the gophers for whom their guest intends her supply of corn balls, the only agricultural term in a triad of which the other two are buffalo fat (hunting produce) and stone beads, which have a vestimentary and not an alimentary connotation.[4] It will be remembered that a triad consisting of vegetable food,

[3] Among the Hidatsa, a stuffed 'mouse' was used as an emblem by associations of young men who, at certain pre-announced periods, undertook to pillage the village houses. All provisions were protected, but not simply as a defensive measure. By making the young men's task difficult, the Hidatsa also believed they were training them for horse-stealing expeditions into enemy country (Bowers 2, p. 134).

[4] The Beckwith version (1, pp. 63–76) presents a triad consisting of corn balls, dried meat, and buffalo fat, which does not contradict the other one since it can be analysed into: *vegetable food, animal food,* and *unguent.* On the other hand, this version gives a different series of helpful animals, namely 1) white-bellied mice; 2) black mice; 3) moles; 4) old badgers. Series such as the following are also found: 1) white-bellied mice; 2) pointed-needle-nosed mice; 3) yellow-bellied mice (Beckwith 1, p. 286); or again: 1) long-nosed mice; 2) red-backed mice with white breasts; 3) nearly black mice; 4) moles (Bowers 1, pp. 287–8). The ethnozoological inventory given in $M_{461}$ illustrates only one formula among several which cannot be elucidated because of taxonomical uncertainties.

adornments and animal food (p. 302 under: 3) is commutable with others reflecting all aspects of Mandan life.

Three strongly marked terms: cultivated seeds, manufactured objects and hunting produce refer, on the other hand, to types of activity not practised by rodents. The latter offer their human guest ground beans of the genus *Amphicarpa*; *Falcata comosa*, a climbing leguminous plant with two kinds of branches, blossoms and fruit. The aerial seeds are so small they are not worth gathering, but the large subterranean beans are eagerly sought as an article of food. As it was hard work harvesting them (cf. the myth), the women on whom this task devolved preferred to pillage the nests of voles (probably belonging to the genus *Microtus* of the *Cricetidae* family), who store up vast hoards of beans. The women of the Dakota tribe, who were neighbours of the Mandan, maintained, however, that they always left some food in exchange: either an equal quantity of corn or some other form of food acceptable to the voles: 'They said it would be wicked to steal from the animals, but they thought that fair exchange was not robbery' (Gilmore 1, pp. 95–6).

It is clear that the mythic story is based on an actual custom, which it in turn justifies. And this custom is deeply significant, since it concerns a type of economic activity half-way between agriculture and hunting: ground beans, a vegetable product, are supplied by animals. Besides, the mouse as the last animal food to be eaten before famine prevails is a frequent mythic theme, and the myth mentions this intermediary activity in connection with a journey which brings together a woman and a man, agriculture and cannibalism; i.e. the extreme poles of a series in which only hunting can play the part of middle term. I have already stated that, between agriculture (with its sociological limit, incest) and hunting (with its sociological limit, war) the Mandan did not conceive of any intermediary term. As a matter of fact, it is difficult to see how a whole tribe could have survived solely on the labours of rodents! Yet however unlikely the hypothesis may be, the myth had even so to refer to it. Without offering a practical solution, it allows a clarification of the exchange norms on the speculative level: a mediatory act which maintains the two extremes in a state of balance, in the absence of a simple state which might replace them. The fact that the exchange appears in the myth in a form so discreet as to pass almost unnoticed, and is carried out with extremely humble partners – the smallest rodents – must not conceal the importance of the theme. It will be seen to play a dominant rôle in myths to be discussed in the last part.

By changing over the wives, the sun's mother makes the reverse of a mistaken choice: the Cheyenne wife, who comes from a hostile community, suits the cannibalistic Sun; and Corn-Silk, a national heroine, is suitable for Moon, in her two-fold capacity as protectress of agriculture and of the Mandan. But for this device, Corn-Silk would not have been able to get away from the Sun, since she needs Moon's help in order to carry out an escape, which fails in all the other versions. But this is not the only difference between $M_{460}$ and $M_{461}$, and so a systematic comparison should be made between them. To simplify matters, I shall refer to the versions as $V_1$ or $V_2$.

According to $V_1$, Moon marries a Mandan girl with strong teeth 'who wolfs her food', and Sun marries a toothless toad-woman.

According to $V_2$, Moon marries Corn-Silk, a Mandan girl, and Sun marries a cannibalistic Cheyenne girl.

If we agree that the Mandan girls in the $V_1$ and $V_2$ are commutable, it follows that when the versions are added together the types of wife can be reduced to two:

$$V_1 + V_2 = \begin{cases} land\ woman: & \begin{cases} \text{Mandan girl} \\ \text{Cheyenne girl} \end{cases} \\ water\ woman: & frog \end{cases}$$

On the other hand, each version keeps only one relevant opposition:

$$V_1 = land\ woman \mid water\ woman$$
$$V_2 = land\ woman(^1) \mid land\ woman(^2)$$

Since it is clear that $V_1$ and $V_2$ are transformations of each other, one of the heroines in $V_2$ must be a transformation of the land woman in $V_1$ and the other must likewise be a transformation of the water woman. The mythic narrative is not very clear on this point, but thanks to the ritual we can supplement its deficiency.

After the defeat of Acting-Foolish, which occurs on the third or fourth day of the Okipa, this evil character, formerly a confirmed bachelor (Maximilian, p. 343), turns into a lewd clown. He imitates rutting buffaloes and pretends to attack the young women. Several times over, he enacts a comical scene with two male dancers dressed as women, one sensible, the other foolish. First he approaches the sensible girl and offers her his corn-husk necklace, but she refuses to have anything to do with him. Then he directs his attention to the other girl, who gladly accepts his offers. These two characters represent Corn-Silk and the Cheyenne woman (Bowers 1, p. 146 and n. 28, 29). Since the latter is ridiculed, we may suppose that, in this respect, the Cheyenne woman in $V_2$ is a transformation of the ludicrous frog in $V_1$. But the toothless frog is incapable of eating noisily.

At this stage, then, the situation would seem to be as follows:

a) (*Silence* : *noise*) :: (*toothless woman* : *woman with teeth*)
   :: (*non-cannibalistic woman* : *cannibalistic woman*).

and consequently, as if it were the Mandan, and not the Cheyenne, woman who was a transformation of the frog. The contradiction disappears when it is noticed that the Mandan heroine combines within herself two terms of the preceding series: she has teeth according to $V_1$ but is non-cannibalistic according to $V_2$. The formula can therefore be rewritten as follows:

b) [*Silence* : *noise*] :: [(toothless) *frog* : *Mandan girl* (with teeth and non-cannibalistic)] :: [*Mandan girl* : *Cheyenne girl*]

which is tantamount to saying, in respect of voracity:

c) *Cheyenne woman* > *Mandan woman* > *frog-woman*.

The Cheyenne woman, being a *cannibal*, is more voracious than the *non-cannibalistic* Mandan woman, who with her sharp wolf-like teeth is more voracious than the *toothless* frog:

|  | Cheyenne : | Mandan : | frog : |
|---|:---:|:---:|:---:|
| *cannibalism:* | + | — | — |
| *teeth:* | + | + | — |

So, in relationship to the stranger-wife and the animal wife, the fellow countrywoman occupies an ambiguous position.

It will be remembered that in the foundation myth relating to the corn rites ($M_{459}$), there was a diametrical opposition between the chthonian ancestors, who emerged from the depths of the earth where they feed on corn, and the celestial people, who were not only carnivorous but cannibalistic. Between these two extremes, water acts as the mediatory term. Yet, in $M_{460}$, which also explains the corn rites, water is the element denoted by the frog. The agrarian myths, then, put forward two independent propositions. On the one hand, water ensures mediation between the sky ($\simeq$ fire) and earth ($\simeq$ vegetation):

a) *earth* < *water* < *sky*.

But, on the other hand, it remains true that:

b) *earth* > *water*.

Consequently, and in spite of the fact that water is the *indispensable mediator*, the mediatory term is *more weakly stressed* than either of the poles that it serves to mediatize. How is this possible? Mandan thought does not manage to evade this problem, which results from the special place it assigns to water, and, as we saw (pp. 311–12), in Mandan thought water plays its mediatory rôle not through interposition but through partially overlapping with the other two elements:

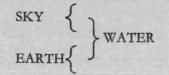

Since the mediatory term is neither superior nor equivalent to the polar terms, but partakes of the nature of both, it shows itself to be superior to the fierce celestial fire, the threat of which it removes, and inferior to the robust earth (as is evidenced by the Indian girl's victory over the frog), although it still remains true that, from the absolute point of view, the sky triumphs over the earth: the People-Above tirelessly persecute humans. In their own way, the myths recognize the ambiguity, since the Sun is mistaken in preferring the frog because the latter can look him straight in the face: objectively, it is the frog who has deceived him, thus manifesting the *power* of water over the sky itself. But although, in this respect, the land-woman is inferior to the water-woman, she is better able, in another respect, to compete with the sky. Thanks to her sharp wolf-like teeth and her noisy chewing, the celestial and cannibal deities *meet their match*. The intransitive structure of the cycle: *earth* > *water* > *sky* (>*earth*) is reduced, as is often the case (L.-S. 5, p. 345, n. 2) to the joint action of two variables which are not made explicit.

It is worth recalling that the Tucuna myth, which I took as my starting point ($M_{354}$), raised a similar problem in connection with a frog-wife. Like the mother-in-law in the Plains myths, the one in the Tucuna myth forces the frog her son has chosen to be his wife to compete in a chewing contest. This frog feeds on *black* beetles (cf. the *black* charcoal which her North American counterpart tries to eat) and she betrays her animal nature when the old woman offers her a highly-spiced dish. So, the North American opposition between the land wife and water wife appears to be congruous with the South American opposition between spiced and unspiced food.

Independently of each other, the myths of both hemispheres link that opposition of the two which they deem relevant to a third, which is the same in both cases: the presence or absence of cannibalism. There is, as it happens, a Tucuna myth ($M_{53}$; RC, pp. 125–6) in which a human hero, who has wandered by accident into the jaguar's house, has to swallow a very spicy stew without complaining, under pain of being eaten himself by the ogre.

So, in both hemispheres, we find an equivalence which should cause no surprise:

    a) *(enemy : compatriot) :: (cannibal : non cannibal)*;

a formula which the Tucuna also change into:

    b) *(human : animal) :: (seasoned food : unseasoned food)*;

which is to say:

    c) *enemy > compatriot > frog*;

whereas the Mandan, for their part, propose:

    d) *(human : animal) :: (good eater : poor eater)*;

which is to say, similarly:

    *enemy > compatriot > frog.*

The comparison is interesting in another respect. It stresses the constancy of the inversion that has already been noted between the myths of both hemispheres which deal with table manners. Like the Timbira hero in $M_{10}$ (cf. p. 306), the Tucuna hero in $M_{53}$ must not make a noise while eating, although the meat is too crisp in the one instance and too hotly spiced in the other. The heroine of the North American myths about the quarrel between the sun and the moon must, on the contrary, chew noisily. In this she differs from her rival, the frog, who has a South American counterpart in the person of a frog in the other Tucuna myth ($M_{354}$). And if, in this Tucuna myth, there had been some reference to her table manners (which unfortunately is not the case) mention would doubtless have been made of her crying out in pain, since it is at least made clear that the spices burn her throat.

In order to escape from the cannibalistic jaguar ($M_{53}$) or from his equally voracious wife ($M_{10}$), the human hero must eat in silence. Only in this way can he hope to mediatize the opposition between nature and culture.[5] But the Mandan heroine plays a much more cautious game. Without becoming a cannibal, she tries to show the sun, the possessor of the sources of life, that although man comes from the bowels of the earth and relies for his survival on water, he can take sides with the sun, against water. Consequently in North America there is a de-mediatizing process, which is in opposition to the mediatizing process. The same point can be expressed in a different way: the Timbira prescribe silence while eating with the jaguar, the master of terrestrial, constructive fire, whereas those Plains Indians, whose mythology contains the sun and moon story, prescribe noisy mastication when eating in the presence of the sun, the master of celestial, destructive fire. After all, the reason why the female visitor to the celestial people has to prove she is a vigorous and noisy chewer is that, as the ambassadress of the human species, she has to show these cannibals that she is *as good as they are*.

---

[5] In the one instance ($M_{53}$), the human hero represents culture and the cannibalistic jaguar nature. In the other ($M_{10}$), the opposite is the case, since the story takes place at a time when men ate their food raw and when the jaguar was the sole possessor of cooking fire. But the relationship of symmetry remains, since the human hero changes into a jaguar at the end of $M_{53}$, whereas at the end of $M_{10}$ the 'jaguar' undergoes the same transformation when he hands over cooked meat to humans, thus becoming himself a true jaguar, an eater of raw flesh.

# PART SIX   AN EVEN BALANCE

*No society can exist without exchange, no exchange without a common standard, and no common standard without equality. It follows that the first law of any society is some agreed equality of men or of things.*

J.-J. Rousseau, Emile, Book III

# 1   *Groups of Ten*

What hidden motives lie behind the complicity suggested by the Mandan myths between the People-Above, who are persecutors, and humans, their victims?

The question is particularly important, since it cannot be dissociated from another, which I have not so far broached. In Part Five, I put forward as an acceptable prototype of the porcupine redaction a myth belonging to the Algonquin of the Great Lakes area ($M_{447}$). It will be remembered that the porcupine redaction developed in an area where the porcupine is rare or non-existent. But if the episode in which Moon changes into a porcupine were to represent an inversion of another myth from a region where the rodent is common, we should be able to understand how the image of the animal survived in an area where the only existence that can be claimed for it is of a metaphysical order. However, this does not explain the link, observable over an unbroken stretch of the Central Plains, between the porcupine redaction and the quarrel between the sun and moon. It is not enough, then, to say that the porcupine redaction is a reversal of a mythological theme occurring elsewhere and that some of the tribes concerned may have been acquainted with it since they came from areas where the theme still persists. They must also have had in their immediate vicinity a prototype of the quarrel between the sun and moon, so that an original combination occurred through its fusion with the porcupine story, the latter having undergone a similar transformation.

I worked out a tentative solution to this problem in 1963-4, but did not include it in my lectures at the College de France, since the evidence in its favour seemed inadequate. Since then, Bowers's monumental work on the social and ceremonial organization of the Hidatsa (2) has been published, and many details are to be found in it which not only confirm my argument but allow me to present it in a more condensed form. I propose, therefore, to begin with this issue.

The Mandan and the Hidatsa used to celebrate almost identical winter

328 THE ORIGIN OF TABLE MANNERS

rites (Maximilian, p. 378) for the purpose of luring the buffalo close to the villages which, at that time of year, were established down in wooded valleys. These rites, which were known as 'Painted Red Stick', were also intended to ensure military victory for the celebrants and long and successful lives (Bowers 2, p. 452). The foundation myth (Mandan: M463, cf. above p. 315; Hidatsa: M464, Bowers 2, p. 452) tells how buffalo bulls agreed to save the Indians from famine – represented by a small ogress in the Mandan version – on condition that the Indians gave them corn balls and other vegetable products, and handed over their wives, wearing no clothes except their buffalo robes. For the purpose of the rite, village elders impersonated buffalo bulls. They were chosen from among men who had distinguished themselves in hunting or war, and who, in their youth, had acquired by similar means their right to pray for the buffalo. The ritual copulation with 'daughters-in-law', immediately transformed into 'granddaughters', ensured the transfer of the supernatural powers from the elders to men of a younger generation. These powers would have gradually deteriorated if rising generations, instead of possessing them in their own right, had been content to exercise them by right of descent (*ibid.*, p. 455).

In theory, it was the wives who took the initiative 'for men have less willpower than women in sexual matters', but sometimes they were overcome by shyness. The young wife would then consult her brothers and her mother, who explained to her the importance of the act expected of her: 'It will', they said, 'be all the better for you, since it is like giving you to the gods to care for' (*sic*: = to be cared for). It sometimes happened that the old man declined the proposition and merely handed the woman his emblem, a painted red stick, which she rubbed against her bare breast while the possessor of the emblem prayed for her and her husband. But it was not the same thing. An informant maintains that he could always tell the difference, because when the real act had been consummated, 'his wives seemed to have new life' (*ibid.*, pp. 454–60).

Bowers gives a second version of the foundation myth, belonging to the Awaxawi sub-group. Although, on the whole, it coincides with the one recorded by Beckwith (1, pp. 181–5), it is full of new details particularly worthy of study since the officiants undertook to play and mime the parts of mythic characters in the course of the ceremony:

*M465. Hidatsa. 'The helpful buffaloes'*

A short, fat and rather ill-looking stranger once challenged the

Mandan to a gambling match. The villagers constantly lost. The Buffalo Woman, who was living in the village at this time, explained that the gambler was the Sun. As soon as he had won all the property, enemies under his protection would attack the village and kill all the inhabitants. There was only one way to change their luck: the young men had to call on the gods and let them enjoy their wives. Otherwise, warriors from twelve villages, already in league, would exterminate the population.

Buffalo Woman was not content just to arrange the ceremony. She asked Moon to be there and to invite Sun, who would be attracted by the promise that a pretty, young Indian woman might give herself to him. But Sun held back. Twice Moon described what a good time they would have eating and making love, but Sun would not go beyond the edge of the village. On the third night Buffalo Woman went to Moon and told him to warn Sun that if he did not make up his mind his lover might go out with someone else. This time Sun came to the village and stood near the ceremonial lodge, and on the fourth night he stepped inside. As soon as he did so, Buffalo Woman said, 'I am your granddaughter ... you are the greatest god'. Sun did not want intercourse with her, claiming that she was already his 'granddaughter'. But he could not refuse in such a situation. So Buffalo Woman became Sun's 'granddaughter' again, against his will.

The effect of the sex act was to be as follows. Willy nilly, the Sun would relinquish his supernatural powers to the Indians, who had become his 'sons' through the 'son's wife' who, prior to the sex act, was a 'daughter-in-law', and afterwards was addressed as 'granddaughter' (Bowers 2, p. 455). So Buffalo Woman had the right to demand that he should deliver the twelve enemy villages into the hands of the Mandan. Sun was sad, saying ... 'I do not like to see you kill off those people, for my "son" is there ... Now I will have to eat him along with the slain warriors.'

The Sun was placed on the west side of the lodge, which was the weakest side (cf. $M_{458}$) 'for the Sun represented bad luck' (*ibid.*, pp. 456, 457). When Buffalo Woman told the people that Sun was eating, the people struck blows on him with sticks, as they did to their enemies. Then the people set fire to the ceremonial lodge at many points so that the light shone over the whole world.

The twelve villages of enemies came and the Sun's 'son' was the leader. The enemies were all killed, including the leader. When the leader was killed, they found that his spinal cord was choke-cherry wood (*Cornus* sp.) and they had difficulty in cutting the head off. The leader was the hundredth killed, so the head was offered to the snake at the point where the Knife River enters the Missouri. Sun came down from the sky and demanded the head, but the snake refused to give it up. Sun found a puff-ball (*Lycoperdon* sp.) and white sage to use for head and hair. But Sun was unable to give life to this artificial replacement and went off crying. The people had won their game (Bowers 2, pp. 452–4).

This myth calls for several comments. Firstly, it will be noticed that it reproduces in part the foundation myth about the rites connected with the People-Above ($M_{461}$), but reverses the foundation myth relating to the Mandan rite for the luring of buffalo between June and August, that is, in summer (Bowers 1, p. 108). Reference has already been made to this myth ($M_{462}$, pp. 315–16) in which, contrary to what happens in $M_{465}$, the Buffalo Woman plays the part not of an endogamous but of an exogamous, wife, who lures her husband into territory occupied by distant enemies instead of defending him against them. In $M_{462}$, Corn-Silk, an endogamous wife (to the extent of appearing as a transformation of her husband's mother), hands over her husband to the Buffalo Woman, so that he should become a master of hunting once he has overcome certain ordeals in distant lands imposed on him by the Buffalo Woman's parents. In $M_{465}$ and the corresponding rite, the reverse occurs: in order to win the same advantage, the hunters, encouraged by their parents-in-law, hand their wives over to the buffaloes, who occupied the village at that time. Consequently, myths featuring buffaloes have a transformational relationship with each other and can be said to form a set. Moreover, the opposition between summer and winter buffalo rites is brought out by the fact that the portable sacred bundles used in the celebration of the former also figure in the liturgy of the okipa, which was a summer ceremony (Bowers 1, p. 271).

But a transformational relationship also appears between this group and the one containing the quarrel between the sun and moon, and can be demonstrated in two ways. Firstly, $M_{465}$ tells the story of a quarrel between the sun and moon: Moon wants to bring Sun to the ceremony, but the latter is wary and reluctant, and is only persuaded to attend after Moon has lied to him. He is tricked, for instead of the beautiful young girl he had been promised he finds a former mistress, with whom he cannot avoid renewing their former intimacy. It should be noted in this connection that the Mandan, if not the Hidatsa, set such great store by the charms of newness that among the women handed over to the buffaloes first place was given to those who had experience of no men other than their husband. It sometimes happened that a woman tried to usurp this envied position, but, thwarted by the jeers of a former lover, the insolent creature had to take her place at the end of the procession (Bowers 1, p. 317). Consequently, as in the myths containing the quarrel between the sun and moon, Sun chooses the wrong wife and the animal creature he finds himself with is devoid of charm. In both cases, although in different ways, marriage between Moon and humans allows the humans to come off best.

Secondly, several remarkable similarities should be noted between $M_{465}$ and one of the Mandan versions of the myth containing the quarrel between the Sun and Moon ($M_{461}$). On each occasion, Sun's marriage to a 'non-human' – a female buffalo *which* the Mandan eat, or a Cheyenne female *who* eats the Mandan – is accompanied by the introduction of games of chance which are a form of warfare, and marks the beginning of a real war against enemies, who are either ten in number (the brothers of the Cheyenne woman) or twelve (the associated villages). On each occasion, the Sun's son engages in combat with these enemies, dies and is beheaded. Finally, it is clearly stated in $M_{461}$ that Moon helps the Mandan by assuming the form of a thunder-bird, and the two myths end with the severed head being offered to a water-snake. These points need to be examined separately.

Let us begin with the figures. In this respect, the myths under consideration belong to a vast group, stretching from the Atlantic to the Pacific, and featuring characters who form a team, usually with ten members. These myths present a difficult problem, because the number sometimes varies and it is uncertain whether the discrepancies are accidental or whether versions which differ on this one point only belong to different categories. The simplest case is provided by the myths of the north-western area of North America, in which regular combinations based on five abound: $5$, $2 \times 5 = 10$, $2 \times 10 = 20$; such combinations are found from the Bella Coola to the Shasta, and especially among the Modoc.

Here are a few examples taken from myths, to which I do not propose to give an index number since several will appear in greater detail in the next volume. Certain Modoc or Klamath heroines have 5 brothers (Curtin 1, pp. 17–26, 95–117; Barker 1, p. 47). One Modoc hero meets 2 sisters who kill 10 deer every day. He himself kills 11, sets off on a hunting expedition and, on 11 successive days, he bags 11 beasts. After killing these 110 animals, he slays 100 others at the rate of 10 a day, then 200 at the rate of 20 a day (Curtin 1, pp. 24–6), i.e. a series of numbers arrived at by the following operations: $10 \times 2 = 20$; $10 + 1 = 11$; $11 \times 10 = 110$; $10 \times 10 = 100$; $20 \times 10 = 200$. In another myth, the demiurge Kumush gives his granddaughter a trousseau of 10 dresses to be worn in the following sequence: as a young girl, for the maturity (puberty) dance (which lasts 5 days and 5 nights), on the day the dance ends, on the 5th day after the dance, as a common everyday dress, for getting wood, when digging roots, when on a journey, for a ball game and the 10th, as her burial dress (ibid., pp. 39–40). One myth describes the partial destruction or dispersal of 10 sickness-brothers who live in the east, and 10 sun-brothers who live in the west (ibid., p. 51). When the hero Moon wants to marry, he rejects 10 frog-sisters one after the other, in spite of their beauty and elegance, and chooses the 11th candidate, an ugly, dirty and ragged green frog, whose form can today be seen as the spots on the moon and who brings him back to life every time he is eaten up by the monsters responsible for eclipses (ibid., pp. 81–2; cf. Spier 2, p. 141). Wus, the fox, experiences all kinds of misadventures in a village in which 10 basket-brothers, 10 fire-drill brothers and 10 red-ant brothers are living in 6 huts in groups of 5 (ibid., pp. 191–3). Another village houses 10 fox-brothers and 10 wolf-brothers. Each one has a wife and 5 daughters, except the youngest fox who is unmarried. The foxes also have a sister who is carried off by enemies, after the latter have wiped out the whole community. The young fox, the sole sur-vivor apart from his mother, asks her to make 10 pairs of moccasins; each pair lasts him 10 days. He arrives at the enemy village and frees his own people; each moccasin given to the freed women becomes a pair and, as he travels back, the hero finds his own tattered moccasins he had thrown away on the outward journey (ibid., pp. 343–9). Other myths list 5 eagle-brothers, 5 rat-sisters, 5 stone-brothers, 5 worm-brothers, 5 hawk-brothers with 5 eagle-brothers, 5 wild-cat brothers, 5 marten-brothers, 5 bear-brothers ... (ibid., pp. 153–90, 207–12, 268–71, 280, 284, 293–4, 319, 321–32 and passim).

Along the Pacific coast, from British Columbia to California, count-ing in fives or tens occurs with the same regularity. The Bella Coola, who are northern Salish, have a group of 10 divinities composed of 9 brothers and one sister. The dancers who personify them wear masks representing the full moon (the 2 elder brothers), the half-moon (the 3rd and 4th brothers), the stars (the 5th and 6th brothers), the rainbow (the 7th), the flower of the American mulberry tree (the 8th), the king-fisher (the 9th and youngest), and the walrus-bladder (the sister, cf. Boas 12, pp. 33–4 and pl. IX, figs 1–9). The myths of the Nez Percé Indians, who are inland Sahaptin, constantly refer to groups of 5 and 10: 5 sisters, 5 brothers, 5 daughters, 10 buffaloes, 5 female grizzly-bears and 5 male black bears, 5 beaver-brothers and 5 musk-rat brothers, 5 wolf-brothers, 5 or 10 days, 10 children, 5 frog-sisters, 5 wolf-brothers, 5 bear-sisters and 5 goat-sisters, 5 geese-brothers and 5 mountains (Spinden 1, pp. 21, 151–4; Phinney, pp. 52, 61, 69, 70, 86, 88, 227, 306, 408, 457 and *passim*). It would be easy to list similar examples in the myths of the Athapaskan of the lower Yukon (Chapman, p. 183) as well as in those of the Chinook (Boas 5, 7, *passim*), the Shasta (Dixon 1, p. 14), the Hupa (Goddard, *passim*) and the Yana (Sapir 3, p. 228).

The Mandan units of 10, to which I have drawn attention, un-doubtedly belong to this group, especially since many similar examples can be found among these same Indians: in $M_{462}$, the buffalo woman's mother has 10 grandchildren (Bowers 1, p. 278), who form a counter-part to the Cheyenne woman's 10 brothers in $M_{461}$. Maximilian refers to a longevity contest between the 2 demiurges which lasted 10 years. 10 masks are involved in the okipa. To see 11 geese together is a sign of spring (*loc. cit.*, pp. 362, 376, 378). In the Plains, counting in fives and tens can be observed among the Arapaho, with series of 1, 5, 10 buffaloes, and 100 robes in which all the quills inserted into the embroidery work have to be counted (Dorsey–Kroeber, pp. 239 47); among the Kiowa, who tell how the body of their cultural hero was cut up into 10 parts, each endowed with magic properties (Nye, p. 56); among the Kansa, who had 5 hereditary chiefs, 5 main clans, and 5 outer wrappings for sacred objects (Skinner 12, pp. 746, 748). Moving north-wards, I propose to leave aside the central Algonquin, with whom I shall deal later, and to conclude this rapid inventory with the Iroquois, whose mythology mentions 10, or sometimes 12, brothers, that is, 10 present and 2 absent (Curtin 2, pp. 229–42, 482–6).

The fluctuation between groups of 10 and 12 brings us back to the problem I raised earlier. When the Yurok of North Carolina refer to the 10 or 12 thunderers (Spott–Kroeber, p. 232), have we to conclude that this was a slip on the part of the informant, or that there were two dis-tinct numerical systems? So far, the problem has been very much neglected in the case of the New World, but specialists in the history of the Old World are quite familiar with it (for China, cf. Granet, p. 7, n. 2, p. 154, n. 1 and *passim*; for Rome, Hubaux). On the other hand, do the myths in which the participants are arranged in groups of 9, 8, or 7 regard these figures as the lower limits of the 10 group, or do they attribute an intrinsic value to them, as is usually the case when the group prefigures a constellation, such as the Pleiades or the Little or the Great Bear? Similarly, 8 could be explained as $2 \times 4$ (a number held to be sacred almost everywhere in North America) just as well, if not better than, as $10 - 2$. The values of 9 and 11 seem to be more easily reducible to the 10 group: Corn-Silk has 9 brothers (Bowers 1, p. 272); so together they make 10. However, the Cheyenne girl in $M_{461}$ has 10 brothers and together they make 11. The number 12 remains puzzling; should it be regarded as a combinatory variant of 10, as would seem to be suggested by the switching from the 10 enemy brothers in $M_{461}$ to the 12 enemy villages in $M_{465}$, or as the product of $6 \times 2$? Bowers (2, pp. 454–5) puts forward a strong argument in support of the second hypothesis: originally there would appear to have been 6 officiants, but the drop in population caused by the smallpox epidemic of 1837 may have forced 2 villages to link up and put together their sacred bundles. As each bundle consisted of 6 emblems, the number would thereby be increased to 12.

While I am ready to follow Bowers's interpretation in this particular instance, I would nevertheless point out that if 2 sacred bundles or 2 rites can be combined, the reverse can also happen: a sacred bundle or a rite may be duplicated. In some instances, it was even a normal procedure for preserving the rule of descent on the female side, while at the same time strengthening the conjugal bonds: the sacred heritage was divided between a sister and her husband (Bowers 1, pp. 270–71). So, when we have concrete evidence that a group of 12 is the result of adding 2 lots of 6 units each, we cannot rule out the possibility that these lots themselves came into being through the division of an older group of 12. The same argument is valid in the case of the groups of 10.

Even in the mythology of the Modoc, where groups of 5 and 10 tend to invade the whole field, and where, for reasons which will become clear later, their predominance cannot be questioned, combinations based on $10+2$ are to be found. Perhaps the transition from 10 to 12 can be explained by the need to vary the initial homogeneous, and therefore inert, group in order to give it some dynamic imbalance on which the outcome of the plot depends. A Menomini myth ($M_{472a}$; Bloomfield 3, pp. 409–19) presents a series of 10 brothers, whose only occupation is hunting. In order for something to happen, the brothers must first of all have a sister, who will then choose a husband, who becomes the other men's affine, and assumes either a positive or a negative function towards them. In respect of the group of 10 men, it can therefore be said that the formula: (10 men + 1 woman) allows the 10 group to be opened up to the sociological realm, and the formula $[(10 + 1) + 1]$ to become the point of articulation with it.

Whatever the truth of this interpretation, it seems impossible to explain recurrent series of 10 terms – when it is a feature of a great many myths distributed over so vast an area as the one under consideration – by reference in every case to local incidents. Even though, throughout North America, 4 is usually considered as a sacred number, with 3 or 5 as less frequent alternatives, it is an undeniable fact that, in a vast family of myths, these numerical bases are multiplied by 2 or 3. In my view, this 'diploid' or 'triploid' character – to use the terminology of the geneticists – seems to constitute a structural property of the family, and an explanation must be found for it. Probably, there is nothing accidental about the fact that the Mandan, with regard to whom I mentioned the phenomenon in the first place, should use the same coefficient in multiplying the number of canoe passengers, the total being established in their myths, as we shall see later, at 8 or 12.

Several myths of the same family, which make do at first with a lower number, introduce additional units in the course of the narrative, until they arrive eventually at the group of 10. I shall return to these myths later, but for the time being I am concerned purely with their arithmetical aspect. In an Arapaho myth ($M_{466}$; Dorsey-Kroeber, pp. 181-9), the initial situation involves 6 brothers and one sister: $6 + 1 = 7$. The brothers perish one after the other, leaving the sister alone. She swallows a pebble which fertilizes her. She gives birth to a son who grows up and resuscitates his uncles, who had been killed by a sorceress: $6 + [1 (+1)] = 8$. After this happy event the young woman marries a stranger, the 9th person in the story, by whom she has a daughter: $6 + [1 (+1) + 1 (+1)] = 10$. A Crow myth ($M_{467}$; Lowie 3, pp. 128-32) begins with 7 brothers and 1 sister: $7 + 1 = 8$. The latter miraculously conceives a son, who brings his 7 uncles back to life; there is also a stranger whose only rôle in the story would seem to be to make up the group of ten: $7 + [1 (+1)] + 1 = 10$. Again in a Crow myth ($M_{468}$; ibid., pp. 165-9), the hero is in opposition first of all to 3 sisters with toothed vaginas, then to their 7 brothers, who are no less hostile: $3 + 7 = 10$. The Mandan variants ($M_{469a,b}$; Beckwith 1, pp. 149-54; Bowers 1, pp. 286-95) mention 3 sisters with toothed vaginas, a 4th sister, harmless because she is partly human, and 7 hostile brothers:

$[(3+7) + 1] = 11$. Given the ambiguous nature of the 4th sister, it is
clear that 11 is being seen as a limit of 10. The presence of a Gros-
Ventre myth ($M_{470}$: Kroeber 6, pp. 97–100) in the same group as $M_{466}$
similarly shows that a group of 9 characters – 7 brothers, 1 sister and
her miraculously conceived son – is considered as a limit of 10.

What value is being attributed, then, to the ten set? Although the
present state of knowledge of Indian numerical systems leaves much to
be desired, it is nevertheless a well-known fact that, except among the
Caddo who had a quinary-vigesimal system, decimal systems prevailed
in North America to the east of the Rockies. On the other hand, to the
west of the Rockies various systems existed side by side: quinary-
vigesimal, quinary-decimal, pure decimal and quaternary even, among
the Yuki.

In Mexico and in Central America, quinary-vigesimal, decimal-
vigesimal or pure vigesimal systems generally took 20 as the complete
number. It was referred to by a word meaning 'a body' in Yaqui, 'a
person' in Opata, 'a man' in Maya-Quiché and also in Arawak, so that
the practice extended also to the northern regions of South America.

If we leave out of account the cultures of the savannah and the
tropical forest, whose very rudimentary numerical systems were never
more than quinary, and sometimes not even that, we cannot but be
struck by the reversal, in South America, of the geographical distribution observable in North America. In the Andean plateaux, that is in
the western part of the continent, predominantly decimal systems prevailed, whereas the eastern part was divided between various systems:
quinary-vigesimal, simple quinary, or even more rudimentary types.

As has been emphasized by certain of the authors from whom I have
taken these observations (Nykl, Dixon–Kroeber), many systems defy
all attempts at classification. They make up certain numbers by aggrega-
tion and change the formula according to whether the numbers are less
than or equal to 10, between 10 and 20, or over 20. Some seemingly
identical systems build up the numbers from 6 to 9 and those expressing
tens, either by addition or subtraction. The Yaqui, in spite of the fact
that they use a quaternary system, used to count on their fingers (cf.
below, pp. 349–50), a practice which was long thought to be the origin
of quinary systems only.

For these, and other, reasons, traditional cyclical typologies have
been discredited: two systems using the same cycle may be different in
structure. It has therefore been suggested (by Salzmann) that numerical

systems should be classified according to three criteria: their make-up, distinguishing between irreducible and derivative terms; the cycle, defined by the periodic return of the basic terms; and lastly the operational mechanics, that is, the table of arithmetical procedures governing derivation. Other writers have objected that this improvement still allows too much latitude for subjective interpretations. Often the mechanics of derivation prove elusive. Thus, certain languages of the north-west of North America, geographically close to each other, but belonging to separate families – Eskimo, Athapaskan and Penutian – use different terms for the numbers 1 to 6, but strange as it may seem, they form 7 by derivation from 6 + 2, 8 by derivation from 6 + 3, and 9 by derivation from 6 + 4 (V. D. Hymes). I have referred briefly to these purely linguistic and mathematical problems because a useful lesson is to be drawn from them. In the field of numerology, as in other fields, the spirit of each system must be determined independently of the observers' own categories, and account must be taken of the arithmetical philosophy implicit in the given practices and beliefs, always bearing in mind that these practices and beliefs may themselves be in agreement with, at variance with, or even in contradiction with, the nomenclature. In one region which, considering the scale of the continent as a whole, is not far removed from the location of the aberrant derivations I have just quoted, the myths illustrate calculations similar to these derivations. Curtin's collection (1, pp. 318–54) includes a set of myths which conjoin or disjoin 2 groups of men, one consisting of 5 brothers, the other of 2, through the intervention of a woman, the sister of one group or the other. It is as if the addition of 5 + 2, the subtraction of 7 − 5 or 7 − 2 required a third term to function as operator. In this sense, it might almost be said that, in the arithmetic of the myth, 8 is calculated as 5 + 2.

These myths belong to southern Oregon and northern California, adjoining regions which I singled out as being those in which the groups of 5 and 10 occurred with the greatest frequency and regularity. The Klamath and the Modoc had a quinary-decimal system, in which verbal forms such as *tonip* 'five' and *tewnip* 'ten' served as bases for a great many derivations: '5 plus the preceding number', '5 times 5', 'less than 10', '10 at once', '10 times 10', etc. (Barker 2). To form numbers higher than 20, counting was done in tens, and the intermediary numbers consisted of so many tens plus the digits. A special word *na'sat*, meaning all ten fingers and all ten toes, was used for counting in twenties (Spier 2, p. 223).

Until recently linguists were in the habit of linking the Klamath and Modoc with the Sahaptin family, of which the Nez Percé are also representatives. A certain myth belonging to this tribe ($M_{472b}$; Spinden 1, p. 16) describes a mystic use of the group of 10; the log-worm had 10 fire-pokers and he counted these sticks all day long ... thus, he would count all the pokers 'on one side and then on the other'.[1] Curiously enough, this detail is reminiscent of the discovery of 'stray' number systems for counting up to ten or in tens, found among very different tribes which used to live next to each other in the south-east of the United States, that is, as far away as possible from the Sahaptin group. Recorded examples come from the Oneida, the Cherokee, the Creek and the Natchez. According to the informants, 'the numbers were not used singly ... but the sets were always recited in their entirety, either for the counting of objects by tens ... or as a little game or ritual of some kind' (Lounsbury, p. 675).

These practices, occurring in communities geographically remote from each other, suggest that the group of 10 not only had an arithmetical function, but also denoted other categories. It will become clear in the next volume how great is the strategic importance of the Klamath of southern Oregon and their Modoc kinsmen and neighbours of north California for the completion of my interpretation of the vast mythic entity on which this whole enquiry is centred. These tribes used a calendar consisting of 10 or 12 lunar months named after the fingers. They would say the name of each finger twice and, if they wanted to count 12 months, they would say the names of the thumb and forefinger thrice (Spier 2, pp. 218–20). This digital counting suggests that the 10-month calendar represents the basic form and that, in this particular part of America, the total year consisted of a set of 10 months, the product of the addition of 5 winter months and 5 summer months. Besides, had the number 6 been taken as an original base, 6 or 12 ought to have generated 60, a number not found in the myths. It is better, then, to regard 6 as a limit of 5, and 11 or 12 as a limit of 10.

The numeral type of calendar, in which the series of months or particular months were referred to by means of figures and not descriptive terms, used to be found along a continuous area of the Pacific coast, from the Aleutian Islands and adjacent lands to northern California; inland, the area included part of the River Columbia basin. The

---

[1] Compare, in Wishram mythology (Sapir 1, p. 294), 'Two old, blind sisters each possessed five large fire-brands which they counted and re-counted over and over again,' and cf. Jacobs 1, p. 115.

Ahtena had 15 short months designated by numbers; the Chilkat counted all their months without using descriptive terms. The Lilloet, the Shuswap and the Thompson did the same up to the 10th or 11th. The eastern Pomo and the Huchnom had a series of named months, followed by others which were known simply by the names of the fingers. The Yurok did the opposite: they counted the months from 1 to 10 by means of figures and used descriptive terms for the remaining 2 (Cope, p. 143).

So, groups of 10 or 5 often played a part in these systems. According to one witness, the Eskimo of Point Barrow used a 9-month calendar: 'during the rest of the year, there was no moon, only sun'. The Copper Eskimo made no distinction between the months, but had 5 seasons (Cope, pp. 123, 132, 135). A major division of the year into 5 seasons also existed among the Menomini (Skinner 4, p. 62), and among several tribes of the south-east of the United States (Swanton 5, p. 257). The old calendar used by the Nez Percé consisted of 9 months, 4 winter months and 5 summer months.

These instances, taken from widely scattered areas, acquire greater coherence when they are linked with other features. Firstly, the short calendars composed of 9 or 10 months often take no account of certain periods of the year: for instance, the Klamath disregard moonless days (Spier 2, p. 218) and the Bella Coola the solstitial periods, each of which lasts about 6 weeks.

In addition to counting 9 lunar periods, both the River Columbia tribes and the Maidu of California evened out the year by inserting an extra period (Cope, pp. 138–9). In all these instances, a discontinuous calendar was evolved, as it were, through the perforation, at one or several points, of the original continuum.

Secondly, the examples quoted show that the short calendars were accompanied more often than not by a division of the year into two groups of months. We have seen that, among the Klamath, the second series reproduces the first. The same formula recurs a long way away, in the south-west and south-east of the United States where twelve-monthly calendars prevailed. Thus, the south-western tribes distinguished between two series of months separated by the solstices, and sometimes they repeated the same names for each series, unless the second series consisted simply of 'nameless months' (Cope, p. 146; Harrington, pp. 62–6; Cushing, pp. 154–6). The complex system used by the south-western Indians (Swanton 5, p. 262) has several features suggesting a repetitive structure: the name of the 1st month 'Much

Heat' is contrasted with the name of the 12th 'Little Warmth'; those of the 2nd and 3rd, 'Little Chestnut' and 'Big Chestnut', echo those of the 8th and 9th: 'Little Spring' and 'Big Spring'; lastly the pair formed by the 5th and 6th, 'Big Winter' and 'Little Winter', is contrasted with the one formed by the 1st and 12th.

The Yurok, a coastal tribe neighbouring on the Modoc and the Klamath, believed the group of ten to be a reflection of the natural order: pregnancy lasts 10 lunar months, the ideal family for a woman is 10 daughters and 10 sons (Erikson, pp. 266, 290). On the other hand, most of the tribes who possess a short calendar with a repetitive structure, and often also their neighbours, regard the group of 10 as a victory over hostile powers which would have liked to multiply the basic number 5 (or 6) by 2. According to the Shasta, there were once 10 moons in the sky. Consequently, winter lasted too long. In order to shorten it by half, Coyote, the demiurge, killed half the stars ($M_{471a}$; Dixon 1, pp. 30–31). The Klamath tell how Coyote's wife created first of all 24 moons, which prolonged the duration of winter to 12 months ($M_{471b}$; Gatschet, part 1, pp. 105–6; 10-month variant in: Spier 2, p. 220). Another myth ($M_{471c}$; Curtin 1, pp. 51–7) begins at a time when the first ancestors, who were unacquainted with fire, ate raw meat. Fire belonged to 10 sickness-brothers who lived in the east, and to 10 sun-brothers who lived in the west. It was stolen from them, and this made the sicknesses decide to scatter and live everywhere in the world. Then 5 suns were killed, and 5 others were spared: 'Everybody was glad, because now there was a winter and a summer instead of only clouds and storms.' The length of the seasons still had to be fixed: 'If there are 10 months of cold,' so the demiurges argued, 'the people will starve to death; they cannot lay up roots and seeds enough. Let us rather have 5 months.' The demiurges, man's predecessors, then contemplated their work and rejoiced: 'We have got fire for them; we have killed 5 of the sun-brothers; we have made winter short; they will be thankful.'

Several neighbouring tribes, belonging to different linguistic families, refer to a period when time passed too quickly. Various versions of this story have been recorded: Carrier and Kato (Athapaskan family), Yurok (Algonquin family), Shasta and Pomo (Hokan family). The following is a version belonging to the Joshua Indians, who used to live in the State of Oregon and who belonged to the Athapaskan family:

$M_{471d}$. *Athapaskan (Joshua). 'The supernumerary stars'*

In very ancient times, the calendar went along post haste and foods belonging specifically to each season were all eaten together at the same time: for instance, dried salmon, a winter food, and fresh eels, part of the summer diet [the Shasta version, which refers to salmon and deer meat, explains that at the beginning of each season, food stored during the previous months must be thrown away]. Suspecting that the sun was fooling him, and being mocked by his wife, the demiurge, Coyote, called all the animals together and asked them to help him to kill the sun. But the sun appeared to be too far away from them. 20 times in succession, Coyote shortened the distance separating them from the rising sun. At the 21st attempt, he decided to attack the sun at sundown. He made 10 successive attempts to obtain help from the water animals. At the 11th attempt, he learned from the mice that there were 100 suns and 100 moons, which were one and the same people, the various members taking it in turn to appear in the sky.

Coyote and his companions set up an ambush in a sweat-house. 4 times each luminary tried to enter, then withdrew. But at the 5th attempt, it went in and was killed; the griffon-vultures ate the corpse.

In this manner, 50 suns and 50 moons were killed, but after the first 25, the birds became satiated and could not eat any more. The abandoned corpses fouled the air and the other suns and moons became suspicious. A drawn battle ensued with 'the sun and moon who caused great noise and wind'. The animals settled the length of the year, dividing it into 12 months, and since then the suns and moons who were spared have never dared disobey (Frachtenberg 2, pp. 228–33; Shasta version, *ibid.*, pp. 218–19).

We must not forget the enigmatic sun and moon which, by urinating, 'caused great noise and wind'. They will be encountered again presently in the myths of the central Algonquin, but in a transformation which will elucidate the mystery. It is enough to note for the moment that, in this instance, the drawn battle fulfils an arithmetical function: it makes possible the adjusting of the product $2 \times 25 = 50$, which would have obtained otherwise, to the calendar that is promulgated by the myth, a calendar consisting of 12 months each lasting 4 weeks. This method of dividing up the year was not unknown in America. The Kutenai, who constituted an independent linguistic family in the north-west of the

Rocky Mountains, divided the 24-hour day into 7 periods, and declared that they had always been familiar with the division of the month into weeks and had respected it by dancing every 7 days. Denig (p. 416) notes that the Assiniboine, although they had no conception of the week, divided each lunar period into phases – new moon, increasing moon, round or full moon, an 'eaten' moon, half-moon, and a dead or invisible moon. Much further south, the Zuni of New Mexico divided the month into three sections, which they called 'a ten'. Each lunar period was divided into 4 parts by the Plains Cree, into 9 parts by the Malecite, and into 6 by the Wyandot (Cope, pp. 126–8).

The link between the groups of ten and various forms of calendarial or astronomical diploidal structure is all the more worthy of note in that the groups of ten also occur in the north-west of Amazonia and in the sub-Andean regions of tropical America. The Baniwa state that the number of individuals in primordial humanity was 'more than 10' (Saake 3, p. 90). They also distinguish between 10 different kinds of sacred flutes played in pairs, that is $10 \times 2 = 20 + 1$, because there are 3 instruments of the kind called uari (Saake 1). A Cavina myth refers to a team of 10 hunters; a Tumupasa myth specifies that the number of rods placed end to end in order to reach and capture the stars was 20 (Nordenskiöld 3, pp. 288, 301). In Tacana mythology, the ocelot hands over 10 fowl as the price of his journey to the sky. The demiurge, Deavoavai, is the youngest of a family of 9 children, consisting of 8 brothers and one sister; the latter marries a monkey-man; $(8+1) + 1 = 10$, by whom she has a son Chibute: $(8+1) + 1 + 1 = 11$. The demiurge taught the Indians 10 kinds of basket-work. Elsewhere, 10 priests or 10 men form a team ... (Hissink–Hahn, pp. 77–9; 95–6, 155–62). Readers of the previous volume will remember ($M_{300a}$; HA, pp. 336–7) that Deavoavai, through the intermediary agency of his wife, the black Tapir, has a connection with the phases of the moon. The mythology of the Tacana, like that of the Cavina, shows traces of Andean influences, and I emphasized above (p. 327) that this area of South America, in respect of its cosmological themes, has considerable affinities with the northern and western regions of North America.

The Blackfoot, who bring us closer to the Mandan again, reason in a manner which has a two-fold resemblance to Oregon mythology. Not only does their myth also establish an opposition between two demiurges who are husband and wife (cf. $M_{471b, d}$); it adds that the husband wanted to provide men with ten-fingered hands. His wife protested, saying that this would be too many and that all these fingers would 'get in the way of each other'. It would be better 'if there should be four fingers and one thumb on each hand' (M₄₇₁e; Wissler–Duval, p. 20). It will have been noticed that twice the number of fingers would have given seasons twice as long in a calendar of the type used by the Klamath, in which, for each season, the number of lunar months is equal to the number of fingers. Here too, consequently, the number 10 denotes *plenitude*: 10 months make 2 seasons, that is 1 year; 10 fingers make 2 hands, that is 1 person. But it would be wrong if the initial reduplication based on 5 gave rise to a second, and the operation thus became recurrent, since, in that case, food stocks would not last until the end of a prolonged winter, and a 10-fingered hand would be paralysed by its own complexity. These two eventualities are sufficiently alike to justify the choice of a calendar lasting 10, rather than 12 or 13 months, although its users (Spier 2, pp. 218–19) were aware that, in practice, it did not correspond to observed phenomena.

I pointed out a few pages earlier that numerical systems, in which the number 20 denotes plenitude, are found in Mexico, Central America and further south (pp. 335–6). But, as it happens, this was not so in Klamath-Modoc, in which 20 is expressed as *labni tewnip*, 'twice ten' (Barker 2), nor is it so, generally speaking, in the languages of the Penutian group, which express 20 as 'two tens' (Shafer, p. 215). In fact, the whole of Klamath and Modoc mythology could be defined by means of a common armature, arithmetical in type, in which a base of 2 divides a base of 10, multiplies a base of 5, or is added to it. The fact that multiplication by 2 has a baleful connotation is made clear in the myth explaining the origin of war. There was a woman who produced too many children and always two at a time: 'the house was full of children ... soon they got to quarrelling and fighting ... Hereafter, one half of the people of this world will fight with the other half. There will be no more peace' (M₄₇₁f; Curtin 1, p. 142). The myth suggests that mankind would have avoided this disastrous outcome, if the woman had given birth to one child at a time instead of twins ... On the other hand, division by 2 has a beneficent connotation. The ordeals imposed on the bride can be overcome because 2 sisters share the tasks. The elder succeeds partially, but the younger finally achieves what the other claimants were unable to accomplish alone (M₄₇₁g; Curtin 1, pp. 306–7).

As I have just shown, a Blackfoot myth played a decisive part in my interpretation. It would seem that the Blackfoot had the same type of calendar as the Klamath, probably comprising 14 months instead of 10, apparently for ritualistic reasons. However, their calendar also divided the months up into two parallel series, one for winter and one for summer. The first and fourth month of each series had identical or very similar names. In addition, it used to be the practice to refer to the months more often by numbers than by descriptive names (Wissler 4, p. 45).

The details are of particular interest, since the Blackfoot are the most westerly representatives of the Algonquin linguistic family, with the exception of the Yurok and the Wiyot, small isolated communities living along the Pacific coast and who, as has already been indicated, use the groups of ten and give them the usual cosmological overtones. The Kutenai, who were neighbours of the Blackfoot to the west, had a similar belief in a 12-month winter, before the length of the seasons had been reduced by half (Boas 9, pp. 179–83). The Kutenai constitute an isolated linguistic unit but, from the geographical and cultural point of view, they form a bridge between the Blackfoot, who still belong to the Plains culture, and the Salish-Sahaptin group, which extends from the western slopes of the Rockies to the coast, and in which the Klamath and Modoc can be included. In the opposite direction, that is to the east, the Blackfoot themselves ensure a link-up with the Algonquin tribes, who are similar in speech, if not in way of life, and who thus occupy a continuous area from the eastern foothills of the Rockies to the Atlantic coast. In the heart of this vast territory, the concept of the groups of 10 is prominent in myths widely recorded among central Algonquin tribes, such as the Cree, the Ojibwa, the Fox and the Menomini.

In these tribes, the concept appears chiefly in a story which varies from group to group, and the transformations of which are not easy to follow, but which can always be identified through the name of a leading character; this is Mûdjêkiwis in Menomini, and has similar forms in the other languages. There are strong and weak variants of the story, which is concerned with 8 or 10 or 11 unmarried brothers and a mysterious female stranger, who comes one day to look after their household. The youngest brother marries her. The eldest, who is called Mûdjêkiwis, becomes jealous and injures his sister-in-law; she flees and her husband sets out to look for her. After various adventures, he finds her, and brings her back again, together with her sisters, who happen to be equal in number to the hero's brothers. He is thus able to give a wife to each brother.

Sometimes, events take a more tragic turn. The Ottawa of the Great

Lakes area, who are close kinsmen and neighbours of the Ojibwa, whose myth I have just summarized ($M_{473a,b,c}$; Jones 1, pp. 372–5; 2, part 2, pp. 133–50; Skinner 3, pp. 293–5), say that the beautiful stranger has a brother, whose head has been severed. Everywhere she goes, the girl carries the head, which protrudes from a leather pouch tied round the neck. It was the brother himself who ordered his sister to amputate his gangrened body, after she had contaminated him with her first menstrual blood. The young girl uses the Gorgon's head to terrify a giant bear, who is wearing a precious necklace and whom the 10 brothers have rashly attacked. The brothers are subsequently killed during a war expedition; their enemies capture the head and torment it. The heroine retrieves the trophy, brings the brothers back to life and finds wives for them all; the wives manage to revive the severed head and to put it back on its body. The brother and sister change into chthonian spirits, while the 10 brothers ascend into the sky where they become the winds ($M_{474}$; Schoolcraft in: Williams, pp. 46–57).

In an Ojibwa version ($M_{475a}$, *ibid.*, pp. 124–34), the youngest of three brothers is sent in search of a lost arrow which has injured a red swan. The bird changes into the daughter or sister of a sorcerer, whose skull has become bloody ever since enemies seized his wampum-adorned scalp. The hero goes off to war, retrieves the scalp and wins women, whom he gives to his brothers. But the latter, far from showing gratitude, develop a hatred of their younger brother, whom they suspect of having raped the young girls during the return journey. Under the pretext that he must find the lost arrow, they send him to the country of the dead, being confident that he will perish there. From this ordeal, too, the hero emerges triumphant.

In the Menomini version ($M_{475b}$; Bloomfield 3, pp. 418–29), the brothers are 11 in number and their jealousy would have been justified, since their youngest brother actually did sleep with his future sisters-in-law. But they are prompted by a different motive: they lust after the prettiest and youngest of the girls, whom the hero has kept for himself. They kill him by cutting the rope while he is swinging. The women flee and the 10 killer brothers revert to their unmarried state.

In the Fox version ($M_{476}$; Jones 4, pp. 79–101), the brothers' jealousy drives them to kill the youngest. They cut off his head, then cut up his body and roast his flesh. The severed head comes back, devours the killers and their wives and is carried round in a bag by his widow (cf. $M_{474}$). Having been warned by a chickadee (cf. $M_{479}$) that the head intends to eat her, the woman runs away, after spilling and scattering some raccoon oil. The head stops to lap up the oil of which it is particularly fond (cf. $M_{374}$). Meanwhile, the wife takes refuge in a mountain inhabited by underground spirits who finally succeed in eating the head, after it has passed through the bodies of several of them and re-emerged from their anuses.

A whole book would be needed for the analysis of these versions, which dissolve into barely recognizable forms along the periphery of their area of distribution. I propose to dwell at considerable length on certain of their aspects; for the rest, I shall content myself with two observations.

Firstly, the magic wampum necklace and the severed head in $M_{474}$, the head in $M_{476}$, and the wampum-encrusted head or scalp in $M_{475a,b}$ obviously constitute combinatory variants of the same mytheme. Its valency, which is positive in $M_{474}$, becomes negative in $M_{476}$, but in both cases the severed head is, as it were, assimilated by chthonian spirits: either it takes its place among them, or they ingest it. And the necklace in $M_{474}$, which is an inversion of the head or scalp, comes from a bear, an animal which plays the part of a chthonian spirit among the central Algonquin. When retrieved from enemies, the head or the scalp supplies wives ($M_{474-475}$); but when it is the result of a destructive act on the part of kinsmen, it causes the death of both the wives and their husbands ($M_{476}$), deaths which might have been avoided if the husbands had not given way to jealousy.

Secondly, $M_{474}$ begins with an episode at the end of which a young woman accidently contaminates her brother with her first menstrual blood. As the swelling and paralysis move upward through his body, the young man is only able to go on living with his sister, provided he is reduced to a severed head. The same type of configuration can be discerned in $M_{475}$, where the red swan, the *injured* daughter or sister of a man whose scalp has been removed, once more becomes available as a wife when her father or brother has recovered his hair. As it happens, the weaker Ojibwa versions ($M_{473a,b,c}$) make it possible to consolidate this link. In his fury at the fact that their supernatural housekeeper has chosen the youngest brother to be her husband, the eldest wounds the young woman in the side or the arm-pit. The girl dies and then revives; when her husband finds her in the lodge where she has taken refuge, she explains that they will have to remain apart for a number of days, which varies between 4 and 10 according to the versions. The impatient hero comes back before the prescribed time, thus causing his wife to flee, and he has to undergo many ordeals before he can find her again.

That this episode is a discreet version of the story, in the early part of
M₄₇₄, about the origin of monthly periods, appears to be confirmed by
the fact that, shortly after this incident, the heroine becomes pregnant
and gives birth to a son (M₄₇₇d). In other words, she has become fertile.
It is worth noting that, among the central Algonquin, the period of
seclusion imposed on young girls on the occasion of their first monthly
periods generally lasted for 10 days, but that the time was subsequently
reduced to 2 or 3 days, or until menstruation was over (Skinner 4, p. 52
and n. 1; 14, p. 54).

The point can be demonstrated *a contrario*, thanks to the existence, in
Menomini mythology, of a series which is both symmetrical with, and
opposed to, the previous one, and which can be illustrated by a summary of one of its versions.

*M₄₇₅c. Menomini. 'The women of the eastern sky'*

Ten sisters lived in the sky with their mother. Their custom was to
go down to earth in order to seduce men, whose hearts they stole
and ate.

At this time, there was only one Indian woman living on earth
with her young brother. She looked after him, and when he reached
puberty, she kept him carefully secluded so that he could not be
carried off by the cannibalistic women. However, the women
arrived, followed by nine captive lovers who were shivering with
cold and almost dying of hunger as a result of their mistresses' ill-
treatment of them. In one version (M₄₇₅a; Bloomfield 3, p. 459), the
young hero manages to warm them by puffing hot breath into the
air. He chose as his wife the woman who seemed the oldest, but who
was really the youngest and prettiest; the most tender-hearted, too,
since she told her husband about the secret place in the braids of their
head-dresses where her sisters hid the hearts stolen from the prisoners.
He took the hearts and gave them back to their owners.

After this the hero and his young wife fled. The sisters went after
them; the hero succeeded in keeping ahead by breaking the eldest
sister's leg. He then returned to the wigwam, and assembled the nine
men who were brothers, so that together they could pursue their
wives. They scaled a steep cliff at the foot of which they saw a vast
number of bones – the bones of the human people already slain by
the ogresses, and reached the home of the mother of the ogresses,
where the latter had arrived ahead of them. The old woman looked
for the hearts in her daughters' hair-braids. The hero had replaced

them by lumps of snow which melted in the cooking-pot and
flooded the hearth.

Feigning various illnesses, the old woman claimed she would
recover if she sent the hero, who had become her son-in-law, to
obtain certain cures from evil monsters who ought to have got the
better of him. But the hero killed them all one after the other.

Then it was the hero's turn to feign sickness. He sent his mother-
in-law to look for his guardian spirits, who clubbed her to death.

The hero advised the nine brothers, who proved to be thunderers,
to leave their wives. They sent them off to the east, while they themselves took up their abode in the west (Bloomfield 3, pp. 455–69;
other versions: $M_{475d}$, *ibid.*, pp. 452–5; $M_{475e}$, Hoffman, pp. 165–71;
$M_{475f}$, Skinner–Satterlee, pp. 305–11).

Without giving a detailed analysis of this group, I would like to
emphasize certain features, which reproduce the other group, but in an
inverted form. A team of 10 brothers, the eldest of whom is called
Mûdjêkiwis, is dominated by a team of 10 sisters, the eldest of whom is
called Matsikihkwäwis in Bloomfield's transcription, Mä'tshiwiqk-
wawis in Hoffman's, and Mûdjikikwéwic in the version given by
Skinner and Satterlee. Among the Menomini, this was a common name
for the eldest of several sisters, and in other myths it is given to a silly,
rather mad, elder sister (Bloomfield 3, p. 359, n. 2) who corresponds to
the mad girl with the silly laugh in certain Cree myths (Bloomfield 1,
pp. 228–36). In Menomini the meaning of the word could be 'she who
governs' (Hoffman, p. 165), and the equivalent Mudjekwäwis in Ojibwa
mythology 'the bad woman' (Skinner–Satterlee, p. 397).

The 10 brothers are looking for wives, whereas the 10 sisters are
looking not for husbands but for men whom they can devour. First of
all, to turn the men into slaves, the sisters remove their hearts and
conceal them in their own hair-braids – a striking inversion of the
severed heads or stolen scalps, which figure prominently in the other
series. In one series, an old woman feigns illness as a pretext for getting
rid of an affine, while in the other a young woman turns her monthly
periods into an excuse. Finally, the youngest of the men breaks the leg
of the eldest woman who is pursuing him, whereas in the symmetrical
group, the eldest man pierces the side of the youngest brother's wife,
whom he is pursuing.

Since the two patterns stand in such exact opposition to each other,
it has to be accepted that the youngest menstruating sister and the

eldest, who has been rendered lame, form a pair. In the preceding volume (*HA*, pp. 459–64) and on the basis of different data, I made the suggestion that limping symbolized some failure in seasonal periodicity, which at times was desired and at other times feared. We now have confirmation of this hypothesis, since a woman experiencing her first monthly periods, i.e. who has been made periodic, is placed by the myths in opposition to, and correlation with, a lame woman, i.e. an aperiodic creature. It will be remembered that the Tereno myth ($M_{24}$), which led me to discuss the problem of limping, attributed the infirmity in a man to the effect of his wife's menstrual blood, which she was using to poison him. Consequently, both in South and North America, the two terms are linked. This observation provides a suitable occasion for pointing out that, in spite of its northern area of distribution, this myth, in which the dramatic interest springs from the jealousy felt by an elder brother towards a younger, to the point of injuring the wife they shared and thus bringing about the appearance of monthly periods, is also found in Tierra del Fuego, among the Yamana ($M_{475g}$; Gusinde, Vol. 2, pp. 1169–72).

The first consequence of the preceding remarks is that, in the story featuring the unmarried brothers, the heroine with the injured side or arm-pit represents a menstruating woman, and the second is that this mytheme is in opposition to that of the woman who is made lame in the symmetrical series. Lastly, I have suggested (p. 346) that, in the identical series, there is a link between the menstruating woman, i.e. stained with blood below, and the scalped man, i.e. stained with blood above. If this hypothesis is acceptable, it follows that the scalp or severed head of a male kinsman conquered by enemies constitutes a combinatory variant of the menstruating woman, who has been retrieved by her kinsmen from the group of men whose affine she had become, because these men have proved to be too possessive about her. The interpretation thus suggested may appear strange. I shall justify it later (p. 398). For the time being, I propose to deal mainly with the arithmetical aspect of the myths.

In the peripheral variants found both to the south and north of the Great Lakes the number of unmarried brothers is reduced to 8 or 4. In the north of Manitoba, the Swampy Cree refer to 4 brothers ($M_{477a}$; Cresswell, p. 405), while among the Sweet Grass Cree, 10 brothers are mentioned ($M_{477b,c}$; Bloomfield 1, pp. 221–36, 245). In the mythology of the Plains Ojibwa, there are 8 brothers.

The Oglala Dakota, a Siouan-speaking tribe who tell the myth in a very different form (M₄₈₇: Beckwith 2, pp. 396–7; Wissler 1, pp. 200–202; Walker, pp. 173–5), accept a compromise between 4 and 8: there are 4 brothers, the youngest of whom obtains the help of 4 men in order to win 8 sisters; he marries one of them, and shares out the rest, giving 4 to his protectors and 3 to his brothers. But there can be no doubt that it is the same myth, since, like M₄₇₄, it refers to the origin of the west wind, a harbinger of storms; I shall come back to this point later.

The Dakota had a predilection for the figure 4: they distinguished 4 cardinal points, 4 measures of time, 4 parts to each plant, 4 categories in the animal kingdom, 4 kinds of celestial bodies, 4 categories of divinities, 4 ages of life, and 4 cardinal virtues. But they were also perfectly capable of reducing 5 to 4 and 10 to $8 = 2 \times 4$, whenever they came across empirical groups of 5 or 10: they explained that 'mankind had 4 fingers on each hand, 4 toes on each foot and the thumbs and great toes of each taken together are 4' (Walker, pp. 159–61). So there is no need to feel dismay, if the tens characteristic of the central versions of the myths under consideration change into fours or eights in zones peripheral to those in which counting in tens occupies the position I indicated at the beginning. The example of the Dakota shows that what is taking place is, in fact, really a conversion. Furthermore, certain variants quote 5 brothers instead of 4 (Walker, pp. 177–9, 179–81).

A preliminary examination of the notion of 10 suggested that it expressed plenitude. This plenitude is, however, full of ambiguities. Although the number 10 is intellectually satisfying, since each hand has 5 fingers and a summer and a winter each lasting 5 months make up one year, it is nevertheless disquieting in so far as it is the result of $5 \times 2$. Once this method of reckoning has been tried out, it may well become an accepted and recurrent practice; what would be the fate of mankind, if each hand had 10 fingers instead of 5, and if winter lasted twice as long? As I have shown (see above, pp. 337–42), this is the way the Indians reason. Even if we look no further than the versions already summarized (M₄₇₃–₄₇₇), it is quite clear that the Mûdjêkiwis myths do not rest content with the concept of the group of 10: they manipulate it skilfully so as to make it produce more complex sets.

Let us take the Fox myth (M₄₇₆) as an example, since it combines rhetorical devices characteristic of other versions, but in less systematic fashion, and picking out certain features only. The youngest of 10 brothers sets off to look for a lost arrow. He travels for 10 days and every night is given hospitality by a family who offer him a daughter in marriage. 'Very good,' he replies, 'when I am on my return, then I will stop and take her away.' In this manner, he builds up a reserve first of one wife, then 2, then 3, etc., up to 9. When he reaches his destination, he obtains a 10th wife, whom he takes back with him. During the return journey, he adds to her the 9th, the 8th etc., so that, after starting off with one wife, he proceeds to acquire 2, 3, 4 and so on, until he has 10. He arrives at his lodge with all these women, and marries them off in turn to all his brothers, giving the eldest woman to the eldest man, the second oldest woman to the second oldest man, and keeping the last and youngest woman for himself. So once again, from 1 marriage, we go on to 2, then 3, then 4 etc., until there are 10 marriages in all.

What does this mean? On three successive occasions, the story raises the series of the first ten natural numbers to their arithmetical sum of base 1. It is as if the number 10, already considerable in itself, was significant not only because of its own value, but because, by reason of its relative importance, the result of an initial operation, it provided the means of undertaking a still more complex operation with a much higher product. I would hesitate to use as evidence the fact that the arithmetical sum is equal to $\frac{10(10+1)}{2} = 55$, in other words, a figure approximately equal to the number of weeks in the year, if I had not already established the existence, in several regions of America, of a 'finely divided' year, and if the number 50 did not occur explicitly in a myth which, for independent reasons, I included in the same group ($M_{471d}$, p. 341).

But that is not all. The arithmetical sum ensures a kind of mediation between ordinal and cardinal numbers, since it enables the numbers both to appear separately and in succession, and yet to be present altogether simultaneously. In the myth featuring the unmarried brothers, the eldest one is well aware of this, and it even explains the cause of his jealousy. The 10 sisters form a group, the elements of which do not spontaneously link up with those in the group constituted by the 10 brothers, which is on the same level. The sisters are first of all totalized by one of the brothers, who later proceeds to de-totalize them. But what did he do in the interval? At least one version ($M_{475b}$) gives an answer. The eldest brother, being convinced that he has been cuckolded, stirs up feelings of bitterness in his brothers and, with one accord, all nine agree to kill and dismember the youngest. The latter's head returns to the lodge the following night. But before eating each brother, it gives each in turn a detailed account of everything, omitting none of the various operations that have been effected since the beginning of the story. Consequently, the series of the first 10 numbers, which has already been raised to its arithmetical sum, is itself multiplied by 10 (in actual fact, by 9, but in keeping to 10, I believe I am being faithful to the spirit of the story), so that the myth builds up a comprehensive family to the 10th power. If I may venture a rather homely image, I would say that the myth has the complex aspect of a rail capable of holding 10 coat-hangers, each of which can occupy 10 positions, and from which are hanging the same number of sequences, themselves consisting in turn of 10 elements. Whereas, a little while ago, the mythic rhetoric made us aware of the concept of the arithmetical sum, it is now bringing us extraordinarily close to the concept of 'cardinal', in the sense that set theory gives to the term.

No doubt, 10, as a cardinal number, does not define the family of all the 10-term sets conceivable in the absolute. But at least it defines all those conceivable in the mythic universe. In *La Pensée Sauvage*, I drew attention to the difference between scientific thought and mythic thought: one works with concepts, the other with significations, and whereas the concept can be seen as the operator which opens up the set, signification can be seen as the operator which reorganizes it (L.-S. 9, p. 30). It remains to be shown how, in this particular instance, although the mythic universe may at first sight appear to be modest in extent, it nevertheless coincides with the universe as a whole. This will emerge from the Menomini versions, which seem to occupy a position of prime importance in the group.

### $M_{478}$. *Menomini. 'The ten Thunderers or Thunderbirds'*

The youngest of ten brothers, the Thunderers, was captured one day by chthonian spirits. He had a wife, a young son and an older daughter. The uncles ordered the children to go away and live as best they could. The sister taught the boy everything, and he very quickly became an expert hunter. She had forbidden him to go near a neighbouring lake. Tired of always following the same path, the hero moved nearer and nearer to the lake, where he met a boy of his own age, who became his friend.

The stranger was the son and nephew of the two horned Snakes, who were holding the Thunderbird prisoner. Thanks to his friend, the hero was able to visit his father. Their meeting was so distressing that the young Snake begged his father and his uncle to release their

victim, but the father would not agree. So the young Snake decided
to betray his own people.

He told his friend about the place in the mountain where the
mountain-side was thinnest, just above the prison-dungeon. The
sister at once sent the hero to their uncles, the Thunderers. The latter
prepared themselves for war. They arrived rumbling from the west.
A terrible battle began between them and the horned Snakes, who
were beaten and lost their prisoner. The young snake had two sisters,
one friendly towards his companion, the other hostile. So he decided
to leave her. Meanwhile, the Snakes were preparing their revenge.
Warned by his faithful friend who changed into a terrestrial snake,
the hero managed to escape to the west with his sister (Skinner-
Satterlee, pp. 342–50).

Another version ($M_{478b}$; Bloomfield 3, pp. 368–79), which is almost
identical with the one just given, adds that after the Thunderers' victory
the hero marries the young Snake's sisters. However, the eldest sister
plots with her own people who seize and imprison the hero, just as
they had imprisoned his father. The younger sister, the mother of a
small boy, frees her husband, who is recaptured. In a lacrosse match
played between the Snakes and Thunderers, the latter gain a provisional
victory. However, the young Snake explains to his protégés that they
are still in danger, and that his sister, brother-in-law, sister-in-law and
nephew will only be safe if they turn into people. Consequently, just as,
in both versions, the son of the chthonian snakes changes into a terrestrial (underground) serpent, a mixed group composed of a male
Thunderer and a female Thunderer, a Snake-woman and a child born
of a marriage between the two races, assume human form and settle on
the earth's surface, that is, at equal distance from the Thunderers and
the Snakes.

Here is another myth, also belonging to Menomini mythology:

### $M_{479}$. Menomini. 'The Thunderbirds and their niece'

Once upon a time, there was a young girl who lay asleep, not knowing anything. All at once she came to consciousness. Never having
had any parents, she merely awoke and knew her beginning. She rose,
looked around and started walking away and wondering ... and
catching sight of a river, she realized from the current in what direction it was flowing, and chose to follow its course upstream, as she
knew there must be some living people somewhere.

She kicked a stump which was so rotten it fell over and she knew it had been cut long ago. Another stump looked fresher to her. She came to a third stump, which appeared to have been newly cut. Next, she found three different heaps of deer guts, which she picked up, throwing away the first lot and keeping the second, then throwing away the second and keeping the third, which looked freshest of all. Hunters and woodcutters must be living nearby.

A trail led her to a long lodge. A young boy asked her in, and adopted her as his niece. He explained that he was the youngest of ten brothers. Soon his elder brothers would return from their hunt. They would all come into the lodge one after the other, the eldest first.

The brothers warmly welcomed the young girl, and after due deliberation they decided to confirm her in her status as adoptive niece. They ordered her to cover her head while they ate. She peeped through the coverings and saw that, in order to eat, her uncles had changed into large birds with crooked copper bills.

Then autumn came and the brothers began to think of leaving before the cold season. But who would look after their niece during the winter? They refused in turn the raven and the winter hawk, and accepted the offer made by the chickadee, which at that time was a large bird. For the chickadee told the truth; it had a good warm home and picked up particles of flesh and fat the hunters always left behind when they killed any kind of game.

The little girl lived comfortably with her new uncle all winter. The latter warned his niece to be careful about an unruly man, with whom she should not enter into conversation. If she should answer one word, the man who tries to catch women would get her and take her back to his wicked old wife, who would try to drown her, for the wife had a brother under the spring. He was the black hairy water-snake. The poor little girl forgot the warning and became the sorceress's drudge. The latter sent her after dead hemlock bark for firewood, hoping that she would be killed by falling bark, but because the little girl herself had magic powers she emerged unscathed. She was less successful when she went to draw water from the stream. The hairy snake caused her to lose consciousness and drew her down underneath the spring. When she revived, she found herself in a long lodge seated between an old man and an old woman, who were surrounded by their sons, the ten hairy snakes, who were waiting to eat her up.

For several days, the old woman managed to protect the prisoner, for she was afraid of the girl's uncles. The young girl then remembered that the Thunderers had promised to come to her aid whenever she called them. She sang sacred songs; her uncles heard her and set off to find her. They struck with lightning the high mound of rock which held the girl prisoner. Nine snakes died in this terrible battle: only the aged parents and one of their sons were spared, because they had shown compassion.

Having set their niece free, the Thunderers went to the house of the chickadee, who had cried so much that he had shrunk to a tiny little bird. What were they to do with their niece? They chose to place her in the fork of a tree, where she would stay until the end of the world. When she sang, her uncles would hear her. They would rush to her and rain would begin to fall ... For the heroine had changed into a tiny silken green creeping toad (*Hyla versicolor*), always up in the trees and a harbinger of rain. And, as it happened, she had cried for her uncles at the latter part of winter, which explains why storms occur in February or March; for she had arranged things this way (Skinner–Satterlee, pp. 350–56; there is another shorter version, $M_{479b}$, in: Bloomfield 3, pp. 379–83. Cf. also Skinner 13, pp. 161–2).

The two myths belong to different categories. $M_{478}$ would seem to belong to a private tradition, since it explains why the members of the Thunderbird clan are particularly liable to death by drowning (or, as in $M_{478b}$, to be involved in military disasters). $M_{479}$ could be a foundation myth of the Menomini ritual for the invoking of rain and storms in times of prolonged drought, and which consisted in a feast offered to the Thunderbirds (Skinner 7, pp. 206–10). Although one is a clan myth and the other a religious brotherhood myth, $M_{478}$ and $M_{479}$ are nevertheless extraordinarily symmetrical in structure, a circumstance which can perhaps be explained by the fact that one describes the end of the stormy season and the other its return. The most striking opposition is connected with the female character, who is either an eldest sister or a very small girl who has emerged from nowhere, and who is the reverse of the other in these two respects. A man cannot marry his sister, nor do the brothers in $M_{479}$ have any intention of marrying the total stranger, whom they accept as their adoptive niece before turning her into a frog. In this connection, the Menomini versions are different from those that I discussed first in which the plot centres around a marriage between the youngest son and the visiting stranger, then between his brothers and the stranger's sisters. $M_{478b}$ is the only myth to repeat this theme, although in an altered form, which brings it more into line with the symmetrical series illustrated by $M_{475c}$. The earlier versions referred to severed heads and matrimonial alliances, themes not found in the Menomini myths just summarized, where they are replaced by seasonal periodicity.

Let us pause for a moment to consider these transformations, a complete inventory of which can only be made at the level of the group. We know that the myth featuring the unmarried brothers comprises several types. Firstly, the story of Mûdjêkiwis, which, as has been seen, exists in both strong ($M_{474}$) and weak forms ($M_{473a,b,c}$); then the story featuring the women of the eastern sky ($M_{475c}$), which is both symmetrical to, and in opposition to, the previous one. And then there are the two Menomini versions just quoted, echoes of which can be found in the mythology of the central Algonquin, both in the story of the Snake's prisoner ($M_{478}$) and in the story of the ten Thunderers and their niece ($M_{479}$).

Whereas the Mûdjêkiwis series and its opposite are concerned with trophy-heads and matrimonial alliances, the other series deal rather with seasonal periodicity. But they do not do so in the same way: $M_{479}$ heralds its end, which is the opposite to its return; and it can be said that $M_{475c}$ describes the reverse of the opposite, since it decrees the removal eastwards of women who are in turn the opposite of the Thunderers, masculine beings inhabiting the western sky. To form a group of the kind which has recently been shown by M. Barbut to have a possible field of application in the social sciences, all that is lacking is a fourth term, namely, the reverse of the theme. It will be seen later (p. 381 *et seq.*) that the strong forms of the Mûdjêkiwis story also have a meteorological connotation, which remains in a latent state. But it can be noted here and now that whereas $M_{478b}$ ends with a union between humans and celestial or chthonian spirits, $M_{474}$ – which I chose to illustrate the strong forms – on the contrary ends with the disjunction of both upper and lower spirits, who establish their respective abodes at equal distances from humans.

The quadripartite structure of a Klein group is even more applicable to the transformations undergone by the heroine. According to the particular version, the heroine takes the form of a *young wife* ($M_{473}$, $M_{475a,b}$), a *non-wife* ($M_{479}$), an *older sister-instructress* ($M_{475c}$), a *younger misbehaving sister* ($M_{474}$). Let us look at these transformations more closely. In respect of periodicity, the *young wife* in $M_{473}$ takes care to remain secluded at the time of her first monthly periods, which is what the *misbehaving sister* in $M_{474}$ fails to do. Through negligence, she contaminates her brother with her menstrual blood (whereas in $M_{473}$, the husband contaminates himself, in spite of the precautions taken by the heroine).

There is no reference anywhere to the *sister-instructress's* monthly periods. Yet she is careful to seclude her brother at the time of the puberty rites ($M_{475c}$). In other words, like the young wife, she ensures seclusion instead of failing to ensure it, in the manner of the misbehaving sister. However, she differs from both these women in that her action concerns her brother and not herself.

Nor does $M_{479}$ describe the physiological functions of the *non-wife*, although for an entirely different reason: the heroine in $M_{475c}$ and $M_{478}$ is already an adult, older than her brother, able to teach him, and therefore the repository of traditional knowledge; the heroine of $M_{479}$ is a little girl with neither parents nor family and whose mind, according to the myth, is a complete blank. Since such an infantile creature is not marriageable, the brothers make her their adoptive niece, 'the most highly regarded and honoured relative'. Actually, she never reaches adolescence, since she is changed into a frog, which forecasts rain and the return of spring. This lack in the heroine makes possible, then, a shift from physiological to seasonal periodicity.

That is not all. Actively or passively, the myths describe the *sister-instructress* and the *misbehaving sister* in terms of masculine tasks: one teaches her little brother the art of hunting, the other receives the same instruction from her elder brother, when he is paralysed by gangrene: she has to hunt for two. Also actively or passively, the complementary myths describe the *wife* and the *non-wife* in terms of feminine tasks. As soon as she is married, the *young wife* sets about demonstrating her domestic virtues. The *non-wife* on the other hand is completely excluded from household tasks: $M_{479}$ mentions only one meal, which she is not even allowed to witness. Hence a cultural lack or deficiency, in addition to the already mentioned natural lack, and which, like the latter, allows a dialectical development, since the meal has more than just an alimentary value: it would seem to constitute the prototype of the sacrifice offered by men to the Thunderbirds in order to hasten their return (see above, p. 355).

The mythological system featuring the unmarried brothers occurs, then, in the form of four quadripartite structures, which are homologous and interlocking. If arranged in a logical order, they can be said to articulate, respectively, kinship links, biological or cultural behaviour patterns, and lastly certain links between man and the universe, as represented by the sequence of the seasons. Yet these interlocking relationships are not static in character. Far from being separate from the others, each structure conceals an imbalance, which can only be corrected through recourse to some term borrowed from the adjacent structure. A diagram illustrating the total configuration would be less like a series of squares inscribed one within the other than like a Greek key-pattern: *non-wife* is not a kinship term; the non-existence of monthly periods demands that, for periodicity to be defined, it has to be moved from the physiological to the seasonal level; the reverse of the end of one season is not equivalent to the return of the other; and the consummation of a sacrifice is not to be confused with the consumption of a profane meal prepared by a diligent cook. Within the myths, the argument, controlled by an irrefutable dialectic, progresses from kinship to social functions, from biological rhythms to cosmic rhythms and from technical and economic occupations to acts of religious observance.

The feature of this mythic universe I am chiefly concerned with is seasonal periodicity, since this theme, which was introduced by the last two Menomini myths ($M_{478, 479}$), offers a solution to the problem of the groups of ten.

The myths use two groups of ten: there are ten Thunderbirds, as well as ten chthonian Snakes. At the same time, in both $M_{478}$ and $M_{479}$, the eldest of the Thunderers is called Mûdjêkiwis and in $M_{479}$, the youngest is called Pêpakitcisê.

As it happens, these names are titles that were given to Menomini children according to their order of birth. The eldest son was given the name Mûdjêkiwis (Mûdjikiwis, Matsihkiwis) meaning 'Brother to the Thunderers', and the youngest Pêpakitcisê (Pûpäkidjise), 'Little Pot Belly'. But – and this is of prime importance – there were only 5 ordinal terms for boys (3 for girls), and they were respectively: 'Brother to the Thunderers', 'Next to him', 'Next to this one', 'Middle one' and 'Little Pot Belly' (Skinner 4, p. 40). In terms of social practice, the Menomini myths are undoubtedly diploidal, as I postulated at the beginning of the discussion (p. 334). While the eldest brother called Mûdjêkiwis deserves this title, the youngest occupies the 10th, not the 5th position. Consequently, the brothers are twice as numerous as they should be.

Figure 33. Menomini Thunderers. (From Skinner 14, pl. LXX, p. 262.)

Moreover, there exists a version belonging to the Cree of the Plains, and therefore peripheral ($M_{477d}$; Skinner 8, pp. 353–61), which differs from the others in that it contains 2 curious, and probably interlinked, anomalies: on the one hand, the unknown female visitor chooses the 5th and not the 10th brother; on the other hand, there are 2 Mûdjêkiwis, one the eldest of 10 brothers, the other the eldest brother of 10 Thunder-birds who have 10 women as sisters. Not only do the Cree set a group of 10 Thunderers in opposition to a group of 10 chthonian spirits, which are either feline or reptile; they also introduce, between the 2 opposing sides, a group of 10 humans, the 10 brothers, who act as mediators: the brothers kill the chthonian monsters on behalf of the Thunderers, and are given wives in exchange ($M_{477b}$; Bloomfield 1, pp. 228–36). Consequently, the multiplication of terms on one level is accompanied by their division on another. The Plains Cree possess a complex vocabulary for differentiating between age groups, but there is no mention of their using ordinal terms (Mandelbaum, pp. 241–3).

It would be appropriate to look carefully, and in the same spirit, at those cases in which the brother called Mûdjêkiwis or by some equivalent term, occupies the position not of the eldest, but of the second eldest (Schoolcraft version of $M_{475a}$ in: Williams, pp. 124–34), or of the third eldest ($M_{474}$). $M_{474}$ stops the series of 10 brothers after the 3 eldest whereas, in $M_{477d}$, the series is cut short after the 3 youngest, who are rejected by the heroine immediately before she accepts the offer of the 5th.

Let us keep to the Menomini, since their myths can be directly related to real-life customs. We have seen that the sociological series of 5

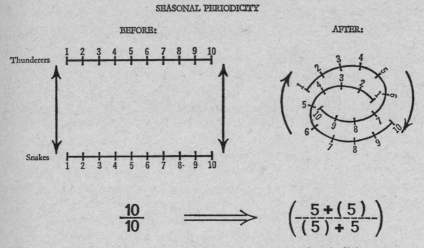

Figure 34. Before and after the introduction of periodicity

ordinal terms is doubled in order to form a mythic series which, had it any counterpart in real life, would give rise to a situation as inextricable as the one conjured up by the anatomical image of the human hand with ten fingers, used by the Blackfoot. It is just such a catastrophic possibility that will be avoided by the introduction of seasonal periodicity at the end of $M_{479}$. For if, instead of perpetually confronting each other in a pitched and inconclusive battle, the powers of good and evil, that is of summer and winter, operate alternately, each will reign for one half of the year, in other words, their numerical strength will in future be divided by two. Five thunderers will be in control during the summer season, and five snakes during the winter season, the other members of

GROUPS OF TEN 361

the troop disappearing behind the half of the other troop, to which it is giving way. There is development, then, from a static opposition with a coefficient of $2 \times 10$, to a dynamic periodicity with a coefficient of $2 \times 5$ (Figure 34).

Thus, the long winter is cut by half, a more beneficial improvement than a lengthening of summer, since winter was a dangerous period, during which the Menomini anxiously awaited the arrival of the spring storms. Like the Bûngi (Plains Ojibwa) and the Plains Cree, who celebrated a thunder ritual instead of a sun-dance (Skinner 5, p. 506; 6, p. 287; cf. Radin 3, pp. 665-6), the Menomini believed that the Thunderers were friendly to humans. They felt uneasy when they had not heard them for a long time. At the first rumble, they would joyfully exclaim: 'Hai, Mûdjêkiwis is heard.' And the eldest son bore the name in honour of the Thunderers (Skinner 4, pp. 73-4; cf. André in: Keesing, p. 61).

This onomastic link between a mythic series and a sociological series completes my demonstration; the Menomini pantheon, being unlike the myths on this point, consisted of five and not ten thunderers.[2] Mûdjêkiwis, their chief, sat in the middle, flanked on his north side by Mûkomais, 'The Inventor of Hail' and by Wi'sikapo, 'the Stationary Bird'; and, to the south, by Wapinämäku, the 'White Thunder' and by Sawinämäku, the 'Red (or Yellow) Thunder'. The two northern thunders brought cold weather and storms, the southern ones warm rains (ibid., p. 77). It is thus confirmed that when the myths refer to the group of ten, they do so only to discard it again in favour of the group of five, which had become the only real group since 'once upon a time', when the transformation of a little girl into a frog, the harbinger of rain (cf. $M_{241}$, HA, p. 184), allowed the establishment of seasonal periodicity.

---

[2] It will perhaps be objected that Skinner (14, pp. 49-50) quotes 16 'Titles of the Thunderers', which the Indians used as names. Mûdjêkiwis comes at the beginning of the list and Pepäkidjisê at the end. But the same character may be called by more than one name. For instance, in $M_{479}$, Pepäkidjisê (Pepakitcisê) 'Little Pot Belly', is also called Mosa'na'sê, which means 'The Terrible' or 'The Destroyer', a title to which is sometimes added that of 'Thunderer-Man', because this divinity liked to assume human form (ibid., p. 50). Also, there is a painted skin showing several thunderers, but their chief and the 'true thunderers', who stand out from the rest, number 5 in all (Skinner 4, p. 104). The other celestial divinities are eagles, masters of lightning, and birds who are servants of the thunderers (ibid., pp. 105-6). A distinction has to be made, then, between the minor thunderers and the major or chief thunderers. 'These are the five great Thunderers; the others are all of lesser rank' (Skinner 7 pp. 74-5, 77).

Light is thus thrown on the nature of the groups of 10, and it becomes clear why some myths contain totals which are unusually large in comparison with the more modest figures, such as 2, 3 or 4, that peoples without writing are normally content with. The groups of 10 represent *saturated sets*, which the dialectic of the myths is concerned to reduce, while at the same time emphasizing this feature by dramatic inventions. The more slowly the hero travels, the shorter the journey seems to him ($M_{477c}$). The 10 or 11 ogresses in the eastern sky ($M_{475c}$) starve their respective lovers with a greater or lesser degree of cruelty: the eldest sister eats all the food, the 2nd to the 5th give nothing, the 6th gives very little, the next 4 share, while the 11th and last gives almost everything. Several versions of the Mûdjêkiwis story ($M_{473c}$, $M_{477c}$) establish a major opposition between the youngest brother, who is married, and the eldest brother who remains unmarried the longest: the youngest begins by assembling all the women and then shares them out amongst his brothers, starting with the one closest to him in age and continuing, in inverse order of seniority, until he comes to the eldest: 'It is queer', exclaimed the latter, 'that the youngest brothers get married first!' (Skinner 3, p. 295; cf. Bloomfield 3, p. 235).

Thus, the long interval is gradually filled in by the systematic addition of the smallest intervals compatible with the argument of the myth, that is, by a procedure which is the reverse of the one I described, almost in the same terms, when the problem of long and short intervals was first encountered (RC, pp. 50–55, 298–9). I showed then that the continuous, which is the reign of short intervals, stood in opposition both to the synchronic discontinuity of the biological species and to the diachronic calendrial discontinuity of the days and seasons. Moreover, during the day, the continuous is manifested by the chromatism of the rainbow and, during the starless, moonless night, by the total darkness which threatens to bring man into contact with hostile forces. The whole mythic presentation of the problem, which I formulated on the basis of South American examples, reappears in the northern regions of North America. In connection with the alternation of the days and the seasons ($M_{479c}$; Bloomfield 3, pp. 317, 335), the Menomini say that the striped squirrel (*Eutamias*) proposed that the other animals should take the markings on his coat as a model: winter and summer would each last six months, six being the number of stripes on his back. He won his case against the bear, who wanted winter and night to prevail continuously. Since the bear has a uniformly black coat, were night to prevail, man would have to hunt by groping about in the dark, and the inevitable contiguity between man and savage beast would be to the advantage of the latter.

We are dealing, then, with an extremely large body of myths, but one in which those using the groups of ten can be distinguished by a feature which is peculiar to them. Instead of doing the usual thing, which is to establish the reign of large intervals where short intervals previously prevailed, these myths appear to be trying to engineer the creation of the continuous by increasing the number of protagonists up to ten, in so far as ten represents the number beyond which discrete units, becoming too numerous, no longer tolerate being separated by distinctive gaps and so fuse together, as it were, to allow the power of the continuous to prevail over that of the numerable. From this point onwards, the myth proceeds to destroy the continuous again by reducing the groups of ten to lower-powered units, which divide the tens by two. In this respect, the only difference between the Menomini versions featuring the Thunderers ($M_{478}$, $M_{479}$) and the group about the unmarried brothers is that the former have recourse to seasonal periodicity to obtain a result also achieved by the other myths in the group, but by devices the nature of which must now be determined, so that they may all, if possible, be related to the same principles.

Before going on to the next myth, the reader is advised to look again at $M_{479}$, which is the second Menomini variant.

### $M_{480a}$. Blackfoot. 'Red-Head'

Once there was a man, who lived alone with his mother, without any relations and far away from other people. He had a head of hair as red as blood. A young girl who had made a long journey came one day to his lodge. She had just been created and came out of the ground; she did not as yet know how to eat or drink or in fact do anything. Red-Head told her to go out and leave him alone. The young woman, who was very much afraid, took refuge in an ant-hill and called upon the insects for help. She begged for some kind of power to secure the good-will of Red-Head.

The ants took pity on her and asked her to bring two strips of buckskin stolen from the lodge. Then they sent her away until the next day. When she returned to the ant-hill, the heroine found that the strips of buckskin had been beautifully embroidered with porcupine quills. This was the origin of quillwork, since the ants were the first embroiderers (cf. above, p. 254). Next, the ants worked Red-Head's mother's robe, and told the heroine to put it next to the old woman's leggings, after first of all decorating the leggings with the buckskin strips. Then she was to hide in the bush and wait and see what happened.

When Red-Head and his mother returned, they were greatly surprised to see such nice work. Convinced that the young woman must have done it, Red-Head asked his mother to go and find her, give her food and ask her to make some embroidered moccasins for him. The heroine agreed to do the work, but explained that no one should watch her while she was busy on it. All she did was to hand over the moccasins to the ants who, by the following day, had them already embroidered. Using the same ruse, she had the hunter's shirt decorated on the front and the back with embroidered patterns in the form of discs, and with strips over the shoulders and on the sleeves. The discs represented the sun, from which the young girl derived part of her powers. A weasel (whose fur provides much appreciated trimming) gave the young woman instructions as to the designs the ants should work. The stripes on the robe would represent the trails followed by the weasel, and the bands on the moccasins the place where the weasels tramped down the snow.

Won over by gifts which he thought were the young woman's work, Red-Head decided to marry her, but the weasel told the girl not to accept. He advised her to take a very sharp bone and to kill the man in his sleep. She did as he directed and then ran away to the Indians and taught them how to make quillwork (Wissler–Duvall, pp. 129–32).

This heroine with neither family nor past, and who emerges from the void in complete innocence, is similar to other girls we have already encountered. Like the girl in $M_{479}$, she can be defined negatively by an absence of kinship links. The heroine of $M_{479}$ was unsuitable for marriage, and the girl in $M_{480a}$ is averse to marriage: both are non-wives. Being incapable of doing anything for herself, to the extent of not even knowing how to eat or drink, the heroine of $M_{480}$ is also the opposite of the sister-instructress in $M_{478}$. So she is both a non-wife and a non-sister. This interpretation can be confirmed with the help of the Mandan and Hidatsa versions, in which the sister of $M_{478}$ who is faithful to her brother, and the perfidious non-sister of $M_{480}$ who kills the man whom she does not want to marry, are transformed into a sister who behaves treacherously towards her brother, with whom she has been left alone in the world, as happens in $M_{478}$. The Mandan heroine, after being initially her young brother's instructress ($M_{481}$; Beckwith 1, pp. 96–102; Bowers 1, pp. 312–14, 366–9; Hidatsa version, pp. 370–73), becomes a cannibal. She attacks the inhabitants of the celestial world and takes their scalps to arrange them in regular rows on her robe. But one place in front of her left shoulder remains empty, and only the brother's scalp can fill it. In this way, so the murderess argues, she will be able to keep her beloved brother on her heart, and since food is carried to the mouth with the left hand, she will be able to feed her brother first. The hero, warned by a guardian spirit, takes to flight. The ogress pursues him and he wounds her with an arrow which sticks in the right side of her chest but does not kill her. Before ascending into the sky, she gives the hero her robe, which is adorned with scalps and shells. Henceforth, this was to become part of a sacred bundle at which the owner and his wives would worship in order to obtain success in war.

At the same time, then, as the *non-productive sister* in $M_{480}$ changes, in $M_{481}$, into a *destructive sister*, we pass from a myth describing the origin of quillwork to a myth explaining the origin of scalps. Furthermore, the transformation takes place at the very heart of Blackfoot mythology, since in another version of Red-Head ($M_{480b}$: Josselin de Jong 2, pp. 97–101), the heroine becomes a widow who has been inconsolable ever since Red-Head killed her husband. She rejects several suitors, and finally agrees to take one of them, but only on condition that he first avenges the murder.

The young man obtains the help of supernatural protectresses, who turn him into a pretty Indian girl, in which guise he presents himself to Red-Head. The latter orders him to embroider his moccasins and leggings before nightfall: should he fail to do so, he will be killed. The false heroine disappears into the bush and hands over the work to the ants. Red-Head is so delighted with the result that he marries her, although warned by his tame magpies that the so-called woman has the eyes of a man. While her husband is asleep, the false wife inserts into his ear an awl made from the antlers of a deer, and she hammers on it with a stone until she pierces his skull. Then she scalps her victim and flees to the home of one of her protectresses, to whom she gives half the scalp, and who in return changes her back into a man. The hero arrives at the village, where he celebrates the first war-dance. He hands the half-scalp over to the widow with whom he is in love and who agrees to marry him.

This second Blackfoot version occupies an intermediary position between the first Blackfoot version and the Mandan version, since it retains the embroidery theme, while relegating it to the background. The subject is no longer the origin of quillwork, the craft being taken as already known, but – as in the Mandan version – the origin of head-hunting and warlike rites.

$M_{480b}$ links the offering of the scalp and the war-rites with marriage. Through this approach, an initial affinity appears between the two groups $\{M_{479}-M_{480a,b}\}$ and $\{M_{473}-M_{476}\}$, with which the discussion began: this latter group already established a link between matrimonial alliances and trophy-heads. But the affinity with the third group $\{M_{478}-M_{479}\}$ is no less obvious. The Blackfoot call the heroine of $M_{480a}$ 'Woman-after-Woman', by which they mean that she has the power always to come to life again (Wissler–Duvall, p. 132, n. 1). She is a periodic creature, like the frog responsible for the alternation of the seasons in the Menomini myth ($M_{479}$), and which, as its scientific name implies (*Hyla versicolor*), has the power to change colour.

In addition to her ability to bring people back to life, the heroine of $M_{480}$, as we have seen, has another, which is the ability to assume the appearance of either a woman or a man. In some versions she is female, in others male; in the latter case, the man turns into a woman in order to deceive and seduce the enemy. The Blackfoot in some instances even present their heroine as a man disguised as a woman and sent to earth by the Sun in order to kill Red-Head (*ibid.*). She then becomes indistinguishable from the hero of the famous Scarface cycle, which must now be studied.

According to one Blackfoot version ($M_{482a}$: McClintock, pp. 491–9; Spence, pp. 200–205), this hero was none other than the offspring of the union between a luminary and a human female in the cycle that was discussed at length in Part Four. In the other Blackfoot versions $M_{482b,c,d,e}$; Wissler–Duvall, pp. 61–5 [2 versions]; Grinnell 3, pp. 93–103; Josselin de Jong 2, pp. 80–82; Uhlenbeck, pp. 50–57), the hero is a young Indian disfigured by a scar, who asks for the hand of a village girl. The latter gives the ironic reply that she will marry him as soon as the ugly disfigurement has disappeared. The boy is very much hurt and decides to go away. He finally arrives at the Sun's abode and becomes friendly with the Morning Star, the Sun's son, and thus obtains the protection of Moon, the Sun's wife. Mother and son intercede on his behalf. Sun, although not easily moved, takes pity on him, cures him, and makes him look so like his own son that even the mother cannot distinguish between them.

Although forbidden to do so by the Sun, the hero one days sets off westwards with his companion. He meets and kills seven cranes, swans or wild ducks, and brings back their severed heads. This was the origin of scalping and, ever since, warriors have displayed them as proof of their exploits. The Sun is delighted to be rid of his enemies, teaches his protégé the rites of war, and gives him a magic pipe the sound of which will charm the girls (Wissler–Duvall, p. 66, n. 1). When he returns to his own people, the hero institutes sweat baths. Then he rises into the sky, where he becomes a star which is often confused with the Morning Star ($M_{482h}$). According to another version ($M_{482d}$), he marries the girl he loves; both live until they reach a ripe old age and have a great many children. Or, as in $M_{482e}$, he goes to bed with the cruel girl and then drives her out to punish her for her wickedness.

There exist certain Sioux variants of this myth, which retain its aetiological function, with certain shades of variation. In the mythology of the Oglala Dakota, the story of a lover whom an unsociable young girl subjects to a certain test before accepting him as a husband also concerns the origin of the scalp knife. The hero is sent by his sweetheart to find an unknown object, called ptehiniyapa, and discovers it thanks to two old women who are the sun and moon. But when he returns with his trophy, the girl changes into a wood-deer and runs away from him; hence, the alimentary taboo concerning this kind of game ($M_{483}$; Beckwith 2, pp. 401–5; cf. Wissler 1, pp. 128–31). This unexpected conclusion presents a problem which will be solved later (p. 386 *et seq.*). The symbolic representation, in $M_{483}$, of the scalp-knife as a buffalo's red horn makes it possible to extend the group to the Winnebago, a Siouan-speaking tribe who lived to the south of the Great Lakes. A complicated myth about the origin of the sacred weapons and the war rites of the Thunderbird clan ($M_{484}$; Radin 2) has as its hero the youngest of 10 brothers, known as Red-Horn. The reference to Thunderbirds on the one hand, and the insistant repetition of the groups of 10 on the other (10 brothers, 10 nights, 10 scalps), suggest that the curve we have been following since $M_{473}$ might well come full circle in Siouan mythology. The myths of the Crow Indians, who also form part of this linguistic family, will complete the proof. But before leaving $M_{483}$, it is worth noting that when the hero sets off to look for the unknown object, he is accompanied by his youngest brother and a friend: in other words, by two people, one of whom is *less than a brother*, the other *more than a brother*. The Dakota treated their last-born with contempt (Beckwith 2, p. 401, n. 3), but in their view the bond of

368 THE ORIGIN OF TABLE MANNERS

ceremonial friendship known as hunka surpassed all others (Walker, pp. 122–40). Therefore, instead of the category of 'brother' becoming exhausted through extension, as in the Mûdjêkiwis cycle, the supererogatory formula of the groups of 10 exhausts it in this instance through comprehension. This logical transformation is probably caused by the predominance in Dakota mythology of the number 4 (already referred to, p. 350), and which may well have prompted this tribe to exclude the groups of 10 in favour of smaller groups.

At the beginning of this discussion, I made use of two Crow myths ($M_{467}$–$M_{468}$, p. 335), considered from the point of view of their arithmetical properties. I do not propose to dwell on them further, except to emphasize that, in one myth, the hero triumphs over a chief who is appropriating all the food and all the women and that, in the other, he triumphs over 7 brothers and 3 cannibalistic sisters, all 3 of whom, except the youngest, have toothed vaginas (Lowie 3, pp. 132, 167–8). These myths, therefore, postulate a homology between a man who appropriates women and food, women who destroy men, and cannibals. The last named are Thunderbirds (they are cannibalistic buffaloes in the parallel Mandan versions already quoted – $M_{469a,b}$ – and to which I shall return, pp. 371–2).

So, once again, the Sioux versions bring us back to our starting point and, in this connection, we cannot but be struck by the fact that the Crow, who have a myth about the origin of scalping similar to those of the Blackfoot and the Dakota, also tell a story about a scar-faced man in terms which are extraordinarily close to those of the myths about the origin of seasonal periodicity, already encountered in Menomini mythology:

$M_{485}$. *Crow. 'Red-Hair'*

Before accepting a suitor, a young girl demanded that he should bring her some of Red-Hair's hair. The hero set off and encountered supernatural protectors, whose help he obtained in exchange for the gift of different species of deer (or animals considered as deer in the native zoological system): wild sheep, elk, deer or American antelopes. A white-tailed deer-woman [*Dama virginiana*] and a female ant (cf. $M_{480a,b}$) helped him to disguise himself as a girl, and the wolverine changed him into a woman.

By turning into an ant, the hero slipped through Red-Hair's guards, who were, in order, the crane, the coyote, dogs, the wolf and the snake. He resumed his female form and proposed to Red-Hair, who married him/her, in spite of the fact that his brothers had warned him against the so-called woman, who had a scar on 'his' arm and a man's smell.

Taking advantage of the fact that 'her' husband was asleep, the false woman killed him and cut off his hair, leaving him bald. Having once again assumed male form, he fled. The brothers pursued the hero who escaped with the help of protectors, stationed all along the way. He gave Red-Hair's hair to his future wife and their marriage was celebrated (Lowie 3, pp. 141–3).

Let us now look at the other story:

### $M_{486}$. Crow. 'Scarface'

There was once an Indian who had fallen into the fire while playing when he was a little boy. He hated the burnt half of his face and decided to go away. Supernatural protectors made him swear to ask for help from an eagle who lived a long way away. The bird promised to help him on condition that he protected the young eaglets from water spirits who were devouring them one after the other. The hero agreed to do so and the eagle introduced him to the Sun, whose children cured him by means of a magic looking-glass, and to whom he taught several games as a demonstration of his thanks. After twenty days,[3] the Sun sent his guest back to the eagle, making him promise that, henceforth, he would look straight at the Sun without making faces.

The eagle warned the hero that fog would soon descend, heralding the attack by the water-spirits. A monster rose out of the water and the hero killed him by hurling red hot stones into his mouth. The monster was a 'long otter', a mythic creature which replaces horned or hairy snakes in Crow demonology. The thunder took its corpse away.

When the eaglets had grown up, the Sun ordered the eagle to make his son take the hero back to his home. After the first snow-fall, the bird put the man on his back and returned with him to the village where he married the pretty young girl who had said she would take him as a sweetheart, if he did not have a burnt face. Henceforth, the hero had the power of predicting changes in the weather (Lowie 3, pp. 152–6).

[3] This is the period during which the sun and moon move across the sky, one behind the other, cf. Hoffman, pp. 209–10.

In this myth the hero, in alliance with the eagles, triumphs over a long otter and acquires the power to predict the weather, whereas, in another version ($M_{486b}$; Lowie 3, pp. 144–9), the water-spirits merely force him to resume his human state and to stop interfering in the great conflict between the upper and lower powers. In other words, as in Menomini mythology, the only means of humanizing the conflict, since it cannot be resolved, consists in the establishment or discovery of seasonal periodicity, embodied by a character who brings about changes in the weather ($M_{479}$), forecasts them ($M_{486}$), or is endowed with so many lives that he himself becomes a changing, periodic being ($M_{480}$).

It is clear, then, that from the beginning of this discussion we have been pursuing two lines of enquiry, corresponding to parallel or convergent mythic formulae. They have a common denominator in the form of a two-fold character – handsome on one side, ugly on the other – who, according to one formula, imposes alternation on over-numerous and opposed teams, or, according to the other formula, alternates with himself by changing sex, and, through the institution of scalping and war rites, regulates the relationships between formations of a new kind: between fellow-tribesmen and enemies, instead of between the supernatural powers of the upper and lower regions. In all cases, the teams form series which the myths set about totalizing or detotalizing. They totalize them, allocating a wife to each member of a family of ten brothers ($M_{473-477}$). They detotalize them by redistributing wives monopolized by one man ($M_{467}$), or by the sharing out of scalps taken from enemies. A scalp brought back makes possible marriage between members of the same tribe ($M_{480b}$, $M_{482-486}$), just as a scalp won back from enemies allows marriage with women foreign to the tribe ($M_{474-475}$).

So far, the detotalizing or retotalizing operations have concerned women, scalps, or both together. There remains to be examined a transformation belonging to the same group but in which, by reversing the Mûdjêkiwis cycle on the one hand, and the Red-Head cycle on the other, the detotalization and retotalization concern men.

### $M_{487}$. Oglala Dakota. 'Stone Boy' (1) [cf. $M_{489}$]

There were once four unmarried brothers who gave hospitality to an unknown female visitor. As she kept her face hidden in her robe, the youngest of the brothers changed into a bird in order to spy on her. He saw that her face was covered with hair. She was a sorceress, who coveted the scalps of the four brothers in order to finish her robe

GROUPS OF TEN 371

which was decorated with similar trophies. She succeeded in killing the three eldest, but the youngest brought them back to life after beheading the ogress.

A second female visitor, who was spied upon in the same way, was pure in heart and only wanted to make moccasins for the brothers. However, after a certain time, the latter disappeared one by one.

Now that she was the only person left on earth, the woman swallowed a small smooth pebble which fertilized her, and before long she gave birth to a son. When he grew up, he set off to look for his uncles and found their skeletons in front of a wicked sorceress's hut. She tried to kill him too, but his stone body made him invulnerable. He killed the old woman and brought his uncles back to life.

When winter came, the hero met some young girls who, assuming he would be crushed against the rocks, made him take part in a sliding competition on the snow-covered slopes. He killed the girls too. They were buffalo who had changed into women, and then, in order to be revenged, all the buffalo attacked the brothers. The brothers won the fight and this is how men came to obtain buffalo as game (Wissler 1, pp. 199–202; for an eastern version, cf. McLaughlin, pp. 179–97).

Although the scalp theme is present, the myth refers chiefly to winter hunting-rites. Among these same Dakota, the symbolism of the sacred pipe is, moreover, an illustration of the link between head-hunting and buffalo-hunting. The pipe represents a red untouchable virgin, who reduces her attackers to skeletons but who gives the buffalo to men who respect her, along with a calumet to be decorated with scalps: 'She directed them to bring in the scalps of their enemies and to celebrate the victory dance, eating the meat of the buffalo' ($M_{487b}$; Wissler 1, p. 203). This pipe, which was also called 'white robe', 'bowl' or 'shell', brings us back, as did $M_{487}$, to the Mandan myth ($M_{481}$) about the origin of a sacred robe which, according to the mythic narrative, is decorated with scalps but which in fact was covered with shells, as is clear from the name of the portable altar (Shell Robe Bundle), in which it was kept.

In the Mandan foundation myths concerning the rites of the winter hunt ($M_{469a,b}$, cf. above, p. 368), the hunt is also linked with the origin of scalping. A young and unlucky eagle-trapper has to win the head of an ogre whose hair is of four different colours. A white-tailed deer-woman (cf. $M_{485}$) rubs her naked body against his, thus changing him into a young girl, but she allows him to keep his own legs so as to remain a good runner. He (she) arrives at the home of the ogre, whose sister is a cannibalistic bird, and inveigles the ogre into marriage. At the first opportunity, the phoney woman kills her husband and cuts off his head. Then, pleading the onset of menstruation, she goes into seclusion and flees.[4]

After various adventures, during which he kills the cannibalistic sister and takes possession of her head, the hero meets three deer sisters [*Dama virginiana*; *Dama hemionus*; *Cervus* sp.], all with toothed vaginas, as well as a fourth sister, a harmless buffalo whom he marries. She protects him against her seven brothers, who are cannibalistic warrior-divinities. After seizing their magic weapons, he decides to go back to his own people.[5] His wife agrees to his departure, but warns him that jealousy will prompt her to kill the first four Indian women whom he subsequently marries. He, therefore, chooses women of socially inferior rank, who all die in turn, and only then the chief's daughter, although she had been offered to him by the father immediately on his return (Beckwith 1, pp. 149–54; Bowers 1, pp. 286–95). This jealous woman, the eleventh member of a group of ten, is an ambiguous creature, half buffalo, half-human who institutes recurrent widowhood: 'To this day it is believed that when a man loses many wives, it is due to the jealousy of the woman [in the myth]' (Bowers 1, p. 295). It should be remembered that, because of the material circumstances, winter hunting, which took place near the village and sometimes even inside it, had a domestic and almost endogamous connotation, from the sociological point of view, whereas summer nomadic hunting had adventurous, warlike and exogamous associations. This is why the foundation myths relating to

[4] It would be worth making a comparative study of the myths about winter-hunting belonging to the Plains Siouan. In an Omaha variant ($M_{469c}$; J. O. Dorsey 1, pp. 185–8), the Mandan ogre with four different shades of hair is replaced by four thunder-ogres, who have respectively white, red, yellow and green hair. On the other hand, in two Crow myths already referred to ($M_{467, 468}$), there is a character who is the protégé of a dwarf. The Mandan foundation myth relating to the winter hunting rite, which is known as 'the snow owl' rite, mentions that the protective bird is a dwarf ($M_{469}$; Bowers 1, p. 286) and, in the Crow myth $M_{468}$, the chthonian spirit's wife is an owl. The bird appears again in Hidatsa mythology, in the form of a chthonian spirit, but one clearly associated with summer hunting, because mention is made of the ritual known as 'Earth naming'. In the foundation myth of this ritual ($M_{469d}$; Bowers 2, pp. 433–4), three Indian women are saved by a stranger who treats them as sisters, whereas, in $M_{469}$, the three female strangers try to kill an Indian, using marriage as a pretext. On the subject of the symmetrical relationships between Mandan and Hidatsa myths dealing with winter hunting and summer hunting, cf. L.-S. 19.

[5] The acquisition of the magic weapons is the result of a deceptive choice, a theme that we encountered first in an Arikara myth, which also deals with the origin of scalping ($M_{439}$, p. 240) and of which there are Mandan and Hidatsa variants (Will 1, 2).

the winter hunting rites are concerned with the theme of jealousy: jealousy may assert its claims, as in $M_{469}$, or, on the contrary, it may have to yield before the Red Stick rites ($M_{463-465}$), in which the young men surrender their wives to the village elders. In parallel fashion, the foundation myth relating to the summer rites explains the origin of inconstancy: 'this was also the beginning of the custom of a man parting with his wife and child and thinking little about it' ($M_{462}$; Bowers 1, p. 381; cf. L.-S. 19).

In order to reassure the reader who may well be wondering where all this is leading, let me recall that Mûdjêkiwis, the eldest of 10 or 11 brothers (just as the heroine of $M_{469}$ is the youngest of 11 brothers and sisters), instituted menstrual periodicity through jealousy. Mûdjêkiwis is also an ambiguous character, at least in his functional aspect, since, there being no wife, it falls to him to keep house for the unmarried brothers. Almost all the versions indicate this, but the Cree variants ($M_{477a-d}$) do so more specifically. On greeting the unknown female visitor, Mûdjêkiwis joyfully exclaims: 'So now we won't have to sew for ourselves!' (Bloomfield 1, p. 230). Or else he explains the situation in these terms: 'I could not cook for them, and I could not provide my relatives with moccasins ...' (Skinner 8, p. 354). In certain myths he is presented as an idiot and a simpleton; in others, he alternates between bravado and cowardice. It is not difficult to find an element of comparison between the state of a widower and the situation in which a man finds himself when his wife is menstruating. But I propose to leave this question on one side for the moment.

Since the course of the argument has brought us back to the Mandan, it is preferable to give a recapitulation of their hunting rites, which make it possible to establish an additional link between all the myths under discussion. The Mandan and the Hidatsa had three major hunting rites: the Red Stick rite, to which I referred in connection with the foundation myth $M_{464-465}$ (p. 328), the Snow Owl rite, which has just been mentioned ($M_{469}$), and the Small Hawk rite, the foundation myth of which has also been described ($M_{462}$, p. 315). The first two are winter rites, and the third a summer rite. In spite of this difference, they can be arranged in a continuous series according to the place occupied in the myths by the Buffalo Woman, who acts as an invariant term. In $M_{464-465}$, the Buffalo Woman is a fellow-Indian who helps the Indians to conquer the 10 or 12 enemy villages – a threatening, compact and saturated entity, which they thin out by cutting off 100 heads. It has just been noted that, in $M_{469}$, the Buffalo Woman is an ambiguous creature, a mediator between an ambassador of the human species and her own family, consisting of homicidal sisters and war-like, cannibalistic brothers. In $M_{462}$, on the contrary, the Buffalo Woman is in league with her own people, and takes her human husband to live with them, thus exposing him to the gravest dangers:

WINTER $\begin{cases} \text{Red Stick:} & \textit{fellow-tribesmen}, \text{BUFFALO WOMAN} \dots \text{\textit{enemies}} \\ \text{Snow Owl:} & \textit{fellow-tribesmen} \dots \text{BUFFALO WOMAN} \dots \text{\textit{enemies}} \end{cases}$
SUMMER  Small Hawk: *fellow-tribesmen* ...... BUFFALO WOMAN, *enemies*

The transfer, thus accomplished, of the Buffalo Woman from the fellow-tribesmen's camp to that of the sworn enemies recalls another case of an identical kind of transfer (see above, p. 224). In the present instance it can be explained by the particular structure of each myth. The Red Stick makes success in war a function of success in hunting: it is thanks to the help given by the buffalo that the Indians conquer their enemies. The Snow Owl, also a winter hunting myth, retains the same formula, but reverses it: it is, in the first place, a myth about the origin of scalping; only after establishing this rite can the hero triumph over the Buffalo Woman's brothers, who at that time were warrior gods. As might be expected, the summer hunting foundation myth adopts a different view-point: after conquering the buffalo, the hero obtains agriculture into the bargain, thanks to the constancy of his wife who is the embodiment of it – in other words, thanks to her lack of jealousy. The Mandan and Hidatsa began hunting on the plains when the corn was knee-high, and sometimes they encountered enemy bands during these expeditions; they would return to the villages for the harvest. So, a complex system of rites and myths can be reduced to three formulae:

a) $\quad$ (war) $\quad = \quad f(\text{hunting})$
b) $\quad$ (hunting) $\quad = \quad f(\text{war})$
c) (agriculture) $\quad = \quad f-1 \, (\text{hunting} \equiv \text{war})$

If we now remember that, also in Mandan and Hidatsa mythology, a frog involuntarily becomes (through $M_{460, \, 461}$) the cause of a quarrel between the sun and moon, which in $M_{465}$ is instigated by a Buffalo Woman, we can grasp the operative value, within this mythological system, of an affinity between the Buffalo Woman and the frog; and this makes it all the easier to establish a link between the function of the one in the Mandan myths and of the other in the Menomini myths; both are mediators, the frog between winter and summer, thanks to the rain it causes, and the Buffalo Woman between hunting and war because of the scalps[6] she incites men to go hunting for, or the victorious capture of which will ensure them success when they come to hunt the Buffalo Woman herself and all her kin.

---

[6] For the relatedness of scalps and rain and dew, cf. L.-S. 5, pp. 249–50; Bunzel 3. p. 527; 1, pp. 674–89.

## 2   *Three Adornments*

We have thus found our way back to the quarrel between the sun and moon, but after following a long, roundabout route which allows us to understand why the myths which begin in this way link up the story either to the porcupine episode or to the theme of the groups of ten, but not to both at once. We already knew that the porcupine character represents seasonal periodicity in action, and we have learned since that the formula of the groups of ten excludes the actual existence of periodicity: for the latter to be introduced, the groups of ten have to give way to smaller totals. Consequently, in the one case the myths start off with periodicity; in the other, they start with its opposite and then set about generating periodicity.

In Part Four, I approached the study of the quarrel between the sun and moon through the Arapaho versions ($M_{425-428}$); it is significant, then, that Arapaho mythology should now provide the variants which will make it possible to wind up this long argument. These variants illustrate the two series, sometimes parallel and sometimes convergent, that I have classed under the respective headings of 'Red-Head' and 'Stone Boy'.

### $M_{488}$. *Arapaho*. 'Red-Head'

There was once a very handsome young man, but he was lazy and could not get up in the mornings. Sometimes he even stayed in bed all day. In the end, his father reluctantly decided to admonish him. But to no effect: the boy persisted in his laziness. However, he had secretly resolved to attack the cannibals that his father had told him about.

He went to make enquiries from an old woman, who told him that the cannibals lived a long way away towards the east. The hero set off. The first evening, he threw into the fire sinews he had brought with him and which, as they shrivelled up in the flames, made the earth contract, and this brought him nearer to his destination. The next day he repeated the same procedure. An old couple directed him to the spot where the cannibals' wife lived, and advised him to beg for her assistance. The wife yielded to his entreaties, allowed the hero to take on her physical appearance and sent him, in her stead, to her seven husbands on the pretext that he was bringing moccasins, which ensured him a warm welcome. The youngest husband pointed out, to no avail, that this woman had a man's arms.

The hero, while pretending to delouse the eldest brother, cut off his head and fled. Roused by their guardian geese, the other brothers went after him. He took refuge in his protectress's iron tent [sic]. His pursuers soon arrived and threatened her. She made as if to let them in, but shut the metal door again so quickly that it cut off their six necks (cf. M241). The woman kept her husband's head for herself, and allowed the hero to take the others. Their hair was a vivid red.

Having returned home during the night, the hero went silently to bed. The next morning his father was about to drive away the stranger who was occupying his son's bed, when he recognized him and welcomed him warmly. That was the end of the cannibals, but stories about them are still told to boys who sleep late in the morning (Dorsey-Kroeber, pp. 126–33; var. pp. 133–5).

I shall discuss this myth together with one illustrating the other series:

$M_{466}$. *Arapaho*. 'Light-Stone' (cf. above, p. 335)

Six brothers lived alone with their sister. One day the eldest decided to go and visit another camp-circle. On his way he discovered an unknown tent, in which an old woman was lying. She explained that she had a bad back and asked the traveller to tramp on her back to ease the pain. But the old woman's last rib stuck out like a spike and killed him. The sorceress staked the corpse to the ground with tipi pins, and she put the ashes from her pipe on his eyes, mouth and chest.

Each brother in turn underwent the same fate. Sad and lonely, their sister began a wandering life. One evening, she put into her mouth a small, round, translucent stone which had taken her fancy. Soon she gave birth to a son who, before long, grew up and was called Light-Stone. On seeing his mother weep, he decided to set off in search of the lost brothers. He arrived at the old woman's tent; she invited him to administer the usual treatment. But the hero's body was made of stone and it crushed that of the sorceress. He placed the corpse on a pile of burning logs and reduced it to ashes. Then he brought his six uncles back to life and all the family was reunited.

One day another old woman turned up, carrying a bag full of clothes and an iron digging stick. As she refused to open her bag in front of her guests, Light-Stone turned into a woodpecker and spied on her [cf. M₄₈₇]. He saw her spread out seven men's costumes and one woman's garment, the fringes of all of which were made of pubic hair. The sorceress was talking to herself, and he realized that she intended to kill him, as well as his mother and his uncles, in order to remove their pubic hair, which she needed to complete her embroidery-work.

On the pretext of sending her to dig up willow potatoes, they got the old woman out of the way and burnt her bag. Warned by the smoke, she came running back and managed to extract from the fire, with her iron stick, a head-dress decorated with two testicles and an iron shield, the leather cover of which was already burnt. Thus armed, she began fighting the young men: her opponents' arrows bounced back from the shield without wounding her. However, she fell dead when Light-Stone hit the centre of the two testes with an arrow. They burnt her corpse on the wood fire.

After these adventures, the family decided to join the tribe's main camp. An Indian soon began courting the sister, who married him and gave him a pretty little daughter. Light-Stone, for his part, won many hearts but could not decide to marry any one of the young girls who came to share his bed night after night [cf. M₄₈₄].

Excited by her elder brother's success, the sister fell in love with him. On several successive occasions, she passed herself off as one of his nocturnal visitors. The hero was surprised by the persistent silence of this particular partner and put a paint mark on her shoulder. On waking he recognized her, and was so ashamed that he stayed in bed all day. Children, who had somehow discovered what was going on, revealed the incestuous situation. When night came, Light-Stone went up onto a hill and bewailed his fate. Four times his mother tried to coax him to come home, but in vain. He resolved to cease being a human being and turned into a stone, because he thought that this was the only way he could prevent himself ever seeing his sister again [cf. M₄₈₁]. And, on the hill, he became a stone, so light that it could be seen from a distance (Dorsey–Kroeber, pp. 181–9).

At this point, I will merely recall in passing a Gros-Ventre version ($M_{470}$; Kroeber 6, pp. 97–100), which is shorter and appears to be intermediary between the Crow and Arapaho versions of the same myth ($M_{467}$, $M_{466}$): instead of running away from his sister, the hero rapes the wife of a chief, who is presumably the same chief as the one in $M_{467}$ since in that myth his main wife is similarly treated, in order to punish him for having appropriated all the marriageable girls, an action which, in respect of matrimonial alliances, constitutes an abuse which is the reverse of incest.

In connection with the medical treatment demanded by the sorceress in $M_{466}$, and mention of which can be found in other myths in areas as far away as Tierra del Fuego (Lothrop, pp. 100–101), it should be noted that the Arapaho belong to the Algonquin family, in which this kind of osteopathic cure was practised: 'If a child is born feet first he is gifted with curing powers for people with sore backs: they let him jump on the patient's back' (Speck 7, p. 80). The link up is all the more plausible in that, according to the myth, the deadly rib is the lowest one, that is, according to the Omaha, the one the head of the foetus rests against. Consequently the meat from this rib, as well as the foetus, are among the special taboos respected by one of the Omaha clans (Fletcher–La Flesche, p. 175). As for the abnormal birth feet first, it raises such vast problems that I shall refrain from embarking on them.

Nor do I propose to discuss the reference in the myths to iron objects – a tent, door or digging stick – since it is not known which native raw material was being replaced by iron; it was probably stone, which figures in other versions. From the functional point of view, it is obvious that iron stands in opposition to leather, as is indicated by the shield episode: one is heat-resistant, the other not. This reference to the distinctive properties of leather or skin, as well as the mention of pubic hair, which the Arapaho were not the only North American tribe to use, to make fringes for robes and leggings, leads on to a Dakota variant, more sophisticated than the other variant ($M_{487}$), and of which I give a much abridged version, limited to certain features of the whole:

$M_{489}$. *Oglala Dakota*. '*Stone Boy*' (2) [cf. $M_{487}$]

Four brothers lived all alone together, and so they did the woman's work. The eldest hurt his foot and noticed that his big toe was beginning to swell. He cut it open and took out a baby girl. When she grew up, she kept house for the unmarried brothers, who treated her like a sister. To stay with them, she refused all the many young men who proposed marriage.

The brothers disappeared one after the other. One day, the young girl was fertilized by a smooth, white pebble, which she had put into her mouth to soothe her thirst. Her son was born, and became a young man and she taught him everything. And although his flesh was as hard as stone, she was afraid he would go away and never return.

Moved by his mother's tears, the young man nevertheless decided to go in quest of his uncles. After a long and difficult journey, he discovered Iya's den. This was an ogre, who had changed into a little old woman, and who tried in vain to kill him. It was Iya who had killed his uncles in order to tan their skin. The hero brought them back to life, and successively fought the old woman who, in the course of the struggle, resumed the form of a giant. He next succeeded in reviving the ogre's innumerable victims by the thick smoke produced through burning the pubic hair with which his virgin brides had decorated his head-gear and moccasins at the time of his departure. Before returning to the camp with his uncles, the hero warned Iya that he was going to tread her arms out flat like a piece of dried skin. The ogre caught stone-boy's feet between his (her) teeth. The latter succeeded in freeing himself but lost a moccasin which could not be found, because in the meantime Iya had made himself (herself) invisible (Walker, pp. 193–203).

Let us pause to dwell for a moment on this myth, which is one of the finest, richest and most dramatic in the whole of American oral literature: I have resigned myself to summarizing it in such a way as to make it unrecognizable, being convinced that only a special study could do it justice. In uttering his curse against the ogre, the hero expresses himself in these terms: 'I will tread your head and arms out flat like a dried skin, and you shall remain forever out in this evil valley, where there is no tree, nor grass, nor water and where no living thing will ever come near you. The sun shall burn you, the cold shall freeze you. You shall feel and think and be hungry and thirsty but no one shall come to you' (*ibid.*, p. 202). Thus spread out to the farthermost confines of the horizon, the ogre is synonymous with a desert-like area, at the same time as he embodies seasonal extremes causing famine, which explains why, in other versions, he is represented as a devouring, cannibalistic monster, the god of gluttony (Beckwith 2, pp. 434–6; cf. the pretty little girl in the Mandan myth [M463], who proves to be an ogress personifying winter famine).

The same rhetorical device, which consists in comparing the earth to a mantle or robe is found in a Dakota version of the unmarried brothers' story, in which it is clearly stated that each brother personifies a wind (M489c: Walker, pp. 176–9. Cf. M489b,d; *ibid.*, pp. 173–6, 179–81; M489e: Beckwith 2, pp. 394–6). The unknown woman visitor marries the south wind. The eldest brother, the north wind, importunes her with his attentions. She hides under his cloak, which she stretches out to the far ends of the earth, and under which she remains a prisoner. Ever since, the north wind and the south wind have been engaged in a never-ending battle over the cloak: sometimes the cold wins, and the cloak freezes and hardens: sometimes the gentle heat of the south wind warms and softens it, and the woman can thrust her multicoloured adornments and finery up to the earth's surface.

This rather philosophical version, given by informants who were Siouan priests, throws light on the Algonquin versions of the Mûdjê-kiwis myth, at the end of which the brothers turn into winds, and in which the eldest, who has an unstable temperament and is by turns a braggart or a coward, represents the west wind in M475 (the Schoolcraft version in: Williams, pp. 124–34); his name, in Ojibwa, may mean 'the bad or sinister wind' (Skinner 14, pp. 49–50). Provided we make the adjustments rendered necessary by geographical distance and climatic differences, I would be tempted to compare this name with the one given to the equivocal sun called the sun of 'the week of the wind', in an Athapaskan myth of the Pacific coast (M471d, see above, p. 341), especially since the myth featuring the unmarried brothers exists in a distinct but clearly recognizable form in the same region, in Chinook mythology (Boas 5, pp. 172–5).

If the Dakota heroine personifying the earth decks her robe with adornments in spring, we should no doubt opt for a similar interpretation of an incident in the myths of the Great Lakes area which, on the basis of the recorded versions, could be read in several different ways. In M474, the heroine paralyses a chthonian bear by scattering in front of him the talismans she finds at the bottom of the leather pouch (a transformation of the cloak), which is tightly fastened round the neck of her brother's severed head. In M475a, on the other hand, the hero's brothers try to hand him over to the chthonian spirits, not only because he has lost a sacred arrow, but also because, in his haste, he has scattered the magic charms contained in his elder brother's bag. A previously mentioned Winnebago myth ($M_{484}$, see above, p. 367) tells how a princess from afar, while pursuing the hero to his village, loses all her garments one by one so that when she eventually arrives she is completely naked. Lastly, one of the heroes of the Dakota myth relating to winter hunting ($M_{487b}$; see above, p. 371) dies in an attempt to divest the red virgin of her clothes: his behaviour is similar to that of the north wind in $M_{489c}$, who, during his reign, divests his sister-in-law of her ornaments.

It was, therefore, no mistake to suppose (p. 356) that the strong versions of the Mûdjêkiwis myth also have a meteorological connotation, although it remains latent in the mythic texts. Contrary to what can be observed in the other versions, it concerns neither the return nor the conclusion of the storms ensured by the regular alternation of the seasons, nor the separation of the cosmic forces which is necessary if the alternation is to take place peacefully. Here, the connotation expresses the violent conflict between these forces. Within the quadripartite system, the structure of which I outlined above, leaving one space provisionally blank, it adequately illustrates the reverse of the theme: in the reverse of the opposite ($M_{475c-f}$), the male and female powers, associated respectively with west and east, separate from each other and return to the celibate state, whereas here male powers, associated respectively with the south and the north, fight incessantly over the same wife.

Other considerations too, in addition to those just put forward, confirm that, in spite of the superficial differences between them, all these myths are interlinked and belong to the same set. In a Dakota version about the origin of buffalo herds ($M_{489f}$; Schoolcraft in: Williams, pp. 34–8), the team of seven brothers who are killed by a giant is transformed into a team of six giants who kill the hero's parents. But whereas in the Scarface story, the man who kills the giant turns into a female seducer in order to achieve his ends, in the Dakota myth it is the last of the giants doomed to be killed who turns into a female seducer in order to escape his inevitable fate. Consequently we are again dealing with a structure involving four elements, the other two of which consist of the transformation of a giant into an old, homicidal sorceress, an antiseductive figure, or of a young woman into a giantess – when she spreads out her cloak until it covers the whole earth – to escape from a seducer ($M_{489c,d}$).

That is not all. In the story of Scarface, the hero, having turned into a woman, obtains the giant's head as a trophy. In $M_{489f}$, the giant, who has undergone the same metamorphosis, seizes a white feather, the hero's magic head-dress, thus causing the hero's transformation into a dog. I shall return to this episode in connection with certain Menomini versions (M$_{493a,b}$, p. 390 *et seq.*). Confining myself for the moment to the transformation: *trophy-head* ⇒ *feather head-dress*, I note that the hero of the Gros-Ventre myth (M$_{470}$) also wears a white feather on his head, and that the hero in M$_{481}$ (Mandan version: Beckwith 1, pp. 96–102; Hidatsa version: Bowers 1, pp. 370–73) is called 'Feather-on-Head'. A feather also adorns the head of the real sister in M$_{481}$, and of the adoptive sister in M$_{487}$, whereas the sister in M$_{489}$, a wicked sorceress, like the other two, has testicles attached to her head-dress. The fact that this is a transformation is clearly confirmed by one detail: to render his sister innocuous, the hero of M$_{481}$ has to aim his arrow at the central rib of the feather and split it down the middle, just as his counterpart in M$_{489}$ kills the sorceress by splitting the testicles apart. Lastly, the ogres live in the west (M$_{483}$) or in the east (M$_{488}$), in symmetrical myths which can also be seen to be akin through the fact that the hero, to make the earth shrink, uses the method of shrivelling thin strips of leather (sinew: see above, p, 201, n. 1), whereas, in other myths belonging to the same group, the heroine makes herself inaccessible by stretching out her leather robe to the ends of the earth.

The Oglala Dakota are close neighbours of the Arapaho to the north. On the southern side, the immediate neighbours of the Arapaho are the Kiowa, who have their own version of the story of Red-Head:

### M$_{490}$. *Kiowa. 'Red-Head'*

An Indian had an only son who could not manage to wake up in the mornings. 'When you have killed a man with hair dyed red', his father said to him, 'you may stay in bed as long as you want.' The boy set out to look for the seven red-headed men. An old woman helped him to dress as a woman. He managed to get past the birds who guarded the ogres. The eldest brother fell in love with the pretty young girl, and in order to put her to the test ordered her to dry some meat, for only women know how to carry out this operation. The hero threw the meat on to an ant-hill, as the old woman had told him to do, and the insects went to work and dried the meat. The meat was so nicely prepared, without any cuts or irregularities, that the eldest ogre refused to listen to his brothers who maintained that the woman had a man's elbow.

On the pretext of searching her husband's head for lice, the false woman stabbed him and cut off his head. The birds gave the alarm. The brothers pursued the hero as far as the hut where his old protectress lived. The latter said she would hand over the murderess who was pretending to pull back. But she shut the door so quickly that she cut off the six heads. The old woman picked them up and took off the scalps. She told the young man that she had wanted these scalps for a long time. She divided them into two lots, keeping half for herself and giving half to the young man. The hero returned home during the night and fixed each scalp on the end of a rod. When the Indians woke up, they saw a shining red light; it was the hair from the scalps. Even the sun looked golden-red. The father told his son that from then on he could stay in bed as long as he wanted. The guardian birds flew away, because there was nobody for them to watch over, and there have been no birds since at the ogres' camp (Parsons 2, pp. 78–80).

At the risk of inflicting a somewhat wearisome intellectual exercise on the reader, I have constantly had to move back and forth between the story of the Red-Heads and the one about Stone-Boy. The reason is that, from tribe to tribe, the two series recur in strictly parallel form or undergo transformations through crossing-over or translocation. I now propose to recapitulate the argument to clarify the relationships.

It will have been noticed that the Arapaho and Kiowa versions of Red-Head are transformations of the initial situation described in the other versions. The hero, instead of being a bashful lover, becomes a lazy son. Two other differences can be added to this first one: the bashful lover's face is handsome on one side and ugly on the other, because of a disfiguring scar or burn; the lazy son's face is so faultlessly handsome that his parents are intimidated by his beauty: 'for he had such a splendid face the parents would not bother him ... for everyone thought so much of him' (Dorsey–Kroeber, pp. 126–7).

Secondly, the rôle of the scalp-obsessed woman is transferred from a fellow-tribeswoman (the hero's fiancée) to a female stranger (a solitary old woman in $M_{490}$, or the wife of the cannibals in $M_{488}$). This stranger who may even be an enemy at the same time as she is the hero's accomplice, plays the ambiguous rôle which seems to be an invariant feature of the group, but which in other myths devolves on one or several brothers, reduced to acting as housewives ($M_{473-477}$), and one of whom even gives birth to a child ($M_{489}$); or on a hero with a two-sided face, who becomes half a woman (since his incomplete transformation nearly gives him away).

In the Arapaho and Kiowa myths, as in those of the Mandan, the rôle is played by an ambiguous protectress. The resemblance suggests that the Arapaho and Kiowa versions should be placed in the second of the categories I formulated on p. 374 for the classification of the Mandan hunting rites. From which can be concluded that these versions make success in hunting (which, however, they do not mention) dependent on success in war, as if they were asserting by pretermission that the latter inevitably produces the former. It is not at all surprising, then, that the conqueror of the red-headed cannibals should allow himself to get up late!

Through the ant episode, the Kiowa version links up with the Blackfoot versions of the same myth ($M_{480}$), although in the Kiowa myth the insects are masters of dried meat, not of quillwork. For meat to dry in the open air without being salted or sprinkled with pickling brine, it had to be cut into thin, even slices, without gashes or irregularities. This delicate operation, while applying to meat (which eventually begins to look like leather), is similar to the preparation of skins for tanning and to the removal of the scalp from a dead warrior's head. And a scalp can be said to be similar in kind both to dried meat and to a precious skin. This is explicitly stated in $M_{474}$, where enemies claim to be reducing the head of a loved one to the condition of dried meat (Williams, p. 53).

It will be remembered that the Blackfoot versions not only invert a Menomini myth ($M_{479}$; cf. above, pp. 363–6) but also themselves occur in two forms, one straight the other inverted. $M_{480a}$ is concerned with the origin of quillwork, while $M_{480b}$ deals with the origin of scalping. Consequently, it can be inferred that native thought posits a correlational and oppositional connection between scalps and embroidered skins. Furthermore, one cannot but be struck by the fact that the myths refer chiefly to embroidered leggings and moccasins. Thus, the opposition between the technique of scalping (a scalp has its own natural adornment of hair) and that of embroidery (which adorns a skin artificially with the 'hair' of the porcupine, so that the animal, too, is scalped) is accompanied by another opposition between the feet and the head, the high and the low. When the hero of $M_{489}$ loses one of his moccasins in the ogre's jaw, he has, as it were, had his foot scalped.

Another internal opposition, this time in the Arapaho myths, corresponds point by point, to the opposition between scalping and quillwork in the Blackfoot myths. $M_{488}$ is a myth about the origin of head-hunting, but $M_{466}$, in which an ogress collects pubic hair instead of scalps, is concerned with a third kind of trophy. It follows that scalps, quill-embroidery and pubic hair fringes form a system. The scalp is a trophy consisting of human skin to which hair is still attached; the fringes are a trophy made from human pubic hair added to animal skin (garments made from deer-skin); quillwork is a trophy made from animal hair added to animal skin:

|  | scalp | fringe | embroidery |
|---|---|---|---|
| (hair) attached/added | + | — | — |
| (skin) human/animal | + | + | — |

It should be added that the scalps were taken from men, the embroidery was the work of women, while the pubic hair could come from either sex. It is well-known that most American Indians removed all body hair; but before doing so, the young men would organize competitions to see who could display the longest body hairs. The Dakota myth, $M_{489}$, tells how the young girls, to whom the hero had promised marriage, decorated him with their pubic hair. This provides a new dimension to complete the system I am now describing; if, as was shown in Part Four, porcupine quills constitute a periodic trophy on the temporal axis, on the spatial axis (and on the temporal axis, too, since there was a war season which coincided with the nomadic hunting season), the other two trophies have periods of opposite cycles: the scalps come from *distant* enemies; the pubic hair from the body of the actual person wearing the fringes, or from the bodies of very *close* women relatives, such as sisters, wives or fiancées. One type of trophy, then, is exogamous, the other endogamous, and so, in an unexpected context, we rediscover the dialectic of the near and the far, which I am using as a guide-line throughout this work, as well as its temporal mediation, thanks to the periodicity of the quills, since it reproduces, in terms of ornamentation, the periodicity of the major cosmic cycles, which served as our first approach to the general problem.

I would like to digress here for a moment to elucidate a point of detail which is not without its importance. It will have been noticed that all these myths concerning the origin of scalping assign a special place to deer: they are helpful in Crow mythology ($M_{485}$), hostile in Mandan mythology ($M_{469}$) and ambiguous in the Dakota myths, in which the hero wins the scalping knife but loses the girl who had offered to marry him as a reward for this feat; she changes into a wood deer and disappears – hence the alimentary taboo on deer meat ($M_{483}$; Beckwith 2, p. 405, cf. above, p. 367). As it happens, deer also have a relevant function in relation to the triple system of trophies I have just defined. Throughout North America, from the Alaskan Eskimo in the west to the Algonquin of the mouth of the Saint Lawrence and New England in the east, and including the tribes of the basin of the Mackenzie River and the Great Lakes area, there existed a kind of deer-hair embroidery, using mainly the hair of the elk and the caribou, which must have dated from very ancient times, since it is also present in Siberia (Speck 9; Driver–Massey, p. 324 and map No. 110; Turner). This practice involved pulling out the hairs from their natural base, in the same way as quills were removed from the porcupine and pubic hair from the human body. But the northern Indians sometimes left the hair on the skins in order to make the adornments known as roach head-dresses, at which the Sauk were the most adept, and which they supplied even to distant tribes (Skinner 9, part 3, pp. 127–31). These crests of dyed hair, which replaced the natural hair removed from the shaved heads of the wearers, were virtually wigs and therefore inversions of scalps. The Kansa were probably aware of the connection, since they stipulated that the head-dress should be worn to celebrate the taking of the first scalp (Skinner 12, pp. 752, 757).

Along one axis, these deer-hair adornments were symmetrical with scalps and, along another, with pubic hair fringes. In a symbolical yet quite intimate way, the fringes effected a conjunction between the sexes, when the warrior wore a garment displaying pubic hair taken from a close female relative: a sister, wife or fiancée. The deer-hair adornments seemed chaste by comparison. This being so, they should perhaps be compared to the 'marriage blankets', or robes that were also sacred objects among the Algonquin of the Great Lakes area. These were made from deer hide (buckskin), beautifully painted and ornamented, and with a single perforation in the middle. Their purpose was to prevent contact between the skin of males and females during copulation. Only certain persons were granted the right to possess these robes, and they rented them out in exchange for some form of payment. If the user soiled the robe which had been entrusted to him, an indemnity was demanded by the owner. These sacred objects, which were used by the Menomini, Sauk, Mascouten, Ojibwa and Shawnee – and sometimes had little bells attached to them, so that the time and circumstances of their use could not pass unnoticed – were thought to prevent men being weak in battle and to obviate any deformity in children conceived with their help (Skinner 4, p. 30; 9, part I, p. 32; 10, part I, p. 37). Thus these marriage blankets prevented the two misfortunes the threat of which is suggested by the 'deer' myths: a later-riser would be a poor warrior and hunter; and Scarface's deformity dated from childhood.

In the case just referred to, the deer-skin caused disjunction of the sexes, in the sense that it alone could come into contact with the two partners, but not they with each other. In support of this interpretation, it may be recalled that the hero of a Crow myth ($M_{485}$) persuades a doe/protectress to change him into a woman by rubbing her naked body against his, and that, in a Dakota myth ($M_{483}$), the transformation of a woman into a deer disjoins a couple who were to have been conjoined by the conquest of the scalping knife. It would seem, therefore, that certain Siouan tribes formulate in their myths the same notions as are expressed in rites by their Algonquin-speaking neighbours. I have already, in another work, drawn attention to such instances of symmetry (L.-S. 5, ch. XII; 19), and I now propose to put forward an additional argument to substantiate them.

Against the above interpretation it might be objected that, among the Plains Sioux, and more especially among the Dakota, deer played an opposite rôle to the one I am trying to attribute to them. Fraternities of dancers and magicians, representing various species of deer, specialized in amorous intrigues, of which these animals were supposed to be the patrons (Skinner 14, p. 264; Wissler 6, pp. 87–8). However, in societies where the seduction of married women was tantamount to an institution, it is clear that 'women stealing', of which the deer associations claimed the monopoly, took place at the expense of lawful marriages. So, the conjunction of lovers encouraged by the deer was the counterpart of a *temporary* disjunction affecting husband and wife. On the sociological level, the result remains comparable to the *partial* disjunction which the use of marriage blankets created between the same spouses, to the advantage, as it were, of a deer, represented in a form at once metonymical and metaphorical by its skin alone, but a skin rendered seductive through being sumptuously adorned. The same complex of problems is to be found at the other extremity of the continent, among the Californian Hupa, who merely gave it another form. They too were deer hunters, and refrained from any sexual intercourse with their wives during the hunting season (Goddard, p. 323, n.).

Let us return to the Arapaho. The myth which enabled me to establish the existence of a triple set of adornments – scalps, quillwork and pubic-hair fringes – does more than merely effect a transformation between the first term and the third. It also introduces an episode, which is missing from the other versions of the Stone Boy story, and which is concerned with the incestuous schemes of the hero's sister and his subsequent metamorphosis into stone.

However, two of the myths I have previously used contain this episode at least in embryonic form. The hero of $M_{466}$ decides to change into a stone, in order, so he maintains, to avoid ever seeing his sister again (see above, p. 378). The cannibalistic sister in the Mandan myth ($M_{481}$) gives the opposite reason for wanting to scalp her brother and attach the trophy to her robe on the vacant place over her left breast: 'I have always loved my brother. On this vacant spot I wish to place his scalp so as to have him always with me' (Beckwith 1, p. 99). Less explicitly, $M_{474}$ had put forward the same argument: the hero, contaminated by his sister's menstrual blood and eaten up by gangrene, tells the young girl that he will die, unless she cuts off his head and keeps it near her. Thus, both the brother himself ($M_{474}$) and the sister ($M_{481}$) see his transformation into a trophy-head as the only means of their remaining together.

The recurrence of the theme would seem to make it possible to postulate the existence of a group. In a good way or a bad way, the trophy-head or scalp of the man conjoins a brother and a sister, who are disjoined by the transformation into stone of the same man, contaminated in one context by menstrual blood, in the other by an incestuous embrace. It follows that $M_{466}$ carries out two operations on the other myths of the group: it *transforms* the scalp into a pubic hair fringe, then, in a second stage, it reverses it into *stone*; but this is no ordinary stone.

In telling the story of the incestuous sister, $M_{466}$ introduces nothing new. The plot is borrowed from the pan-American origin myth relating to the sun and the moon ($M_{165-168}$; $RC$, pp. 296–7; $M_{358}$, see above, p. 42; $M_{392}$, p. 94), in which the sister stains the face of her nocturnal visitor who, once he is discovered, is changed into the moon with its spots. It is nevertheless clear that $M_{466}$ reverses the rôles in the story it has borrowed: it is the sister and not the brother who takes the initiative, with the result that it is her shoulder (and not his face) which is stained. So, in order for the aetiological intention to be respected, it is the sister who should change into the moon (and not into the sun, as in the other versions). $M_{466}$, however, adopts a different solution: it leaves the sister aside and changes the brother into an anti-moon. The stone placed at the top of a hill, and so light in colour that it can be seen from afar, corresponds to the idea of a moon that is terrestrial instead of celestial, and aperiodic instead of periodic, and all the more since the hero of whom it is a transformation was himself conceived through the operation of a smooth, translucid, rounded stone.

But, if the final episode of $M_{466}$ brings into play an implicit opposition: *moon*/(*stone* = *moon*$^{-1}$) which in turn is derived from the explicit opposition: *sun*/*moon*, which rightly belongs to other myths, of which $M_{466}$ is no more than a transformation, we can construct the triad: *sun, moon, white stone* and see it as standing in opposition to the triad of adornments that we were previously discussing.

As it happens, the central and eastern Algonquin have a myth which, as it were, hooks one triad onto the other, and which echoes even into Mandan mythology, where I have already mentioned an instance of it ($M_{458}$, p. 297). This is the story of the young boy who is furious with the sun for having singed his beautiful robe, or done him some other mischief. He decides to ensnare the sun and to hold him prisoner. Of the twenty-one versions recorded by Luomala, seven describe him as using a noose made with *one of his sister's pubic hairs* to capture the luminary, which is the sun in all versions, except for one single instance where it is the moon. Apart from the Dog-Rib myth, these versions all come from neighbouring communities, Cree, Ojibwa, Menomini, and Naskapi ($M_{491a,b}$: Skinner 1, pp. 102–4; Cresswell, p. 404; $M_{492a,b}$: Schoolcraft in: Williams, pp. 256–7; Jones 1, p. 376; $M_{493a,b}$: Hoffman, pp. 181–2; Skinner–Satterlee, pp. 357–60; $M_{494}$: Speck 4, p. 26). I propose to pay close attention only to the Menomini versions, which throw light on several problems already touched upon.

$M_{493a}$. *Menomini.* 'The sun caught in a snare' (1)

A family of Indians consisted of 6 persons: the father, the mother, and 4 children, 3 sons and 1 daughter. The 3 sons decided to go hunting 3 days in succession: they brought back 1 bear but the father said he used to get 2 bears: then 2 bears, but the father said he used to get 3 bears; then 3 bears and the father said he used to get 4 ... Leaving the youngest brother at home, the 2 elder sons started off to hunt, and were captured by the bears. The father and then the mother set off to look for them, but were killed by the bears.

The youngest son remained alone with his little sister. He tried to find his elder brothers, and arrived at the bears' abode, where he killed them by burning them to death, thanks to the help of the animals' sister whose attitude was ambiguous, to say the least. And he restored his brothers to their former condition, for they had been given bears' paws and legs.

As a reward for these achievements, the hero's sister made him a fine robe of beaver skins, trimmed with coloured porcupine quills. But one day, the boy fell asleep while the sun was high in the sky and the heat of the rays burned spots upon the robe. The boy wept violently, and asked his sister for one of her pubic hairs, and made a snare with it which half strangled the sun. It became dark. Several animals came along in response to the sun's cry for help. Finally, a mouse succeeded in cutting the string (Hoffman, pp. 175–82).

The story goes on to relate the elder brother's adventures, which are more or less the same as those of the Dakota hero in $M_{489f}$ (see above, p. 382). It will be remembered that this Dakota myth is an inversion of the Scarface story. The differences between the Menomini and Dakota versions lie mainly in the fact that the Menomini hero marries two wives, one wicked, the other good, who replace two similarly defined sisters in the Dakota version, who are respectively the wives of the usurping ogre and of the hero. In addition, the Dakota hero is changed for a time into a dog; in the Menomini version, a dog brings the hero back to life, in other words, changes the hero, who has become a corpse, back into his former self.

In another Menomini version ($M_{493b}$: Skinner–Satterlee, pp. 357–60), the hero has no brothers. After his parents have been killed by the bears, he remains alone in the world with his elder sister, who acts as his instructress. In the absence of brothers, the hero has a pet eagle who advises him to use a pubic hair not to make, but to bait, a snare with which to capture the sun, who has been guilty of burning his blanket. In a third version (ibid., pp. 360–61), a hawk proves to be an even more effective ally.

The myth goes on to describe the destruction of the bears, who live at the bottom of a lake, then relates the story of the women in the eastern sky, almost in the same terms as those already quoted ($M_{475c}$, see above, p. 347). It is clear, then, that at least in Menomini mythology, there is a definite link between the myth featuring the ensnared sun and the cycle featuring the groups of ten. This empirical connection confirms the validity of the method I am using, since the same conclusion had already been arrived at by a process of deductive reasoning.

The first version, in which the respective ages and rôles of the brother and sister are reversed, also refers us back to the cycle of ten, but indirectly, through the original way in which it deals with the problem of the arithmetical total. The hunter-brothers in the myth can choose between two routes, one leading to the right, the other to the left. On the first day, the two elder brothers took the road to the right: they encounter a bear who kills the eldest brother; along the road to the left, the youngest brother finds nothing. On the second day, the brothers adopt the same procedure; the two elder brothers find a bear which kills the second brother, while the third brother, who has taken the road to the left kills a bear. On the third day, all three brothers are together where the two roads meet, and each of them kills a bear (the youngest by himself first of all, then the two older ones, then all three acting in concert). But although the number of bears increases by one unit per day, the father complains every time that there is one short. We are dealing, then, with a series made up of actual numbers and virtual numbers (expressed by the father's desire): $1$, $[1 \, (+1)]$, $2$, $[2 \, (+1)]$, $3$, $[3 \, (+1)]$, a series which runs parallel to that of the successful hunters: (1st, o, o), (o, 2nd, 3rd), [(3rd), (2nd, 1st), (3rd, 2nd, 1st)]. The variable distribution of the brothers along the two roads adds a geometrical coordinate to the two preceding coordinates, both of which are arithmetical in character, but one relating to the cardinal number, the other to the ordinal number.

The rôle of the tame eagle in the second version is particularly worthy of attention, since, as I have said, this version includes the story of the women of the eastern sky which, in Bloomfield's account (3, p. 469), ends abruptly with the releasing of an eagle and the formulation of a taboo on keeping eagles in captivity. Let us pause for a moment to consider this point.

The Menomini, who are descendants of the oldest established Algonquin group in the Great Lakes area, and whose language also appears to be the most isolated (Callender), used to have a complex cosmology. They believed in the existence of four levels on either side of the earth's surface. Bald eagles and other birds of prey reigned over the first of the upper worlds, golden eagles and white swans over the second, thunderers over the third, and the sun over the fourth and last. In the other direction, that is, under the earth, there came first of all horned snakes, the masters of the first of the lower worlds, then, in order, large deer, panthers and bears – the masters of the second, third and fourth worlds, respectively. The term 'panthers' referred to mythic

Figure 35. Menomini 'panthers'. (From Skinner 14, pl. LXXI, p. 263. The smallest pattern represents an ordinary puma.)

creatures (Figure 35), similar to pumas but horned like buffalo (Skinner 4, pp. 81, 87; 14, pp. 31, 263).

In the Hoffman versions, which run together in a long saga myths which occur as separate stories in other contexts, the fight against the chthonian bears, which the hero wins with the help of his dog, is followed by a fight with the sun in which, according to $M_{493b}$, the hero is victorious thanks to his tame eagle. Next comes an account of the eldest brother's adventures among the large deer, contrasting versions of which are to be found in the Hoffman (pp. 186–96) and Skinner and Satterlee (pp. 399–403) collections: in the latter version, the man triumphs over the caribou in alliance with the moose; in the former, the man triumphs over the moose in alliance with the elks. But each time the conquered people changes into the homonymous zoological species. Last come the adventures of the youngest brother who is pursued by bears: he escapes from them and the exhausted and hungry monsters resign themselves to retaining their animal state (Hoffman, pp. 196–9).

It is as if the myths sometimes effect a coalition between humans and real or mythical animals and sometimes set them in opposition to each other, to carry out a series of operations producing various balanced states of the cosmos. A human plus an eagle triumphs over the sun, who occupies the highest position in the upper world; but the sun, plus the mouse or the mole, which are weak chthonian animals living just under the surface of the ground, triumphs over humans. A human plus a dog (the position of which on the earth is symmetrical with the mouse's position below the earth) triumphs over the bears who occupy in the lower world a position which is symmetrical with that of the sun in the upper world. Whereas the addition (*human + eagle*) results in the sun being dominated (cf. $M_{486a}$), the subtraction (*human − eagle*) leads to reconciliation with the thunderers, as is very explicitly indicated in $M_{475c}$. Thus, the eagle, which (contrary to the custom of other tribes) must not be tamed, so that there should be no encroachment on the first two of the upper worlds of which the bird is master, forms a correlational and oppositional pair with the dog, which humans can turn into their domestic animal, thus encroaching on the first of the lower worlds, where the horned snakes have a dog as their servant.

In order to get a closed group, it would be necessary to include the myths featuring panthers. I shall not attempt to do so, because they seem exceptionally complex and difficult to isolate. It is better to defer discussion of the problem, while offering a few indications to future research-workers of the way in which it might be approached. There exist two versions of a Menomini myth in which panthers play an important part ($M_{493c}$: Skinner–Satterlee, pp. 317–27; $M_{493d}$: Bloomfield 3, pp. 469–83). Curiously enough, this myth inverts almost all the themes I have listed: the scalp or head captured by enemies is changed into legs; the robe imprudently exposed to the sun and burnt is replaced by garments which are put away so as to be protected from bad weather; the sun, instead of being trapped with the result that darkness spreads over the world, is slowed down in its course by the hero in order to prolong daylight ... The theme of jealousy appears at the end of the myth, as an explanation of the dangers to which the hero has been exposed. We thus rediscover, in a symmetrical form, the Mandan foundation myth relating to summer hunting ($M_{462}$), in which a jealous buffalo-woman lures her human husband to the abode of her own people in order to expose him to the gravest dangers; here, however, jealous sisters pursue the hero to the abode of his own people, to be precise, to the house of his grandfather, who is just as homicidally disposed as the buffalo woman's kinsfolk in the other myth. In other respects, $M_{493c,d}$ reproduces $M_{489f}$, but we know that the latter myth itself occupies an inverted position within the group as a whole.

These peculiarities of the Algonquin 'panther' myths present an interesting problem. It will be remembered that I reduced the Plains porcupine redaction to an inversion of the Algonquin myths about the animal, an inversion made necessary by the absence or scarceness of the porcupine in the Plains, where the myths transform it from a symbolic into an imaginary animal. The Menomini were in a similar situation in respect of buffaloes as the Mandan or Arapaho with regard to porcupines: they were not unacquainted with buffaloes, but had to go a long way away in order to hunt them (Skinner 14, p. 120). Consequently, we may wonder if the chthonian panthers with buffalo horns are not a transposition, on the imaginary level, of the buffaloes which were exotic animals for the Menomini, just as the celestial porcupine in the Plains myths is a transposition of an animal which is absent from that area, but real and terrestrial elsewhere. This would make it comprehensible why a Menomini myth about panthers should be an inversion of a Mandan myth about buffalo-hunting, just as certain Plains myths are an inversion of myths of the Great Lakes area about porcupine-hunting.

Like all the myths so far examined, the myth about the ensnared sun is concerned with the establishment of a certain kind of periodicity. This characteristic is brought out prominently in numerous versions. The periodicity is seasonal in Bûngi mythology where the sun and the hero agree about the length of winter, and also in Chipewyan mythology, where the sun agrees to lengthen the days which are too short. More often, daily periodicity, which has been threatened by the reign of eternal night, is restored when the sun is set free (Montagnais, Ojibwa, Cree, Menomini, Fox, Iowa, Omaha). Even the Naskapi version ($M_{494}$), which seems at first sight to be a deviation, falls into place when interpreted in this way. This is the version in which the moon is trapped, instead of the sun. However, the myth states explicitly that the moon and the sun formerly travelled across the sky together: consequently, perpetual daylight then prevailed. In relation to the other versions, and considering that they too are concerned with ensuring the regular alternation of day and night, the myth respects the following transformation:

$$\left[ \left( \text{Ensnared sun} \right) \Rightarrow \left( \text{Ensnared moon} \right) \right] \quad \overset{f}{=} \quad \left[ \left( \begin{array}{c} \text{danger of} \\ \text{perpetual} \\ \text{night} \end{array} \right) \Rightarrow \left( \begin{array}{c} \text{danger of} \\ \text{perpetual} \\ \text{day} \end{array} \right) \right]$$

These general properties must not cause us to lose sight of the fact that this myth was introduced on the basis of those few versions, in which the hero makes a snare with pubic hair. I do not propose to broach the problem raised by the existence of this story in the myths of the South Sea Islands, which often use the same terms; several versions recorded in Tahiti and the Tuamotu archipelago specify that the pubic hair is taken from a close female relative – mother, sister or wife (Luomala, pp. 26–7). It is for specialists in Polynesian mythology to determine whether these versions lend themselves to an interpretation analogous to the one I am putting forward or whether, in the two different areas, similar elements are being used in different combinatory systems.

However, if we limit ourselves to the American data, we cannot ignore the fact that Luomala (p. 18), after studying the distribution area of the variants, concludes that the pubic hair theme, which presents this type of hair as being preferable to any other substance, must constitute a recent development, as must also the hero's anger at the sun's destruction of his robe. But this is not the first time that structural analysis finds itself unable to endorse the conclusions reached by the historical method; we had a previous instance in connection with the myth about the wives of the sun and moon. It is clear that, in my interpretation, the pubic hair snare occupies a fundamental position, a point I will not try to justify by conjectural history. I am struck not so much by the relative rarity of the theme and its concentration near the hypothetical centre of the diffusion, as by the frequent presence of a sister of the hero. This is a feature of fifteen out of the twenty-six versions, and in two others the sister is replaced by a mother. Unlike the practitioners of the historical method, I cannot accept the idea that myths might contain gratuitous and meaningless themes, especially when the same detail is given a prominent place in several versions. The persistent reference to the sister, which is at once an instance of periphrasis, synecdoche and litotes, draws attention to, at the same time as it discreetly veils, a tenuous but infinitely significant product of her body. In fact, the themes of the singed robe and the pubic hair snare are the two elements which make it possible to work out the interconnections between a vast body of myths so as to show that they form a coherent system.

I do not propose to discuss the robe episode in detail, although it is no doubt significant that, with one exception, the versions which mention what the robe is made of should specify deer fur or deer hide (see above, p. 387 *et seq.*), or birds' feathers, birds being the 'watchers' or guardians of the solar ogres in several myths already discussed. The choice of the pubic hair, which is often tenaciously insisted upon in spite of the sister's frequent reluctance to part with it, is the essential point in relation to the fact that, according to fourteen versions, the sun's capture was followed by a long night (Luomala, p. 11). The myth is referring, then, to a disjunction between the sun and the earth and certain versions explain the disjunction by the use of a pubic hair. But we already know that the scalp plays the reverse rôle of conjoiner of the sun and the earth: the first scalps came from ogres whose hair was as red as fire and emitted a glow which intensified and embellished the light of day ($M_{490}$). Unlike the Mandan and the Hidatsa – in whose mythology the system undergoes a partial transformation for reasons I have indicated (pp. 285, 293, 307–8) and shall elucidate in the last part of this volume – the other tribes of the Siouan family as well as the central Algonquin regarded the scalp as the symbol of their alliance with the sun: 'It is in his honour that battles are fought and scalps taken ... The [Menomini] warrior licked the blood while the scalp was fresh to symbolize the devouring of the enemy by the sun. The old men say that all men who are killed in battle are devoured by the sun' (Skinner 4, pp. 79, 116; 11, p. 309).

It results from the foregoing that, within the category of trophies, pubic hair connotes the disjunction of the sun and humanity, whereas the scalp connotes their conjunction. It is thus possible to consolidate the two triads the triad of cosmic objects and the triad of adornments – by looking upon them as triangles with opposing vertices. At the vertex of one, we can place pubic hair, while the sun stands at the vertex of the other, since, according to the group $\{M_{491}-M_{494}\}$, it is the function of a pubic hair to *capture* the sun. As the study of myths $M_{466}$ to $M_{490}$ suggested in advance, this capturing function makes it possible to reduce the complex body of myths we have been exploring to a system (Figure 36).

In spite of the apparent simplicity of the diagram, the system it illustrates is extremely complex. It will be noted in the first place that, in the right-hand triangle, the sun, the moon and the stone (the latter being a mode of the earth) constitute *terms*, and that these terms are not all the same distance away in relation to man: the sun is a long way away, the stone is near, and the moon occupies an intermediary position.[1] Between these terms and man, the entities inscribed in the

---

[1] Not in terms of spatial distance, of which the Indians had no conception. But I am not counting on ethnography to supply this datum in the form of empirical knowledge. I am postulating it as necessary for the coherence of the system. Nevertheless, in practice, it

left-hand triangle play the part of *mediators*. As the preceding discussion has shown, the scalp is a positive mediator with regard to the sun, and the pubic hair a negative mediator: one conjoins, the other disjoins. And the distinct preference for moccasins in the myths shows that they are seeking primarily to mediate the relationship between man and the earth by means of embroidered garments. But, at the same time, these mediators themselves are positioned at different distances: the scalp comes from an enemy, that is, from afar; the pubic hair comes from the wearer's own body or from the body of a kinswoman; quillwork occupies a middle position: it is made by a 'close' female relative, using 'distant' materials.

It might be said, almost without any punning intention, that the myths, according to their arrangement in relationship to the diagram, link up the most remote of the *cosmic terms* – the sun – with the nearest of the *cosmetic factors* – the pubic hair – while at the same time respecting the clearly discernible links between the term, or factor, and the other correlated terms or factors. It has just been shown that the application

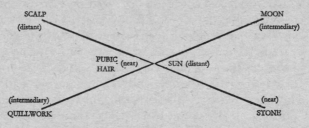

Figure 36. Reciprocal adjustment of the two triads

of this method of analysis brings out an immediate relationship in the myths between quill-work, as represented by the moccasins, and the earth, as represented by the stone. So, for the system to be coherent, an immediate relationship should be apparent between the third term and the third factor, that is, the moon and the scalp respectively.

In fact, this logical requirement is so indispensable for all the myths in the group that the stories they tell are chiefly concerned with providing a commentary on it. Whereas the myths dealing with the origin of the sun and of moon spots, as well as those dealing with the wives of the sun and moon, concur in proclaiming that the moon spots symbol-

---

coincides with the observable data in so far as the moon's phases, being more marked than those of the sun, and with more clearly visible details, create an affinity between the moon and terrestrial objects, which does not exist to the same extent in the case of the sun.

ize menstruation, it was shown at the beginning of this discussion (p.394) that the myths about the origin of scalping establish an equivalence between scalps and menstruating women.

Not only in North America, but also throughout the world, the philosophy of head-hunting, either ritually or by direct representation, suggests the same tacit affinity between trophy-heads and the female sex. In this respect, the particular technique of scalping must not be allowed to deflect our attention from the general phenomenon: scalping may well have been a recent phenomenon in North America, deriving from a kind of head hunting, similar to that practised widely in South America, in former times in Peru, and up to the present historical period among the Jivaro and the Mundurucu. The myths we have been dealing with refer as often to severed heads as to scalps, if not more often; and their noticeably archaic character is emphasized by the fact that the Mandan and part of the Hidatsa, from whom I took several of my examples, attached special value to the skulls of their enemies, as well as to those of illustrious ancestors, which they placed in their sacred bundles (Maximilian, pp. 381–2; Bowers 2, pp. 331–2).

Keeping to North America, I remind the reader that over almost the whole of the area, scalps were immediately handed over to women, or to men whose kinship with the winner of the scalp was through the female line. Among the forest-dwelling Algonquin, as well as among the Plains tribes and the Pueblo Indians, the women performed the scalp dance, with blackened faces and often dressed as male warriors; at the end of the dance, they would take possession of the trophies (Skinner 4, p. 119; 5, p. 535; 12, p. 757; J. O. Dorsey 3, p. 330; Wissler 5, p. 458; Murie, p. 598; Ewers, p. 207; Lowie 9, p. 650; Stephen, Vol. I, pp. 97–9; White, pp. 97–101; etc.). 'If a brave man takes you for his woman,' the Dakota Indian tells his daughter, 'you may sing his scalp song and dance his scalp dance' (Walker, p. 147).

In areas where very strict taboos prevailed in respect of parents-in-law, as for instance among the Algonquin living to the west of James Bay and in the Plains, such taboos could only be lifted by the gift of a scalp (Wissler 4, p. 13, n. 1, where he quotes the Blackfoot, the Mandan, the Assiniboine and the Cree; Lowie 2, p. 30). 'A Hidatsa who wants to talk to his mother-in-law brings her a scalp he has captured in battle and says: "Here is a cane to be used by an old woman." And he offers her the lock as if it were a cane. The mother-in-law has then the right to carry the scalp in the victory dance' (Beckwith 1, p. 192, n. 92).

A distinction should perhaps be made between those cases in which the scalps are given to warriors' wives or to their wives' relatives (Ojibwa, Omaha, Kansa) and those in which they go to blood relatives, such as the warrior's mother, aunt or sister (Cœur d'Alêne, Menomini, Winnebago, Iowa, Pawnee, Zuni). The information available is not always sufficiently precise and detailed to offer a basis for reliable conclusions. The most that can be said is that the difference does not seem to derive from the rule of descent, but rather from the respective positions of takers and givers of women in the particular society. By offering his sister a scalp, a man reinforces her affinity with spilt blood; he neutralizes this affinity in respect of his wife when he makes up for the fact that she was given to him as a gift by handing over a scalp to her kinsfolk, who have become his affines. Let us say that, in the one instance, he transforms his sister into a perpetually menstruating woman, thus symbolically taking her away again from her husband, although in fact he has given her to the husband, while in the other instance, he himself, as a husband, recognizes that a wife is never given without some hope of return: each month, during the space of a few days, menstruation deprives the husband of his wife, as if her relatives were reasserting their rights over her, and as if the tension between givers and takers, correlative to this re-appropriation, could be resolved by the presentation of a blood-stained trophy in exchange for that other blood-stained trophy, a menstruating wife.

This equivalence is no mere postulation; it is clearly stated in the myths themselves. After cutting off the ogre's head, the false wife makes menstruation the excuse for leaving the hut and absconding with the trophy: 'As she (he) walked, the blood dripped from the head and she (the victim's mother) thought it was from sickness' ($M_{469b}$: Bowers 1, p. 291). When the hero of the Winnebago myth $M_{484}$ retrieves his father's scalp from the enemies who have killed him, he presents it to his mother and to a co-wife and urges them to put the precious relic in their bed. They protest that they cannot make love with a scalp, thus adopting an attitude symmetrical with that of a man whose wife is menstruating. In order to validate this interpretation, it is enough to quote a previous episode from the same myth, in which the leader of a war-like expedition, who originates the capture of scalps, stipulates that the first four trophies should come from two young married couples, who are so much in love that they have left the village in order unduly to prolong their respective honeymoons. What clearer way could there be of saying that married couples never belong completely to each other, and that if society is unable to exercise its authority over them, were it only by enforcing the periodic gap placed by nature between husband and wife, it undertakes to separate them by an even bloodier intervention?

This is the message suggested by the myths, when they bring together in the same story the origin of scalping and that of menstruation or when, as in $M_{474}$, they make menstruation responsible for the first trophy-head. Significantly enough, the trophy-head or scalp ($M_{475a}$) may be allowed to rejoin the body or head of its owner, and is thus similar to a woman who, after a few days of menstruation, becomes whole again. But, if native thought likens head-hunting to hunting for women (among the Plains Indians war had both purposes), and if correspondingly it likens a menstruating wife to a scalp which has been temporarily wrested by the givers from the takers, it must also see a direct equivalence between war and marriage. There is no lack of evidence suggesting that this is so, and it will suffice to quote one instance. Among the Kansa, only tattooed warriors, that is those who had received the highest military honours, were allowed to play the part of go-betweens in matrimonial transactions. The warrior (mezhipahai) engaged by the suitor's parents would choose three other confirmed warriors to accompany him to the young girl's house. If the girl's parents were favourably disposed, the mezhipahai would recite the list of his exploits, after which his assistants would do likewise. On their way back to the youth's house, they would stop at intervals to repeat the process. If, however, their errand had been unsuccessful, they would return in silence ... During the marriage feast, the young couple were seated back to back and did not look at each other (Skinner 12, pp. 770–71).

Thus it happens that structural analysis can throw sudden and un-expected light on aspects of rites and customs which had so far remained obscure, but which must have some fundamental significance, since they recur in identical form in regions of the world very remote from each other. It is worth remembering, as being methodologically instructive, that it was the discussion of the arithmetical nature and scope of the groups of ten which led me, without any previous intention on my part, to propose an explanation of the connection between trophy-heads and females, common to very diverse cultures, and of the wide-spread North American practice of presenting scalps to women, or allowing women to take charge of them.

Yet at the same time we can understand why, in all the myths under consideration, the origin of scalping and of menstruation involves hermaphroditic characters: 'There were four brothers who lived alone together, and so they did the woman's work. One day, the eldest was gathering wood when something ran into his big toe ... which swelled up until it became as big as his head. Having thus become pregnant, he gave birth to a little girl' ($M_{489}$: Walker, p. 193). These male house-wives ($M_{473, 477}$) have a counterpart in myths in which heroes become women or disguise themselves as women ($M_{480, 482, 483}$ etc.), ambiguous heroines ($M_{469, 493}$) or men with two-sided faces ($M_{482, 486}$).

Characters of this type existed not only in the myths; in some instances, they had real-life counterparts who carried out ritual func-tions. The Cheyenne, for instance, entrusted the organization of the scalp dances to a small group of individuals known as 'half-man, half-woman', who were dressed like old men. These were men who had a female style of life and whose voices seemed to be halfway between male and female. Moreover, each of them had two names, a man's name and a woman's name. The young people were very fond of them, because they acted as intermediaries in arranging marriages, and en-couraged the love affairs for which the scalp dances provided an opportunity. During one section of the dances, each female dancer pre-tended to capture her male partner, and the latter's sister had to buy his freedom with gifts (Grinnell 4, pp. 306–10).

There seems to be a striking contrast here with the Kansa customs I described above. In one instance, the rôle of go-between is played by warriors, and this emphasizes the opposition between the sexes, which are likened respectively to fellow-tribesmen and enemies; in the other case, the same function is performed by composite characters and this minimizes the opposition between the sexes, between which they act as mediators. The Hidatsa for their part, looked upon the careers of war-rior and 'man-woman' as being two alternatives; an adolescent who refused to accept the one had perforce to choose the other (Bowers 2, p. 220). But, in matrimonial exchanges, the different formulae cor-respond to different degrees of tension between groups of affines. And if the scalp effects mediation between the paternal and maternal groups, it is only to be expected that the mythic character who institutes scalp-ing should be partly male and partly female. We shall come soon to a Menomini myth, in which a hermaphrodite has precisely this function ($M_{495}$, p. 406).

Lastly, it should be pointed out that the scalp and menstrual blood, the only two elements that have figured in this discussion, belong to a more complex group involving four terms. The myths in this group bring into play two other terms: dandruff from a wife's head, which might be called mini-scalps, and an animal's liver which a greedy and spiteful wife insists on eating. I have already referred to the belief, widely recorded among the American Indians, that menstrual blood comes from the liver ($HA$, p. 365). If the relations between a man's scalp and woman's dandruff is metaphorical in character, it follows that the relations between liver and menstrual blood is metonymical; added to which, a woman who is young but fond of liver behaves as if she had already passed the age of the menopause: 'Women do not eat the part of the buffalo over the liver until they are over age for child-birth, as it is considered harmful before that period' (Beckwith 1, p. 302, n. 141). From the Modoc and the Salish to the Micmac (Curtin 1, p. 126; Phinney, p. 137; Rand, p. 68), the myths of North America provide innumerable examples of the liver as old people's food.

But that is not all. The possession of a scalp ensures success in war, while the ingestion of female scurf leads to lack of success in hunting. According to $M_{493b}$, the non-ingestion of the liver is the pre-condition of the husband's success in hunting (Hoffman, pp. 182–5; Skinner–Satterlee, pp. 399–400). Lastly, menstrual blood causes lack of success in fighting: the Plains Indians would remove the sacred bundles used for military rites from a tent where there was a menstruant woman. We thus arrive at a kind of Klein group, if we give the values $x$, $-x$, $\dfrac{1}{x}$, and $-\dfrac{1}{x}$ to the scalp, the dandruff, the liver and the menstrual blood respectively.

The preceding remarks go some way towards answering the questions that were raised at the beginning of the present section, Part Six (p. 327). They would suggest, then, a less pessimistic conclusion than that expressed by Lowie (3, p. 9): 'In my opinion, the quest of this primeval mythology is as fruitless as that of primeval Siouan culture. No doubt the undifferentiated Siouan tribes had both a culture and a mythology. But after the thousands of years that have elapsed ... nothing is now left of which we can confidently affirm that it represents the ancient heirloom, rather than the result of mutual borrowings or borrowings from like sources.' This may well be true, but it does not exclude the possibility of going quite far back into the past.

After setting out to find some plausible explanation of the origin of the porcupine redaction, I gradually became involved in the study of a mythology relating to head-hunting, the archaic nature of which was evident from certain of its intrinsic features and from its area of distribution. At the root of this mythology I discovered two homomorphic triads, between which the myths establish a functional relationship. On the one hand, three types of adornments or trophies: scalp, quill-work and pubic hair fringe; on the other, three types of cosmic entities: sun, moon and stone. The scalp belongs to the category of the far, and the pubic hair to that of the near, just as the sun occupies a distant place in the sky and the stone a nearby place on the earth. The myths exploit the parallelism by making the trophy-head the means whereby a brother and a sister can stay near to each other, and the stone the means whereby the opposite result is achieved. Yet they also state that the sun and the moon are at the right distance from each other, as is also the case with the man and the woman when the latter, instead of coveting her partner's scalp or pubic hair, devotes herself to embroidering moccasins for him.

Furthermore, the myths establish a connection between this system and a philosophy of menstruation. One hero ($M_{474}$), when contaminated by menstrual blood, can only stay with his sister provided he changes into a trophy-head; another hero, who is contaminated by his sister's embraces, has to change into a stone in order to be sure of remaining sufficiently far away. I have shown the reason for this dialectic: a menstruating woman, who has to remain in temporary seclusion, keeps her husband *at a distance*, so that during this period, metaphorically at least, it is as if she had gone back to be *near* her own people. Consequently, we can understand how it is that the same group of myths deals simultaneously with the origin of menstruation, conjugal jealousy and widowers (see pp. 371-2). The jealous husband is the victim of an illusion, if he imagines that a wife is given once and for all. The occurrence of menstruation revives a kind of right of repossession; if the matter is looked at from this angle, which is one of periodic unavailability rather than indisposition, it becomes clear that the man's state as a widower results from the wife's unavailability, which already existed in a temporary form because of menstruation, and which has been merely rendered definitive by death. Consequently, being a widower and being jealous represent extreme conditions, between which the living, but periodically diminished woman, occupies the middle place; the same is true of the scalp and the fringe of pubic hair, extreme adornments between which stands quillwork, the symbol of feminine virtues. Lastly, the same is also true of the sun and the stone since, between the sun's daily periodicity and the stone's lack of periodicity, the moon illustrates periodicity in more complex and varied forms.

We need only study the diagram in Figure 36 to verify that, while the porcupine, for reasons already explained, must play the part of a metaphysical animal, it has a place already marked out for it in the system: near the moon with which it is identified in the myths. Like the moon, the porcupine is a periodic creature. And its quills are used for embroidery, which – one might almost say in anticipation – occupies an intermediary place between the scalp, which is congruous with the sun, and the fringe of pubic hair. Obviously, the pubic hair is not congruous with the stone, the antithesis of the sun, in the same way as the scalp and the sun are congruous with each other. We know, however, from $M_{466}$, that the stone is a transformation of the moon by virtue of the same operation which made the quills a transformation of pubic hair. This phenomenon of torsion should cause no surprise, since it consti tutes a particular instance of a law I have enunciated in other contexts (L.-S. 5, p. 252; *HA*, p. 249).

The link between the porcupine and the moon having thus been validated (in myths which, it must not be forgotten, already dealt with the origin of menstruation, cf. above, p. 346), one problem still remains to be solved: why do all the myths involving the porcupine redaction begin with the quarrel between the sun and moon?

I must first of all remind the reader that Sun and Moon play a part in some of the foundation myths relating to scalping and its rites. Moon, Sun's wife, intercedes with her cruel husband on Scarface's behalf ($M_{482b}$). Or alternately, the hero obtains the help of two old women who are, in fact, the Sun and the Moon ($M_{483}$). The reason why I included these myths in my argument was that I regarded them as transformations of myths belonging to the central Algonquin ($M_{473-477}$), the Menomini in particular ($M_{478-479}$), and of which the Mandan and Hidatsa myths ($M_{464-465}$) were already transformations, and it was in these latter myths that the problem of the groups of ten first arose. It will now be seen that, in order to solve the outstanding problem, the reverse procedure has to be carried out. To understand the part played by the sun and the moon in the myths concerned with the origin of scalping, it will be necessary to move back from the Plains myths we have been dealing with to those of the Menomini, which in turn will lead us, although by a different route, to the Mandan and Hidatsa myths which were our starting-point. Here, then, is the myth about the origin of scalping as told by the Menomini:

## $M_{495}$. Menomini. 'Red-Head'

There was once an Indian who was much abused by his wife. He was a worthy hunter, but the insatiable wife carried back the animals as fast as he killed them. What is more, she behaved badly. He became sad and planned to desert her. As he was possessed of a sacred power, he enlisted the aid of a white-coated deer he had just shot. While the body of the accommodating animal which he had hung from a tree dodged this way and that to prevent the wife getting hold of it, he departed.

Although she had been kept a long time by the deer who was fooling her, the woman discovered her husband's flight and set off after him. At first, he managed to keep ahead by creating magic obstacles; then he came upon a man roasting meat whose help he begged, since his persecutor was gaining on him.

Without paying much attention to him, the stranger invited the hero to start eating the end of a long piece of gut, which he himself would start eating at the other end while, between them, they stretched it out as far as possible. But the wicked wife was approaching. Being frightened, the hero hurriedly finished his half of the gut and the mouths of the two eaters met just in time for the stranger, now replete, to get up, put the bear he had just slain on his back, and command the hero to get on top of the bear to make it easier for him to carry them both together.

They rose skyward just as the wife arrived on the scene. She shouted to her husband's rescuer: 'It is not because your sister is good that you are taking my husband, when I intended to kill both of you. I am bitterly jealous!'

The stranger was none other than the Sun, or daylight. He lived in the sky with his sister who was not at all welcoming to the hero, although the Sun had brought him to bear them company. When the Sun was away, she abused the poor young man because she did not like his looks.

One day the man could not stand it any longer and went off on a little trip. He met a supernatural protector who informed him that Sun's sister had ten lovers; this was why she did not want him about. He offered to help the hero to fight the lovers, if the hero would carry him on his back for, as he said, he was only half a man – a hermaphrodite and a cripple. The two allies slew one of the lovers who had red hair. They removed and prepared the scalp, then the hero went back to the Sun's house. He had hardly entered when the Sun's sister began to make fun of him: 'How ugly you look with your guts inside of you! I can see them lying there all coiled up.' The Sun heard her and rebuked her and said he had not brought the man there for her to abuse but for himself to have as a friend.

The Indian went out hunting and brought back game every time he was not carrying the cripple on his back. He also slew five of the red-headed lovers and took their scalps. The cripple rubbed his protégé's body with fat from the slain lovers and told him to give the scalps to his friend the Sun. The latter uttered cries of joy and said they would make the greatest blanket in the world. Thus adorned, he could now offer the most marvellous sight to the assembled multitudes. His gratitude increased when he was given the scalps from the last five lovers. His sister shook with rage, but said nothing, for she feared her brother.

The cripple warned the hero that the sister would try and coax him to make love to her, but that he should resist her, since she was trying her utmost to be revenged. But the flesh is weak: he fell under her spell and married her. They had a son and a daughter. One day, the Sun advised the couple to go and visit the husband's relatives on earth, but added that he would like their little boy to be left with him. He gave his sister all manner of advice about how she should behave with the Indians.

The couple stayed away for a long time. Meanwhile their son grew up to be a youth, and the Sun decided that the young man should take his place. For a time all went well, but one day the youth disobeyed his uncle's orders and cut straight across, instead of following the usual trail all the way round. The Sun was sad, because he had spoiled things for all time for humans. The winter days would be shortened, and they would never get through their work.

The Sun was also anxious to know how his sister was behaving. To begin with, she had paid no attention to the tattlings and slanderous remarks of the other women who were jealous because her husband was a powerful hunter. Then she forgot what her brother had told her and glared at the women with such intense feeling that they died. The Sun was displeased and recalled her, her husband and daughter back to the sky. And he brought the dead women back to life. That is what happened, when the Sun and Moon took the form of human beings and became half-human (Skinner–Satterlee, pp. 371–6).

In another Menomini version ($M_{495b}$: Bloomfield 3, pp. 531–7), the hero's nature is reversed. He changes from an adult, unhappily married though a skilful hunter, into a useless adolescent who resists initiation. This transformation is clearly homologous with the one in the Scarface cycle, which replaces the ugly, unfortunate lover by a handsome, lazy son; and, if we go still further back, with the transformation of the wife into a non-sister in the unmarried brothers' cycle. When the hero of $M_{495b}$ finally decides to fast in order to communicate with his guardian spirit, Moon offers him her protection. She carries him off to the sky, introduces him into the house of her brother, the Sun, and marries him. Soon they have a son who grows up very quickly and who, so his uncle the Sun decides, must replace him. As in the preceding version, the boy chooses a short cut and the Sun reprimands him for having shortened the length of the days.

The Sun then invites his human brother-in-law to accompany him on his daily course. About midday, they see in a village a man who cuts himself accidentally while busy on some piece of work or other, and who faints at the sight of his own blood. The Sun asks the humans to offer up a dog as a sacrifice, probably in order to cure the wounded man. In the afternoon, the celestial travellers see men waging war on each other; the one favoured by the Sun is victorious. When they finally return in the evening they discover that Moon, Sun's sister and the human's wife, is unwell: this is the origin of menstruation.

I would like to digress at this point in order to note the triple transformation: [wound (not a war-wound) suffered by a man ⇒ (war-wound)] ⇒ [wound (not a war-wound) suffered by a woman]. By extending this transformation, we come back to the unmarried brothers' cycle, in which the origin of monthly periods is masked by the metaphor of a *war wound* inflicted on a *woman*. In the above myth, logical necessity takes precedence over physiological necessity, since the moon has her first period after the birth of her son. In another Menomini myth (Bloomfield 3, p. 559), a man faints, like the man in $M_{495b}$, not at the sight of his own blood while he is engaged on some peaceable task, but because a menstruating (bleeding) woman looks at him.

$M_{495b}$ continues along exactly the same lines as the first version, and both have the same ending. But there are myths belonging to tribes relatively close to the Menomini, in which the leading characters switch positions. The Ottawa ($M_{496}$: Schoolcraft 2, pp. 228–32 and Williams, pp. 249–51) relate how Moon, Sun's sister, captures an Indian who becomes her husband. She allows him to climb back down to earth tied to the end of a chain, but forbids him ever to take a human again as his wife (cf. M₃₈₇c).

In Pawnee mythology (M₄₉₇; G. A. Dorsey 2, pp. 194–6), both the Ottawa myth and the Menomini myth are reversed. The Pawnee tell the story of a certain Sun-Ray, who starves his young wife and forces her to remain in seclusion. She makes several attempts to escape, but each time her persecutor discovers her whereabouts and treats her worse than before. Finally, the inhabitants of a village where she has taken refuge accuse Sun-Ray of being a celestial creature, and of having wrongly taken a woman from earth as his wife. Upset by these reproaches, he says he will go back to the Sun and take his place among the Sun's rays. Never again will he marry an earth woman ...

This variant has its counterpart in Mandan mythology (M₄₉₈: Maximilian, p. 365), where there is a story of an Indian who tries to usurp the identity of the 'Lord of Life', in order to seduce a human woman enamoured of this god. The latter discovers the fraud and lets down two ropes, which he uses to hoist the young girl into the sky. The presence of this version in Mandan mythology is particularly worthy of attention, since all the myths to which I have just referred revolve around the theme of conjugal jealousy. So does a previously discussed myth from the same area, which ends with the transformation of jealous wives into wild sun-flowers, thereafter subject to a double taboo: they have neither to be dug up nor urinated upon (M₄₈₁: Bowers 1, p. 373). The second part of the taboo, a transposition of the one decreed by Moon to her own advantage in a myth that I am about to discuss, suggests an oppositional structure: *moon/sun-flower*, *urine/ menstrual blood*, etc., which would deserve further investigation.[2]

---

[2] In order to avoid any misunderstanding, I must point out at once that, in the Siouan languages, the sunflower is not named after the sun, as is the case in French and English. Cf. in Mandan *mapèho-sedèh*, 'seeds for grinding' (I would like to offer my special thanks to Professor H. C. Conklin of Yale University who, at my request, was kind enough to obtain this information directly from a Mandan lady): in Dakota *wahcha zizi*, 'yellow flower'; in Omaha-Ponca, *zha-zi*, 'yellow grass'. The reason for the taboo may lie elsewhere: the tribes of the Upper Missouri used to cultivate sunflowers, which also grew wild (Maximilian, p. 346; Heiser, p. 435), and it seems significant that the taboo decreed by M₄₈₁ should explicitly relate to the wild plants which, if treated disrespectfully, might appear to be being denied the possibility of also being considered as cultivated plants. If this hypothesis is correct, the sunflower is an ambiguous entity, like the moon, quill-embroidery and the hermaphrodite in the other triads of the group. We have already come across similar conceptions in South America, in connection with a solanaceous plant, half-way between the wild and the cultivated growths, and deserving special consideration for this reason (*HA*, pp. 313–14).

The description given by Henry (Coues, p. 323), which dates from the very beginning of the 19th century, provides apt confirmation of the above interpretation. He says that

I said I was about to quote a myth, chiefly as a source of transformations which would make it possible to elucidate certain points that the
other versions leave unresolved.

### $M_{499}$. Ojibwa. 'The two moons'

A young Indian called Red-Stocking lived alone with his cousin (his
father's sister's son). As neither had a wife, they did the cooking
themselves as well as getting in fire-wood. This pleased the cousin
who greatly shocked Red-Stocking by expressing the hope that they
should never get married.

Shortly afterwards, however, the Indian who had spoken so rashly
met a pretty young woman in the forest several times and fell in love
with her. She gave him a look and a smile and then ascended into the
air and disappeared from view. Red-Stocking, out of pity for his companion's despair, set out to look for the woman; he discovered her,
cut the cord with the help of which she used to return to the sky, and
brought her back with him. The cousin married her; she proved to
be a perfect housekeeper for the two men.

Winter came. One day, while the cousins were out hunting, a
stranger who had taken on the appearance of Red-Stocking went into
the hut and abducted the young wife. In spite of her resistance, he
carried her off to a distant village where everything was red, and
hunchbacks dressed in rags worked like women, pounding corn in
mortars. The abductor, who had a skull for a head, explained to the
heroine that these hunchbacks were none other than the husbands of
the wives he had captured [cf. $M_{479}$]. And he shut her up in a large
long-lodge full of completely bald women. Horrified at the idea that
she would undergo the same fate, for she had very beautiful hair, the
heroine tried to keep from falling asleep; but towards morning she
fell asleep for a little while, and when she awoke her hair had gone.

She ran out of doors weeping, and walked blindly until she collapsed
from fatigue and despair. The Sun, who was passing by, questioned
her and restored her hair with balsam drops mixed with grease and
dissolved in water.

He asked her to follow him, but warned her that his wicked old
wife, the Moon, might take advantage of his absence and slay her;

---

sunflowers grow fairly profusely without any special cultivation a short distance away from
the fields, wherever seed has been blown by the wind. However, the natives do not gather
these flowers, since they are inferior to those which have been sown and carefully tended.

for they were ever travelling and were rarely in their abode together. Night was falling when the Sun arrived with his protégée. Soon after, the Moon left them. From high up in the sky, she saw below an Indian woman making maple sugar and pouring the syrup into a kettle. While she was busy, the woman felt a sudden desire to make water and went outside with her sap pail still in her hand. As she relieved nature, she gazed steadily at the Sun-by-Night. This unseemly behaviour angered the Moon and she tied up the culprit and put her into her pack with the sap-pail. In order to punish his wife for always inflicting harm on people, the Sun forced her from now on to carry her victim; this is the origin of the spots on the moon, which are still identifiable as the woman and the pail.

During his absences, the Sun never failed to warn his god-daughter to be on her guard, but the Moon made several attempts to kill her. She almost succeeded by means of a swing which plunged the heroine into a kind of natural well. However, the girl remembered that she had been blessed by the thunderers. She beseeched them to help her and they came and rescued her [cf. $M_{479a,b}$]. When she returned to the hut, she asked the Sun whether he really loved his wife. And when he replied in the negative, she handed the sorceress over to the thunderers who ate her up. The Sun was delighted to have got rid of her with so little trouble, and he asked the heroine to take the place of the nocturnal planet and to become a friend to humans.

Once while they were resting together (i.e. during a moonless night), the man with a skull for a head tried to get his prisoner back, but the Sun set his dogs after him.

Red-Stocking's cousin had in turn set out to look for his wife. He followed her trail and arried at the glade where the hunchbacks warned him that he would share their fate. The demon threw him in a wrestling match, broke his back and turned him into a hunchback clad in rags and, carrying a pestle and a bag of maize seed, the poor wretch was made to do hard labour.

Red-Stocking, for his part, was ruminating on the curse that his cousin had levelled against marriage, and also, it seems, on the sacrifice he himself had made in not marrying the beautiful stranger. This, he thought, was the source of all their troubles. And when a charming woman proposed marriage to him, he rebuffed her and set off to look for the two missing people.

He arrived at the house of the wicked spirit, beat him in a wrestling match, broke his spine and lengthened his face. Then he exiled him to the chthonian world. Next he straightened the hunchbacks' spines, set the wives free, reunited husbands and wives and sent them all back to the places from which they had set out (Jones 2, part 2, pp. 623-53).

This myth is extremely interesting on several counts. First of all, it enables me to settle a question I raised at the beginning of the present volume, on encountering an Ojibwa myth (M$_{347}$, p. 62) almost identical with another, of South American origin, which I discussed at length in the previous volume. This was a Warao myth (M$_{241}$), belonging to a cycle concerned with wild honey, a product which is absent from the northern regions of North America where, on the nutritional level at least, maple sugar occupies a corresponding position. But does it follow that the myths of North and South America deal with sugar and honey in the same way? If the answer were in the affirmative, this would be tantamount to having instituted a genuine experiment, the results of which would validate *a posteriori* the hypotheses about the semantic function of honey which I put forward on the basis of purely South American data. This experiment can now be carried out, thanks to M$_{499}$.

In the course of the preceding volume, I gradually brought to light a philosophy of honey, inspired by the analogy between this natural product and menstrual blood.[3] Both are elaborated substances, which result from a kind of infra-cooking, vegetable in the one instance (since

---

[3] The present volume was already with the printer when my colleague, Gérard Reichel-Dolmatoff of the University of Bogotá, kindly sent me the unpublished text of a conversation with an informant from the Choco, which presents a whole theory identifying wild honey with sperm. This extraordinary inversion of a system which I have shown to be characteristic of a vast territory stretching from Venezuela to Paraguay does not contradict my interpretation, but instead gives it an additional dimension, and allows the completion of the Klein group, of which, so far, the fourth term was missing. Sperm is *that which ought* to be transmitted from husband to wife; menstrual blood is *that which ought not* to be transmitted from wife to husband. As I showed in *From Honey to Ashes*, honey is something which has to be transmitted by the husband to the wife's relatives and which, consequently, goes in the same direction as sperm, but further. Similarly, it has been established in the present volume (see above, p. 399) that scalps also, are transmitted from husband to wife, and more often to the wife's relatives. We thus obtain a generalized four-term system, in which there is a correspondence between menstrual blood and sperm on the one hand, and between scalps and honey on the other. The husband transfers the sperm to his wife, and, through the intermediary agency of his wife, he transfers the honey to his parents-in-law, as compensation for the wife he has received from them. Unless she is a sorceress (cf. M$_{24}$), the wife does not transfer menstrual blood to her husband. The husband, for his part, transfers the scalp to his wife's relatives in order to prevent the non-transference of menstrual blood taking on the significance of a non-transference of the woman herself by her parents, as if they were repudiating the agreement implicit in the marriage.

the South American Indians classify honey as a vegetable), and animal in the other. Furthermore, honey can be healthy or poisonous, just as a woman is a 'honey' when she is in her normal state, but secretes a poison when she is menstruating. Finally, we have seen that, in native thought, the search for honey represents a kind of return to nature, imbued with an erotic appeal transposed from the sexual to the gustatory register, and which would sap the very foundations of culture if it lasted too long. Similarly, the custom of the honeymoon would be a threat to public order if husband and wife were allowed to enjoy each other indefinitely and to neglect their duties towards society.

To show how maple sugar fits in, we must first of all look at its mode of production. In the maple tree (*Acer saccharum*, *Acer saccharinum*) and in other species from which sugar is sometimes extracted (*Acer negundo*, *Hicoria ovata*, *Tilia americana*, *Betula* sp., etc.), the rising of the sap takes place in early spring, when there is still snow on the ground. At this period of the year, which was marked by the return of the migratory crows, the Indians of the Great Lakes area would leave their villages, and each family would go off to camp in the maple groves belonging to it. The preparation of the sugar was carried out chiefly by the women, while the men went hunting. The women set up the shelters, inspected their birch-bark receptacles, of which there might be between 1,200 and 1,500 and which often needed to be repaired or replaced by new ones. Early spring was also the season when the birch-bark could be easily loosened from the trunks and cut, bent and sewn. The stitching was made water-tight by being impregnated with the resin of the balsam fir (*Abies balsamea*). The colour and quality of the sugar depended on the whiteness and cleanliness of the receptacles (Densmore 1, pp. 308–13; Gilmore 1, pp. 74, 100–101; Yarnell, pp. 49, 52). As the resin of the balsam has a bitter flavour, whereas maple-tree sap is sweet, and since fat was mixed in with the syrup to improve its quality, we see at once that the hair lotion, prepared by the Sun in $M_{499}$ from small quantities of balsam mixed with fat, is connected with the same series of technological operations as the preparation of maple sugar, with which the myth is also concerned.

The preparation of the sugar demanded great care and constant effort, day and night, until the process was completed. Incisions were made in the trunks, and the sap collected. Several boilings in different receptacles changed the sap, first into a thick syrup and then into a granular substance which was stirred with a wooden paddle. This was the sugar proper, and the Indians were no doubt familiar with it before the introduction of iron pots or kettles, since they knew how to boil liquids without burning the bark receptacles. In historic times, they used to make sugar in enormous quantities and keep it all through the year, both to sweeten their food and to tide themselves over during periods of famine. They also used to make 'wax sugar', a much appreciated sweet-meat, by pouring the boiling syrup into snow, which made it congeal in the form of a soft paste.

It is already clear that the quest for maple sugar closely resembled the quest for honey, another wild product. Both activities demanded a temporary return to a state of nature, involving a nomadic or semi-nomadic mode of life in the depths of the forest, at a period in the year when food was scarce, or at any rate all foods except honey or sugar, the delights of which sated the senses; but, however delicious, this restricted diet could not be adhered to for a prolonged period without producing harmful effects and a feeling of weariness.

The Indians of both North and South America reacted similarly to this double paradox, at once sociological and alimentary. They had two methods of consuming the delicious food: either immediate consumption involving no rules, or deferred consumption, subject to all kinds of formalities which supposed connivance between the natural substance and the supernatural order, and made it possible to overcome the contradiction caused between the demands of culture and those of nature by its harvesting, according to whether or not the harvesting was followed by processing.

Just as the South American Indians placed no restrictions on the consumption of freshly gathered honey, but had rules about the consumption of fermented honey, so their North American counterparts observed a similar distinction in respect of maple syrup. In its fresh state, they drank it freely and uninhibitedly in place of water. At the beginning of the 17th century, the (Micmac) Indians used to drink the sap from the tree in order to quench their thirst (Wallis 2, p. 67). The Iroquois regarded the freshly drawn sap as a favourite drink (Morgan, Vol. 2, p. 251). On the other hand, as soon as the preparation of the sap began, consumption was taboo. Among the Sauk, 'the sugar could not even be tasted until it was absolutely ready'. Then a dog was offered as a sacrifice, and eight people were invited to consume a bowlful of sugar without touching a drop of water (Skinner 9, part 3, p. 139). Consequently, although the sap, when fresh, was like water, during the ritual period at least, the prepared sap excluded water. A myth, common to the Huron and the Wyandot (M$_{500}$: Barbeau 1, pp. 110–11; 2, p. 17), relates how, in olden times, the spirit of the maple tree transformed the sap flowing from the tree into a sugar-loaf. An Indian woman engaged in sugar-harvesting wanted to eat the loaf, but the spirit appeared before her and explained that she had to keep it very carefully in a box as a kind of talisman. Generally speaking, the sugar-harvest – *le temps des sucres*, as it was called by French Canadians – and the camp life among the maple groves were marked by ceremonies and rites: the Menomini performed a dog dance, also known as the beggars' dance (Skinner 7, pp. 210–11), and the Iroquois a warrior dance, the purpose of which was to hasten the arrival of warm weather and the rising of the sap (E. A. Smith, p. 115). Since beggars and ceremonial clowns play the part of mediators in North American rites, it would be interesting to determine whether there is not some affinity between the warrior-beggar opposition here and the warrior-hermaphrodite opposition in the Plains matrimonial rites, for which I have suggested an interpretation (pp. 401–2). There were other ritualistic prescriptions governing the harvesting. The Menomini required the sap to be collected daily during a period of an hour or an hour and a half before dusk. If the sap was allowed to stand longer, it became bitter and unusable. Nor had it to be wasted or spilt, since 'the Powers below would be offended and foul weather ensue. In case this occurs, the contents of the catching dishes are turned out and the dishes inverted until the snow or rain ceases' (Skinner 14, p. 167).

There is a second analogy between maple sugar and honey. We know that honey can be sweet or sour, healthy or poisonous, according to whether it comes from bees or wasps, or from various species of bees, or even according to the period at which it is gathered and the time which elapses before it is eaten. The North American Indians carefully noted similar differences with regard to maple sugar. First of all, they distinguished between the species: the Iroquois word for maple sugar means 'sweet juice', and it was immediately extended to honey, when the Iroquois became acquainted with bees. On the other hand, they considered the sugar from the wild cherry-tree as bitter (Waugh, pp. 140–44). But we have just seen that maple sugar itself could be either bitter or sweet, according to the time it took to collect, and the greater or lesser degree of care given to its preparation. I drew attention earlier to a major opposition between maple sap and fir resin, which form a technological pair, although one is sweet and the other bitter. To this must be added the fact that the rising of the sap was characterized by annual periodicity, whereas in Canada it was falsely believed, no doubt in imitation of Indian views, that resin flows during the full moon (Rousseau–Raymond, p. 37). Thus sap and resin can be said to be opposed to each other both as regards taste and as regards the pattern of their respective periodicities. However, the sap too can become bitter. This leads to a certain ambivalence, which a Menomini myth resolves by combining sap and urine:

$M_{501a}$. *Menomini*. *'The origin of maple sugar'* (1)

The attention of the demiurge Mänäbush was one day attracted to a maple tree which was not one of his creations, but was made by some other hero. Mänäbush was displeased for the sap was pure syrup and ran very slowly. Harvesting it would be long and tedious, he thought; and he urinated into the tree, which made the sap thinner. Men will realize that it is a far better way to get their sugar, concluded the demiurge. It will be more difficult for them, and they will have to work for it by their sweat; but they will have more sap this way, even if they have to prepare it (Skinner 14, pp. 164–5; cf. Ojibwa variant, Kohl, p. 415).

The most immediately striking feature of this myth and of the one which follows is their resemblance with the South American myths about the origin of honey ($M_{192}$, $192b$, *HA*, pp. 70–74). The argument is the same in both contexts. In the beginning, both honey and sugar were available to mankind in great quantities and in an immediately consumable form. However, this availability might have led to over-indulgence. So cultivated honey had to become wild, and the syrup, which occurred in nature as if already processed, had to be changed into sap which would henceforth involve a long and tedious operation. This regressive movement, common to the myths of widely separated communities facing similar problems in different environments, is even more pronounced in another Menomini version, which in addition inverts urine into menstrual blood: the one *causes* the appearance of the sap while the other is a *consequence* of its appearance. But at this point I must digress again for a moment.

I have already pointed out (p. 393) that, in Hoffman's collection, the Menomini myths are linked together to form a long saga consisting of a series of episodes illustrating the demiurge's adventures. This being so, one often wonders whether the headings inserted by the author reflect native divisions, or whether they were added later to indicate where the reader might pause. Thus, Hoffman entitles the myth with which we are at present concerned: 'The origin of maple sugar and menstruation', in spite of the fact that there appears to be no link other than a temporal one between the two events. I propose to show that the divisions have a rational basis, by bringing out a connection which remains latent in the mythic text.

$M_{501b}$. *Menomini. 'The origin of maple sugar'* (2)

Mänäbush, the demiurge, went out hunting and came back empty-handed. Nokomis, his grandmother, and he gathered together all their effects and built a new home among maple trees. The old woman invented vessels from birch-bark and collected the sap which poured out like a thick syrup. Mänäbush tasted it and found it sweet, but said it would not do to have the trees produce sap so easily. It would make humans lazy. It was better that they should have to boil the sap for several nights; this would keep them occupied and stop them acquiring bad habits.

He climbed to the very top of one of the trees and shook his hand all over the maples like rain, so that the sugar should dissolve and flow from the trees in the form of sap. This explains why humans have to work hard when they want to eat sugar.

Later Mänäbush was surprised to see that his grandmother was taking great pains with her appearance. He spied on her and caught her making love with a bear. The demiurge took a piece of very dry birch-bark, lit one end of it and hurled the burning bark at the bear, striking him on the back just above the loins. The bear rushed to the river in order to put out the flames but he fell dead before reaching the water. Mänäbush carried the carcass back and offered a piece to his grandmother. As she recoiled from it, he threw a clot of the bear's blood at the old woman, hitting her on the abdomen. She declared that because of this act women would always have trouble every moon and give birth to such clots as this one. Mänäbush then ate all he wanted of the meat and put the rest aside (Hoffman, pp. 173–5).

I shall return to the theme of the lascivious grandmother in the next volume, when I deal with myths belonging to the north-west of North America, in which it plays a prominent part. Here it presents a special interest, since it occurs immediately after the origin of maple sugar. In *From Honey to Ashes* (pp. 122–3, 296–305), I established, with the help of South American myths, the existence of a connection between honey, a seductive food, and the figure of an animal seducer; i.e. two embodiments, one alimentary, the other sexual, of the ascendancy exercised by nature, an ascendancy expressed literally in the one instance and figuratively in the other. The same connection is to be found here, but this time it is established between maple sugar and the animal seducer, thus confirming the semantic homology between sugar and honey. In $M_{401b}$, the torch incident establishes a subtle link between the two episodes, since birch-bark occurs twice in the story: first as a means of making receptacles for sap which will flow *like water*, then as an improvised torch which burns *like fire*. And it is a fact that birch-bark possesses the two-fold property of not catching fire when it contains water, even boiling water, and of providing the best kindling when it is dry (Speck 10, pp. 100–101). By stressing the ambivalent nature of birch-bark, the myth confirms the parallel between the two episodes which it narrates in sequence.

But the most important point is that $M_{501a}$ and $M_{501b}$ bring us back to $M_{499}$, while at the same time throwing new light on the latter myth. To show this, I must first recall that the two Menomini versions dealing with the origin of maple sugar are symmetrical: in one, male urine is an *antecedent* of sap; in the other, blood (of the type which can only come from a woman) is a *consequent* of this same sap. In this sense, the two myths are inversions of $M_{499}$, in which a woman interrupts the making of sugar in order to go and make water; having been caught with her pailful of sap, she comes to represent the spots on the moon, which other myths, reflecting what one might call the lesson of the American Vulgate, interpret as being stains due to menstrual blood. Consequently, $M_{499}$ and $M_{501b}$ both posit a close link between the origin of maple sugar and that of menstruation. The only difference between them in this respect lies in the fact that in the one instance, the link is an internal one of similarity, whereas in the other it is an external one of contiguity.

The demonstration can be consolidated by an observation of quite a different order. The Ojibwa, like the Plains Indians, held a great annual ceremony, but it was dedicated to the thunderers, not to the sun, and they maintained that this was a form of ritual older than the other (Skinner 5, pp. 506–8). The Plains Ojibwa or Bûngi, who had perhaps taken over this ceremony from the Cree, celebrated it in autumn with a four-day feast followed by songs and lamentations. At the end, bark goblets filled with maple syrup were passed round and the participants drank in turn. It is impossible not to be reminded of the 'sweet-water' passed round by the Arapaho during the Sun-dance and which symbolized menstrual blood, endowed for once with a positive virtue as a sign of fertility. I underlined this feature (see above, p. 213; cf. Dorsey 5, pp. 177–8), the exceptional nature of which would become explicable if, as sometimes happens between neighbouring tribes, the Plains rite were an inversion of an older northern rite and revived – the natural product being absent in a different environment – a symbolism which the relevant myths left in a latent state. Like the celestial porcupine, which was a metaphysical reflection of a real animal from a more northerly habitat, the 'sweet-water' could well be maple syrup, moved by force of circumstance into an imaginary drink.

It follows from the preceding remarks that the analysis of the mythology of sugar in North America corresponds point by point to the analysis of the mythology of honey in South America, as presented in Volume Two of *Introduction to a Science of Mythology*. In one context it is honey, in the other maple syrup, which has an affinity with menstrual blood, an affinity linked to the fact that these animal and vegetable secretions are said respectively to be responsible for the spots on the moon. Maple syrup, like many South American varieties of honey, comes from a tree; and, in the myths of tropical America, honey coincides with menstrual blood when the negative value attributable to honey is carried to the extreme limit.

That is not all. According to the North American myths, the first syrup was changed back into sap by the addition of male urine. And it was urine, too, but feminine urine, which caused the syrup to take on the metaphorical function which normally devolves on menstrual blood: that of representing the spots on the moon. To these three terms, the myths add a fourth: the resin of the balsam, which is bitter like urine and is secreted monthly like menstrual blood. Two secretions are animal in origin, the other two vegetable. Furthermore, $M_{499}$ introduces an oppositional relationship between resin and a woman's bald head, since the resin, when applied to the head, acts as a hair-restorer. Indians did not scalp women, so it could be said that in the case of a female, a bald head corresponds to a scalped head. We already know, however, that the myths also see an equivalence – except for the change of sex – between a scalped man and a menstruating woman. It follows, then, that menstrual blood is opposed to resin and, as I have postulated, is the equivalent of maple sap, which itself is opposed to resin.

I have not yet given a complete account of the points of articulation of the system. We know from $M_{475c}$ that a woman with a broken leg (and therefore lame) stands in opposition to a menstruating woman (see pp. 348–9). If we now consider that $M_{499}$ contains men with broken spines (and who are consequently hunchbacks), we can deduce that they are opposed in the same way to the wounded and bleeding man in $M_{495b}$, who is a transformation of the Moon in $M_{495a}$, the first woman to menstruate. We can thus extract from the myths a new four-term group: *lame woman, hunchbacked man, menstruating woman, wounded man*, which confirms, in a most curious way, a diagonal relationship found among the Navajo Indians, although they are far removed from the central Algonquin. They say that a husband must not beat his wife while she is menstruating, because this might damage his back-bone. Similarly, a man who had sexual intercourse with a menstruating woman would be in danger of breaking his back-bone (Ladd, pp. 424–5).

It is also striking that the inverted forms just listed should appear in $M_{499}$ alongside several others. Not only does the Ojibwa myth transform the lame women into hunchbacked men and the scalped men into bald women, in relationship to previously studied myths, it also transforms a Red-Head, the hero's opponent, into a hero called Red-Stocking, whose opponent's head is reduced to a skull: in other words, the rival head has no red hair or hair of any other colour ... it also transforms a large team of brothers into a pair of cross-cousins, and a wife, sister, or non-sister, into a non-wife, since the only link between the hero and heroine lies in the fact that he could have married her.

In order to understand these inversions and their systematic nature in a myth which entrusts to maple syrup the function which, in other contexts, devolves on menstrual blood, we must look carefully at certain technical details. I mentioned earlier that the sugar, which was 'easy to digest ... with a pleasant, slightly acid flavour' (Chateaubriand 1, p. 139), varied in taste from sweet to bitter according to the species from which the sap was taken, the degree of whiteness and cleanliness of the receptacles, the time of day at which the sap was collected and the amount of care given to its preparation. The Indians, however, also distinguished between two qualities of sugar determined by climatic conditions: 'It is said that the best sugar is made when the early part of the winter has been open, allowing the ground to freeze deeper than usual, this being followed by deep snow. The first run of sap was considered the best. A storm usually followed the first warm weather, and afterwards the sap began to flow again. This sap, however, grained less easily than the first and had a slightly different flavour. Rain produced a change in the taste of the sugar, and in thunder-storms it is said to have destroyed the characteristic flavour of the sugar ... The last run of sap also had a different taste from the first. This was boiled as thickly as possible and placed in bark containers. These were sometimes buried in the ground and covered with bark and boughs to keep the contents cool during the summer, and so that they would neither become sour nor freeze' (Densmore 1, pp. 309, 312–13). These variations must have been of considerable importance, since Chateaubriand himself was careful to note them: 'The second harvest takes place when the sap in the tree has not enough body to solidify. This sap is reduced to a kind of treacle which, when mixed with spring water, provides a cooling drink during the summer heat' (*ibid.*). Chateaubriand's remarks are all the more interesting in that he follows them up almost immediately with the extremely valuable information that the Indians regarded the woodpecker as the master of sap; that is, they attributed to it the rôle it plays in the South American myths in respect of honey (*HA*, p. 116).

Among these various details, the one I would like to draw particular attention to is the loss of flavour after a spring storm. We are familiar with the character who embodies this particular meteorological phenomenon in the myths of the central Algonquin: he is none other than Mûdjêkiwis, who is anxiously awaited and joyfully greeted by the Menomini when, after the long winter, they hear the first rumble of thunder: 'Hai! here comes Mûdjêkiwis!' (see above, p. 360). Even as late as 1950, 'the Ojibwa welcomed the March gales, harbingers of spring ... for they associated Mûdjêkiwis with springtime and rain' (Coleman, pp. 104–5). However, we have seen (p. 381) that, in their language, the name of this divinity probably meant 'the wicked or evil wind'.

But we can also understand the reason for this ambiguity, which the myths express in their own way by presenting Mûdjêkiwis as an equivocal character: an elder or eldest brother forced to do women's work; simple-minded yet jealous and resentful; a temperamental character, excited and depressed by turns. The explanation is that spring storms, driven by the west wind, herald fine weather but can also cause havoc. According to their angle of approach, the myths and rites emphasize one or other of the two aspects: mainly the positive one in the Mûdjê-kiwis cycle which deals with seasonal periodicity, but more the negative one in the myths dealing with 'the sugar season', when the early arrival of spring storms causes irreparable damage to the quality of the sap. Since the valency of the west wind is reversed in these myths, all the themes they borrow from the other group in which the same meteorological phenomenon occurs must also be reversed.

In support of this interpretation, it may be recalled that, in one Ojibwa version of the Mûdjêkiwis story (Schoolcraft, in: Williams, pp. 65–83), the character, the eldest of ten brothers, is changed into Kabeyun, the west wind, the father of three sons, respectively the north, south and east winds. Furthermore, Kabeyun fertilizes a woman, the Moon's granddaughter, who dies in giving birth to the north-west wind, the latter being none other than Manabozho who later engages his father in fierce combat. Manabozho corresponds, in Menomini mythology, to Mänäbush, the master of maple syrup whose enemy, as we have just seen, is the west wind. The Timagami Ojibwa explained the hostility between the west wind and the demiurge, whom they called Nenebuc, by saying that too much wind makes fishing impossible in summer and causes famine, but that if the west wind does not blow, the water becomes heavy and stagnant with equally disastrous results ($M_{502}$: Speck 7, pp. 30–31). Here too, then, the west wind has an ambiguous character and the demiurge's task is to keep it under control.

The Ojibwa myth $M_{499}$, some aspects of which have been discussed, calls for additional comment, but I do not propose to carry the analysis any further, for two reasons. Firstly, I do not feel prepared to make use of an obscure myth – also of Ojibwa origin – ($M_{374c}$; Schoolcraft, in: Williams, pp. 84–6), in which a hunchback obtains a wife for his brother, who then travels far to the south and takes up his abode with an effeminate community whose way of life he adopts. However, it will be remembered that $M_{499}$ features hunchbacks who are compelled by their master to perform feminine tasks. Equally tantalizing but no less obscure is the similarity between the bald women in $M_{499}$ and a community of shaven-headed 'public women' or prostitutes, mentioned by the Northern Athapaskan (Petitot 2, pp. 91–2). Secondly, a special study would have to be made of the conflict between the old moon and the young moon which occupies an important place in North American mythology and which I have barely touched upon. It should, however, be noted that this theme is simply a transformation of the coupling of a celestial and a terrestrial character in the myths under discussion: No-Tongue and the Sun's son in the Arikara myth about the origin of scalping ($M_{439}$); Scarface and the morning-star, also a son of the Sun, in the Blackfoot myths ($M_{482}$); and Sun and his nephew in the Menomini myths ($M_{495a,b}$). This nephew, the Moon's son, who behaves rashly and perhaps with deliberate harmfulness towards humans, when the Sun takes him as a collaborator, is reminiscent of Moon's son in $M_{461}$ whom his uncle, Sun, tries to turn into a cannibal.

In the next volume, I shall return to some of the myths devoted to the quarrel between the two Moons, but to consider them from a different angle. Without broaching the problem of the group as a whole, I would like, in passing, to emphasize one aspect of it. After starting from a quarrel between the Sun and the Moon involving a human woman with 10 hostile brothers, we eventually arrived, after a long and

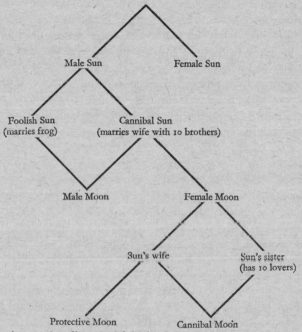

Figure 37. A tentative diagram of the interconnections between the semantic valencies of the sun and the moon

circuitous route, at $M_{495a}$ which contains the same quarrel, involving this time a woman (the Moon herself) who has 10 hostile lovers. Consequently, either the Sun's wife has 10 brothers or her sister has 10 mates. In both cases, the quarrel breaks out as a result of one or several marriages between 'the People-Above' and humans.

Furthermore, the arithmetical problem posed by the number of brothers led us to study other groups of 10, then myths about the origin of scalping and finally myths about the captured sun and the long night. It so happens that the Menomini myth we have finally arrived at

(M$_{495a}$) revives the last two themes but expresses them in an inverted form. On the one hand, it explains the origin of the shortened winter days, which no doubt create a kind of prolonged night, as being the normal result of seasonal periodicity, whereas, in M$_{491-493}$, the long night was presented as being abnormal and scandalous. On the other hand, the episode of the bear's intestine eaten from both ends, which reappears in a gluttony contest in Cree mythology (Bloomfield 1, pp. 251–2), takes on a much deeper significance in M$_{495a}$ if we can accept it as being a symmetrical image of the snare: the *stretched* strip of gut finally unites the Sun and his friend; it becomes the symbol of the latter's *release* and of his *elevation* into the sky, whereas the *tightened* snare leads to the Sun's *capture* and his *lowering* to earth by the very person whose friendship he had rejected, according to a myth (M$_{458}$) concerned with the autumn equinox, and which is in correlation with, and in opposition to, M$_{495a,b}$, a myth about the winter solstice and the shortest days in the year. Like pubic hair, the stuff of which the snare is made, and like porcupine quills and human head hair, strips of dried bear intestine were used to decorate clothes (Beckwith 1, p. 107).

It follows from all these points of comparison that, within a system in which, for different reasons, I showed that a place was always reserved, as it were, for the porcupine redaction, the quarrel between the sun and the moon was also included. The truth is that the only originality of the porcupine redaction is that it opens up a particular path, in so far as it is allowed to do so by pre-existing limitations which compel this path to be different from those already taken by the other myths of the group. It thus renders still more complex a network of relationships that has been only partially uncovered even in the course of this too lengthy investigation. The Sun can be male or female; if male, it is either foolish (and the husband of a frog) or cannibalistic (and the husband of a Cheyenne woman). In both of these cases, the moon may be male (the husband of a human woman), and in the second case only, a female, wife or sister of the Sun. The wife may be either protective or hostile, whereas the sister is always hostile (Figure 37).

Furthermore, through the theme of the quarrel between Sun and Moon, M$_{495a,b}$ make it possible to link up the Algonquin myths featuring the groups of ten (M$_{473}$–M$_{479}$) with the Mandan myths featuring the wives of the Sun and Moon (M$_{460}$–M$_{461}$), which in their turn connect up, as has already been shown, with several other myths forming a system (Figure 38). The myths featuring the groups of ten convert a spatial and moral axis (high and low, good and bad) into a temporal and calendrial axis, which survives in the myths about the wives of the Sun and Moon, while at the same time generating a second temporal axis. The latter introduces physiological instead of seasonal periodicity, and links it up with war, that other bloody and periodic activity, and also with scalp-hunting which, within the compact mass of the enemy, creates discontinuities comparable to those which had to be introduced into the long year if humans were not to be vanquished by the rigours of an interminable winter. Thus it is that a long dialectical itinerary curves back upon itself, bringing our investigation round to the point from which it started.

The fact that $M_{495a}$ acts as a pivot in this system is also the result of considerations of another kind. This myth shares the same armature as those with which our enquiry began. $M_{495a}$ combines within a single narrative two stories which, when I was considering them from the point of view of their South American modalities, I had to present as standing in a transformational relationship to each other: as if the South American myths, starting from $M_{495a}$ or some equivalent story, had divided the task between them, each relating half of the story, while preserving the memory of their common origin by striving to maintain the parallelism between them.

$M_{495a}$ begins like a Tereno myth, also concerned with a wicked wife, who soon turns into an ogress and from whom her husband manages to escape with the connivance of some elusive form of game (a deer carcass dangling evasively from a tree, or young birds thrown from the top of a tree and fluttering out of range). $M_{24}$ is a transformation of $M_{7-12}$ (RC, pp. 106–8; HA, pp. 37, 437), which in turn are transformations of $M_1$, and it is a remarkable fact that the continuation of $M_{495a}$ should be a reproduction of this first group. The hero of $M_{495a,b}$ pays a visit to the good Sun and the wicked Moon; the hero of $M_{7-12}$ and his persecutor have an indirect link with the sun and moon, since as brothers-in-law they belong to two different moieties, related respectively to the sun and the moon in the Serenté social and religious systems. And the two leading characters in $M_1$ also have relationships, although less obvious ones, with celestial entities, which could be the Crow constellation in the case of the one, and the Pleiades in the case of the other (RC, pp. 227–9, 243–6).

In $M_{7-12}$, as well as in $M_{495a}$, a man persecuted by a male or female affine is saved by a supernatural protector (in the latter case the Sun, master of celestial fire, in the former the jaguar, master of terrestrial, cooking fire), who takes him to his abode, i.e. takes him in an upward

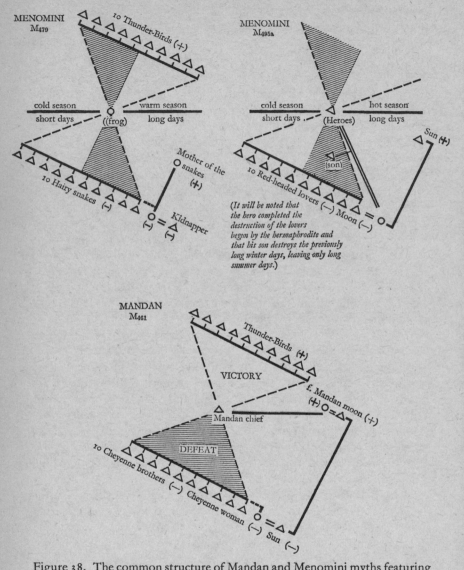

Figure 38. The common structure of Mandan and Menomini myths featuring groups of ten

or downward direction (the hero of $M_1$, $M_{7-12}$ was stranded in the beginning at the top of a tree or a rocky cliff), and who adopts him, thus inadvertently exposing him to persecution by his (the protector's) sister or wife, who thinks he is ugly and *cannot stand the way he eats*: she is repelled by the sight of his coiled digestive tube ($M_{495a}$) or she is irritated ($M_{10}$) by the noise he makes when chewing grilled meat: which is tantamount to saying that, in the one case, from the anatomical, and therefore natural, point of view, and in the other from the point of view of good manners, which are a cultural feature, the Sun's sister and the Jaguar's wife consider that the messenger of the human species does not satisfy his alimentary needs with sufficient discretion. In the myth about the wives of the Sun and Moon, on the contrary, the female human visitor wins the esteem of the celestial people both because of her sharp teeth, which are a gift of nature, and because of her manner of eating, which she owes to culture.

There are even two tiny incidents of $M_{7-12}$ which reappear unchanged in the North American versions. Like the Jaguar in the Ge myths, the Sun in the Algonquin myths is constantly warning his male or female ward to be on guard against his wicked wife or sister. In $M_{499}$, the heroine questions the Sun to find out whether he loves his elderly wife. Encouraged by the Sun's negative reply, she kills the wife, and the Sun, on learning he is a widower, makes no secret of his relief. I drew attention earlier to the same 'profession of indifference' on the part of the Jaguar in the Ge myths, and I showed that it did not occur as a contingent incident in the development of the narrative (RC, pp. 81-3).

Secondly, the supernatural protectors in $M_8$ and $M_{495a}$ transport the hero in the same way: they make him sit astride the animals they already have on their backs: in the one case a bear, in the other a wild pig. The importance of this detail in the South American myth has already been noted (RC, pp. 84-8): because of its position in other myths, the wild pig appears as the appointed mediator between the human kingdom and the animal kingdom. In Menomini mythology, the bear occupies exactly the reverse position; furthermore he is interchangeable with felines, large deer and horned snakes, since all are chthonian spirits, whose irreducible character is emphasized by the fact that they are clearly assigned to the fourth and last of the lower worlds: in fact, no two terms in the Menomini pantheon are further removed from each other than the Sun and the bear, nor any further removed from humans than either (see above, p. 391). Among the central Algonquin and the Iroquois, the dog occupies a position homologous to that of the wild pig in South America; the dog, too, once belonged to the human world, but lost his human status through indiscreet behaviour (Skinner 14, p. 179). This duality in the character of the dog is in keeping with the functions assigned to it in the myths that have been discussed.

It is not difficult to understand why the North American myths replace the mediatory animal by a bear, which is given the same part to play although in principle it has the opposite function. These myths are the foundation myths of scalping, an activity which, among the central Algonquin at least, was inseparable from the cannibalism they practised in respect of their enemies. The Menomini stories present a picture of particularly ferocious behaviour, and give lavish descriptions of the impalement, mutilation and devouring of victims (Bloomfield 3, pp. 87–93, 107–11, 115–23). These Indians, in fact, practised a kind of ritualistic cannibalism out of bravado. Often, when setting out on a war expedition, they made it a point of honour not to take provisions. As soon as they killed an enemy they removed long strips of flesh from the thighs of the corpse and tied them to their belts. In the evening, they would roast this meat and make scornful remarks about individuals who had not had the foresight to stock up with such supplies, or about the squeamish ones who could not stomach such fare ... ' "I am brave, I can eat anything," was their boast as they swallowed their horrible meal.' Similar customs have been noted among the Cree, the Sauk and the Fox (Skinner 4, p. 123).

Unlike their Tupi neighbours who, in this respect, were no less ferocious than the central Algonquin, the Ge tribes were not cannibalistic, and in their myths fire is stolen by a human from a wild animal, a future cannibal, in order to establish the institution of cooking, that is, the norm of a regulated form of feeding. It will also be remembered that, in Bororo mythology, these same myths are inverted and deal with the origin of water instead of fire.

As already pointed out (see pp. 318–23), between the two fomulae of the cannibalistic feast and a more sober form of cooking, the Mandan myths adopt a compromise solution which springs from an ambiguous attitude both to fire (celestial in this case) and water. By chewing noisily, the female human visitor proves to the cannibalistic Sun, the owner of all sources of life and master of the powers of nature, that man may come from very far away, even from the depths of the earth, and depend on water for the cultivation of his food, yet still know how to adapt the celestial forces to his purpose. Man needs celestial water to protect his plants from the Sun ($M_{459}$); but the celestial people and humans are willy-nilly *in league with each other* against water which, when terrestrial, can also become destructive.

I shall justify these statements at the beginning of the next chapter. In concluding the present one, I would like briefly to call attention to the curious similarity between the arithmetical and calendrial philosophy of the North American Indians and that of the ancient Romans, as mentioned in various sources (there are also, of course, differences).

'Romulus', says Ovid, 'laid down that twice five months should be counted in his year ... Ten months are enough to allow the child to emerge from the mother's womb ... The wife too, after her husband's death, wears the sad garments of her widowhood for ten months' (*Fasti* I, V, 28–36). This calendar would seem to be similar in type to the one I have noted in several regions of North America and which I used as the starting point for the interpretation of the groups of 10, instances of which can also be found in ancient Rome. The analogy becomes even clearer, when we observe that the Roman calendar of 10 months was obtained by the multiplication of 5 by 2 and that, like the one in America, it had a numerical form: only the first 4 months were given names, after Mars, Venus, Terminus or old age and Juventas or youth, following each other in that order. The other months had only a number (*ibid.*, V, 39–42). Many other American examples will be found above (pp. 288–90).

It is said that it was Numa who inserted the months of January and February between December and March, thus extending the calendar to 12 months. It is a fact that the Roman system of numeration often juxtaposed groups of 10 and 12, thus betraying an uncertainty which is common in several parts of the world, and which I have also mentioned as existing in America. One ancient belief made use of a duodecimal formula, but it resulted, like the decimal formula of the primitive calendar – *menses quinque bis* – from the multiplication of an arithmetical base by 2.

At the time of the founding of Rome, Remus and Romulus studied the portents. The former saw 6 vultures on the Aventine; the latter saw 12 fly over the Palatine: this was the beginning of their disagreement (Reinach, Vol. 3, pp. 302–3; Hubaux, p. 2). This method of using reduplication to arrive at what I have called the saturated set seems to correspond to the American approach to the problem. In America, as in ancient Rome, the human mind seized on the concept of recurrence to create sets of a higher order. The Roman idea of the 'great months', each lasting a century, like that of the 'great year' made up of 365 years with days each lasting a year, belongs to a family of sets generated by a similar series of operations. The Romans followed the same line of reasoning when they later tried to interpret the legend. In causing 12 vultures to appear to Romulus, the gods could not have meant to promise that the recently founded city would last 12 months, or even 12 years; such a brief period would not have justified so solemn a message. 120 years after the founding of the city, the obvious conclusion was that the number of vultures had foretold that Rome would last for 1,200 years. This explains the dejection into which the Romans were plunged when Alaric threatened their city in 402–3 and their even greater despair when Genseric conquered and sacked the city in 455. Since the founding was officially said to have occurred in 753 B.C., it had to be accepted that the ancient prediction was being fulfilled (Reinach, *loc. cit.* pp. 304–7).

So, like the North American Indians in certain myths I have discussed at great length, the Romans began by multiplying a base by 2. Then they used the product to denote collections made up of complex elements of a similar order, and then made collections of these collections. But it is also clear that the same logical procedure was given opposite meanings in the Old World and the New. For the Indians, the possibility of including within the same family comparably ranked but increasingly compact sets, constituted an awesome and even terrifying phenomenon. And if they gave it expression in their myths, this was always because of a desire to reverse the process. The sets of sets encountered in the myths do not indicate a fact of experience, but rather what might have happened, to the greater detriment of mankind, if things had not evolved in the other direction, towards a gradual reduction of the larger sets. The reduction is achieved only by a return to the original base, which, through being multiplied by 2, had supplied a numerical product the magnitude of which offers an anticipatory vision of even more monstrous magnitudes which the first would inevitably have generated, if left to itself.

This power of multiplication, feared by the Indians as a deadly threat, was regarded by the Romans as offering them their chance of survival. For them, there was something exhilarating in the procedure which consists in repeating the same operation several times on the product of the preceding operation. They were intoxicated by the vistas of the future opened up by the progressive gradation of the groups: 12 days, 12 months, 12 years, 12 groups of ten years, 12 centuries. In short, from a yet static formula, they derived the hope of a process of historical evolution, whereas the Indians, unable to tolerate any events other than those they encapsulated within the already enacted time of myth, wanted those events to have a finished character which would guard them against any possibility of development, apart from the repetitive development of periodicity.

This difference in attitude with regard to high numbers admirably reflects the contrast between a society which is already determined to be historical, and others which are also historical no doubt, but most unwillingly, since they believe that they will lengthen their duration and increase their security by excluding history from their being. It is an old saying that nature abhors a vacuum. But might it not be said that culture, in the primary form in which it opposes nature, abhors a plenum? This, at least, is the conclusion suggested by the preceding analyses. my proposed interpretation of the groups of ten, as illustrating the concept of the saturated set, links up with the interpretation of short intervals and chromatism proposed in the first volume of *Introduction to a Science of Mythology* (*RC*, pp. 50–55, 256–82), and which is the theme of various passages in the second volume.

But if this brief comparison between Roman and American beliefs[4] has a meaning, it suggests the possibility of going still further. We ought to say that it is the function of history to serve as a mediator between the antithetical tendencies which are in conflict within man because of his dual nature. History would then be truly defined by its own peculiar dynamism, in the sense that this dynamism allows it to be at once destructive and constructive.

By rejecting and fragmenting nature, culture strives in the first place to put a vacuum where there has been a plenum. And when it opens itself to change, it allows itself the complementary possibility of putting a plenum where there was a vacuum; but at this point, it must bow to the inevitable and use for its purposes forces which it formerly condemned, since history, which provides it with the means of this reversal, intervenes in culture as a kind of second nature: that nature which men secrete during the historical process, as they cover up the past with ever new layers and press the old layers ever further down, as if to fill in the yawning gap between themselves and a world that nature itself, now plundered and enslaved, is on the point of abandoning.

[4] A. K. Michels's recent work: *The Calendar of the Roman Republic*, Princeton, 1967 appeared too late for me to make use of it. However, it makes little reference to the forms of calendar which existed before the 5th century B.C.

# PART SEVEN THE RULES OF GOOD BREEDING

*This great universe (which some multiply as Species under one Genus) is the true looking-glasse wherein we must looke, if we will know whether we be of a good stamp or in the right byase. To conclude, I would have this worlds-frame to be my Schollers choise-booke: So many strange humours, sundrie sects, varying judgements, diverse opinions, different lawes and fantastical customs teach us to judge rightly of ours, and instruct our judgement to acknowledge his imperfections and naturall weaknesse, which is no easy an apprentiship: ...*

The Essayes of Michael Lord of Montaigne, Book I, Ch. XXIV, translated by John Florio, 1603

*The Susceptible Ferryman*

'*Des héros de roman fuyez les petitesses.*'
(*Avoid the petty behaviour of the heroes of novels.*)
Boileau, *Art Poétique, Chant III*

The ambiguous position of water in the natural philosophy of the
Mandan emerges clearly from one of their myths, the foundation myth
of the rites in honour of the 'great birds', that is, the thunderbirds,
whose chief function was to ensure success in war.

$M_{503}$. *Mandan. 'The visit to the sky'*

This account goes back to the time when villages were near the
mouth of Heart River. There lived a great chief who was the father
of two sons born of different mothers. The elder, who was sensible,
was called Black Medicine; the younger, who was called Grows-in-
Lee-Places in some versions or Sweet-scented-Medicine in others,
was a little foolish and something of a mischief maker.

One day, while they were hunting, the brothers were surprised to
find no more game. Soon they came to a lodge out of which a man
walked with something on his back, and without paying any attention to the two hunters. The two brothers walked into the lodge
which looked very snug. Ribs, tongues and legs of meat were being
roasted over the fire. After waiting in vain for the owner to appear,
they ate and drank their fill, then fell asleep.

The next morning they set off in a south-easterly direction, which
was the way their host had gone. They saw no game of any kind.
They went back to the lodge, and the same man with something on
his back passed them without looking at them or speaking.

The following day, the brothers, determined to clear up the
mystery, were careful to approach the camp away from the wind, to
prevent the man smelling them. When he came out they seized him.
His bundle was thrown to the ground, making such a noise that

people a long distance away could hear it. The bag burst and all game animals ran all over the earth, for it was he who had been holding them in his power.

The two heroes remained in the hut overnight, and went on in the morning. All at once they saw something white on the ground. It was bubbling up and the foolish one shot arrows into it, but Black Medicine objected and thought they ought to leave it alone. The thing was a tornado which exploded and carried them off into the air. They just had time to lash themselves together with the sinews of their bows [in the Beckwith version, with their snares]. They flew over Great-River in Arikara territory and landed on an island among many islands, with water as far as the eye could see.

The next day they set off to see what the island was like. They came to a path which led them to a large earth lodge, and saw corn-fields and gardens on all sides of them. A woman, who was the Old-Woman-Who-Never-Dies [cf. above, p. 292] was glad to see them and offered them mush (maize porridge) from a tiny but inex-haustible pot. The brothers were also hungry for meat and went hunting. They did not go far until they saw a buck and shot it. The old woman agreed to make dried meat of it, although she did not eat that kind of food herself. When she got the deer outside, she told it to run away. The brothers could hunt deer if they wanted to, pro-vided they cooked and ate them in the woods; for it was these animals which looked after the gardens for her.

One day the old woman told the brothers not to go hunting but to hide near the wall of the lodge. They saw young women go into the hut one by one. They were carrying offerings of dried meat or cooked meat dishes. These women were the ears of corn (corn divinities) who, every autumn, sought refuge with the old woman until spring returned. Before long, each woman turned into an ear of seed corn, and the old woman put them away in different places, according to the kind of corn they were. She took the meat to use during the winter.

The brothers grew weary of this lazy life and said they were getting homesick for their own country. The old woman agreed that they should go, and handed them a meal of 'four-in-one' cornballs, made of corn, beans, sunflower-seeds and boiled pumpkin, to be given to the snake who would take them across the water. This long-horned snake, with grass, sage, willows and cotton-wood on his head, would be one of a team of four ferrymen, the first three of whom the heroes had to be careful to reject. Of these three, one would have a single horn, the second forked horns and the third head with two horns and a growth of young plants between them [Beckwith version: 1) a serpent with one sharp horn; 2) a serpent with horns like antlers; 3) a serpent with sandbanks on top of his head and 4) a monster with his head covered with the dirt in which cotton-wood trees grew]. She urged the brothers to ask the snake to put his head close to the shore. They should take advantage of this moment to jump down.

Everything happened just as the old woman had said and the snake, refreshed by the corn balls, managed to reach the other bank. However, it was unable to put its head down on dry land; Black Medicine jumped but the snake nearly swallowed him. His brother was determined to reach the bank by using the snake as a landing-stage, but when he reached the nose the monster swallowed him [Beckwith version: Black Medicine jumped to one side; Sweet Medicine straight ahead]. Sweet Medicine, comfortably installed in the monster's huge jaw, urged his elder brother to join him. But the prudent Black Medicine refused and wept. This went on for three days. On the fourth night, Black Medicine saw in the water the reflection of a man standing beside the shore, and wearing his coat with the hair side out. The man asked the cause of all the crying each night, and explained that the snake came close to the shore because he liked cornballs. Black Medicine replied that he had none left. His protector gave him a cornball made from sun-flower seeds pounded with a lot of rabbit dung and very little corn. On the morning of the fourth day, the hero offered it to the snake, begging it to open its jaws wide so that he could have one last glimpse of his brother. The snake agreed but refused to put his head on the shore. He asked if there were black clouds in the sky. Black Medicine claimed that there were none, seized his brother by the wrist and pulled him out. At that moment a long flash of lightning killed the big snake.

The unknown protector, a thunderbird, brought the brothers, who had been knocked unconscious, back to their senses and took them away to his earth lodge. He had a wife and two daughters [Beckwith version: bashful girls with light-coloured hair], who at once got busy cutting up the snake into small pieces. But the wife remained in her bed all day long. Noting that his guests were very active and endowed with more powers than ordinary Indians, Thunderbird offered them his daughters in marriage, the older boy to take the older girl, and the younger boy the younger girl [Beckwith version: Sweet Medicine, the elder brother in this context, insisted unreasonably on taking the younger daughter]. In spite of their father-in-law's warnings, the two heroes embarked upon a series of dangerous adventures, from which they emerged victorious after destroying certain monsters who were terrorizing the birds. And they also cured their mother-in-law who had been injured and crippled by a long porcupine quill in her foot. This had prevented the birds setting off on their spring migration to the west [Beckwith version: the mother had been injured because she had flown down to get a porcupine and a quill had stuck in her foot].

One day, Thunderbird asked his sons-in-law to hide in a corner of the earth lodge because he was expecting some relatives. Ravens, crows, hawks and eagles arrived in succession, and each one took up its position according to its species or variety. After eating the meat of the double-headed snake, the last of the monsters slaughtered by the heroes, Thunderbird publicly gave them credit for having killed the game, and introduced them to his own people whom he then dismissed, for it was now autumn: they would all meet again and travel together the following spring.

The birds went off to their old nests for the winter. When spring returned and it was time to migrate upstream, the birds assembled and decided to turn the two young men into birds so that they could all fly off together. They changed them into eggs, from which the young men were reborn in the form of bald eagles and quickly learned to fly. They all set off together and flew up the Missouri valley. Obeying the wise counsel given them by their wives, the brothers chose the oldest and most cracked of the swords offered them by the birds, for these were the weapons which possessed the magic power of creating lightning and killing snakes. When the flock flew over the Mandan village, the heroes' father was giving a feast in honour of all the big birds, as he always did at this time of year.

The two men wanted to return to their own home and they invited their wives to follow them. The latter declined the invitation, fearing that they would feel ill at ease among humans, and they gave their husbands magic feathers which would represent them in the rites which from now on the Indians should perform in the autumn too, when the birds went south (Bowers 1, pp. 260–69; Beckwith 1, pp. 53–62).

There is   great deal to be said about this myth, and I shall begin by making a number of random observations of differing importance, but all of which may help, in their various ways, towards an understanding of the story.

Firstly, the episode of the woman with the injured foot provides a link between $M_{503}$ and those myths containing the quarrel between the Sun and Moon which belong to what, following Thompson, I have referred to as the 'porcupine redaction'. In fact, this central episode is simply a reversal of the initial episode in the porcupine redaction. In that context, a marriageable girl is made mobile by a porcupine which she covets for cultural reasons: she wants to enable her mother to finish some quillwork; and which entices her upwards from the earth into the sky (from low to high), where she marries a celestial husband. In $M_{503}$, a mother with marriageable daughters is rendered immobile by a porcupine which she had coveted for natural reasons: she wants to eat it (being herself an eagle), and which brings her down from the sky to the earth (from high to low), where her celestial daughters marry terrestrial husbands. The link appears even more obvious when it is pointed out that, in another Mandan myth, a version of the quarrel between the sun and moon takes the place of the visit to the birds' domain, and comes after the sojourn of the two brothers with the Old-Woman-Who-Never-Dies and their adventures with the snake ($M_{460}$, see above, p. 312). In this myth, which is very similar to certain Hidatsa variants which will be referred to later ($M_{503b,c}$, p. 443), the snake episode precedes another relating how the foolish brother is transformed into a water-snake through eating the flesh of a second reptile (two-headed, in the Hidatsa versions), the body of which has been cut open by the heroes. This type of incident is also described in $M_{503}$ (Bowers 1, p. 266), with beneficent instead of maleficent consequences (since eagles eat snakes), and takes place during the heroes' stay with the thunderbirds. The meaning of this episode will become clear later (p. 456); being a reversal like the porcupine episode, and recurring as it does in both mythic series, it reinforces their symmetry.

Although the myth is a foundation myth relating to war rites, both the Mandan version and the Hidatsa versions were associated with eagle-trapping (Bowers 1, p. 226, n. 5: 2, pp. 361, 363), the rites of which involved head-rests shaped like snakes (cf. above, Figure 32) and sticks hung with offerings for the birds. It is, moreover, known that snakes concealed in the pits used as traps were extremely dangerous to the hunters (Bowers 1, p. 241, n. 33). Yet $M_{503}$ is also associated with ordinary hunting rites, since the myth opens with a description of the release of game held captive by a figure who in this particular myth remains undefined but who is referred to as Hoita, the speckled eagle, in the okipa foundation myth (see above, p. 309, cf. Bowers 1, p. 349). The triple association of war, profane hunting and sacred hunting can be explained by the fact that the Plains Indians thought of war as an extreme form of hunting in general, of which eagle-trapping combined all the symbols and sublimated all the properties.

It will also be noted that the foolish brother in $M_{503}$ adopts a similar behaviour to Oxinhede, 'Acting-Foolish' of the okipa dances. One invites his brother to join him in the chthonian monster's jaws; the other invites his father the Sun, who is an ogre, to move closer to humans. So, in both cases, foolishness consists in being partial to a state of things which excludes mediation.

But let us return to the myth itself. One of the brothers is called Black Medicine, the name of a medicinal plant with haemostatic properties, which is used to cure wounds caused by eagles and also snake-bites (Beckwith 1, p. 259, n. 126; Bowers 1, p. 261). We have already encountered (p. 65) this ranunculaceous plant, *Actaea rubra*, a close relative of the baneberry (*A. spicata*), which occupies an important place among popular herbal remedies in Europe. Directly or periphrastically, the other brother's names also designate a herb, which could be *Actaea arguta*, a plant 'good for the blood' according to the Cheyenne, who call one of their cultural heroes after it (cf. Grinnell 2, Vol. 2, p. 174 *et seq.*). One of the plants is black, the other brown, just as the mythical bears which used to have their eagle-trapping pits on either side of the Missouri were black and brown respectively (cf. Bowers 1, pp. 261 and 214–15). The river flows along a north-west/ south-east axis, which divides the universe into two moieties: a western one (including the south) and an eastern one (including the north). Different demiurges saw to the creation of beings and things in each region (Maximilian, pp. 362–3; Will–Spinden, p. 139). In Mandan mythology, the moieties associated respectively with the west and the east perpetuated the memory of this basic duality (Figure 39). The heroes of $M_{503}$ – whose oppositional and correlational relationships are even more strongly marked when they appear in other myths as *Lodge Boy* and *Thrown Away* (cf. above, p. 287) – travel first of all towards the south-east, the home of the Old-Woman-Who-Never-Dies and the goal of the autumn migration of the birds. In the spring, they will accompany the birds in their north-westerly flight. But in order to go from east to west, they will first of all have to cross the river. The latter has

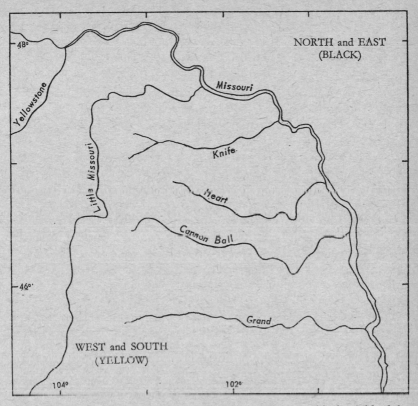

Figure 39. A diagrammatic representation of the geographical world of the
Mandan

both a dividing and a unifying function; it marks the frontier between
two worlds and yet, by following its course as they fly up or down the
Missouri valley during their seasonal migrations, the birds can pass
without difficulty from one world to the other.

The mythic narrative is not only located in space; it also unfolds in
time. The initial seasonal cycle begins with a tornado or a cyclone, both
of them meteorological phenomena which the Mandan and Hidatsa
associate with the north-east (cf. Beckwith 1, p. 62: 'As a boy,' one
informant said, 'I never heard of a cyclone here, but only in the east').
The brothers, who have tied themselves together, are borne horizontally by the cyclone towards the island-home of the Old-Woman-Who-
Never-Dies, where they spend the summer, autumn and winter. They

set off again on their travels in the spring, and just after their separation from each other a personified storm carries them vertically up into the sky, where they remain for a further year until the following spring. This mythic sequence of events is in keeping with the facts. The most important ceremonies were performed in the spring, when the 'big birds' – eagles, hawks, ravens and crows – flew towards the north-west, to the 'bad lands' and the Rocky Mountains. The object was to honour the birds so that they would pass near the villages and bring the rains necessary for fields and gardens. The ceremonies coincided with the first spring storms, and came after the rites associated with the Old-Woman-Who-Never-Dies, the reason being that the water birds, of which she was the owner and which the Indians honoured in conjunction with the female spirits of corn described in $M_{503}$, made the migration northwards while there was still snow on the ground; the eagles and other large birds followed later. On the other hand, the fall or autumn rites for birds of prey were performed first, since these birds were believed to fly southward in leisurely fashion along the Missouri, hunting as they went, whereas water birds – such as geese, swans and ducks – only set out after the onset of cold spells (Bowers 2, p. 363).

There were, then, two series of rites for the big birds. The first celebrated their arrival in the spring, and the second marked their departure in the autumn. It will have been noticed that $M_{503}$ is less concerned with explaining the absolute origin of these rites than with their seasonal repetition. The spring rites must already have been in existence, since the heroes' father is performing them when the birds fly over his village. But, before bidding farewell to their husbands, the daughters of the thunderbirds order them henceforth to perform the same rites in the autumn as well.

This is an important point, because the Hidatsa versions ($M_{503c,b}$; Bowers 2, pp. 359–62; Denig, pp. 613–17 – this version was supplied by an Assiniboine chief who, however, attributed it 'to the Gros-Ventre', that is, to the Hidatsa, cf. *ibid.*, p. 403) differ from $M_{503}$ in several respects. Either the visit to the birds is retained, but it is one of the birds' sons and not a wife who is lame, his injury being due to a deer's antler and not to a porcupine's quill; or the visit to the sky is replaced by a trip westwards to visit the great snake, the owner of buffaloes, whom the heroes deceive. In both cases, the foolish brother commits the error of eating the snake's flesh and turns into a large reptile at the bottom of the Missouri river. At least one of the Hidatsa versions ($M_{503c}$, Bowers 2, p. 361) deals explicitly with the founding of the spring rites: 'He (the hero) announces that he is going to give the ceremony for the big birds and notifies the people that the weather in early spring will be cloudy and rainy for four days, after which the birds will arrive in groups from the south.' It would seem, therefore, that, as we move from the Mandan to the Hidatsa, the aetiological function of the myth is reversed in relation to the ceremonial calendar, at the same time bringing about, in stories which remain similar in all other respects, the transformations to which I have already drawn attention (cf. L.-S. 19).

The fact had to be recalled, since I have already noted the existence in Mandan mythology of a story, identical with the Hidatsa versions, but which is used by the Mandan to introduce the quarrel between the sun and the moon ($M_{460}$). This confirms, by a different type of approach, the hypothesis put forward on p. 439 that $M_{503}$ and $M_{460}$ stand in a relationship of inverted symmetry to each other. This conclusion results from the fact that $M_{503c}$ is an inversion of $M_{503}$ on the calendrial axis, while $M_{503c}$ goes with $M_{460}$, which consequently is also an inversion of $M_{503}$. Besides, is it not the case that the story of the quarrel between the sun and moon centres on a visit to the sky? The plots may seem very different but we are still on familiar ground.

Further echoes of $M_{503}$ can be found beyond Mandan mythology. The Thunderbird's wife is a cripple and her infirmity prevents the birds starting off on their spring migration. In other Hidatsa myths $M_{503d,e}$ (Bowers 2, pp. 304-8, 439), the hero's father-in-law is lame and the two brothers cure him with the help of *Actaea rubra*, thus allowing the Indians to embark on their seasonal migration from their winter to their summer village; they cure in the same way a lame Buffalo woman, who cannot get to the summer grazing grounds. The explanation of ritual limping which I put forward in the previous volume (*HA*, pp. 459–66) on the basis of different myths, as well as the one suggested in the course of a discussion of the subject in the present volume (pp. 348–9), are thus given further confirmation.

Several details of $M_{503}$ are also reminiscent of a Warao myth ($M_{28}$; *RC*, pp. 109–16 and *passim*; *HA*, pp. 453–8), in which two brothers, one wise and one foolish, fall victim to an aquatic ogress. She devours the one who comes too near the bank and whose reflection she has glimpsed in the water; this is the same process of discovery as that which is attributed in $M_{503}$, to the prudent brother when he perceives his celestial saviour, after taking care not to approach too close to the bank where he too would have been swallowed up by an aquatic ogre. So, in both instances, the hero who survives is the one who realizes the discontinuous nature of the transition from water to land, or from land to water; the other hero perishes through having had recourse to short intervals in the vain hope of cancelling out the discontinuity.

I would like to draw particular attention to the episode during which the heroes cross a river on the back of a snake-monster. It is found very frequently in North America and also occurs in South American myths too, as is shown by a series of myths which were discussed in *The Raw and the Cooked* ($M_{124}$, $M_{139}$) and in the second part of the present volume ($M_{402}$–$M_{404}$). When I first pointed out the theme of the susceptible ferryman (*RC*, p. 253, n. 24), I did no more than emphasize its importance; it is now time to unravel its meaning.

It is important, in the first place, because of the fact that the myths of both North and South America tell the story in almost the same terms. After re-reading the Mandan myth ($M_{503}$), let us go back to a Mundurucu myth, of which I gave only a brief summary (above, pp. 121–2).

$M_{402}$. *Mundurucu. 'The adventures of Perisuát'* (extract)

Perisuát's uncle, who had changed into a tapir, explained to his nephew before he left that in order to reach the village he would have to meet the three giant alligators which were in the river at this point, and the largest of which was named Uäti-pung-pung. The first two would offer their services as ferrymen, but Perisuát should reject them and wait for Uäti-pung-pung to appear, who would have imbauba trees (*Caecropia* sp.; cf. *HA*, p. 364) growing on his back.

So the hero refused the services of the first two alligators and asked the third to take him across the river. But since the alligator did not come close enough to the bank, Perisuát could not mount him. Finally he was able to grab an overhanging branch and swing aboard. He thus avoided being eaten by the beast.

In midstream, the alligator said that he was going to sound his horn, and he uttered a deep grunt accompanied by a bad smell. Perisuát had been warned by his uncle not to spit in disgust, so he told the alligator that he smelt nice.

When they got near the farther shore, the alligator tried to persuade the boy to swim to the bank so that he could eat him. Perisuát, however, asked the alligator to approach closer and finally he was able to swing off the alligator's back by a branch. Once safe on dry land, he called out that the alligator's breath was maddeningly bad. 'Why did you not say this in the middle of the river?' asked the ferryman. He then thrashed about in a rage and broke all the trees growing along his back (Murphy 1, pp. 96–7).

In an Assiniboine version ($M_{504}$; Denig, p. 611), the ferryman, who in this instance is a crane, also wants to be complimented on the sweetness of his breath. A Kickapoo myth ($M_{505}$; Jones 3, p. 85) relates how a fish agrees to ferry the hero across on condition that the latter strikes him every time he slows down; a vulture had had to give up the idea of rendering the same service because it emitted such a vile stink that its passenger could not help vomiting during the crossing. In the myths of the eastern Algonquin, chiefly in variants of $M_{437}$, $M_{438}$ (Prince, pp. 68–9; Leland, pp. 152–4; Rand, pp. 164–5, 312–13, 320), it is the supposed physical beauty of a crane which is acting as ferryman, that has to be praised; or (Leland, pp. 184–5, 325–6, 328–9) the ferryman is again a saurian: a horned alligator, which is also blind and irascible.

All these features are retained in other South American versions: in $M_{124}$, for instance, the hero mocks the saurian because of its repellent appearance; in $M_{139}$ and $M_{403a,c}$, the animal wants its passenger to insult it (since it is looking for an excuse to eat him), or alternatively, as in $M_{404}$, it accuses him of not being sufficiently respectful.

Such striking similarities in mythic variants of the same story, originating from areas which are geographically very far apart, present a problem. Is there a logical armature capable of explaining the persistence of the theme in spite of its transference to areas far removed from some hypothetical place of origin, or its independent emergence in widely divergent societies? Whichever of the three hypotheses we start from, it is impossible to avoid postulating the existence of some internal necessity as a pre-condition of the other two.

We have already gone half way towards finding an answer by noting (pp. 439–43) that $M_{503}$, containing the susceptible ferryman episode, also includes another which can be interpreted as an inversion of the porcupine incident in the sun and moon cycle. For, although the two cycles are symmetrical, it must be remembered that the cycle concerned with the quarrel between the sun and the moon emerged in connection with the discussion of problems raised by a different motif, namely the canoe journey made by the sun and moon. So the internal necessity of the susceptible ferryman episode might well result from the fact that it too constitutes an inversion of the canoe motif.

The hypothesis has only to be formulated for its validity to be obvious. The canoe journey, in both directions – upstream and down-stream – takes place along the river axis: the trip on the ferryman's back is perpendicular to this axis, since it involves crossing the river. But there is more to it than that. In certain North American versions, the crane stretches out its leg to form a foot-bridge. In both North and South American mythology, the snake-ferrymen have horns between which lie sand banks overgrown with luxuriant vegetation: they are floating islands, such as can be seen at flood time in the rivers of both North and South America. This was particularly true of the Missouri river: 'In the spring, huge pieces of land break away from its banks: these floating islands drifting down the Missouri river, with their trees still covered with leaves or blossom, some still erect, others half collapsed, provide a wonderful spectacle' (Chateaubriand 1, p. 95; cf. Matthews, p. xxii; Neill, p. 383).

Bridges and islands are both similar to, and dissimilar from, boats, although not exactly for the same reasons: an island and a canoe are floating bodies, one belonging to the natural order, the other a creation of culture; and although the few bridges built by the American Indians may look like natural gangways, owing to the crudeness of their construction, they are fixed, not movable, and perpendicular to the current, not parallel to it. Lastly, the canoe journey involves two passengers who, as we have seen, must remain at the right distance from each other, whereas the crossing of the river creates a state of intimate conjunction between two travellers: the ferryman and his passenger.

Various mythic texts bear witness to the objective reality of the transformation. When the hero of $M_{403b}$ makes his request, the alligator, whose one thought is to gobble him up, replies untruthfully that its shoulders form a large canoe capable of supporting the weight of one passenger (Wagley–Galvão, p. 141). A Salish myth ($M_{506}$; Adamson, p. 270), in which the ferryman displays his unpleasant nature by repeating the appeals for help instead of replying to them, ends with the assurance that 'hereafter no one shall act as a canoe and drown people'. The Oglala Dakota ($M_{507}$; Walker, pp. 205–6) relate how a fallen trunk changed into a magic canoe: ' ... it rolled over, and as it rolled became more and more like a boat with a head, two great eyes and a tail ... people had to get in quickly or it would leave without them'.

The fact that the aquatic monster is an anti-canoe is also clear from a Dakota myth, which is closely related to the Hidatsa versions of $M_{503}$ and a Mandan variant ($M_{460}$; cf. Maximilian, pp. 380–81; Bowers 2, pp. 199–200).

*M₅₀₈. Dakota. 'The large fish'*

A chief's daughter, who was against marriage, finally agreed to accept a poor young man on condition that he did something noble. The man organized a war party but could find no one of the enemy. On their way home, the Indians met a gigantic turtle, onto whose back they all climbed, except the hero and his friend. The beast dived into the lake and the five over-venturesome men were drowned [cf. M₃₈₅].

The two survivors went on until, worn out with fatigue, the lover had to stop in order to rest. Meanwhile, his companion searched everywhere to see if he could find some dead fish, because at this time of year the high water might have left some stranded on the shore. He found one, cleaned and cooked it and then asked the lover to share the meal. The latter at first refused, then accepted on condition that his friend promised to fetch him all the water he could drink.

However, he proved to have an insatiable thirst, and the friend grew weary of fetching the water in the only receptacle they had. The hero crawled to the river, sprang in and lying down drank straight from the stream. Gradually, he changed into a huge fish which barred navigation.

When she learned of the tragedy, the chief's daughter swore to be faithful to her fiancé, who had been lost 'for love of me'. She made men's clothing for a whole year, asked to have a bark canoe built and then floated slowly down to where the fish was. She handed over her gifts, swearing that she would never marry in memory of his sacrifice, on condition that 'the Indians could once more descend the river in their canoes'. Slowly the great fish sank to the bottom, and the waters of the Sainte-Croix (Stillwater River) were free (McLaughlin, pp. 23–8; cf. the Arikara version, Dorsey 6, pp. 79–80; Creek version, Swanton 1, pp. 32–3; etc.).

Whereas an island and its mythic equivalent are the reverse of a canoe, a canoe, when wrongly handled, can become an island, as is shown by a South American myth:

*M₅₀₉. Arawak. 'The origin of islands'*

In the course of their peregrinations, travellers visited a country where the inhabitants could travel in their corials (canoes) only with the tide. They had paddles, but held them edgewise instead of broadside to the water. This method of progression entailed always having to travel with a very long pole. When the tide turned against them they would drive this pole into the bottom of the stream and make fast their corial ...

The old leader who was a medicine man changed into a bunia bird and yelled out: tarbaran! tarbaran! which means 'the broadside'. 'And what would you say,' retorted the ignorant paddlers, 'if we were to take the broadsides of our paddles and hit you on the head with them?' Finally they decided to turn their paddles round and found they could travel three times as fast and that they could go up and down stream quite independently of the current (Roth 1, p. 221).

To this myth, which is reminiscent of beliefs found not only among the Salish, where they have the same form as in Guiana (Adamson, pp. 40, 420), but also among the Karaja (first paddles held by the blades, Baldus 6, p. 215), Roth adds the comment that an island on the Essequibo River is called hiarono-dulluhing, i.e. 'woman's pole', because Arawak women, who had not yet been instructed in canoe management, drove a pole into the mud in order to moor their canoe at high tide. But they pushed it in so far that they were unable to pull it out. Sand piled up round it, and grass and trees grew there, forming the sort of island which can be seen today. The island, an inversion of the canoe, thus reconstitutes the image of the ferryman whose back is covered with sandbanks bristling with vegetation.

If my interpretation (p. 145) of the Tikal bone engravings is correct, they will appear as illustrating the two stages of the transformation. The canoe with animal passengers can sometimes take on the appearance of a hairy snake (Figure 40), a mythic creature, considered as a doublet

Figure 40. A canoe in the shape of a hairy snake. Tikal bone engraving. (From Trik, fig. 5. Photo, University Museum, Philadelphia.)

of the horned snake by the Waiwai of Guiana (Fock, p. 91), as well as by the Cheyenne (Grinnell 2, Vol. 2 *passim*) and the Menomini (Skinner–

Satterlee, p. 354). In some Mandan myths ($M_{512-515}$, pp. 459–60) we shall presently discover a boat which can alternatively play the part of a reliable canoe or an untrustworthy ferryman, according to whether the number of passengers is, or is not, *measured*, i.e. calculatedly moderate.

Let us pause and examine this point. We know that the canoe journey made by the sun and moon is governed by the concept of balance; this was established in Part Three. On the other hand, the data I have assembled regarding the susceptible ferryman episode indicates a lack of control on the part of both the leading characters, who vie with each other in guile, untruthfulness and insulting behaviour. Now, we came to the conclusion that the canoe journey motif connoted circumstances of an equinoctial type. Does it not follow that the susceptible ferryman motif, in so far as it is symmetrical with, and in opposition to, the canoe-journey motif, must connote circumstances of a solstitial type?

It would be easy to answer this question if we could discover some correlation between the rituals associated with either motif and these particular periods in the calendar. Unfortunately, in spite of Bowers's extraordinary achievement, his research into Mandan society was done at a time when the ancient culture survived only in the memory of a few old men and women, and so the ceremonial calendar remains hazy and difficult to interpret. The picture which emerges, however uncertainly, is still more complex than the one I have just proposed as a working hypothesis. It would seem that the Mandan ceremonial calendar was based on several oppositions, none of which would appear to be exactly translatable into the terms of a solstice/equinox opposition.

An initial opposition exists between the big bird rites, the origin of which is described in $M_{503}$, and all the others. The latter, of which there were some twenty (cf. Bowers 1, p. 108), took place either on a single occasion or on several, but always within a continuous period of time, which might last for one or several months or even a whole year. The big bird rites, on the other hand, took place only in April and November. Consequently, they belonged to the category of those ceremonies which were performed discontinuously, at two distinct periods in the year. These periods, occurring as they did in spring and autumn, coincided more or less with the equinoxes. Significantly enough, the offerings to the Missouri, the origin of which is indicated in the variants of $M_{503}$, also took place twice a year (see below, p. 456).

Let us now look at the buffalo-hunting rites, the complexity of which has been mentioned (pp. 311–12, 373–5). They can be divided into two groups: on the one hand, the great tribal feast of the okipa, the

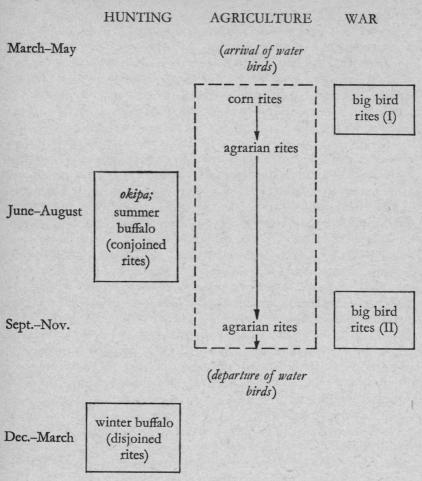

HUNTING          AGRICULTURE          WAR

March–May                    (*arrival of water birds*)

corn rites

big bird rites (I)

agrarian rites

June–August    *okipa;* summer buffalo (conjoined rites)

Sept.–Nov.                   agrarian rites

big bird rites (II)

(*departure of water birds*)

Dec.–March    winter buffalo (disjoined rites)

purpose of which was to increase the buffalo herds, and which took place during the hottest months (Bowers 1, p. 122), and, on the other hand, various village rites connected with winter hunting, which were performed during the coldest months. Consequently, the two periods fall about the time of the solstices (*ibid.*, pp. 315 and 325, 326: 'in the winter during the shortest days'; and Bowers 2, p. 59: 'the rites to the winter herds began with the winter solstice').

So, the bird rites and the buffalo rites stand in a correlational and oppositional relationship to each other along several axes. The bird rites, which were all identical, were repeated at different periods; the buffalo rites, which differed from each other (in that the okipa was made up of several rites and there were at least three distinct rites relating to the winter buffalo: the 'Snow Owl', the 'Red Stick', and the 'White Buffalo Cow') took place, as far as each cycle was concerned, during a single period in the year. Lastly, the bird rites coincided more or less with the equinoxes, the buffalo rites with the solstices.

In contrast to these clearly defined oppositions, the agrarian rites began with the arrival of the water birds at the beginning of spring, and were spaced out at intervals during the year. The ceremonial calendar, in a much simplified form, can be presented diagrammatically (p. 450).

We know that the two groups of rites which are furthest apart in the diagram were incompatible. If the winter hunting rites were performed in the spring when the seedlings were showing, the frosts could well return and kill all the plants (Bowers 1, p. 327). On the other hand, the big bird rites and the agrarian rites were compatible, since the former fulfilled the subsidiary function of attracting the spring rains necessary for agricultural prosperity (see above, p. 311).

This point having been established, a problem arises through the fact that the susceptible ferryman episode occurs at least thrice in Mandan mythology. It appears not only in the myth featuring the big birds ($M_{503}$), but also in the foundation myth relating to the corn rites ($M_{460}$); and in the Snow Owl myth which is a foundation rite intended to attract the winter buffalo ($M_{469a,b}$). In other words, the episode creates an affinity between two incompatible series: winter buffalo and corn, and two compatible series: corn and big birds. It is as if it were meant to perform a bonding function at a point in the system that is particularly weak through relationships of incompatibility and compatibility occurring together there in a marked position.

As it happens, subtle differences can be observed between the three stories. The Winter Owl myth is by far the most complex, since it contains the incident in which the hero persuades the snake to move in closer and closer to the bank so that he can make his jump by clinging to the branches growing on the monster's back. These details are described in exactly the same terms in the Mundurucu story about Perisuát ($M_{402}$). Furthermore, $M_{469}$ is a transformation of $M_{503}$ in two respects: the hero feeds the snake with eight corn balls instead of four and, fearing that he may be devoured, he throws them into the water a long way from the monster and not straight into its jaws.

The corresponding episodes in $M_{503}$ and $M_{460}$ also stand in opposition to each other, but on different axes. In the first place, whereas the snake in $M_{503}$ actually swallows one of the brothers, and the serpent in $M_{469}$ is prevented from doing so, his counterpart in $M_{460}$ has no such sinister intentions. He is anxious to be of service, and merely requires to be fed during the crossing to keep up his strength. The food consists of four balls of 'four-in-one', with the addition of a piece of dried meat which the hero has the good luck to find in his pocket just when the snake is about to stop through exhaustion.

From this detail it is clear that $M_{460}$ and $M_{503}$ are symmetrical, since in the latter myth too mention is made of a fifth item of food: the ball supplied by the thunderbird, and made of sunflower seeds pounded with rabbit dung and a very small quantity of corn. Thus, in one instance, the snake is given meat, a more sustaining food than cornflour balls; and in the other, a pseudo-food composed mainly of dung.[1]

We can say, then, that $M_{460}$, $M_{469}$ and $M_{503}$ feature respectively a helpful ferryman, an untrustworthy ferryman whose plans are foiled, and an untrustworthy ferryman who almost achieves his aim. The hero rewards the first, masters the second and deceives the third. The two extreme situations relate to the rites performed about the time of the equinoxes: the spring equinox in $M_{460}$ and the autumn one in $M_{503}$, while $M_{469}$ is a foundation myth relating to rites performed about the time of the winter solstice. The rites are concerned either with agriculture, or hunting or war, which is a series also constituting a progression:

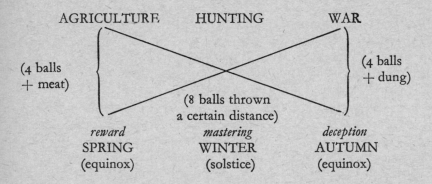

---

[1] The analysis is not complete since, during the return journey, the hero also has to feed the snake with flesh from his own thigh ($M_{469b}$; Bowers 1, p. 291). I propose to leave this incident aside, since the Snow Owl myth is the only one in which the ferryman plays a part during both the outward and the return journeys. It should therefore be analysed separately, and this would take me too far afield, especially since Mandan mythology is virtually inexhaustible in its richness and complexity. Here I can do no more than scratch the surface.

The diagram clearly illustrates the contrapuntal character typical of every mythic and ritual system since, while the two series: *agriculture, hunting, war* and *spring, winter, autumn* are one progressive and the other regressive,[2] they harmonize together with what might appropriately be called a *basso continuo*, expressing the regular alternation of an equinox and a solstice. But, if the analysis is taken further, it becomes clear that the dialectical development of the myth ($M_{503}$ in this case) tends to transform this initial and static opposition into a dynamic progression. It should be recalled that $M_{503}$ is not a foundation myth relating to the 'big bird' rites in general, but one which explains how rites which were first performed in spring only, came to be repeated in the autumn. However, when they are considered from a logical point of view, the two equinoxes depend originally on an identical transformation: $(day = night) \Rightarrow (night = day)$; and, experientially, both are relevant in respect of the birds. But it is precisely for this reason that the conceptual imbalance, which would have occurred if the mythic narrative had been content to sanction one and not the other, would have been even greater than the imbalance between the hunting rites accompanying the two solstices: for ceremonies are performed at each solstice – the okipa in summer and special rites in winter – and these ceremonies may remain dissimilar since – contrary to the equinoxes – the solstices too are in opposition to each other: $(day > night) \neq (night > day)$. The theoretical situation referred to in $M_{503}$, where the myth supposes a time when Indians celebrated the big bird rites only in the spring (in the autumn, according to the Hidatsa versions), would present – if I may be allowed the expression – a hyper-solstitial character, with an even greater degree of imbalance than the opposition between the solstices. The myth seems, then, to rest on the implicit equivalence:

$$(a\ single\ marked\ equinox) : (solstice) :: (solstices) : (equinoxes)$$

At the same time it becomes clear why the episode of the susceptible ferryman, the 'solstitial' character of which I postulated, happens to be transferred to a seemingly equinoctial circumstance. For, owing to the fact that the circumstance was not repeated, it violated a demand for symmetry created by the very concept of the equinox itself.

---

[2] The progressive character of the first series results from the fact that, in $M_{460}$, the dried meat comes after the balls made from a vegetable food, and from the fact that the dried meat in $M_{460}$ stands in opposition to the ball composed of vegetable food and dung in $M_{503}$; the regressive character of the second series arises directly from the calendrial time sequence, since in the latter winter succeeds autumn and spring winter.

This interpretation is valid for $M_{469}$, which refers objectively to the winter solstice, and for $M_{503}$ as I have just shown. In order to establish a ritual balance between the equinoxes, the myth has recourse to an initial model in a state of imbalance and which, logically, is situated on the side of the solstice. But is it also valid for $M_{460}$? Apparently not, since this myth is the foundation myth of the Old-Woman-Who-Never-Dies rites, which were performed in the spring to open the series of agricultural ceremonies that would continue until the autumn, but could not be prolonged beyond that point, since they were strictly incompatible with the winter hunting rites.

In order to solve this difficulty, we must look at the forms taken by the susceptible ferryman episode in Mandan mythology from a different angle. Several different forms have been noted: a very weak form in $M_{460}$, where the use of the adjective 'susceptible'[3] is justifiable only in the literal sense, since the snake would not accomplish its mission if its strength were maintained by the food to which it is susceptible; a stronger form in $M_{469}$, where the snake intends to devour its passengers, and an even stronger one in $M_{503}$ where it actually succeeds in swallowing one of them. Nevertheless, there seems to be a striking difference between, on the one hand, the Mandan and Hidatsa versions and, on the other hand, all the other versions with which I have established a comparison: instead of the passenger or passengers repaying the monster with flattering but insincere words, with insults or even with blows, the Mandan heroes feed him: openly and frankly in $M_{460}$, cautiously in $M_{469}$, and, in $M_{503}$, frankly at first then deceitfully, when the surviving brother gives him a ball made of dung as a substitute for real food. Consequently, only this last mentioned incident, which occurs only in this one Mandan myth, belongs to the most common type. It can be said that, within the susceptible ferryman group to which they belong, the Mandan and Hidatsa myths illustrate a local transformation which, as regards this particular point, even concludes with an inversion.

Is it possible to find a reason for this? Yes, no doubt, thanks to $M_{503}$, the impeccable construction of which has a demonstrative value, which also explains why I chose this myth as the starting point of my discussion.

[3] TRANSLATORS' NOTE: It should perhaps be pointed out here that *le passeur susceptible* has had to be rendered literally, because the author intends a punning exploitation of the adjective. But the play on words is less successful in English, because the first meaning tends to be 'easily impressed or seduced', whereas the first meaning in French is rather 'touchy, irascible'.

After the episode about the releasing of the game animals, the purpose of which, as I have shown is to connect up the celebration of the birds with the okipa, $M_{503}$ continues with three sequences relating to the heroes' supernatural adventures. The first takes them to the home of the Old-Woman-Who-Never-Dies, where they stay for one year; the second describes how they crossed the river on the snake's back; the third takes them to the home of the thunderbirds where they also spend one year. The first and third sequences seem to follow an exactly similar pattern: identical duration of stay, lapse of one seasonal cycle, visit of supernatural spirits during whose arrival the heroes have to remain hidden, division of plants and birds according to species or varieties, etc. In what way, then, are they different from each other? The first sequence describes a *terrestrial* sojourn at the home of an *agricultural* divinity, and during which the heroes have to behave with *moderation*: they can hunt deer, although these animals are the spirits of the gardens, but only on condition that they behave with restraint and observe a certain number of rules: they must kill, cook, and eat the game in the forest, keeping well away from the cultivated and inhabited areas.[4] On the other hand, at the home of the birds, and therefore in a *celestial* setting, the heroes' behaviour is characterized by a *lack of moderation*. They *boldly hunt* the monsters and pay no heed to the cautious advice they are given; and they dazzle their supernatural hosts by their daring deeds.

It is clear, then, in what way the second sequence differs both from the first and the third. It is concerned with *travelling* and not with *residing*; it takes place on *water* and not on *land* or in the *sky*. Lastly, the heroes' behaviour towards the snake is strictly intermediary between the *moderation* and the *lack of moderation* they display when with the agrarian goddess or the war-like gods: they *bargain* about the price of the crossing and distribute their food payments in instalments, which they only hand over at the end of each stage, in exchange for services already rendered. Towards the horned snake, then, the heroes behave with a mixture of boldness and caution, and the ambiguous aspect of this policy is also brought out by the fact that the wise brother manages to get himself carried across, whereas the monster swallows the adventurous brother. Lastly, it will be noted that, while staying with the mother of corn, the heroes *receive*, whereas when they stay with the birds they *give* (*ils paient de leur personne*, as the French saying has it, i.e. risk

[4] The same taboo is found among the Wintu of California (cf. Du Bois–Demetracopoulou, p. 343).

heir own skins in order to procure food, hunting weapons and ritual objects for their hosts) and, when dealing with the horned snakes, they *negotiate* their crossing by means of food balls not all of which are genuine but which nevertheless make it possible to deceive the other party. Bargaining is not far removed from guile, and guile verges on deception.

The various modalities of the susceptible ferryman episode illustrate a gradual transition leading from payment in kind to payment in the form of encouraging words, lies, insults and blows. *So the ferryman has to be susceptible*: sometimes in the sense of being physically sensitive, as in several North American versions in which he cannot bear his neck or sore knee to be touched, however lightly, but more often in the psychological sense; otherwise guile and bargaining, which effect the mediation between the other two kinds of behaviour, could not be introduced into the myths as an original solution to the problem which they raise. But if this ambiguous behaviour appears in the myth as the only appropriate attitude towards the monster whose function it is to embody the aquatic element forming a triangle with the earth and the air, is it not because, in such a system, water itself plays an ambiguous rôle? Certain versions of $M_{503}$ state this clearly: after the heroes have burnt a way through the two-headed monster's body (thus inverting the one-headed snake going through water: ([*snake*] *traversing water* ⇒ *traversed by fire*), the foolish brother commits the sacrilegious act of eating the monster's flesh and changes into a snake, owner of the Missouri (cf. $M_{508}$ and Bowers 1, p. 199; 2, p. 360). Henceforth, according to whether or not the Indians make offerings to him twice a year – when the water freezes over in November or the ice breaks up in April (Will–Spinden, p. 127; Bowers 2, p. 373) – he will either help them to cross the river, or he will cause storms, torrents and floods which make the river impassable and destroy the crops. 'For', as he explains to the people, 'I am no more a man. I am either your friend or your enemy' ($M_{503b}$; Denig, pp. 613–17).

So, the power of water oscillates between two extreme modes: on the one hand, the mode illustrated by the canoe whose course regulates the passage of time, the alternation between day and night and the return of the seasons, provided the travellers remain at a reasonable distance from each other, that is, establish an *internal* interval inside their boat; on the other hand, storms and floods which upset the natural course of things and which result from a failure to respect an *external* interval

between the traveller and the aquatic monster. The susceptible ferryman character illustrates a middle position. Instead of travelling by
water, he crosses it; and the inevitable contiguity between his body and
that of the passenger involves a mortal danger, which the hero can only
avert by making sure that, when he is moving from land to water or
from water to land, the interval to be bridged is neither too small nor
too great; this is tantamount to shifting the standard of reasonable
distance from inside the boat to outside.

It is therefore necessary to amplify our provisionally accepted, but
too simple, concept of a relationship of inversion between the ferryman
and the canoe. In reality, these two terms pre-suppose a third, which we
have just seen emerging in Hidatsa mythology: the flood, during which
the water, which was mastered by the canoe journey, goes out of control; the successful crossing, on the other hand, takes on the appearance
of a prize obtained at the price of a dialogue which is also a duel, between calculating man and hostile water:

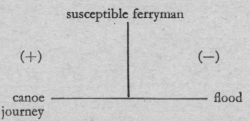

The Mandan and Hidatsa origin myths, in which the flood occupies
an important place, will make it possible to confirm the accuracy of
these propositions.

Neither tribe considers the possibility that mankind may have
emerged from water, although they look upon water as being the
primeval element. This is significant enough in itself, but it becomes
even more so when we see that the myths seem uncertain about whether
to opt for a terrestrial or a celestial origin. They combine the two
theses and the Hidatsa sages illustrated the system by drawing a kind of
Y: the two arms of the fork represent the emerging of some of their
ancestors who lived in the underworld, and the descent from the sky
of the others; the convergence of the two lines represent the adventures
of both groups after they had converged and cooperated (Bowers 2,
p. 304). The Mandan hold even more complex views about their mythic
origin. They believe that there were a large number of primeval communities, such as fish people, eagle people, bear people, corn people,

and buffalo people, etc. (Bowers 1, pp. 26, 365), from which three races stand out as playing a part in the myths. In the case of both the Mandan and the Hidatsa, these myths, fifteen or more of which are extant, vary a great deal and appear to preserve separate village traditions. To avoid an excessive use of letters of the alphabet, I propose to number these myths separately, except for the Mandan group already referred to as $M_{459}$, and of which I distinguish three variants, a, b and c (Bowers 1. pp. 156–63; 194–6; 196–7). I am using the numbers 510 and 511 for the oldest known versions (Maximilian, p. 364; Catlin, pp. 369–70), and 512 to 522 for the versions in Beckwith 1 and in Bowers 1 and 2, which belong partly to the Mandan and partly to the Hidatsa.

It is probably because they were once divided into moieties that the Mandan accord a special place in their myths to the corn people, who emerged from the underworld, and to the buffalo people, who were fashioned by the demiurge Lone-Man at a time when he was the sole representative of the human species. Like the eponymous peoples, the moieties were associated respectively with corn and buffalo, east and west, war and peace, the male principle and the female principle, the stem and bowl of the pipe, running water and stagnant water, hilly or wooded ground and open ground, etc. (on the subject of this systematic dualism cf. $M_{515}$; Bowers 1, pp. 353–61). The two peoples met and amalgamated roughly about the same time as the division into moieties was established. Some versions concentrate on the corn people, others on the buffalo people, while others deal with both. They do not all pay equal attention to the celestial people who came down to earth to join the other two peoples. However, the okipa rites, to which the group as a whole is linked, demonstrate the importance of a ternary system. Eagles and hawks, personified by dancers, fight against 'antelopes' (*Antilocapra americana*), which Indian terminology puts into the same category as deer, the spirits of the gardens; and the antelopes try to steal food from the buffaloes and the bears (Maximilian, p. 376; Bowers 1, pp. 144, 146, 153). So, the techno-economic triangle – agriculture, hunting and war – corresponds exactly to the tripartition of primeval mankind into corn people, buffalo people and celestial people, to whom three demiurges also correspond: Lone-Man and First-Creator, who shared the creation or the organization of space on the opposite banks of the Missouri, and Hoita, the speckled eagle, who played no part in terrestrial creation, since he is exclusively the representative of the 'People-Above' (cf. Bowers 1, p. 120). The transition from the binary to the ternary system is therefore accomplished by integrating two oppositions: between Lone-Man and First-Creator, then, after the latter has changed into a coyote, between Lone-Man and Hoita.

A comparative analysis of Mandan and Hidatsa origin myths would require a great deal of effort and would probably not yield great results. Each version, in emphasizing certain particular aspects of the narrative and leaving others in the background, seems to be prompted by the memory of historical adventures peculiar to one particular clan or village and which we are not in a position to reconstitute. I propose therefore to restrict myself to bringing out the pattern common to all the versions. After the emergence of the corn people and their convergence with the buffalo and celestial peoples, the ancestors lived near a stream called 'The Unknown' or 'The Stranger'. After a migration lasting several years, they arrived at an estuary. There, on the opposite bank or – according to some versions – on an island in the middle of a lake, they saw a large village, the chief of which was called Maniga, a word probably formed in some way from a root meaning water. All the versions have this episode in common and develop it as follows:

$M_{512-515}$. *Mandan. 'Origin myth'* (fragment: *the flood*)

The ancestors used to cross the water to trade for shells of which there was an abundance on the shores of this distant island. Maniga's people allowed them to come and gather shells, in exchange for rabbit skins and yellow meadowlark breasts. Yet these strangers never came to visit the Mandan: in order to carry out the exchange the latter had to make a dangerous crossing in a magic boat that went by its own power, provided it carried a fixed number of passengers.

After the Mandan had succeeded in crossing the stormy waters, further hardships awaited them. First of all, the willows along the bank turned into warriors with whom they had to wrestle before they could moor their boat. Then Maniga would supply so much food, water, tobacco and women that many of the Mandan died of excessive indulgence. Only those who had overcome all the ordeals could fill their bags with shells and go back. But such was the passion of the Mandan for these pearly jewels that they set off in search for them every summer, even though the hardships they encountered always killed several of the party.

Thanks to the help of the demiurge called Lone-Man or South-Wind, the Mandan at last succeeded in deceiving their opponents. Lone-Man had the idea of using a tube, made from a hollow sunflower-stem or a rush or a reed, which the Indians pushed through their bodies and by means of which they sent the food, drink and smoke down into the fourth world. According to other versions, Lone-Man enlisted the help of three medicine-men, one able to over-eat, the other to drink too much and the third to smoke too much. The Mandan learned how to overcome the final ordeal by using a buffalo's tail from which the hair had been removed in place of their natural organs. It is also said that Lone-Man took it upon himself to deal with all the women, for, although he remained chastely un-married while he was in the tribe, he acquired extraordinary powers when he was in a foreign land.

Furious at being defeated, Maniga broke with the Mandan by falsely accusing them of killing a dog. He created a flood, from which Lone-Man was able to protect his people: 'A thick mist will fall; it will last four days and four nights. Then you will know that they are coming to destroy you. But it will only be water.' As he said, the waves could reach no higher than the cedar tree, protected by a belt of water willow which the demiurge had ordered the Mandan to plant (Beckwith 1, pp. 4–7; Bowers 1, pp. 132, 340–41, 347–53, 360–61, etc.).

The nature of the exchanges is sufficiently indicative of the spirit of the myth. In return for the shells from which they would make drinking bowls ($M_{459a}$; Bowers 1, p. 156) or earrings ($M_{513}$; Beckwith 1, p. 12),[5] the Mandan offered the pelts of animals such as rabbits (skunks, accord-ing to $M_{514}$; Bowers 1, p. 351), as well as meadowlarks. The shells came from the river: rabbits and skunks sleep underground and live at ground level; it will be remembered that meadowlarks build their nests on the ground and fly low (see above, p. 237). So, as far as the Mandan are concerned, we are dealing with two intersections: *underground ∩ surface of the earth*, and *surface of the earth ∩ atmospheric sky*, integrating, in binary form, the triad of primeval peoples. In the process of exchange earth and sky together are set over against water.

According to an old version, the magic boat originally carried only eight people ($M_{510}$: Maximilian, p. 364), according to other versions twelve ($M_{512}$: Beckwith 1, p. 4; $M_{514, 515}$: Bowers 1, pp. 347–61), and sometimes thirteen when the demiurge embarked as an extra passenger without causing the boat to capsize ($M_{512, 514}$). Since Mandan boats only held one or two persons, and since the canoe in which the sun and moon travelled also had only two passengers, it seems likely that we have here

[5] In historical times, the Mandan were skilled in the making of beads from pounded glass which was melted in ovens (Maximilian, pp. 338, 340, 348; Will–Spinden, pp. 115–16).

one of those instances of mythic 'polyploidy', other examples of which have already been noted among the Mandan and Hidatsa, and allowed me to introduce the concept of the saturated set (above, pp. 349–61). According to $M_{512-513}$ (Beckwith 1, pp. 4, 12), this boat was called i-ci-he 'Go-by-itself', since it moved in obedience to commands. $M_{515}$ states that the Indians lost it because a foolish boy said to it in fun: 'Go on your way!' when it was empty; the boat sailed away and never returned (Bowers 1, p. 361). These unfortunate words recall the wrong use of oars in $M_{509}$.

The trees which turn into warriors and which protect the village against flooding, could be water willows (*Salix interior*), according to indications given by Bowers (1, p. 162: '*water willow*' and pp. 351, 361), later to be replaced by cotton-trees. By forcing his guests to imbibe enormous quantities of food, drink and smoke, Maniga is obviously trying to turn the forces of land, water and air against them. The trick whereby these substances are sent down into the fourth underworld recalls the Mandan belief in four skies arranged in tiers above the earth, and four worlds below it.

When considered from a more general point of view, the myth is seen to present an aetiological character: it proposes a theory of floods based on a two-fold explanation: they result from a conflict between the terrestrial people and the water people, and they are a manifestation of the seasonal cycle.

Let us begin by analysing the seasonal aspect. The Mandan named the months of the year according to meteorological conditions: e.g. 'little cold' or 'seven cold days'; or according to certain features of animal and vegetable life: 'the rut of wolves', 'sore eyes', 'ripe corn', 'fall of the leaves', etc. Two periods, corresponding roughly to April and November, were given symmetrical names indicating thaw or the formation of ice, which were important events on two counts: on the one hand, the thaw preceded, and the frosts followed closely after, the period May–October which was the time for agricultural work; on the other hand, the breaking up of the ice heralded the heavy floods which occurred in late spring and which, as we have just seen, occupied an essential place in religious conceptions (Will–Spinden, pp. 117–20, 127).

However, it is not possible to dissociate the spatial aspect of the myth from its temporal aspect. For the Mandan, a change of season meant also a change of abode. They used to establish their summer villages on promontories overlooking the river, so that they only had to protect them on one side by means of a ditch or fence. This relatively high elevation – about 20 or 30 metres – was still further emphasized by the fact that the fields and gardens lay in hollows, where the soil was fertile and easy to work. Seven varieties of corn were grown, as well as four kind of bean, five kinds of gourd, and three kinds of sunflower. After the seeds had been sown, the ground had to be weeded regularly during the summer months.

When the cold weather arrived, the river froze over and there was no longer any fear of flooding. The Mandan would then move to their winter camps in wooded, sheltered places in the valleys. During historical times at least, the Hidatsa followed the same custom: each winter village had its corresponding summer village, the former being perched on some grassy terrace overlooking the Missouri, while the latter lay down by the river on wooded ground. Each type of abode had its own separate political organization, since the powers of the 'winter chief', which were absolute while they lasted, came to an end with the return to the summer village (Bowers 1, p. 251; 2, p. 61).

The Mandan summer village included an area of beaten earth about fifty metres in diameter, at the centre of which stood a cylindrical construction made of planks bound together with branches and with a central pole made from the trunk of an American juniper (*Juniperus virginiana*). About 1930, traces of such a construction still remained in one village (Bowers 1, fig. 19). The tree-trunk represented the demiurge Lone-Man and the wooden wall the fortifications which he erected to protect the village from the flood (see above, p. 446). It was here that the main okipa rites were performed. These commemorated the Mandan victory over Maniga and the destructive power of water (see illustration on back cover of the French edition). The 'aquatic' aspect of the ceremony is also brought out by the fact that the sacred drums, which were always repaired in a boat in the middle of the river, were 6 in number, and 3 were struck 'toward the upstream' and 3 'toward the downstream direction' (Bowers 1, pp. 121, 128, n. 18, 151, 360).

The Mandan referred to the wooden structure, which they regarded as their sacred ark, by a word meaning 'the big boat' (M$_{511}$; Catlin, pp. 350, 353, 369). So, the opposition between village and canoe, which it was possible to deduce from South American myths, is replaced in Mandan mythology by an opposition between the winter village and the summer village; one close to water when it is frozen, and consequently immobile; the other set back from the water when the river is in flood and thus becomes too mobile. Between the frozen river and the thawed-out river, immobilized water and unleashed water, the summer village fulfils a function analogous to that of the canoe which transcends the opposition between the journey downstream, when the natural movement of the water increases speed, and the journey upstream, which reduces speed. And just as the canoe's celestial passengers must remain at the right distance from each other – neither too close nor too far apart – to ensure the exact regulation of the length of the days and nights and of the seasons, so the summer village, unlike the winter village, must be established at a reasonable height in respect of the river: not too far from the cultivated fields below which still have to be attended to during the summer, yet high enough for the flood water to stop at the base of the symbolic rampart and so spare the houses. In this sense, and as the Mandan themselves recognize by calling their ark 'big boat', the summer village *is* a canoe, since it enables them to overcome the perils of water.

That is not all. It will be remembered that the South American myths assign a rôle to the mythic canoe: in it and through it a kind of arbitration is effected between the near and the far, incest and celibacy, conjunction and disjunction. With the two polar terms between which it mediates, it forms, then, a ternary system. We have already seen that the dualism of Mandan thought can also accommodate imaginary triads, and we are now about to understand how this comes about. If the summer village occupies a half-way position, it can only do so in relation to two extreme limits: the sky and the earth. From this point of view, there is a diametrical opposition between the celestial village, where part of the ancestors lived, and the winter village, which is more 'terrestrial' (since it is lower) than the summer village, whose rôle as mediator has already been recognized, for quite different reasons.

The Hidatsa myths, which put the *sky/earth* opposition in the foreground, stress the motives which prompted the ancestors to leave their celestial abode and come down to earth: they could find no more game, and it was while searching in all directions that they discovered the buffalo herds below them ($M_{520}$; Beckwith 1, pp. 22–3; $M_{522}$; Bowers 2, p. 304). The Mandan myths, by attributing the disappearance of game to spite on the part of the demiurge Hoita, the personification of the celestial people, provide a symmetrical illustration of this idea ($M_{514}$; Bowers 1, p. 349). In both cases, the reference to the sky denotes the absence of game.

In so far as they are rites intended to increase the buffalo herds, the okipa dances merely reverse the relationship: they appoint birds to guard buffaloes whose food is being stolen by the spirits of the gardens (see above, p. 458). We can say, then, that in respect of the sky hunter and game are disjoined.

It is significant that the Hidatsa myth describing the descent from the sky should continue with the seasonal migration from the summer village to the winter village. It is chiefly in winter that the relationship between hunter and game appears as the reverse of that which, according to the myths, prevails in the sky. From the beginning of winter until the spring, the Mandan and Hidatsa relied for their source of food on the buffalo herds which came to find grazing grounds and shelter down in the valleys. In fact the Indians used to set up their villages in those very localities frequented by the animals. All social and religious activity tended therefore to encourage the conjunction of man and game, within the village itself. The entire population fasted and prayed assiduously. If the herds approached, it was strictly forbidden to cut wood or light fires or to make the slightest noise. The 'Black Mouths' were on constant guard to see that no person hunted prematurely, for the buffalo herds were easily startled in the river bottoms and had to be left undisturbed for a few days to get settled in their new environment. The Indians found it very hard to restrain themselves, particularly when the children were crying from hunger and cold. Yet everybody stayed indoors and the buffaloes could often be seen walking between the lodges (Bowers 2, pp. 56–63).

The fact that the close proximity of hunter and game was a necessary precondition for avoiding famine no doubt explains why sexual promiscuity held such an important place in the winter buffalo rites (see above, pp. 327–8). In its technical aspects, the winter hunt has an endogamous, even an incestuous, connotation. The conjunction it implies is in concrete opposition to an abstract disjunction which could only be depicted in the myths, since in practice Indians hunted at all seasons.

But the summer hunt represents an intermediary case between these extreme forms, one real, the other imaginary. It took place in the plains, far away from the village. The hunter went to the buffalo, instead of waiting for the buffalo to come to him. I have already drawn attention (p. 315) to this contrast, which is comparable, on the economic level, to the socially instituted opposition between exogamous marriage and endogamous marriage, on condition, however that the former takes place a reasonable distance away: otherwise it would be in danger of not taking place at all, and this would lead to a disjunction. By posing the problem of arbitration between the near and the far in different terms, Mandan thought thus links up with the conceptions of the Indians of tropical America. The transformation: (*mobile canoe* / *immobile water*) ⇒ (*immobile village* / *mobile water*) being granted, Mandan thought simply puts the summer village in the place of the canoe, since it also protects its occupants against dangerous waters and is symbolized by a sacred ark, significantly called 'big boat'. In both instances along a vertical or a horizontal axis which is also in both cases temporal, the same formula can serve to express the properties of the two mythemes, the formula which allowed me on pp. 193–4 to define the canoe as the intersection between union and disjunction, and which can now be applied to the summer village: $(\cap) \cup (//)$.

For the second time, we have come full circle, since it was the myth discussed at the very beginning of the present volume ($M_{354}$), the story of the hunter Monmanéki's marriages, which confronted us with the image of the canoe. In order to interpret this image, I had recourse, in the first instance, to certain North American myths which illustrated its converse in the form of a quarrel between the sun and the moon; by reversing the latter theme, we encountered the lodge for the ritual eagle hunt, the abode of the reconciled sun and moon ($M_{458}$), and the symbolism of which already led back to the canoe.

Following a fresh itinerary, we then moved from the canoe motif to that of the susceptible ferryman, and from the journey along the river to the business of crossing it; through a reversal which is also sub-stantiated by the myths, this last theme brought us to the flood, which makes rivers impassable. Finally, the neutralized flood led us back once more to the canoe, in the form of the sacred ark or tabernacle of the summer village.

Among the Mandan and the Hidatsa, the eagle-trapping lodge can be said to have the same relationship with the summer village and the winter village as the summer village itself (being situated at a half-way point) has with the celestial village (above) and the winter village (below). It so happens that the place of eagle-trapping in the seasonal cycle is between the summer buffalo hunt and the winter buffalo hunt, and we have seen that these two forms of buffalo-hunting are opposed to each other from all points of view: technical, economic, social, moral and religious. The opposition holds good in the other case too and is even intensified, since the summer village plays a mediatory rôle be-tween the disjoined hunting (in the sky) and the conjoined hunting (on low ground).

But it is clear that our second return to our starting point supposes a change of direction. This fact emerges at once from a comparison of the two 'bass parts' on which I construct the harmony of $M_{458}$ and $M_{503}$. In the first case, I set it down as:

| summer solstice | autumn equinox | winter solstice |

which is to be read from left to right (p. 302); whereas, in the second case, I set it down as:

| spring equinox | winter solstice | autumn equinox |

which is to be read from right to left (p. 453).

A little reflection will show that the two itineraries are complementary and that together they define a closed set. In connection with the first, a study of certain South American myths yielded the clinging-woman motif, the paradigm of which I could only establish by extending the enquiry as far as North America, to the myths of the Plains Indians which brought me back to the canoe by way of the quarrel between the sun and the moon. During a second stage, the study of certain North American modalities of the canoe motif brought to light the susceptible ferryman motif, the paradigm of which I could not have established without the help of South American examples; finally, it was these examples which brought me back to the canoe. If this is a correct statement of the course that has been pursued, it must follow that a symmetrical relationship exists between the clinging-woman motif and the motif of the susceptible ferryman (Figure 41).

This already seems obvious, even if we consider the matter from the semantic point of view only. In either case, we are dealing with two characters, one of whom climbs on the other's back in order to undertake a journey over land or water. The clinging-woman tries to remain as long as possible on the back of her husband, for whom she represents a mortal danger; the travelling hero wants to remain as short a time as possible on the back of the ferryman, who represents an equally mortal danger for him. The actual slave of the clinging-woman gets rid of her with the help of water, since she cannot swim; the virtual prey of the cannibalistic alligator gets rid of the monster with help of land (earth), on which the alligator cannot set foot. Finally, whereas the ferryman is susceptible (sensitive), the clinging-woman is not so at all. She has no scruples about bespattering her husband's back with excrement ($M_{354}$),

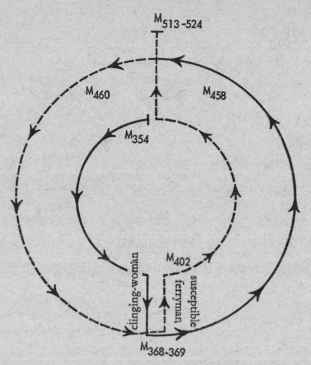

$M_{513-524}$

$M_{460}$

$M_{458}$

$M_{354}$

clinging-woman

$M_{402}$

susceptible ferryman

$M_{368-369}$

Inner circle:   South American itinerary
Outer circle:   North American itinerary
Solid line:     'outward' journey
Dotted line:    'return' journey

Figure 41. The journey through the mythic field accomplished in the course of the present volume

whereas one of the ways in which the ferryman shows his susceptibility is by threatening to devour the traveller, should he be taken short and commit an indiscretion on the monster's back ($M_{403a}$; Nordenskiöld 3, p. 288).

At the same time, textual analysis of the myths supplies empirical confirmation. We know that the clinging-woman motif can be reversed in two ways: on the one hand, it can become a rolling head which pursues its victims until they find refuge in water and, on the other, a diving tortoise which drags its victims down into water where they drown. Now, in most cases, the myths connect the susceptible ferryman motif with one of these two inversions of a motif which, as I postulated, is itself an inversion of the former along a different axis. This is so in the North American variants of the susceptible ferryman story, where the crane stretches out his foot to form a bridge to help the hero in his flight from the rolling head (Waterman, p. 43); and in $M_{508}$ (the first episode of which is a repetition of $M_{385}$, which I used as an introduction to the deadly tortoise motif). In South America, certain versions of the susceptible ferryman story conclude with a clinging-son motif ($M_{403b}$, Wagley–Galvão, pp. 140–41), which is a transformation of the clinging-woman along two axes: *woman* ⇒ *man*, and *wife* ⇒ *son* (whereas the rolling head theme is usually a transformation *wife* ⇒ *mother*).

So complicated a journey through the mythic field, along roads which sometimes proceed in the same direction, but follow courses which are far apart while remaining parallel, or intersect and even turn back upon themselves, would be incomprehensible if we did not realize that it has allowed us to carry out several tasks simultaneously. This volume presents the development of an argument in three dimensions – ethnographical, logical and semantic; and, if it has any claim to originality, this will be because, at every stage, it has shown how each dimension remains inseparable from the others.

First, from the ethnographical point of view, it has been necessary to cover immense distances, and to overcome the multifarious differences in way of life, social organization and beliefs which divide the Indians of tropical America from the Plains Indians of North America. I had set the first two volumes of *Introduction to a Science of Mythology* so definitely within the – to me – more familiar area of South American ethnography that this change of objective is almost tantamount to exploring another planet. By limiting the present volume to myths of the central regions of North America, I have, however, chosen, as it were, to put my space-ship into a parking orbit until the next and last volume offers it the opportunity of a fresh departure towards regions situated even further to the north and west where, granted the existence of transformations that would inevitably result from a change in hemisphere – even supposing the cultures were identical, which they are not – we shall be able to recognize a mirror image of the very first myths with which our investigation began.

In this respect, the comparison on p. 305 between $M_{428}$ and $M_{10}$ is simply a foretaste of the proof I hope to provide of the fact that a mythological system, however extensive its area of distribution, is always a closed system.

Moving on now to the formal point of view, I propose to distinguish three aspects of the development of the argument. In the first place, over and beyond the oppositions brought into play by the first myths to be studied, and which were situated mainly along a vertical, cosmic and spatial axis: high and low, sky and earth, sun and mankind, etc., I moved towards myths belonging to a different system defined by oppositions situated along a horizontal, social and temporal axis; here and there, near and far, endogamous and exogamous, etc. Whereas the first axis appears to develop in absolute space, the second appears to develop in relative time.

This observation highlights another aspect. The first oppositions were constructed by means of polar or mediatory terms of which it could always be said, in the absolute, that they were present or absent, conjoined or disjoined. On the contrary, the oppositions I have been dealing with throughout this volume involve, as their primary elements, not *terms* but *relations* perceived between these terms, according to whether they appeared too close together, too far apart, or at the right distance from each other. In other words, conjunction, disjunction and mediation, each illustrated by empirical modalities to which only approximate values can be given, while they still no doubt remain definable as relations, at the same time become the terms of a combinatory system operating on a higher level than the other, and which can be seen as the beginning of a veritable logic of propositions, a development of the logic of forms demonstrated in the second volume, and which itself was a development of the logic of sensible qualities dealt with in the first volume. By persistently going over and over the same myths, or through the incorporation of myths that are new (but belong, from the formal point of view, to the same set, in so far as they can be shown to be transformations of the preceding ones) structural analysis follows a spiral course. It seems to be going round in circles, but the aim is always to reach ever deeper layers of the mythic substance, into the heart of which it probes and all the properties of which it gradually permeates.

With the transition from discrete quantity to continuous quantity, or at least from long seasonal intervals to those lesser intervals formed by the lunar months and the succession of the days, we eventually saw how a novel-like form is gradually substituted for the mythic structure, thus giving rise to what might be called a mythology of fluxions, since it sets out to interpret those small periodic oscillations which cause alternation between night and day, upstream and downstream, ebb and flow, freezing over and thawing out, and the rising and falling of river water-levels.

The semantic aspect still remains to be examined. Here, too, a transformation has been seen to occur. The opposition between the raw and the cooked which provided the title of the first volume was an opposition between the *absence* or *presence* of cooking. In the second volume, I took the presence of cooking as given, in order to examine its *periphery*: the customs and beliefs concerning honey, on the hither side of cooking, and, on the far side, those relating to tobacco. Proceeding along the same lines, this third volume has been concerned with the *outer limits* of cooking which have a natural aspect, namely, digestion, and those with a cultural aspect, and which extend to table manners by way of recipes. The latter, as it happens, belong to both categories in that they prescribe the cultural elaboration of natural substances, whereas digestion stands in a correspondingly symmetrical position, since it consists in the natural elaboration of substances previously treated by culture. As for table manners, they belong to what might be called a secondary cultural elaboration, in which the manner of eating is compounded with the method of preparation. It remains to be shown, by way of conclusion, in what sense and to what extent the myths studied in this volume articulate a triple theory of digestion, recipes and table manners.

# 2 *A Short Treatise on Culinary Anthropology*

> PAUL: *I think that means. that Mummy and auntie intend to go to America.*
>
> SOPHIE: *But there's nothing terrible in that; on the contrary, it'll be great fun. We'll see tortoises in America.*
>
> PAUL: *And magnificent birds: red, orange, blue, mauve and pink ravens, not like our horrid black ravens.*
>
> SOPHIE: *And parrots and humming-birds. Mummy told me there were lots in America.*
>
> PAUL: *And there are black, yellow and red savages too.*
>
> SOPHIE: *Oh, but I would be afraid of savages, they might eat us.*
>
> Comtesse de Ségur, The Misfortunes of Sophie, Ch. XXII

Let us return for a moment to the Mandan and Hidatsa origin myths, one aspect of which I omitted from my analysis. In the Hidatsa myths chiefly, but also in the Mandan myths, the vengeful behaviour of the Water-People does not always seem to be the cause of the flood. Several versions connect its origin with other events, which took place before the visits to Maniga ($M_{459a}$). Moreover, $M_{518}$, $M_{519}$ and $M_{521}$ do not even mention these visits (Bowers 1, pp. 156–63; Beckwith 1, pp. 18–21, 155–8; Bowers 2, pp. 298–302). They relate instead how, in former times, when the birds returned in the spring, a hunter, furious at finding only one bird caught in the net, sent it back to its own people, after plucking it and sticking one of its wing feathers into its nostrils as a gesture of contempt. This is the version in $M_{519}$, which describes the incident in very similar terms to those of the Tucuna myth discussed in the previous volume ($M_{240}$, *HA*, p. 179).

Later, the Indians committed another foolish action. They had killed a female buffalo and taken the calf; as a joke, they put the mother's intestines (already blown up with air to hasten drying, according to $M_{459a}$) on the young animal's head and sent it back, thus adorned, to the buffalo herd. The animals, enraged by such insulting behaviour, unleashed torrential rain. A flood ensued, from which, as in the other stories, the demiurge Lone-Man protected his people. This is the same flood, but in this case it is caused by rain, i.e. water of celestial origin, and not by the thawing out of the rivers.

Thoughtless actions on the part of hunters probably belong to a pattern of taboos relating to animals, about which taboos unfortunately little is known, although a Cheyenne story ($M_{523}$; Grinnell 6, p. 176) throws some light on them: an Indian warns his daughter not to say: 'my poor animal' when she sees a captured buffalo calf or a captured bird; for one ought not to express pity for these suffering creatures. However, one day while some children were torturing a calf, the young girl could not conceal her feelings, as a result of which the game disappeared.

My intention is merely to define the spirit underlying these reprehensible actions. By sticking a feather into the bird's beak, the hunters are putting in front something which should be behind, and inside something which should be outside. Conversely, when they placed the mother's entrails on the calf's head, they were putting outside what should have been inside. It would seem that the behaviour of the Indians in Maniga's country in the other version of the flood story belongs to a formal structure of the same type. By means of the hollow pipe ruse, the visitors succeed in putting inside, by seeming to ingest it, food which, because of its superabundance, ought in the ordinary course of events to have remained outside.[1]

The winter hunting rites testify in a different way to the relevant function of the dialectic of outside and inside in Mandan and Hidatsa philosophy. As was prescribed in the foundation myth ($M_{464}$; see above, p. 328 *et seq.*) the officiants, whose rôle it was to embody the helpful

---

[1] French is probably not the only language containing expressions such as *mettre dedans* (literally, 'to put inside', i.e. to take in, deceive). If I might venture to generalize the paradigm, it could be said that the two heroes in $M_{503}$, who find themselves confronted with water, 'take in' the aquatic monster, while at the same time they themselves (literally) manage to remain outside the monster's belly and outside the water in which they nearly drowned, before running the risk of being devoured.

animals, held painted red sticks to which they had tied lungs, hearts and windpipes. These emblems represented the buffaloes (Bowers 1, pp. 315–16, 332; 2, p. 457) thus *mis à nu* (stripped bare) one might say, borrowing Marcel Duchamp's words, by the hunters. The reference is less incongruous than it might seem since, during the performance of these rites, the wives, who from the start were clad only in fur robes, were soon '*mises a nu par des célibataires même*' (stripped bare by unmarried men): 'Often a small group of three or four clansmen, widowers who no longer participated in the active events of the day, would send for a distant "son" whose young wife met their fancy and offer to bring the young man luck if he would leave his wife to them.' Since Whites were supposed to possess greater supernatural powers than Indians, the traders who called at the villages soon learned to pray for their 'sons', whenever the latter had pretty wives. 'Not only did they spend many pleasant nights with young women, but also received rich rewards in robes and even horses from the husband in return for promises of success' (Bowers 2, pp. 462–3).

Let us return to the visceral offerings. Before swimming across the Missouri, the Assiniboine used to tie to a stick some pieces of buffalo guts, grease and bladder and put it into the water, saying: 'That is to enable me to cross without accident; let no wind blow nor pain take me in crossing' (Denig, p. 532). It would be interesting to verify whether or not, in the Plains liturgy, this typical offering formed an oppositional pair with the decorated and painted buffalo head to which prayers were addressed so that the animal should not gore (that is, eviscerate) the hunter.

Although the owner of the waters appreciated intestines as offerings, especially pieces from the large intestine (Bowers 2, pp. 360, 373), the dreaded arrival of the flood water had at least one beneficial effect: it brought dead buffaloes down with it, of which the Mandan were particularly fond and which they preferred to fresh meat (Neill, p. 383). They used to hang the game until the flesh was half decomposed. Even their dried meat was high (Coues, Vol. I, p. 325; Will–Spinden, p. 121). A myth ($M_{515}$, Bowers 1, p. 355) confirms the importance attributed by the Indians to this preliminary process of digestion, which occurred outside the body since it took place in water. When the demiurge Lone-Man thought he ought to be born again in the tribe, he had great difficulty in finding a suitable young woman to be his mother. After various schemes had failed, he succeeded in the following way: a thirsty young girl who was working in her field in the hot sun ran down n to the river to get a drink. The water was up to the willow-trees and a dead buffalo came floating by. Its back was cut open and the young girl wanted to have the kidney fat, which she could see sticking out. She pulled the animal on to the bank, and ate the fat which made her pregnant.

We must not forget that the trick whereby the Indians in $M_{514-515}$ replace their digestive tracts by a hollow stem thanks to which the food passes through their bodies without remaining there, that is, without undergoing the process of digestion, parallels, but in the beneficial mode, a pathological condition with which we have been familiar since the beginning of this enquiry. In the Bororo story ($M_1$) which remains our basic reference myth and which is still being commented on as it were, in this third volume, the hero is famished and incapable of feeding himself, because he has no posterior, and the food passes through his body without being digested. The comparison is all the more imperative in that this hero, a victim of his own people's wickedness, becomes the master of storms and rain, which he uses to punish them. Symmetrically, in $M_{514-515}$, the Indians who are the victims of the wicked master of the flood, overcome their enemy by avoiding the organic necessity of digestion. But is it not the case that, unlike the human body, water, being the medium most favourable to putrefaction, achieves *externally* a natural transformation of food in a way comparable to the transformation achieved *internally* by the human body through the digestive process?

During the course of this enquiry, we have often encountered pierced or blocked characters, such as the one who occurred at the beginning of the present volume in the person of the pierced wife of Monmanéki, the hunter, who bespatters her husband's back with excrement ($M_{354}$); later, there was the primeval couple in a Yabarana myth ($M_{416}$), and here now is another Guiana myth which maintains that the blocked state was common to the first race of humans.

*$M_{524}$. Taulipang. 'The origin of digestion'*

In former times, neither men nor animals had anuses, and they excreted through the mouth. Pu'iito, the anus, used to walk slowly among them, break wind in their faces and then flee. The angry animals discussed what should be done. They pretended to be asleep and when Pu'iito approached one of them, with the intention of behaving in the usual way, they chased him, seized him and cut him up into pieces.

Each animal was given its share, which was greater or smaller in accordance with the size of the orifice it has today. This is why all living creatures have an anus; otherwise they would be forced to excrete through the mouth, or would burst (K.-G. 1, p. 77).

It is true that, according to other traditions, certain animals retain their former state; the ant-eater is said to be one, and the Tacana maintain that this is why it has to feed on small insects (Hissink–Hahn, pp. 165–76; cf. *HA*, pp. 132–5, 202–4); and the Barama River Carib (Gillin, pp. 203–4) believe that the sloth has had no anus since the time when it had to be blocked with earth in order to prevent it continually breaking wind. On the other hand, the guariba monkey, which defecates incessantly, is too open a character (cf. *HA*, pp. 396, 428–9).

A separate volume would be necessary to draw up a typology of these characters, who are blocked or pierced, above or below, in front or behind, who are unable to ingest anything except liquids or smoke (and sometimes have to be satisfied with allowing liquids or smoke to pass over the surface of their bodies) and who, being devoid of either mouths or anuses, have no digestive functions. They exemplify, on the alimentary level, a series for which there are other parallels: on the sexual level, there are the characters who either have no penis or a long penis, no vagina or a large vagina (i.e. various conditions which make them non-piercing or too piercing, non-pierceable or too pierceable); or again, in terms of daily activities, characters without eyes or joints and who therefore can neither see nor move about. If we restrict ourselves to the first series, as being the only one which concerns us at this point, it is clear that the characters who cannot ingest (above) or excrete (below), or who ingest or excrete too much or too quickly, are used in mythic thought to express certain fundamental notions; otherwise it would be difficult to understand why they recur in widely separated places and at different periods. 'Along the borders of India, there exist men whose bodies are entirely covered with feathers like birds, and who take no other food apart from the scent of flowers which they inhale through the nose' (Aulus-Gellius, *Noctes atticae* IX, iv; cf. Pliny, *Nat. Hist.*, VII, ix). In a work which my colleague, Dr George Devereux, kindly brought to my notice, Lucian refers to people without anuses who live on a juice extracted from the air, like dew, who cannot defecate and who copulate in the bend of the leg with boys (*Vera Historia*, Loeb Classical Library; Lucian, Vol. I, p. 277).

Among the Northern Tupi, Huxley (pp. 160–73) discovered an

implicit physiology in which digestion becomes a natural counterpart of cooking. Cooking effects mediation between what, in another context, I called the burnt world and the rotten world. The presence of the digestive tract fulfils the same function in relation to the absence of mouth or anus. In the first instance, food could only take the form of smoke; in the second, it would be taken in and eliminated through one and the same orifice, and would become confused with excrement.

During digestion, the organism temporarily retains food before eliminating it in a processed form. Digestion therefore has a mediatory function, comparable to that of cooking which suspends another natural process leading from rawness to rottenness. In this sense, it may be said that digestion offers an anticipatory organic model of culture. However, this model also has a more general significance; a rapid review of the major mythic themes that have been expounded in this volume will show that they can also be interpreted in this way. In the star-husband cycle, Moon's human wife who fails in her function as mediatory agent between sky and earth, dies while pregnant in her attempt to cross the frontier separating the two worlds, after she has removed the stopper preventing communication between them. Symmetrically, the water frog can remain permanently stuck on the body of her celestial affine: she also fails in her function as mediator, because she herself is pierced either above or below, being incontinent in respect of either saliva or urine. Consequently, the failure of the two female mediators can be explained by the fact that the first *goes through the obstacle while she is full*,[2] (i.e. pregnant, therefore solid) whereas the second *adheres* while she is *hollow*, thus illustrating two contradictory solutions in relation to the outside and the inside.

The basic character of this systematization also emerges from the correlations, found in various parts of the world, between the opening and closing of the different orifices of the body. In the myths of the Sanema of Southern Venezuela, there is a community of subterranean dwarfs (oneitib), who eat and speak with extreme rapidity, because, having neither intestines nor anuses, they are perpetually hungry, swallow meat raw and eat young women who, as sometimes happens, try to conceal the onset of menstruation to avoid being forced into marriage. In other words, characters who are open from the alimentary point of view punish others who, although sexually open, maintain untruthfully that they are closed. The woman-eating oneitib often visit

[2] TRANSLATORS' NOTE: The French word *plein, pleine* has the three meanings: full, pregnant, and solid (the opposite of *creux, creuse*, hollow).

humans and make them ravenously hungry: they thus open them too much above, in an alimentary respect, instead of punishing them for claiming to be too closed below, in a sexual respect ($M_{525}$; Wilbert 8, p. 234).

Finally, it should be emphasized that the theory of orifices exploits the possibilities of a combinatory system which, varying as it does at different times and in different places, often reverses the significance of its operations. When the Yurok of California declare that a woman in childbirth must keep her mouth shut so that the child may emerge more easily from the vagina (Erikson, p. 284), their views coincide with ancient European beliefs recorded by Pliny (*Nat. Hist.*, B., VII): 'To yawn during childbirth is fatal, and sneezing at the moment of conception causes abortion.' In the case of a caesarian birth, however, the mouth and vulva of the mother had to be kept open (Parker). But the Arapaho had a different approach: they would tickle the throat of a woman in labour with a feather, so as to cause sickness or vomiting which was meant to hasten the birth and the evacuation of the placenta Hilger 2, pp. 16, 17, 19). As in other semantic fields, only the form in which the problem is posed remains constant, not its content.

Certain beliefs of the Menomini provide a convenient transition to the theory of recipes, since these particular Indians prohibited the eating of fried or grilled (broiled) food by pregnant women for fear the placenta might stick and cause the mother's death (Hilger 1, p. 163). In any case, the major transformation which led us back from the myths featuring the quarrel between the sun and the moon to those dealing with the birds'-nester (and more especially back to $M_{10}$ from $M_{428}$, see above, p. 305) has its origin in an implicit culinary doctrine which establishes a correlational and oppositional link between the over-broiled meat which the hero of $M_{10}$ must chew in silence and the boiled intestines which the heroine of $M_{428}$ must masticate noisily.

The only type of oven known to the Ge Indians – $M_{10}$ is a Ge myth – was the baking oven. When they could not use the baking technique, which they considered to be the only noble one, they would expose the meat directly to the heat of the fire. Consequently, their cooking methods made no clear distinction between broiling (grilling) and roasting. As in the case of most so-called primitive peoples, broiling for them was simply a mode of roasting, the only difference being that the meat was placed nearer to the fire. Consequently, for the time being I propose not to consider grilling or broiling as a special technique, but to see the relevant opposition as being between roasting and boiling.[3] No doubt, the opposition is part of the much broader system, to which the first volume of *Introduction to a Science of Mythology* was almost entirely devoted. Food presents itself to man in three main states: it may be raw, cooked or rotten. In relationship to culinary operations, the raw state constitutes the unmarked pole, whereas the other two are strongly marked, although in opposite directions: the cooked being a cultural transformation of the raw, and the rotten its natural transformation. Underlying the main triangle, there is, then, a double opposition between *processed / non-processed*, on the one hand, and *culture / nature*, on the other.

Considered in themselves, these categories are no more than empty forms which tell us nothing about the cooking methods of any particular society. What each society understands by 'raw', 'cooked' and 'rotten' can only be determined through ethnographical observation, and there is no reason why they should all be in agreement about the definitions. The recent increase in the number of Italian restaurants in France has given French people a taste for raw food in a much 'rawer' state than was traditional with us: the vegetables are simply washed and cut up, without being prepared with an oil and vinegar dressing, according to the usual French custom – except for radishes, which, however, are significantly felt to require a generous accompaniment of butter and salt. Through Italian influence we have, then, extended our category of the raw. Certain incidents which occurred after the Allied landings in 1944 show that American soldiers had a broader conception of the category of the rotten than the French; under the impression that the Normandy cheese dairies stank of corpses, they sometimes destroyed the buildings.

It follows that the triangle formed by the *raw*, the *cooked*, and the *rotten* defines a semantic field, but only from the outside. In all forms of cooking, the food is not just cooked; the process must be carried out in some particular way. Nor does there exist any pure state of the raw: only certain foodstuffs can be eaten raw, and even then only after having been washed, peeled, cut up, and frequently seasoned. Lastly, even those traditions which most readily accept rottenness, only tolerate it in certain spontaneous or controlled forms.

In *The Raw and the Cooked*, I deliberately ignored these shades of difference. On the basis of South American examples, my aim was to

---

[3] A first draft of the following remarks was published under the title: 'Le Triangle culinaire' in *L'Arc*, no. 26, 1965 (re-issued in 1967 and 1968).

define the culinary triangle in its most general manifestation and to show how, in every culture, it could be used as a formal framework to express other oppositions, either cosmological or sociological. Having thus characterized it from the inside by the analysis of its internal properties, I proceeded, in *From Honey to Ashes*, to approach it from the outside and to study its 'neighbourhood'. Still keeping to the formal point of view, I sought to define the raw, the cooked and the rotten, considered no longer simply in themselves or from the angle of oppositional systems comparable to the one they constitute, but in relation to peripheral functions: the more-than-raw, that is honey, and the more-than-cooked, that is tobacco. Although certain modalities of the cooked, such as the roast and the boiled, were met with in the course of the enquiry (*HA*, p. 339, n. 32), I deliberately refrained from discussing them.

The time has now come to do so, since the myths studied in this third volume go beyond the oppositions between the raw, the cooked and the rotten to establish a deliberate contrast between the roast and the boiled, which, in a great many cultures, represent the basic modes of cooking. Along with other no less genuine oppositions, they figure in a French work of the 12th century which deserves to be quoted at the beginning of this discussion. In a concentrated form, which gives a denser meaning to each term, it outlines the possibility of a structural analysis of the language of cooking: 'Others devote too much vain study to preparing meats, excogitating infinite kinds of decoctions, fryings and seasonings; craving, like women great with child, now soft, now hard, now cold, now hot, now boiled, now roast, now with pepper, now with garlic, now with cinnamon, now with savoury salt' (Hughes de Saint-Victor, *De Institutione Novitiarum,* in Franklin, p. 157). This passage establishes a major opposition between food and seasoning; and it distinguishes between two extreme forms of the preparation of foods: boiling and frying, which in turn have several modalities classifiable in pairs: soft and hard, cold and hot, boiled and roast. Lastly, it also classifies seasonings in contrasted pairs: pepper and garlic on the one hand and cinnamon and salt on the other, by opposing – along one axis – pepper and what, a century later, were still called in French *les aigruns* (garlic, onions, shallots, etc. cf. Améro, Vol. II, p. 92); and, along the other axis, sweet spices and salt.

What, then, constitutes the opposition between the roast and the boiled? Roasted food, being directly exposed to fire is in a relationship of *non-mediatized conjunction*, whereas boiled food is the product of a two-fold process of mediation: it is immersed in water and both food and water are contained within a receptacle.

So, on two counts, the roast can be placed on the side of nature, and the boiled on the side of culture. Literally, since boiled food necessitates the use of a receptacle, which is a cultural object; and symbolically, in the sense that culture mediates between man and the world, and boiling is also a mediation, by means of water, between the food which man ingests and that other element of the physical world: fire.

The simplest way of conceiving of the opposition postulates that the more primitive technique appeared first: 'In ancient times men roasted everything', was the Greek view, as expressed by Aristotle. He adds that, consequently, it is permissible to boil meat that has been previously roasted, but not to roast meat that has been previously boiled, since that would be to run counter to history (*Problemata*, III, 43; quoted by Reinach, Vol. V, p. 63). His conclusion is far from being universally accepted, but its premises are found among widely differing communities. The natives of New Caledonia who were acquainted with the use of pottery before the arrival of the French (contrary to the indication given in the first printings of *L'Arc, loc. cit.*, p. 21, through a faulty transcription of my notes) were all the more inclined for this reason to stress that, once upon a time, 'people only broiled or roasted, "burnt" as the natives say ... The use of the cooking pot and the eating of boiled tubers are proudly considered ... as proofs of ... civilization' (Barrau, pp. 57–8). An Omaha origin myth ($M_{526}$; Fletcher–La Flesche, pp. 70–71) relates how men first invented fire and ate their meat roasted; but they grew tired of this daily diet and wondered how they could prepare meat differently. So they invented pottery, put water in the pot, meat in the water and the whole lot on the fire. In this way they learned to eat their meat boiled. The Micmac also harked back to primitive customs, but to justify their predilection for roast meat (Wallis 2, p. 404).

The opposition by virtue of which roast is on the side of nature and boiled on the side of culture and which is implicit in the preceding examples, is underlaid by another opposition between non-processed and processed food. It should, however, be recognized that this last opposition can take on very different values, since not all societies define the boiled and the roast in the same way.

The Plains Indians, whom I have so frequently referred to in the preceding chapters, provide an excellent illustration of the divergencies. Some tribes cook their food for a long time, others only for a little while, or they may prescribe very different cooking times, according to whether the meat is to be boiled or roasted. The Assiniboine, for instance, preferred roast meat to boiled meat, but in either case they liked it underdone (Denig, pp. 581–2). Their neighbours, the Blackfoot, who cooked their meat for a long time when they roasted it, reduced boiling to what our cooks call blanching, that is, they plunged the meat into boiling water for a few seconds, until it lost its external colouring (Grinnell 5, n. 205). These two cooking styles contrasted with the method practised by the Kansa and Osage, who liked their food to be overcooked (Hunter, p. 348), as well as with the practice of the Ingalik of Alaska: they believed that fish should be eaten either well-cooked or raw, or dried or rotten, but never half-cooked, since fish, when half-cooked, was not considered to be well prepared (Osgood, p. 165).

Turning finally to South America, we find that, according to Armentia (p. 11), the Cavina used to eat overboiled food which they allowed to cook slowly from 6 o'clock in the evening until 2 o'clock in the morning and then left to stand until daybreak, before serving. No doubt it was from the Indians that the settlers of Dutch Guiana got their recipe for the 'pepper pot', kept going from day to day by putting the remains of the last meal into the pot, along with a little freshly-made sauce. This stew improved with age. One example is quoted of a stew – a prized domestic possession, like a certain famous French *cassoulet* – which lasted for thirty consecutive years without the pot ever being cleaned (Schomburgk, Vol. I, p. 96).

I would not maintain, then, that all societies must necessarily put the boiled into the category of the processed and the roast into the opposite category. It would be more accurate to say, in the first place, that the opposition between roast and boiled seems to be operative in all contexts, however diverse its empirical content may be, and secondly that this particular way of formulating it seems to be more frequent than the other way. As a matter of fact, in many societies a double affinity can be observed: that of the roast with the raw, i.e. the non-processed, and that of the boiled with the rotten, which is one of the two modes of the processed.

The affinity of the roast with the raw results from the fact that, more often than not, it is compatible with incomplete cooking, this incompleteness even being a sought-after effect in our West European societies. Incompleteness occurs whenever roast meat is unevenly cooked, either on one side or the other, or on the outside in relation to the inside. A Wyandot myth ($M_{527}$; Woodman, p. 8) emphasizes this paradoxal nature of roast meat: 'The Creator caused fire to gush forth and directed the first man to put a portion of the meat on a stick and to roast it before the fire. But the man was so ignorant that he let it stand until it was burnt on one side, while it was raw on the other.' The Pocomchi of Mexico regard roasting as a compromise between the raw and the burnt. After the universal conflagration (M528; Mayers, p. 10), that which had escaped the fire became white, and that which had been burnt, black. That which had been merely singed became red. This explains the various colours of corn seeds and beans. Among the Waiwai of British Guiana, the shaman must never eat roast or fried meat. However, the Waiwai rarely resort to these methods of cooking and 'prefer to boil or cure their meat' (Fock, p. 132); nor must he come into contact with the colour red or with blood, a detail which also suggests an affinity between the roast and the raw. Aristotle rated boiling higher than roasting, on the ground that it was more effective in destroying the rawness of meat: 'roast meat being rawer and drier than boiled meat' (quoted by Reinach, *loc. cit.*).

The affinity between the boiled and the rotten is indicated in several European languages by expressions such as *pot-pourri* or *olla podrida*, which refer to different kinds of meat seasoned and cooked with vegetables; there is also the German expression *zu Brei zerkochtes Fleisch*, 'meat cooked until rotten'. Certain American languages indicate the same affinity, and it is significant that this should be so among the Siouan communities, neighbours of the Mandan, who, as we have seen, were extremely fond of 'gamey' meat, to the point of preferring the flesh of a dead animal which had been a long time in the water to that of a freshly-killed buffalo. In the Dakota language, the verb i-ku-ka conveys both the idea of decomposition or deterioration caused by some external influence, and that of boiling food which has been cut into pieces and mixed with other ingredients (Riggs, p. 196). The Mandan verb na'xerep here, 'to boil', seems to imply prolonged cooking until the meat falls off the bones (Kennard, p. 12).

These distinctions by no means exhaust the complexities of the contrast between the roast and the boiled. Boiling takes place inside (a receptacle), whereas roasting is cooking from the outside: one suggests the concave, the other the convex. Thus, the boiled often belongs to what might be called 'endo-cooking', intended for private use and for a small closed group. This is most forcefully expressed in the Hidatsa language, where the same word mi dá ksi is used for the fence surrounding the village, the cooking pot and the pan, since all three delimit an enclosed space (W. Matthews, p. 126). The roast, on the contrary, belongs to 'exo-cooking', the kind that is offered to strangers. In France in the old days, *la poule au pot* (boiled fowl) was a family supper dish, whereas roast meat was reserved for banquets, where it enjoyed pride of place. It always came after the boiled meat and herbs which were served at the beginning of the meal, and was accompanied by rare fruit, such as melons, oranges, olives and capers: 'The roast is set down on the table while the boiled food and the entrées are being cleared away ... But the time to serve the fish is towards the end of the meat course, between the roast and the dessert' (Franklin, pp. 221–3).

The same opposition is found in non-European societies, although they do not formulate it in the same way. Among the Kaingang of Southern Brazil, widows and widowers are forbidden to eat boiled meat, and so is someone who has killed an enemy (Henry 1, p. 184, and n. 15). Boiled meat could thus connote a strengthening of family and social ties, and roast meat a weakening of these ties.

The opposition between the roast and the boiled may occur on other levels too, not only in myths and ritual, but also in daily life. Several American tribes associate the roast with living in the bush and masculinity, the boiled with village life and femininity. The Amazonian Yagua boil or smoke their meat. The first process is carried out only by the women, but the smoking may be done by the men when they are out hunting, and in the village itself if the women are absent (Fejos, p. 44). Karsten explains (2, p. 115) that the Jivaro boil meat in an earthenware pot or roast it in front of the fire. They use the second method when they are camping away from the village to hunt, fish or perform other tasks, and it is the only method that a man may decently employ. In the village, boiling is carried out exclusively by the women; a man never boils anything apart from decoctions of tobacco and other magic plants. Goldman (p. 79) states that the Cubeo adopt 'the common tropical forest pattern: women boil, the men bake and broil'.[4] In Trumaï villages, according to Murphy and Quain (p. 30), 'the men did all the roasting, although it was permissible for the women to help. However, most foods were prepared by boiling, and the burden of cooking thus fell on the women'.

The Ingalik of the north-western part of the northern hemisphere divided food-stuffs into two categories, according to whether they had to be boiled or broiled: 'the boiling of food is the standard method of

[4] However, the terms 'bake and broil' do not seem to be very consistent with 'the common tropical forest pattern', which is based rather on roasting and smoking.

cooking when food is prepared in the house ... and ... broiling, except for certain fish, is limited to the travelling camp' (Osgood, pp. 276–7). On the other hand, the Tanana, their easterly neighbours, who ate almost all their food boiled, nevertheless made cooking a purely male task. This unusual practice was, it seems, shared by other northern Athapaskan tribes, such as the Ahtena, the Tanaina and certain Kutchin communities, although groups such as the Chandalar-Kutchin and the Loucheux who were closely related to them in respect of habitat, language and culture, entrusted cooking to the women (McKennan, pp. 41–6). But among the Sahaptin of the Columbia River, it was the men who did the cooking (Garth, p. 52).

As was noted above, the Siouan-speaking Assiniboine reversed the usual connotations of the roast and the boiled in their culinary procedures. It is consequently all the more curious to find them adopting attitudes similar to those of the Athapaskan to which I have just referred: 'when the men were at war ... they ate their food boiled. The women never used this method: their normal method consisted in roasting the meat on a spit tilted over the fire ... formerly they used to make and cook with earthenware receptacles ... but only the men used them' (Lowie 2, p. 12). A group of Menomini myths ($M_{475c-f}$) follows the same system: contrary to the real-life practice, they present the women as roasting the meat, and the men as boiling it; but the women in these myths are ogresses. The attribution of boiling to men and of roasting to women also seems to occur in certain East European countries; I shall return to the point later.

The existence of these deviant systems poses a problem. It suggests that the semantic field of recipes includes a greater number of dimensions than I indicated at the beginning of my discussion. No doubt, the communities among whom these inversions occur are thinking in terms of different oppositional axes. In this respect, I can make one or two tentative suggestions. For instance, boiling provides a method of preserving all the meat and its juices, whereas roasting involves destruction or loss. One suggests economy, the other waste; the second is aristocratic, the first plebeian. This aspect of the matter is obvious in societies which stress status differences between individuals or classes. Among the ancient Maori, a nobleman was allowed to roast his own food, but he avoided all contact with cooking utensils and baking-ovens, which were looked after by slaves and low-class women. To compare someone with a 'steaming oven' was, moreover, to proffer a deadly insult. Nothing, it was thought, was more likely than steam to spoil the physical and mental attributes of a highly born person, or of nature in its wild state: birds disappeared from the forests when people got into the habit of taking boiled food there. When white settlers introduced pots and pans into New Zealand, the natives believed that these were infected utensils, like the hot stones of their ovens (Prytz-Johansen, pp. 46, 89, 208–11). These attitudes represent a striking reversal of those already noted among the Kanaka of New Caledonia.

Similar observations can be made about European societies, in which attitudes towards the roast and the boiled have evolved in the course of time. The democratic spirit which inspired the compilers of the *Encyclopédie* in the 18th century is reflected in their vindication of boiled food: '... one of the most succulent and nourishing foods available to man ... It might be said that the boiled is to other dishes as bread is to other kinds of food' (see under 'bouilli'). Fifty years later the dandy, Brillat-Savarin (*Physiologie du Goût*, VI, § 2), was to take the opposite view: 'Professors[5] never eat boiled food out of respect for principles, and because they have proclaimed *ex cathedra* the following incontestable truth: Boiled meat is flesh without the juices ... This truth is beginning to gain ground and boiled meat has disappeared from the menus of truly elegant dinner parties; it is replaced by a roast tenderloin of beef, a turbot or a fish stew.' The reason why the Czechs look upon boiled meat as a man's food may be that their traditional society was more democratic in character than that of their Slovak or Polish neighbours. A similar interpretation might be suggested for the contrasting attitudes of the Romans, the Greeks and the Hebrews towards the roast and the boiled, which have been recently described by Professor Piganiol.

Elsewhere, the opposition may take a different form. Since boiled meat is prepared without loss of substance and within a closely confined space (see above, p. 482), it may seem a fitting symbol of cosmic totality. The Arawak of Guiana had a rule that the meat of animals killed in the hunt should be gently boiled in a pot without a lid, which had to be constantly watched in case it boiled over. Should it do so, all animals of that species would leave the area and could no longer be hunted (Roth 1, p. 295). At the other extremity of the continent, in the Great Lakes area of North America, the Fox observed the same rule for the cooking of ceremonial food: 'Should it boil over, then all life would all go outside.' There was also a rule that nothing must be

---

[5] TRANSLATORS' NOTE: The original has 'professeurs', which is ambiguous, but probably means 'experts in matters of cooking'.

dropped into the pot during cooking; while the contents were being eaten, not even the tiniest scrap could be left, or dropped (Michelson 5, pp. 249, 261).

Boiled food is life, roast food death. Folklore the world over offers countless examples of the cauldron of immortality; but there is no indication anywhere of a spit of immortality. A rite performed by the Cree Indians of Canada conveys very clearly the cosmic totality attributed to boiled food. The Cree believed that the Creator told humans that the first berries to be picked had to be boiled. Then the bowl had to be held first towards the sun, 'who was asked to ripen the berries, then towards the thunder who was asked for rain, and finally towards the earth, who was asked to bring forth her fruits' (Mandelbaum, p. 285). For the Ojibwa too, boiled meat had a relationship to the order of the universe; although they usually cooked squirrels by spitting the carcases and roasting them in the flames, they purposely boiled them when rain was needed (Speck 7, p. 80). In this case, the roast and the boiled are given differential functions and their combination constitutes a culinary universe, which is a miniature reflection of the cosmos. Perhaps a similar interpretation would be appropriate for the unusual Welsh recipe which involved stuffing roast goose with boiled ox-tongue and then encasing it in a layer of forcemeat, inside a pastry crust; the dish was supposed to last all through Christmas week (Owen, p. 34).

Here we find a link-up with the symbolism of the most remote Indo-European past, as it has been reconstituted by Professor Dumézil (p. 60): 'To Mithra belongs that which breaks of its own accord, that which is steamed, that which is properly sacrificed, milk ... and to Varuna that which is cut with an axe, that which is sealed in the naked flame, soma, the intoxicating liquid.' It is not a little surprising, but extremely significant, to find certain genial philosophers of cooking of the mid-19th century showing the same awareness of the contrast between knowledge and inspiration, serenity and violence, moderation and excess, symbolized in like fashion by the opposition between the boiled and the roast: 'Cooking is an acquired art, but roasting is a gift' (Brillat-Savarin, *loc. cit.* aphorism 15); 'Roasting is both nothing at all and absolutely everything' (Marquis de Cussy, *L'Art Culinaire*, in: Améro, Vol. I, p. 367).

Within the basic triangle formed by the categories of the raw, the cooked and the rotten, we have, then, inserted two terms, the roast and the boiled, which, in most cases, can be placed, one in the vicinity of the raw and the other in the vicinity of the rotten. Still missing, however, is a third term, illustrating the concrete modalities of the form of cooking which most resembles the abstract category of the cooked. This modality, I suggest, is smoking, which, like roasting, implies a non-mediatized operation (involving neither a receptacle nor water), but which, unlike roasting but in the manner of boiling, is a slow form of cooking, and so both thorough and steady.

In the process of smoking, as in that of roasting, nothing is interposed between the fire and the meat, apart from air. But the difference between the two techniques lies in the fact that, in one case, the layer of intervening air is reduced to a minimum whereas, in the other, it is increased to the maximum. The South American Indians, whose favourite method is smoking, build a wooden frame about 1·5 metres high to lay the meat on, and keep a very low fire going underneath for about 48 hours. Consequently, while the two techniques have one constant feature – the presence of intervening air – there are differential features which can be expressed by the oppositions: *near/far* and *fast/ slow*. A third differential is the absence of a utensil in the case of roasting (any stick can be used as a spit), whereas the Indian barbecue-frame is a man-made construction and consequently a cultural object.[6]

In this last respect, smoking is no doubt akin to boiling, which also requires a cultural instrument, namely the receptacle. However, a major difference can be observed between the two kinds of receptacle. Or rather, the difference is instituted by culture in order, as it were, to stress the opposition which might otherwise have remained too weak and thus failed to take on significance. Pots and pans are utensils which are carefully looked after and preserved. They are cleaned and put away after use, so as to be made to last as long as possible. The barbecue frame, on the contrary, *must be destroyed immediately after use*; otherwise the animal would take its revenge by coming to barbecue the hunter. Such, at least, is the belief held by the Indians of Guiana (Roth 1, p. 294), who – as has already been noted – also hold the obviously symmetrical belief that if a badly watched pot boils over, the reverse penalty will ensue: the game will flee beyond the hunter's reach, instead of attacking him. Lastly, as has already been observed, the boiled clearly

---

[6] Yet in this instance, too, it would be rash to generalize, since the Indians of Oregon treated with special respect the pointed wooden sticks they used as spits, whereas the receptacles used for boiling were often just roughly shaped pieces of bark heated by means of hot stones. I shall return to this point in the next volume.

stands in opposition to both the smoked and the roast in respect of the presence or absence of water.

But let us return for a moment to the opposition between perishable and durable utensils, which has just been noted among the Indians of Guiana in connection with the smoked and the boiled. This opposition, as it happens, will allow me to solve a difficulty connected with the system I am proposing, a difficulty which has no doubt not escaped the reader's attention. At the beginning, I defined one of the oppositions between the roast and the boiled as expressing the opposition between nature and culture. Yet, a little later, I suggested an affinity between the boiled and the rotten, at the same time as I defined the rotten as the processing of the raw by natural means. Is it not contradictory that a cultural technique should lead to a natural result? In other words, what philosophical significance is to be attributed to the invention of pottery (and consequently of culture), if, in native thought, boiling is compared to decay which, in the state of nature, is the condition to which raw food evolves spontaneously?

The technique of smoking, as it is conceived of by the natives of Guiana, involves a similar paradox. On the one hand, smoking, of all modes of cooking, is the one which most resembles the abstract category of the cooked; and since the opposition between the raw and the cooked appears to be homologous with that between nature and culture, smoking represents the most cultural mode of cooking; in practice it is also the most highly regarded by the natives. Yet, on the other hand, the barbecue frame, the cultural instrument of smoking, must be destroyed immediately after use. Here we can see a striking parallel with boiling, the cultural means of which, the receptacles, are preserved, while the boiling itself is considered as a process of spontaneous destruction. The boiled, at least in native terminology, is frequently the equivalent of the rotten, although the function of cooking is rather to prevent or delay decay.

Can any reasons be suggested to explain the parallelism? In so-called primitive societies, cooking in water and smoking have in common the fact that both are connected with time – one in respect of the means used, the other in respect of the results obtained. Cooking in water is carried out by means of earthenware receptacles (or wooden ones in communities among whom pottery is unknown, but who boil water by plunging hot stones into it); in either case, these receptacles, which are kept clean, carefully looked after and repaired from generation to generation, are amongst the most durable of cultural objects. As for smoking, it preserves foodstuffs for much longer than any other form of cooking. It would seem as if the prolonged enjoyment of a cultural product involved, sometimes on the level of ritual and sometimes on that of myth, a corresponding concession in favour of nature: when the result is long-lasting, the means must be precarious, and vice versa.

This ambiguity, which, as can be seen, is characteristic of both the smoked and the boiled, although it works in different directions, is the same as the one which seemed to be linked to the most widespread conception of the roast. Roast meat, which is burnt on one side and raw on the other, or grilled on the outside and red inside, embodies the ambiguity of the raw and the cooked, of nature and culture which the smoked and the boiled must illustrate in their own way, if the structure is to be coherent. But the reason which compels them to do so is not a purely formal one: by means of the ambiguity, the system demonstrates that the art of cooking is not entirely situated on the side of culture. Since it corresponds to the demands of the body, and is determined in each of its modes by the particular way in which, in various contexts, man fits into the world, cooking, being situated between nature and culture, has as its function to ensure their articulation one with the other. It belongs to both domains, and reflects this duality in each of its manifestations.

But it cannot always do so on the same level. The ambiguity of the roast is intrinsic, that of the smoked and the boiled extrinsic: it does not appertain to the things themselves, but to the way in which they are referred to or to the attitudes adopted towards them. For, here again, a distinction has to be made: the characteristic of being natural, which language often confers on boiled food, belongs to the category of metaphor: the boiled is not the rotten; it merely resembles it. Conversely, the transfiguration of the smoked into a natural entity is not a result of the non-existence of the barbecue, but of its deliberate destruction. This transfiguration therefore belongs to the category of metonymy, since it consists in acting as if the effect had no need of a cause and could consequently fulfil both functions simultaneously. Even when the structure, in order to overcome some imbalance, changes or becomes more complex, it can never do so without creating some new imbalance on a different level. We observe once again that it is the unavoidable dissymmetry of the structure which gives it its power to create myth, which is precisely an attempt to correct or mask this inherent dissymmetry.

Let us return to the culinary triangle. I inscribed within it another triangle concerned with cooking processes, or at least with those of the simplest kind, since I restricted my observations to three ways of preparing food: roasting, boiling and smoking. The smoked and the boiled stand in opposition to each other in respect of the element interposed between the heat and the food: in the one instance it is air, in the other, water. The smoked and the roast are in opposition through the greater or lesser volume of air involved; the roast and the boiled through the presence or absence of water. The dividing-line between nature and culture, which can, according to one's preference, be drawn parallel either to the axis of air or to that of water, places the roast and the smoked on the side of nature and the boiled on the side of culture, *in respect of the means used*; and the smoked on the side of culture and the roast and the boiled on the side of nature, *in respect of the results obtained* (Figure 42).

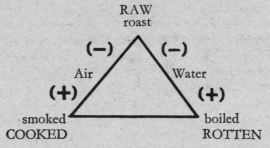

Figure 42. The culinary triangle

It should not be thought, however, that I am naïvely asserting that all cooking systems conform to this model for the same reasons and in the same way. I have taken it as an example, because it reflects one aspect of the system current in our own society (the complete analysis of which would require the exploration of additional dimensions), and also, I think, of several other systems. But it is clear that the diagram illustrates only one of many transformations taking place in an infinitely vast set, which will no doubt never be apprehended in more than fragmentary fashion, because adequate data about culinary practices in various parts of the world is lacking, anthropologists having paid little attention to the subject.

Confining my observations to the deviant systems of certain Plains tribes to which I referred earlier (pp. 480–81, 484), I would like to point out first that these communities were either unacquainted with the technique of smoking or chose not to employ it (Figure 43). They

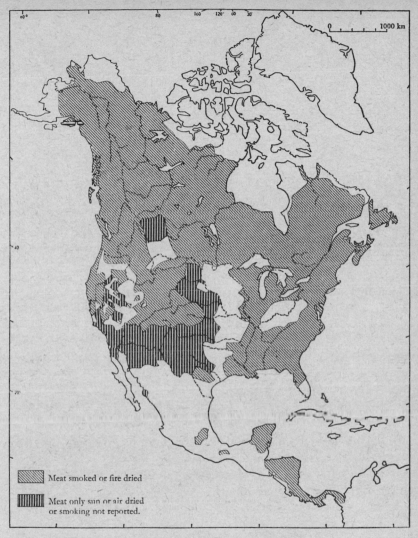

Figure 43. Dried and smoked meat in North America.
(From Driver and Massey, map 53.)

cut the meat up into very thin slices, which were dried by exposure to the air, a method I myself often used in Brazil, where the result is known as *carne de vento*. Meat prepared in this way is very tasty, but it goes bad much more quickly than meat which has been previously salted or smoked. This is why the Blackfoot, the Cheyenne and the Oglala Dakota Indians carried the process a stage further. After preparing thin slices of hard, dried meat, they laid them directly on a bed of glowing embers, first one way up then the other. Next, they beat them as with a flail to break them up into small pieces, which were mixed with melted buffalo fat or marrow; they then packed the preparation tightly into leather bags, taking care to see that no air was left inside. After the bags had been sewn up, the women jumped up and down on them to make the contents homogeneous. When each bag and its contents had become a compact mass, it was exposed again to the sun to complete the drying process (Grinnell 3, p. 206; Beckwith 2, p. 431, n. 1; Berthrong, p. 31).

In so far as the technique of preparing pemmican replaces smoking, it is normal that it should lead to a split in the polar term which stands in opposition to the boiled and the roast in the culinary triangle, and should replace it by a pair of terms which are both correlative with, and in opposition to, each other: *drying*, on the one hand, which is further removed from the cooked than the roast and the boiled are, since it dispenses with fire, and on the other hand *preserving*, which presupposes drying, but differs from it through bringing the meat into direct contact with the fire, and thus represents a superlative form of cooking.

The Blackfoot seemed to me to present a problem, because their culinary system places the boiled on the side of the almost raw and the roast on the side of the more-than-cooked. As it happens, we have additional information in their case. First, Grinnell (*loc. cit.*), one of the best observers of the Blackfoot Indians, explains that the grilling of dried meat, which is one stage in the preparation of pemmican, was carried out on two adjacent hearths. The burnt meat made each fire unusable for a time, because the pungent smoke would have given an unpleasant taste to the next batch of meat-slices. So two fires were in operation alternately, to allow the organic matter in each to be burned away before it was next used. It could well be that in this kind of system, where over-combustion was seen as having a corrupting effect, the category of the burnt replaced that of the rotten: the commutation is all the more likely, since considerations quite foreign to the present argument have already indicated that the two categories form a pair of correlative and opposite terms (*RC*, pp. 176-8, 292-5, 334-9). The inversion of the rotten into the burnt could have involved, as a concomitant phenomenon, the inversion of the boiled and the roast, in relation to the poles of the raw and the cooked.

But the most important factor is that the Blackfoot lived at a meeting-point of languages and cultures, where various influences merged or came into conflict. There were the woodland Algonquin, with whom the Blackfoot were linked linguistically; the Plains tribes whose way of life they shared; and the north-western Algonquin and the Plateau Indians, with whom they had commercial links. This cosmopolitan atmosphere also had repercussions on their culinary system. Like the other Plains tribes, the Blackfoot knew how to boil meat in makeshift cauldrons, by lining the sides of small pits with a piece of rawhide, and then filling them with water into which they plunged hot stones. At the same time, they seem to have been the only Plains Indians to make stone receptacles (Grinnell 3, p. 202),[7] probably under the influence of the various Plateau cultures, from which they had also learned a very complicated technique for rendering edible the bulbs of a certain liliaceous plant (*Camassia quamash*): these bulbs were cooked for several days in succession in an earth oven, then dried in the sun and preserved in bags.

For the purposes of boiling, the Blackfoot had, then, a very wide range of receptacles at their disposal, from rawhide cauldrons to stone vessels, by way of soft leather bags and bowls made of wood or, once upon a time, of earthenware: that is, perishable utensils, such as those made of untanned hide, or lasting ones such as stone dishes. This dualism in the technical means of boiling had as its counterpart a dualism in the reverse culinary method (reverse in the sense that it excludes water), in respect of the results obtained: meat dried by exposure to air is perishable, but the pemmican into which it is transformed is not. Lastly, the four main culinary methods used by the Blackfoot – the preparation of pemmican, the cooking of bulbs in ovens, the blanching of meat in boiling water and the drying of meat through exposure to the air – seem to be reducible to pairs of correlative and opposite terms. The first two are complex, the last two simple. The first and last take place in the open air, the second and third below the level of the ground in pits with or without water. The chthonian oven, used for cooking vegetable foods, is opposed to animal flesh,

[7] At least, this is what Grinnell says. Evidence indicating that the Crow Indians may have done so too comes mainly from the myths (cf. Lowie 11).

which is suspended at a certain height above the ground, just as, within the category of animal foods, pemmican, which is packed into dried and hermetically sealed hide-bags, is opposed to meat which is blanched in a piece of rawhide, opened out and filled with water. It is not surprising that this extended four-point system, in which two terms represent the *almost raw* (dried or scalded meat) and two the *more-than-cooked* (pemmican and plant bulbs, that is, preserved animal and vegetable foods), should require two internal points of support in order to be firmly anchored to the simple valencies of the *raw* and the *cooked*, implied indirectly by the other four points. And, as we know, the Blackfoot often ate the viscera of game, such as the intestines and liver, raw, whereas, as I have already said, they insisted on roast meat being overcooked.

This is one example of a transformation of the model; there are others. In a culinary system in which the category of the roast subdivides into the roast and the (broiled) grilled, it is the second term (denoting the smallest distance separating the meat from the fire) which stands at the apex of the triangle of cooking methods, while the roast – still on the air axis – is to be placed half-way between the grilled and the smoked. The procedure is similar, if the culinary system under consideration makes a distinction between boiling and steaming: the latter method, which separates the water from the food, is then to be placed half-way between the boiled and the smoked.

In order to introduce the category of the fried, we must have recourse to a more complex transformation. The culinary triangle has to be replaced by a tetrahedron which supplies a third axis, in addition to those of air and water: that of oil. The grilled remains at the apex, but oven-roasted meat (with the addition of oil or fat) which is opposed to spit-roasted meat (without the addition of oil or fat) should be placed in the middle of the line linking the smoked and the fried. Similarly, braising (cooking in a shallow mixture of water and fat), which is opposed to steaming (cooking without fat and with a gap between the food and the water), and also to oven-roasting (which involves the addition of a little fat, but no water), takes its place on the line linking the fried and the boiled. The axis of the fried is rarely encountered in America.[8] But there is an instance in a Menomini myth ($M_{476b}$; Bloomfield 3, pp. 434–5) where the heroine gets rid of the rolling head by giving it a steam bath in which boiling oil replaces water. This episode

[8] Frying did occur, however, among the Iroquois (Waugh, pp. 137–8) and among the West Coast tribes (Elmendorf, pp. 133–4; Haeberlin–Gunther, p. 23).

is a reversal of the one in the Fox myth ($M_{476}$), where the heroine halts the pursuit of the same ogre by giving him raw oil to lap up.

If necessary, the model could be made still more complex by opposing animal and vegetable foods in all cases where these require cooking methods exclusive of each other's use, and by distinguishing, within the category of the vegetable, between cereals and leguminous plants: the former can be simply grilled, whereas the latter require the addition of water or fat, and sometimes both; unless, of course, the cereals are subjected to fermentation, a process which requires water for its completion, but excludes fire (cf. Anderson–Cutler, Aschmann, Braidwood). Lastly, condiments can take their place in the system, according to the kind of combinations considered possible or impossible with each type of food, and according to the nature of the contrast which each culture establishes between the two categories. One cannot but be struck by the fact that most American communities regard rotten food as the prototype of pre-cultural food, and consider hot peppers, their main condiment, as a disjunctive agent between nature and culture. On the other hand, one African society, the Dogon, describes pre-cultural food in the form of sand seasoned with sesame sauce (Dieterlen–Calame-Griaule), that is, as a condiment combined with a non-food.

If further dimensions were added to the model, it could be made to include diachronic aspects, such as the order and presentation of meals, and behaviour during them. Extremely interesting, in this connection, is the tentative comparison made by Elmendorf–Kroeber (pp. 139–40, 146) between the meal patterns of two communities belonging to the West Coast of the United States, the Twana and the Yurok. A whole series of contrasts emerges: irregular or regular meals, the serving of dishes one after the other or simultaneously, the compatibility or incompatibility of certain types of food, eating contests in one tribe contrasting with wealth-accumulating contests in the other, etc. There can be no doubt that such contrasts are superimposable on many others, which are not alimentary in nature, but sociological, economical, aesthetic and religious: men/women, family/society, village/bush, thrift/extravagance, nobles/commoners, sacred/profane ... Thus we can hope to discover how, in any particular society, cooking is a language through which that society unconsciously reveals its structure, unless – just as unconsciously – it resigns itself to using the medium to express its contradictions.

# 3 *The Moral of the Myths*

*Farewell, Paris: we are searching for love, happiness and innocence: never can we be far enough away from you.*

J.-J. Rousseau, *Emile*, Bk IV

The digression in the preceding chapter was justified, if it has shown the wealth and fecundity of oppositions, such as the one between the roast and the boiled, which we encountered in the myths. But those myths are not content merely to contrast these methods of cooking or to associate them respectively with two kinds of meat, the fleshy parts and the viscera, in keeping with a culinary style of which other examples are to be found in America (*HA*, p. 348 and n. 37); they also relate the roast and the boiled with certain distinctive forms of behaviour which are obligatory or forbidden during meals.

In a myth belonging to the Timbira Indians of Central Brazil ($M_{10}$), a boy, who is not strongly marked sexually since he has not reached puberty, and who is the guest of a male being and his pregnant wife, must refrain from making a noise while chewing grilled meat. In a myth belonging to the Arapaho Plains Indians of North America ($M_{425-428}$), a woman, who is strongly marked sexually, since several versions specify that she is extremely beautiful, who, according to all versions, is pregnant or about to become so, and who is welcomed into a domestic family consisting of elderly parents and their two sons, has to make a noise while eating a piece of boiled viscera.

The coincidence cannot be accidental, since in both cases the semantic context is the same. The Plains story begins with an error on the part of the sun, who is misled about the physical appearance of humans. Because they cannot bear to look directly at him, he cannot know what their faces are really like. Now, according to the myths and rites of the Ge Indians, the conjunction of the sun and mankind, of the sky and the earth, would be catastrophic for this world and its inhabitants. Considered from this point of view, the grimaces of the humans dazzled by the sun would seem to be premonitory signs of a fatal proximity which, if it were to be increased, would lead to drought and a conflagration.

On these matters, the Plains Indians held views very similar to those of the Ge. In both cases, the sun is presented as a cannibalistic monster; the Mandan, who were crop-growers, performed rites to ward off drought which were almost as rigorous as those of the Serenté, because they were afraid the sun would burn up their gardens. They thought that no close communion was possible between the sun and man.

The initial pattern of the Plains series coincides, then, with the one I have detected as lying behind the Ge myths about the origin of cooking. And what follows is unmistakably a culinary episode, or rather a story about table manners – rather shocking manners, according to our standards, since the behaviour recommended is noisy eating. But have we ever wondered why we attach such extraordinary importance to quiet eating? In European society, it serves as a criterion, and any stranger who failed to conform to it would be labelled irredeemably as ill-bred.

In order to define the behaviour of the human heroine in the Arapaho series or that of her counterpart in the Mandan series, I pointed out that the character occupies an ambiguous position in both contexts. Earth people are milder in their behaviour than the celestial cannibals but although water acts as a mediatory term between sky and earth, the earth element is stronger than the water element. So, the sun makes a mistake in marrying the frog, on the ground that only she can look straight at him; although the earth woman is inferior to the water-sprite in this respect, in another respect she is better equipped to deal with the sky. Because of her sharp wolfish teeth and her noisy chewing, she is, as I have already said, a match for the cannibalistic sun.

It is clear now why the Ge hero must chew in silence and the Plains heroine noisily. In the first instance, it is a question of ensuring the transition from raw food to cooked food, of turning the act of eating into a cultural and mediatized process. Because he was the first to try to do this, the Timbira hero deserves to become the patron saint of all those civilized little children whose parents are constantly warning them 'not to make a noise while eating'. On the other hand, and in a double respect, chewing noisily with an open mouth conjoins forces which, as a rule, it is preferable to keep disjoined. But the reason is that the problem arises here in the same terms as were stated on pages 323 and 428: it is a question of demonstrating to the cannibalistic sun that man can assimilate part of the hostile forces, become their accomplice and win them over. Although noise would seem to be reprehensible when one is eating with the master of cooking fire, it is, on the contrary, obligatory when one is eating with the master of celestial fire.

However, one difficulty remains, in that the myths of both North and South America prescribe different kinds of behaviour according to the particular circumstances, whereas in our European societies only one kind is permitted on all occasions: everywhere and at all times, the European code of politeness rules out the possibility of eating noisily. This difference is not attributable to the normal discrepancy between mythic presentation and actual behaviour, since in everyday living the American Indians accepted the fact that behaviour should be appropriate to the particular circumstances. Thus the Omaha scolded children who made noises or faces while eating: 'But silence with the lips when eating was not exacted, except from the chiefs when they were taking their soup. This act must be done very quietly. It was said there was a religious reason attached to this custom, but just what could not be definitively ascertained' (Fletcher–La Flesche, p. 336). The Ingalik had more prosaic motives. They usually ate quietly, but smacked their lips a little if they did not like the taste of the food. When this was done the woman got 'shy' (Osgood, p. 166), i.e. felt ashamed of her cooking.

It would seem, then, that in one sense, the table manners of so-called primitive peoples formed a kind of adjustable code, the terms of which could be combined in such a way as to transmit different messages. But such was also the case, until recent times, in European society. In the 19th century, the French accepted the Spanish habit of belching, as a gesture of politeness, at the end of a copious meal. Furthermore, our ancestors interpreted the differences in eating habits they observed between themselves and foreigners as if they were tantamount to a language: 'The Germans eat with their mouths closed and think it is unseemly to do otherwise. The French, on the contrary, half open their mouths and find the German practice rather disgusting: The Italians eat delicately, the French more vigorously, so that they find the Italian practice too refined and precious. And so each nation has something peculiar to it and different from others. This is why a child learns to eat according to the place where it happens to be and the customs of that place' (from a French imitation of Erasmus's *Civilitas*, by C. Colviac, 1560, quoted by Franklin, pp. 201–2). As can be seen, the French, not so very long ago, might well have behaved like the heroine in the Indian myth!

We have changed our table manners, then, and adopted others, the norm of which at least has been generalized throughout the Western world, where different ways of chewing no longer denote national or local traditions; they are merely either good or bad. In other words, and contrary to what we have observed in exotic societies, eating habits, for westerners, no longer constitute a *free code*: we opt for some habits and prohibit others, and we conform to the first in order to transmit a *compulsory message*.

This subtle change in social functioning is accompanied by another, which I can illustrate by an example. If a sample of parents were asked at the present time why they do not allow their young children to drink wine, they would all no doubt reply in the same terms: wine is too strong a drink; it cannot safely be given to young and tender constitutions, which only tolerate foods suited to their delicate nature. But this explanation is a very recent development; from ancient times up to the Renaissance, and perhaps until even later, the reason given for not allowing children to drink wine was exactly the opposite: it was not the vulnerability of young constitutions to aggression from without, but the virulence of vital phenomena within those constitutions: hence the danger of bringing into conjunction explosive forces, both of which require rather the addition of a tempering element. Instead of wine being considered too strong for children, children were thought to be too strong for wine, or at least as strong. A passage in the French imitation of Erasmus's *Civilitas*, to which I have already referred, formulates the idea quite explicitly: 'The drink given to children should be wine so diluted as to be no more than water, for, as Plato says in this connection: "one must be careful not to heap fire upon fire", which is what would happen if children (who are all heat and fire) drank pure or insufficiently watered wine, or any kind of beer. Furthermore, here is the punishment which awaits children who drink insufficiently watered wine, or too strong beer: their teeth become yellow, black, or rust-coloured, their cheeks sag, their eyes become rheumy and their intelligence dulled and vacant' (quoted by Franklin, p. 197).[1] The Platonic precept comes from *Laws* (II, 666a). It may also have been in Plutarch's mind when he reversed the idea to justify old men's fondness for undiluted wine: 'Since their temperature has become weak and feeble, it

[1] The original text by Erasmus runs as follows (1, p. 67): 'Wine and beer, which is just as intoxicating as wine, harm children's health and corrupt their morals. It is more suitable for hot youth to drink water ... Otherwise, those who have a passion for wine will find they are rewarded with black teeth, sagging cheeks, rheumy eyes, a sluggish intelligence and premature old age.'

needs to be deliberately stimulated and fired' (*Table Talk*, question seven: 'Why do elderly people prefer undiluted wine?'). It follows, then, that we regard children as having the same nature as was ascribed to the elderly in the ancient world, but we forbid children to drink wine for the very reason which once caused it to be recommended to the elderly.

However, as regards moral training, we continue to respect the traditional model: more often than not, we behave as if our aim were to control disorder and violence coming from within, whereas, in matters of hygiene, we are anxious to protect weakness, also internal in origin, and an as yet uncertain balance, against aggression from without. Nothing could be more diametrically opposed to the philosophy of education that we have encountered in $M_{425-428}$ and in other myths, where the human female wards learn, at one and the same time, how to use domestic utensils, how to cook, and how to control their physiological functions; to prove their feminine virtues, they must show their skill in house-keeping, menstruate regularly, and give birth punctually at the appointed time.

According to the myths discussed in this volume, it was boys in South America and girls in North America who, at the onset of puberty, were the first repositories of these rules of good behaviour, which have to be understood simultaneously on the physical and the mental level; it is as if, in the history of civilization, the prototype of the 'exemplary little girls' was first thought of in the form of menstruating maidens.

And indeed, what condition could better demonstrate that boiling up of internal forces, which was, or still is, used, even in our European societies, as a justification for the rigours of education, since these forces are thought to be uncontrollable, unless hemmed about by various rules? Let us keep for the moment to America, since it is our chosen field of enquiry, although Africa or the South Sea Islands could supply exactly comparable data. When a young Indian woman from the Chaco or the surrounding areas first began to menstruate, she was laced up in a hammock and remained suspended for a period which varied from three days among the Lengua to two months among the Chiriguano. Equally strict seclusion was also the rule among the Southern Guarani (Colleville–Cadogan, p. 50; Cadogan 5, p. 6), in the Amazonian basin and in Guiana. Throughout the west and north-west of North America, a girl menstruating for the first time was not allowed to touch the ground with her feet, nor to look at the sun. To ensure the first prohibition, the Carrier Indians conveyed her bodily from point to point. Among other tribes, the second was achieved by covering her head with a hood, a mat or a basket, or sometimes by tying an eye-shade made of feathers around her forehead (Dixon 7, pp. 457-8). The Algonquin of the Great Lakes area merely required her to keep her eyes lowered. Any contact between her hands and her body or domestic utensils would have been fatal. Among several Athapaskan tribes (Carrier, Tsetsaut), she wore mittens, used a scratcher for her head and back, and sometimes even for her eyelids, drank through a tube and picked up her food with a sharpened bone (unless some other girl was given the task of putting the pieces into her mouth one by one). Among the Lilloet, the prohibitions remained in force for at least a year, and sometimes for as long as four.

Although the alimentary taboos imposed on young girls were extremely variable (cf. Frazer 4, Vol. 10, pp. 22-100; Driver 1), certain common denominators can be worked out. In the west and north-west of North America, where these taboos were most in evidence, menstruating girls could drink neither hot nor cold beverages, only tepid ones. Their solid food also had to be luke-warm; it could not be raw (in the case of the Eskimo who often ate their food raw), nor under-cooked, in the case of the Shuswap, nor fresh, in the case of other tribes; nor boiled, in the case of the Cheyenne. The Klikitat, for their part, forbade the eating of rancid food. So what did the secluded girl eat? Leaving aside the taboo concerning the heads of certain animals, which applied to all persons in a critical condition, and the curious distribution of which throughout the New World would be worthy of special study,[2] we can say, in the first place, that she ate very little and only very well-done, or even dried, food. The Twana of the State of Washington, for instance, insisted on meat, fish, shell-fish, vegetables

---

[2] In the North American tribes: Tsimshian (Boas 2, p. 110); Tanana (McKennan, pp. 137, 141-2); Wintu (C. DuBois, p. 9); Menomini (Skinner 14, p. 194). In the South American tribes: Guayaki (Clastres, MS source); Jivaro (Karsten 2, p. 515); Kachúyana (Frikel 1, passim); Hixkaryâna (Derbyshire, p. 167). Certain tribes justified the taboo through the fear that a defect of the animal might be transmitted to the eaters, if they were too prone to contamination. Amongst other tribes, it would seem to result from the preference shown by adults or old people for the head, which was held to be a delicacy. I myself have childhood memories of meals, during which some elderly person, usually the hostess, would give herself the fish's or the rabbit's head which, had it been offered to the young people around the table, would in any case have filled them with uncontrollable disgust. It would be interesting to carry out research to see if there is any general evidence of this custom, and to determine the motives behind it. They would, no doubt, appear neither simple nor pure.

and fruit all being dried (Elmendorf–Kroeber, p. 440). After the introduction of civilized techniques, which offered the natives simple and
elegant solutions to the taboo problem while allowing the traditional
rules to be respected, they sometimes adopted such solutions with
alacrity. For instance, a Wisconsin Chippewa Indian girl recalls her
32-day period of seclusion in the following terms: '... my grandmother
also brought me a pail of water. She had not got it from the lake either;
she got it from the pump. I was not allowed to eat anything that came
from the ground, no vegetables, potatoes or anything. My grandmother ... gave me bread ... oranges and candy ... and canned corn.
That was alright since it came from a can. But she could not have given
me fresh corn. I could also eat canned salmon and sardines' (Barnouw,
pp. 118–19).

The fact that traditional customs can so easily make use of our
modern culinary techniques and thus become more accessible to
observation, helps us to understand their significance. All the taboos
that have just been listed are homologous. The menstruating girl can
drink neither hot nor cold liquids, for the same reason that she is not
allowed to eat fresh or tainted food. She is subject to a violent internal
commotion, which would become even more violent if her organism
ingested solids or liquids that were, in one sense or another, strongly
marked. The aim, in feeding her with preserved foods, of either native
or commercial origin, or with preparations similar to such foods, is to
supply her with inert or, as it were, stabilized substances.

A form of cooking which handles nature gingerly, either with the
intention of preserving its attractions or suspending its work of destruction, is always in danger either of leaving food a little short of the
point of equilibrium desired by culture so that it may remain in its
given state, or of carrying it beyond. In short, the Indians feed their
pubescent girls on a diet of preserved food to keep them away from
rawness and rottenness (cf. RC, pp. 334–8). This motive does not, of
course, rule out others, prompted purely by convenience; but taken
together, they all may be very similar to the reasons which encourage
American housewives (soon to be imitated, no doubt, by others) to
feed their families on preserved food.

So, without any deliberate intention on my part, a dialogue has been
initiated between past and present, and between the foreign and the
familiar. Yet, in this case too, native philosophy preserves its originality. If we put the question: what dangers are being envisaged in either
case for such rules of behaviour to be evolved? – the modern house-

wife would reply: risks for oneself and for one's family, since she prefers preserved food to fresh food because she thinks the latter may be either under-ripe or over-ripe. But the savages, with impressive unanimity, give the answer: risks affecting other people.

The Guiana Indians maintain that they starve their menstruating wives and daughters to allow their bodies to get rid of the poison which would cause vegetation to wither and men's legs to swell, everywhere the women walked (Roth 2, p. 680). The Chinook, who lived at the other end of the continent, held similar views. Old people tell how in the old days, menstruating women refrained from visiting the sick: 'they said, if the menstruating person were to see the sick person, he (the patient) would become even more ill. Or if she gave him some food, or she looked at what he was to eat, then he would become even sicker' (Jacobs 2, part 2, p. 496). According to the Salish of the Cowlitz River, a menstruating girl must not look at old people, or at boys whatever their age, or even up at the sky, for fear of exposing them to grave dangers (Adamson, pp. 261–2). The Tlingit of Alaska prescribe the wearing of broad-brimmed hats on the grounds that it will prevent the young girl looking up at the sky and thus polluting it (Krause, p. 153). We have seen that the northern Athapaskan impose very rigorous taboos on their menstruating women; 'they believe that this natural female infirmity causes sickness and death in man' (Petitot 2, p. 76). The Hupa of California lump together under the heading 'bad persons' those mourning recently dead persons, women during menstruation, after childbirth or a miscarriage. They also include gravediggers, whose sad, tragic situation is illustrated by their traditional prayer: 'I am suffering from that evil (death) which has been left to us of the Indian world. The people are afraid of me. I do not have a fire where the others have their fire. I have a fire by myself. And besides, what the rest eat I do not eat. Furthermore, I do not look at the world. So much my body frightens them ...' (Goddard, p. 266, n., p. 357).

It would be possible to add many more such examples, testifying to the total opposition between the reasons for good manners believed in by so-called primitive people and ourselves. We wear hats to protect *ourselves* from rain, cold and heat; we use forks to eat with, and wear gloves when we go out, so as not to dirty *our* fingers; we drink through a straw in order to protect *ourselves* from the coldness of the beverage, and we eat preserved foods to make things easier for *ourselves* or to defend *ourselves* from the theoretical dangers associated with rawness or rottenness. Yet in other societies, today as in former times, hats, gloves, forks, drinking tubes and preserved foods are meant as barriers against an infection emanating from the body of the user. Whereas we think of good manners as a way of protecting the internal purity of the subject against the external impurity of beings and things, in savage societies, they are a means of protecting the purity of beings and things against the impurity of the subject.

This formulation must, however, be tempered by one observation. Any violation of the taboos affecting menstruating girls also involves a danger for them, but whatever the society we care to study, we always find that it defines the danger in the same, or in very similar, terms. The culprit will become a wizened skeleton, say the Zulus; to quote another African example, the Akamba and the Baganda believe either that she will remain sterile or that her children will die in infancy, or that her own life will be cut short. Similarly, in America, the northern Athapaskan thought that if a menstruating girl or a woman who had just given birth failed to respect the taboos, they would have weak muscles, be afflicted with haemorrhages and die in the prime of life. Within the Athapaskan group too, the Tanana believed that drinking hot or cold, instead of luke-warm, liquids would cause the hair to fall out in the first case and the teeth in the second; and if a woman looked at the sun while menstruating, her hair would go prematurely white (McKennan, pp. 143, 167). The Twana of Puget Sound maintained that if a woman in seclusion touched her head with her fingers, it would at once rot away. Her hair would cease to grow, and what does a woman desire more than a long, thick head of hair? (Elmendorf–Kroeber, p. 440). The Chinook believed that premature wrinkling and white hair would be the lot of the widow who touched her face with her hand (the same held true for widowers); and, according to these same Indians, adolescents who showed little respect for good manners and greedily seized the biggest pieces of meat would later only obtain an ageing marriage-partner (Jacobs 2, pp. 501, 530). Far away from the Chinook, in the very heart of tropical America, the Bororo believed that anyone who, while eating or drinking in the sacred enclosure of the men's house, committed a breach of etiquette by emptying all the dishes, would be afflicted with premature old age: his eye-brows would become white and impossible to pluck (*EB*, Vol. 1, p. 371). It will be remembered that the 16th-century French text quoted above (p. 499) warns that children allowed to drink unwatered wine will suffer from various ailments, all of which are disabilities generally associated with advanced age.

The taboos affecting menstruating girls – and sometimes also women who have just given birth, widows and widowers, murderers, grave-diggers, and officiants in sacred or profane rites – can only have a meaning through the integration of the two aspects I have described separately. The violation of food taboos, the failure to use table utensils or toilet accessories, the carrying out of forbidden actions, all these things pollute the world, ruin harvests, frighten away game and expose *others* to sickness and famine; and as regards *oneself*, shorten the normal span of human life by bringing on symptoms of premature senility. Yet the system would remain incomprehensible, if we failed to notice that the two types of sanctions are mutually exclusive. A menstruating woman or one newly delivered of a child, who fails to obey the rules, grows old herself, but she does not cause ageing in others. So the dangers arising from her behaviour differ according to the parties concerned. For the woman herself, the dangers lie in an *acceleration* of the course of life, springing from internal factors. For others, they involve an *interruption* in the course of life, produced by external factors, such as infection and famine.

This dualism can only be explained if we recognize that a seemingly heterogeneous set of taboos and prohibitions becomes coherent, when viewed simultaneously according to two different perspectives. From the spatial point of view, they serve to prevent a conjunction that would be dangerous because of the high potential prevailing at the two poles of the same axis: the axis of natural forces where this situation is normal, and on which a particular individual happens to find himself or herself, through being subjected to a violent commotion caused by physiological or sociological circumstances which are bringing about a change of state. Between the social person and his or her own body, in which nature is unleashed, between the body and the biological and physical universe, table or toilet utensils fulfil an effective function as insulators or mediators. Their intervening presence prevents the occurrence of the threatened catastrophe. This point was already emphasized in *The Raw and the Cooked* (p. 334), where I adopted for my own purposes an interpretation first put forward by Frazer, and which deserves to remain a classic of its kind, because of the wealth of data involved and the rigour of the analysis.

But we see now that this interpretation is incomplete, since it accounts for only one half of the facts. Puberty rites are not situated merely on a spatial axis, 'between heaven and earth', as Frazer rightly suggested by the wording of the title of the first chapter of the concluding volume of *The Golden Bough*. They are also situated on a temporal axis, which it would be misleading to regard as merely internal to the individual concerned. For, as was shown in the first part of *Introduction to a Science of Mythology*, the myths use the theme of ageing ($M_{104}$, RC, p. 177 and p. 176 *et seq.* of the present volume; $M_{149a}$ *ibid.*, pp. 139–40) to introduce a fundamental category, that of periodicity, which modulates human existence by assigning it a certain duration, and by establishing, within this duration, the major physiological rhythms which have their seat in the female organism. We have also learned from other myths ($M_{425-428}$; $M_{444-447}$ etc.) that the education of girls is mainly achieved by the mental and biological interiorization of periodicity.

We now see that the absence of mediatory utensils such as combs, head-scratchers, mittens and forks, between the subject and her body, causes the hair to turn white, the skin to wrinkle, etc. The reason must be that only the establishment of regular periodicity, mediatized, as it were, by itself, wards off a two-fold threat; on the one hand, the danger of the absence of periodicity, which is so often described in the myths in terms of continuous day or continuous night; and, on the other hand, the danger of too rapid periodicity, which, in practice, would come to the same thing, as can be illustrated by the analogy of an alternating electric current, the practical effect of which becomes indistinguishable from direct current, provided its period is made short enough.

The reason why women are most in need of education is that they are periodic creatures. Because of this, they are perpetually threatened – and the whole world with and through them – by the two possibilities that have just been mentioned: their periodic rhythm could slow down and halt the flow of events, or it could accelerate and plunge the world into chaos. It is equally conceivable that women might cease to menstruate and bear children, or that they might bleed continuously and give birth haphazardly. But in either case, the sun and the moon, the heavenly bodies governing the alternation of day and night and of the seasons, would no longer be able to fulfil their function. Through their hopeless quest for a perfect wife, the myths say they would be perpetually absent from the sky, and engaged on an endless search.

It follows, then, that food taboos, good manners and utensils used for eating or for personal hygiene, are all mediatory agents fulfilling a dual function. As Frazer realized, they no doubt play the part of insulators or transformers which abolish or reduce the tension between poles, the respective charges of which are, or were, abnormally high.

But they also act as standards of measurement, in which case their function becomes positive, instead of remaining negative. Their 'obligato' use assigns a reasonable duration to each physiological process, and to each social action. For, in the last resort, correct behaviour requires that what must be, should be, but that nothing should be brought about too precipitately. And so it is that, in spite of the humble functions assigned to them in daily life, such apparently insignificant objects as combs, hats, gloves, forks or straws through which we imbibe liquids, are still today mediators between extremes; imbued with an inertia which was once deliberate and calculated, they moderate our exchanges with the external world, and superimpose on them a domesticated, peaceful and more sober rhythm (cf. *HA*, p. 145). Used by each one of us and adapted to the modest scale of the human body, they nevertheless perpetuate the mythic image of the celestial canoe, with which we have been dealing in the present volume: it too is a technical object, but one which brings out clearly the function which, in the last analysis, must perhaps be seen as characterizing all technical objects, as well as the culture which produces them: the function of separating and uniting entities which, if too close together or too far apart, would leave man exposed to powerlessness or unreason.

It remains to be seen whether man's victory over his powerlessnessl when carried to a state out of all proportion to the objectives with which he was satisfied during the previous millennia of his history, will not lead back to unreason. The first two volumes of this series were concerned with bringing to light the hidden logic behind mythic thought, in its dual aspect as a logic of qualities and a logic of forms. We now find that mythology also conceals an ethical system, but one which, unfortunately, is far more remote from our ethic than its logic is from our logic. If the origin of table manners, and more generally that of correct behaviour, is to be found, as I think I have shown, in deference towards the world – good manners consisting precisely in respecting its obligations – it follows that the inherent ethic of the myths runs counter to the ethic we profess today. It teaches us, at any rate, that the formula 'hell is other people',[3] which has achieved such widespread fame, is not so much a philosophical proposition as an ethnographical statement about our civilization. For, since childhood, we have been accustomed to fear impurity as coming from without.

When they assert, on the contrary that 'hell is ourselves', savage

[3] TRANSLATORS' NOTE: *L'enfer, c'est les autres,* a quotation from Jean-Paul Sartre's play, *Huis Clos.*

peoples give us a lesson in humility which, it is to be hoped, we may still be capable of understanding. In the present century, when man is actively destroying countless living forms, after wiping out so many societies whose wealth and diversity had, from time immemorial, constituted the better part of his inheritance, it has probably never been more necessary to proclaim, as do the myths, that sound humanism does not begin with oneself, but puts the world before life, life before man, and respect for others before self-interest: and that no species, not even our own, can take the fact of having been on this earth for one or two million years – since, in any case, man's stay here will one day come to an end – as an excuse for appropriating the world as if it were a thing and behaving on it with neither decency nor discretion.

Paris, February 1966 – Lignerolles, September 1967

# Bibliography

In the numbered entries, works already listed in the Bibliographies of the preceding volumes retain their original numbers; works appearing here for the first time are added at the end of the entry, regardless of date of publication.

## ABBREVIATIONS:

| | |
|---|---|
| *AA* | *American Anthropologist* |
| *APAMNH* | *Anthropological Papers of the American Museum of Natural History* |
| *ARBAE* | *Annual Report of the Bureau of American Ethnology* |
| *BBAE* | *Bulletin of the Bureau of American Ethnology* |
| Colb. | Colbacchini, A. |
| *CUCA* | *Columbia University Contributions to Anthropology* |
| *EB* | Albisetti, C. and Venturelli, A. J., *Enciclopédia Bororo*, Vol. I, Campo Grande, 1962 |
| *FHA* | Lévi-Strauss, C., *From Honey to Ashes*, London, 1973 |
| *HSAI* | *Handbook of South American Indians*, BBAE 143, 7 vols, Washington D.C., 1946–59 |
| *JAFL* | *Journal of American Folklore* |
| *JRAI* | *Journal of the Royal Anthropological Institute of Great Britain and Ireland* |
| *JSA* | *Journal de la Société des Américanistes* |
| K.-G. | Koch-Grünberg, Th. |
| L.-N. | Lehmann-Nitsche, R. |
| L.-S. | Lévi-Strauss, C. |
| *MAFLS* | *Memoirs of the American Folk-Lore Society* |
| Nim. | Nimuendaju, C. |
| *RC* | Lévi-Strauss, C., *The Raw and the Cooked*, London, 1970 |
| *RIHGB* | *Revista do Instituto Historico e Geografico Brasiliero* |
| *RMDLP* | *Revista del Museo de la Plata* |
| *RMP* | *Revista do Museu Paulista* |
| *SWJA* | *Southwestern Journal of Anthropology* |
| *UCPAAE* | *University of California Publications in American Archaeology and Ethnology* |

ABBEVILLE, Cl. d'. *Histoire de la mission des pères Capucins en l'isle de Maragnan et terres circonvoisines*, Paris, 1614.

ABREU, J. Capistrano de. *Rã-txa hu-ni-ku-i. A Lingua dos Caxinauas*, Rio de Janeiro, 1914.

ADAMSON, T. 'Folk-Tales of the Coast Salish', *MAFLS*, Vol. 27, New York, 1934.

ADNEY, E. T. and CHAPELLE, H. I. *The Bark Canoes and Skin Boats of North America*, Smithsonian Institute, Washington D.C., 1964.

AMÉRO, J. *Les Classiques de la table*, new ed., 2 vols, Paris, 1855.

ANDERSON, E. and CUTLER, H. C. 'Methods of Popping Corn and their Historical Significance', *SWJA*, 6, 3, 1950.

ARMENTIA, N. 'Arte y vocabulario de la Lengua Cavineña', *RMDLP*, Vol. 13, 1906.

ARNAUD, E. 'Os Indios Galibi do rio Oiapoque', *Boletim do Museu Goeldi, n.s., Antropologia 30*, Belém-Pará, 1966.

ASCHMANN, H. 'A Primitive Food Preparation Technique in Baja California', *SWJA*, 8, 1, 1952.

AUDUBON, J. J. *Scènes de la nature dans les États-Unis et le nord de l'Amérique*, trans. E. Bazin, 2 vols, Paris, 1868.

BALDUS, H. (2) *Lendas dos Indios do Brasil*, São Paulo, 1946.

——. (6) 'Karaja-Mythen', *Tribus, Jahrbuch des Linden-Museums*, Stuttgart, 1952-3.

BALLARD, A. C. (1) 'Mythology of Southern Puget Sound', *Univ. of Washington Publications in Anthropology*, Vol. 3, No. 2, 1929.

BARBEAU, M. (1) 'Huron and Wyandot Mythology', *Memoir 80, Anthropol. Series no. II, Geological Survey of Canada*, 1915.

——. (2) 'Huron-Wyandot Traditional Narratives', *National Museum of Canada, Bull. no. 165*, Ottawa, 1960.

BARBUT, M. 'Le sens du mot "structure" en mathématiques' in 'Problèmes du Structuralisme', *Les Temps Modernes*, 22e année, No. 246, Nov. 1966.

BARKER, M. A. R. (1) 'Klamath Texts', *University of California Publications in Linguistics*, Vol. 30, Berkeley, 1963.

——. (2) 'Klamath Dictionary', *ibid.*, Vol. 31, Berkeley, 1963.

BARNOUW, V. 'Acculturation and Personality Among the Wisconsin Chippewa', *Memoir Number 72, AA* 52, 4, 2, 1950.

BARRAU, J. *L'Agriculture vivrière autochtone de la Nouvelle-Calédonie* (Commission du Pacifique Sud), Nouméa, 1956.

BARRÈRE, P. *Nouvelle relation de la France équinoxiale*, Paris, 1743.

BARRETT, S. A. (1) 'The Cayapa Indians of Ecuador', *Indian Notes and Monographs, Museum of the American Indian, Heye Foundation*, 2 vols, New York, 1925.

——. (2) 'Pomo Myths', *Bulletin of the Public Museum of the City of Milwaukee*, Vol. 15, 1933.

BEALS, R. L. 'The Contemporary Culture of the Cáhita Indians', *BBAE 142*, Washington D.C., 1945.

BECHER, H. (1) 'Algumas notas sôbre a religião e mitologia dos Surára', *RMP*, n.s. Vol. 11, São Paulo, 1959.

——. (2) 'Die Surára und Pakidái. Zwei Yanonámi-Stämme in Nordwestbrasilien', *Mitteilungen aus dem Museum für Völkerkunde in Hamburg*, Vol. 26, 1960.

BECKER-DONNER, E. 'Nichtkeramische Kulturfunde Nordwestargentiniens', *Archiv für Völkerkunde* VIII, Wien, 1953.

BECKWITH, M. W. (1) 'Mandan–Hidatsa Myths and Ceremonies', *MAFLS*, Vol. 32, New York, 1938.

BECKWITH, M. W. (2) 'Mythology of the Oglala Dakota', *JAFL*, Vol. 43, 1930.

BENNETT, W. C. 'Numbers, Measures, Weights, and Calendars', *HSAI*, Vol. 5, 1949.

BERTHRONG, D. J. *The Southern Cheyennes*, Norman, Oklahoma, 1963.

BLOOMFIELD, L. (1) 'Sacred Stories of the Sweet Grass Cree', *Bulletin 60, Anthropological Series no. 11, National Museum of Canada*, Ottawa, 1930.

——. (2) 'Plain Cree Texts', *Publications of the American Ethnological Society*, Vol. 16, New York, 1934.

——. (3) 'Menomini Texts', *Publications of the American Ethnological Society*, Vol. 12, New York, 1928.

BOAS, F. (2) 'Tsimshian Mythology', *31st ARBAE* (1909–10), Washington D.C., 1916.

——. (4) ed. 'Folk-Tales of Salishan and Sahaptin Tribes', *MAFLS*, Vol. 11, 1917.

——. (5) 'Mythologie der Indianer von Washington und Oregon', *Globus*, Vol. 43, 1893.

——. (6) 'Traditions of the Ts'Ets'ā'ut', *JAFL*, Vol. 10, 1897.

——. (7) 'Kathlamet Texts', *BBAE 26*, Washington D.C., 1901.

——. (8) 'The Eskimo of Baffin Land and Hudson Bay', *Bulletin of the American Museum of Natural History*, Vol. 15, New York, 1901–7.

——. (9) 'Kutenai Tales', *BBAE 59*, Washington D.C., 1918.

——. (10) 'Chinook Texts', *BBAE 20*, Washington D.C., 1894.

——. (11) 'Property Marks of the Eskimo', *AA*, n.s., Vol. 1, 1899.

——. (12) 'The Mythology of the Bella Coola', *Memoirs of the American Museum of Natural History*, Vol. 2, 1900.

BOGORAS, W. G. (1) 'The Folklore of Northeastern Asia as compared with that of Northwestern America', *AA*, n.s., Vol. 4, 1902.

——. (2) 'The Chukchee', *Memoirs of the American Museum of Natural History*, Vol. 11, 1904–9.

BOWERS, A. W. (1) *Mandan Social and Ceremonial Organization*, Chicago, 1950.

——. (2) 'Hidatsa Social and Ceremonial Organization', *BBAE 194*, Washington D.C., 1965.

BRAIDWOOD, R. J. *et al.* 'Symposium: Did Man Once Live by Beer Alone?', *AA*, 55, 4, 1953.

BREHM, A. E. (1) *Brehms Tierleben. Allgemeine Kunde des Tierreichs*, Leipzig und Wien, 10 vols, 1890–93.

——. (2) *La Vie des animaux*, 4 vols, Paris, s.d.

BRETT, W. H. (1) *The Indian Tribes of Guiana*, London, 1868.

——. (2) *Legends and Myths of the Aboriginal Indians of British Guiana*, London, (1880?).

BRIDGES, E. L. *Uttermost Part of the Earth*, London, 2nd edn, 1950.

BRIGHT, W. 'The Karok Language', *University of California Publications in Linguistics*, Vol. 13, Berkeley, 1957.

BRINTON, D. *Native Calendars of Central America and Mexico*, Philadelphia, 1893.

BRUNER, E. M. 'Mandan–Hidatsa Kinship terminology', *AA*, 57, 4, 1955.

BULLEN, R. P., ed. 'Caribbean Symposium', *American Antiquity*, 31, 2, part 1, 1965.

BUNZEL, R. L. (1) 'Introduction to Zuni Ceremonialism', *47th ARBAE* (1929–30), Washington D.C., 1932.

——. (3) 'Zuni Ritual Poetry', ibid.

BURT, W. H. *A Field Guide to the Mammals*, Cambridge, Mass., 1952.

BUSHNELL, Jr, D. I. 'Tribal Migrations East of the Mississippi', *Smithsonian Miscellaneous Collections*, Vol. 89, No. 12, Washington D.C., 1934.

CADOGAN, L. (4) 'Ayvu Rapyta. Textos míticos de los Mbyá-Guarani del Guairá', *Antropologia, no. 5, Boletim no. 227, Universidade de São Paulo*, 1959.

——. (5) 'En torno al BAI ETE-RI-VA y el concepto guarani de NOMBRE', *Suplemento Antropológico de la Revista del Ateneo Paraguayo*, Vol. I, No. 1, Asunción, 1965.

CALLENDER, C. 'The Social Organization of the Central Algonkians', *Milwaukee Public Museum, Publications in Anthropology*, No. 7, Milwaukee, 1962.

CARDUS, J. *Las misiones Franciscanas entre los infieles de Bolivia*, Barcelona, 1886.

CATLIN, G. *See* Donaldson, Th.

CHAMBERLAIN, A. F. 'The Maple amongst the Algonkian Tribes', *AA*, o.s. 4, 1891.

CHAMBERLAIN, L. S. 'Plants Used by the Indians of Eastern North America', *American Naturalist*, Vol. 35, Jan. 1901.

CHAPMAN, J. W. 'Athapaskan Traditions from the Lower Yukon', *JAFL*, 16, 1903.

CHATEAUBRIAND, F. de. (1) *Voyages en Amérique, en Italie, au Mont Blanc*, new edn, Paris, 1873.

——. (2) *Mémoires d'Outre-Tombe*, ed. de la Pléiade, 2 vols, Paris, 1951.

——. (3) *Génie du Christianisme*, ed. Garnier-Flammarion, 2 vols, Paris, 1966.

CLASTRES, P. *La Vie sociale d'une tribu nomade: les Indiens Guayaki du Paraguay*, Paris, 1965 (typescript).

COLEMAN, B., FROGNER, E. and EICH, E. *Oiibwa Myths and Legends*, Minneapolis, 1962.

COLLEVILLE, M. de and CADOGAN, L. 'Les Indiens Guayaki de l'Yñaro̅', *Bulletin de la Faculté des Lettres*, TILAS 3, 4, Strasbourg, 1963–4.

COOPER, J. M. 'The Araucanians', *HSAI*, Vol. 2, *BBAE 143*, Washington D.C., 1946.

COPE, L. 'Calendars of the Indians North of Mexico', *UCPAAE*, Vol. 16, Berkeley, 1919.

CORNPLANTER, J. *Legends of the Longhouse*, Philadelphia–New York, 1938.

COUES, E., ed. *Manuscript Journals of Alexander Henry and of David Thompson*, 3 vols, New York, 1897.

COUTO DE MAGALHÃES, J. V. *O Selvagem*, 4ª ed. completa com *Curso*, etc., São Paulo–Rio de Janeiro, 1940.

CRESSWELL, J. R. 'Folk-Tales of the Swampy Cree of Northern Manitoba', *JAFL*, Vol. 36, 1923.

CULIN, S. 'A Summer Trip among the Western Indians', *Bulletin of the Free Museum of Science and Art*, Philadelphia, Jan. 1901.

CURTIN, J. (1) *Myths of the Modocs*, Boston, 1912.

——. (2) *Seneca Indians Myths*, New York, 1922.

CURTIN, J. and HEWITT, J. N. B. 'Seneca Fiction, Legends and Myths. Part 1', *32nd ARBAE* (1910–11), Washington D.C., 1918.

CUSHING, F. H. 'Zuñi Breadstuff', *Indian Notes and Monographs, Vol. 8, Museum of the American Indian, Heye Foundation,* New York, 1920.

DANGEL, R. 'Bear and Fawns', *JAFL,* Vol. 42, 1929.

DEETZ, J. 'The Dynamics of Stylistic Change in Arikara Ceramics', *Illinois Studies in Anthropology,* No. 4, Urbana, 1965.

DEMPSEY, H. A. 'Religious Significance of Blackfoot Quillwork', *Plains Anthropologist,* Vol. 8, 1963.

DENIG, E. T. 'Indian Tribes of the Upper Missouri. Edited with notes and biographical sketch by J. N. B. Hewitt', *46th ARBAE* (1928–9), Washington D.C., 1930.

DENSMORE, F. (1) 'Uses of Plants by the Chippewa Indians', *44th ARBAE* (1926–7), Washington D.C., 1928.

——. (2) 'Chippewa Customs', *BBAE 86,* Washington D.C., 1929.

DERBYSHIRE, D. *Textos Hixkaryâna,* Belém-Pará, 1965.

DIETERLEN, G. and CALAME-GRIAULE, G. 'L'Alimentation dogon', *Cahiers d'études africaines,* 3, 1960.

DIXON, R. B. (1) 'Shasta Myths', *JAFL,* Vol. 23, 1910.

——. (?) 'Maidu Myths', *Bulletin of the American Museum of Natural History,* Vol. 17, 1902–7.

——. (3) 'Maidu Texts', *Publications of the American Ethnological Society,* 4, 1912.

——. (7) 'The Shasta', *Bulletin of the American Museum of Natural History,* Vol. 17, 1902–7.

DIXON, R. B. and KROEBER, A. L. 'Numeral Systems of the Languages of California', *AA,* Vol. 9, No. 4, 1907.

DONALDSON, Th. 'The George Catlin Indian Gallery', *Annual Report ... of the Smithsonian Institution,* part II, Washington D.C., 1886.

DORSEY, G. A. (1) 'Traditions of the Skidi Pawnee', *MAFLS,* Boston–New York, 1904.

——. (2) 'The Pawnee. Mythology', *Carnegie Institution of Washington,* Publ. No. 59, 1906.

——. (3) 'The Mythology of the Wichita', *Carnegie Institution of Washington,* Publ. No. 21, 1904.

——. (4) 'The Cheyenne. I. Ceremonial Organization', *Field Columbian Museum, Publication 99, Anthropol. Series, Vol. IX, No. 1,* Chicago, 1905.

——. (5) 'The Arapaho Sun Dance; the Ceremony of the Offerings Lodge', *Field Columbian Museum, Publ. 75, Anthropol. Series,* IV, Chicago, 1903.

——. (6) 'Traditions of the Arikara', *Carnegie Institution of Washington,* Publ. No. 17, 1904.

——. (7) 'Sun Dance' in Hodge, F. W., ed. 'Handbook of American Indians North of Mexico', *BBAE 30,* 2 vols, Washington D.C., 1910.

DORSEY, G. A. and KROEBER, A. L. 'Traditions of the Arapaho', *Field Columbian Museum, Publ. 81, Anthropol. Series,* Vol. V, Chicago, 1903.

DORSEY, J. O. (1) 'The Çegiha Language', *Contributions to North American Ethnology,* Vol. VI, Washington, 1890.

——. (2) 'A Study of Siouan Cults', *11th ARBAE* (1889–90), Washington D.C., 1894.

——. (3) 'Omaha Sociology', *3rd ARBAE* (1881–2), Washington, 1884.

DRIVER, H. E. (1) 'Culture Element Distribution: XVI. Girls' Puberty Rites in Western North America', *Anthropological Records*, 6, 2, Berkeley, 1941.
——. (2) 'Geographical-Historical *versus* Psycho-Functional Explanations of Kin Avoidances', *Current Anthropology*, Vol. 7, No. 2, April 1966.
DRIVER, H. E. and MASSEY, W. C. 'Comparative Studies of North American Indians', *Transactions of the American Philosophical Society*, n.s., Vol. 47, part 2, Philadelphia, 1957.
DUBOIS, C. 'Wintu Ethnography', *UCPAAE*, Vol. 36, No. 1, Berkeley, 1935.
DUBOIS, C. and DEMETRACOPOULOU, D. 'Wintu Myths', *UCPAAE*, Vol. 28, 1930–31.
DUBOIS, C. G. 'The Religion of the Luiseño Indians', *UCPAAE*, Vol. 8, Berkeley, 1908.
DUMÉZIL, G. *Les Dieux des Germains, essai sur la formation de la religion scandinave*, Paris, 1959.
EGGAN, F. 'The Cheyenne and Arapaho Kinship System' in Eggan, F. ed., *Social Anthropology of North American Tribes*, Chicago, 1937.
ELMENDORF, W. W. 'The Structure of Twana Culture [with] Comparative Notes on the Structure of Yurok Culture [by] A. L. Kroeber', *Research Studies, Monographic Supplement 2*, Pullman, 1960.
ENDERS, R. K. 'Observations on Sloths in Captivity at Higher Altitudes in the Tropics and in Pennsylvania', *Journal of Mammalogy*, Vol. 21, 1940.
ERASMUS, L. F. (1) *La Civilité puérile*, French trans. of Latin text by Alcide Bonneau, Paris, 1877.
——. (2) *Declamatio de pueris statim ac liberaliter instituendis*, trans. with commentary and critical study by J. C. Margolin, Genève, 1966.
ERIKSON, E. H. 'Observations of the Yurok. Childhood and World Image', *UCPAAE*, Vol. 35, Berkeley, 1943.
EWERS, J. C. 'The Horse in Blackfoot Indian Culture', *BBAE 159*, Washington D.C., 1955.
FARABEE, W. C. (1) 'The Central Arawak', *Anthropological Publications of the University Museum*, 9, Philadelphia, 1918.
——. (2) 'Indian Tribes of Eastern Peru', *Papers of the Peabody Museum, Harvard University*, Vol. 10, Cambridge, 1922.
FARON, L. C. (1) 'Mapuche Social Structure', *Illinois Studies in Anthropology*, No. 1, Urbana, 1961.
——. (2) 'The Magic Mountain and other Origin Myths of the Mapuche Indians of Central Chile', *JAFL*, Vol. 76, 1963.
——. (3) *Hawks of the Sun*, Pittsburgh, 1964.
FARRAND, L. 'Traditions of the Quinault Indians', *Memoirs of the American Museum of Natural History*, Vol. IV, New York, 1902.
FEJOS, P. 'Ethnography of the Yagua', *Viking Fund Publications in Anthropology*, Vol. 1, New York, 1943.
FENTON, W. N. 'An Outline of Seneca Ceremonies at Coldspring Longhouse', *Yale University Publications in Anthropology*, No. 9, New Haven, 1936.
FERNALD, M. L. and KINSEY, A. C. *Edible Wild Plants of Eastern North America* (Gray Herbarium of Harvard University, Special Publication), Cornwall-on-Hudson, 1943.
FISHER, M. W. 'The Mythology of the Northern and Northeastern Algonkians in Reference to Algonkian Mythology as a Whole' in F. Johnson,

ed.: *Man in Northeastern North America, Papers of the R. S. Peabody Foundation*, Vol. 3, Andover, Mass., 1946.

FLANNERY, R. 'The Gros Ventres of Montana; Part I, Social Life', *The Catholic University of America, Anthropol. Series*, No. 15, Washington D.C., 1953.

FLETCHER, A. C. and LA FLESCHE, F. 'The Omaha Tribe', *27th ARBAE* (1905–6), Washington D.C., 1911.

FOCK, N. 'Waiwai. Religion and Society of an Amazonian Tribe', *Nationalmuseets skrifter. Ethnografisk Roekke, VIII*, Copenhagen, 1963.

FONTANA, B. L. (Letter of December 11th, 1963).

FRACHTENBERG, L. J. (1) 'Coos Texts', *CUCA*, Vol. 1, New York–Leyden, 1913.

——. (2) 'Shasta and Athapaskan Myths from Oregon (Collected by Livingston Farrand)', *JAFL*, Vol. 28, 1915.

FRANCISCAN FATHERS. *An Ethnological Dictionary of the Navaho Language*, Saint Michaels, Arizona, 1910.

FRANKLIN, A. *La Vie privée d'autrefois. Les repas*, Paris, 1889.

FRAZER, J. G. (4) *The Golden Bough*, 3rd edn, 13 vols, London, 1923–6.

FRIKEL, P. (1) 'Morí-A Festa do Rapé. Indios Kachúyana; rio Trombetas', *Boletim do Museu Paraense Emilio Goeldi*, n.s., *Antropologia*, No. 12, Belém-Pará, 1961.

——. (2) 'Ometanímpe, os Transformados', *Boletim do Museu Paraense Emilio Goeldi*, n.s., *Antropologia*, No. 17, Belém-Pará, 1961.

FULOP, M. 'Aspectos de la cultura tukana: Cosmogonia; Mitología, Parte I', *Revista Colombiana de Antropologia*, Vols 3, 5, Bogotá, 1954, 1956.

GARTH, Th. R. 'Early Nineteenth Century Tribal Relations in the Columbia Plateau', *SWJA*, 20, 1, 1964.

GATSCHET, A. S. 'The Klamath Indians of South-Western Oregon', *Contributions to North American Ethnology*, Vol. II, two Parts, Washington, 1890.

GILIJ, F. S. *Saggio di storia americana*, etc., 4 vols, Rome, 1780–84.

GILMORE, M. R. (1) 'Uses of Plants by the Indians of the Missouri River Region', *33rd ARBAE* (1911–12), Washington D.C., 1919.

——. (2) 'Notes on Gynaecology and Obstetrics of the Arikara Indians', *Papers of the Michigan Academy of Science, Arts and Letters*, Vol. 14 (1930), 1931.

——. (3) 'Months and Seasons of the Arikara Calendar', *Indian Notes*, Vol. VI, No. 3, *Museum of the American Indian, Heye Foundation*, 1929.

GODDARD, P. E. 'Hupa Texts', *UCPAAE*, Vol. 1, No. 2, Berkeley, 1904.

GODEL, R. *Les Sources manuscrites du Cours de linguistique générale*, Genève, 1957.

GOEJE, C. H. de. (1) 'Philosophy. Initiation and Myths of the Indians of Guiana and Adjacent Countries', *Internationales Archiv für Ethnographie*, Vol. 44, Leiden, 1943.

——. (2) 'De inwijding tot medicijnman bij de Arawakken in tekst en mythe', *Bijdragen tot de taal-, land- en Volkenkunde*, 'S-Gravenhagen, 101, 1942.

GOLDER, F. A. 'Tales from Kodiak Islands', *JAFL*, Vol. 16, 1903.

GOLDMAN, I. 'The Cubeo Indians of the Northwest Amazon', *Illinois Studies in Anthropology*, No. 2, Urbana, 1963.

GOLDSCHMIDT, W. 'Nomlaki Ethnography', *UCPAAE*, Vol. 42, 4, Berkeley, 1951.

GRANET, M. *Danses et légendes de la Chine ancienne*, 2 vols, Paris, 1926.

GRINNELL, G. B. (1) 'Falling Star', *JAFL*, Vol. 34, 1921.

——. (2) *The Cheyenne Indians*, 2 vols, New Haven, 1923.

——. (3) *Blackfoot Lodge Tales*, New York, 1892.

——. (4) 'Coup and Scalp among the Plains Indians', *AA*, Vol. 12, 1910.

——. (5) 'Cheyenne Woman Customs', *AA*, Vol. 4, 1902.

——. (6) 'Some Early Cheyenne Tales', *JAFL*, Vols 20-21, 1907-8.

GUALLART, J. M. 'Mitos y leyendas de los Aguarunas del alto Marañon', *Peru Indigena*, Vol. 7, Nos 16-17, Lima, 1958.

GUNTHER, E. 'Ethnobotany of Western Washington', *University of Washington Publications in Anthropology*, Vol. 10, No. 1, Seattle, 1945.

GUSINDE, M. *Die Feuerland Indianer*, 3 vols, Mödling bei Wien, 1931-9.

HAAS, M. R. 'Addenda to Review of Bloomfield's "The Menomini Language"', *AA*, Vol. 68, 2, 1, 1966.

HAEBERLIN, H. 'Mythology of Puget Sound', *JAFL*, Vol. 37, 1924.

HAEBERLIN, H. and GUNTHER, E. 'The Indians of Puget Sound', *Univ. of Washington Publications in Anthropology*, Vol. 4, 1, 1930.

HAGAR, S. 'Weather and the Seasons in Micmac Mythology', *JAFL*, Vol. 10, 1897.

HALL, E. R. and KELSON, K. R. *The Mammals of North America*, 2 vols, New York, 1959.

HARRINGTON, J. P. 'The Ethnogeography of the Tewa Indians', *29th ARBAE*, Washington D.C., 1916.

HAVARD, V. (1) 'Food Plants of the North American Indians', *Bulletin of the Torrey Botanical Club*, 22 (3), 1895.

——. (2) 'Drink Plants of the North American Indians', *Bulletin of the Torrey Botanical Club*, 23 (2), 1896.

HEISER, Jr., Ch. B. 'The Sunflower among the North American Indians', *Proceedings of the American Philosophical Society*, Vol. 95, No. 4, Philadelphia, 1951.

HENRY, J. (1) *Jungle People. A Kaingáng Tribe of the Highlands of Brazil*, New York, 1941.

HENSHAW, H. W. 'Indian Origin of Maple Sugar', *AA*, o.s. 3, 1890.

HEWITT, J. N. B. (1) 'Iroquoian Cosmology', *21st ARBAE* (1899-1900), Washington D.C., 1903.

——. (2) 'Iroquoian Cosmology – Second Part', *43rd ARBAE* (1925-6), Washington D.C., 1928.

HILGER, I. M. (1) 'Menomini Child Life', *JSA*, t. 40, 1951.

——. (2) 'Arapaho Child Life and its Cultural Background', *BBAE 148*, Washington D.C., 1952.

HISSINK, K. and HAHN, A. *Die Tacana, I. Erzählungsgut*, Stuttgart, 1961.

HOFFMAN, W. J. 'The Menomini Indians', *14th ARBAE* (1892-3), Washington D.C., 1896.

HOLTVED, E. (1) 'The Eskimo Legend of Navaranâq', *Acta Arctica*, 1, Copenhagen, 1943.

——. (2) *The Polar Eskimos Language and Folklore*, 2 vols, Copenhagen, 1951.

HUBAUX, J. *Les Grands Mythes de Rome*, Paris, 1945.

HUMBOLDT, A. de and BONPLAND, A. *Voyage aux régions équinoxiales du nouveau continent*, 23 vols, Paris, 1807–35.

HUNTER, J. D. *Manners and Customs of Several Indian Tribes Located West of the Mississippi*, reprinted, Minneapolis, 1957.

HUXLEY, F. *Affable Savages*, London, 1956.

HYMES, V. D. 'Athapaskan Numeral Systems', *International Journal of American Linguistics*, Vol. 21, 1955.

IHERING, R. von. *Dicionário dos animais do Brasil*, São Paulo, 1940.

IM THURN, E. F. *Among the Indians of Guiana*, London, 1883.

JABLOW, J. 'The Cheyenne in Plains Indian Trade Relations, 1795–1840', *American Ethnological Society Monographs*, 19, New York, 1951.

JACOBS, E. D. *Nehalem Tillamook Tales*, Eugene, Oregon, 1959.

JACOBS, M. (1) 'Northwest Sahaptin Texts', *CUCA*, Vol. 19, 1–2, New York, 1934.

——. (2) 'Clackamas Chinook Texts', *International Journal of American Linguistics*, Vol. 25, 1–2, 1958–9.

JENNESS, D. 'Myths and Traditions from Northern Alaska', *Reports of the Canadian Arctic Expedition*, 1913–18.

JETTÉ, Fr. J. 'On the Superstitions of the Ten'a Indians', *Anthropos*, Vol. 6, 1911.

JONES, W. (1) 'Ojibwa Tales from the North Shore of Lake Superior', *JAFL*, Vol. 29, 1916.

——. (2) 'Ojibwa Texts', *Publications of the American Ethnological Society*, Vol. 7, 2 parts, 1917–19.

——. (3) 'Kickapoo Tales ... translated by T. Michelson', *Publications of the American Ethnological Society*, Vol. 9, Leyden–New York, 1915.

——. (4) 'Fox Texts', *Publications of the American Ethnological Society*, Vol. 1, Leyden, 1907.

JOSSELIN DE JONG, J. P. B. (1) 'Original Odzibwe Texts', *Baessler Archiv*, 5, 1913.

—— (2) 'Blackfoot Texts', *Verhandelingen der Koninklijke Akademie van Wetenschappen te Amsterdam, Afdeeling Letterkunde Nieuwe Reeks*, Deel XIV, No. 4, 1914.

KARSTEN, R. (2) 'The Head-Hunters of Western Amazonas', *Societas Scientiarum Fennica. Commentationes humanarum litterarum*, t. 7, No. 1, Helsingfors, 1935.

KEESING, F. M. 'The Menomini Indians of Wisconsin', *Memoirs of the American Philosophical Society*, 10, 1939.

KENNARD, E. 'Mandan Grammar', *International Journal of American Linguistics*, Vol. 9, 1, 1936–8.

KENSINGER, K. 'The Cashinahua of Southeastern Peru', *Expedition*, Vol. 7, No. 4, 1965.

KILPATRICK, J. F. 'The Wahnenauhi Manuscript: Historical Sketches of the Cherokees', *Anthropological Papers*, Nos 75–80, *BBAE 196*, Washington D.C., 1966.

KINGSLEY NOBLE, G. 'Proto-Arawkan and its Descendants', Publ. 38, *Indiana University Research Center in Anthropology, Folklore and Linguistics, International Journal of American Linguistics*, Vol. 31, No. 3, part 2, 1965.

KLEIVAN, I. 'The Swan Maiden Myth among the Eskimo', *Acta Arctica*, 13, Copenhagen, 1962.

KOCH-GRÜNBERG, Th. (1) *Von Roroima zum Orinoco. Zweites Band. Mythen und Legenden der Taulipang und Arekuna Indianer*, Berlin, 1916.
——. (2) *Zwei Jahre bei den Indianern Nordwest Brasiliens*, new edn, Stuttgart, 1921.
——. (3) *Indianermärchen aus Südamerika*, Iena, 1921.
KOHL, J. G. *Kitchi-Gami. Wanderings Round Lake Superior*, new edn, Minneapolis, 1956.
KRAUSE, A. *The Tlingit Indians*, trans. E. Gunther, Seattle, 1956.
KRICKEBERG, W. *Felsplastik und Felsbilder bei den Kulturvölkern Altamerikas*, etc., 2 vols, Berlin, 1949.
KROEBER, A. L. (1) 'Handbook of the Indians of California', *BBAE 78*, Washington D.C., 1925.
——. (2) 'Arapaho Dialects', *UCPAAE*, Vol. 12, Berkeley, 1916.
——. (3) 'The Arapaho', *Bulletin of the American Museum of Natural History*, Vol. 18, parts 1, 2 and 4, New York, 1902–7.
——. (4) 'Cheyenne Tales', *JAFL*, Vol. 13, 1900.
——. (5) *Cultural and Natural Areas of Native North America*, Berkeley, 1939.
——. (6) 'Gros Ventre Myths and Tales', *APAMNH*, Vol. I, part 2, New York, 1907.
KRUSE, A. (2) 'Erzählungen der Tapajoz-Munduruku', *Anthropos*, t. 41–4, 1946–9.
LADD, J. *The Structure of a Moral Code*, Cambridge, Mass., 1957.
LATCHAM, R. E. (1) 'Ethnology of the Araucanos', *JRAI*, Vol. 39, 1909.
——. (2) *La Organización social y las creencias religiosas de los antiguos araucanos*, Santiago de Chile, 1924.
LEHMANN-NITSCHE, R. (8) 'El Caprimúlgido y los dos grandes astros', *RMDLP*, Vol. 32, 1930.
——. (9) 'La Cosmogonía según los Puelche de la Patagonia', *RMDLP*, Vol. 24, 2nd part, 1918.
——. (10) 'El viejo Tatrapai de los Araucanos', *RMDLP*, Vol. 32, 1929.
——. (11) 'El Diluvio según los Araucanos de la Pampa', *RMDLP*, Vol. 24 (2nd series, t. 12), 1916.
LELAND, Ch. G. *The Algonquin Legends of New England*, London, 1884.
LENZ, R. 'Estudios araucanos', *Anales de la Universidad del Chile*, Vol. 91, 1895.
LÉVI-STRAUSS, C. (5) *Anthropologie structurale*, Paris, 1958.
——. (9) *La Pensée sauvage*, Paris, 1962.
——. (10) *The Raw and the Cooked*, London, 1970.
——. (13) 'Résumé des cours de 1960–1961', *Annuaire du Collège de France*, 61st year, 1961–2.
——. (14) 'The Deduction of the Crane', in P. and E. K. Maranda, eds. *Structural Analysis of Oral Tradition*, Philadelphia, 1971.
——. (15) *From Honey to Ashes*, London, 1973.
——. (16) 'Guerre et commerce chez les Indiens de l'Amérique du Sud', *Renaissance, revue trimestrielle publiée par l'École libre des hautes études*, Vol. I, fasc. 1 et 2, New York, 1943.
——. (17) 'Résumé des cours de 1964–1965', *Annuaire du Collège de France*, 65th year, 1965–6.
——. (18) 'Le Sexe des astres', *Mélanges offerts à Roman Jakobson pour sa 70ᵉ année*, La Haye, 1967.
——. (19) 'Rapports de symétrie entre rites et mythes de peuples voisins'

in T. O. Beidelman, ed. *The Translation of Culture. Essays to E. E. Evans-Pritchard*, London, 1971.

LOTHROP, S. K. 'The Indians of Tierra del Fuego', *Contributions from the Museum of American Indian, Heye Foundation*, Vol. 10, New York, 1928.

LOUNSBURY, F. G. 'Stray Number Systems among Certain Indian Tribes', *AA*, n.s., Vol. 48, 1946.

LOWIE, R. H. (1) 'The Test-Theme in North American Mythology', *JAFL*, Vol. 21, 1908.

——. (2) 'The Assiniboine', *APAMNH*, Vol. 4, part 1, New York, 1909.

——. (3) 'Myths and Traditions of the Crow Indians', *APAMNH*, Vol. 25, part 1, New York, 1918.

——. (4) 'Shoshonean Tales', *JAFL*, Vol. 37, 1924.

——. (5) 'Studies in Plains Indian Folklore', *UCPAAE*, Vol. 40, No. 1, Berkeley, 1942.

——. (6) 'A Few Assiniboine Texts', *Anthropological Linguistics*, Nov. 1960.

——. (7) 'The Religion of the Crow Indians', *APAMNH*, Vol. 25, part 2, New York, 1922.

——. (8) 'Sun Dance of the Shoshoni, Ute, and Hidatsa', *APAMNH*, Vol. 16, part 5, New York, 1919.

——. (9) 'Societies of the Arikara Indians', *APAMNH*, Vol. 11, part 8, New York, 1915.

——. (10) 'The Tropical Forests: An Introduction', *HSAI*, Vol. 3.

——. (11) 'The Material Culture of the Crow Indians', *APAMNH*, Vol. 21, New York, 1922.

LUOMALA, K. 'Oceanic, American Indian and African Myths of Snaring the Sun', *Bernice P. Bishop Museum Bulletin 168*, Honolulu, 1940.

McCLINTOCK, W. *The Old North Trail*, London, 1910.

McGREGOR, S. E. (Letter of November 22nd, 1963).

McKENNAN, R. A. 'The Upper Tanana Indians', *Yale University Publications in Anthropology*, 55, 1959.

McLAUGHLIN, M. L. *Myths and Legends of the Sioux*, Bismarck, N. D., 1916.

McNEISH, R. S. 'The Origin of New World Civilization', *Scientific American*, Vol. 211, 5, 1964.

MANDELBAUM, D. G. 'The Plains Cree', *APAMNH*, Vol. 37, part 2, New York, 1940.

MATHEWS, C. *The Indian Fairy Book*, New York, 1869.

MATTHEWS, W. *Grammar and Dictionary of the Language of the Hidatsa*, New York, 1873.

MAXIMILIAN, Prince of Wied. *Travels in the Interior of North America*, trans. H. E. Lloyd, London, 1843.

MAYERS, M. *Pocomchi Texts*, University of Oklahoma, Norman, 1958.

MECHLING, W. H. 'Malecite Tales', *Memoirs of the Canada Department of Mines, Geological Survey*, Vol. 49, Ottawa, 1914.

MEDSGER, O. P. *Edible Wild Plants*, New York, 1939.

MÉTRAUX, A. (5) 'Myths of the Toba and Pilagá Indians of the Gran Chaco', *MAFLS*, Vol. 40, Philadelphia, 1946.

——. (8) 'Mythes et contes des Indiens Cayapo (groupe Kuben-Kran-Kegn)', *RMP*, n.s., Vol. 12, São Paulo, 1960.

——. (15) 'Tribes of Jurua-Purus Basins', *HSAI*, Vol. 3, *BBAE 143*, Washington D.C., 1948.

MICHELSON, T. (1) 'The Narrative of a Southern Cheyenne Woman', *Smithsonian Miscellaneous Collection*, 87, No. 5, Washington D.C., 1932.
——. (2) 'The Narrative of an Arapaho Woman', *AA*, n.s., Vol. 35, 1933.
——. (3) 'Some Arapaho Kinship Terms and Social Usages', *AA*, n.s., Vol. 36, 1934.
——. (4) 'Micmac Tales', *JAFL*, Vol. 38, 1925.
——. (5) 'The Mythical Origin of the White Buffalo Dance of the Fox Indians', *40th ARBAE*, Washington D.C., 1919.
——. (6) 'Notes on the Buffalo-Head Dance of the Thunder Gens of the Fox Indians', *BBAE 87*, Washington D.C., 1928.
——. (7) 'The Proto-Algonquian Archetype of "Five" ', *Language*, Vol. 9, 1933.
MONTOYA, A. R. de. *Gramatica y diccionarios (Arte, vocabulario y tesoro) de la lengua tupi o guarani*, new edn, Vienna–Paris, 1876.
MOONEY, J. (1) 'Myths of the Cherokee', *19th ARBAE* (1897–8), Washington D.C., 1900.
——. (2) 'Calendar History of the Kiowa Indians', *17th ARBAE*, part 1 (1895–6), Washington D.C., 1898.
——. (3) 'The Cheyenne Indians', *Memoirs of the American Anthropological Association*, I, 1907, part 6.
——. (4) 'The Ghost-Dance Religion', *14th ARBAE* (1892–3), part 2, Washington D.C., 1896.
MOONEY, J. and OLBRECHTS, F. M. 'The Swimmer Manuscript. Cherokee Sacred Formulas and Medicinal Prescriptions', *BBAE 99*, Washington D.C., 1932.
MORGAN, L. W., *League of the Ho-de-no sau-nee or Iroquois* (Reprinted by Human Relations Area Files), 2 vols, New Haven, 1954.
MURIE, J. R. 'Pawnee Indian Societies', *APAMNH*, Vol. 11, part 7, New York, 1914.
MURPHY, R. F. (1) 'Mundurucú Religion', *UCPAAE*, Vol. 49, 1, Berkeley–Los Angeles, 1958.
——. (2) *Headhunter's Heritage*, Berkeley–Los Angeles, 1960.
——. (3) 'Matrilocality and Patrilineality in Mundurucú Society', *AA*, 58, 1956.
MURPHY, R. F. and QUAIN, B. 'The Trumaí Indians of Central Brazil', *Monographs of the American Ethnological Society*, 24, New York, 1955.
NEILL, E. D. 'Life Among the Mandan and Gros Ventre Eighty Years Ago', *The American Antiquarian and Oriental Journal*, Vol. 6, 1884.
NIMUENDAJU, C. (2) 'Sagen der Tembé-Indianer', *Zeitschrift für Ethnologie*, Vol. 47, 1915.
——. (3) 'Bruchstücke aus Religion und Überlieferung der Šipaia-Indianer', *Anthropos*, Vols 14–15, 1919–20; 16–17, 1921–2.
——. (5) 'The Apinayé', *The Catholic University of America, Anthropological Series no. 8*, Washington D.C., 1939.
——. (6) 'The Šerenté', *Publ. of the Frederick Webb Hodge Anniversary Publication Fund*, Vol. 4, Los Angeles, 1942.
——. (8) 'The Eastern Timbira', *UCPAAE*, Vol. 41, Berkeley, 1946.
——. (13) 'The Tukuna', *UCPAAE*, Vol. 45, Berkeley, 1952.
——. (15) *Wortliste der Tukuna-Sprache*, Belém do Pará, 1929 (typescript of *Museu Nacional*, Rio de Janeiro).

NORDENSKIÖLD, E. (1) *Indianerleben, El Gran Chaco*, Leipzig, 1912.
——. (3) *Forschungen und Abenteuer in Südamerika*, Stuttgart, 1924.
NYE, W. S. *Bad Medicine and Good. Tales of the Kiowas*, Norman, Oklahoma, 1962.
NYKL, A. R. 'The Quinary-Vigesimal System of Counting in Europe, Asia and America', *Language*, Vol. 2, 1926.
ORCHARD, W. C. 'The Technique of Porcupine-quill Decoration among the North-American Indians', *Contributions from the Museum of the American Indian, Heye Foundation*, Vol. 4, No. 1, New York, 1916.
OSBORN, H. A. (1) 'Textos Folkloricos en Guarao', *Boletín Indigenista Venezolano*, Años III–IV–V, nos 1–4, Caracas (1956–7), 1958.
——. (2) 'Textos Folkloricos en Guarao II', *ibid.*, Año VI, nos 1–4, 1958.
——. (3) 'Warao II: Nouns, Relationals, and Demonstratives', *International Journal of American Linguistics*, Vol. 32, 3, part 1, 1966.
OSGOOD, C. 'Ingalik Social Structure', *Yale University Publications in Anthropology*, 53, 1958.
OWEN, Trefor M. *Welsh Folk Customs*, Cardiff, 1959.
PALMER, R. S. *The Mammal Guide. Mammals of North America North of Mexico*, New York, 1954.
PARKER, H. 'The Scobs Was in her Lovely Mouth', *JAFL*, Vol. 71, 1958.
PARSONS, E. C. (3) 'Kiowa Tales', *MAFLS*, Vol. 22, New York, 1929.
——. (4) 'Micmac Folklore', *JAFL*, Vol. 38, 1925.
PETITOT, E. (1) *Traditions indiennes du Canada nord-ouest*, Paris, 1886.
——. (2) *Monographie des Déné-Dindjié*, Paris, 1876.
PETRULLO, V. 'The Yaruros of the Capanaparo River, Venezuela', *Anthropological Papers no. 11, Bureau of American Ethnology*, Washington D.C., 1939.
PHINNEY, A. 'Nez Percé Texts', *CUCA*, Vol. 25, New York, 1934.
PIGAÑIOL, A. 'Le Rôti et le bouilli', *A Pedro Bosch-Gimpera*, México, 1963.
PREUSS, K. Th. (1) *Religion und Mythologie der Uitoto*, 2 vols, Göttingen, 1921–3.
——. (3) 'Forschungsreise zu den Kagaba', *Anthropos*, Vols 14–21, 1919–26.
PRICE, R. 'Martiniquan Fishing Magic' (unpublished; shown to the author in 1964).
PRINCE, J. D. 'Passamaquoddy Texts', *Publications of the American Ethnological Society*, Vol. 10, New York, 1921.
PRYTZ-JOHANSEN, J. *The Maori and his Religion*, Copenhagen, 1954.
RADIN, P. (1) 'The Winnebago Tribe', *37th ARBAE* (1915–16), Washington D.C., 1923.
——. (2) 'The Thunderbird War Club, a Winnebago Tale', *JAFL*, Vol. 44, 1931.
——. (3) 'Ethnological Notes on the Ojibwa of Southeastern Ontario', *AA*, Vol. 30, 1928.
RAND, S. T. *Legends of the Micmacs*, New York–London, 1894.
RASSERS, W. H. 'Inleiding tot een bestudeering van de Javaansche Kris', *Mededeelingen der Koninklijke Nederlansche Akademie van Wetenschappen; afdeeling letterkunde, Nieuwe Reeks deel 1*, No. 8, 1938.
RAY, V. F. (2) 'Sanpoil Folk Tales', *JAFL*, Vol. 46, 1933.
——. (3) *Primitive Pragmatists. The Modoc Indians of Northern California*, Seattle, 1963.

REICHARD, G. A. (2) 'Literary Types and the Dissemination of Myths',
*JAFL*, Vol. 34, 1921.
——. (3) 'An Analysis of Cœur d'Alene Indian Myths', *MAFLS*, Vol. 41,
1947.
REICHEL-DOLMATOFF, G. (1) *Los Kogi*, 2 vols, Bogotá, 1949–50 – 1951.
——. (2) 'Mítos y cuentos de los Indios Chimila', *Boletín de Arqueología*,
Vol. 1, No. 1, Bogotá, 1945.
——. (3) 'The Agricultural Basis of the Sub-Andean Chiefdoms of Columbia',
in Wilbert, J., ed., *The Evolution of Horticultural Systems in Native South
America. Causes and Consequences. A Symposium*, Caracas, 1961.
REINACH, S. *Cultes, mythes et religions*, 5 vols, Paris, 1905–23.
REINBURG, P. 'Folklore amazonien. Légendes des Zaparo du Curaray et de
Canelos', *JSA*, n.s., Vol. 13, 1921.
RIGGS, S. R. 'A Dakota–English Dictionary', *Contributions to North American
Ethnology*, Vol. VII, Washington D.C., 1890.
ROBINET, F. M. 'Hidatsa I, II, III', *International Journal of American Linguistics*,
Vol. 21, 1955.
RODRIGUES, J. Barbosa. (1) 'Poranduba Amazonense', *Anais da Biblioteca
nacional de Rio de Janeiro*, Vol. 14, fasc. 2 (1886–7), Rio de Janeiro, 1890.
ROLLAND, E. *Faune populaire de la France*, tome II, 'Les Oiseaux sauvages',
Paris, 1879.
RONDON, C. M. da Silva. 'Esbôçô grammatical e vocabulário da lingua dos
Indios Boróro', *Publ. no. 77 da Commissão ... Rondon*; *Anexo 5, etnografia*,
Rio de Janeiro, 1948.
ROTH, H. L. 'American Quillwork: a Possible Clue to its Origin', *Man, 23*,
1923, pp. 113–16.
ROTH, W. E. (1) 'An Inquiry into the Animism and Folklore of the Guiana
Indians', *30th ARBAE* (1908–9), Washington D.C., 1915.
——. (2) 'An Introductory Study of the Arts, Crafts and Customs of the
Guiana Indians', *38th ARBAE* (1916–17), Washington D.C., 1924.
ROUSSEAU, J. (letter of June 25th, 1964).
ROUSSEAU, J. and RAYMOND, M. 'Etudes ethnobotaniques québécoises',
*Contributions de l'Institut botanique de l'Université de Montréal*, No. 55, 1945.
SAINTYVES, P. *L'Éternuement et le bâillement dans la magie, l'ethnographie et le
folklore médical*, Paris, 1921.
SAAKE, W. (1) 'Die Juruparilegende bei den Baniwa des Rio Issana', *Proceed-
ings of the 32nd Intern. Congress of Americanists*, Copenhagen (1956), 1958.
——. (3) 'Aus der Überlieferung der Baniwa', *Staden-Jahrbuch*, Bd 6, São
Paulo, 1958.
SALZMANN, Z. 'A Method for Analyzing Numerical Systems', *Word*, Vol. 6,
No. 1, New York, 1950.
SAPIR, E. (1) 'Wishram Texts', *Publications of the American Ethnological Society*,
Vol. 2, Leyden, 1909.
——. (2) 'The Algonkin Affinity of Yurok and Wiyot Kinship Terms', *JSA*,
Vol. 15, 1923.
——. (3) 'Yana Texts', *UCPAAE*, Vol. 9, 1, Berkeley, 1910.
SAUSSURE, F. de. 'Notes' in *Cahiers Ferdinand de Saussure*, 12, 1954.
SCHAEFFER, Cl. E. 'Bird Nomenclature and Principles of Avian Taxonomy
of the Blackfeet Indians', *Journal of the Washington Academy of Sciences*,
Vol. 40, No. 2, 1950.

SCHAUENSEE, R. M. de. (1) *The Birds of Colombia*, Narberth, Pennsylvania, 1964.

——. (2) *The Species of Birds of South America and their Distribution*, Narberth, Pennsylvania, 1966.

SCHOMBURGK, R. *Travels in British Guiana 1840–1844*. Trans. and ed. W. E. Roth, 2 vols, Georgetown, 1922.

SCHOOLCRAFT, H. R. (7) *Oneóta, or Characteristics of the Red Race of America*, New York, 1845.

——. (2) *The Myth of Hiawatha*, Philadelphia, 1856.

——. (3) *Historical and Statistical Information Respecting ... the Indian Tribes of the United States*, 6 vols, Philadelphia, 1851–7.

SCHWARZ, H. F. (2) 'Stingless Bees (Meliponidae) of the Western Hemisphere', *Bulletin of the American Museum of Natural History*, Vol. 90, New York, 1948.

SHAFER, R. 'Notes on Penutian', *International Journal of American Linguistics*, 18, 4, 1952.

SILVA, P. A. Brüzzi Alves da. *A Civilização Indigena do Uaupès*, São Paulo, 1962.

SIMMS, S. C. 'Traditions of the Crow', *Field Columbian Museum, Publ. 85, Anthropol. Series, Vol. 2, No. 6*, Chicago, 1903.

SIMPSON, R. de E. 'A Mandan Bull-Boat', *The Masterkey*, 23, 6, 1949.

SKINNER, A. (1) 'Notes on the Eastern Cree and Northern Saulteaux', *APAMNH*, Vol. 9, New York, 1911.

——. (2) 'Some Aspects of the Folk-Lore of the Central Algonkin', *JAFL*, Vol. 27, 1914.

——. (3) 'Plains Ojibwa Tales', *JAFL*, Vol. 32, 1919.

——. (4) 'Social Life and Ceremonial Bundles of the Menomini Indians', *APAMNH*, Vol. 13, part 1, New York, 1913.

——. (5) 'Political Organization, Cults, and Ceremonies of the Plains-Ojibway and Plains Cree Indians', *APAMNH*, Vol. 11, part 6, New York, 1914.

——. (6) 'The Sun Dance of the Plains-Cree', *APAMNH*, Vol. 16, part 4, New York, 1919.

——. (7) 'Associations and Ceremonies of the Menomini Indians', *APAMNH*, Vol. 13, part 2, New York, 1915.

——. (8) 'Plains Cree Tales', *JAFL*, Vol. 29, 1916.

——. (9) 'Observations on the Ethnology of the Sauk Indians', *Bulletin of the Public Museum of the City of Milwaukee*, Vol. 5, Nos 1, 2, 3, 1923–5.

——. (10) 'The Mascoutens or Prairie Potawatomi Indians', *Bulletin of the Public Museum of the City of Milwaukee*, Vol. 6, Nos 1, 2, 3, 1924–7.

——. (11) 'War Customs of the Menomini', *AA*, Vol. 13, 1911.

——. (12) 'Societies of the Iowa, Kansa, and Ponca Indians', *APAMNH*, Vol. 11, part 9, New York, 1915.

——. (13) 'Sauk Tales', *JAFL*, Vol. 41, 1928.

——. (14) 'Material Culture of the Menomini', *Indian Notes and Monographs, Museum of the American Indian, Heye Foundation*, New York, 1921.

SKINNER, A. and SATTERLEE, J. V. 'Folklore of the Menomini Indians', *APAMNH*, Vol. 13, part 3, New York, 1915.

SMITH, E. A. 'Myths of the Iroquois', *2nd ARBAE*, Washington D.C., 1881.

SMITH, H. H. (1) 'Ethnobotany of the Ojibwe Indians', *Bulletin of the Public Museum of the City of Milwaukee*, Vol. 4, No. 3, 1932.

——. (2) 'Ethnobotany of the Forest Potawatomi Indians', *ibid.*, Vol. 7, No. 1, 1933.

SPARKMAN, P. S. 'Notes on California Folklore. A Luiseño Tale', *JAFL*, Vol. 21, 1908.

SPECK, F. G. (2) 'Reptile-Lore of the Northern Indians', *JAFL*, Vol. 36, 1923.

——. (3) 'Penobscot Tales and Religious Beliefs', *JAFL*, Vol. 48, 1935.

——. (4) 'Montagnais and Naskapi Tales from the Labrador Peninsula', *JAFL*, Vol. 38, 1925.

——. (5) 'Bird-Lore of the Northern Indians', *Public Lectures of the University of Pennsylvania*, Vol. 7, 1921.

——. (6) *Naskapi. The Savage Hunters of the Labrador Peninsula*, Norman, 1935.

——. (7) 'Myths and Folk-Lore of the Timiskaming Algonquin and Timagami Ojibwa', *Canada Department of Mines, Geological Survey, Memoir 71, No. 9, Anthropol. Series*, Ottawa, 1915.

——. (8) 'Some Micmac Tales from Cape Breton Island', *JAFL*, Vol. 28, 1915.

——. (9) 'Huron Moose Hair Embroidery', *AA*, n.s., Vol. 13, 1911.

——. (10) *Penobscot Man*, Philadelphia, 1940.

SPENCE, L. *The Myths of the North American Indians*, London, 1916.

SPENCER, R. F. 'The North Alaskan Eskimo', *BBAE 171*, Washington D.C., 1959.

SPIER, L. (2) 'Klamath Ethnography', *UCPAAE*, Vol. 30, Berkeley, 1930.

——. (3) 'Notes on the Kiowa Sun Dance', *APAMNH*, Vol. 16, part 6, New York, 1921.

——. (4) 'The Sun Dance of the Plains Indians: its Development and Diffusion', *APAMNH*, Vol. 16, part 7, New York, 1921.

SPINDEN, H. (1) 'Myths of the Nez Percé Indians', *JAFL*, Vol. 21, 1908.

——. (2) 'A study of Maya Art', *Memoirs of the Peabody Museum of American Archaeology and Ethnology*, Vol. 6, 1913.

SPOTT, R. and KROEBER, A. L. 'Yurok Narratives', *UCPAAE*, Vol. 35, No. 9, Berkeley, 1942.

SPRUCE, R. *Notes of a Botanist on the Amazon and Andes ...*, 2 vols, London, 1908.

STAMP, H. 'A Malecite Tale: Adventures of Buckchinskwesk', *JAFL*, Vol. 28, 1915.

STEPHEN, A. M. 'Hopi Journal, edited by E. C. Parsons', 2 vols, *CUCA*, Vol. 23, New York, 1936.

STERN, Th. 'Klamath Myths Abstracts', *JAFL*, Vol. 76, 1963.

STIRLING, M. W. 'Historical and Ethnographical Material on the Jivaro Indians', *BBAE 117*, Washington D.C., 1938.

STOCK, C. de B. 'Folklore and Customs of the Lepchas of Sikkim', *Journal of the Asiatic Society of Bengal*, Vol. 21, 1925.

STRADELLI, E. (1) 'Vocabulario da lingua geral portuguez-nheêngatú e nheêngatú-portuguez, *etc.*', *RIHGB*, t. 104, Vol. 158, Rio de Janeiro, 1929.

STRONG, W. D. (1) 'Aboriginal Society in Southern California', *UCPAAE*, Vol. 26, Berkeley, 1929.

——. (2) 'From History to Prehistory in the Northern Great Plains', in

*Essays in Historical Anthropology of North America, Smithsonian Miscellaneous Collections*, Vol. 100, Washington D.C., 1940.

STURTEVANT, W. C. 'The Significance of Ethnological Similarities between Southeastern North America and the Antilles' in S. W. Mintz, ed. 'Papers in Caribbean Anthropology', *Yale University Publications in Anthropology*, Nos 57–64, New Haven, 1960.

SUSNIK, B. J. 'Estudios Emok-Toba. Parte Iᵃ: Fraseario', *Boletín de la Sociedad Científica del Paraguay*, Vol. VII, 1962, *Etno-linguistica*, 7, Asunción, 1962.

SWANTON, J. R. (1) 'Myths and Tales of the Southeastern Indians', *BBAE 88*, Washington D.C., 1929.

——. (3) 'Some Neglected Data Bearing on Cheyenne, Chippewa and Dakota History', *AA*, Vol. 32, 1930.

——. (4) 'Southern Contacts of the Indians North of the Gulf of Mexico', *Annaes do XX Congresso Internacional de Americanistas*, 1922, Rio de Janeiro, 1924.

——. (5) 'The Indians of the Southeastern United States', *BBAE 137*, Washington D.C., 1946.

TASTEVIN, C. (2) 'Nomes de plantas e animaes em lingua tupy', *RMP*, t. 13, São Paulo, 1922.

——. (3) 'La Légende de Bóyusú en Amazonie', *Revue d'Ethnographie et des Traditions populaires*, 6th year, No. 22, Paris, 1925.

——. (4) 'Le fleuve Murú. Ses habitants. Croyances et mœurs kachinaua', *La Géographie*, Vol. 43, Nos 4–5, 1925.

——. (5) 'Le Haut Tarauacá', *La Géographie*, Vol. 45, 1926.

TAYLOR, D. 'The Dog, the Opossum and the Rainbow', *International Journal of American Linguistics*, Vol. 27, 1961.

TEIT, J. (1) 'The Shuswap', *Memoirs of the American Museum of Natural History*, Vol. IV, Leiden–New York, 1909.

——. (2) 'Traditions of the Lilloet Indians of British Columbia', *JAFL*, Vol. 25, 1912.

——. (3) 'Cœur d'Alêne Tales'. Cf. Boas, F. (4).

——. (4) 'Traditions of the Thompson River Indians', *MAFLS*, Vol. 6, 1898.

——. (5) 'Mythology of the Thompson Indians', *Memoirs of the American Museum of Natural History*, Vol. XII, Leiden–New York, 1912.

——. (6) 'The Salishan Tribes of the Western Plateaus', *45th ARBAE* (1927–8), Washington D.C., 1930.

——. (7) 'Tahltan Tales', *JAFL*, Vol. 32, 34, 1919–21.

——. (8) 'Kaska Tales', *JAFL*, Vol. 30, 1917.

TERRELL, R. H. 'Petroglyphs, Huge Honey Combs Found in Sonora, Mex.', *Press-Enterprise*, February 20th, 1966.

THOMPSON, J. E. (1) *The Civilization of the Mayas*, Chicago, 1927.

——. (2) *The Moon Goddess in Middle America. With Notes on Related Deities*, Washington, Carnegie Institution of Washington, 1939.

THOMPSON, S. 'The Star-Husband Tale' (Liber saecularia in honorem J. Qvigstadii), *Studia Septentrionalia*, 4, Oslo, 1953.

THOMSON, Sir A. L. *A New Dictionary of Birds*, London, 1964.

TRIK, A. S. 'The Splendid Tomb of Temple I at Tikal, Guatemala', *Expedition*, Vol. 6, No. 1, Fall, 1963.

TROWBRIDGE, C. C. 'Meeãrmeear Traditions', *Occasional Contributions from the Museum of Anthropology of the University of Michigan*, Ann Arbor, 1938.

TURNER, G. 'Hair Embroidery in Siberia and North America', *Pitt-Rivers Museum Occasional Papers in Technology*, Vol. 7, Oxford, 1955.

TURNEY-HIGH, H. H. 'Ethnography of the Kutenai', *Memoirs of the American Anthropological Association*, Vol. 56, 1941.

UHLENBECK, C. C. 'Original Blackfoot Texts. A New Series of Blackfoot Texts', *Verhandelingen der Koninklijke Akademie van Wetenschappen te Amsterdam*, *Afdeeling letterkunde*, *Nieuwe Reeks*, Deel XII, 1; XIII, 1, Amsterdam, 1911–12.

UHLENBECK, C. C. and VAN GULIK, R. H. 'An English-Blackfoot and Blackfoot-English Vocabulary', *ibid.*, Deel XXIX, 4; XXXIII, 2; 1930–34.

VOEGELIN, E. W. 'Kiowa-Crow Mythological Affiliations', *AA*, Vol. 35, 1933.

WAGLEY, Ch. and GALVÃO, E. 'The Tenetehara Indians of Brazil', *CUCA*, Vol. 35, 1949.

WALKER, J. R. 'The Sun Dance and other Ceremonies of the Oglala Division of the Teton Dakota', *APAMNH*, Vol. 16, part 2, New York, 1917.

WALLIS, W. D. (1) 'Beliefs and Tales of the Canadian Dakota', *JAFL*, Vol. 36, 1923.

——. and WALLIS, R. S. (2) *The Micmac Indians of Eastern Canada*, Minneapolis, 1955.

WASSÉN, S. H. (1) 'Some General Viewpoints in the Study of Native Drugs Especially from the West Indies and South America', *Ethnos*, t. 2, Stockholm, 1964.

——. (2) 'The Use of Some Specific Kinds of South American Indian Snuff and Related Paraphernalia', *Etnologiska Studier*, 28, Göteborg, 1965.

WASSÉN, S. H. and HOLMSTEDT, B. 'The Use of Paricá, an Ethnological and Pharmacological Review', *Ethnos*, 1, Stockholm, 1963.

WATERMAN, T. T. 'The Explanatory Element in the Folk-Tales of the North-American Indians', *JAFL*, Vol. 27, 1914.

WAUGH, F. W. 'Iroquois Foods and Food Preparation', *Canada Department of Mines, Geological Survey, Memoir 86*, Ottawa, 1916.

WAVRIN, Marquis de. *Mœurs et coutumes des Indiens sauvages de l'Amérique du Sud*, Paris, 1937.

WEDEL, W. R. (1) 'An Introduction to Pawnee Archaeology', *BBAE* 112, Washington D.C., 1936.

——. (2) 'The Great Plains' in Jennings, J. D. and Norbeck, E., eds. *Prehistoric Man in the New World*, Chicago, 1964.

WHIFFEN, Th. *The North-West Amazons*, London, 1915.

WHITE, L. A. 'The Acoma Indians', *47th ARBAE* (1929–30), Washington D.C., 1932.

WILBERT, J. (7) 'Erzählgut der Yupa-Indianer', *Anthropos*, Band 57, 1962.

——. (8) *Indios de la región Orinoco-Ventuari*, Caracas, 1963.

——. (9) 'Warao Oral Literature', *Instituto Caribe de Antropologia y Sociologia, Fundación La Salle de Ciencias Naturales*, Monograph no. 9, Caracas, 1964.

——. (10) 'Zur Kenntnis der Yabarana', *Naturwissenschaftliche Gesellschaft, Antropologica, Supplement-band no. 1*, Köln, 1959.

WILL, G. F. (1) 'No-Tongue, a Mandan Tale', *JAFL*, Vol. 26, 1913.

——. (2) 'The Story of No-Tongue', *JAFL*, Vol. 29, 1916.

WILL, G. F. and SPINDEN, H. J. 'The Mandans. A Study of their Culture. Archaeology and Language', *Papers of the Peabody Museum of American Archaeol. and Ethnol., Harvard University*, Vol. 3, part 4, Cambridge, Mass., 1906.

WILLIAMS, M. L., ed. *Schoolcraft's Indian Legends*, East Lansing, Mich., 1956.

WILSON, E. W. 'The Owl and the American Indian', *JAFL*, Vol. 63, 1950.

WILSON, G. L. 'Hidatsa Eagle Trapping', *APAMNH*, Vol. 30, part 4, New York, 1928.

WIRZ, P. 'The Social Meaning of the Sept-house and the Sept-boat in Dutch and British New-Guinea', *Tijdschrift voor Indische Taal-, Land- en Volkenkunde*, Deel LXXIV, Afl. 1, Batavia, 1934.

WISSLER, C. (1) 'Some (Oglala) Dakota Myths', *JAFL*, Vol. 20, 1907.

——. (2) 'Sun Dance of the Plains Indians; General Introduction', *APAMNH*, Vol. 16, New York, 1921.

——. (3) 'Indian Beadwork', *Guide Leaflet* No. 50, *American Museum of Natural History*, 2nd edn, New York, 1931.

——. (4) 'The Social Life of the Blackfoot Indians', *APAMNH*, Vol. 7, part 1, New York, 1911.

——. (5) 'Societies and Dance Associations of the Blackfoot Indians', *APAMNH*, Vol. 11, part 4, New York, 1913.

——. (6) 'Societies and Ceremonial Associations in the Oglala Division of the Teton-Dakota', *APAMNH*, Vol. 11, part 1, New York, 1912.

WISSLER, C. and DUVALL, D. C. 'Mythology of the Blackfoot Indians', *APAMNH*, Vol. 2, New York, 1908.

WOODMAN, J. J. *Indian Legends and Tales of Captivity*, Boston, 1924.

WOOD, R. 'An Interpretation of Mandan Culture History', *River Basin Surveys Papers*, No. 39, *BBAE 198*, Washington D.C., 1967.

YARNELL, R. A. 'Aboriginal Relationships between Culture and Plant Life in the Upper Great Lakes Region', *Anthropological Papers, Museum of Anthropology, University of Michigan*, No. 23, Ann Arbor, Michigan, 1964.

*Index*

# Index of Myths

Numbers in boldface indicate complete myth

1. Myths listed in numerical order and according to subject-matter

*a. New Myths*

c. *References to Other Myths from Volumes I and II*

## 2. Myths listed by tribe

# Index